American Women Writers to 1800

D0067373

American Women Writers to 1800

EDITED BY *Sharon M. Harris*

NEW YORK   OXFORD   OXFORD UNIVERSITY PRESS

1996

Oxford University Press

Oxford   New York
Athens   Auckland   Bangkok   Bombay
Calcutta   Capetown   Dar es Salaam   Delhi
Florence   Hong Kong   Istanbul   Karachi
Kuala Lumpur   Madras   Madrid   Melbourne
Mexico City   Nairobi   Paris   Singapore
Taipei   Tokyo   Toronto
and associated companies in
Berlin   Ibadan

Published by Oxford University Press, Inc.
198 Madison Avenue, New York, New York 10016

Oxford is a registered trademark of Oxford University Press

Library of Congress Cataloging-in-Publication Data
American women writers to 1800 / edited by Sharon M. Harris.
p. cm.   Includes bibliographical references (p.) and index.
ISBN 0-19-508453-5
1. American literature—Women authors—History and criticism.
2. Women and literature—United States—History—18th century.
3. Women and literature—United States—History—17th century.
4. United States—Intellectual life—18th century.
I. Harris, Sharon M.
PS149.A44   1995   810.9'9287—dc20   94-48119

1 3 5 7 9 8 6 4 2

Printed in the United States of America
on acid-free paper

Acknowledgments

Over an eight-year period, the number of individuals to whom I have become indebted is far too numerous to list. It is my sincere hope that they know who they are and that I have extended my appreciation throughout the years in which I have been engaged with this project. Friends, other scholars, colleagues, and students alike deserve my deepest thanks. Four individuals do deserve special mention: Carla Mulford, for her abiding support; Lydia Kualapai, for her expert research assistance; Elizabeth Maguire, an editor whose support and patience have been notable; and Dana Nelson for her astute reading at an early stage.

I wish to acknowledge several institutions from which I have received support for this project: a National Endowment for the Humanities Travel to Collections Grant; the Maude Hammond Fling Summer Research Grant from the University of Nebraska Research Council; and a Summer Research Grant from Temple University.

I also wish to thank the following individuals and institutions for their support and/or permissions to publish materials included in the anthology: the American Philosophical Society; The British Library (MSS/CMH/1224, 1963); The Cincinnati Historical Society; Colonial Society of Massachusetts; The Quaker Collection, Haverford College; the Corbit-Higgins-Spruance Papers, Historical Society of Delaware; Georgia Historical Society Library; the Hatfield Historical Society and Mr. and Mrs. Roswell S. Billings; the Simon Gratz Manuscripts Collection, the Society Collection, the Bartram Papers, the Logan Papers, the Pemberton Papers, the Parrish Collection, Sarah Wister Journal, and the Drinker-Sandwith Papers, Historical Society of Pennsylvania; the Library Company of Philadelphia; the Library of Congress; Mary K. Goddard Papers, MS. 1517, Maryland Historical Society; the Massachusetts Historical Society; the Moravian Historical Society; the National Archives of Canada; New Hampshire Historical Society, Josiah Bartlett Papers; the Van Rensselaer Manor Papers (7079), The New York State Library; The Oyster Bay Historical Society; the South Carolina Historical Society; Durrett Collection, Department of Special Collections, the University of Chicago Library; the University of New Mexico Press; the Virginia Historical Society; the Hillhouse Family Papers, Yale University Library; and *The Adams Family Correspondence* (3: Apr. 1778–Sep. 1780), eds. L.H. Butterfield and Marc Friedlaener (Cambridge, MA: Belknap P of Harvard UP, 1973), reprinted by permission.

Contents

Note on the Text

Whenever possible, original manuscripts have been used as have first known or extant editions of published texts. Early practices of capitalization, spelling, punctuation, and the like, have been retained; exceptions include changes for clarification, in which case brackets have been used, and the long "s" has been changed to modern usage as have u's and v's.

American Women Writers to 1800

Introduction

"And their words do follow them"—The Writings of Early American Women

In 1736 when Jonathan Edwards preached the funeral sermon for his grand-mother, Esther Warham Mather Stoddard, he chose "And their words do fol-low them" as scriptural doctrine to commemorate Stoddard's extraordinary contributions to the community. Throughout her life, she led sanctioned prayer groups for women, used the meetings to comment on religious writings, con-cluded her sessions with prayers, and was "[r]umored to have been even more forceful and learned than her husband," the renowned minister Solomon Stod-dard.[1] This act of prayer leadership places Esther Warham Stoddard in a long history of Euro-American women religious activists in America, beginning in the Puritan community with Anne Hutchinson (whose leadership of prayer groups and outspokenness against the clergy's practices led not to a sermon in her honor but to humiliation and banishment) and including later activists in the eighteenth century such as Sarah Haggar Osborn (for whom responses to her actions blended the success of her predecessors and the disdain of most of the established clergy). Although no writings by Warham Stoddard are ex-tant, her "words" and work in the community were recognized by her grand-son as worthy of commemoration, and—as this anthology demonstrates—the words *and* works of many women, including Warham Stoddard's great-grand-daughter, Esther Edwards Burr, warrant similar recognition. Leading prayer groups represents only one of the numerous literary and activist patterns[2] that

1. *The Journal of Esther Edwards Burr, 1754–1757*, eds. Carol F. Karlsen and Laurie Crumpacker (New Haven: Yale UP, 1984), p. 6; see also Mary Sumner Benson, *Women in Eighteenth-Century America* (New York: Columbia UP, 1935).

2. While "patterns" may be an insufficient term in many senses, I wish to avoid the term "traditions"—first, because it is too easily essentialized; second, because much further study of the field of early women's writings will be necessary before we can begin to discern any such traditions, if they exist; and third, because to speak accurately of traditions we will need a compendium of preceding adjectives to distinguish exclusivity as well as inclusivity. That is, how can we speak of the "tradition" of early women's poetry without distinguishing Native and European differences; oral and written differences; class, regional, racial, and age differences?—the list is immense and far too important to be limited by the search for "traditions." Further, "patterns" also asserts a link between this section of the introduction and the third section that addresses questions about women writing as well as writings by women.

3

emerge in the study of early American women's texts, but virtually all of the patterns, however diverse, synthesize work and words. That indelible link is crucial to understanding women's lives and the aesthetics that shaped their writings. Before I postulate a theoretical perspective on one of the patterns in these texts (a poetics of interruptability that is formulated as what I term *discours décousu*) and ways in which late-twentieth-century feminist theories may enchance our understanding of early women's lives and their writings, let me suggest some reasons that an anthology such as this is needed in early American studies.

When I was a Master's student in 1983, I (rather innocently in those days) asked my professor why our Early American Literature course included only three women writers—Anne Bradstreet, Mary Rowlandson, and Sarah Kemble Knight. His reply was that very few women in colonial America were literate and thus we had only these rare literary works by women. When I was a doctoral student at another university in 1985, I (with no innocence) asked my professor why the only woman writer in our Early American Literature course was Anne Bradstreet. His reply was that very few women in colonial America were literate and thus we had only a few "significant works by women." Neither professor was maliciously hoarding information (although the latter was certainly implying specific aesthetic and literary values through the term "significant"); they had merely been taught the myth of early women's literary productions and, importantly, they adhered to traditional ideas of aesthetics and of what constituted literature (diaries and letters, for instance, would typically be excluded).

In the last decade, early American literary studies have been rapidly expanding through scholars' reassessments of longheld but narrowly focused assumptions about Native American traditions, explorations of the "New World," European settlement of the continent, the War for Independence, and the formulation of America (as a nation and as a concept); yet relatively little research has been devoted to women's cultural and literary contributions before 1800.[3] Most of the research that has been published about early American women has been produced by historians; their research has certainly encouraged those of us who are literary scholars, but, of course, their work does not always address the same cultural and theoretical implications as a predominantly literary perspective.

This anthology seeks, therefore, to advance the process of filling that documentary and intellectual gap in American cultural and literary history and especially to encourage further explorations in the field. A majority of the texts included in the anthology have not been reprinted since their original publication or, in the case of most letters and diaries, have never been published. I offer the anthology as a sampler of the available writings by women in this period, recognizing that as critics have greater access to the materials, our perceptions about women's writings will broaden and change. I do, however, ap-

---

3. Notable exceptions are the work of Annette Kolodny, Cathy N. Davidson, and two series at Oxford University Press: the Early American Women Writers Series, and Women Writing in English before 1830 Series in conjunction with Brown University's Women Writers Project.

proach the texts in this general introduction and in the section and biographical introductions (as well as in the selection process) from the perspective of a feminist scholar and theorist.

The primary criteria for inclusion were the literary and cultural significance of a text. In the postmodern 1990s we should, of course, recognize both of these significations as highly subjective, but the discovery and analysis of the texts themselves were, for me, instrumental in redefining what constitutes literature (and thereby reshaped my aesthetic evaluations of these texts and others) and further elucidating cultural issues, always broadening and sometimes challenging what I "knew" about early America.[4] Let me use an extreme example, one that might raise questions about its inclusion: the letters of Deborah Read Franklin. Her writings evidence borderline literacy,[5] yet the tonal qualities are impressive (one hears her voice in phrases such as "I am set down to Confab a littel with my dear child" and "we have an ox arosteing on the river"). What is unquestionable is that Read Franklin's letters are historically significant. She records a frontline view of political actions—and reactions—in Revolutionary Philadelphia, which sometimes resulted in the need for her to confront citizens' often violent responses to her absent spouse's negotiations. More important, her letters act as a life-text symbolizing, on the one hand, her individual struggles and accomplishments, and, on the other hand, the disparity between the opinions and opportunities of the dominant culture in Revolutionary America and those of many women and other oppressed members of that society whose futures offered little hope for reform but ample opportunity for hardship and increased marginalization. Thus this anthology should provide a means of further interrogating our own literary and cultural assumptions—about early America and in general.

The anthology will be most useful to and best understood by its readers if they recognize that it has been shaped around the goal of acknowledging (cultural and individual) diversity and difference: that is, the rationale for inclusion reflects the growing interest in gender, geographic, racial, class, thematic, generic, and aesthetic diversity in early American studies. Let me reiterate here that I believe it is far too early—if ever necessary—to establish a canon of early American women writers; the discipline of early American studies in gen-

4. As to definitions, I should note my own discomfort with the term "American" literature and culture in this book. In later periods, I prefer "United States" as a means of designating the geographic boundaries of my study and of acknowledging that the United States does not constitute all of the Americas. In this study, however, only the last twenty-five years of the period being examined can accurately be termed "United States" literature, and "North American" is inaccurate because, for limitations of time and space, the study indeed examines only those writers who lived in what is now the continental United States. Undoubtedly, this issue will continue to present its complexities as we delve further into the earliest periods of existence in this region, but for the present, I have unimaginatively settled for "American."

5. Like Read Franklin, many early American women wrote almost phonetically, suggesting (ironically in Read Franklin's case, considering her husband's occupations) that they had little access either to printed texts or, perhaps equally important, to a critical group. There was no female version of the American Philosophical Society; however, see the section in this anthology on "Epistolary Exchanges" and biographical introductions to writers such as Hannah Griffitts for the ways in which the emergence of informal groups aided women's literary development. See, too, David Shields's recent attention to literary salons in early America.

5

eral is currently engaged in what might be called critical flux (a very healthy condition, I would argue) and deserves much more research and development before such considerations come under debate. I should also emphasize that, while the selection process sought to capture diversity and difference, my goal was *not* to use diversity as a means of erasing or suppressing opposition, contradiction, and struggle among alternative significations and/or subjectivities. Thus while it was tempting to create a text that included only strong feminist voices (and there are many), I ultimately determined that early American studies in general and feminist studies in particular are better served by a selection of texts that foregrounds ideological conflict and opposition struggles in early women's texts.

The most evident sense of diversity in this anthology is, of course, gender. This element is addressed both in the terms of sex (focusing exclusively on women writers, who themselves need to be written back into early American literary history) and of accultured attitudes toward and by women. Although I believe emerging feminist issues are evident throughout these writings, I have not attempted to limit my selections to a particular perspective by women. Texts that at times perpetuate dominant-culture ideologies must be studied carefully: first, because *all* women—acquiescent or radical—had to struggle with those ideologies; second, as a means of better understanding the conditions (ideological and material) under which women produced their texts; and third, because those ideologies are often subverted textually. We are accustomed to a writer's use of irony, for instance, as a subversive literary technique, but less commonly recognized avenues of subversion converge with irony in many of these texts. I have included, for instance, several "introductions" or "prefaces" to published works (most notably to spiritual autobiographies; see the writings of Bathsheba Bowers, for example) because that is a highly contested space in early women's writings. Many women writers' prefaces are steeped in apologia for the hubris of writing and publishing their ideas; yet the preface is also where some early women authors otherwise locate themselves in relation to their literary endeavors and assert their right to a public presence. Thus the introductory statements, separated as they are from the main text, become an ironic representation of women's cultural marginalization. A central focus of the selections is also the ways in which many women writers challenged those accultured attitudes.

The three women writers (Bradstreet, Rowlandson, Knight) traditionally included in early American studies were all residents of Massachusetts; this anthology, however, follows recent trends in the field and recognizes geographic diversity by including other New England women's writings, writers from the mid-Atlantic and southern colonies, and those writers who explored the regions to the west of the original states. This extended geographic perspective also makes available several selections from African-American authors and numerous transcriptions of Native American legends and oral narratives that focus upon women's lives. Economic class differences are explored through the inclusion of writings by slaves, indentured servants, and members of the mercantile class as well as of the upper-class.

Thematically, the included texts both complement and extend earlier thematic studies of early American literature. Those women writers who have been included in the canon have attained their status because they addressed themes that were critically acknowledged in the writings of their male counterparts: natural features and resources of the "New World," spiritual awakenings, relations between Native Americans and European settlers, patriot or loyalist sympathies, and what it means to be an American. All of these themes are evident in the selections included here as well. Other issues raised by these writers, however, should encourage new or varied intellectual engagements with themes such as women's education; the social and psychological complexities of girlhood, courtship, marriage, childbirth, and later life; sexuality; the legal status of women; domestic economies and women's work (especially as Native American narratives interrogate limited definitions of domesticity); the existence of subcommunities that support alternative ideologies to the dominant culture's laws and political theories; and the rise of abolitionist and feminist philosophies at the end of the eighteenth century as it became evident that the newly formed government did not afford equality to all of its citizens.

In some ways, however, this anthology's most significant contributions to the field may be rooted in the diversity of genres that it includes. While some nontraditional genres such as diaries and letters have always been studied by early Americanists, they have typically been limited to texts by authors such as John Winthrop or Thomas Jefferson who are initially recognized for their writings in traditional literary genres; thus the diaries and letters of these writers are seen as supplements to their primary writings and have rarely been examined as literary documents themselves. In contrast, this anthology includes authors for whom these nontraditional genres were their *primary* means of literary expression. A text's inclusion in one section does not preclude it from appropriately fitting into several other categories as well; sections are intended as a guide, not as a restriction. For instance, Abigail Abbott Bailey's *Memoirs* certainly constitutes a spiritual autobiography, but it may be equally well studied as a jeremiad or, as Ann Taves has astutely noted, in the tradition of captivity narratives (Taves 15–19); it is included here in the section on domestic records because of its unusual incorporation of accounts of violence within the domestic setting. Further, a few notable women—such as Judith Sargent Murray and Margaretta V. Bleecker Faugères—were gifted in many genres and thus selections from their bodies of work are dispersed throughout the anthology.

The process of recovering early women's voices has resulted in a treasury of writings from a broad spectrum of genres: letters, diaries and journals, memoirs and autobiographical narratives, legends, sermons, hymns, conversion narratives, petitions and other political documents, histories, essays, poetry, dramas, novels, and scientific tracts.

While acknowledging my indebtedness to several recent feminist historians who are re-educating all of us in early American and feminist studies, I would also assert that we have not yet even begun to acknowledge the extraordinary range of women's written or oral texts, the differences in their lives, and their prolific contributions to our early history. In my research for this anthology, I examined the lives and works of nearly four hundred women; it is impossible to reflect their diversity and accomplishments, their strengths and struggles, their successes and failures in one text. I hope that the excerpts in *American Women Writers to 1800* will encourage further study into the writers who are not included as well as those who are. Before outlining some facets of women's lives and writings in early America, let me comment on the organization of the anthology. As several feminist historians have recently argued, traditional studies of early societies and the organization of anthologies around exploration expeditions and wars are major factors in the exclusion of women; nor, in patriarchal cultures, do such events necessarily represent the most important elements of women's experiences. Certainly—and to a greater extent than is often acknowledged—women were a significant part of these endeavors, and I have included extensive sections on women's writings during the Revolution and other national events. But the richness of women's lives—in both their private *and* public facets—may best be appreciated by recognizing the conditions and processes under which they came of age, the vital role that the (extensive) domestic arena played in their lives and in the development of the Six Nations and the United States, and the many ways in which women inscribed for themselves priorities that at times supported but often differed from and challenged their male counterparts' visions. Thus I have organized this anthology into three major sections and sixteen subsections. While chronicity is acknowledged within each subsection and within this general introduction, it is not given the priority so evident in most anthologies. Chronicity breeds linear thinking, at the expense of many other ways of knowing. What interests me here, if I can excerpt an idea from Kristeva, is "less chronology than a *signifying space*, a both corporeal and desiring mental space" (214). In "Women's Time," Kristeva posited an emergent third-generation feminist "attitude":

> It seems to me that the role of what is usually called 'aesthetic practices' must increase . . . to demystify the identity of the symbolic bond itself, to demystify, therefore, the *community* of language as a universal and signifying tool, one which totalises and equalises. In order to bring out—along with the *singularity* of each person and, even more, along with the multiplicity of every person's possible identifications . . . —the *relativity of his/her symbolic as well as biological existence,* according to the variation in his/her specific symbolic capacities.[6]

It seems to me that, if we are to encourage any such new attitude, we will be well served by examining, to the extent possible, signifying spaces from the past in order to enhance future feminist explorations. So, Part I begins with "The Ages of Women," intended as a means of capturing such spaces and as a challenge to traditional scholarship, which has readily cast much of early American "aesthetic practices" in the prism of "The Age of Man." Part II, "Emerging Feminist Voices," is a bridge between women's lives as rendered in

---

6. Julia Kristeva, "Women's Time" in *The Kristeva Reader,* ed. Toril Moi (New York: Columbia UP, 1986), pp. 187–213.

8

Part I and the thematic and generic focus of Part III, "Origins, Revolutions, and Women in the Nations." Emphasizing the rise of feminist voices in early America, Part II suggests that it is out of women's lived experiences that feminist beliefs, literature, politics, and culture evolve. While a detailed introduction is given for each of the three parts of the anthology, the following discussion presents more broadly a view of women in early America.

To observe that women existed in North America long before Puritan immigrants arrived on the continent is barely to tap into a significant aspect of American women's history. Many of the highly developed and diverse cultures of the earliest Native Americans were matriarchal and/or worshipped female spirits such as Thought Woman whose "potentiality is dynamic and unimaginably powerful."[7] The creation stories of numerous tribes center on a Creatrix, and First Woman (unlike Christianity's Eve) is typically depicted as strong, confident, and culturally powerful. Women were valued "tale-spinners" in many early tribal societies:

> In tribal culture, anyone could make songs, women as well as men. Although in some societies women sang primarily to win power or protection for their men, song-making was also a way for a woman to achieve status in the tribe. A sort of unofficial copyright system prevailed in many areas, making the song the property of the person who composed and sang it.[8]

While we can no longer trace particular song-poems to an individual, we do have access to many ancient songs, legends, and histories that reveal cultural attitudes toward Native American women's places in society and that record their communal experiences as a means of passing their customs to the next generations. Although the natures of native and European settlers' cultures are in most ways strikingly different, in this sense these native "spinsters"[9]— weavers and tale-spinners alike—have much more in common with their early Euro-American counterparts than has often been recognized: whether by deed

7. Paula Gunn Allen, *The Sacred Hoop: Recovering the Feminine in American Literary Traditions* (Boston: Beacon, 1986), p. 15.

8. Jane B. Katz, ed., *I Am the Fire of Time: The Voices of Native American Women* (New York: E. P. Dutton, 1977), pp. xv–xvi. For other accounts of early American Indian women's cultural and literary lives, see Gunn Allen; Gretchen M. Bataille and Kathleen Mullen Sands, *American Indian Women: Telling Their Lives* (Lincoln: U of Nebraska P, 1984); Rayna Green, *Native American Women: A Bibliography* (Wichita Falls, TX: Ohoyo Resource Center, 1981); and Beverly Hungry Wolf, *The Ways of My Grandmothers* (New York: William Morrow, 1980).

9. Originally, a "spinster" was a woman who was adept in the culturally valued skills of spinning, weaving, and sewing. As Marta Weigle has discerned, this term devolved in European traditions and in the transposition of those traditions into North America until it denoted either the pejorative connotation of the single woman or was linked to witchcraft (*Spiders & Spinsters: Women and Mythology* [Albuquerque: U of New Mexico P, 1982], pp. 27–28). Chapter One of Weigle's text is an impressive collection of the mythology of "Spiders & Spinsters" throughout history and concludes with poems on the subject by Rose Terry Cooke and Adrienne Rich. For other feminist commentaries on the ways in which the meaning of "spinster" has moved from a valued position to one of denigration in patriarchal societies and the ways in which feminists have attempted to recover the positive meaning of women's work/words, see, for example, Mary Daly, *Gyn/Ecology: The Metaethics of Radical Feminism* (Boston: Beacon, 1978), and Susan Hill and Judy Chicago, *Embroidering Our Heritage: The Dinner Party Needlework* (1980).

or word, early women wove the fabric of American life and "letters" as surely as did their male counterparts.

The early explorer Richard Hakluyt details the presence of Native American women in his account of the first voyage to Virginia in 1584. On a journey up the Occam River to the island of Roanoke where a Native American village was well established, Hakluyt observes:

> When we came towards it, standing near unto the water's side, the wife of Granganimeo the king's brother came running out to meet us very cheerfully and friendly. Her husband was not then in the village; some of her people she commanded to draw our boat on shore . . . [and] having five rooms in her house, she caused us to sit down by a great fire, and after took off our clothes and washed them, and dried them again.[10]

Although Hakluyt fails to name the woman whose kindness so comforted him, he does recount her actions in memorable detail.

For centuries to follow, we will find this pattern of the European explorer/settler's rendering of Native American life far more prevalent than accounts by native peoples themselves. This is due in part to issues of orality, but equally (if not more) so to nineteenth- and twentieth-century critical practices. Yet there is a vast body of literature that can capture Native American perspectives on women's roles and teachings in early tribal communities. Selections in this anthology, for example, include the legend of "The First Ship," a Chinook account of a woman who sighted the first Spanish explorers in her region and warned her community of the impending danger; "Two Sisters and the Porcupine" (Menomini) and "The Ignorant Housekeeper" (Cherokee), which act as cautionary tales for female conduct; and "The Seven Stars," which represents the numerous narratives that explain natural phenomena. One of the striking elements of any body of Native American texts is the strong and integrated role that women had in early (especially precontact) tribal societies. While I have included Native American texts throughout the anthology, in the belief that no study of *American* literature can be complete without such texts, I wish to be explicit in the fact that I am not advocating all texts be read through one lens. Native American literatures must be examined in the same way that a colonial Georgian writer must be examined within the context of her own culture and not, say, from the same perspective as a Calvinist Puritan writer would be. But I also believe that there are theoretical means of examination that do not erase differences and that those means may be applicable to all people's (con)texts.

Mexican, European, and African women's histories in North America are of much briefer duration than those of Native American women, but they too arrived on the continent long before the English Puritans. In the fifteenth century, Christopher Columbus was authorized "to recruit for the [1492] expedition thirty women who received neither pay nor keep but were expected to work their passage and marry upon arrival."[11] In the next century, the Lady

---

10. Richard Hakluyt, *Voyages to the Virginia Colonies*, ed. A. L. Rowse (London: Century, 1986), pp. 71–72.

11. Samuel Eliott Morison, *The European Discovery of America*, 2 vols. (New York: Oxford UP, 1971, 1974), p. 2:142. The women were among the 100 convicts aboard ship.

of Cofitachique (fl. 1540) was ruler of the area where Georgia and South Carolina now conjoin. Taken captive by Hernando DeSota, she and an African slave escaped their captivity with the Spanish and returned to her village where she continued to rule. Also in the sixteenth century, a Mexican woman, Doña Ana de Zaldivar y Mendoza (fl. late 16th c.), like Queen Isabella of Spain, helped support explorations into New Mexico. Doña Ana and her spouse, Juan Guerra de Resa, funded Don Juan de Oñate's colonization of New Mexico, a colonization that strengthened Spanish and Mexican influences in the region but decimated many Native American tribes. In an agreement dated January 27, 1598, they stated:

> I, Doña Ana, by virtue of the authority given and granted to me, which I accept and use; and I, Juan de Guerra Resa—and we, husband and wife, in common agreement and full accord, . . . authorize the pledging of the amount that may be determined in order that the expedition and discoveries shall not be abandoned or delayed for lack of means.[12]

Many early Spanish and Mexican women of renown have been recovered by scholars in those fields of study (most notably, Sor Juana Inez de la Cruz), but—to date—I have been unable to identify other writings by Spanish-American or Mexican-American women. Undoubtedly this lack says more about our own critical moment than it does about literary history.

"Isabella" is the first known African woman to be brought to mainland America (although if we consider the West Indies, the Spanish system of plantation slavery there had begun as early as 1502). When Isabella arrived in Jamestown in August 1619, she was one of "20. and odd Negroes" who had been purchased several months earlier from the Dutch in exchange for provisions; about four years later, Isabella gave birth to a son, the first American-born African child. Although it would be several years before the American slave trade was fully established, women were ensnared in this destructive system from its beginning.[13] Yet the writings of African Americans included in this anthology suggest many ways in which women struggled for an individual voice and respect for their race. Phillis Wheatley (c. 1753–1784) is, of course, the most renowned pre-twentieth-century African-American poet in literary history, and her poetry has recently begun to receive the critical attention that it deserves. But the one extant poem by Lucy Terry (1730–1821), Wheatley's poetic predecessor, also deserves considerable attention, not only for the details of the poem itself but for the satirical humor that she brings to her quite divergent vision of the captivity narrative tradition.[14] And "Belinda" (fl. 1782), a slave

12. Quoted in George P. Hammond and Agapito Rey, eds., *Don Juan de Oñate, Colonizer of New Mexico 1598–1628*, 2 vols. (n.p.: U of New Mexico P, 1953), pp. I:375–376.

13. For accounts of early African-American history, see Lerone Bennett, Jr., *Before the Mayflower: A History of Black America*, exp. ed. (New York: Penguin, 1982), especially ch. 2; John B. Boles, *Black Southerners 1619–1869* (Lexington: UP of Kentucky, 1984), ch. 1; Joanne M. Braxton, *Black Women Writing Autobiography: A Tradition Within a Tradition* (Philadelphia: Temple UP, 1989), introduction; and Marion Wilson Starling, *The Slave Narrative: Its Place in American History* (Boston: G. K. Hall, 1981).

14. See Sharon M. Harris, " 'Oh lack-a-day!': Lucy Terry's Satire of the Captivity Narrative Tradition" (forthcoming).

who narrated a petition, also warrants recognition; her text begins the African-American women's autobiographical tradition, and it links her in several ways with other women: as an oral rendering, her work should be understood in the long tradition of marginalized women's oral narratives; and as a petition, this text aligns her with one of the earliest forms of nontraditional written protest among early American women of all races.

In the same group of Jamestown colonists that included Isabella were Caucasian women who apparently came to Virginia as indentured servants. The early records of the Virginia Company note that a law was enacted on August 4, 1619, to control the activities of these women, especially in terms of marriage: "No maide or woman servant, either now resident in the Colonie or hereafter to come, shall contract herselfe in marriage without either the consent of her parents or of her M^r or M^{ris}, or of the magistrate and minister of the place both together."[15] After early difficulties in the colony, the leaders decided that marriage would create an atmosphere of community and restraint that was badly needed if the colony was to thrive. Thus in 1621, the directors of the Virginia Company sent to the colony

> as many maide & yong weomen as will make upp the number of fiftie, wth those twelve formerly sent in the Marmaduk; wch we hope shalbe received wth the same Christian pietie and charitie as they are sent from hence; the providinge for them at theire first landing, and disposinge of them in Mariage (wch is o^r cheife intent) we leave to yor care & wisdome. . . ."[16]

Although the Company's leaders obviously viewed these early women as little more than disposable goods, they did caution this time that the women should be provided "fitting services, till they may hapne uppon good matches," and charged the colonists to allow a woman to "fondly bestow her self" if she chose, "for the libertie of Mariadge we dare not infrindg."[17] However, if a woman did select her own marriage partner, a "quantitie of tobacco proporconed" was to be paid to the colony, a stipulation which only reinforced the sense of women slaves, indentured servants, and free women as commodities for exchange in early Virginia.

American studies have centered on English settlers in the colonies, but colonists from many other regions settled in America as well. Within two years (1619–1621), for example, the marriageable English women noted above arrived in Virginia, the Pilgrims settled in Plymouth Plantation, and the Dutch established New Amsterdam. The Dutch settlement offers a quite different view of women's lives in early America from that of either of its contemporaries. Throughout the seventeenth century (even after the English conquered them in 1664), the Dutch settlers developed a prosperous and far more egalitarian community than the Massachusetts Puritans or the Virginia settlers, at least within the upper-classes. Comparing the lives of two Dutch colonists suggests the diversity of opportunities for women within that community. It is notable

---

15. *The Records of the Virginia Company of London*, ed. Susan Myra Kingsbury (Washington, D.C.: U.S. Government Printing Office, 1933), pp. 3:173–174.

16. Ibid., p. 3:505.

17. Ibid.

that, unlike the English property laws that prevailed in Massachusetts Bay Colony and elsewhere, the Dutch laws allowed a woman to decide at the time of marriage how she wanted her property to be handled. Under *manus*, her property became her husband's; under *usus*, however, she retained full control of her own property. *Usus* also allowed her to go into business for herself if she chose. This law was maintained by the Dutch settlers in New Amsterdam; it was repealed only when the English took over the region in the late seventeenth century. Maria van Cortlandt van Rensselaer (1645–1689), a second-generation settler who married into the aristocratic leading family of Rensselaerwyck Colony, was a woman whose widowhood thrust her into the position of a temporary administrator of the colony. It was not a role that she would have chosen for herself, as her letters attest, but she struggled to do justice to the community as a whole and to ward off intrusions of the English whenever possible. Born only a decade later, Alida Schuyler Livingston (1656–1727) lived a quite different life. Her first husband was a van Rensselaer, but she found her true satisfactions in her second marriage where she was able to establish an egalitarian relationship and develop her talents as a businesswoman. Whereas Maria had seen her leadership role as a burden, Alida embraced such responsibilities, willingly undertook the management of the family estate while her husband was absent, and eventually took on the role of manager of their Albany properties both before and after her husband chose to retire.

Even in our studies of New England Puritan women's culture, many traits of daily life inscribed in their texts suggest the need to reconsider the assertions of rampant illiteracy among women. What *is* evident is the patriarchal culture's centuries-long opposition to women's devotion to learning. As Adrienne Rich has observed, the disorder created by Anne Hutchinson's resistance to the theology of the Massachusetts Bay leaders led John Winthrop in 1645 to write his now infamous statement that the "sad infirmity" of a young woman in the colony must be attributed to "her giving herself wholly to reading and writing"; Winthrop asserted that these activities had resulted in her "loss of understanding, and reason."[18] Anne Bradstreet (1612–1672) of Massachusetts Bay Colony is, of course, well recognized for her education and literary talents; many other women also wrote with great skill and made known their estimation of education. Although the Winthrop women did not receive formal educations, they all could read and write, and they produced a significant body of correspondence. Lucy Winthrop Downing (1600/01–1679) raised concerns about the availability of university education only for her son,[19] but Winthrop Downing's own writing talents reveal her extensive education and adept means of expression. In the neighboring Pilgrim community, as early as the 1650s women like Judith

---

18. Quoted in Adrienne Rich, "Anne Bradstreet and Her Poetry" in *The Works of Anne Bradstreet*, ed. Jeannine Hensley (Cambridge: Belknap, 1967), p. xiv; see also *Winthrop's Journal: A History of New England, 1630–1649*, ed. James Kendall Hosmer (New York: Scribner, 1908), p. 2:225.

19. Winthrop Downing makes no mention of concern about education for young women; this may be most readily attributed to prevailing attitudes about an appropriate women's sphere, but it may also reflect the strained relations between Winthrop Downing and her stepdaughter, who was sent to the colony before Winthrop Downing and her husband made the journey. See the entry in "Epistolary Exchanges" for details.

Smith, Ann Atwood, and Elizabeth Pole purchased several books and established private libraries in their homes.[20] These libraries were undoubtedly sparse—records detail only the value not the quantity of books in an individual's estate and only Atwood's collection seems at all on a par with the libraries of her far better educated compatriots Miles Standish and William Bradford—but they suggest that many women who have not been included in our historical accounts of the early Puritans were at least capable of reading and certainly valued the written word.[21] In subsequent eras, too, several distinguished women poets appeared: Anna Thompson Hayden (1648–post-1720), Jane Dunlap (fl. 1771), Phillis Wheatley (c. 1753–1784), Sarah Wentworth Morton (1759–1846) and Margaretta V. Bleecker Faugères (1771–1801), among numerous others. Although this period also experienced a proliferation of women's spiritual autobiographical narratives, most of the extant writings by New England women before the Revolution are in nontraditional genres, such as letters and diaries.

The literature of New England in the early period of American literary history is a rich and diverse body of work, but other areas on the continent were also rapidly developing, and with geographic and economic advancement, there emerged numerous writers of significance. From the southern colonies, we have an extraordinary body of women's writings that denies the still too-prevalent stereotype of the plantation Southern belle and instead reveals women like Mary Stafford (fl. 1711), Margaret Brett Kennett (fl. 1723–25), and Eliza Lucas Pinckney (c. 1722–1793) whose courage, imagination, and hearty strength led them into activities far beyond the norm and shaped their diverse writings. In the mid-Atlantic states, Quaker writings dominate the literary and cultural scene. Although the Quaker leader John Woolman is well known, few women in that culture have received similar attention; this is unfortunate, since Quaker women's early exposure to education and a community willingness to have women's opinions voiced allowed for the emergence of numerous texts of literary, cultural, and historical significance. Hannah Callowhill Penn (1671–1726) is representative of the blending of Quaker women's propensity for participation in religious and civic community endeavors; her extant writings are letters only, but other Quaker women produced a vast body of literature in epistolary and other genres.

The influence of religion in early American culture and in the development of women's literary history cannot be overestimated. Puritan Calvinism and its contending counterparts in New England were, paradoxically, both a means for women's oppression and for their movement toward a more public voice in the community. The hierarchical nature of Calvinist tenets—God/man/woman and child—certainly determined the limited scope of women's opportunities in early New England, but the emphasis upon salvation as a personal experience that was abetted by written explorations of the status of one's soul offered women

---

20. Thomas Goddard Wright, *Literary Culture in Early New England, 1620–1730* (1920; rpt., New York: Russell & Russell, 1966), pp. 28–29.

21. See *Reading in America: Literature and Social History*, ed. Cathy N. Davidson (Baltimore: Johns Hopkins UP, 1989), for a broader discussion of literacy in early America, and especially E. Jennifer Monaghan's article in that collection, "Literacy Instruction and Gender in Colonial New England," pp. 53–80 (originally published in *American Quarterly* 40 [Mar. 1988]: 18–41).

an opportunity to write not only poetry and letters but also spiritual autobiographies, diaries, and occasionally to make public theological statements. In the struggle toward salvation, language did not have to be so rigidly tempered, and although the Self must always be understood as dangerous and necessarily subjected to God's will, subjectivity did emerge in tentative forms that opened avenues of exploration for later writers.

One of the most overlooked areas of women's literary development is the advent of the Great Awakenings in eighteenth-century America. Typically understood only in terms of figures such as Jonathan Edwards, Charles Chauncey, and George Whitefield (and more recently, to include marginalized figures such as the converted Mohegan, Samson Occom), these religious revival periods throughout the eighteenth century garnered for women extraordinary moments of access to public expression and, often, to the publication of their literary endeavors. Religious poetry flourished. The sisters Jane Colman Turell (1708–1735) and Abigail Colman Dennie (1715–1745) offer a study in contrasts that emerged at this time: daughters of a Calvinist minister, Colman Turell was recognized for her piety and the poetry she wrote that complied with Calvinist traditions, while Colman Dennie rejected patriarchal conceptions of "filial duty" in her poetry as in her life. (It should be noted that because Colman Dennie resisted cultural traditions, her poetry was not valued and only one of her poems is now extant, whereas Colman Turell's life and writings were honored and published after her death and have been recently reproduced in a facsimile edition.) Sarah Parsons Moorhead (fl. 1741–42), on the other hand, used poetry as a means to openly address James Davenport and Gilbert Tennent, leaders of the 1740s revival; while Parsons Moorhead adhered to Calvinist theology, she counseled the two leaders on their methodology. A few women also recognized the Awakenings as an opportunity to expand their religious roles. As noted earlier, Sarah Haggar Osborn (1714–1796) is an interesting counterpart to Anne Hutchinson. Although Haggar Osborn did not challenge the tenets of her Newport, Rhode Island, community leaders, she did follow Parsons Moorhead's pattern of challenging the methods by which the leaders practiced those tenets. Like Hutchinson, Haggar Osborn organized prayer groups within her home; in the 1760s, she challenged Calvinists' separatist ideologies by having men and women participate together in the groups and, most notably, by also including freed and enslaved African Americans in her home sessions.

The revivals also encouraged a new interest in the publication of women's essays and autobiographies. The *Devotional Papers* of Sarah Prince Gill (1728–1771) appeared shortly after her death. Late in the century, books were published by Susanna Anthony (1726–1791), Martha Wadsworth Brewster (fl. 1757), Jenny Fenno (fl. 1791), and many other women. The impact of the Awakenings continued well into the next century, as evidenced in the diaries and the conversion work of the Cherokee religious activist Catherine Brown (1800–?).[22]

But, as scholars have long discerned, New England Calvinism was by no

---

22. One of the notable elements of finding Native American autobiographies, like those by African Americans, is that a writer's work was much more likely to be published and preserved if she or he had converted to Christianity, like Brown or Samson Occom, among others.

means the only religion to thrive in early America. The Society of Friends (Quakers) afforded women quite liberal expression of their opinions and experiences, and many Quaker women published their religious narratives. Bathsheba Bowers (c. 1672–1718) published a spiritual autobiography in 1709, and she chose to live an unconventional life that was nourished by her religious independence; Jane Fenn Hoskens (1694–?) and Sophia Wigington Hume (1702–1774), like many other Quaker women, became traveling ministers whose works spread throughout the colonies and to Europe as well; and later writers such as Hannah Griffitts (1727–1817), a letter-writer and poet, and Hannah Callender (1737–1801), a diarist, represent the numerous women activists and writers whose outspokenness and style challenge the passive stereotype of early American women. Although the Calvinists and Quakers constitute the largest bodies of women religious writers in the early period, it should also be noted that Elizabeth Ann Bayley Seton's (1774–1821) work in the late eighteenth century resulted in the establishment of the Catholic Sisters of Charity organization, and Bayley Seton herself became America's first Catholic saint. Women religious activists were instrumental in the establishment of many religious sects in early America; among them were Barbara Ruckle Heck (1734–1804, Methodist), Ann Lee (1736–1784, Shaker), the Catholic activists Philipine Duchesne (1769?–1852) and Sister Marie Tranchepain (?–1733), Abigail Levy Franks (1696–1756, Jewish), Jemima Wilkinson (1752–1819, Quaker), and Judith Sargent Murray (1751–1820, Universalist).

It was the American Revolution, however, that opened numerous avenues for women's public and literary expression and allowed them more freedom in addressing secular as well as religious issues. Not only did women like Margaret Hill Morris (1737–1816) of New Jersey act as nurses, or like Esther deBerdt Reed (1747–1780) and Martha Dandridge Custis Washington (1731–1802) form organizations such as the Ladies Association to support and supply the troops, women were also often instrumental in preserving family estates and certainly in maintaining the local agrarian economies. The letters of Mary Bartlett (?–1789), for instance, reveal one woman's endeavors to maintain the family lands as productive entities while her husband attended the Continental Congresses; she acted as overseer and managed the planting and harvesting of crops while raising a large family and giving birth to a child in her husband's absence. These early activities—and the subsequent denial of women's status as citizens in the new nation—were instrumental in the development of early movements for women's equality.[23] In the years preceding and during the American Revo-

23. It is interesting to note, in contrast, the long history of patriarchy's subjugation of women in society and yet their equally prevalent pattern of using female analogies for the problems within their societies. Cotton Mather's *Magnalia Christi Americana*, for instance, is a hagiography of the men who (he asserts) founded America. Other than in reference to the witchcraft trials (and with a few brief exceptions, such as a passing reference to Anne Bradstreet), women are excluded from this process. However, when Mather begins to lament the degeneracy of later generations, he writes: "Religion brought forth prosperity, and the daughter destroyed the mother" (*Magnalia Christi Americana, or the Ecclesiastical History of New England*, ed. Raymond J. Cunningham [New York: Frederick Ungar, 1970], p. 27). As Margaret Olofson Thickstun has astutely recognized, such analogies are deeply rooted in the Pauline theological tradition; see *Fictions of the Feminine: Puritan Doctrine and the Representation of Women* (Ithaca: Cornell UP, 1988).

lution, women recorded their opinions about war and the culturally fracturing political disputes of the eighteenth century in striking commentaries, both in private journals and letters as well as in published texts. Their publications included broadsides (such as "The Sentiments of an American Woman," 1780), poetry (see Ann Eliza Schuyler Bleecker [1752–1783] and Mercy Otis Warren [1728–1814], among others), and political tracts and petitions (see, for instance, texts by the African-American slave Belinda [fl. 1782], and the Euro-American colonist Letitia Cunningham [fl. 1783]). What emerges is women's significant engagement with the philosophical issues of the era, including the appropriate political order for a new nation. Currently recognizable voices, such as Abigail Smith Adams (1744–1818) and Judith Sargent Murray (1751–1820), were joined herein by Lydia Minturn Post (fl. 1776–1783), Patience Lovell Wright (1725–1786), and Mary Willing Byrd (1740–1814), among many others.

Although the conclusion of war forced most women to return to traditional roles, it would be erroneous to assume that, until the nineteenth century, women passively accepted their marginalized position in society. From a twentieth-century perspective, it is too often assumed that women's dissent began at Seneca Falls, but women's challenges to systems of oppression and subjugation in America begin with the earliest known existence of women on the continent. As Jane B. Katz has discerned, "There is, in the oral literature, a tradition of independence, even of dissent."[24] Nor was Anne Hutchinson the only seventeenth-century woman to resist Puritan authorities. When Roger Williams was banished to Rhode Island, several of his followers remained in Salem, Massachusetts, but refused to be silenced. Jane Verin,[25] Margery Reeves, and Margery Holliman "refused to worship with other members of the congregation, the latter two because they denied that the churches of the Bay were true churches of Christ."[26]

Most important, the desire to write remained a compelling influence in many Euro-American women's lives. Diaries and correspondence abound in the early federal years, and they reveal both the oppressive nature of women's lives (e.g., Abigail Abbott Bailey [1746–1815]) as well as the rise of independent voices (e.g., Eliza Southgate Bowne [1783–1809]). The publication of women's writings also increased rapidly in these years: we have extraordinary works by Mercy Otis Warren (1728–1814), a poet, dramatist, and letter-writer; novels by Susanna Haswell Rowson (1761–1824) and, most notably, by Hannah

24. Katz, p. xvii. As Katz observes, "In a Cheyenne legend, Corn Woman left an abusive husband. Ordered by her brother to return she did so but told her husband: 'Don't ever try to beat me again. If you do, I'll fight you with whatever is at hand. I don't care if you kill me' " (xvii). As is evident in this episode, however, the abuse itself is not socially condemned. On this point, women of all races and classes were, unfortunately, equalized. In seventeenth-century Rhode Island, for instance, Jacob Verin was censured for not allowing his wife freedom of conscience in her religious practices (Ola Elizabeth Winslow, *Master Roger Williams: A Biography* [New York: Macmillan, 1957], p. 140); Verin was not censured, however, for the force and brutality he used in his attempts to control his spouse. See also Abigail Abbott Bailey's endurance of brutality in the excerpt from her journal included in the "Domestic Lives" section.

25. See note 24 above.

26. Philip Gura, *A Glimpse of Sion's Glory: Puritan Radicalism in New England, 1620–1660* (Middletown, CT: Wesleyan UP, 1984), p. 43.

Webster Foster (1758–1840), who admonished the double standards for men and women in American culture; and the profound writings of Judith Sargent Murray, whose feminist essays, poetry, and dramas demanded the "equality of the sexes." Although we are most familiar with the "republican motherhood" process of reacculturation after the Revolution, the 1790s was in fact a decade of public debate on women's cultural roles. The interest of so many American women in the writings of Catherine Macauley and, more cautiously, of Mary Wollstonecraft reflects their concerns with women's rights and expanded roles in the so-called Enlightenment era.[27] It was an era in which women's roles were advocated in such diverse scopes as the True Woman (see below) and woman as man's equal. If such discussions rarely move beyond a concept of women as "Woman," under whatever guise of limitation or liberty, the nature of women's roles and responsibilities in American culture would never again be considered uncontestable.

From the time of the Puritans through the end of the eighteenth century, when written texts were more prevalent and modern scholars more interested in processes of preservation and assessment, our knowledge about women's lives and writings rapidly increases in comparison with the sparse accounts of the earliest women on the continent. From Alice Morse Earle at the end of the nineteenth century and Julia Cherry Spruill in the early twentieth century, women scholars have made significant inroads in the recovery and reassessment of early American women's contributions to the development of our national literature and history. As we recover, assess, and theorize women's early writings, we must also expand our cultural understandings of early America. A brief and highly selective notation of the fields pursued by some early women will suggest the diverse landscape that was early American culture: the colonial leader Lady Deborah Moody (1600–1660); the African-American woman known only as "Alice," one of our earliest oral historians; artists such as Laetitia Sage Benbridge (?–c. 1780), Henrietta Johnston (?–1729), and Mary Roberts (?–1761); inventors including Mary Peck Butterworth (1686–1775) and Sybilla Masters (?–1720); actresses such as Susanna Haswell Rowson (1761–1824) and Sarah Hallam Douglass (?–1773); numerous printers, most notable of whom was Mary Katherine Goddard (1738–1816); teachers such as Sarah Pierce (1767–1852), Rebecca Jones (fl. 1770s–80s), and Anna Caritas Nitschmann Zinzendorf (1715–1760); interpreters and/or agents, including Elizabeth Wooley Davenport (?–post-1660), Coosaponakessa or "Mary Musgrove" (fl. 1734), and Catherine Montour (c. 1684–c. 1752); businesswomen who explored many avenues of enterprise, including Anna Rutter Savage Nutt (1686–1760), who owned an iron foundry, "Anna Nutt and Company"; Mar-

27. For a discussion of the intellectual debates of the Enlightenment era and the means by which they engaged but most often excluded women or presupposed women's irrationality, see Linda K. Kerber, *Women of the Republic: Intellect and Ideology in Revolutionary America* (New York: Norton, 1980, 1986), ch. 1; Donovan, *Feminist Theory: The Intellectual Traditions of American Feminism*, exp. ed. (New York: Continuum, 1992), ch. 1; and for the impact of the new sciences on women through the issue of witchcraft, see Carolyn Merchant, *The Death of Nature: Women, Ecology, and the Scientific Revolution* (New York: Harper, 1980). What is too often ignored, as well, is the erasure of racial issues in Enlightenment philosophies.

garet Hardenbroek de Vries Phillipse (?–1690), who was a shipowner and merchant; and Maria de Peyster Schrick Spratt Provoost (?–1700), who was also a merchant.[28]

To the nineteenth- and early twentieth-century historians noted above and their contemporary heirs (including Linda Kerber, Nancy F. Cott, and Laurel Thatcher Ulrich in history and Cathy Davidson, Annette Kolodny, and Amy Schrager Lang in literature, and *many* others), I owe an inestimable debt, and it is my hope that this anthology will spur many other feminist scholars to pursue research in this field. Indeed, in the eight years during which I researched, compiled, and edited this volume, there has been a significant (if still relatively small) output of published essays and books on early American women's writings. It is a promising beginning.

The process of revising canons should never be limited to the mere inclusion of additional texts; at their best, revisionist activities allow us to interrogate longheld beliefs and to reassess our own criteria of evaluation. As Mary Jacobus has argued,

> The rediscovery of a female literary tradition need not mean a return to specifically "female" (that is, potentially confining) domains, any more than the feminist colonizing of Marxist, psychoanalytic, or poststructuralist modes of thought necessarily means a loss of that alien and critical relation which is one aspect of women's inheritance. Rather, they involve a recognition that all attempts to inscribe female difference within writing are a matter of inscribing women within the fictions of one kind or another (whether literary, critical, or psychoanalytic); and hence, that what is at stake for both women writing and writing about women is the rewriting of these fictions—the work of revision which makes "the difference of view" a question rather than an answer, and a question to be asked not simply of women, but of writing too.[29]

I was trained in the era of the transition from New Critical to Postmodern theories and now embrace transatlantic feminist theories.[30] Luce Irigaray reminds us that women's languages will remain "inaudible for whoever listens to them

28. See the selected listing of "Notable Early American Women" at the end of this anthology for a more detailed description of early women's writings and activities.

29. Mary Jacobus, "The Difference of View" in *The Feminist Reader: Essays in Gender and the Politics of Literary Criticism*, ed. Catherine Belsey and Jane Moore (New York: Basil Blackwell, 1989), pp. 61–62.

30. I understand transatlantic feminism to be a tenuous locale, but its very tenuousness seems to capture the richness of the present unfixed moment of feminist thought in which flexibility and openness are necessary modes of engagement. Naomi Schor has identified this locale as the locus of the trickster, but as she asserts, "If we are to go beyond the current split (when it is not an impasse) in feminist literary criticism, we will have to recognize that, to a degree that has perhaps not been sufficiently measured, *history inhabits sexual difference*" ("Reading Double: Sand's Difference" in *The Poetics of Gender*, ed. Nancy K. Miller [New York: Columbia UP, 1986], p. 267). It is my belief that transatlantic feminism will discern many other "inhabitancies" that have the potential not only to recognize diacritical processes such as *discours décousu* (discussed below) but also to move feminist theory out of the impasse—which is necessary especially in these days of rampant backlash.

with ready-made grids."[31] Close examination of nontraditional genres, where aesthetic standards have not been established and thus do not as readily condition our responses, can at times bring a reader to the quite exciting position of having to find an alternative discourse as a means of explaining—to herself and to others—what she values in these texts. Let me suggest, through a discussion of the development of one facet of women's poetics, one of the many ways in which my own work with early American women's diaries has encouraged me to reconsider certain aesthetic judgments.

A recognition of what I will term the "associativeness" of women's writing needs to be a central facet of the ongoing evaluation of women's poetics. While in part this may be understood in the context of Hélène Cixous's assertion of *feminine écriture*'s fluidity and the connections of that fluidity with women's physiology, it is, to my mind, much less biologically than experientially induced. Josephine Donovan, in setting forth what she identifies as "six structural conditions" integral to shaping women's experiences and thereby their aesthetic judgments, has denoted that because women have most often "been confined/consigned to the domestic" sphere, "traditional women's consciousness" has been shaped by the "non-progressive, repetitive, and static" nature of that work. A women's poetics, then, Donovan asserts, will have to consider "the cyclic experience of women's lives," and she expands on this through example.[32]

In passing, however, she remarks also on the "fundamental 'interruptibility' " of domestic work, including women's practice of writing within that arena. As I indicated at the beginning of this introduction, women's writings and their other forms of work are indelibly linked in the early period. Donovan perceives the interruptibility of domestic work as "contribut[ing] to a consciousness that is aware of contingency, that perceives itself bound to chance, not in total control."[33] I would agree that this fundamental facet of women's experiences shapes their consciousness and their writing styles and valuations, but I would argue that, rather than resulting in a perception of loss of control (with the negative connotations Donovan applies to such a loss[34]), some of the best early American women writers have often taken interruptibility and made it their own.

This interruptive mode of discourse is most often reflected in women's private writings through what has traditionally been viewed as fractured syntax.

31. Luce Irigaray, *This Sex Which Is Not One*, trans. Catherine Porter (Ithaca: Cornell UP, 1985).

32. Josephine Donovan, "Towards a Women's Poetics" in *Feminist Issues in Literary Scholarship*, ed. Shari Benstock (Bloomington: Indiana UP, 1987), pp. 101–102.

33. Ibid., p. 102.

34. "Control" conveys a highly masculinized concept of dominance and rigidity. Comparing the differing models of reading espoused by George Poulet and Adrienne Rich, Patrocinio Schweickart has noted "that the metaphors of mastery and submission, of violation and control, so prominent in Poulet's essay, are entirely absent in Rich's essay. . . . In the paradigm of reading implicit in [Rich's] essay, the dialectic of control (which shapes feminist readings of male texts) gives way to the dialectic of communication" ("Reading Ourselves: Toward a Feminist Theory of Reading" in *Speaking Gender*, ed. Elaine Showalter [New York: Routledge, Chapman and Hall, 1989], p. 36). While models of reading and writing are not simply interchangeable, the cultural conditioning behind these dialectics of reading are certainly applicable to our understanding of differences in discursive modes as well.

But if we think of Emily Dickinson's exquisite use of dashes and line breaks, we can begin to understand that interruptibility can be taken to extraordinary literary and philosophical heights. Numerous women writers before Dickinson used similar writing techniques; appropriately, this most often appears in private writings in which the writer felt less restricted in expressing her thoughts. As Elizabeth Ann Bayley Seton, founder of the Sisters of Charity and the first American Catholic saint, observed when writing to her closest friend, Julianna Scott, "Why do I tell you all this? How is it that never can I preserve any constancy in a letter to you, but always involuntarily express my thoughts as they arise? I write some letters where the words drop so heavily that I can scarcely form them at all; but when I begin 'Dear Julia,' they flow faster than the pen can write them."[35] In reading early eighteenth-century American women's diaries and journals, I am often struck by the proliferation of parenthetic remarks, of bracketed phrases, of dashes and ellipses, of marginalia that sometimes act as a dialogue with the author's first thoughts, and of the extended sentences through which we can visualize the author's "mental optics" (to borrow Phillis Wheatley's phrase) as a flight of many intellectual take-offs and prosperous landings.

This is not discontinuity; it is associativeness born of interruptibility. The best of these writers does not want to tie down her thoughts to a linear pattern (a pattern often misconstrued as an absolute for logic). She allows her mind to rove through multiple associations and—importantly—when these texts are written to be shared with another, she assumes that her reader will be willing and able to engage in these same fast and fluent mental shifts, grasping the complexity and infiniteness of the ideas engaged and the contiguousness of meaning which her style conveys.

Because of these interruptive and nontraditional associative patterns, women's private writings might easily be dismissed as "nonliterary." Such a dismissal, however, would be a failure of comprehension on our part rather than a failure of style in their writings. Though it needs to be reiterated, it is certainly not a new idea that the incorporation of a marginalized group's literature into mainstream critical consciousness will alter both our understanding of a body of literature and its aesthetic valuations. In 1895 Victoria Earle Matthews, fiction writer, essayist, and cofounder of the National Association of Colored Women, published an essay in which she asserted the same concept: "when the literature of our race is developed," Earle Matthews prophesied, "it will of necessity be different in all essential points of greatness . . . from what we may at the present time, for convenience, call American literature."[36] This is equally true if we think in terms of gender as well as race. An analysis of early American women's pre-Revolutionary diaries, then, offers an apt example of how a feminist reconsideration of women's poetics may enhance our understanding of these texts.

35. Elizabeth Seton, *Letters of Mother Seton to Mrs. Julianna Scott*, ed. Joseph B. Code, 2nd ed. (New York: Father Salvator M. Burgio Memorial Foundation in Honor of Mother Seton, 1960), letter dated October 28, 1798.

36. Quoted in Henry Louis Gates, Jr., "Foreword: In Her Own Write," *Iola Leroy, or Shadows Uplifted* (New York: Oxford UP, 1988), p. xv.

Let me begin with a few examples of what I mean by interruptive techniques, and then I will explore how some women converted this environmentally determined writing style into an intellectual and philosophical aesthetic. Mary Wright Cooper's diary of the 1760s reflects both the domestic interruptibility of her life on a Long Island farm and yet also a glimpse of talent for alliteration, descriptive adjectives, and such. During the following entries, several relatives have been visiting and the toll it has taken on Wright Cooper is evident:

> *Tuesday [March 7, 1769].* Cole. O, I am dirty and tired allmost to death cooking for so many peopel, freted almost to death. New moon at 1 a'clok this night. Begins [ ] snow.
>
> *Wednsday.* Snow afternoon. Clear bu[t] cold. Tabethia here.
>
> *Friday.* Clears with a harde north west wind. Extreme cold. Jo Cooper winnowing wheate. Black squall clouds and a most frightfull wind this night.
>
> *Saterday.* Extreeme high wind. Col. [Fr]eeses all day long. O, I am tired most to death, dirty and distressed. have no cloths to weare to meeten. extremely distrest. I se no [ ] in these days. My darkness [? is gre]ate. . . . Black att hearte, oh Lord. . . .

The "harde north west wind" becomes a leitmotif in Wright Cooper's diary, reflecting both her internal and external worlds. Yet as exhausted as Wright Cooper obviously was, it is equally apparent that she felt compelled to jot down—however cursorily—fragments of her life and thoughts.

Anna Green Winslow's life could not, in most ways, have been more different from Wright Cooper's. From a well-to-do family, Anna was sent as an adolescent to a finishing school in Boston; while there, she resided with an aunt and uncle. Her diary was kept as a letterbook for her mother. (I will discuss more fully below the question of the so-called private nature of these writings.) Yet the domestic demands on an upper-class, twelve-year-old girl are evident even here, and her diary entry for February 22, 1772, reflects the manner in which interruptibility can begin to be a means of second-voice commentary on one's own writing:

> I have spun 30 knots of linning yarn, and (partly) new footed a pair of stockings for Lucinda, read a part of the pilgrim's progress, coppied part of my text journal (that if I live a few years longer, I may be able to understand it, for aunt sais, that to her, the contents as I first mark'd them, were an impenetrable secret) play'd some, tuck'd a great deal (Aunt Deming says it is very true) laugh'd enough, & I tell aunt it is all human *nature*, if not human reason. And now, I wish my honored mamma a very good night.

Her aunt's comments, which she records parenthetically in her text, act as acculturizing controls which Anna resists primarily through humor; this pattern is maintained throughout her three-year diary.

If we look to a complex figure such as Sarah Haggar Osborn, an extremely pious Calvinist, and the diaries she maintained in the 1750s and 1760s, we can begin to understand how the construction of the self as subject in nontraditional autobiographical narratives such as diaries and letters aligns itself with the associativeness of interruptibility in many women's texts. Paradoxically, in Calvinist theology, the self must be the focal point for explorations of the status of one's soul, and yet there must be no aggrandizement of the self. Humility and self-discovery rarely go hand in hand—to the modern mind; but the Puritans believed that it was the ego or the will (the self) that acted as a wall between the communicant and God's enfusing grace. How, then, to write one's life, especially on a daily basis? It was, as Haggar Osborn understood it, a study in denying the external life so that one's "eyes may be with the cherubims fix'd turning inwards."[37] Author/ity of self must be denied, but authority is often unwittingly harbored in the commands that the "sinner" casts toward God to take up His rightful role of power—do this to me, to our congregation, "for thy own Honour," Haggar Osborn repeatedly commands. This process forces the diarist to gain a decentered sense of power at best (which was typical for all Puritans in their religious meditations), but that "power" then demands *for itself* subjugation and repression in the guise of salvation (and women's roles, unlike men's, in public matters demanded acts of subjugation and repression as well). Thus, for women, the balance between humility and activism under patriarchy was always at odds with self-discovery (subjectivity) and thus with salvation. This process surely abetted so many New England women's adherence to the cult of domesticity.[38] But the subtle, perhaps unconscious struggle for subjectivity also suggests where the longstanding impetus to resist that "cult" ideology arose.

Humility was always a struggle for an activist such as Sarah Haggar Osborn. She repeatedly desires that God "clothe me with Humility," as if it were a garment she could put on to mask her natural assertiveness. She ultimately finds two means of maintaining her activism and yet aiming for humility. One means is to speak of herself in the third person, especially when she is under attack from the church elders for holding prayer groups in her home—"the poor distressed oppressed one she is the work of thy Hands &c and now all yt should be for Her are against Her I pray thee appear for Her Help preserve her from any dreadful thing and snatch Her as a brand out of the burning. . . ."[39] This entry constitutes a clear marginalization of herself in the face of authority; so, too, does her second means of synthesizing activism and humility, but it is a means that affords her much more comfort: she aligns herself with marginalized groups, most often with a women's community. The following entry follows several days of attempting to find humility, which ultimately Haggar Osborn attains only through a promise to "yield pasive when I cant yield active obedience":

> [Friday, April 10, 1767] blessed be God after Lying down to rest a while God graciously recruited my strength and spirits and kindly carryd me to His House and

---

37. Sarah Haggar Osborn, 1767 diary, p. 130. All page numbering for Haggar Osborn's unpublished diaries follow her own pagination.

38. Barbara Welter's classic essay, "The Cult of True Womanhood: 1820–1860" (*American Quarterly* 18 [Summer 1966]), sets specific nineteenth-century dates for True Womanhood and the cult of domesticity. In the nearly thirty years since this essay was first published, analyses of formerly unknown texts by and about earlier women have demanded a recognition that the origins of True Womanhood be moved back into at least the mid-eighteenth century.

39. Haggar Osborn, 1767 diary, p. 151.

in a degree engag'd me there brot 27 of us together in the afternoon and graciously engag'd my whole soul in prayer my dear Susa Mrs Henshaw and Mrs
Peabody our Grand Place was for Heart Holiness the subduing of our Lusts and
corruptions for strength from Heaven to be and do what God would Have us be
and do and for the outpourings of Gods spirit upon all the world especially upon
our isle our town our churches our Ministers our Minister church and congregation our Society all dear to us by the bonds of Nature grace our friendship. . . .[40]

The "Society" she refers to is made up of the twenty-seven women who have
come together in her home, in friendship, to pray and discuss scripture under her tutelage. What occurs in this passage is a movement from the universal ("the world") to the local ("our isle . . . our Minister") to the women's
community ("our Society") that allows her the comfort of spiritual sistership
and a means within her diary of expressing the sense of self she gains through
this connectedness with other women. Her desire for activism is evident also
in her prayers, not only to be what God desires but to *do* his work as He desires. Haggar Osborn harbored a fundamental difference in style from that of
the clergy: she wished to convert souls by rousing them to an awareness of
danger not, as the clergy did, by "exciting them to fly from the wrath to come"
but rather by suggesting that God offered them a "cradle of security" in which
they could attain peaceful sleep.[41]

Haggar Osborn's use of interruptive discourse is most notable in her use of
marginalia. At the end of each year (and sometimes during the year), she
rereads her text and comments on past thoughts or records additions to the
knowledge that she had at the time of her original entry. By this means, she
allows herself an opportunity to "loop back" on her life, retaining her identity as recorded in the first entry but reshaping that identity by filling in the
changes and additional knowledge of herself and her culture that she has
gained over time.

If we understand women's discourses as often reflecting a fluid and multiple
self,[42] we can also begin to understand the aesthetics of private writings wherein
the writer feels both the pressures of the external *and* a sense of *jouissance* (as it
were) at confronting those demands. It is a struggle between social constructions
of women (Woman) as Other and a resistant self (more accurately, selves) that
desire(s) recognition. I will use Esther Edwards Burr's journal of 1754–1757 as
an example for the remainder of my discussion on the associativeness integral to
a poetics of interruptibility as a discursive mode frequently used by women in
pre-Revolutionary America. Edwards Burr maintained her diary entries with a
specific audience in mind, her longtime friend Sarah Prince. On the rare occasions when they could locate a traveler who could be entrusted with their writings, they exchanged their personal reflections. Edwards Burr was far better educated than most women of her era but was not, by any means, educated on a
par with the male members of her extensive and renowned family. One of the
great difficulties in studying women's private writings remains the accessibility

40. Ibid., pp. 131–132.
41. Ibid., 1757 diary, p. 10.
42. Reference the works of Hélène Cixous, Mary Daly, and Luce Irigaray, among others.

of original manuscripts. Carol F. Karlsen and Laurie Crumpacker's edition of Edwards Burr's journal is a testimony to careful and thoughtful scholarship, yet even in such a text the commonplace of publishing—to standardize style—could not be completely resisted. A typical entry in Edwards Burr's journal reads as follows:

> In the Morning Mr Whitefield preached (I could not go out myself.) Mr Burr saw Mr Cumming and determined as soon as Meeting was out he would speak to 'em, but when it was out sombody spoke to Mr Burr about business and put it quite out of his mind. I knew then they would be offended—Next Morn by 7 they rode by our house going home without so much as calling—but the wind was so high that Mrs Cumming dare not go . . . and with a deal of trouble we got em here to dinner.[43]

In spite of the extensive interruptive modes used in this short excerpt (the ellipsis is Edwards Burr's as well), the editors note that they "eliminated her superfluous dashes, those accompanying other punctuation or used decoratively at the end of a line" (x). While Karlsen and Crumpacker were obviously careful to avoid changes that would alter content, in many other editorial cases there seems to be a complete failure to recognize what we assume is well known: that style and content are not separable.

With authors such as Haggar Osborn and Edwards Burr, however, where original texts and precise transcripts are available, we can study the process of how interruptibility develops into associativeness. Edwards Burr's life was a nonending schedule of domestic responsibilities, many of which were related to her husband's prominent position within the community, and her writings often have a breathless tonal quality. Although in her November 9, 1754, entry, she assumes that the exhausting pace of her life in the first few months of residency in New Jersey is only a momentary condition, it was in fact representative of what would become the norm for her increasingly prominent life:

> *Saturday P.M.*
> The Governor and Lady just went from here. They drank Tea with me. He is as well as usial. I find in my distress about my friends, and great confusion in the house (this confusion was occasioned by a croud of people here all day, such a day as I have hardly seen since I have been here) I have wrote a most dolefull heap of scrawls as almost all my writing is. But if you cant read it or any other of my letters pray be so good as to put em into the fire. It is no wonder for all the time I do get to write I steal. As for copping, I never do. I am glad I can get time to scratch once, for my writing, and in such haste two, is but scratching. (I dont so much as look over what I send to you. You have my thoughts just as they then happen to be.)[44]

This entry has a tone of apologia similar to the subversive prefaces of spiritual autobiographies noted earlier. Other entries suggest that, although the element of minimal time never faded, there was in fact a reflective nature to Ed-

---

43. Edwards Burr, pp. 46–47.
44. Ibid., p. 61.

wards Burr's writings if we understand the discourse of interruptibility. Issues that particularly interested the two diarists—most often relating to women's experiences or to representations of women[45]—are picked up repeatedly and expanded upon, sometimes over a period of several weeks.

For instance, on the evening of December 1, 1754, Esther wrote, "Saturday in my haste I have made a most Egregious blunder which I never discovered till this minute, but you will pardon this and all others. But I am realy ashamed. (I dont wonder at your surprize but plese to turn it up and you will see *whats the matter.*) I would burn this, but I cant possibly write it over again for want of time."[46] The "Egregious blunder" was that, in her haste, she had written upside down on the page. But she continues to address several issues—a friend's earlier letter, the current actions of the church scholars, the fact that an eighteen-year-old minister-in-training ("Brother Sammy") has begun to reside with them, a dream that Sarah had related, etc.—and then she reflects upon an entry in Sarah's most recently received journal:

> Page. 80. You desire Mr Burrs and my thoughts about what Solomans good Woman kept a candle a burning all Night for, and query whether she did not set up to read, or rather seem to take it for granted that she did.
>
> I have asked Mr Burr for his thoughts, and he will not be serious about it but said in a jest that she kept a candle burning for the reason that Mr Pemberton did, but I intend to ask him again. . . . My thoughts are these—first her Candle goeth not out *by Night* (viz) *as soon as tis Night.* You know tis a common way of speaking, as for instance, such a person *did not get up by day.* We dont mean that he lay aBed *all day*, but he did not get up as soon as the day Broke—our people coming—you shall have more of this subject the first opportunity I can get to write.[47]

Esther was greatly interested in the religious issue of the "good Woman" whose candle was said to burn through the night, but she is unable to return to such contemplative moments for almost two weeks. In between, only brief, exhaustion-ridden entries appear. The December 2nd entry reads in its entirety, "Extreamly hurried prepareing for the Presbytery,"[48] and most of the notations reflect her own day and night labors: "Dined eight Minnisters. In the forenoon a Sermon, in the afternoon the Presbytery sat upon our affairs, and adjourned till some time in Jannawary. Our people are in a great fude, some of em shew a very bad spirit."[49] The next night she prepared dinner for ten more visiting ministers. Finally, on December 12, after quickly not-

---

45. For her time and her position as the spouse of a minister, Edwards Burr was remarkably vocal in her opposition to derogatory comments about women who had gained a place in the public arena. See, for example, her debate with a male guest about the woman-centered themes in Annis Boudinot Stockton's poetry. "My Tongue, you know," she wrote Sarah Prince, "hangs pretty loose" (257).

46. Edwards Burr, pp. 68–69.

47. Ibid., pp. 69–70.

48. Ibid., p. 70.

49. Ibid.

ing that she had called at a neighboring pastor's home and that her husband was absent again, preaching in New York, she returned in her evening notation to the issue of the good Woman:

> But to return to my good Woman which I had like to have forgot. By her Candles not going out by Night, or as soon as Night, May shew her industry, that her business did not cease as soon as night came. She was not in a hurry to lay all aside and go to bed as lazy people do. . . . It could not be that she sat up till two, or three, o' the Clock or great part of the Night as you seem to suppose, for tis said of her Vers 15, "She ariseth also while it is yet Night," etc. . . . Now I query whether tis possible for her to arise so erly (if she sat up so late as you suppose) and live under it, unless she was made of some other sort of *Matter* than we be, which is not very likely, for Solomon speaks of her as one of *US*, and that makes him *wonder so much, and admire her so greatly as to set her price far above Rubies.* I apeal to your own experience. You know you cant get up erly in the Morn if you set up very late, dont you, *say?* But if you have any objections to what I have said, pray let me know it in your next.[50]

Esther and Sarah analyzed this issue over several weeks, recognizing the conditions of women's quotidian existence as a worthy theme for contemplation. Further, the humorous admonishments to Sarah to consider "your own experience" reflect Edwards Burr's concern with the ways in which the good Woman was admired for feats that were impossible for the typical woman to accomplish. It is in the venue of the commonplaces of domestic work, rather than as a national leader, that a woman writer such as Edwards Burr may find herself to be a representative figure. Interruptibility has for centuries been the most prevalent muse for the development of women's poetics.

As noted, Edwards Burr's journal was actually written with her friend Sarah Prince in mind as her audience. This semiprivate nature of diaries is a feature of most (extant)[51] women's "private" writings of this era: they were often letterbooks as much as private diaries—Anna Green Winslow addresses her mother, Sally Wister keeps her diary for her friend Deborah Norris, Nancy Shippen Livingston writes with her infant daughter in mind, and Elizabeth Sandwith Drinker's diary is intended as a record for her adult children. Because of this, the aesthetics of early women's diaries can also be assessed in the context of their relationship to another genre closely linked to women's writing traditions: epistles.[52]

It is from theories of epistolary narratives that our understanding of the aesthetics of early American women's diary writings may most fully benefit. Like letters, diaries are episodic and relate events and thoughts of the moment. Continuity, then, in its traditional sense, is not to be expected. Instead, associativeness is privileged. This distinction has probably been the greatest source of

---

50. Ibid., p. 72.

51. It may, of course, be the fact that such diaries *were* exchanged that helped to preserve them, whereas other, truly private writings did not survive past the writer's lifetime.

52. Catharine Maria Sedgwick coined the term "epistolary journalizing" that captures the conjunctions of the two genres (*Hope Leslie*, p. 97).

the diary's state of neglect in contemporary criticism.[53] Rather than progressing linearly toward a single (however complex) point that constitutes a form of closure—a progression that has been extraordinarily privileged in the twentieth century by critical emphasis on the novel—the associativeness inherent in a poetics of interruptibility is a kind of intellectual looping, episodic and disjunctive in form—what I am going to term *"discours décousu,"* and by which I mean an unstitched pastiche of ideas that yet bears a logical reality of associations in its entirety, even when the text has no closure, no conclusion (except as it constitutes a lack of further notations by the author). Frederick Jameson uses "pastiche" to signify groups that are incapable of communicating with one another. My use of the term in defining *discours décousu* is to signify the very distinct means by which women exercised a model of pastiche, rooted in their labor-distinctive lives, *as* communication. Several feminists have studied the influence of quilting (a traditional form of women's work also rooted in the "spinster" tradition) on women's aesthetics, and the associativeness of this interruptive mode of discourse—its ability to intellectually link various patchwork loops, as it were—once again acts as a complement to women's quilting aesthetic patterns. But the implications, I believe, are much broader. Indeed, Cathy Davidson has defined the picaresque novel (written by women and men) as presenting a "crazy quilt" polis, "stitche[d] together . . . [by] no more than certain satirical thread or tone, a comic energy or movement."[54] *Discours décousu* complements the Bahktinian theory of patchwork, but addresses how women's environments, especially the work patterns necessary in early American domestic life, made this discursive style an especially viable mode of expression. *Discours décousu* need not be for women writers only but is frequently engaged by them as most appropriate to their literary productive needs. *Discours décousu* is dependent to a degree upon concepts of quilting raised by Elaine Hedges and Elaine Showalter, but their studies do not address what I believe are necessary theoretical questions. For instance, Showalter asserts, "American women's tradition of piecing, patchwork, and quilting has consequences for the structures, genres, themes, and meanings of American women's writing in the nineteenth and twentieth centuries."[55] Such an assertion leaves unproblematized the very concepts that, I believe, *discours décousu* challenges: structures, genres, themes, and meanings. Further, I have opted for the French phrase in an attempt to make explicit my own theoretical location—that which recognizes the value in both U.S. and French feminisms and yet that which also feels that alone, and as diverse as each school of feminist thought may be, they remain inadequate. It is when the strengths of these various theories are integrated (perhaps, in what is currently termed "transatlantic feminism"[56]) that,

53. In coming to this and the following conclusions, I am indebted to the recent proliferation of studies of epistolary narratives, most notably Elizabeth J. MacArthur's *Extravagant Narratives: Closure and Dynamics in the Epistolary Form* (Princeton: Princeton UP, 1990). While critical attention has been focused on fictional (and mostly English) epistolary works, much of the discussion has implications for nonfiction epistles and diaries-as-letterbooks.

54. Cathy N. Davidson, *Revolution and the Word: The Rise of the Novel in America* (New York: Oxford UP, 1986), p. 164.

55. Elaine Showalter, "Piecing and Writing" in *The Poetics of Gender*, p. 223.

56. See note 30 above.

to my mind, we have the most fruitful inquiries, interrogations, explorations. *Discours décousu* does not (as U.S. and British feminisms tend) erase the problematics of language and subjectivity, nor does it (as French feminisms tend) erase an enormous body of work by women over time.

Perhaps it is the fascination itself with genres that conform to some system or awareness of closure (even when that constitutes an intentional progression to nonclosure) and the aesthetics that have been privileged within the context of that fascination that needs to be interrogated, since women so often neglect this tradition in their private writings. Elizabeth J. MacArthur has conjectured that "the fascination with closure" may be connected "to a fear of deviance and a desire for stability."[57] These are, of course, necessary traits of conformity that the dominant group in any hierarchical culture must demand if it is to retain its position. It is little wonder, then, that members of marginalized groups—in this instance, but certainly not limited to, early American women diarists—may be drawn to alternative (subversive) forms. The diary genre is perfect for such alternatives because its restricted nature (its insistence upon privacy) undermines the overt control of authority figures other than the author herself. Patriarchal systems and ideologies may be *momentarily* abandoned, challenged, or supplanted. Thus while the diarist explores multiple facets of subjectivity, she can simultaneously engage in acts of creating meaning for herself. As Irigaray reminds us, " 'other meaning' [is] always in the process of weaving itself"; such language is never merely identical with an already known meaning, "rather it is contiguous."[58]

Discours décousu is equally important in considering writings by women of color in early America. As Alice Walker has described the history of African-American women's artistry, quilting was a means of expression but also a means of negotiating subjective space in a landscape that threatened not only voice but life itself. Their "bits and pieces" of "rags" were woven into a powerful "language" of resistance and selfhood.[59] That sewn language may not have been readily recognizable to their oppressors, but that failure of recognition by the dominant culture in no way diminished what *had been said* through art. *Discours décousu*, then, is simply a way of teasing out the threads of discursive patterns to reconstruct (rather than simply deconstruct) the multivalence of representation encoded in early women's texts. There is no "women's pattern" to be deciphered; rather, *discours décousu* is a means of interrogating a particular text produced by a particular author in a particular historical moment. For instance, Phillis Wheatley used conventional poetic forms and subverted conventionality by aligning the American political leaders' resistance against tyranny with the need to resist racial tyrannies as well. In her letters, however, Wheatley demonstrates a somewhat less conventional form, depending upon her audience. In letters to Sir John Thornton or the Countess of Huntington, Wheatley produced texts following standardized formal letter-writing codes. In letters to her friend and equal Obour Tanner, she increas-

57. MacArthur, pp. 15–16.
58. Irigaray, p. 29.
59. Alice Walker, *In Search of Our Mothers' Gardens: Womanist Prose* (New York: Harcourt Brace Jovanovich, 1983), p. 239.

ingly relaxed formalities. Undoubtedly, her letters to Obour were not private, since both were slaves. But even within the context of scrutinized texts such as these, Wheatley demonstrates a less rigid discursive process. It is in the final extant letter to Obour, after Wheatley has been freed, that she expresses herself most freely:

> tho' I have been silent, I have not been umindful of you, but a variety of hindrances was the cause of my not writing to you. But in time to come I hope our correspondence will revive—and revive in better times—pray write me soon, for I long to hear from you—you may depend on constant replies—I wish you much happiness. . . .[60]

It should not be surprising, then, that diaries and letters proliferated during the American Revolution. As the dominant culture contemplated a new political order, women's diaries and letters constituted the "fomenting [of] a rebellion" little suspected by the country's leaders. These private writings opened the way for women's intellectual development, for a philosophical exchange of ideas with other women, and eventually—for the most bold among them—a movement into the public arena of national life and debate. Interruptibility remains a facet of women's experiences, and the associativeness of a poetics of interruptibility as signified in women's private writings through *discours décousu* may be studied in nineteenth- and twentieth-century literatures as well. *Discours décousu*'s dialectics of process may be evidenced, for instance, in an impressively wide range of women's texts: from Esther Edwards Burr's diary to Catharine Maria Sedgwick's *Hope Leslie* in which narrative digressions are integral to Sedgwick's discourse; to Caroline Kirkland's *A New Home—Who'll Follow?*, in which, for example, domestic interruptibility shapes how Mrs. Danforth narrates her personal history; to Margaret Fuller's *Summer on the Lakes in 1843*, in which the author uses the metaphor of threading to describe her discursive pattern;[61] to Emily Dickinson's poetry, in which patterns and poetics exemplify *discours décousu*:

> The Perished Patterns murmur—
> But His Perturbless Plan
> Proceed—inserting Here—a Sun—
> There—leaving out a Man   (P #724)

For all of its potential, *discours décousu* is only one means of rethinking early women's writings. It is my hope that this anthology will provide all of us who are students of early American literatures with many avenues for further exploration.

---

60. Phillis Wheatley, *The Collected Works of Phillis Wheatley*, ed. John Shields (New York: Oxford UP, 1988), pp. 186–187.

61. In *Summer on the Lakes, in 1843* (Chicago: U of Chicago P, 1991), Margaret Fuller asserted, "I wish I had a thread long enough to string on it all these beads that take my fancy" (148). Her discursive style in the text is a threading of her own thoughts as they swiftly move from one subject to another, as well as a compendium of other writers' thoughts intricately strung among her own "fancies."

The Ages of Women

art I of this anthology presents a view of women's lives as written by themselves and most often for other women. The five sections of Part I correspond to major stages in early American women's lives: their development from youth to young womanhood; their education (informal and formal); their domestic lives; their participation in work outside the domestic arena; and their final thoughts as they neared death.

Probably no issue crosses the stages of women's lives with such importance as does that of education. In tribal societies, education for young women was skill-oriented. In Plains tribes dominated by the buffalo culture, knowing how to tan and dress hides was as important as cooking. A young woman's tools were as likely to be a scraper (to clean the inside of the hide) and a flesher (to work the hide into the proper thickness) as a ladle or a kettle. In pueblo societies (which have existed in the Southwest for more than 3,000 years), farming was the central focus, and the skills of harvesting corn and producing meal for a variety of dishes were a necessary part of a girl's education. In all tribes, women and men alike were expected to learn the spiritual and cultural customs of their society. For many Native American women, the act of passing to the next generation the legends and origin stories as well as events at council meetings and other community gatherings was an integral facet of home education. In a community with no written language, the oral traditions passed down by native women were equivalent to Euro-Americans' editorials, essays, poetry, and fiction. They were the perpetuators of culture; although individual women's names may be lost to us, a study of various tribes' legends reveals what behaviors by women were valued or admonished and how girls and young women were educated to participate in their culture.

For most Euro-American women, there were similar attitudes about education—the learning of household duties and spiritual and cultural customs was the first stage of their educational process. However, because the colonists were linked to a culture that emphasized the written word, issues of literacy pervade the history of Euro-American women's education. Because the European settlers believed that women's intellect was inferior to men's, women's education was often neglected in pre-Revolutionary America. Yet it was not completely absent. When girls in middle-and upper-class families learned to read and write, it came almost exclusively through home education. Occasionally, a tutor would be brought into the home, but most often it remained the province of parents (and especially fathers, who had greater access to literacy than did mothers) to educate their children. But educational requirements—or the complete lack thereof—varied from community to community. In Massachusetts Bay Colony, for instance, where many of the male leaders had been Cambridge educated, there was greater emphasis upon literacy for both sexes, although males' education was always privileged. In 1642, a court order was enacted that required (white) parents to educate all of their children, which meant to teach them to read, write, and do basic arithmetic. Since not all parents could afford private tutors, by 1647 towns of more than fifty families were required to establish schools. For young girls, this meant the early dame schools; while they were an important beginning to women's education, they most often emphasized sufficiency rather than proficiency. Even with the early laws advocating the education of all white children, there was an evident hierarchy of priorities: schools could be used for girls' education only when not being used for the boys, which, in many communities, meant only in the summer.

The establishment of female academies first occurred in New England in the 1760s. In the northern colonies, organized systems emerged earlier than in the south, where the plantation economy made establishing schools less feasible and private tutoring the longstanding preferred practice. Julia Cherry Spruill has noted that "Old Field Schools" were also popular in the education of southern Euro-American girls and boys. In the upper classes, young women were sometimes sent to England for their education; for example, two seventeenth-century Virginian sisters, Susan and Ursula Byrd, were educated in England, and in the next century Mary Wayles Jefferson and Thomas Jefferson followed the same practice for their daughters. In the mid-Atlantic colonies, Philadelphia led the way in establishing academies for girls, with schools like that established by Anthony Benezet appearing in the 1750s. The majority of women in the colonies, however, remained nonliterate. It was both the changing ideologies invoked by the Revolution and the insistence upon giving women an opportunity to read the Bible that led the way for changes in women's educational opportunities.

The post-Revolutionary years evinced a radical change in women's education. The concept of Republican Motherhood was, paradoxically, one avenue for advancement. Republican Motherhood was an ideology intended to return women to the private sphere after the end of the war. Since women had taken on a multitude of unusual roles during the war—including supporters traveling with the troops, spies, managers of family properties, and heads of households—the male leaders of the new nation needed to suggest the rewards of turning women's political consciousness toward a more limited sphere of personal activity. They found that ideology in Republican Motherhood, which argued that the greatest contribution a woman could make to her country was to maintain a stable household and to educate her sons to become responsible, productive citizens. As the historian Linda Kerber has observed, many women embraced this conservative vision of women's role in the polis, but many other women used this vehicle as a means for expanding women's education. If sons were to be educated, the next generation of daughters must also be educated so they could offer the best possible educations to *their* sons. Diaries of this period also note the changing status of early home education; diarists often refer to such practices as a school or the mother-teacher as "holding school," thus awarding mother-teachers a new status as well.

Some women, however, were more adamant about the diversity of contributions well-educated women could make to the new nation. Abigail Smith Adams (1744–1818), for instance, insisted, "If we mean to have Heroes, Statesmen and Philosophers, we should have learned women." Judith Sargent Murray (1751–1820) published several essays in which she argued for a new vision of women's lives: "I expect to see our young women forming a new era in female history," she asserted. And a few young women, such as Priscilla Mason (fl. 1793), demonstrated their newly gained education in public addresses. Although Mason sought in her valedictory speech to assuage her audience's fears about women's increased opportunities for education, she also offered "a few thoughts in vindication of female eloquence." Writing only a year after the publication of Mary Wollstonecraft's *Vindication of the Rights of Woman* (a text that is referenced repeatedly in American women's letters and diaries), Mason was undoubtedly conscious of the implications of her choice of wording.

Yet significant disparities remained between boys' and girls' educations. While boys' schools varied between college-preparatory (especially Latin and logic) and skill-oriented programs, girls' schools usually emphasized accomplishments, especially such traits as would increase upper-class girls' opportunities for marriage. Instruction of females tended to emphasize drawing, embroidery, and French and English language skills. Further, education remained a class- and race-bound opportunity for decades to come. Middle-class girls were more often apprenticed to individual families to learn housekeeping skills; if they learned to read and write, it was for the purpose of account-keeping.

While Quaker Philadelphia was notable for its School for Negro Children, founded in 1758, it was not until the 1810s that schools would be established by women for African-American children and impoverished children of all races, and it would not be until after the Civil War that any systematized program of education for African-American children would emerge, and even then tenuously. For most African-American girls, education was limited to the skills necessary for back-breaking field work and, for a few, housekeeping skills employed for the benefit of their owners. These limitations, however, too often erase the skill with which African-American women practiced these trades and the ways in which they sometimes subverted the system to share their talents by educating their daughters to the art of field labor or housekeeping. In a letter to her master, Judith Cocks (fl. 1795), a slave who had been indentured to another master for her owner's increased profit, demonstrates her literacy and a recognition of her value as a laborer. Elizabeth Sandwith Drinker (1734–1807), a Euro-American woman who took in indentured servants and slaves in order to train them in household skills, often remarked upon the notable talents of these two classes of women under her (forced) tutelage. The extraordinary abuses inherent in these class systems (evidenced unwittingly in Sandwith Drinker's diary, for example) should not be ignored; nor should the ways in which some women were able to find a means of expressing their talents, even under such oppression. Further, not all African Americans were enslaved. While the vast majority were, the 1790 census of the original thirteen states indicates more than 5,000 heads of households were African-American men, and 513 households were headed by African-American *women*. In a period in which enslaved African Americans numbered more than half a million, it is a small, but notable, figure.

As noted, free schools for poor Euro-American children did not emerge until the end of the eighteenth century. Ann Parrish (1760–1800), a Pennsylvania philanthropist and educator, founded the first charitable educational organization for and by women in the new nation. In 1785, Isabella Marshall Graham (1742–1814) came to New York City and began a school for children in the poorer sections of the city, and in 1796 she founded an early women's organization, the Society for the Relief of Poor Widows with Children. In the southern colonies, attention to women's education had lagged behind advances in the northern and middle colonies. By 1700, some 75 percent of southern women still could neither read nor write. Yet free schools for Euro-American children had been evident in the South since the early eighteenth century. In Georgia, for example, free schools were begun as early as 1743, and the Reverend George Whitefield established in that colony the Orphan House, which was designed to educate girls as well as boys. For the upper classes, however, private schooling remained the norm in the South.

New educational opportunities did emerge throughout the newly formed states, but the consequences for a female who sought such opportunities were never without risk. A learned woman, especially a woman who sought to express her wisdom outside the role of motherhood, was often deemed an "unsexed" or "masculinized" woman. As the anonymous "Aspasia" (fl. 1776–89) noted, many men seemed to fear that "the more a woman's understanding is improved, the more apt she will be to despise her husband." Early advice literature, such as that published by the prolific Eunice Smith (1757–1823), often used female biblical types to reinforce a highly conservative view of woman's sphere, and curricula at many of the female academies were highly gendered. Yet resistance did not always come in public, vocalized manners. Some women began to envision different lives for their daughters than they themselves had experienced, and out of that parental desire came many individual but collectively significant changes. In Anne Shippen Livingston's (1763–1841) record, for instance, we discover a young woman's struggle against the didacticism of advice literature and a determination to define new opportunities for her daughter. Rejecting the conventional idea that "Women are only born to suffer & to obey," Shippen Livingston recorded the directions she preferred to take with her daughter, including, "Observe strictly the little seeds of reason in her & cultivate the first appearance of it diligently."

Most often change came regionally—Quakers and Moravians had long believed that females as well as males should be educated and that women should be trained as public teachers as well as mother-teachers. A few women, like

Sarah Pierce (1767–1852) of Litchfield, Connecticut, and Mary Vial Holyoke (1737–1802) and Susanna Haswell Rowson (1761–1824), both from Massachusetts, established rigorous female academies that embraced new visions of what a "proper" female education might entail. Both Pierce and Haswell Rowson, frustrated with the limited number and debatable quality of published texts for girls' educations, wrote their own texts—sometimes full-length manuscripts, such as Rowson's numerous textbooks, at other times, short texts that met the teacher's daily demands of her students, such as Pierce's short dialogues to be read or performed by her students. Marriage was not eliminated as young women's primary career goal, but it was redefined as an institution that demanded educated, self-reliant partners of *both* sexes.

In addition to the normal learning processes, early schools for girls in post-Revolutionary America emphasized for the first time the importance of advancing females' writing abilities, even in schools that retained conservative curricula. In more experimental educational environments, such as Sarah Pierce's Litchfield academy for girls, writing was emphasized in a variety of ways. Pierce's requirements were that each girl must write sixty lines a week. The extant journals of her students (see Charlotte Sheldon) suggest that Pierce offered her students a wide range of topics for writing—school subjects and sermons, as one would expect, but also personal feelings, records of everyday events in their lives, family issues: in other words, writing as expression in its fullest sense. It is out of this kind of radical new vision for women's voices that we see the extraordinary proliferation of women's writings after the Revolution.

This change also included the move into critiques of the written word. If the novel was deemed a dangerous influence on female behavior (see Part III), young women in female academies were encouraged to note *and critique* the texts they were reading, for school and for pleasure. It is notable how often the practice of literary criticism was retained in adulthood. Elizabeth Sandwith Drinker's fifty-year diary is rife with entries about her love of reading and her desire to record and analyze the texts she read. In the letters exchanged between women we can also observe that this kind of critique was a way of sharing—and honing—one's critical opinions. (See also "Epistolary Exchanges" in Part III.) A few women moved these skills into the public arena: Judith Sargent Murray, Mercy Otis Warren, and Susanna Haswell Rowson. Such women laid the foundation for the rise of women's published literature and criticism in the nineteenth century.

No section of this anthology so amply displays the diversity of experiences, desires, and accomplishments of early American women as does the following collection of women's accounts of their quotidian existence. From Native American legends that define a young woman's obligations to and accomplishments within her community, to letters and diaries that record everyday struggles and rewards of various Euro-American women, to memoirs that reveal intimate details of domestic relations, the texts included in "Domestic Records" capture for the twentieth-century reader what early American women felt were significant aspects of their everyday lives. (While "Domestic Records" is presented as a separate grouping in Part I, in order to emphasize the significance of this aspect of women's lives, in fact the domestic arena is portrayed in women's writings throughout the anthology.) These accounts also remind us of the differences between women, even those of similar classes and beliefs. Thus we see Elizabeth Sandwith Drinker who found much to celebrate as an older woman who had attained the role of matriarch of her family. In contrast, Rebecca Dickinson, who was single, lamented her age and the passing of an opportunity for such status as marriage afforded women. Certainly not all single women lamented not marrying (see Hannah Griffitts, for example), and some women were beginning to challenge the derogatory nature of the term "old maid." Judith Sargent Murray, for instance, challenged the idea of a woman being "stigmatized with that dreaded title, an Old Maid." Rather than being taught to fear "descending down the vale of life in an unprotected state," she argued that young women ought to be educated to "a reverence of self." For all of these challenges to relational identifications of women, however, marriage and motherhood remained important signifiers in women's lives for decades—perhaps centuries—to come.

Equally important is the way in which such records force us to reconsider our definition of what we mean by "domestic." Because there has been a longer history of studying nineteenth-century "woman's sphere" (and challenges to that culturally determined arena), "domestic" has, come to be narrowly defined as "within the household." In early American studies, however, "household" itself must be called into question. For Native American women raised in a nomadic culture, for instance, one's household was what could be easily carried to each new locale. (See, for example, Mary Rowlandson's captivity narrative for a description of the minimal material goods owned by Native Americans and the necessity of being able to carry their belongings in packs upon their backs.) Even in non-nomadic Native American communities, "domestic" duties entailed the planting, harvesting, and production of food; preparation of clothing; childrearing; and numerous community responsibilities, including (as noted above) relating tribal legends to children as a means of perpetuating the rituals and values inculcated in those legends.

For early Euro-American settlers, domestic responsibilities also moved far beyond a woman's duties within the home. It sometimes meant helping to run the family business, be it a colony (as in the case of Maria van Cortlandt van Rensselaer) or, more often, a farm (as with Mary Wright Cooper). In a preindustrial society, women's contributions to the agrarian economy were required for the survival of the colony as well as of the individual. The processes of indentured servitude (see Elizabeth Sprigs's and Elizabeth Sandwith Drinker's accounts) or slavery (see Judith Cocks's letter) appropriated women laborers as means of profit for owners and as integral to the functioning of economic orders.

If terms such as "domestic" and "household" need redefining, they also remind us of the flexibility of language itself and how language can be used either to acknowledge or denigrate women and women's work. Words such as "gossip" and "spinster" have altered meanings radically over time. "Gossip" originally was derived from "god-sibling," referring to someone who acted as witness at the birth and baptism of a child; in the seventeenth century, a gossip was a woman who aided another woman at childbirth. Thus, a gossip was not a derogatory term for someone who spread rumors but rather was a precursor to the midwife and was aligned in meaning with the concept of a supportive woman friend. Similarly, "spinster" has become synonymous with "old maid"; its original meaning, however, was to signify a person who worked a spinning wheel. Again, then, a term that was intended to designate a particular form of work became a denigrating term aligned only with women and meant to create a gap in social status between married and single women. It is notable that both terms were originally meant to align women with work and yet became aligned with concepts of protection (either protecting oneself from the dangers of idle rumors, or with the necessity of marriage to protect a woman believed to be incapable of surviving on her own). In examining the meanings of words such as "domestic" or "spinster," it is always vital to ask, "Who benefits from the change in meanings?"

When women's writings do take us within the home, they often present a far different picture of early American family dynamics than has typically been presented by the nearly exclusive study of men's writings, which either ignore women's distinct lives or exclude the household arena entirely. In the writings of Abigail Abbott Bailey (1746–1815), Susan Livingston Symmes (?–post-1808), and Elizabeth Sandwith Drinker, interpersonal relationships predominate. Not surprisingly, the more detailed the writer is about her personal life, the more likely it is that she is writing a private document to be seen only by a trusted friend or family member or herself alone. It is important to recognize, too, that the writings we do have from early America are highly class-dictated, since for most of this period, many women (of all races) had no access to literacy. In the poorest families, young children were bound to the upper classes to work and help support their impoverished families. Most often, bound children were between five and ten years of age, and their indentureship ranged from a few years to until they reached adulthood. However, some children were bound out as infants. Julia Cherry Spruill has identified several infant females who were separated from their families at astonishingly early ages: Margaret Brannum of Virginia was apprenticed in 1722 when she was not yet two years old; baby Kenmore was apprenticed by her mother, Mary, when she was only nine months old. Such indentured servitude often meant a deprived and cruel existence with little opportunity for any but the most rudimentary forms of education; therefore, we rarely hear anything from individuals of this class. Even Elizabeth Sprigs, who had been indentured for disobeying her father, had been taught to read and write, unlike the majority of her counterparts.

Whether Native American, Dutch, Puritan, or Quaker and whether literate or nonliterate, most women were expected to live androcentric lives; that is, they were to dedicate (and thereby sublimate) their lives to the care and well-being of male authority figures—fathers, brothers, husbands, sons. What these records reveal, however, is that circumstances often demanded that women take on the role of provider and protector; when this occurred, their writings reveal the psychological struggle such women confronted in maintaining a culturally defined "womanliness" while at the same time accomplishing "manly" deeds. In early America's patriarchal societies, women's contributions to the economic and personal livelihood of their homes and communities were culturally discounted by inscribing "feminine" as "other" and "lesser" than "masculine." Women who were forced into or chose nontraditional roles bore double burdens: they carried the entire responsibility for their own or their family's survival, and they faced social disparagement and sometimes ostracism for having the courage to do so. Yet many women continued to do just that, to act as they saw fit according to their circumstances. In so doing, they began the process of challenging, consciously or unconsciously, the definition of "woman's sphere" in early America.

In "Businesswomen's Writings," we see the breadth of this process of redefining. Traditionally, colonial studies have asserted that women did not participate in the economic and business facets of early American life; however, as the following entries reveal, women from various backgrounds did participate in the economic development of the tribal societies, the colonies, and the new nation. Their primary role in supporting the economy was, of course, maintaining nuclear family households and agrarian economies. Yet we cannot fully understand the complexities of women's work in early America unless we comprehend the diverse avenues that such work actually took. Planting, harvesting, hunting, cooking, cleaning, and childrearing may have been the most prevalent work performed by early women, but it certainly was not the only work. If Deborah Read Franklin's (1708–1774) work remained within the household, it was dramatically shaped by her husband's political activities, to the extreme extent of having to physically defend her home against angry opponents of Benjamin's political practices. Martha Daniell Logan (1704–1779) and Eliza Lucas Pinckney (c. 1722–1793) pushed the boundaries of the domestic realm to include scientific experimentations that advanced botanical and crop-production knowledge. Other women took on public roles. The Lady of Cofitachique (fl. 1540), for instance, was the ruler of Cofitachique, an area that covered what is now Georgia and South Carolina; little is known of her life, but she negotiated with Hernando De Soto when he was exploring the area, was taken captive by De Soto because of her knowledge of the region, and eventually escaped with an African slave of De Soto's. It is believed both the Lady of Cofitachique and the African eventually returned in safety to her community. Many colonial women were tavern owners or proprietors of general stores. Margaret Brent (1601–1671) was a successful attorney in seventeenth-century Maryland, and Hannah Callowhill Penn (1671–1726) was responsible for numerous legal transactions in colonial Pennsylvania. Some women were also engaged in the maritime industry. In colonial New Amsterdam, Cornelia De Peyster delivered the first cargo of salt to her colony; it was a woman, Margaret Phillipse (?–1690), who operated the first packet between the colonies and England; and Martha Smith (fl. 1718) owned a whaling business. In the late seventeenth century, Alida Schuyler van Rensselaer Livingston (1656–1727) managed her family's extensive properties and ran their New Amsterdam colony for several years. In the early eighteenth century, Madame Montour (c. 1684–c. 1752), of French and Seneca heritage, acted as an interpreter and agent between the Iroquois and New York colonists; and Coosaponakessa (Mary Musgrove, 1700–post-1760) held the same roles of interpreter and agent in Georgia in the pre-Revolutionary years. At the end of the century, Mary Katherine Goddard (1738–1816) became a renowned publisher, printer, and bookstore owner.

Women's work was integral, in all of its varying facets, to the survival of tribal societies and the colonies as well as to the establishment of the United States—and importantly, many early women understood their contributions in that context, both before and after the Revolution.

Early women's lives were never easy. For most women, comforts were few, demands were plentiful, and recognition of their accomplishments was minimal. While some women wrote diaries or poetry throughout their lives, many women wrote only occasionally. For some, the prospect of death itself was the harbinger which moved them to express their final thoughts. The recording of deathbed declarations, a well-known tradition in early European societies, was carried to the "New World" by most religious sects. In the quite disparate examples of women's contributions to the genre included here, we find samples not only of specifically woman-centered statements but of the evolution of the tradition from almost exclusively spiritual acclamations to the inclusion of a variety of secular assertions, including defenses of aberrant life histories. Sarah Whipple Goodhue (1641–1681) and Hannah Hill Jr. (1703–1714) both adhered to restrictive roles for Puritan women; yet Whipple Goodhue desired to leave a record of her thoughts for her children (a pattern going back at least to Anne Dudley Bradstreet), and Hill sought a broader audience for her words of advice. Yet too often, women's lives and especially their final accounts have been romanticized by later readers. The life of Rebekah Chamblit, a young woman who was executed in Boston in 1733 for infanticide, reminds us of the varied nature of early women's existences—and of the consequences for women who stepped outside the norm. When Chamblit became pregnant outside of marriage, she was faced with a community that would, at the least, ostracize her. Out of fear and humiliation, she committed the horrifying act of killing her newly born infant. Although her testimony was forced by her interrogators, it also reveals her awareness of the few options she saw for herself under the circumstances. In each of these writers' testimonies, the conventionalism of their form is superseded by the individual personality brought to bear upon that form.

Chamblit's text also raises another important issue—the extraordinary silencing of Euro-American women's sexuality that prevailed in early America. This is nowhere so evident as in the gendering of art forms in early America. Painting was (with few exceptions) the venue of males, and as the historian Laurel Thatcher Ulrich has observed, painting emphasized young women at the moment of their coming to adulthood. If paintings represented an idealized sexuality, needlework—the venue of females—emphasized domesticity and marriage. Needlework sometimes addressed courtship, but never sexuality itself. Throughout this anthology, we will see women struggle to suppress what is not to be spoken, and we can recognize the few strong voices that sought, to some degree, to break the silence. In all three parts of the anthology, women struggle to find means of writing what they saw as the realities of their lives. If at the end of the eighteenth century, the struggle is ongoing—in the form of novels as well as death-bed testimonies—it is equally important to recognize the impact these early struggles had on the opportunities for later women to more fully express both their outrage at the repressive nature of American life as well as celebrations of their multifaceted lives as women.

Youthful Reflections

The Seven Stars (Blackfoot)

Originally located in Canada, the Blackfoot moved some time before the seventeenth century into the western regions of what is now the continental United States, settling in the Montana area. The Blackfoot constitute an alliance of three Algonquian tribes— the Sisikas (who have retained the Blackfoot name), the Bloods, and the Piegans. Although farther west than most Plains tribes, the Blackfoot tribes of early America lived in tipis and hunted buffalo. The "Seven Stars" narrative, like many Native American texts, conveys both the image of a strong and defiant young woman and the story of how natural phenomena came into existence.

Bibliography: Wissler and Duvall.

The Seven Stars

Once there was a young woman with many suitors, but she refused to marry. She had seven brothers and one little sister. Their mother had been dead many years and they had no relatives, but lived alone with their father. Every day the six brothers went out hunting with their father. It seems that the young woman had a bear for her lover, and, as she did not want anyone to know this, she would meet him when she went out after wood. She always went out for wood as soon as her father and brothers went out to hunt, leaving her little sister alone in the lodge. As soon as she was out of sight in the brush, she would run to where the bear lived.

As the little sister grew older, she began to be curious as to why her older sister spent so much time getting wood. So one day she followed her. She saw the young woman meet the bear and saw that they were lovers. When she found this out, she ran home as quickly as she could, and when her father returned, she told him what she had seen. When he heard the story, he said, "So, my elder daughter has a bear for a husband. Now I know why she does not want to marry." Then he went about the camp, telling all his people that

41

they had a bear for a brother-in-law, and that he wished all the men to go out with him to kill this bear. So they went, found the bear, and killed him.

When the young woman found out what had been done, and that her little sister had told on her, she was very angry. She scolded her little sister vigorously, then ordered her to go out to the dead bear, and bring some flesh from his paws. The little sister began to cry, and said she was afraid to go out of the lodge, because a dog with young pups had tried to bite her. "Oh, do not be afraid!" said the young woman. "I will paint your face like that of a bear, with black marks across the eyes and at the corners of the mouth; then no one will touch you." So the little sister went for the meat. Now the older sister was a powerful medicine-woman. She could tan hide in a new way. She could take up a hide, strike it four times with her skin-scraper and it would be tanned.

The little sister had a younger brother that she carried on her back. As their mother was dead, she took care of him. One day the little sister said to the older sister, "Now you be a bear and we will go out into the brush to play." The older sister agreed to this, but said, "Little sister, you must not touch me over my kidneys." So the big sister acted as a bear, and they played in the brush. While they were playing, the little sister forgot what she had been told, and touched her older sister in the wrong place. At once she turned into a real bear, ran into the camp, and killed many of the people. After she had killed a large number, she turned back into her former self. Now, when the little sister saw the older run away as a real bear, she became frightened, took up her little brother, and ran into the lodge. Here they waited, badly frightened, but were very glad to see their older sister return after a time as her true self.

Now the older brothers were out hunting as usual. As the little sister was going down for water with her little brother on her back, she met her six brothers returning. The brothers noticed how quiet and deserted the camp seemed to be. So they said to their little sister, "Where are all our people?" Then the little sister explained how she and her sister were playing, when the elder turned into a bear, ran into the camp, and killed many people. She told her brothers that they were in great danger, as their sister would surely kill them when they came home. So the six brothers decided to go into the brush. One of them had killed a jack-rabbit. He said to the little sister, "You take this rabbit home with you. When it is dark, we will scatter prickly-pears all around the lodge, except in one place. When you come out, you must look for that place, and pass through."

When the little sister came back to the lodge, the elder sister said, "Where have you been all this time?" "Oh, my little brother mussed himself and I had to clean him," replied the little sister. "Where did you get that rabbit?" she asked. "I killed it with a sharp stick," said the little sister. "That is a lie. Let me see you do it," said the older sister. Then the little sister took up a stick lying near her, threw it at the rabbit, and it stuck in the wound in his body. "Well, all right," said the elder sister. Then the little sister dressed the rabbit and cooked it. She offered some of it to her older sister, but it was refused, so the little sister and her brother ate all of it. When the elder sister saw that the rabbit had all been eaten, she became very angry, and said, "Now I have a mind to kill you." So the little sister arose quickly, took her little brother on her back, and said, "I am going out to look for wood." As she went out, she followed the narrow trail through the prickly-pears and met her six brothers in the brush. Then they decided to leave the country, and started off as fast as they could go.

The older sister, being a powerful medicine-woman, knew at once what they were doing. She became very angry and turned herself into a bear to pursue them. Soon she was about to overtake them, when one of the boys tried his power. He took a little water in the hollow of his hand and sprinkled it around. At once it became a great lake between them and the bear. Then the children hurried on while the bear went around. After awhile, the bear caught up with them again, when another brother threw a porcupine-tail on the ground. This became a great thicket, but the bear forced its way through, and again overtook the children. This time they all climbed a high tree. The bear came to the foot of the tree, and looking up at them, said, "Now I shall kill you all." So she took a stick from the ground, threw it into the tree and knocked down four of the brothers. While she was doing this, a little bird flew around the tree, calling out to the children, "Shoot her in the head! Shoot her in the head!" Then one of the boys shot an arrow into the head of the bear, and at once she fell dead. Then they came down from the tree.

Now the four brothers were dead. The little brother took an arrow, shot it straight up into the air, and when it fell one of the dead brothers came to life. This he repeated until all were alive again. Then they held a council, and said to each other, "Where shall we go? Our people have all been killed, and we are a long way from home. We have no relatives living in the world." Finally, they decided that they preferred to live in the sky. Then the little brother said, "Shut your eyes." As they did so, they all went up. Now you can see them every night. The little brother is the North Star. The six brothers and the little sister are seen in the Great Dipper. The little sister and the eldest brother are in a line with the North Star, with the little sister being nearest it because she used to carry her little brother on her back. The other brothers are arranged in order of their age, beginning with the eldest. This is how the seven stars[1] came to be.

Two Sisters and the Porcupine (Menomini)

The early Menomini were a prairie tribe and, like the plains tribes, have many cultural narratives that link the human and animal worlds. This story of the two sisters parallels the Iroquois figures of the twin brothers—that is, one human who acts in accordance

---

1. The constellation Ursa Major.

with the natural world and one who does not. In all such Native American narratives, the consequences of disharmony with animals and nature in general is vividly rendered.

Bibliography: Hoffman, W. J.

Two Sisters and the Porcupine

There was once a village in which dwelt two sisters who were considered the swiftest runners in the Menomini tribe. Toward the setting sun was another village, though so far away that an ordinary walker would have to travel two days to reach it. Once these two sisters decided to visit the distant village; so, starting out, they ran at great speed until nearly noon, when they came to a hollow tree lying across the trail.

Snow was on the ground, and the sisters saw the track of a Porcupine leading to the hollow of the trunk. One of them broke off a stick and began to poke it into the cavity to make the Porcupine come out, saying, "Let us have some fun with him." "No, my sister," said the other. "He is a ma'nido, and we had better let him alone." The former, however, continued to drive the Porcupine farther and farther through the trunk until at last he came out, when she caught him and pulled all the long quills out of his body, throwing them in the snow. The other remonstrated such cruelty, for she thought it was too cold to deprive the Porcupine of his robe. Then the girls, who had wasted some time and still had a great distance to travel, continued their running toward the village for which they were bound.

When they left the hollow log, the Porcupine crawled up a tall pine tree until he reached the very top, where he faced the north and began to shake before his breast his small tshi'saqka rattle, singing in time to its sound. Soon the sky began to darken and the snow to fall, while the progress of the girls, who were still running along, became more and more impeded by the constantly increasing depth of snow.

One of the sisters looked back and saw the Porcupine on the treetop, using his rattle. Then she said to her little sister who had plucked out his quills, "My sister, let us go back to our own village, for I fear some harm will befall us."

"No, let us go on," replied her companion, "we need not fear the Porcupine." As the depth of the snow impeded their progress, they rolled up their blankets and continued the journey.

The day was drawing to a close and the sisters had not yet reached a point from which they could see the village they were striving to reach. Traveling on, they came to a stream which they recognized as being near the village, but night had come on, and the snow was now so deep that they were compelled by exhaustion to stop. They could hear the voices of the people in the village, but could not call loud enough to be heard. So they perished in the snow which the Porcupine had caused to fall. One should never harm the Porcupine, because he is a tshi'saqka and a ma'nido.

Mary Downing (fl. 1630s)

As the daughter of Anne Ware and Emmanuel Downing, Mary Downing was born into a well-to-do English Puritan family. Her mother died when Mary was quite young, and her father married Lucy Winthrop (*q.v.*). It was customary in the seventeenth century to place children as domestics in other homes; since Mary's parents were concerned about the worsening conditions for Puritans in England, they sent her and one or two other siblings to reside in Boston in 1633, five years before the Downings themselves came to the colonies. During her early years in Boston, Mary resided with her aunt and uncle, Margaret Tyndal (*q.v.*) and John Winthrop. In spite of the influence of these exemplars of Puritan piety, Mary's correspondence with her father exposes the changes in the younger generation's attitudes that were already occurring in the mid-seventeenth century. By revealing a rueful attitude toward the conservatism of her elders and by expressing a desire to wear the latest fashions, Mary was treading on slippery ground; in little more than a decade, Nathaniel Ward would publish his renowned attack on women's fashions in the *Simple Cobler of Aggawam* (1647). The patriarchy's fear was that the allurement of fashion would lead young women into immoral ways and away from their traditional duties of piety and subservience.

Works: Correspondence. *Bibliography*: *Winthrop Papers*.

Mary Downing's Letter

November 27, 1635

Worthy Sir, Deare Father, The continuall experience that I enjoy of your tender love and care to a child, though I confesse an underservinge one [yet] your love emboldens mee to present my humble duty and respect I owe and shall render with my might and power to your selfe soe longe as it pleaseth the Lord to continue my life. I have found soe much your love and see that neither time nor distance of place doth diminish or blast the same. . . . Father I trust in him who hath the harts and the disposinge of them in his hand, that I have not provoked you to harbor soe ill an opinion of mee as my mothers lettres do signifie and give me to understand, the ill opinion and hard perswasion which shee beares of mee, that is to say, that I should abuse your goodnes, and bee prodigall of your purse neglectfull of my brothers bands and of my slatterishnes and lasines. for my brothers bands I will not excuse my selfe, but I thinke not worthy soe sharpe a reproofe, for the rest I must needs excuse, and cleare my selfe If I may bee beleived. I doe not know my selfe guilty of any of them. for myne owne part I doe not desire to bee myne owne judge, but am willinge to be judged by them, with whom I live and sees my course, whether I bee addicted to such thinges or noe   for my habitt, it is meane, for the most as many servants, and if I had not had money which I had for some thinges here I might have wanted many necessaries which I could not have bin without, except I should have made you a scoare[1] here, which I was not willinge to doe: I writt to my mother for lace not out of any prodi-gall or proud mind but onely for some crossecloathes,[2] which is the most al-lowable and commendable dressinge here. Shee would have mee weare dress-ings which I did soe longe as they would suffer mee, whilest the elders with others intreated mee to leave them of; for they gave great offence and seeinge it hath pleased the Lord to bringe mee hither amongst his people, I would not willingly doe any thinge amongst them that should be displeasinge unto them, but for myne owne part since my sendinge for things gives such offence I will be more sparinge in that kind hereafter but leave it to the Lord to deale with mee according to his mercy earnestly desireinge him to give mee an hart to bee content with my porcion, knowinge that nothinge can beefall mee but that, that hee hath appointed   I may take that verse in the 106th Psalme 17th verse, fooles because of their transgressions and their iniquities are afflicted soe I thinke that just it is, whatsoever affliction shall come unto mee. Deare Father I am farr distant from you, and know not how longe it will please the Lord to continue it soe, but howsoever I desire to rest satisfied with his will and doe earnestly desire to submitt my selfe in all duty and obedience as be-longeth unto a child to your selfe and my mother, as if I were with you. Fa-ther I perceive by your lettres that you would very willingly to have mee change my condition[3] which I must confesse I might soe may with divers if the Lord pleased to move my hart to accept any of them, but I desire to wayte upon him that can change my hart at his will. thus with my humble duty to your selfe and my mother craving pardon of you both and of her If I have given her any offence, and soe desiringe your prayers to him, who is able to give wisedome and direccion to me in all thinges I rest: Your obedient Daughter till death

Mary Downinge

Sarah ("Sally") Eve (1749/50–1774)

Sarah Eve was one of thirteen children born to Anne Moore and Oswell Eve; only six children survived to adulthood. Sarah's father was a wealthy sea captain and commander of the *George*. While the sons went to sea with their father, Sarah and her mother re-

---

1. A debt.
2. Linen cloths that women wore across their foreheads.
3. That is, to become one of the "Saints" through conversion.

mained at their family home in the Northern Liberties area of Philadelphia. Red-headed Sarah was well educated and, according to local legend, known for the brilliance of her imagination as well as her charitable acts. Eve was engaged to Dr. Benjamin Rush, but she died on December 4, 1774, three weeks before the scheduled marriage. A memorial tribute to her, entitled "A Female Character," appeared in the *Pennsylvania Packet* after her death, with the observation that "She was cut off in the 24th year of her age by a painful and lingering illness." In 1772–73, Sarah Eve had maintained a journal so her father could "form a pretty just idea of the melancholy winters that we have had since he went away." While she occasionally reverts to this original purpose, her journal more accurately presents a thoughtful, educated young woman's life and mind in pre-Revolutionary America.

Works: Journal. *Bibliography*: Earle, *Colonial Dames*; Jones; *Pennsylvania Packet* (12 Dec. 1774).

From the Journal of Sarah Eve

February 15th. [1773]— . . . This evening Isabel planted peas, concluding like the Young Man in the Fable, from the exceeding fineness of the day, that summer was come; and as the death of the swallow and coldness of the weather which was so pleasant but the other day, convinced him of his mistake in prematurely selling his *cloathes*, so I fancy will the rottenness of the peas satisfy her that had they been planted six weeks later, it had been much better. However, as this haste only proceeds from an anxiety of having them before our neighbors, it may be termed an innocent, if not a laudable emulation.

March 12th.— . . . After dinner Mama went up with Mrs. C[lifford] to her garden: the peas that were planted under the glasses are up, and they say, look beautifully. I never once thought of it before I heard Mrs. Clifford mention it, why such an exemplary man as Mr. Duche[1] should sit every day and have his hair curl'd and powder'd by a barber. Since, I have thought about it *greatly*, and would like to hear *his* sentiments on this subject. But, my dear ma'am, what would a Parson be without *powder*, it is as necessary to *him* as to a *soldier*, for it gives a more significant shake to his head, and is as *priming* to his words & looks. As to having his hair curled, he perhaps thinks it of little or no consequence, since curled or uncurled locks will turn so gray, or perhaps he may look upon it as more humiliating to wear his own hair than a wig, as then his head must serve as a *block* on which the barber must dress it.

In the evening Nancy & Hannah Mitchell came up to see us. I ask Rose's pardon, I really came near forgetting we had the pleasure of seeing her black lady ship in the afternoon, but as our girl was not at home we could not prevail upon her to stay to Tea. "Farewell, my dear missey, my love to ye girl, d'ye hear!"

1. The Reverend Jacob Duche was a minister of the United Churches in Philadelphia.

March 23rd.—A most fine day indeed, but as this is not uncommon at this season, I dare say, in a week it will be entirely forgotten, as in general it is only the rare occurences that make impressions on the memory. In this year we have had as yet but one day rendered memorable by its temperature, and that was the 21st of February, the extreme coldness of which made it so. Scarcely a day but you hear it referred to; it was "that cold Sunday" that such an one caught their cold . . . another, attributes the death of a friend to "that cold Sunday" . . . and so on! It puts me in mind of those lines of our poet Godfrey:[2]

> "Curiosity's another name for Man;
> "The blazing meteor streaming thro' the air,
> "Commands our wonder, and admiring eyes
> "With eager gaze we trace the lucent paths
> "Till spent at last, it shrinks to native nothing,
> "While the bright stars which ever steady glow
> "Unheeded shine and bless the world below."

The weather certainly may be said to be an emblem of mankind; there are few men in an age that are remembered after they are dead, and those few for being remarkable, like the days of the year, extreme in something, man for his goodness, wisdom, or ambition, for the service or disservice he has done a community, in common, with the weather only pleases or displeases for the present, all is forgotten when no more. It seems ingratitude so soon to forget those whose whole lives were made eminent by their social virtues, when perhaps another will be remembered and his name handed down to posterity for having been the best hair-dresser, or the best fiddle-maker of his time.

April 4th.—I think for the future I will not be so particular about the weather, and will only notice what is rather uncommon. . . . and yet upon second thought, I don't know but it would have been best, for I need only to have collected a few recipes, old sayings & scraps of poetry, and in a year or two I might have published as good an almanack as Father Abraham's, Poor Richard's, or even Mr. Taylor's.[3] "But now," says mama, "*we* have *no* such almanacks as *his* was!"

May 1st.— . . . This day is five years since my dear father left us; I am persuaded that had we known that morning we parted with him, that he was to have been absent so long, we should have thought it impossible to have existed for one half the time; nay, I know not at that time whether we should have wished it. Happy mortals are we, that we cannot dive into futurity! if we could, how pleasure would be anticipated until it became tasteless, and the knowledge of distant evil would render us utterly insensible to the joys of present good.

June 3rd.—In the morning I went to Mrs. Smith's, met with B. Trapnal who had just received a letter for me from my brother *Ose*,[4] in Georgia dated May 15th;

2. Thomas Godfrey, a Philadelphia poet and dramatist; his works were published in 1765. The quote that follows is from "The Prince of Parthia, A Tragedy."

3. "Poor Richard's" was Benjamin Franklin's satirical almanac (1732). "Father Abraham's," although supposedly authored by "Abraham Weatherwise," was another of Franklin's pseudonymous publications; Jacob Taylor's *Taylor Almanac* preceded Franklin's by thirty years.

4. Oswell Eve was at sea with his father and his brother, John.

we had flattered ourselves that before that time they were in Jamaica, but meeting with their usual luck they had been detained. Will fortune never cease to persecute us? but why complain! for at the worst what is poverty![5] it is living more according to nature—luxury is not nature but art—does not poverty always bring dependence? No, a person that is poor could they divest themselves of opinion is more independent than one that is not so, as the one limits his wants and expectations to his circumstances, the other knows no bounds therefore is more dependent in many senses of the word—"happy is the man that expects nothing for he shall not be disappointed." Poverty without pride is nothing, but with it, it is the very deuce! But seriously there must be something more dreadful in it than I can see, when a former acquaintance and one that pretended a friendship for another, such as Nancy T—— did [one of that money loving family of the F——][6] will almost run from you as though poverty were realy infectious. The lady I mentioned will cut down an alley or walk herself into a perspiration rather than acknowledge she has ever seen you before, or if it so happens she can not help speaking to you, it is done in so slight a manner and with so much confusion, that, were it not for this plague "Pride" I should enjoy it above all things. However, I have the satisfaction to feel myself, in many respects, as much superior to her as she to me in point of fortune. And yet for years, I may say, we were almost inseparable, there was scarce a wish or thought that one of us had, that was not as ardently desired by the other.... People when deprived of the goods of fortune are apt, I believe, to be jealous . . . and often fancy themselves slighted when, perhaps, it was never intended. But nothing, I now think, could ever tempt me to renew our former acquaintance.

August 30th.—This morning I went to see my aunt, and then to Mr. Mitchell's to spend the day; but hearing that Mr. John Penn was to be proclaimed Governor, curiosity led Deby Mitchel and I to go see him. For my part I had rather be his brother than he, the one possesses the hearts of the people the other the Government. Yesterday he made a public entry into Town with a large train.[7]

Elizabeth Sprigs (fl. 1756)

Elizabeth Sprigs's brief but informative letter to her father, John Sprigs, is one of the rare records we have of a female servant's assessment of her working conditions in mid-eighteenth-century

---

5. Prior to the period covered by Eve's journal, her father had experienced severe financial difficulties which still haunted her and her mother as they struggled to maintain the household in his absence; the consequences to their social position are evident in Eve's entry for this date.

6. Eve's bracketed insertion.

7. John Penn had come to Philadelphia on this day from New York to be reappointed as Governor; his first tenure (1763–1771) had been an unpopular one. His brother Richard had governed with immense popularity after the end of John's first term. Richard and John's animosity toward one another was evident to the community.

America. Approximately 350,000 servants were brought to the colonies in the pre-Revolutionary years, with Virginia and Maryland making the greatest use of indentured servants' labor. While many Europeans agreed to a period of indentured labor as a means of coming to America, the system also encouraged the export of criminals and, in rarer cases such as Sprigs faced, the use of such labor was a means of parental control. Sent to America by her father as punishment for "undutifullness," Elizabeth struggled to survive a cruel employer and impoverished living conditions. Her account reminds us of the extreme consequences for young women in early America who dared to abandon the requirements of "female behavior."

Works: Correspondence. Bibliography: Calder.

Elizabeth Sprigs's Letter

Honred Father   *Maryland Sept'r 22'd 1756.*[1]

My being for ever banished from your sight, will I hope pardon the Boldness I now take of troubling you with these, my long silence has been purely owning to my undutifullness to you, and well knowing I had offended in the highest Degree, put a tie to my tongue and pen, for fear I should be extinct from your good Graces and add a further Trouble to you, but too well knowing your care and tenderness for me so long as I retaind my Duty to you, induced me once again to endeavour if possible, to kindle up that flame again. O Dear Father, belive what I am going to relate the words of truth and sincerity, and Ballance my former bad Conduct [against] my sufferings here, and then I am sure you'll pitty your Destress Daughter, What we unfortunat English People suffer here is beyond the probility of you in England to Conceive, let it suffice that I one of the unhappy Number, am toiling almost Day and Night, and very often in the Horses druggery, with only this comfort that you Bitch you do not halfe enough, and then tied up and whipp'd to that Degree that you'd not serve an Annimal, scarce any thing but Indian Corn and Salt to eat and that even begrudged nay many Negroes are better used, almost naked no shoes nor stockings to wear, and the comfort after slaving dureing Masters pleasure, what rest we can get is to rap ourselves up in a Blanket and ly upon the Ground, this is the deplorable Condition your poor Betty endures, and now I beg if you have any Bowels of Compassion left show it by sending me some Relief, C[l]othing is the principal thing wanting, which if you should condiscend to, may easely send them to me by any of the ships bound to Baltimore Town Patapsco River Maryland, and give me leave to conclude in Duty to you and Uncles and Aunts, and Respect to all Friends

Honred Father
Your undutifull and Disobedient Child
Elizabeth Sprigs

1. John Sprigs was still in London at the time this letter was written.

Anna Green Winslow (1759–1779)

Born in Nova Scotia, Anna Green Winslow was a descendant of Mary Chilton, who was among the first Pilgrims to settle in New England. Anna's father, Joshua Winslow, was a Loyalist during the American Revolution, and his exile caused a separation of several years from his wife, Anna Green, and his daughter. Anna died, probably from consumption, before the family could be reunited. Winslow's diary, written to keep her parents informed of her progress and probably as a school assignment, details her upper-class life from 1771 to 1773 when she was attending "finishing school" in Boston. While the diary depicts the harsh preachings of the Puritan ministry at the Old South Church, it also employs a style that captures the typically quixotic thoughts of a young girl's self-absorption.

Works: Diary. *Bibliography*: Earle, ed., *Diary of Anna Green Winslow*.

From the Diary of Anna Green Winslow

Nov[r] 18th, 1771.[1]—Mr. Beacons[2] text yesterday was Psalm cxlix. 4. . . . Mr. Beacon ask'd a question. What is beauty—or, wherein does true beauty consist? He answer'd, in holiness—and said a great deal about it that I can't remember, & as aunt[3] says she hant leisure now to help me any further—so I may just tell you a little that I remember without her assistance. . . . He said he would lastly address himself to the young people: My dear young friends, you are pleased with beauty, & like to be tho't beautifull—but let me tell ye, you'l never be truly beautifull till you are like the King's daughter, all glorious within. . . . while you are without holiness, your beauty is deformity—you are all over black & defil'd, ugly and loathsome to all holy beings, the wrath of th' great God lie's upon you, & if you die in this condition, you will be turn'd into hell, with ugly devils, to eternity. . . .

30th Nov. [1771]—My company yesterday were Miss Polly Deming, Miss Polly Glover, Miss Peggy Draper, Miss Bessy Winslow, Miss Nancy Glover, Miss Sally Winslow[,] Miss Polly Atwood, Miss Han[h] Soley[4]. . . . We made four couple at country dansing; danceing I mean. In the evening young

1. Winslow is addressing her mother in these entries.
2. The Reverend John Bacon, successor to Joseph Sewall at the Old South Church in Boston.
3. Sarah Winslow West Deming (1722–1788), Winslow's paternal aunt, was a gentlewoman with whom young girls from established families could board while attending finishing schools in Boston.
4. Polly Deming, Winslow's cousin; Mary (Polly) Glover (1758–1842), daughter of Anne Simpson and Nathaniel Glover, wealthy Bostonians; Elizabeth (Bessy) Winslow (1760–1795), another cousin; Anne (Nancy) Glover (1753–1797), Mary's sister; Sarah (Sally) Winslow (1755–1804), a third cousin; Hannah Soley (1762–?), daughter of Hannah Carey and John Soley. The remaining members of the party remain unidentified.

Mr. Waters[5] hearing of my assembly, put his flute in his pocket and played several minuets and other tunes, to which we danced mighty cleverly. But Lucinda[6] was our principal piper. . . .

Valentine day.—My cousin Sally reeled off a 10 knot skane of yarn today. My valentine was an old country plow-joger.[7] The yarn was of my spinning. Aunt says it will do for filling. Aunt also says niece is a whimsical child.

Feb. 21 [1772]—. . . I have made the purchase I told you of a few pages agone, that is, last Thursday I purchas'd with my aunt Deming's leave, a very beautiful white feather hat . . . I have long been saving my money to procure for which I have let your kind allowance, Papa, lay in my aunt's hands till this hat which I spoke for was brought home. As I am (as we say) a daughter of liberty[8] I chuse to wear as much of our own manufactory as pocible. . . .

Feb. 22[d]. [1772]—. . . I have spun 30 knots of linning yarn, and (partly) new footed a pair of stockings for Lucinda, read a part of the pilgrim's progress, coppied part of my text journal (that if I live a few years longer, I may be able to understand it, for aunt sais, that to her, the contents as I first mark'd them, were an impenetrable secret) play'd some, tuck'd[9] a great deal (Aunt Deming says it is very true) laugh'd enough, & I tell aunt it is all human *nature*, if not human reason. And now, I wish my honored mamma a very good night.

Monday noon Feb. 25th. [1772]—. . . Dear mamma, I suppose that you would be glad to hear that Betty Smith who has given you so much trouble, is well & behaves herself well & I should be glad if I could write you so. But the truth is, no sooner was the 29th Regiment encamped upon the common[10] but miss Betty took herself among them (as the Irish say) & there she stay'd with Bill Pinchion & awhile. The next news of her was, that she was got into gaol for stealing: from whence she was taken to the publick whipping post. The next adventure was to the Castle, after the soldier's were remov'd there, for the murder of the 5th March last. When they turn'd her away from there, she came up to town again, and soon got into the workhouse for new misdemeanours, she soon ran away from there and sit up her old trade of pilfering again, for which she was put a second time into gaol, there she still remains. About two months agone (as well as I can re-

5. Josiah Waters, Jr.

6. Lucinda was Sarah Winslow Deming's slave. Her date of birth is unknown, although a Winslow family member noted that she was only about seven years old when she was bought by Winslow Deming, and she was given her freedom upon her mistress's death in 1788. Thereafter, Lucinda lived at the home of one of Winslow Deming's nephews, General John Winslow.

7. Tradition held that the first member of the opposite sex to be seen on that day became your valentine.

8. As Morse Earle notes, "Boston was at that date pervaded by the spirit of Liberty." Many young women used their domestic skills to produce memorabilia to liberty and often declared themselves "tea-totlers" until the British tax had been lifted from that commodity.

9. To tuck is to finish cloth after it comes from the weaver. Aunt Deming's pun is that to tuck can also mean to upbraid or rebuke. This kind of playful banter between aunt and niece runs throughout the diary.

10. British troops had been quartered in Boston since 1770. On March 5, 1772, the troops fired on unarmed Bostonians; Daniel Webster asserted that this slaughter of several citizens was the beginning of the separation from England.

member) she & a number of her wretched companions set the gaol on fire, in order to get out, but the fire was timely discovered & extinguished, & there, as I said she still remains till this day, in order to be tried for her crimes. I heard somebody say that as she has some connections with the army no doubt but she would be cleared, and perhaps, have a pension into the bargain. Mr. Henry says the way of sin is down hill, when persons get into that way they are not easily stopped.[11]

March 21.— . . . (P.M.) Mr. Hunt call'd in to visit us just after we rose from diner. . . . Aunt told him that *his name* went frequently into my journals together with broken & some times whole sentences of his sermons, conversations &c. He laugh'd & call'd me Newsmonger, & said I was a daily advertiser. He added, that he did not doubt but my journals afforded much entertainment & would be a future benefit &c. Here is a fine compliment for me mamma.

May 25.— . . . After making a short visit with my Aunt at Mrs Green's . . . yesterday towards evening, I took a walk with cousin Sally to see the good folks in sudbury Street, & found them all well. I had my HEDDUS roll on, aunt Storer said it ought to be made less, Aunt Deming said it ought not to be made at all. It makes my head itch, & ach, & burn like anything Mamma. This famous roll is not made *wholly* of a red *Cow Tail*, but is a mixture of that, & horsehair (very course) & a little human hair of yellow hue, that I suppose was taken out of the back part of an old wig. . . . [Aunt] took up her apron & mesur'd me, & from the roots of my hair on my forehead to the top of my notions, I mesur'd above an inch longer than I did downwards from the roots of my hair to the end of my chin. Nothing renders a young person more amiable than virtue & modesty without the help of fals hair, red *Cow tail*, or D—— (the barber).[12] Now all this mamma, I have just been reading over to my aunt. She is pleas'd with my whimsical description & grave (half grave) improvement, & hopes a little fals English will not spoil the whole with Mamma. Rome was not built in a day.

Eliza Southgate Bowne (1783–1809)

The third of Mary King and Robert Southgate's twelve children, Eliza was born September 24, 1783, in Scarborough, Maine. Her mother came from one of the wealthiest families in the region, and her father was a successful physician. An exceptionally observant and intelligent young woman, Eliza was fortunate to be raised in a family that valued education. She first attended school in Scar-

11. On May 16, 1772, Winslow noted: "Last Wednesday Bet Smith was set upon the gallows. She behav'd with great impudence." This is Winslow's entire response to Betty Smith's punishment; the remainder of her diary for that day talks about a school dance in which she participated.

12. Hair rolls, sometimes reaching great heights and weighing as much as fourteen ounces, were the height of fashion in prewar Boston.

borough, then briefly attended a finishing school near Boston before being transferred to the excellent boarding school run by the author and educator Susanna Haswell Rowson (*q.v.*).

In 1803, Eliza married Walter Bowne and settled in New York. She gave birth to two children—Walter (b. 1806) and Mary (b. 1808). Eliza's second pregnancy was a difficult one, however, and her health continued to fail thereafter. Upon medical recommendation, she and her sister Octavia Southgate Browne and Octavia's husband sailed for Charleston, South Carolina, where it was believed the warm weather would have a healing effect. The journey was treacherous, however, and Eliza died in Charleston on February 20, 1809, before her husband could join her. Her letters to family members constitute a detailed depiction of upper-class life for a "finished" young woman in eighteenth-century Maine.

Works: Correspondence. *Bibliography*: Cook; Fizer.

The Letters of Eliza Southgate Bowne

Honored Parents: *Medford, May 12, 1797.*[1]

With pleasure I sit down to the best of parents to inform them of my situation, as doubtless they are anxious to hear,—permit me to tell them something of my foolish heart. When I first came here I gave myself up to reflection, but not pleasing reflections. When Mr. Boyd[2] left me I burst into tears and instead of trying to calm my feelings I tried to feel worse. I begin to feel happier and will soon gather up all my Philosophy and think of the duty that now attends me, to think that here I may drink freely of the fountain of knowledge, but I will not dwell any longer on the subject. I am not doing anything but writing, reading, and cyphering. There is a French Master coming next Monday, and he will teach French and Dancing. William Boyd and Mr. Wyman[3] advise me to learn French, yet if I do at all I wish you to write me very soon what you think best, for the school begins on Monday. Mr. Wyman says it will not take up but a very little of my time, for it is but two days in the week, and the lessons only 2 hours long. Mr. Wyman says I must learn Geometry before Geography, and that I better not begin it till I have got through my Cyphering.

We get up early in the morning and make our beds and sweep the chamber, it is a chamber about as large as our kitchen chamber, and a little better finished. There's 4 beds in the chamber, and two persons in each bed, we have chocolate for breakfast and supper.

Your affectionate Daughter
Eliza Southgate.

1. Eliza is at Mrs. Wyman's boarding school at Medford, Massachusetts. Because of the school's cramped conditions and possibly because of the limited curriculum, the Southgates quickly removed Eliza from the school and placed her with Susanna Haswell Rowson.

2. Joseph Boyd was the husband of Isabella Southgate Boyd, Eliza Southgate's eldest sister.

3. Wyman was the spouse of the school's headmistress.

Hon. Father: *Boston, February 13, 1798.*

I am again placed at school under the tuition of an amiable lady,[4] so mild, so good, no one can help loving her; she treats all her scholars with such a tenderness as would win the affection of the most savage brute, tho' scarcely able to receive an impression of the kind. I learn Embroidery and Geography at present and wish your permission to learn Musick. You may justly say, my best of Fathers, that every letter of mine is one which is asking for something more; never contented—I only ask, if you refuse me, I know you do what you think best, and I am sure I ought not to complain, for you have never yet refused me anything that I have asked, my best of Parents, how shall I repay you? You answer, by your good behaviour. Heaven grant that it may be such as may repay you. A year will have rolled over my head before I shall see my Parents. I have ventured from them at an early age to be so long a time absent, but I hope I have learnt a good lesson by it—a lesson of experience, which is the best lesson I could learn.

I have described one of the blessings of creation in Mrs. Rawson, and now I will describe Mrs. Wyman as the reverse: she is the worst woman I ever knew of all that I ever saw; nobody knows what I suffered from the treatment of that woman—I had the misfortune to be a favorite with Miss Haskell and Mr. Wyman, she said, and she treated me as her own malicious heart dictated; but whatever is, is right, and I learnt a good lesson by it. . . . May it please the disposer of all events to return me safe home to the bosom of my friends in health safely. I never was happier in my life I think. . . .

To Moses Porter.[5]

My most charming Cousin! . . . As I look around me I am surprised at the happiness which is so generally enjoyed in families, and that marriages which have not love for a foundation on more than one side at most, should produce so much apparent harmony. I may be censured for declaring it as my opinion that not one woman in a hundred marries for love. A woman of taste and sentiment will surely see but a very few whom she could love, and it is altogether uncertain whether either of them will particularly distinguish her. If they should, surely she is very fortunate, but it would be one of fortune's random favors and such as we have no right to expect. The female mind I believe is of a very pliable texture; if it were not we should be wretched indeed. Admitting as a known truth that few women marry those whom they would prefer to all the world if they could be viewed by them with equal affection, or rather that there are often others whom they could have preferred if they had felt that affection for them which would have induced them to offer themselves,—admitting this as a truth not to be disputed,—is it not a subject of astonishment that happiness is not almost

4. Susanna Haswell Rowson.
5. Porter was the son of Mary King Southgate's sister, Pauline, and her husband, Aaron Porter; he was one of Eliza Southgate's favorite correspondents. This letter was written sometime around October 1800, three years before Southgate's own marriage, which, according to her letters, was indeed a union of "equal affection."

banished from this connexion? Gratitude is undoubtedly the foundation of the esteem we commonly feel for a husband. One that has preferred us to all the world, one that has thought us possessed of every quality to render him happy, surely merits our gratitude. If his character is good—if he is not displeasing in his person or manners—what objection can we make that will not be thought frivolous by the greater part of the world?—yet I think there are many other things necessary for happiness, and the world should never compel me to marry a man because I could not give satisfactory reasons for not liking him. I do not esteem marriage absolutely essential to happiness, and that it does not always bring happiness we must every day witness in our acquaintance. A single life is considered too generally as a reproach; but let me ask you, which is the most despicable—she who marries a man she scarcely thinks *well* of—to avoid the reputation of an old maid—or she, who with more delicacy, than marry one she could not highly esteem, preferred to live single all her life, and had wisdom enough to despise so mean a sacrifice, to the opinion of the rabble, as the woman who marries a man she has not much love for—must make. I wish not to alter the laws of nature—neither will I quarrel with the rules which custom has established and rendered indispensably necessary to the harmony of society. But every being who has contemplated human nature on a large scale will certainly justify me when I declare that the inequality of privilege between the sexes is very sensibly felt by us females, and in no instance is it greater than in the liberty of choosing a partner in marriage; true, we have the liberty of refusing those we don't like, but not of selecting those we do. This is undoubtedly as it should be. But let me ask you, what must be that love which is altogether voluntary, which we can withhold or give, which sleeps in dulness and apathy till it is requested to brighten into life? Is it not a cold, lifeless dictate of the head,—do we not weigh all the conveniences and inconveniences which will attend it? And after a long calculation, in which the heart never was consulted, we determine whether it is most prudent to love or not.

How I should despise a soul so sordid, so mean! How I abhor the heart which is regulated by mechanical rules, which can say "thus far will I go and no farther," whose feelings can keep pace with their convenience, and be awakened at stated periods,—a mere piece of clockwork which always moves right! How far less valuable than that being who has a soul to govern her actions, and though she may not always be coldly prudent, yet she will sometimes be generous and noble, and that the other never can be. After all, I must own that a woman of delicacy never will suffer her esteem to ripen into love unless she is convinced of a return. Though our first approaches to love may be involuntary, yet I should be sorry if we had no power of controlling them if occasion required. There is a happy conformity or pliability in the female mind which seems to have been a gift of nature to enable them to be happy with so few privileges,—and another thing, they have more gratitude in their dispositions than men, and there is a something particularly gratifying to the heart in being beloved, if the object is worthy;

it produces a something like, and "Pity melts the heart to love." Added to these there is a self-love which does more than all the rest. Our vanity ('tis an ugly word but I can't find a better) is gratified by the distinguished preference given us. There must be an essential difference in the dispositions of men and women. I am astonished when I think of it—yet—But I have written myself into sunshine—'tis always my way when anything oppresses me, when any chain of thoughts particularly occupies my mind, and I feel dissatisfied at anything which I have not the power to alter,—to sit down and unburthen them on paper; it never fails to alleviate me, and I generally give full scope to the feelings of the moment, and as I write all disagreeable thoughts evaporate, and I end contented that things shall remain as they are. When I began this it absolutely appeared to me that no woman, or rather not one in a hundred, married the man she should prefer to all the world— not that I ever could suppose that at the time she married him she did not prefer him to others,—but that she would have preferred another if he had professed to love her as well as the one she married. Indeed, I believe no woman of delicacy suffers herself to think she could love any one before she had discovered an affection for her. For my part I should never ask the question of myself—do I love such a one, if I had reason to think he loved me— and I believe there are many who love that never confessed it to themselves. My Pride, my delicacy, would all be hurt if I discovered such *unasked* for love, even in my own bosom. I would strain every nerve and rouse every faculty to quell the first appearance of it. There is no danger, however. I could never love without being beloved, and I am confident in my own mind that no person whom I could love would ever think me sufficiently worthy to love me. But I congratulate myself that I am at liberty to refuse those I don't like, and that I have firmness enough to brave the sneers of the world and live an old maid, if I never find one I can love.

Lucinda Lee (fl. 1787)

Only a fragment of Lucinda Lee's journal is extant; however, the manuscript, which covers less than two months, reveals significant details about the upper-class social life of a young woman born into the distinguished Lee family of Virginia. Addressed to her friend Polly Brent ("Marcia," "Lavinia"), the journal details Lee's activities during a visit to various Lee and Washington families in Virginia who were her relatives. The journal is also an example of the "female world of love and ritual" that Carroll Smith-Rosenberg has identified.

Works: Journal. *Bibliography*: Earle, *Colonial Dames*; Mason, Emily V.; Smith-Rosenberg, 53–76.

From the Journal of Lucinda Lee

The Wilderness, September 16, [1787][1]

I hear you say, "The Wilderness! where in the world is that, Lucy?" It is the name of this place. I can't say I was much struck with the situation of the House; but they are as kind, good People as I ever saw. . . .

I have spent the morning in reading; and, much to my satisfaction, old Mrs. Gordon[2] is just come to spend the day here. Lucy Gordon and myself are just returned from walking out. I was delighted: we walked to a river—they call it here; but it is very narrow. The banks of it are beautiful, covered with moss and wild flowers; all that a romantic mind could form. I thought of my Polly, and thought how delighted she would have been had she been a Spectater of the scene; and how much more pleased would your Lucy have been, how more delighted if she could have had her Polly to point out the Beauties too, and make her observations: but her dear Company was denied. Lucy Gordon is a truly good Girl, but nothing of the romance in her. So much the better, say I; she is much happier without. I wish to Heaven I had as little. . . .

September 20. I have spent this morning in reading *Lady Julia Mandeville,* and was much affected. Indeed, I think I never cried more in my life reading a Novel: the stile is beautiful, but the tale is horrid. I reckon you have read it. Some one just comes to tell us A Mr. Masenbird and Mr. Spotswood is come. We must go down, but I am affraid both Sister's and my eyes will betray us. Adieu. I will describe the Gentlemen on my return.

Mr. Spotswood is the Gentleman we visited the other day. I think him handsome. Mr. Masenbird is an Englishman, and single, that has settled in this part of the World. I had heard he was a very uncouth creature, but he is quite the reverse—very polite, not handsome.

Interrupted again. They are come to tell me a Mr. Grimes and his Lady are come to wait on us. I must throw aside my pen, and go down to be introduced. Adieu. I will write more when we retire to dress.

Mrs. Grimes is very handsome, though appears to be a little proud. Sister is almost drest; I shall have but little time to smart myself. Adieu. My Great-Coat shall be my dress today. . . .

September 22. To-day we dine with old Mrs. Gordon. Lucy and myself are going to walk over now; Sister and Mrs. Gordon will not go this hour. Adieu. I will carry my Journal with me.

We had a very pleasant walk; got a number of grapes and nuts in our way. Lucy and myself are going to walk in the Garden, to get some pink-seed I am anxious to have. The Gentlemen dined to-day at Mr. Masenbird's. Mrs. Gordon and sister are come: they have proposed cards, and I am called to join them. Adieu.

I would have staid to-night with old Mrs. Gordon, but expected to go down

---

1. "The Wilderness" is the residence the John Grymes family. The 1871 edition of Lee's journal presents its dates as 1782; correct dates are September 16 to November 12, 1787.

2. A neighbor, whose daughter, Lucy Gordon, is described by Lee as "very clever, though not a Beauty."

to-Morrow. Lucy and myself had a pleasant walk back. The married folks went on before.

We have supped, and the gentlemen are not returned yet. Lucy and myself are in a peck of troubles for fear they should return drunk. Sister has had our bed moved in her room. Just as we were undress'd and going to bed, the Gentlemen arrived, and we had to scamper. Both tipsy!

To-day is Sunday. Brother was so worsted by the frolick yesterday, we did not set off to-day. Old Mrs. Gordon dines here to-day. Lucy and myself are going to walk to the river, and get a nosegay of wild flowers.

September 24. . . . Well, my dearest Lavinia, I am arrived at *Belleview*,[3] a good deal fatigued, where we found Mr. Bushrod Washington and his lady, on their way down. She is fonder of me than ever; prest me to go with her to Maryland this Winter. Mr. Phil Fitzhugh is likewise here. He said, at supper, he was engaged to dance with one of the Miss Brents at a Ball in Dumfries, but that it was only conditionally. Mammy has just sent me word she has a letter for me—it is from Nancy, I am sure. Adieu.

It was, and one for you enclosed in it. Nancy writes me her Sister Pinkard is at *Chantilly*.[4] It must be a great acquisition to her happiness to have so amiable a companion as I have heard she was.

The Company is all gone, and I have seated myself to converse with my Polly. Mrs. A. Washington has lent me a new Novel, called *Victoria*.[5] I can't say I admire the Tale, though I think it prettyly told. There is a verse in it I wish you much to read. I believe, if I a'n't too Lazy, I will copy it off for you: the verse is not very butifull, but the sense is, I assure you.

To-day I have spent in putting my cloaths to rights—a dreadful task, you will say. I am going to take a little airing this evening. Adieu: the horses are at the door. . . .

October 3 [at Chantilly]. I am just up, and am going to seat myself for Sibby to crape my hair.

Cousin Nancy and myself have just returned from taking an airing in the Chariot. We went to *Stratford*:[6] walked in the Garden, sat about two hours under a butifull shade tree, and eat as many figs as we could. How did we wish for our dear Polly, and think that was the only thing we wanted to compleat our happiness! . . .

October 4. To-day I have been busy making a cap. I don't think it clever, though I have spent a good while about it. Nancy and myself have been locked up stairs by ourselves all day. She is better to-day than she was yesterday.

Oh, my Marcia, how hard is our fate! that we should be deprived of your dear company, when it would compleat our Felicity—but such is the fate of

3. Residence of the Thomas Ludwell Lee family.
4. Home of Richard Henry Lee family. Richard Henry Lee (1732–1794) was a leader in the American Revolution, served in the Continental Congress, signed the Declaration of Independence, and became a U.S. Senator from Virginia in 1789.
5. Susanna Haswell Rowson's (*q.v.*) first novel, published in 1786.
6. Residence of the Philip Ludwell Lee family.

Mortals! We are never permitted to be perfectly happy. I suppose it is right, else the Supreme Disposer of all things would not have permitted it: we should perhaps have been more neglectful than we are of our duty.

October 6. I wish, my Polly, you could see Mrs. Pinkard. You would be delighted with her. She is, I think, among the finest Women I have seen; and is thought very beautifull.

I have been very agreeably entertained this evening, reading a Novel called *Malvern Dale.* It is something like *Evelina,*[7] though not so pretty.

I have a piece of advice to give you, which I have before urged—that is, to read something improving. Books of instruction will be a thousand times more pleasing than all the novels in the World. I own myself, I am too fond of Novel-reading; but, by accustoming myself to reading other Books, I have become less so, and I wish my Polly to do the same.

October 8. . . . I have been very busy to-day working a little screne, to hold in my hand to prevent the fire from burning my face. I think it will be beautifull.

I have seated myself in my rapper to scribble a little. Mr. Pinkard has been reading a Play[8] all evening to Nancy and myself. We were much pleased with it. Nancy grows better and better every day—which I am delighted at. Adieu: sleep has closed my eyes.

October 11. Hannah[9] and myself were going to take a long walk this evening, but were prevented by the two horred Mortals, Mr. Pinkard and Mr. Washington, who seized me and kissed me a dozen times in spite of all the resistance I could make. They really think, now they are married, they are prevaliged to do any thing.

October 12. I am going to tell you a piece of a secret; but you must never mention it. Nancy had an admirer lately—who do you think it is? No other than Mr. Newton. He got his discard yesterday.

It is in the evening. Nancy and myself have been to visit our little garden. We were so unfortunate as to make it on the side of the hill, and it is wash't very much. Do you visit our dear pledge, and think of your Lucy? How often do I think with rapture on the happy hours we spent sitting on the fence, singing and looking at the river with the Moon shining on it. Oh, how beautiful it look't! Adieu.

October 15.[10] . . . We have retired to dress for dinner. Shall I tell you our dresses? I hear you say "Yes." Mrs. P. wears a brocade; Cousin M. her pink Great-Coat, and I my pink. Adieu. Mrs. P. is going to dress my hair.

Every moment I can spare from the Company I dedicate to you. Two Beaux dined here. Mr. James Thomson and Mr. Ford. In the evening two more came— Mr. Beal and Mr. Joe Thomson. We are all preparing to dance. Adieu: I hear the Fidle.

7. A 1778 novel by the English writer Fanny Burney (1752–1840).
8. The play was *Belle's Stratagem* by Hannah Cowley.
9. Hannah Lee, daughter of Richard Henry Lee.
10. Lee is now at Pecatone, the residence of Mrs. Turberville.

October 16. We spent last night very agreeably. Danced till Eleven. My partner was Mr. Beal. This is a beautiful situation—the Garden extends from the House to the river. I have been takeing a very agreeable walk there. An airing is proposed this morning. We are all in Mr. Turberville's Coach. Adieu: it is at the door.

I don't know when I've been happier than I am now. Every thing conspires to make me so. Cousin Turberville is so Affectionate. She does every thing in her power to make her Company happy. I had forgot to tell you Cousin Hannah's dress yesterday. It was a blue lute-string habit, taffety apron and handkerchief, with the most butiful little hat on the side of her head I ever saw.

We are dressing for dinner: this is a ceremony always practiced here. I wear my Great-Coat.

We are just done tea; and are to have the same Gentlemen to dance again to-night.

I begin to want very much to see my Polly. Ah! what would I not give to obtain that [happiness]. It appears a year since the morning I parted from you, and how long, very long will it be before I clasp you to my breast. I am deprived even the consolation of hearing from you. Adieu, my love. I must return to the Company.

October 17. We danced last night, and every one appeared to be happy. I can answer for your Lucy: her partner was Mr. James Thomson—one of the best dancers I most ever saw. Early this morning came one of the Miss Ballendine's—truly Amiable, I believe, but not handsome. But how prefarable is good sense and affability to Beauty: more pleasing a thousand times!

. . . The old man being sick that plays the Fidle, we have diverted ourselves playing *grind the bottle* and *hide the thimble*. Our time passed away agreeably enough.

October 22. We return this morning to *Pecatone*.[11] Adieu.

We are at *Pecatone*, and dressing. There are several Gentlemen to dine here. Mr. Thomson has invited this Family and ourselves to drink tea with him this evening. He has had a New Cargo of tea arrived. We intend going, and I shall not scribble again to-night.

October 23. We went to Mr. Thomson's; returned, and danced at night. Mr. Turberville and Mr. Beal each made us all a present of a pound of Powder. I really have a great Affection for Mrs. Pinkard. She always chooses my headdress, dresses my hair, and is the best Creature in lending you any thing. If you just say you want a thing, if she happens to have it, she will insist on your wearing it. Cousin Hannah has a quantity of Cloaths. She has put on every day since I have been here a different dress of muslin, and all handsome. Adieu, my best beloved. I have but little time to scribble, and that is only when we retire to dress.

October 27.[12] When we got here we found the House pretty full. Nancy was here. I had to dress in a great hurry for dinner. We spent the evening very

---

11. They had spent four days at Mr. Ballandine's estate.
12. The travelers are now at Bushfield, the residence of Lee's cousins the Washingtons.

agreeably in chatting. Milly Washington is a thousand times prettyer than I thought her at first, and very agreeable. About sunset, Nancy, Milly, and myself took a walk in the Garden. We were mighty busy cutting thistles to try our sweethearts, when Mr. Washington caught us; and you can't conceive how he plagued us—chased us all over the Garden, and was quite impertinent.

I must tell you of our frolic after we went to our room. We took it into our heads to want to eat; well, we had a large dish of bacon and beaf; after that, a bowl of Sago cream; and after that, an apple pye. While we were eating the apple pye in bed—God bless you! making a great noise—in came Mr. Washington, dressed in Hannah's short gown and peticoat, and seazed me and kissed me twenty times, in spite of all the resistance I could make; and then Cousin Molly. Hannah soon followed, dress'd in his Coat. They joined us in eating the apple pye, and then went out. After this we took it in our heads to want to eat oysters. We got up, put on our rappers, and went down in the Seller to get them: do you think Mr. Washington did not follow us and scear us just to death. We went up tho, and eat our oysters. We slept in the old Lady's room too, and she sat laughing fit to kill herself at us. She is a charming old lady— you would be delighted with her. . . .

On Women's Education

How Women Learned to Grind (ZUNI)

Since in many tribes the preparation of corn was a vital aspect of a young woman's training—and of the survival of a tribe (see, for example, "Corn Grinding Song" in the "Poetry" section, Part III)—young women were trained in the arts of grinding and preparing corn. Among the Zuni, the following legend became an integral part of female education processes and was included in late-eighteenth-century ceremonies celebrating the process.

Bibliography: Cushing; Niethammer.

How Women Learned to Grind

Once, many generations ago, there lived a beautiful goddess of the ocean—the "Woman of the White Shells," younger sister of the Moon. This goddess was the special patroness of beauty and grace and she imparted an attractiveness almost equaling her own to those into whose hearts she deigned to breathe. So that she would not be defiled, she lived in a cave.

One day when some maidens were passing near the mountain, suddenly the beautiful goddess appeared to them, sitting high up in the rocks, dressed in sparkling white cotton garments. She beckoned to the maidens to approach her, reassuring them with her friendly smile.

"Sit ye down by my side," she said to them, "and I will teach you the arts of women." Then with a sharp-edged fragment of jasper, she chipped out a mealing stone of lava. Next she fashioned another stone of finer rock, long enough to reach entirely across the mealing stone. Taking white shells and white kernels of corn, the goddess ground them together between the stones, demonstrating to her pupils a grace of movement before unknown to women. Now, leaning ever so lightly on her grinding stone and glancing slyly under her waving side-locks, she talked to the watching maidens, teaching them how to tease their lovers; then dashing the hair from her eyes, she turned back to the mealing trough and began to grind, singing meanwhile, in time with her labors, the songs that ever since young women have loved to sing, young men loved yet more to listen to.

She stopped then and picked some long stems of grass which she made into a brush and used to sweep together the flour she had been grinding. Of this she gave to each of the maidens an equal measure.

"Take it," she said, "and remember how I have made it that ye may be blessed with children and make more for them and they for theirs. With it men and women shall cast their prayers to the Beloved and maidens shall beautify their persons." Then she took a little of the flour between her palms and applied it lightly to her face and bosom until her countenance appeared almost as white as her mantle and as smooth as dressed doeskin. And ever since that time women have won the most lingering of lovers with the wiles of the mealstone.

Anne ("Nancy") Shippen Livingston (1763–1841)

Anne ("Nancy") Shippen was born on February 24, 1763, into one of Philadelphia's most prominent families. The Shippen House was the center of social and political activities during the years when Philadelphia was the new nation's capital, and Nancy received the attention of numerous distinguished young men. At age eighteen, she fell in love with a French attaché, Louis Otto; her father persuaded her, however, that it would be best for her to marry Colonel Henry Beekman Livingston, a wealthy New York landowner. When her husband's jealousy led to abusive treatment, Shippen Livingston returned home. Because she was pregnant, she made numerous efforts to reconcile with her husband; after the birth of her daughter Margaret ("Peggy"), she even allowed the infant to reside with the Livingston family for a period of time in the hope that such action would secure her daughter's financial future. Although reconciliation proved impossible, Shippen Livingston was not allowed to renew her relationship with Otto, since her husband would grant her a divorce only if their child remained with him. She refused to give up her daughter, and thereafter led an increasingly reclusive life that centered on her only child. As her journal reveals, she planned for her daughter a decidedly different future from the "tragic drama" of her own life.

Works: Journal. *Bibliography*: Armes.

From Nancy Shippen Livingston's Journal

May 15 [1783]—10 in the morning—I sit down to write now what I intended to write the day before yesterday. I hope I shall not be disturb'd. My baby[1] lies assleep in the Cradle before me—I will write till she awakes—

Do not hope for perfect happiness; there is no such thing in this sublunary state. Your sex is the more exposed to suffer, because it is always in dependence: be neither angry nor asham'd of this dependance on a husband. . . .

Do not hope that your union will procure you perfect peace: the best Marriages are those where with softness & patience they bear by turns with each other. . . .

Do not expect the same degree of friendship that you feel: men are in general less tender than women; and you will be unhappy if you are too delicate in your friendships.

Beg of God to guard you from jealousy: do not hope to bring back a husband by complaints, ill humour, or reproaches. The only means which promise success, are patience & softness: impatience sours & alienates hearts: softness leads them back to their duty. In sacrificing your own will, pretend to no right over that of a husband: men are more attach'd to theirs than Women, because educated with less constraint. They are naturally tyrannical; they will have pleasures & liberty, yet insist that Women renounce both: do not examine whether their rights are well founded; let it suffice to you that they are established. They are masters, we have only to suffer & obey with a good grace.

Thus far Madame de Maintenon must be allow'd to have known the heart of man. I cannot agree with her that Women are only born to suffer & to obey—that men are generally tyrannical I will own, but such as know how to be happy, willingly give up the harsh title of master for the more tender & endearing one of Friend. Equality is the soul of friendship: marriage, to give delight, must join *two minds*, not devote a slave to the will of an imperious Lord.

May 16—Papa told me this morn[g] at breakfast that I must send my darling Child to its Grandmama Livingston;[2] that she had desir'd M[rs] Montgomery[3] to request it of me, as a particular favor. I told him I cou'd not bear the Idea of it, that I had sooner part with my life almost than my Child. He told me it was for the future interest of my baby, that its fortune depended on the old Lady's pleasure in that particular—beg'd me to think of it, & to be reconciled to it. If I know my own heart I never can. When will my misfortunes end! I placed my happiness in her! She is my all—& I must part with her! cruel cruel fate—

May 17—10 oclock at night—I have been so unhappy all day that I have not stir'd out of my room except to dinner. Mamma then ask'd me if I had thought of Mrs L's proposal. I told her, I had thought of nothing else—she ask'd me my determination—I told her I wou'd not part with my Child if I cou'd pos-

---

1. Margaret (Peggy) Beekman Livingston.
2. Margaret Beekman Livingston, Nancy's mother-in-law, after whom her daughter was named.
3. Janet Livingston Montgomery, Nancy's sister-in-law.

sibly help it. She then told me Mrs M.——y did not go to the Manor till the middle of June; that Papa had determin'd that the Child shou'd go at any rate— that he cou'd not be answerable for the Childs losing her fortune which she wou'd certainly do, if I kept her from her Grandmother. I cried all the time she was speaking & then retir'd to my room—which I have not left since. I feel pleased however that I have a month to determine in, & be with my angel Child.—I have kiss'd her a thousand times since.—& find I love her as well as myself. I must think of some thing in order to keep her with me, & yet secure her fortune.

May 19— ... I was much affected at a little annecdote I heard this morn^g of a young Lady who was sacrificed to the avarice & ambition of her parents to a man she hated—& her death was the natural consequence of her misery. She had a soul form'd for friendship—she found it not at home, her elegance of mind prevented her seeking it abroad; & she died a meloncholy victim to the Tyranny of her friends & the tenderness of her heart. It is a painful consideration, that the happiness or misery of our lives are generally determin'd, before we are proper judges of either.

May 20— ... I know not yet how much I shall suffer when the time comes.— O! what a separation! how much I dread it! but I will if possible stay with her. Ah! It will be impossible I'm affraid, because it depends on the *disposition* of her father.—Alass! he will never change.

May 22—I spend so much of my time in caressing & playing with Peggy that I allmost forget I have any thing else to do—I forget to read—to write—to work—in short I neglect the business of the day. At night I sit down to unfold my thoughts on paper—I love it much—me thinks it is allmost as pleasing as telling them to a friend. ...

May 24—Afternoon—I thought seriously this Morn^g about my sweet Childs education. I form'd many schemes which I believe it would be very difficult to put in execution. I wish in some particulars that it may differ from mine. In some respects I wish it may be as good. I have her wellfare at heart more than any earthly object. God grant she may be in every respect what I wish her.—I have met with sentiments on that head that please me. I will insert them here that I may not forget them:

SOME DIRECTIONS CONCERNING A DAUGHTERS EDUCATION

1st.   Study well her constitution & genious.

2d.   Follow nature & proceed patiently.

3d.   Suffer not Servants to terrify her with stories of Ghosts & Goblins.

4th.   Give her a fine pleasing idea of Good, & an ugly frightful one of Evil.

5th.   Keep her to a good & natural regimen of diet.

6th.   Observe strictly the little seeds of reason in her, & cultivate the first appearance of it diligently.

7th.   Watch over her childish Passions & prejudices, & labour sweetly to cure her of them.

8th.   Never use any little *dissembling* arts, either to pacify her or to persuade her to anything.

9th.   Win her to be in love with openness, in all her acts, & words.

10th.   Fail not to instill into her an abhorance of all "serpentine" wit.

11th.   If she be a brisk witty child do not applaud her too much.

12th.   If she be a dul heavy child, do not discourage her at all.

13th.   Seem not to admire her wit, but rather study to rectify her judgment.

14th.   Use her to put little questions, & give her ready & short answers.

15th.   Insinuate into her the principles of politeness & true modesty, & christian humility.

16th.   Inculcate upon her that most honorable duty & virtue SINCERITY.

17th.   Be sure to possess her with the baseness of telling a Lye on any account.

18th.   Shew her the deformity of Rage & anger.

19th.   Never let her converse with servants.

20th.   Acquaint her in the most pleasant & insinuating manner, with the sacred History, nor let it seem her lesson, but her recreation.

21st.   Set before her the gospel in its simplicty & purity, & the great Examples of Antiquity unsophisticated.

22d.   Explain to her the nature of the baptismal san[c]tion.

23d.   Prepare her in the best manner for confirmation.

24th.   Animate, & instruct her for the holy communion.

25th.   Particularly inform her in the duties of a single & married state.

26th.   Let her be prepared for the duties & employment of a city life, if her lot should be among citizens.

27th.   See she be inform'd in all that belongs to a country life.

28th.   Discreetly check her desires after things pleasant, & use* her to frequent disappointments. *Ro[u]sseau[4]

29th.   Let her be instructed to do every thing seasonably & in order, & what ever she is set to do let her study to do it well, & peaceably.

30th.   Teach her to improve everything that nothing may be lost or wasted, nor let her hurry herself about any thing.

31st.   Let her always be employ'd about what is profitable and necessary.

32d.   Let nothing of what is committed to her care be spoil'd by her neglect.

---

4. Shippen's note, as placed in the text.

33d. Let her eat deliberately, chew well, & drink in moderate proportions.

34th. Let her use exercise in the morning.

35th. Use her to rise betimes in the morning, & set before her in the most winning manner an order for the whole day.

When wisdom enters into her heart, & knowledge is made pleasant to her soul, "discretion shall preserve her, & understanding shall keep her."

Hannah Langdon (fl. 1789)

Moravian missionaries first came to America in 1734, eventually centralizing in Bethlehem, Pennsylvania, in 1741. In that same year, Benigna Zinzendorf, the sixteen-year-old daughter of one of the founders, established a school for girls in Germantown with a beginning enrollment of twenty-five pupils. By 1749 another girls' school was established in Bethlehem; the commitment to female education and the involvement of women in administration and teaching at the Moravian schools was integral to the community. The Moravian seminary at Bethlehem became one of the most renowned boarding schools in America, drawing young women from prominent families throughout the country. Girls could attend from age five to age sixteen, and they were taught religious studies and to read and write in English and German. Their training included the traditional sewing crafts—spinning, weaving, all levels of skill in sewing, knitting, and darning—as well as history, geography, and music. Hannah Langdon was a pupil at the Bethlehem seminary in 1789 when she recorded the following journal entry.

Works: Journal. *Bibliography:* Haller.

From the Journal of Hannah Langdon

[Saturday, March 7, 1789]: . . . We had a spinning day. Early in the morning our tutoress, accompanied by the sweet notes of Sister Sulamith's guitar, awoke us with a hymn. After breakfast the room was put in order for the business of the day—the spinning wheels arranged in one row, and the distaffs in two. At nine o'clock our tutoresses presented us with apples. At ten o'clock cakes were handed around. We had several of the sisters from the Sisters' House visiting us throughout the day. In the evening Sister Huebner complimented us with a repast of choclate and pancakes—both rareties

to us—and very acceptable after the labors of the day. We then adjoined in chorus singing:

'To the Giver of all good,
It is He whose blessing raises
All that gives us clothes and food.
Who of you could ever have expected
What on this spinning-day has been effected;
Oh! the pleasure is most sweet
Right to use our hands and feet!

Then the following couplets were recited by the girls, the youngest first: (24 in all)

C. REICHELT:
'I've caused no disturbance, dear misses, so pray
Excuse Caroline's not spinning today.'

E. BEAUMONT:
'I've spun seven cuts, dear companions, allow
That I am yet little, and know not right how.'

P. HECKEWELDER:
'Eleven I've done: and I've been very busy;
Believe, I have sat at my distaff quite easy.'

P. STONE:
'Though my finger was hurt, I've spun eight and ten,
Believe, dear companions, I've tried all I can.'

A. HICKLEY:
'Thirteen I've finished, and, with real delight,
I say I could spin till late in the night.'

E. BEDELL:
'I've spun cuts—they are thirty and three
More than I expected; and this pleases me.'

L. PALMER:
'Two less than Miss Hannah, I've done with delight;
Oh, spinning wheel! to me, what a most pleasing sight!'

The ringing of the bell summoned us downstairs.

—Hannah Langdon

Priscilla Mason (fl. 1793)

Priscilla Mason brought the issue of women's intellectual abilities to public attention when she chose the right of women to a public voice as the topic of a speech she gave on May 15, 1793, as a member of the graduating class of the Young Ladies Academy of Philadelphia. The majority of speeches given by the graduates focused on thanking their teachers and their families for the opportunity to gain an education; rarely did the other women's speeches raise the issue of how they might use their education in the future. In contrast, Mason viewed education as the first step toward equal opportunities for women in law, religion, and all realms of public service, and she argued for the establishment of a federally supported women's congress to set forth an explicitly American pattern of women's rights. Although this congress was designed only for the regulation of "dress and fashions," it is obvious from Mason's speech that she recognized that such a seemingly innocuous confederation would lead to women's "dignity and independence . . . and even authority"—at first in terms of fashion but ultimately in terms of women's "equal participation of honor and office."

Mason's demands were never fulfilled, but her speech was immediately included in the history of the academy, which was published in the following year. "The Salutatory Oration" remains an important document in several ways: it is an example of how widely spread were the ideas associated today with Judith Sargent Murray, Abigail Adams, and Mary Wollstonecraft; it illuminates Mason's alma mater as instrumental in encouraging intellectual pursuits by women and in establishing a curriculum that paralleled that of young men; and it reminds us of one young woman's courage in deciding to practice her philosophy of women's public involvement.

Works: Graduation address. *Bibliography: The Rise and Progress of the Young-Ladies' Academy of Philadelphia.*

The SALUTATORY ORATION,
Delivered by Miss Mason.

Venerable Trustees of this Seminary, Patrons of the improvement of the female mind; suffer us to present the first fruits of your labours as an offering to you, and cordially to salute you on this auspicious day.

Worthy Principal, tutor, friend and parent, all in one! when we recollect our obligations to you, we feel, and would speak, but delicacy forbids.

The stern republican and polish'd citizen, will certainly join e'er long, to banish the barbarous custom of offering open adulation in such a place as this.

We therefore content ourselves with simply saluting you; and wishing the events of the day may speak your praise, in language suitable to your feelings.

Respected and very respectable [audie]nce;[1] while your presence inspires

---

1. The manuscript has several large blotches on this page.

our tender [illegible] with fear and anxiety, your countenances promise indulgence, and encourage us to proceed. In the name of myself and s[iste]rs, therefore, I cordially salute you, [and I] hope you will pardon the defects of an attempt to please you, defects arising in some measure from due respect.

A female, young and inexperienced, addressing a promiscuous assembly, is a novelty which requires an apology, as some may suppose. I, therefore, with submission, beg leave to offer a few thoughts in vindication of female eloquence.

I mean not at this early day, to become an advocate for that species of female eloquence, of which husbands so much, and so justly, stand in awe,—a species of which the famous Grecian orator, Xantippe, was an illustrious example. Although the free exercise of this natural talent, is a part of the rights of woman, and must be allowed by the courtesy of Europe and America too; yet it is rather to be *tolerated* than *established*; and should rest like the sword in the scabbard, to be used only when occasion requires.—Leaving my sex in full possession of this prerogative, I claim for them the further right of being heard on more p[ubli]c occasions—of addressing the reason as well as the fears of the other sex.

Our right to instruct and persuade cannot be disputed, if it shall appear, that we possess the talents of the orator—and have opportunities for the exercise of those talents. Is a power of speech, and volubility of expression, one of the talents of the orator? Our sex possess it in an eminent degree.

Do personal attractions give charms to eloquence, and force the orator's arguments? There is some truth mixed with the flattery we receive on this head. Do tender passions enable the orator to speak in a moving and forcible manner? This talent of the orator is confessedly ours. In all these respects the female orator stands on equal,—nay, on *superior* ground.

If therefore she should fail in the capacity for mathematical studies, or metaphysical profounditites, she has, on the whole, equal pretensions to the palm of eloquence. Granted it is, that a perfect knowledge of the subject is essential to the accomplish'd Orator. But seldom does it happen, that the abstruse sciences, become the subject of eloquence. And, as to that knowledge which is popular and practical,—that knowledge which alone is useful to the orator; who will say that the female mind is incapable?

Our high and mighty Lords (thanks to their arbitrary constitutions) have denied us the means of knowledge, and then reproached us for the want of it. Being the stronger party, they early seized the sceptre and the sword; with these they gave laws to society; they denied women the advantage of a liberal education; forbid them to exercise their talents on those great occasions, which would serve to improve them. They doom'd the sex to servile or frivolous employments, on purpose to degrade their minds, that they themselves might hold unrivall'd, the power and pre-eminence they had usurped. Happily, a more liberal way of thinking begins to prevail. The sources of knowledge are gradually opening to our sex. Some have already availed themselves of the priviledge so far, as to wipe off our reproach in some measure.

A M'Caulley, a Carter, a Moore, a Rowe,[2] and other illustrous female characters, have shown of what the sex are capable, under the cultivating hand of
science. But supposing now that we possess'd all the talents of the orator, in
the highest perfection; where shall we find a theatre for the display of them?
The Church, the Bar, and the Senate are shut against us. Who shut them? *Man*;
despotic man, first made us incapable of duty, and then forbid us the exercise.
Let us by suitable education, qualify ourselves for these high departments—
they will open before us. They *will*, did I say? They have done it already. Besides several Churches of less importance, a numerous and respectable Society, has display'd its impartiality.—I had almost said gallantry in this respect.
With others, women forsooth, are complimented with the wall, the right hand,
the head of the table,—with a kind of mock pre-eminence in small matters:
but on great occasions the sycophant changes his tune, and says, "Sit down
at my feet and learn." Not so the members of the enlightened and liberal
Church. They regard not the anatomical formation of the body. They look to
the soul, and allow all to teach who are capable of it, be they male or female.

But Paul forbids it! Contemptible little body! The girls laughed at the deformed creature. To be revenged, he declares war against the whole sex: ad-
vises men not to marry them; and has the insolence to order them to keep silence in the Church—: afraid, I suppose, that they would say something against
celibacy, or ridicule the old bachelor.

With respect to the bar, citizens of either sex have an undoubted right to plead
their own cause there. Instances could be given of females being admitted to
plead the cause of a friend, a husband, a son; and they have done it with energy and effect. I am assured that there is nothing in our laws or constitution
to prohibit the licensure of female Attornies; and sure our judges have too much
gallantry, to urge *prescription* in bar of their claim. In regard to the senate, prescription is clearly in our favour. We have one or two cases exactly in point.

Heliogabalus, the Roman Emperor; of blessed memory, made his grandmother a Senator of Rome. He also establised a senate of women; appointed
his mother President; and committed to them the important business of regulating dress and fashions. And truly methinks the dress of our country, at
this day, would admit of some regulation, for it is subject to no rules at all—
It would be worthy the wisdom of Congress, to consider whether a similar in-
stituion, established at the seat of our Federal Government, would not be a
public benefit. We cannot be independent, while we receive our fashions from
other countries; nor act properly, while we initiate the manners of the governments not congenial to our own. Such a Senate, composed of women most
noted for wisdom, learning and taste, delegated from every part of the Union,
would give dignity and independence to our manners; uniformity, and even
authority to our fashions.

2. Catharine Macaulay (1731–1791), English historian and Whig radical best known for *Letters
on Education* (1790), in which she argued for the importance of women's education; Elizabeth Carter
(1717–1806), English poet, translator, and correspondent who encouraged other women writers to
focus on women's experiences; Jane Elizabeth Moore (1738–?), English poet and memoirist;
Elizabeth Singer Rowe (1674–1737), English poet and journalist, whose Dissenting religious views
were reflected in her writings, as were her attitudes about men's control of literary traditions.

It would fire the female breast with the most generous ambition, prompting to illustrious actions. It would furnish the most noble Theatre for the display, the exercise and improvement of every faculty. I would call forth all that is human—all that is *divine* in the soul of woman; and having proved them equally capable with the other sex, would lead to their equal participation of honor and office.

Judith Sargent Murray (1751–1820)

For a biography of Murray, see the "Feminist Visions" section, Part II.

Desultory Thoughts upon the Utility of Encouraging a Degree of Self-complacency, especially in FEMALE BOSOMS[1]

Self estimation, kept within due bounds,
However oddly the assertion sounds,
May, of the fairest efforts be the root,
May yield the embow'ring shade—the mellow fruit;
May stimulate to most exalted deeds,
Direct the soul where blooming honor leads;
May give her there, to act a noble part,
To virtuous pleasures yield the willing heart.
Self estimation will debasement shun,
And, in the path of wisdom, joy to run;
An unbecoming act in fears to do,
And still, its exaltation keeps in view.
"To rev'rence self," a Bard long since directed,
And, on each moral truth HE well reflected;
But, lost to conscious worth, to decent pride,
Compass nor helm there is, our course to guide;
Nor may we anchor cast, for rudely tost
In an unfathom'd sea, each motive's lost.
Wildly amid contending waves we're beat,
And rocks and quick sands, shoals and depths we meet;
'Till, dash'd in pieces, or, till found'ring, we
One common wreck of all our prospects see!
Nor, do we mourn, for we were lost to fame,
And never hap'd to reach a tow'ring name;

1. *Gentlemen and Ladies' Town and Country Magazine* (Oct. 1794): 251–253.

Ne'er taught to "rev'rence self," or to aspire;
Our bosoms never caught ambition's fire;
An indolence of virtue still prevail'd,
Nor the sweet gale of praise was e'er inhal'd;
Rous'd by a new stimulus, no kindling glow.
No soothing emulations gentle flow,
We judg'd that nature, not to us inclin'd,
In narrow bounds our progress had confin'd,
And, that our forms, to say the very best,
Only, not frightful, were by all confest.

I think, to teach young minds to aspire, ought to be the ground work of education: many a laudable achievement is lost, from a persuasion that our efforts are unequal to the arduous attainment. Ambition is a noble principle, which properly directed, may be productive of the most valuable consequences. It is amazing to what heights the mind by exertion may tow'r: I would, therefore, have my pupils believe, that every thing in the compass of mortality, was placed within their grasp, and that, the avidity of application, the intenseness of study, were only requisite to endow them with every external grace; and mental accomplishment. Thus I should impel them to progress on, if I could not lead them to the heights I would wish them to attain. It is too common with parents to expatiate in their hearing, upon all the foibles of their children, and to let their virtues pass, in appearance, unregarded: this they do, least they should, (were they to commend) swell their little hearts to pride, and implant in their tender minds, undue conceptions of their own importance. Those, for example, who have the care of a beautiful female, they assiduously guard every avenue, they arrest the stream of due admiration and endeavour to divest her of all idea of the bounties of nature: what is the consequence? She grows up, and of course mixes with those who are self interested: strangers will be sincere; she encounters the tongue of the flatterer, he will exaggerate, she finds herself possessed of accomplishments which have been studiously concealed from her, she throws the reins upon the neck of fancy, and gives every encomiast full credit for his most extravagant eulogy. Her natural connections, her home is rendered disagreeable, and she hastes to the scenes, whence arise the sweet perfume of adulation, and when she can obtain the regard due to a merit, which she supposes altogether uncommon. Those who have made her acquainted with the dear secret, she considers as her best friends; and it is more than probable, that she will soon fall a sacrifice to some worthless character, whose interest may lead him to the most hyperbolical lengths in the round of flattery. Now, I should be solicitous that my daughter should possess for me the fondest love, as well as that respect which gives birth to duty; in order to promote this wish of my soul, from my lips she should be accustomed to hear the most pleasing truths, and, as in the course of my instructions, I should doubtless find myself but too often impelled to wound the delicacy of youthful sensibility. I would therefore, be careful to avail myself of this exuberating balance: I would, from the early dawn of reason, address her as a rational being; hence, I apprehend, the most valuable consequences would result in some such language as this, she might from time to time be accosted. A pleasing form is undoubtedly advantageous. Nature, my dear, hath furnished you with an agreeable person, your glass, was I to be silent, would inform you that you are pretty, your appearance will sufficiently recommend you to a stranger, the flatterer will give a more than mortal finishing to every feature; but, it must be your part, my sweet girl, to render yourself worthy respect from higher motives: you must learn "to reverence yourself," that is, your intellectual existance; you must join my efforts, in endeavouring to adorn your mind, for, it is from the proper furnishing of that, you will become indeed a valuable person, you will, as I said, give birth to the most favorable impressions at first sight: but, how mortifying should this be all, if, upon a more extensive knowledge you should be discovered to possess no one mental charm, to be fit only at best, to be hung up as a pleasing picture among the paintings of some spacious hall. The FLATTERER, indeed, will still pursue you, but it will be from interested views, and he will smile at your undoing! Now, then, my best Love, is the time for you to lay in such a fund of useful knowledge as shall continue, and augment every kind sentiment in regard to you, as shall set you above the snares of the artful betrayer.

Thus, that sweet form, shall serve but as a polished casket, which will contain a most beautiful gem, highly finished, and calculated for advantage, as well as ornament. Was she, I say, habituated thus to reflect, she would be taught to aspire; she would learn to estimate every accomplishment, according to its proper value; and, when the voice of adulation should assail her ear, as she had early been initiated into its true meaning, and from youth been accustomed to the language of praise; her attention would not be captivated, the Siren's song would not borrow the aid of novelty, her young mind would not be enervated or intoxicated, by a delicious surprise, she would possess her soul in serenity, and by that means, rise superior to the deep laid schemes which, too commonly, encompass the steps of beauty.

Neither should those to whom nature had been parsimonious, be tortured by me with degrading comparisons; every advantage I would expatiate upon, and there are few who possess not some personal charms. I would teach them to gloss over their imperfections, inasmuch as, I do think, an agreeable form, a very necessary introduction to society, and of course it behoves us to render our appearance as pleasing as possible: I would, I must repeat, by all means guard them against a low estimation of self. I would leave no charm undiscovered or unmarked, for the penetrating eye of the pretended admirer, to make unto himself a merit by holding up to her view; thus, I would destroy the weapons of flattery, or render them useless, by leaving not the least room for their operation.

A young lady, growing up with the idea, that she possesses few, or no personal attractions, and that her mental abilities are of an inferior kind, imbibing at the same time, a most melancholly idea of a female, descending down the vale of life in an unprotected state; taught also to regard her character ridiculously contemptible, will, too probably, throw herself away upon the first who approaches her with tenders of love, however indifferent may be her chance of happiness, least if she omits the present day of grace, she may never be so happy as to meet a second offer, and must then inevitably be stigmatized with that dreaded title, an Old Maid, must rank with a class whom she has been accustomed to regard as burthens upon society, and objects whom she might with impunity turn into ridicule! Certainly love, friendship and esteem, ought to take place of marriage, but, the woman thus circumstanced, will seldom regard these previous requisites to felicity, if she can but insure the honors, which she, in idea, associates with a matrimonial connection—to prevent which great evil, I would early impress under proper regulations, a reverence of self; I would endeavour to rear to worth, and a consciousness thereof: I would be solicitous to inspire the glow of virtue, with that elevation of soul, that dignity, which is ever attendant upon self-approbation, arising from the genuine source of innate rectitude. I must be excused for thus insisting upon my hypothesis, as I am, from observation, persuaded, that many have suffered materially all their life long, from a depression of soul, early inculcated, in compliance to a false maxim, which hath supposed pride would thereby be eradicated. I know there is a contrary extreme, and I would, in almost all cases, prefer the happy medium. However, if these fugitive hints may induce some abler pen to improve thereon, the exemplification will give pleasure to the heart of CONSTANTIA.

Charlotte Sheldon (1780–c. 1840)

Charlotte Sheldon attended Sarah Pierce's Female Academy in Litchfield, Connecticut, during its first years of existence. Born in 1780, Charlotte was the daughter of a Miss Judson of Washington, Connecticut, and Dr. Daniel Sheldon of Litchfield. Sheldon's mother died when she was four years old. She was an adept student, but in the year following her attendance at the academy, she became an invalid. She died in Hartford, probably in 1840. Although her most common comment about attending school is "Went to school & did what I commonly do there," her notations capture the early curriculum of the academy and her burgeoning critical assessment of texts and sermons.

Works: Diary. *Bibliography:* Vanderpoel.

From the Journal of Charlotte Sheldon

Tuesday May 10th, 1796   the weather was so rainy this morning that I did not expect to set out for Hartford. So I sat down to my knitting and learnt a very good song called "The Mill Clapper," of Philo Roberts. It cleared off this afternoon so we sat off we had some rain but at night it cleared off beautifully.

The air was finely perfumed with the shad and appletree blossoms. I arrived at Farmington just at dark and stopt at Mr. Wadsworth's tavern   Mrs. Beardsley was over there and invited us to Dr. Tods there we directed our march. Tho. I had much rather have staid at Mr. Wadsworths for I was very little acquainted with Mrs Beardsley and was muddied from top to toe. Very soon after I got there I went to bed.

Friday 13th   read in the Moral Tales, tho' I think them rather immoral. . . .

Sunday 15th   Finished "Nanine."[1] went to church in the afternoon it is a very handsome building we heard a flute and bass viol which Becca[2] and I mistook for an organ quite a laughable mistake dressed took a walk down to Uncle Sheldons.

Monday 16th.   Washed and ironed almost all day went a shopping. read in Buffon's Natural History. It has a great number of cuts in it and is very entertaining. I should like to read the whole of it   sung etc., etc.,

Saturday 21st   Sat out again for home found the roading better than I expected, got home about four o'clock went to Miss Sally's[3] to carry a letter my face was so burned, I was ashamed to make my appearance any where felt tired & lazy.

Sunday 22nd,   Went in the forenoon to meeting. read in the American magazine & in the European magazine Miss Pierce's girls spent the evening at our house. . . .

Tuesday 24th,   Read & wrote to the 30th page of the history knit sewed one of the tags of the fringe onto my cloack

Thursday 26th,   Studied geography at school felt very indolent, laughed & gaped the greatest part of the time, knit, finished my short gown.

Sunday 29th,   Attended meeting all day, heard two very indifferent sermons, read in the American Magazine found many good things in it & among the rest an extract from Mrs. Yearsley's poem on the slave trade[4]. . . .

Tuesday, 31st,   Starched my gown and hung it to dry, sewed, Persuer of these pages, know that I, the author of them, am not very well versed in polite literature, thou must expect to find, a dry, uninteresting, inaccurate, parcel of sentences, jumbled together in a hand hardly intelligible—this is no news perchance thou wilt say—

Thursday, [June] 9th,   Aunt [Hopkins] & family departed for Watertown this morning, drew some patterns, worked on my shawl, studied a lesson in Guthrie we got partly through France. . . . Assisted mammy, went up to Miss Pierce's

1. A play by Voltaire.
2. Her friend—and probably cousin—"Becca" appears often in the diary.
3. "Miss Sally" was the title by which students referred to Sarah Pierce.
4. Ann Yearsley (1752–1806), English novelist, poet, and dramatist. Her volume *Poems on Various Subjects* (1787) included a poem on the slave trade.

& borrowed the Robbers,[5] read partly through it. it is an excellent tragedy. The character of Amelia is rather inconsistent in my opinion.

Saturday 17th, Sewed. Parsed. Began to read the Recess,[6] a very good novel. It is founded on the idea that Mary Queen of Scots was privately married to the Duke of Norfolk & had two daughters Ellinor & Matilda who are the heroines of the novel, they were educated in the Recess which was several rooms in an Abbey unknown but to three persons. Matilda was married to the Duke of Leicester who took shelter in the Recess from assassins. Took a walk. Read again the Recess.

Sunday 6th Read again in the Recess. I have finished the first volume. Attended meeting all day, was n't much edified. . . .

Saturday 24th Felt pretty dull, Read the second volume in the Recess, the language was pretty good, I like this volume better than the first, Tho I think it is not possible, that any person could suffer as many misfortunes as Ellinor & Matilda, I like the character of Ellinor better than that of Matilda. there is something very interesting in her character, I wanted to have it end happily. Went a strawberrying with Susan Bird.

Sunday 25th, Read all the forenoon, Attended meeting in the afternoon, heard a very poor sermon. Read in the history of Spain, I think it a very good one, I do not know the name of the author. Picked a large basket of roseleaves.

Monday 26th, Washed a little etc., Made a half handkerchief, took a walk up to Captain Stantons. Read in the history of Spain translated to the 15th page in Rousseau's Emelias. Drew a rose, Read in the history of Spain in the evening.

---

5. Friedrich Schiller's *The Robbers: A Tragedy* (1795).

6. Sophia Lee (1750–1824) published *The Recess; or, a Tale of Other Times: An Historical Romance* in 1783–85.

Domestic Records

The Ignorant Housekeeper and The Wren and the Cricket (Cherokee)

In the precontact period, the Cherokee were one of the most powerful and skilled groups in North America. In the sixteenth century the Cherokee were established in the Eastern Woodlands with a highly developed agricultural culture. A 1750 smallpox epidemic devastated their society, killing almost half of their members. In the nineteenth century, they established themselves as the Cherokee Nation, but their forced remove in 1838—along what came to be known as "the trail of tears"—again destroyed thousands of lives. After settling in Oklahoma the Cherokee reestablished themselves as a noted tribal culture.

The two Cherokee narratives included here reflect cultural expectations of women. "The Ignorant Housekeeper" suggests similarities in gender expectations that cross Native and Euro-American cultures and was probably intended as a cautionary tale, while "The Wren and the Cricket" distinguishes between the sexes' actions but also captures traditional concerns about the relationship between the Cherokees and the natural world.

Bibliography: Mooney.

The Ignorant Housekeeper

An old man whose wife had died lived alone with his son. One day he said to the young man, "We need a cook here, so you had better get married." So the young man got a wife and brought her home. Then his father said, "Now we must work together and do all we can to help her. You go hunting and bring in the meat and I'll look after the corn and beans, and then she can cook."

The young man went into the woods to look for a deer and his father went out into the field to attend to the corn. When they came home at night they were hungry, and the young woman set out a bowl of walnut hominy before them. It looked queer somehow. When the old man examined it, he found that the walnuts had been put in whole.

"Why didn't you shell the walnuts and then beat up the kernels?" said he to the young woman.

"I didn't know they had to be shelled," she replied.

Then the old man said, "You think about marrying and don't know how to cook," and he sent her away.

The Wren and the Cricket

The little Wren is the messenger of the birds, and pries into everything. She gets up early in the morning and goes round to every house in the village to get news for the bird council. When a new baby is born, she finds out whether it is a boy or girl and reports to the council. If it is a boy, the birds sing in mournful chorus: "Alas! the whistle of the arrow! My shins will burn," because the birds know that when the boy grows older he will hunt them with his arrows and roast them on a stick.

But if the baby is a girl, they are glad and sing, "Thanks! The sound of the pestle! At her home I shall surely be able to scratch where she sweeps," because they know that after awhile they will be able to pick up stray grains where she beats the corn into meal.

When the Cricket hears that a girl is born, it also is glad, and says, "Thanks, I shall sing in the house where she lives." But if it is a boy, the Cricket laments, "*Gwe-he!* He will shoot me! He will shoot me! He will shoot me!" because boys make little bows to shoot crickets and grasshoppers.

When inquiring as to the sex of the new arrival, the Cherokee asks, "Is it a bow or a sifter?" or, "Is it ballsticks or bread?"

Maria van Cortlandt van Rensselaer (1645–1689)

Born in New Amsterdam (New York City) on July 20, 1645, Maria was a second-generation Dutch settler, the daughter of Anna Loockermans and Oloffe Stevense van Cortlandt. Little is known of Maria's youth, but when she married Jeremias van Rensselaer on July 12, 1662, she began a life that was to lead to her role as administrator of the Dutch colony (patroonship) of Rensselaerswyck. Jeremias had become director of the colony in 1658, but with his death in 1674, Maria was the only family member available to take charge of the colony.

This was a turbulent era in the colony's history: van Rensselaer's relatives were disputing rights to the colony when the English, under Governor Edmund Andros, were granted rights to the province of New Netherland, an act that threatened the van Rensselaers' historic claim to Rensselaerswyck. With two daughters and four sons, the youngest of whom was born after Jeremias's death, and in spite of her own impaired health that required the use of crutches, van Rensselaer became the sole support of her family. In 1676, hostile relatives in Holland put the colony under the control of Nicholaes van Rensselaer and assigned Maria as treasurer of the estate; since Nicholaes did not reside in the colony, however, Maria had immediate responsibility for the everyday demands of the immense enterprise. After Nicholaes's death two years later,[1] Maria once again was placed in command, a position she retained, with her brother's assistance, until her death in 1689.

As Maria's correspondence reveals, the demands of her domestic situation were far more encompassing than those confronted by most seventeenth-century women. Her knowledge of the intricacies of property rights, of human nature as family members fought for control, and of the realities of the colony's precarious future in the province's transition from Dutch to English control helped her to survive as her lifestyle was transformed from that of upper-class comfort to a struggle for personal survival and the support of her family. Before her death, van Rensselaer accomplished her primary goal—control of Rensselaerswyck, the most valuable land patent in the colony, for her children. That legacy established the van Rensselaers as one of the most powerful families in colonial New York.

Works: Correspondence. *Bibliography*: van Laer; Wilcoxen.

The Letters of Maria van Cortlandt van Rensselaer

[September? 1680]

Dear Brother: Your favor of the 12th of July came duly to hand and from it I saw that you duly received the account of my husband, deceased, your brother, regarding the colony, and that you and your sister were quite shocked when you saw the balance of the account. In answer thereto I shall say that if my husband, deceased, had made up the account himself, there would have been quite a bit more due. Do not think, dear brother, that it is an account which is made up out of my head. God preserve me from doing that. We have taken it from his own writings and if I should include all the expenditures which have been

---

1. Nicholaes's widow, Alida, married Robert Livingston, who made what van Rensselaer regarded as profuse demands upon the estate. See Alida Schuyler van Rensselaer Livingston's history and writings in "Businesswomen's Writings." Translation from the Dutch is by A.J.F. van Laer.

made and charge for all the extraordinary meals, a great deal more would be coming to me. Dear brother, you well know yourself how it went, first upon the arrival of the English, then upon the arrival of the Dutch, and then again upon the arrival of the English, and how, whenever any one of importance came from New York, he had to be entertained to keep up the dignity of the colony. You also well know that brother Jan Baties[t] wrote that one should not be particular about 1000 gl. or two. For whom, then, was it done, except for the colony? . . .

And as to what brother writes about loss on grain, seawan, etc., you also know how the grain has gone up in schepels, to 5 and $6\frac{1}{2}$ schepels to the beaver, which is a great loss to the colony, and the seawan from 20 to 25, 30 and 36 gl. to the beaver. What would have become of us, then, if we had not had something else besides? If you examine the receipts of the colony, you will see that one year with another it could not produce enough to cover the expenses. One has to pay the schout, the secretary, the governor, the councilors, and in addition pay all expenses. If brother will take that into consideration, he can only say that it is true. . . .

You also complain that nothing is being sent over. How can anything be sent over when so many outlays had to be made and must still be made? On the farm called Turckeyen a new house has been built. On the farm of the Vlaming[2] a new house must be built. On the farm of Thunis Dircx a new house must be built. Gerrit Gysbert, at Bettlem,[3] will in the spring build a barn. Jonge Jan must build. Hen[drick] Mase must build. Hendrick van Nes must build a dwelling house and the old grist-mill must be completely torn down. One hears of nothing but expenses and at present there is such a poor harvest that many will not have any grain for bread. Furthermore, much money has been spent on the new mill, as I thought that it would produce some revenue, but now bolting is also prohibited,[4] so that I am at a loss to know where a stiver is to come from to be sent over. . . .

November 12, 1684

Dear Brother: . . . That I have written several times that I should like to own the land and the grist-mill is true, but as you can not consent to it, I shall keep possession of them, for it might happen within a short time that you would not get a stiver from them and that some one else got hold of them. As to your thinking that because the mill stands so near the town it must yield much revenue, that is not so, for there are mills everywhere, so that there is no specially large amount of grinding. Moreover, those of Albany are not allowed to have their grain ground outside, so that it goes badly with us. The other mill stands idle. The old mill must be repaired and it needs two new millstones, for the stones are so old that they are broken and held together by an iron band. Neither I, nor my father and brother doubted but that you would have granted me the mill, as I have no other [means of support and] we can

2. Pieter Winne, who was called "the Fleming."
3. Bethlehem.
4. On January 20 a decree by the governor and council had prohibited the bolting and packing of flour for exportation except at New York.

not [live] in Holland with our father's family. . . . I must say one thing more, namely, that the governor and others have told me that my husband, deceased, had entered into Jacop Janse Flodder's contract, for the grist-mill belonged to Flodder himself, as he had had it built, but as the patroon's mills, which stood on the strand, were carried away by the ice, he had to deliver another mill, which my husband did. I never knew that.

Therefore, I beg you, sell me the small grist-mill which stands next to Spitsenberg's mill, on appraisal by impartial persons. It is conveniently located; I only want it for a stiver on Sundays for the poor, for as you know I can do nothing and I am daily getting weaker. I could manage it with a Negro if there was anything to grind, for I must live and my children are growing up and father, deceased, founded the colony with that idea in mind. . . .

[As to] our inheritance from the estate of brother, deceased, I am much surprised that you take such care to settle his estate, for which even the money must come from the colony. Whence, then, is the other money to come? And if I am to send you a considerable sum of money to satisfy me, where, then, is the rest to come from? Therefore, I beg you to let me have what I have asked for; then the work of sending [money] back and forth will be avoided. You may be quite sure, dear brother, that I should like to see the estate of your brother, my deceased husband, settled just as much as your deceased brother Jan's estate. He left one son and your brother [Jeremias] six children and a sorrowful widow, who with God's help in honor seeks to bring up her children and tries to satisfy every one, which in the sorrowful state in which I am at present often makes me sigh.

On the 5th of April it pleased God suddenly to take out of this world my dear father, while he was in his prayers and in good health, in the presence of myself and of my dear mother, who would have liked so much to keep me with her a while longer, but I had to go up the river. Having been home but a short time, I received a letter that I must come down again. I therefore went down again in all haste. God granted us a favorable wind, so that we arrived at New York the next day, but I found my dear mother in the place where my father's bier had stood. She had died on the 12th of May. You can imagine how I felt and still feel, being a widow with six children and having neither father nor mother, who were such a support to me in all things, but now I have no one. My father took care while he was alive that after his death I should have some property. Should I now not take care to know how my affairs stand, I should be worse than a heathen, for now I have no one and every one looks out for himself. I never thought that my br[other Step]hen[5] would have deserted us so. [According to] father's and mother's will no [accounting was to be demanded of] him whether he had carried out his father's will. . . .

[August? 1687]

[To Richard van Rensselaer:] . . . and whereas my son[6] is now at my house and attends to the affairs of the colony, I shall follow your further instructions

5. Stephanus van Cortlandt had assisted his sister's administration when she was first widowed.
6. Kiliaen van Rensselaer, who became the fourth patroon.

to turn the books over to him. Whatever you may be pleased to write to him he will duly attend to. He is now 24 years of age.

Kasper on the hill[7] requests [permission] to buy the pasture of brother Jan Batist. I have had a talk with him. He is willing to give 100 beavers. The pasture rents for 3 beavers and the old man can not manage it, so his son desires to take it over. Your lot is vacant; no one wants it. . . .

My daughter Anna will write to the friends and send over her will.[8] She is going down to have the will probated and will at York write to Holland for advice from the friends. I never thought that patroon's sister[9] was such a vile woman. May God forgive her. She need not count on what is to be paid out of the colony on account of Brant van Slechtenorst, for he has possession of the farm and furthermore what he borrowed must first be deducted. Brother can tell her that if she wants to get it, she may come and get it here. Fie, she wrote to him as if he were the worst vagabond and grabber in the whole country, so that I was ashamed to read the letter, since he was such a beloved one of the Lord. And even our mother, deceased, had to be dragged in. "Know whom you married," [she wrote,] "an Anna, but you forget that Anna caused our mother, deceased, so much pain and sorrow. But now one howls with the wolves with which one is in the woods," and other ugly words, which I can not and will not write for the sake of peace, but I hope that God will forgive her. If she will agree in love and friendship, there will on my daughter's part be no failure to do so. . . .

Mary Wright Cooper (1714–1778)

Mary Wright was born in Oyster Bay on May 18, 1714, and she lived the remainder of her sixty-four years in that vicinity. One of six children of Elizabeth and William Wright, Mary's early years of comfort ill prepared her for the hard labor that became her daily lot after her marriage in 1728, at the age of fourteen, to Joseph Cooper. The Coopers were not poor, but in an agrarian community such as Oyster Bay, all family members were required to participate in the rigors of field or household production, and Wright Cooper's diary reflects the importance of weather conditions in a farming community. Joseph and his brother Simon owned a large farm at Cove Neck, and Mary's diary, in its sporadic and almost breathless entries, reveals the exhaustion that best defined her quotidian existence.

7. Casper Jacobsen Halenbeck, lessee of the pasture behind the fort.
8. That is, her husband Kiliaen's will.
9. Nella Maria van Rensselaer (de Swart), whose father, Johannes van Rensselaer, had been in litigation with Brant van Slechtenhorst.

The mother of six children, Wright Cooper did not begin keeping a record of her life until she was in her early fifties. A devout woman, she found little joy in her life and looked to the next world for peace and, not surprisingly, for rest. Numerous entries relate the physically (and therefore mentally) exhausting nature of her life: "My feet ach as if the bones was laid bare. Not one day's rest have I had this weeke. I have no time to take care of my cloths or even to think my thoughts. Did ever poore creature lead such a life before" (January 7, 1769). Although the diary has little distinction in terms of literary quality, it is significant for its details about farming and a middle-class woman's life in mid-eighteenth-century New York; yet there are phrases and insights that suggest a latent literary talent, if Wright Cooper had been able to find sufficient time to write. She is representative of literally thousands of anonymous women whose writings remain only in fragments or are completely lost to us.

Works: Diary. *Bibliography*: Cooper.

From the Diary of Mary Wright Cooper

Febeaury the 19, [1769] Sabbath. Fine warme and still as ye[ster]day and more so. I went to the Newlig[ht] meten with greate delight and offer[ed] my self to be a member with them.... but I was sudingly seased with a great horr[or][1] and darkeness.... O, my God, why hast thou forsaken me. Thou knowest that in the sinsarity and uprightness of my hearte I have done this, moved as I did belive by Thy spirit. Evening, I came home before the worship began, much distrest.

Tuesday [March 7]. Cole. O, I am dirty and tired allmost to death cooking for so many peopel,[2] freted almost to death. New moon at 1 a'clok this night. Begins [ ] snow.

Wednsday. Snow afternoon. Clear bu[t] cold. Tabethia here.

Friday. Clears with a harde north west wind. Extreme cold. Jo Cooper winnowing wheate. Black squall clouds and a most frightfull wind this night.

Saterday. Extreme high wind. Col. [Fr]eeses all day long. O, I am tired most to death, dirty and distressed. have no cloths to weare to meeten.[3] extremely distrest. I se no [ ] in these days. My darkness [? is gre]ate.... Black att hearte, oh Lord....

1. Blots cover several letters in the ms.
2. Several relatives were staying with the Coopers, including their youngest daughter, Esther, who would soon separate from her husband and return home (see April 14 entry).
3. Although raised Anglican, Wright Cooper attended a church in Oyster Bay that was free form, often seeming closer to Quaker meetings in practice than Anglican.

[M]arch the 12, Sabbath. Much warmer and like to be a fine day. O, I am try-ing to fit my cloths to go to meeten in as much distres as my heart can hold. Am. L. and Eb Colw. came here. I am forced to get diner and cannot go to meten atall. Alas, how unhappy and meresabel I am. I feele banished from God and all good.

Friday [April 14, 1769]. Some clouds and wind, cold. Easter gone from home on some business. Tabthea come here. Our peopel[4] quriel with her and De-mon Cooper turned her out of doors and threw her over the fence to my greate [gr]ief and sorrow.[5]

April the 16, 1769, Sabbath. Clear but a cold north west wind. The sun shine bright to my sorrow, for had it hid his face it might have hid sorrow from my eyes.

Moonday. A small shower . . . but soon clears. . . .

Wednsday. Like to be a rainey day but clear in the afternoon. I am unwell and up very late.

Thirsday. O, I am so very sik so that I cannot set up all day nor all night. Very cold snow some hours in the day.

Friday. Clear but cold. I feele much beter all day. Evening, I am sik again.

Saterday. Clear but cold. O, I am sik all day long. Up very late but I have got my cloths ironed. . . .

Sabbath, April the 23. Some small showers, but I went to meeten in good sea-son. Sister's tex: what is man and so considered him in his four fold state. Very fine talk. All my young peopel went to meeten and stayed all day.

April the 16, Wednesday. The divideing of land[6] betweene Simon and Jo Cooper is this day finnished, writeings signed and delivered. Si., E.S., Jo. Prue, Salle are all in a pleasant humor, sing all togerther and some dancing.

Friday. Rain all the day long. O, I am much distrest a bout my affairs with Chambes.[7] Freese very harde this night.

May the 1, 1769, Moonday. East wind and rain all day long. a very cold storm. the wind exceeding high all night.

Wednesday. A fine clear morning. The early songsters warbling thier notes and all nature seemes to smile, but a darke cloud hangs continuly over my soul and makes the days and nights pass heavily along.

Thirsday. A fine clear morning. I went frome hom on some buisness. Come home disopinted.

---

4. The term Wright Cooper uses for the family's slaves.
5. Half a page is missing at this point in the diary.
6. Joseph and Simon divided the farmland equally between themselves.
7. Ben Chambers; the basis of the money dispute is unknown.

May the 6, 1769, Saterday. A fine warme day. Cleare and pleasent. I a hurred, dirty and distresed as ever.

Sabbath. I am much distrest. No cloths irond, freted and tired almost to death and forst to stay at home.

Tuesday. Ben Chambers come here. I paid what I owed him throw mercy. I here Isreal[8] is comeing home. Has sold his place. I run to town to perswad his mother[9] to go to se him but she was gone to Seder Swamp. I come home very much tired.

Wednsday. Very hot weather. I am tired and very dirty. I herd sister wants to se mee. I design to go tomorrow.

Thirsday. A harde north east wind. I was going to town but Ester had a mind to go, so I sent her. About noon it began to rain very harde. Jacobe Weekes com here and beged to sell a wheele[10] to pay his house rent.

Friday. Very hot. I went to town. Sister is very uneacy about her sons.

Saterday. Much hard worke, dirty and distrest. This night is our Covnant meeten but I cannot go to my greate surprise. Sister come here this night much distrest about her sons. We seeme to have littel or no sence of any thing but our troubels.

Saterday. I went to town . . . We are much hurred and have not done cleaning the house. Oh, it has been a week of greate toile and no comfort or piece to body or mind.

July the 13, 1769, Thirsday. This day is forty years sinc I left my father's house[11] and come here, and here have I seene littel els but harde labour and sorrow, crosses of every kind. I think in every respect the state of my affairs is more then forty times worse then when I came here first, except that I am nearer the desierered haven. A fine clear cool day. I am un well.

Abigail Abbott Bailey (1746–1815)

Abigail Abbott was born on February 2, 1746, in Rumford (Concord), New Hampshire. At the age of seventeen she became a devout member of the Congregational Church; her faith was a source of strength she would desperately need in the coming years. In 1767 Abigail married Asa Bailey, and the young couple settled in

8. Israel Townsend, Wright Cooper's nephew.
9. Sarah Wright Townsend, Wright Cooper's sister.
10. A spinning wheel.
11. The Coopers had been married forty-one years on May 22. They probably lived with her family for a year before settling at Cove Neck.

Haverhill. During their twenty-five year marriage, Abigail gave birth to seventeen children. But the great tragedy of her life was her husband's abuse, which began shortly after their marriage, and his blatant unfaithfulness: he had an affair with one hired woman and attempted to rape another, who brought charges against him (he was acquitted). Asa remained an accepted member of the Haverhill community; however, after the family moved to Landaff and Asa began incestuous attacks upon their daughter Phebe, both Abigail and the citizens of Landaff recoiled. However, Abbott Bailey's recognition of her husband's resigned indifference to salvation played as great a role in her decision to divorce as did his maltreatment of their daughter. With the support of family and friends, Abigail filed for divorce and claimed property rights in the process. The divorce proceedings were long and arduous, but the divorce was granted in 1793. For the remainder of her life, Abbott Bailey continued to be an active member of her church. She died at her son's home in Bath, New Hampshire, on February 11, 1815.

Works: *Memoirs of Mrs. Abigail Bailey* (1815);[1] diaries. Bibliography: Culley; Taves.

From *Memoirs* of Abigail Abbott Bailey

December 1788. . . . Though all the conduct of Mr. B.[2] from day to day, seemed to demonstrate to my apprehension, that he was determined, and was continually plotting, to ruin this poor young daughter,[3] yet it was so intolerably crossing to every feeling of my soul to admit such a thought, that I strove with all my might to banish it from my mind, and to disbelieve the possibility of such a thing. I felt terrified at my own thoughts upon the subject; and shocked that such a thing should enter my mind. But the more I labored to banish those things from my mind, the more I found it impossible to annihilate evident facts. Now my grief was dreadful. No words can express the agitations of my soul: From day to day they tortured me, and seemed to roll on with a resistless power. I was constrained to expect that he would accomplish his wickedness: And such were my infirmities, weakness and fears, (my circumstances being very difficult)[4] that I did not dare to hint any thing of my fears to him, or to any creature. This may to some appear strange; but with me it was then a reality. I labored to divert his mind from his follies, and to turn his attention to things of the greatest importance. But I had the mortification to find that my endeavors were unsuccessful.

I soon perceived that his strange conduct toward this daughter was to her very disagreeable. And she shewed as much unwillingness to be in the room

1. Probably written in the early 1790s as justification to her church for her actions, the *Memoirs* were published posthumously in 1815.

2. Asa Bailey.

3. Phebe Bailey. As soon as she turned eighteen, Phebe left home to escape her father's sexual abuse.

4. She was pregnant.

with him, as she dared. I often saw her cheeks bedewed with tears, on account of his new and astonishing behaviour. But as his will had ever been the law of the family, she saw no way to deliver herself from her cruel father. Such were her fears of him, that she did not dare to talk with me, or any other person, upon her situation: for he was exceedingly jealous of my conversing with her, and cautioning her. If I ever dropped words, which I hoped would put her upon her guard, or inquired the cause of her troubles, or what business her father had so much with her? if I was ever so cautious, he would find it out, and be very angry. He watched her and me most narrowly; and by his subtle questions with her, he would find out what I had said, during his absence. He would make her think I had informed him what I had said, and then would be very angry with me: so that at times I feared for my life. I queried with myself which way I could turn. How could I caution a young daughter in such a case? My thoughts flew to God for relief, that the Father of mercies would protect a poor helpless creature marked out for a prey; and turn the heart of a cruel father from every wicked purpose.

After a while Mr. B's conduct toward this daughter was strangely altered.... he grew very angry with her; and would wish her dead, and buried: and he would correct her very severely. It seems, that when he found his first line of conduct ineffectual, he changed his behaviour, felt his vile indignation moved, and was determined to see what he could effect by tyranny and cruelty. He most cautiously guarded her against having any free conversation with me, or any of the family, at any time; lest she should expose him. He would forbid any of the children going with her to milking. If, at any time, any went with her, it must be a number; so that nothing could be said concerning him. He would not suffer her to go from home: I might not send her abroad on any occasion. Never before had Mr. B. thus confined her, or any of his children. None but an eye witness can conceive of the strangeness of his conduct from day to day and of his plans to conceal his wickedness, and to secure himself from the light of evidence....

What then is man? What are all our dearest connexions, and creature comforts? How fading and uncertain! How unwise and unsafe it must be to set our hearts on such enjoyments! God has set me an important lesson upon the emptiness of the creature. This he has taught me, both in his word, providences, and in the school of adversity. But I, a feeble worm, can benefit by divine lessons, only in the strength of Christ. But, praised be the God of grace, I think I can say by happy experience, "I can do all things through Christ, who strengtheneth me."[5] I desire to bless God that he prepared me for the trials which have commenced; that he prepared me in some measure, to meet them with resignation of soul to the divine will, and with confidence in God, that he will order all things for his own glory. I was lead earnestly to pray that when any signal trials should commence, I might be blessed with strength and grace according to my day: and I think I did not pray in vain. God has remarkably sustained me....

... Mr. B.[6] as your conduct for a long time has been such, as to force a conviction on my mind, that your remaining in your family could not probably

5. Phil. 4:13.
6. This letter to her husband was written in 1790 and is included in the *Memoirs*.

be of long continuance . . . [and] as I know not how soon this solemn event shall arrive; or whether I shall have much opportunity at that period to tell you my views of your conduct;—under these distressing apprehensions I think I must invent some method to speak to you, and try to do something for the benefit of your *soul*, after you are finally gone from us, and have opportunity for serious reflection. To accomplish this my desire, I have written a few lines, with a view to place them among your things, where you may find them some time after having left us. When I wrote this, I still had some hopes you had not accomplished your most infamous designs. . . .

Could I have believed, when you told me, at the close of your strange conduct for several days, that you had been planning to sell our farm, and move to the westward; expressing a most kind attention to the best interest and future good of our family . . . —could I have thought it possible, O false hearted lover! that under the cover of such pretences, you was then planning the ensuing scenes of infamy, the ruin of a daughter! and the disgrace of your own family! . . .

But though you have thus hardened yourself, and deserted me, I cannot forget the dear connexion, which has been, and which ought faithfully to have been maintained, between you and me.

> Alas, the tortures of my wretched case!
> Just as we see the feeble vine, that needs
> Support, intwining with the pricking thorn.
> She feels the smart; her need she also feels,
> Both of support, and healing for the wound.
> Nor will her hold let go, till forced and torn.
> So I, confiding in a faithless friend,
> By you am torn and wounded to the soul!
> With sorrow, pain, and hopeless grief I sigh,
> And mourn the friendship of a husband lost!

At the time when you read these lines, I shall expect no more aid or friendship from you. But my wish is, that there may be excited in your heart some feeling sense of the miseries and tortures you have occasioned me. . . . You do know your accountability to God for all the deeds done in the body.

Your afflicted and forever deserted wife, A.B.

Judith Cocks (fl. 1795)

Judith Cocks's letter to her master, James Hillhouse, a United States representative (1791–96) and later a senator (1796–1810) from Connecticut, is one of the very few extant documents written by a slave woman before 1800. Although nothing is known of Cocks other than what is revealed in her letter, the letter itself is rich in details of her anguished condition under indenture to a Georgia slaveowner and of her attitudes and feelings under bondage.

Works: Correspondence. *Bibliography*: Blassingame.

Judith Cocks's Letter

Marietta, 8th March 1795.

Sir

I have been so unhappy at Mrs. Woodbridges that I was obliged to leeve thare by the consent of Mrs. Woodbridge who gave up my Indentures and has offen said that had she known that I was so sickley and expensieve she would not have brought me to this Country but all this is the least of my trouble and 1 can truly say sir had I nothing else or no one but myself I am sure I should not make any complaint to you   But my little son Jupiter who is now with Mrs. Woodbridge is my greatest care and from what she says and from the useage he meets with there is so trying to me that I am all most distracted   therefore if you will be so kind as to write me now how long Jupiter is to remain with them as she tells he is to live with her untell he is twenty five years of age   this is something that I had no idea of   I all ways thought that he was to return with me to new england or at longest only ten years   these are matters I must beg of you sir to let me know as quick as you can make it convenient   I hope you will excuse me of troubling you wich I think you will do when you think that I am here in A strange country without one Friend to advise me   Mrs. Woodbridge setts out for connecticut and I make no doubt but she will applay [apply] to buy Jupiter's time wich I beg you will be so good as not to sell to her   I had much reather he wold return and live with you as she allowes all her sons to thump and beet him the same as if he was a Dog   Mrs. Woodbridge may tell you that I have behaved bad but I call on all the nabours to know wheather I have not behaved well and wheather I was so much to blame   she has called me A theif and that I denie   I have don my duty as well as I could to her and all her famely as well as my Strength wold allow of   I have not ronged her nor her family   the nabours advised me to rite you for the childs sake   I went to the Gentlemen of the town for there advise   thay told me I could get back without any dificulty   I entend to return this fall   remember me to all your family if you please   I thank you for sending me word my dauter was well   this is my hand writing   I remain the greatest humlity

you Humble servant   Judith Cocks

please show this to Mrs Woodbridge

Susan Livingston Symmes (fl. 1794–1808)

What is known of Susan Livingston's life might be set against the great romance of the rise of a new nation and the exploration of western territories; her life, however, was anything but romantic. The daughter of William Livingston, a governor of New Jersey, Susan became in 1794 the third wife of the renowned patriot John Cleves Symmes. John had been a leader of New Jersey troops, an associate judge of the the the state supreme court, an elected member of the Continental Congress, and after 1785 was appointed a judge for the newly designated Northwest Territory.

After their marriage, John assured Susan that if she accompanied him to the Ohio frontier region she would be able to return often to her home. It was a promise soon forgotten, and Livingston Symmes quickly realized that her husband assumed she would meet his desires in regard to their place of domicile as well as in financial decisions. The latter was a second promise broken, since John originally had told her that in connection with money she had brought to the marriage she could "receive the interest or transfer the Stock" at her own discretion. However, when she finally insisted upon using that money to repay her sister, Mrs. Ridley, for debts incurred before her marriage, John secretly sought legal control of all of her property. As a visitor once described Livingston Symmes, she was "a lady distinguished by elegance of mind," and rather than acquiesce, she attempted legal action of her own to defend her right to manage her own money. Unfortunately, the judge from whom she sought assistance was a friend of her husband's, and he did not honor her request for confidentiality.

In 1808, after years of living in the North Bend region while John traveled on business, Susan Livingston Symmes left her husband. Although they never divorced, she remained in New York, until her husband's death made the separation final.

Works: Correspondence. *Bibliography*: Bond, Jr.

The Letters of Susan Livingston Symmes

North Bend March 4, 1796[1]

Sir

I feel myself greatly embarrassed, & distressed at addressing a Gentleman so much a Stranger to me, & upon so delicate a subject, & nothing but my confidence in the benevolence of your disposition; & the apparent necessity for vindicating my own & Sisters character should have induced me to trouble you upon

---

1. Addressed to Judge Robert Morris at New Brunswick. Morris was a long-time associate and friend of John Cleves Symmes. The "Mrs. R. business" refers to Livingston Symmes's sister, Mrs. Ridley.

this occasion— Happening to cast my eye this morning over a paper that the Judges's nephew was reading, & observing my own name, it excited a curiosity to join in the perusal, when to my surprise I found it to be a letter from the Judge in answer to one of yours respecting Mrs. R. business; in which I find he labours under several mistakes— It will doubtless appear singular to you, that I should not rather endeavour to convince him than you— & I think myself obliged to assign the reasons, one is, that the Judge has not been pleased to communicate your letter or his answer; tho' the most important is, least the *ungrateful* subject should bring altercation, & interrupt that harmony which I wish ever to maintain—

He asserts that I transferred the 2400 dol. [to Mrs. Ridley] at Phil[adelphia], when on my way thro' to N.Y. with him, (which was some time in June or July)— The fact is they were transferred the preceeding Spring at Baltimore, the certificates being on the books at Annapolis, could not I believe have been transfered at Phil— This transaction *I* acquainted Mr. S. with, no person being *privy* to it, tho I had no objection to its being public, & at the same time shewed him my accounts which was within a very few days after our marriage— & told him that the certificates (on the books of Pennsylvania) which I then shewed him, were Mrs. R. that I must make them over to her before I left the Country. His displeasure was great, he insisting upon it that it was all a gift of mine— There was no more occasion to inform Mr. S. before our union that I pd. Mrs. R. than that I had pd. my other Sisters & Brothers—

... Mr. S. saw the account with the list of the other property I had & yet says I gave Mrs. R. three forths of my property— It was my intention to settle with her whenever stock rose that I could sell to advantage, & either divide the profits (if any accrued) with her or pay her the sums I had received on her account with interest from the time of receiving them. The Spring I made over the 2400 dollars, certificates were selling at 16s & Mrs. R. took them at par, so that she should complain if any one— I never made a mystery of any thing, I always told the Judge that my fortune was inconsiderable, but that Mrs. R. & myself by living together could be comfortable & independent— when conversing about property so shortly after our marriage he told me he had been informed I had six thousand pounds, & was greatly disappointed to find that I had not the half— that was no fault of mine— Certain it is that I have never spent a shilling either of his money or what was mine, but I have been a prudent, industrious, obedient wife, accommodating myself entirely to his manners & way of life, which are very different from what I have been accustomed to before our marriage— The transition was great indeed! & unspeakable is my mortification to find Mrs. R. opinion of the Judge better founded than mine— Mrs. R. is a woman of the strictest veracity; & most rigid honor, & would not lay claim to property which was not her right—

What I have said on this subject to you Sir, I have never hinted to any one of my own family— Your own delicacy will suggest to you the propriety of keeping the contents of this letter a most sacred secret—

I am Sir

With the greatest Respect

Yours—

Susan Symmes—

Feby 10—Baltimore [17]94[2]

Permit me my friend once more to intrude upon your patience & *waste* so much of your time as to endeavor to clear myself of the heavy charges brought against me in your letter of the 4th february.

I never manifested any distrust of your circumstances, in the first letter you wrote me, you said your fortune was sufficient & I had the fullest confidence in your word.— what I proposed respecting mine was merely to relieve a sisters anxiety whose income was insufficient without the addition of mine, and judging it could be no object with you: how this can be construed into self love I cannot see. I think it would have been an act of great generosity in both of us. I am sorry you are obliged to recur to ages back to find love matches. I see them daily among my acquaintances, altho in many cases previous settlements & stipulations take place, either at the request of parents, friends or the desire of the gentleman. doubtless many connections are founded in interest— for my own part I never would give my hand where I was not attached upon any consideration. I think an Union founded on esteem promises the most happiness, as that will remain when passion declines: I am sorry you have so mistaken my Ideas upon the subject, and still more, that having been flattered with your good opinion, I should be so unfortunate as to forfeit it. as to the plan of living at Morris about a twelve month & then to be fetched to the Miamis,[3] and after a few years residence there (to arrange your affairs) to return to Jersey, it was precisely your own plan the morning of your departure do you not recollect that you said you would write to Mr Short[4] to come to Morris & you would protract your stay as long as possible— and when in your last but one you talked of gardening, I presumed you meant at Morris— I have only one proposal more to make, which is that you do just as you wish in the matter. Your will shall be mine. I know not what more I can say. If you *choose* to go alone to the miamis— my best wishes shall accompany you. Indeed my friend your letter has wounded my feelings more than ever I expected they would have been by you. Since mine has offended you forget the contents, and be assured I erred with the best intentions in consequence of a promise made Mrs R. before I thought of changing my situation; However that may be, in this I am clear that I am with esteem

& affection your friend

Martha Laurens Ramsay (1759–1811)

Martha Laurens was born in Charleston, South Carolina, on November 3, 1759. Eleanor Ball and Henry Laurens had thirteen chil-

---

2. Addressed to her husband. Judge Morris did not maintain Livingston Symmes's confidence in these matters as requested. In 1796 John sent copies of this and one other letter from Susan to Morris as proof against his wife's claim that she had the right to transfer her stock to her sister.

3. The Miami Purchase. John Cleves Symmes had been deemed the "patriarchal founder" of that region.

4. Peyton Short, John's son-in-law.

dren, and by the time Martha, their eighth child, was born, they were one of the wealthiest families in the Carolinas, owing to Henry's activities in the rice and slave trades. A precocious learner, Martha was well educated in scholarly and religious fields as well as the skills necessary to become a dutiful housewife. Laurens's father insisted that the domestic life engage all three forms of education. As he indicated in a letter to her when she was fifteen, "When you are measuring the surface of this world, remember you are to act a part on it, and think of a plumb pudding and other domestic duties" (*Memoirs* 56).[1] Laurens's mother died when she was an adolescent, and the relatives with whom she lived traveled in the colonies and abroad, eventually settling in the south of France. She lived in Europe during the American Revolution, returning only after peace had been established. In 1787 she married David Ramsay, a renowned scholar and patriot; they had eleven children.

Martha Laurens Ramsay continued to educate herself, both in religion and in the newer sciences, including the works of John Locke. She was a prolific correspondent and throughout most of her life maintained a diary, which David Ramsay published after her death in Charleston on June 10, 1811. Few women of the eighteenth century so carefully balanced an intellectual and domestic life as did Martha Laurens Ramsay.

Works: Letters, memoirs. *Bibliography*: Ramsay.

The Letters of Martha Laurens Ramsay

Letter to David Ramsay, at Columbia

Charleston, December 17, 1792.

My Very Dear Husband,

You have doubtless heard, by this time, that I am fatherless, and will feel for me in proportion to the great love you have always shown me, and your intimate knowledge of my frame, and the love I had for my dear departed parent. Never was stroke to an affectionate child more awful and unexpected than this has been to me. I had heard from my dear father, that he was somewhat indisposed, but not confined even to the house; however, last Tuesday and Wednesday week I was seized with so inexpressible a desire to see him, that nothing could exceed it, and nothing could satisfy it, but the going to see him.

---

1. The extent to which this paternalistic attitude prevailed in eighteenth-century America is evident in a note appended by Laurens Ramsay's husband (and editor) to this letter when it was published in the *Memoirs*: "The pleasantry about the plumb pudding, had its effect. Miss Laurens made a pudding before she began to make use of her globes, and profited by the hint, that the knowledge of house wifery was as much a part of female education, as a knowledge of geography" (56).

Accordingly, on Wednesday noon, very much against my family and personal convenience, I set out with faithful Tita and little Kitty, and slept that night at Mrs. Loocock's; the next morning it rained, but I could not be restrained. I proceeded to Mepkin, and arrived there at one o'clock, wet to the skin, I found my dear father indisposed, as I thought, but not ill. He conversed on indifferent matters; seemed very much delighted with my presence; told me I was a pleasant child to him; and God would bless me as long as I lived; and at twenty minutes before eight o'clock, retired to rest. The next morning, at seven o'clock I went to his bedside; he again commended my tenderness to him, and told me he had passed a wakeful night; talked to me of Kitty and of you; had been up and given out the barn door key, as usual. At eight I went to breakfast. In about ten minutes I had despatched my meal, returned to him, and thought his speech thick, and that he wavered a little in his discourse. I asked him if I might send for Dr. M'Cormick; he told me if I desired a consultation, I might; but that he had all confidence in my skill, and was better. I asked him why his breathing was laborious; he said he did not know, and almost immediately fell into his last agony; and a bitter agony it was; though, perhaps, he did not feel it. At ten o'clock, next day, I closed his venerable eyes. Oh, my dear husband, you know how I have dreaded this stroke; how I have wished first to sleep in death, and therefore you can tell the sorrows of my spirit; indeed they have been, indeed they are very great. I have been, and I am in the depths of affliction; but I have never felt one murmuring thought; I have never uttered one murmuring word. Who am I, a poor vile wretch, that I should oppose my will to the will of God, who is all wise and all gracious; on the contrary I have been greatly supported; and if I may but be following Christ, am willing to take up every cross, which may be necessary or profitable for me. I left Mepkin at one o'clock on Saturday, as soon as the body of my dear parent was decently laid out, and I was sufficiently composed for travelling. I know, by information, that the awful ceremony[2] was performed last Tuesday. I have never been able to write till this day. Our dear children are well. Eleanor comes to my bedside, reads the Bible fo[r] me, and tells me of a heavenly country, where there is no trouble. Feeling more than ever my dependance on you for countenance, for support and kindness, and in the midst of sorrow, not forgetting to thank God that I have so valuable, so kind, and so tender a friend; I remain, my dear husband, your obliged and grateful wife,

Martha Laurens Ramsay.

From the Diary of Martha Laurens Ramsay

September 22, 1794. Mrs. Petrie died of a six days illness; having been married to Mr. George Petrie, only twelve days. God grant that no such awful and awakening providence, as the removal of a young person, so lately full of life,

---

2. Henry Laurens was cremated; he had long indicated that this was his desire, and Martha Laurens Ramsay had long resolved not to be present at the cremation.

and health, and strength should pass without some serious improvement, some earnest desire to have my loins girt, and my lamp burning.

October 6th. My sister Pinckney[3] died, having been generally delirious from Friday; and her speech so thickened, that though she attempted it in the intervals of reason, she never could make us understand what she wished to say to us. Miss Futerell and myself were constantly with her; but my heart is too full to write on this subject. Lord, thou knowest my groanings, and my sighings are not hid from thee; commisserate thy poor, sinful suffering creature; and fill me with humility and resignation under this exceedingly heavy stroke of thy Providence.

June 2nd [1795]. I can no longer say the skies are darkening, for they are so darkened that I see no light; and I am ready to call myself desolate, forsake, cast off by God: yet, I dare not murmur, I am not in hell, where I deserve to be. Instead of poring on my disappointments, vexations, and sufferings, I would endeavor in this dark dismal night of trial, to praise the Lord that there is a haven of rest prepared for the weary; and to lament my sins, which make such deep sorrows necessary to my sanctification. Oh my Savior, put out thy helping hand, and keep me from sinking in these deep waters; let the billows, instead of overwhelming me, make me cleave closer to the cross; and, Oh my compassionate Father! If it be not thy will, to grant me the prayer, which I believed thou wouldst have done, having had my heart, so drawn out to pray; yet at least keep me from being overwhelmed by temptation, and from being so entirely depressed, as to be useless and worthless in that state of life to which thou hast called me. If I may not record that the Lord hath heard, and granted my request, at least enable me to know and feel, that he hath given brokenness of heart, and let me not dare, while under the frowns of his providence, to sin against him, lest a worse thing come upon me, and my soul be ruined. . . .

Rebecca Dickinson (1738–1815)

The eldest of six children of Anna and Moses Dickinson, Rebecca lived her entire life in Hatfield, Massachusetts. Dickinson remained single and supported herself as a seamstress. Like many single women, "Aunt Bek" (as she was locally known) was an integral part of her extended family—foremost as a companion, but also at times as an unpaid caretaker of her sister and brother-in-law's children (the Billings ran an inn in Hatfield) and of her aging mother. Dickinson began her diary when she was in her thirties but only segments from 1787 to 1802 (from age forty-nine to sixty-four) are

---

3. Mary Eleanor Laurens, who married Charles Pinckney.

extant. A devout and philosophical woman, Dickinson recorded in her journal her extensive ponderings on God's ways and on her own existence as an older single woman. Few documents so poignantly capture the loneliness that a single woman could feel in a society that viewed marriage as a woman's primary career goal; yet her journal is also a testament to endurance and to the recognition that there are many acceptable lifestyles. Rebecca Dickinson died in Hatfield on December 31, 1815, at the age of seventy-seven.

Works: Journal. Bibliography: Sprigg.

From the Journal of Rebecca Dickinson

this is the 25 of july 1787 this Day makes me forty nine years of age   the goodness of god has Suffered me to live in his world   it is god and god only to who I owe the length of my life. . . . he has kept me from those deadly Enemies who have Sought my life   may my Soul never Stray from god but live within the orb [?] with god where Saten and his Emissaries have no Power   my Soul is affraid of Saten and the mallis of wicked men   keep me o my father   may not I be joined with the wicked   I abhor there ways   I would that god would Shelter me under the Shadow of his wing   the last night had a Sad Dreeme wich I hope will never Come to Pass   methought that I was in a Place where I Could not *Escape*   it is a Sad thing to fall into the hands of the wicked   may I never fail but live with god never doubting his power to spend me by night and noon   god has taken a fatherly Care of me for near fifty years. . . .

this is Sunday august 5 Day 1787   this morning here alone in [this] old hous there is the wisdom of god and the goodness of god to be Seen in all the things which Confine me . . . the use of this hous is a gift from god and may my Soul be truly thankfull for the gift   it is good to find that god is a leading our lives with benifit   how god has Preserved me this Sommer when my foolish thoughts Surmised that I Should be very unhappy in this hous alone but that god whose tender Care is over all his works has made it a good habitation to me   there is no Place in the whole world that I Can think on where I Could be So well accomadated for Soul and body which makes me Cry this morning a[t] the wisdom and the Power of god and the goodness of god which gives me life and health and Crowns my brow with Content   there is a great many family blesings which I know nothing of but the gifts of time always bring Sorrow along with them   a numirous family and a great Estate bring a great Confine upon the minds of the owners more then a ballence for all the Comfort that they bring. . . .

this morning of the 25 of august. . . . olliver hastings who has been maried for Some months and brought home his wife the last evening Chery Sills [?] aged eightteen years they have gon into a hous well built . . . no doubt there was forty Coupple who was invited in Some Singel Some marryed Peopel   a very fine Collecttion   all drest out to give them joy in there begining   I Drinked tee with brother and Sister Billing our Courzon the School master Patte Church my litel Cozen josepth billing . . . a great many fine Peopel who was a Crouding in   the ladies with there Silks   the men the happiest who Could get the neerest to them   about Dusk on the Edge of the evining Set out to Come home to this lonely hous where I have lived forty nine years lonesome as Death to Come here to Spend the night alone to reflect on my od life and to ruminate the Strange thoughts and Schemes with which this mind of mine has Surmised to think on the many years Continued by me for a Portion in the world and with the world and like the work but after all have alone as lonely as tho I was Cast out from all the rest of the Peopel and was a gasing Stock for the old and young to gaze at but this morning found all to be right . . .

this is a Saterday evening the 8 of Septempber 1787   the last night Died at hadly the wife of Chester williams aged forty three years   She was lovely in her life and happe in her Death I hope   She has been merried Seventeen years   a most agreable woman   Deserved a better husband then She had but She Profeted for heaven by the husband that She had   God Called her out of the world to follow him for Some years   She has made a Profession of Religion   god has Called her to great tryals the loss of health for the last Seven years of her life the loss of her goods which I hope weaned her from the world her husbend has been in jail for more then a year Past and is Still Confined there   he Could not See her Die . . . She had no more troble then was good for her   may my Soul imitate her in faith and Patients and reap an Eternal reward among the Saints in glory

[September 1787]   this day I have been Contriving for my Self what to doe and where to goe but there is no way for me to Escape from this hous no way which will doe for me   I have Contrived this day to go to hadly but every thing is against me there is work for me to doe here   this morning out of imploy which makes room for my Pen   this week is begun one day is gon and another is a going   how my time flies like the Swift Ships never to return— this week I look for Sister mather from bennington with her too Children   I Shall be glad to See them   I hope to be at home when they Come to town which makes me at a loss about going but my Daily bread Depends on my labour. . . . let what will befall me in this life   my way is hedged in my reason of my Sins which Confine me to this Prison where I now dwell. . . .

[September 22?, 1787] . . .   I looked round me this afternoon to See those who was looking at me as a guilty being one who had not forgave my Enimies . . . this have I Said that the Prosperity of my greatest Enemy Could doe me no harm but god only knows my heart and has Seen the Secret enmity that is loged there   how they have hised and waged the head at me by reason of my Solotary life wondering how I Could Spoend my time here alone in this hous it is indeed a mistry to me . . .

[Late November 1787]   this day there is a Couppel to begin to live together Roger Dickinson and Abagil Feild   they began the world rong by having a Child before a hous   there is great runing to and from this day by all the Peopel young and old   how the times alter in a few years   it is twenty years Since I have kept this hous   a thanksgiving and the day after have hardly [illegible word] over to the nearest neighbour but now forsaken by all my friends and all my acquaintence what a gloome old age draws over all our Comforts but time it is that old age is not a getting time but a Spending day   my frinds are day by day a leaving me many are a going to the grave   how think the leaves fall from the trees in october   So our frinds fail us after fifty   many droop into the grave many are kept from us by Sickness   how few of the Peopel who move round me doe I know they are a generation that I know nothing about nor they dont want to know me nor how lonely I live   this day here alone in his hous have Spent Some of the day on the bed   have had an invitation to goe to hadly to morow but no Strength to move and must be Content with what is ready . . . I would beg of god that my Estate may be a Comfort to me now in the line of old age

this is the 02 of january 1788 . . . the Care of my fathers family lay with great wait on my mind that the Parents of these littl Children might bring them up in the fear of god . . . my Sister ballard had a little Daughter born about the 7 of this month which makes Sixteen Couzens but Six girls   the lord bless them and make them blessings in the world and give them o my father the gifts and graces of thy own Children and that very Portion in this life which will raise there Souls to god   may no Scandal or [illegible] Stain there Connecttins but may Purity of heart and life with the humility be theres   there is too here at this time att the table with me Rebeca ballerd Charels Dickinson it being Sabeth noon and the meeting is now done

this is Sunday the 24 of July [1791] . . . Children and grand Children is the Portion of many of the daughters of adam but god of his faithfullness has Set me by my self   no Childrens Children to be accountible for   no home no habitation of my own but god has Provided an in[n] for me   tho it is not my own yet god knows it is good for me to be here   it is the best hous in the world to leern the Divine mind to leern tru humility   blessed be god for all his loving kindness to me   I am fifty-three yeers of age to morrow   how goodness and mercy has followed me all my life long   no good thing has god withheld from me   light and life has been dayly been with me   o that god would gether me to himself

---

Elizabeth Sandwith Drinker (1734–1807)

Elizabeth Sandwith Drinker's diary, begun in 1757 and continued over the next fifty years until her death in 1807, is one of the most extensive diaries (totaling thirty-six volumes) surviving from the eighteenth century. Sandwith was the daughter of Sarah Jervis and William Sandwith, notable merchants in Philadelphia, where Sandwith lived her entire life. In 1761, she married Henry Drinker

(1734–1809), a shipping merchant. They had nine children, five of whom lived to adulthood.

Sandwith Drinker's life reminds us of the advanced ideas about women's education and opportunities that proliferated in the Quaker community—she was herself educated at Anthony Benezet's renowned school for girls and was committed to education for all of her children. While her diary is a remarkable compendium of personal and national events for the last half of the eighteenth century, it is also the record of an individual. In the latter capacity, Sandwith Drinker's entries also remind us that there was great diversity among Quakers. Whereas Sandwith Drinker was notable for her interest in medicine, she was also quite reclusive, preferring to associate with family more than others within her community; after her children were grown, this prolific reader loved to spend as much time as possible secluded with a book. Sandwith Drinker's diary can be studied from many perspectives—the consequences of religious pacifism during wartime; the everyday life of upper-class Quakers in eighteenth-century America; the use of home remedies for a multitude of illnesses; familial relationships; the changes in a woman's life from the time of courtship through marriage, motherhood, and into her years as the grand matriarch of a family with numerous grandchildren.

Unlike many of her Quaker contemporaries, Sandwith Drinker had highly conflicted responses to the issues of slavery and indentured servitude; she did not consider herself in the same class as slaveowners, but she also would not countenance any talk of ending slavery. The Drinker family engaged in the German servant trade, and many slaves or indentured African Americans were brought to their Pennsylvania properties, where the Drinkers were paid to train them in agrarian and household skills. Sandwith Drinker was in control of several indentured servants and slaves at varying times throughout her life. The entries included here denote her intertwined relationships with two women: Mary Courtney, a poor Quaker woman who resided in the vicinity of the Drinkers' summer farm and whose health had been ravaged by numerous unsuccessful pregnancies; and Sally Brant, an independent-minded woman servant indentured to the Drinker household.

Works: Diary. Bibliography: Cowell; Crane.

From the Diary of Elizabeth Sandwith Drinker

17 June [1794]. . . . yesterday I visited poor John Courtney Wife, she expects some time this summer to lay in with her seventh child, has had but one that was born alive, a fine little girl, now between 3 and 4 years of age, whom they have with them, by her own acc^t, poor woman, she has suffer'd greatly, I feel much for her,—to be sick and poor is hard indeed.

8 [August]. . . . I have been for a week past under great anxiety of mind on acc^t of our poor little and I fear miserable SB[1]—'tis *possible* I may be mistaken, 'tho I greatly fear the reverse.

11. The full moon arose last night very red, which I look'd upon as a mark of dry weather, it occur'd to me while looking at it, that it was to be eclipsed this morning totally for about two hours,—it was late when I retir'd to my Chamber, and later when I went to sleep—the thoughts of the unhappy Child that lay on a matrass at the foot of my bed, who does not appear to feel half so much for herself, as I do for her, keep't me wakeing. . . . H. and ED.[2] had a trying Conversation, if a conversation it could be call'd, with SB—poor poor Girl, who could have thought? . . .

19. . . . Joe Gibbs, was yesterday morning dismiss'd from our service, we suppose he is gone towards New-England, he has left, if we mistake not, a Memorial behind him. . . .

Sepr 17. . . . John [Courtney] came in for liquid ladanem[3] for his wife twenty five drops . . . I went in some time after to see her and gave her, by her own urgent desire 50 drops more in about an hour after the 25—I then left her, in hopes it would still those useless pains that she suffer'd—it appear'd to have little or no effect; the mid-wife inform'd me that le enfant est fort grand, et la mere bient pitit,[4] it was her oppinion que l'enfant mort, that she wish'd I would send for a Doctor. . . . the Doctor confirm'd what the mid wife had said, et avec ses instruments et beaucoup deficility, ill la delivera d'enfant mort,[5] the first male child of seven, a very fine lusty baby—6 of the 7 dead born. . . .

9 [October]. . . . near one o'clock when we retir'd, we were busy'd making habilliment pour la noir au jaun illigetemate. . . .[6]

7 [November]. . . . I settled matters with Mary [Courtney], concerning our poor Sall, who I intend leaving with her, 'till her grevious business is settld, I look on Mary as a well minded and well disposed woman, and who, with our help, will take the proper care of her. . . .

13 [November]. . . . I disclosed to our Sarah my intentions of leaving her with Mary for some time, she wep't and appear'd in trouble but before we left her seem'd reconciled, about four we bid adieu to Clearfield[7] and arriv'd at home to tea. . . .

1. "SB" is Sandwith Drinker's notation for Sally Brant, an unmarried Caucasian indentured servant, who Sandwith Drinker believes is pregnant; Joe Gibbs, an African American, was the father.
2. Henry and Elizabeth Drinker. At this time in the entries, Sandwith Drinker often refers to herself in the third person.
3. Laudanum, a form of opium, was a frequently used pain killer in the eighteenth century.
4. The infant is very large, and the mother very small.
5. And with his instruments and much difficulty, he delivered her of [the] dead infant.
6. Clothing for the black and yellow illegitimate one (Sally Brant's baby).
7. Clearfield was the name given to a farm the Drinkers had recently purchased. Sandwith Drinker refused to allow the pregnant Brant to return to Philadelphia with the family for the winter.

6 *[December]*. . . .   Sister and William[8] went this fore noon to Clearfield—they found S.B. and her bantling well, Sally weep'd when she saw MS—and cover'd her head with the bed-cloaths—The Child is very Yallow for one so young. . . . A Negro boy of the name of Peter Woodard, came this Afternoon to us, from one of the lower Counties, kent I believe it was, sent here by Warner Mifflin, he was raged and lousey, having been for upwards of a week on board the Vessel, and in poor trim before, fifteen pounds is said to be the price for him, WM. writes that he is 11 or 12 years of age. . . .

23 *Dec*[r]. . . .   call'd at John Courtneys just before we came away. S.B. is very well, and in rather too good spirits, everything considered, she had nam'd the Jaune pettet,[9] Hannah G——bs, I disaprovd it, and chang'd it to Catharine Clearfield, with which she appear'd displeas'd. . . .

March 4 [1795]. . . .   —About a mile on this side Clearfield my husband and Sister mett Joe, he had the impudence, as M Courtney told MS. to come up into her room, she ask'd him what he wanted, he reply'd, to see something you have got here, and then look'd into the Cradle—she ask'd him if he own'd it, he say'd No, and further this deponent sayeth not.—If he had not seen the Child, he had all reason to belive it was his, but the colour was convincing, he had frequently boasted of it, but was fearful of the expences that might accrue. . . .

8 *[April]*. . . .   S.B. has form'd an acquaintance with one of Gardners workmen, I fear we shall have more trouble with the bold Hussey. . . .

11 *[April]*. . . .   John Courtney and family mov'd from Clearfield to Philadelphia. Mary left Sall's Child, with Geo. Frys wife. . . . How many vicissitudes do I pass through, in the small sphere in which I daily move. . . .

19 *[April]*. . . .   Sally Johnson[10] here this Afternoon, ask'd if SB could spend a day with her this week, to which I consented, told her of her daughters late conduct wish'd she would take her and Child of our hands, that she had a year to serve from this month, which would have been of more worth to us, had she been a virtuous girl, than any other two years of her time, a girl in her place would cost us 8 or 9/P week, that she is as capable, or perhaps more so, then any one we could hire; I was afraid of her bad example to our other little girl &c—she appeard more angry than griv'd, said she should not care if the childs brains were beat out &c—she would never have anything to do with it—I told her we would make no acc[t] of the expences we had already been at of Sallys laying in and board, the childs nursing since &c. she said she would take her daughter provided they, nither of 'em, should ever have any thing to do with the Child—she went away rather out of humor—when HD. come home we related the above to him, concluded were we to turn her

---

8. Elizabeth's sister, Mary Sandwith (1732–1815), who lived with the family, and her eldest surviving son, William Drinker (1767–1836).

9. Little yellow one.

10. Sally Brant's mother.

off, upon her mothers terms, she would be in the high road to further ruin—
he call'd her into the parlor this evening and talk'd closely to her, told her he
had a right to send her to the work house and sell her for a servent, that it
was in pity to her, and in hopes of her reformation that he did not send Joe
to prison, she had always had a good example in our house, if she did not
mend her conduct she should not stay much longer in it &c. she cry'd but
said nothing—How it will end, or what we shall do with her, I know not,—
set aside this vile propensity, she is one of the most handy and best servants
we have ever had—and a girl of very pritty manners.

15 [May].... George Fry's wife parted with the poor little yallow one, to a
Negro woman in the Neighbourhood 'till we can otherwise dispose of it....

June 29.... HSD.[11] came to town, he informs us, that little Caty Clearfield
is very unwell, her bowels much disordred, I suppose she is teething....

2 [July].... a note from Henry, telling us, that ... poor little Caty was dead—
Jacob Morris, a black boy, whose Mother had her to nurse brought the note,
and came for a—Shroud to bury her in....

5 [July].... I told SB. yesterday, a little while before I left home, of the death
of her Child, and took that oppertunity to talk to her on that and some other
Subjects, she shed a few tears, but all, appeard to be got over in a little time
after....

14 [July].... I paid the black woman, Sally Morris 2"1"3" for nursing little
Caty near 7 weeks at 6/-p week—Henry paid Betsy Fry, some time ago, the
same sum, for the same service, for between 5 and 6 weeks at 7/6p.—many
are, the number of poor little Infants that go out of the world, for want of perticular care, 'tho I have no reason to suppose this child neglected, I paid Mary
Courtney, between 8 and 9 pounds for nursing it &c, she did her duty by it,
I doubt not, and Betsy Fry appear'd to take good care of it—And Sally Morris, I do believe did her best, she has had several Children of her own, her
family were very fond of it and I was told they weep'd much when it died—
I should have taken it home, it suited, and brought it up, or had it brought
up in our family, but a fear of brining the parrents togeather, or reviveing the
former likeing to the sire, as the mother is still in our house, but tis gone, and
no doubt but all's for the best.

---

11. Henry Sandwith Drinker (1770–1824), Elizabeth's youngest surviving son.

Businesswomen's Writings

Martha Daniell Logan (1704–1779)

Martha Daniell was born in St. Thomas Parish, South Carolina, on December 29, 1704, to Martha Wainwright and Robert Daniell, a deputy-governor. Robert Daniell died in the spring of 1718, and Martha married George Logan, Jr., on July 30, 1719; she was fourteen years old. Rather than confining her talents to traditional domestic duties, Daniell Logan recast the domestic arena as a place of business. She ran a boarding house and school in Wando River, South Carolina, on land she had inherited from her father and where she and George had settled after their marriage. Daniell Logan gave birth to eight children, six of whom lived to adulthood. Not only did she run the plantation and boarding school at Wando River, but she also established a boarding school in Charleston after the family moved to that city, and she acted as an attorney for one of her sons in the sale of properties he owned.

Daniell Logan's greatest talents were as a horticulturalist. By 1753 she was placing advertisements in the *South Carolina Gazette*, noting that seeds and roots were available for sale at her home. She corresponded with other botanists, such as John Bartram, and published a "Gardners Kalendar" as early as 1752; it was reprinted several times in various almanacs, the last printing occurring in the 1780s. In 1796, after her death, the most extensive version of her "Gardners Kalendar," and her first signed writing, was published in *The Palladium of Knowledge* and was repeated in issues through 1804. She not only cultivated her own extensive gardens, which supplied other botanists with samples, but she also gathered her roots and seeds from various neighbors' property as well as her own—she mentions Mrs. Bee, Mr. Raper, Mr. Glen, and Mrs. Hopton, among others, as contributors to her naturalist studies.

Works: Letters, "Gardners Kalendar" (1752). *Bibliography*: Earle, *Colonial Dames*.

The Letters of Martha Daniell Logan

Letter to John Bartram, Philadelphia

S^r

   I have recived your faviour with the Bagg of roots for which am much Obligd
& doe now Send you a Smale parsel of Seeds which are Cheafly Natives. Those
with out Names are what a friend of mine Sent me from the Country so that
I Cannot tell what they are. I am in hopes it will be in my Power to Send you
Some Varity which I am to have from the Same hand as Soon, they ripen. the
tops of the Plant you mentioned by the quarter house are now dryed of so
that I Cannot find it till Spring when you Shall Certinly have it if I live till
then. you wire so kinde to ask what woulde be Exceptable to me. the mainy
Shrubs & plants you have be Stowed on me have Succeded so badly that I am
quite dishartned from trying Varity & Shall Confine my desires to what I know
will doe theirefore if you have any Single Hyacinths of Verry Deep blues or
reeds nothing would be moore Exceptable & as I am freequently disappointed
in my Seeds from England Shoulde be verry glad to be Supplyd from y^r Part
with about half a pound good Orang Carrotts & 4 Ounces Parsnips 2 cabage
2 Reed beats 2 good Savoy Cabage for which would be willing to Pay the Cosst
& return the faviour if in My Power. this I Coulde gett done by any Capt of
Vessel but it woulde not be in theire Power to know whither they wire good
or not of theire kindes, so that I might be disappointed, & Perhaps have as
good at home. Elce Should not give you any trouble on this head wheirefore
hope you will Excuse this Liberty in S^r your well wisher & Humble Servt

Martha Logan

   Sep^tr 14 1760
PS my good wishes & Complyments attend your family. I shall be glad of the
Plants you offer

Letter to John Bartram

S^r

   . . . I Doubt not you have many things which I shoulde be glade of, as I am
particularly fond of Double flowers & if you Coulde Send me afue Seeds of
white Stockgilly flowers & yellow Wall flowers which woulde Produce the Double flowers, or any of the Sweet or Other peases of the Like Kinds they woulde
be Much Esteemed. or afue fine Carnations as I have only the Comon
kinds— I was so unluckey this Last Summer to Loose all the Roots of my Ra-
nunialists [?] anemoneys Tulips & fine Double Hyacinths by Laying them in a
Closet to Dry affter they weire taken up, for the mice devoured them before I
had athought of it, If these Seed with you & can Spaire them I shoulde be
Vastly glade to make the any Return for afue. Ither roots or Seeds, Wee have
[off page] Sorts of Bulbas roots & I Coulde Easely Convey them to the if They
woulde be any Adision to your Collection of flowers. I Shoulde be Likewise
glade [blot] your kinde of hesperis as they may differ from mine   alls alittel
Double Chine asster Seed

I doe againe assure you of the truth of my assertion Relating to the Striped Stockgilly Flowers & if the See[d] Should Produce you flowers of asslaine Seed I begg yould not bee Discouraged but make a Second tryal the Next Season by which I am perswaided you will be Convinced of the truth———The Seeds I sent you by the Names of Virgin Stock was the Same Littel flower you so much admired in my Garden & hope they have Succeeded with the but have againe Sent afue moore for fear of any accidents & am with greatest Sincerity

S^r y^r assured friend & Humble Servnt
Martha Logan

Charlestown 20 December
1760
My good Wishes attend y^r family

Letter to John Bartram, accompanied by "a Box of Earth & Plants"

S^r

I Recieved yours Dated 1^d March with with [sic] the Seeds Enclosed & am much Obligd for them. I hope for better sucess with these then those before having never aSeed of the Sweet Sultaine or the Humble plant that Came up. the roots & Seeds you Mention will be Very Exceptable & if the Crocusts are blue I Shall Like them Still better as I have 2 roots of yellow allready———

. . . The yellow Wood bears no Seeds & Grows Wilde when its Propogated, only from its Slips Wheirefore have Sent you Some in a box of Earth (though tis Rather late to move it) but as tis not Difficult to grow hope they Will Live. If not I Can with Ease Send you Some moore Next Winter— . . . allso alist of many things Which I Coulde with ease furnish you . . .

Trees & flowering Shrubs

Oliander. Sweet Shrub. Cassena

Double flowered Pumgranet

Dwarple Pumgraned. Nutmet mirtles . . .

Olive tree

the Catalpa one with white & other reed flowers.

Canary Srub (Purple flowrs)

Flowring bays & Lowrels

English Honey Suckles

Chine Indigo

Pasion flower

the feathered leaf Oine with Scarlet flowrs

Snaile flower

Rose Cashia

Turkey Balm

alloways two Sorts one that flowrs Constantly the other very
   seldom (if Ever)

Ice plant.

White crocusts

grape Hyacinth (blue)

Chine & Turkey pinks. Caldonian Iris.

Gause Narses. Double White Sweet Sented Cypress narses/ Tuby
   roses. . . .

Letter to Ann Bartram, Philadelphia

Madm   *Octr 18 1761*

I Received your faviour by Capt North & am Much Obligd for taking the trouble of Answering Mine in Mr Bartrams absence. I hope he is by this Returned to his family & well. Pray give my Respects to him & thell him I Shoulde be Very glade he would tell Mr Ratlive what the Andromed on the road he mentioned to me is & I will moste Sertinly gett it & Send at a proper Season but I Cannot finde it out from Doc^{tr} Gardens———Mr. Ratlive is my Nighbour & will Enforme me better then any Letter Can I hear with Send him Some roots of the Indian or Worm Pink as the Seeds weire all fallen before I had y^{rs} about them. In the Same Tub is Some Slips of Mrs Bees Littel flowers Least the Seeds Shoulde faile the Berryes on the Trees are not yett Ripe Enough but If I live y^r Spouse may Sertinly Expect them with the Other things. I am with great truth your well wisher & friend

                                Martha Logan   Turn Over

Since I rotte the foregoing part I had a cupple Slips of a shrub & the Cashion rose Sent me. as they wire out of the ground & roome Enough for them in Tub thoughts they might be Exceptable to the. The Shrub is a native of this Province & the beauty not in its flowers but in its Seeds which are very curious & appear Like Scarlett flowers which Cover it in the fall of the year. . . .[1]

Deborah Read Franklin (1708–1774)

Portions of Deborah Read Franklin's life have been a part of American literary history since the eighteenth-century publication of her husband Benjamin's *Autobiography*. Benjamin Franklin detailed their

---

1. Daniell Logan included a "Catalogue of growing Roots of Forest Trees, Shrubs & Plants" that she had prepared for the former Minister of France, "Lieut Gerard." The catalogue included thirty-three notations, given first in Latin, then the number of roots, and finally the English name. Included are samples from cranberry, sassafras, Benjamin, dogwood, snowdrop, and umbrella trees, as well as rose and great mountain laurels.

trouble-laden courtship, Deborah's compatibility as a spouse, and her industrious nature. His emphasis upon her frugal attributes, however, tends to give us only one type of insight into their marriage and her contributions to the development of the new republic.

The daughter of Sarah and John Read, Deborah was born in Philadelphia in 1708. Little is known of her early life, until her meeting with Benjamin when he boarded in the Read home on his arrival in Philadelphia. Deborah and Benjamin had decided to marry before he left for England in 1724, but the temptations of youth and new experiences resulted in what he called one of the most serious "Errata" of his life. After he broke their engagement, Deborah married John Rogers; it was not a happy union, and Rogers left Philadelphia. When Deborah and Benjamin decided to marry in 1730, there was no proof of John Rogers's death; therefore, although she and Benjamin considered themselves married as of September 1, 1730, no legal proceedings occurred.

Read Franklin exemplifies the working-class woman of little formal education whose marriage thrust her into the center of national politics. Yet she also had to contend with the quotidian difficulties of maintaining the family business while her male relatives involved themselves in the politics of the day, and she had to bear the social brunt of her absent husband's political actions.

Works: Correspondence. *Bibliography*: *The Papers of Benjamin Franklin*.

Letters of Deborah Read Franklin to Benjamin Franklin

Aug. 9. 1759[1] . . . I went to hear the Negro Children catechised at Church.[2] There were 17 that answered very prettily indeed, and 5 or 6 that were too little, but all behaved very decently. Mr. Sturgeon[3] exhorted them before and after the Catechising. It gave me a great deal of Pleasure, and I shall send Othello[4] to the School. . . .

My Dear Child[5]   *Philadelphia Jan the 8 1765*
 . . . Salley is Come home[6]   Shee traveled the coldest day I ever felte or that I ever remember and staid at the ferry [?] house till the next day then walked over one half of the river and then in the bote the other half but Shee is att

1. Benjamin Franklin was in London at the time this letter was written.
2. Christ Church in Philadelphia. The children were part of the School for Negro Children, which opened in November 1758.
3. The Rev. William Sturgeon of Philadelphia.
4. "Possibly a child of BF's 'Negro Man Peter, and his Wife Jemima,' the couple to be freed under his will of 1757 . . . or a 'Negrow boy' for whom DF paid 41£ 10s. in June 1757 . . ." (*Papers* 8:425n).
5. This is the salutation with which Read Franklin typically greeted her husband.
6. Sarah (Sally) Franklin, Deborah and Benjamin's daughter, had been in Burlington, New Jersey, at her brother William's home. William was Benjamin's son, born out of wedlock by an unknown mother but raised by Deborah and Benjamin after their marriage.

home Safe now and we air all blocked up Could. I donte think we have had so much Snow this thirtey years   one Can hardly see the Topes of the postes now it is two deep to go a Slaying I am told the river is inhabeyted with Taverens but I have not seen it. Jamey Allin[7] fell in but as mony pepel was on he had presente helpe. I did not hear that he got Cold. . . . The marbel fireplaces is come safe but be Kind eneuef to tell our worthey friend Mr. Collinson that thair was not one Case in ither of the Boxes.[8] I sente for our Cusin Wilkison[9] to take the marbel ought and Stueby to take Care of the bundel of Levess but it was not thair. The Mantel is quite Curis indeed, but I donte remember wather you sed in what room the beste [?] shold be put. Yisterday I Spook to Nabor Headock[10] but he ses thair is no such Thing as painting till next March with ought the wather shold olter verey much so I muste indever to make my slef as esey as I Can but I did raly think I shold a bin allmoste ready to a movesed as soon as this wather has brook up. . . . God bless you my dear Child. I am your afeckshenit wife . . .

Feb th 10, [1765]   I am set down to Confab a littel with my dear child as it Semes a Sorte of a hollow day for we have an ox arosteing on the river[11] and moste pepel semes plesd with the a fair but as I partake of none of the divershons I stay at home and flatter myself that the next packit will bring me a letter from you. . . . We have nothing stiring amoungst us but phamlits and Scurrilitey[12] but I have never sed or dun aney thing or aney of our famely you may depend on it nor shall we. All our good friends Cole [call] on us as yousall [usual] and we have bin asked ought but I have not gon. . . .

September 22 1765

My Dear child . . . You will se by the papers what worke has hapened in other plases[13] and sumthing has bin sed relaiteing to raising a mob in this plase. I was for 9 day keep in one Contineued hurrey by pepel to removes and Salley was porswaided to go to burlinton for saiftey but on munday laste we had verey graite rejoysing on a Count of the Chang of the Ministrey and a preyperaition for binfiers [bonfires] att night and several houses thretened to be puled down. Cusin Davenporte[14] Come and told me that more then twenty pepel

7. William's son, James Allen, who had been studying in London.

8. The Franklins had begun the construction of a new house two years earlier. With the long and frustrating delays and with Benjamin now abroad, the responsibilities for its completion were Read Franklin's.

9. Read Franklin's cousin, Anthony Wilkinson.

10. Eden Haydock, a local glazier, plumber, and painter.

11. "Apprently ox roasting on the Delaware [River] had become quite fashionable during the severe winter of 1765. *Pa.Gaz.*, Feb. 7, 1765, reported such an event on February 5 which 'drew together a great Number of People' " (*Papers* 12:43n).

12. Isaac Hunt and David James Dove had recently published the pamphlet *Exercises in Scurrility Hall*, which attacked Benjamin's political activities. These attacks were probably why Read Franklin did not participate in "the divershons" of the community.

13. Read Franklin is referring to the colonial responses to the Stamp Act of 1765.

14. Josiah Franklin Davenport, Benjamin's nephew.

had told him it was his Duty to be with me. I sed I was plesed to reseve Civility from aney bodey so he staid with me sum time to words night I sed he shold fech a gun or two as we had none. I sente to aske my Brother[15] to Cume and bring his gun all so so we maid one room into a Magazin. I ordored sum sorte of defens up Stairs such as I Cold manaig my self. I sed when I was advised to remove that I was verey shuer you had dun nothing to hurte aney bodey nor I had not given aney ofense to aney person att all nor wold I be maid unesey by aney bodey nor wold I stir or show the leste uneseynis but if aney one Came to disturbe me I wold show a proper resentement and I shold be very much afrunted with aney bodey. . . . I will not stir as I rely donte think it wold be right in me to stir or show the leste uneseyness att all.[16] . . . Mr. John Ross and Brother Swore it is Mr. Saml Smith[17] that is a seting the pepel a-mading by teling them that it was you that had pland the Stampe acte and that you air indevering to get the teste ackte brought over hear but as I donte go much to town I mabey shall be esey for a while after the eleckshon is over but tel that I muste be disturbed. . . .

Eliza Lucas Pinckney (c. 1722–1793)

Eliza Lucas Pinckney is one of the few early American women who has been recognized for her contributions to American history—most notably, for her experiments with indigo. She was born on December 28, 1722(?), in Antigua, West Indies, where her father, Lieutenant Colonel George Lucas, was stationed with the British army; her mother's identity is unknown. Educated at Mrs. Boddicott's in England, Lucas moved with her family in 1738 to their country estate, Wappoo, seventeen miles outside of Charleston, South Carolina. Because of her mother's poor health and her father's commission, which required him to be in Antigua, Lucas took over the management of Wappoo and two other plantations when she was seventeen. Until the age of twenty-one, she maintained the plantations and experimented with growing indigo, a product that eventually became one of South Carolina's major staples. Yet she also read voraciously (from Locke to *Pamela* to legal texts), tutored her sisters as well as two African-American girls whom she wished to become teachers for the other African-American children enslaved on the Pinckney plantations.

From her early youth, Lucas was a decidedly independent person. She refused to consider the men her father selected as viable

15. Probably Read Franklin's brother, John Read.
16. Several townsmen and relatives assisted Read Franklin in guarding her home on the night of September 16, 1765.
17. Samuel Smith, a local merchant.

candidates for marriage, intending to remain single as long as she chose—which was until May 27, 1744, when she married Charles Pinckney, a lawyer and the widower of one of her Charleston friends. She and Charles had been friends for several years, in spite of their age difference (he was twenty years older than she). They discussed agricultural issues and exchanged books (including Locke and Virgil; the latter she acknowledged as the inspiration for the planting of a cedar grove on the family estate). They had three children who survived: Charles Cotesworth, Thomas, and Harriott. From 1753 until 1758 the Pinckneys lived in London, where Charles acted as commissioner to London for South Carolina. Shortly after their return, Charles died of malaria; Lucas Pinckney did not remarry during the decades that followed. She survived the loss of large portions of her property during the American Revolution and spent much of her last years living with her widowed daughter, Harriott Pinckney Horry. Eliza Lucas Pinckney died in 1793 in Philadelphia, where she had gone to seek treatment for cancer.

Works: Letterbook, correspondence. Bibliography: Pinckney.

The Letters of Eliza Lucas Pinckney

To Colonel Lucas, Eliza's Father, Spring 1740

Hond.Sir

. . .

As you propose Mr. L. to me I am sorry I can't have Sentiments favourable enough of him to take time to think on the Subject, as your Indulgence to me will ever add weight to the duty that obliges me to consult what best pleases you, for so much Generosity on your part claims all my Obedience, but as I know tis my happiness you consult [I] must beg the favour of you to pay my thanks to the old Gentleman for his Generosity and favourable sentiments of me and let him know my thoughts on the affair in such civil terms as you know much better than any I can dictate; and beg leave to say to you that the riches of Peru and Chili if he had them put together could not purchase a sufficient Esteem for him to make him my husband.

As to the other Gentleman you mention, Mr. Walsh, you know, Sir, I have so slight a knowledge of him I can form no judgment of him, and a Case of such consiquence requires the Nicest distinction of humours and Sentiments. But give me leave to assure you, my dear Sir, that a single life is my only Choice and if it were not as I am yet but Eighteen, hope you will [put] aside the thoughts of my marrying yet these 2 or 3 years at least.

You are so good to say you have too great an Opinion of my prudence to think I would entertain an indiscreet passion for any one, and I hope heaven will always direct me that I may never disappoint you; and which indeed could induce me to make a secret of my Inclination to my best friend, as I am well aware you would not disaprove it to make me a Sacrifice to Wealth, and I am as certain I would indulge no passion that had not your aprobation, as I truly am

Dr. Sir, Your most dutiful and affecte. Daughter
E. Lucas

To my Father.

Hon'd Sir   *June the 4th, 1741*

Never were letters more welcome than yours. . . . It was near 6 months since we had the pleasure of a line from you. Our fears increased apace and we dreaded some fatal accident befallen. . . .

I simpathize most sincerely with the Inhabitance of Antigua in so great a Calamity as the scarcity of provisions and the want of the Necessarys of life to the poorer sort.[1] We shall send all we can get of all sorts of provisions particularly what you write for. I wrote this day to Starrat for a barrel [of] butter.

We expect the boat dayly from Garden Hill when I shall be able to give you an account of affairs there. The Cotton, Guiney corn, and most of the Ginger planted here was cutt off by a frost. I wrote you in [a] former letter we had a fine Crop of Indigo Seed upon the ground, and since informed you the frost took it before it was dry. I picked out the best of it and had it planted, but there is not more than a hundred buses of it come up—which proves the more unluckey as you have sent a man to make it.[2] I make no doubt Indigo will prove a very valuable Commodity in time if we could have the seed from the west Indias [in] time enough to plant the latter end of March, that the seed might be dry enough to gather before our frost. I am sorry we lost this season. We can do nothing towards it now but make the works ready for next year. . . .

Y.m.obt.and ever D[evoted] D[aughter]
E. Lucas

To Mary Bartlett, c. 1740/41

Dr. Miss B[3]

. . . Why, my dear Miss B, will you so often repeat your desire to know how I triffle away my time in our retirement in my fathers absence. Could it afford you advantage or pleasure I should not have hesitated, but as you can expect neither from it I would have been excused; however, to show you my readiness in obeying your commands, here it is.

In general then I rise at five o'Clock in the morning, read till Seven, then take a walk in the garden or field, see that the Servants are at their respective

---

1. The British and Spanish were battling at Cartagena.
2. Nicholas Cromwell, a dye-maker who made the vats Lucas used in her experiments with indigo.
3. Bartlett had come from England to visit her relatives, the Pinckneys.

business, then to breakfast. The first hour after breakfast is spent at my musick, the next is constantly employed in recolecting something I have learned least for want of practise it should be quite lost, such as French and short hand. After that I devote the rest of the time till I dress for dinner to our little Polly[4] and two black girls who I teach to read, and if I have my paps's approbation (my Mamas I have got) I intend [them] for school mistres's for the rest of the Negroe children—another scheme you see. But to proceed, the first hour after dinner as the first after breakfast at musick, the rest of the afternoon in Needle work till candle light, and from that time to bed time read or write. 'Tis the fashion here to carry our work abroad with us so that having company, without they are great strangers, is no interruption to that affair; but I have particular matters for particular days, which is an interruption to mine. Mondays my musick Master is here. Tuesdays my friend Mrs. Chardon (about 3 mile distant) and I are constantly engaged to each other, she at our house one Tuesday—I at hers the next and this is one of the happiest days I spend at Woppoe. Thusday the whole day except what the necessary affairs of the family take up is spent in writing, either on the business of the plantations, or letters to my friends. Every other Fryday, if no company, we go a vizeting so that I go abroad once a week and no oftener.

Now you may form some judgment what time I can have to work my lappets. I own I never go to them with a quite easey conscience as I know my father has an aversion to my employing my time in that poreing work, but they are begun and must be finished. I hate to undertake any thing and not go thro' with it; but by way of relaxation from the other I have begun a peice of work of a quicker sort which requires nither Eyes nor genius—at least not very good ones. Would you ever guess it to be a shrimp nett? For so it is.

O! I had like to forgot the last thing I have done a great while. I have planted a large figg orchard with design to dry and export them. I have reckoned my expence and the prophets to arise from these figgs, but was I to tell you how great an Estate I am to make this way, and how 'tis to be laid out you would think me far gone in romance. Your good Uncle[5] I know has long thought I have a fertile brain at schemeing. I only confirm him in his opinion; but I own I love the vegitable world extremly. I think it an innocent and useful amusement. Pray tell him, if he laughs much at my project, I never intend to have my hand in a silver mine and he will understand as well as you what I mean.

Our best respects wait on him and Mrs. Pinckney. If my Eyes dont deceive me you in your last [letter] talk of coming very soon by water[6] to see how my oaks grow. Is it really so, or only one of your unripe schemes. While 'tis in your head put it speedily into execution and you will give great pleasure to

Y m o s
E. Lucas

4. Lucas's younger sister, who resided with her and their mother in South Carolina. Lucas's two brothers had remained in England.
5. Charles Pinckney, Lucas's future husband.
6. By water, it was only six miles from Charles Town to the Pinckney estate, as compared to seventeen miles by land.

To Her Daughter, Harriott Pinckney Horry, Spring 1775

Tuesday morning

My dear child,

This is rather a continuation of my letter by Sam as I have but just sealed that. I shall give April some of the Pompion [pumpkin] seed you sent; I would not let him plant any English pease, as you would not be in town to eat them, and the ground may be applyed to things that will be of use in the fall. Your garden has been very useful to me for the little I want, for tho' I should not chuse to use any thing that would not spoiled by standing, those that I knew would run to seed in a short time such as greens and Lettuce, I made free with. I wished you some of the latter as they are all runing to seed and you were unlucky with yours at Hampton. I have desired April to send you up some leaks by the boat. Your people seem to behave orderly and quitely. . . .

Your brother is three months in the year out of town and then I believe he is only a drudge for the rest and for himself also. He went and hired himself the other day to a man who had a barrel of Rice broke at the landing before your brother's door[7] to carry the Rice tyed up in a blanket (no body at home knows any thing of the matter) and the unmerciful wretch gave the fellow such a load to carry to the draw gate that gave him a violent pain in his back and has been rubed with oil of Turpentine. He has been here to day, and has lost his fever. His back is much beter, but not well.

Jones sent me word a few days after I came to town that the stores had been served and he could not get a bit of fine washing pavilion Gause any where; I afterwards sent old Mary with directions not to miss a store, and to let them know it was Cash, and after two or three days serch she got me some coarse stuff for which I payed ready money; but I have been more luckey to day for you; I sent her to Cape (I am glad you mentioned him) and have got 40 yards of fine Pavilion washing gause; 'tis more than your quantity but they wont cut and it will do to mend it. It is 15s. per yd.

A Providence vessel is just arrived which gives me an opportunity to beg your acceptance of a little Turtle in fine order, and some very fine limes. I would send more limes but your boat makes such quick trips I think 50 will be as many as you can use till she returns; and while they are good, i am told the Bananas and oranges are bad, or should not forget my boy.

Capt. Moore of Philadelphia is just come in. Blott has an assortment of paper in him. 'Tis not yet landed. If you do not receive paper for your room by the boat, 'tis because I chuse to see that, before I determine upon one. I am much obliged for the penns, I have now a great stack.

Wednesday

'Tis all a mistake about the paper. They mistook the Vessel, Blot just informs me. In the red trunk is limes, 2 Osnaberg aprons, and your Pavalions, with some book, musling which Tom will be obliged to you to have made into

---

7. Thomas Pinckney's property on East Bay Street included a wharf where this incident apparently occurred.

C[ollar] Bands. The patern is with it inside the pavalion gause, but two bands will be enough at present for the Circuit so dont hurry your self. Send back the patern.

Sally has just informed me your brothers are at Ashley River and will be down to Night. Mrs. William H. Drayton drank tea with me on Sunday, desires her love to you, as does Sally.

A Packet came in on Sunday Night (rained all day on Monday). I did not know it till yesterday to inform you by Sam. Poor Lady Charles Montague is dead, as is Mr. Burn—she dyed at Exeter. I cant tell you much Public News, what I have heard is as follows, That the American affairs at home wear a more favourable Aspect. The King has promised to receive the petition. Jamaica has petitioned, the rest of the Islands are about to do it, as well as the London Merchants; The Trades people clamour extremely. Mr. Fox[8] is not so violent as he used to be against us. Capt. Turner is also arrived and says there is a prospect of the Acts being repealed. Pray God Grant it may prove true.

I sent 9 pieces of paper and borders from Mrs. Fowler. I wish you may like it. There is none in town like the patern you sent. Blot says that these may be more than enough with what he sent up; 'tis of no consiquence for he will take what ever is left again. There is very little Choice in town. What I sent you I think the prettiest. Pray give my love to Mr. Horry and my dear boy. I send him 14 apples and some cakes. There is great plenty of the former in town but such trash they would not keep to Santee. . . .

My dear Harriott's
Most affectionate Mother
Eliza. Pinckney

Coosaponakessa (Mary Musgrove Matthews Bosomworth) (c. 1700–post-1760)

Coosaponakessa was the niece of Brims, a leader of the Creeks at Coweta Town, where she was born. Her parents were believed to be Brims's sister and the explorer Henry Woodward. Coosaponakessa was educated and converted to Christianity at Pon Pon in South Carolina. In 1717 her uncle gave her in marriage to John Musgrove as a pledge of peace in the devastating Yamasee War of 1716 between the Creek and the English. Coosaponakessa, who became known as Mary Musgrove after her marriage, established with her husband one of the most prosperous trading posts in the region at Yamacraw Bluff. Her contributions as interpreter and agent were immeasurable during the strife-ridden 1730s, when

8. The British statesman Charles Fox. Lucas Pinckney is probably referring to Fox's actions during the Tea Act and Intolerable Acts crises.

Georgia was being established and when Carolina and Georgia disputed both the rum trade and trade with Native Americans.

In 1734 a dispute arose over the licensing of traders to both the Creeks and the Choctaws. The original settlers of the Georgia colony numbered only 106 (including 20 women and 17 girls), with an additional 500 settlers arriving within the year. The leadership was minimal, and relations with Carolina and, especially, the indigenous peoples were crucial to their survival. As Musgrove's only extant letter reveals, she sided with the British in Georgia who successfully negotiated with the Choctaws, which Carolina's leaders had been unable to do. Musgrove was the interpreter for Chief Redshoes and the colonial leaders at the 1734 meeting that brought the Choctaws into trade with the Georgia colonists.

General James Oglethorpe, founder of the Georgia colony, greatly admired Musgrove and established close relations with her that lasted throughout the early years of the colony. In 1736, for example, when relations between the English settlers and the Native Americans became strained, Oglethorpe requested that Musgrove serve as interpreter at his crucial meeting with Chigilly, leader of the Lower Creeks, and Malachi, who was to succeed Chigilly (Malachi was Musgrove's cousin and son of Brim). Increasingly, Oglethorpe relied on Musgrove for advice as well as for her interpreting skills; this reliance was sometimes resented by Englishmen, such as William Stephens, a representative of the colony's Trustees who felt that Oglethorpe relied too heavily upon Musgrove's opinion. Throughout her life, Musgrove had to negotiate not only between the Native Americans and colonists but also the double-bind of racial and gender prejudices.[1]

John Musgrove died in 1735; in 1736 Mary married another trader, Jacob Matthews, who had once been the Musgroves' servant. During her second marriage, she not only continued to run the Yamacraw trading post but, at Oglethorpe's request, opened a second post at Mount Venture. In 1742 the Matthews returned to Savannah and Jacob died shortly thereafter. When Oglethorpe left Georgia in the summer of 1743, he promised Musgrove Matthews 100 pounds a year to continue as interpreter. The following year she married Thomas Bosomworth, an Anglican minister who gave up the ministry to work with Mary at Yamacraw.

It is at this point in her life that most historians suggest Mary Musgrove Matthews Bosomworth was misled by her new husband into beliefs of having been wronged by the colonists. But the situation was far more complex. She had continued to act as interpreter for Oglethorpe's successors; she did not become a "problem"

---

1. This is nowhere so evident as in historical accounts that rely solely upon the colonists' vision of matters. When Musgrove challenged the colonists over back pay and property rights, she was deemed by one colonist "a Mad and Frantick Woman" (Temple and Coleman 264), an image that has prejudiced her contributions to early Georgia history.

for the colony until she demanded the back pay of the monies promised her by Oglethorpe. Mary, her husband, and their Creek supporters threatened to stop any further European settlement in regions negotiated under the 1739 Creek-colonial treaty. On August 7, 1749, guns were fired by approximately two hundred Creeks as they entered Savannah in support of Mary Musgrove Matthews Bosomworth. When the colonial leaders sought to negotiate with the Creeks, Mary entered and reportedly threatened the leaders. She was arrested. While that incident soon faded, she did not give up her fight; by 1750 she had the signatures of seven chieftains of the Creek nation in support of her claims to both the past-due money and the lands that she wanted deeded to her and her husband. Her claims were never settled during the period of Trusteeship in Georgia. It was not until 1760 that Governor Henry Ellis sought restitution for Mary's claim. She received 2,050 pounds and a grant for the land on which she lived at St. Catherine's Island.

Works: Letter. *Bibliography*: Coleman; Lane; Spalding.

Letter of Coosaponakessa (Mary Musgrove) to General James Oglethorpe

[Savannah, Georgia, July 17, 1734]

Honoured Sir

I make bold to acquaint You that Thos. Jones is returned from the Choctaws and according to your Honours desire he has brought the Choctaws down and they have received great favours from Col. Bull and Mr. Causton and all the rest of the Colony, and a great deal of Respect shew'd them which they are wonderfully pleased at. And when they came down Mr. Jones brought with him some of the Heads of the Tallooposes which is called the Upper Creeks; The Dog King of the Uphalais Cahuaway by name went with Mr. Jones up to the Choctaws to make peace, and he is mighty glad that he and Mr. Jones did persuade them to come down which is more than ever Carolina could do to get them down before. And the Choctaws are so glad that some white People whom they call'd their Masters has taken such Care of them as to send for them and they was very glad of the good hopes to live as well as the other Indians do, for they had nor have no Trade with the French and their Skins lye by them and rot. When Mr. Thos. Jones came to them at first there was thirty Towns only that had the notice. Before Mr. Jones came away all they gave their Consents for their Coming, but Notice was still sent on farther. And they say that they like the English better than the French, and that they will stand by the English as long as they have one left alive. There was some of the Caupahauches and the Hulbaumors came with them. The Choctaws are all amazed to see the Creeks drink as they do, and they think the Creeks are saucy to the white People. The Choctaw King thinks they are obliged to the white People and thinks they cannot do enough for the white People especially the English.

And since they have been here there has not one of them been disguished in Liquor or any ways saucy upon any Account. They have been here 21 Days for Mr. Causton thought it proper to send for Col. Bull and that was the Reason of their being Detained so long here. Govr. Johnson has sent for them to come to Carolina but Thomas Jones was not willing they should go to Carolina for fear of disobliging your Honour, and as he was sent for them for the Colony he did not Care they should go any where else. Your Honour's Name is spread very much amongst them and they say that when your Honour comes back to Georgia they will be bound to raise a thousand or two at your Honour's Command if desired, and they design to leave the French entirely and then they will come down and pay their Respects to You, and to Govr. Johnson if your Honour desires they should go to Carolina but not without your Honour's Consent. Mr. Thos. Jones does insist of the Trade amongst the Choctaws as your Honour did promise him, and the Choctaws have so very great Respect and Value for Mr. Jones that they had rather have him to trade among them than any body else because he ventured his Life to bring them down to the English.

Honoured Sir, There has been a great Dispute about the Lot that You was pleased to give the Grant of to Thomas Jones, and since You have given it to Mr. Parker Gent. and since to me. Jones is returned home. He finds he had lost it so there has been a Court Business about it, for Mr. Jones does insist upon that very Lot or else none; and the Court has considered upon it and was so good as to give it to him again. The Colony is in good health and I hope your Honour and all your family is in good health and my Husband is the same, and I beg your Honour will take great Care of him, he being in a strange place and not able to take Care of himself and to send him home as soon as possible.[2] Capt. Mackay is not gone up as yet the Creeks nor I do not know when he will. The Indians has expected him these three months ago. The Talloopose King has made great Complaints of the French building Forts amongst them and they did not know where or who to go to so they came to see if the English would protect them.

I remain . . .

Mary Katherine Goddard (1738–1816)

Mary Katherine Goddard was born in New London, Connecticut, on June 16, 1738. The eldest child of Sarah Updike and Dr. Giles Goddard, Mary was educated by her mother, who was noted for her own exceptional education. Mary's first business training also came from her mother. Mary Katherine Goddard's list of "firsts" is remarkable, even in an era that produced many remarkable women. Sarah and Mary moved to Providence, Rhode Island, in 1762 to assist William Goddard, Mary's sibling, in establishing a print shop.

2. John Musgrove was in England, acting as interpreter for Tomo-Chi-Chi and other Native American leaders.

In 1765 William moved to Philadelphia to publish a newspaper in that city; "Sarah Goddard and Company" took over publication of The *Providence Gazette* and Mary became her mother's apprentice. Three years later, the two women again moved to assist William in business. When Sarah died in 1770, Mary took full charge of the *Pennsylvania Chronicle*, and in 1774 she moved to Baltimore to take over the *Maryland Journal*, which William had established the previous year, while her brother traveled throughout the colonies in an effort to establish the postal service.

During the American Revolution, Mary Goddard developed the *Maryland Journal* into one of the most important publications of its era. She was the printer appointed by the Continental Congress to publish the first official printing of the Declaration of Independence; she was the first woman appointed to federal office in her capacity of Baltimore postmistress; and she ran several other businesses (including a bookshop and a bookbindery) while she published the *Journal*. At the end of the war, the *Maryland Journal* had not only survived the difficulties of war but was a highly successful publication.

Just when Goddard's success was most evident, however, sexual discrimination deprived her of the privileges of her success. First, her brother forced her out of the management of the *Journal* so he might return not only to his duties but to the financial rewards of the position. She did not go quietly. She refused to make amends with her brother and published a rival almanac in which she harshly criticized him. Second, in 1789 she was replaced as head of the Baltimore post office by a man. At the time, the latter decision was explained explicitly in terms of her sex: the Baltimore post office would become the supervising office for several branch offices and that expansion would demand travel that, it was assumed, a woman could not be expected to do. Goddard was not alone in her resistance to such discrimination. More than 200 citizens of Baltimore protested her removal, and Goddard herself sought the assistance of President George Washington and petitioned the U.S. Senate to keep her position, but it was to no avail. (Neither the expansion nor the necessary travel occurred after a man was appointed postmaster.) Goddard's 1790 petition attests to her accomplishments and to the discrimination in her removal.

Goddard remained single and supported herself as a bookseller until her death on August 12, 1816. Her will expressed her continuing anger at her brother: rather than leave her property to her only surviving relative, she willed it to a female slave, whom she also manumitted at her death. Certainly, the act had far less to do with her concerns about holding slaves than it did her wish to make clear that she had never forgiven her brother.

Works: Printer, publisher of the *Pennsylvania Chronicle* and *Maryland Journal*, almanac compiler, bookseller, petitioner. *Bibliography*: Beasley and Gibbons; Hudak; Schilpp and Murphy; Wheeler.

Mary Katherine Goddard's Petition

To the Honorable Senate of the United States.

The Representation of Mary Katherine Goddard humbly sheweth, That She kept the Post Office at Baltimore from the Dissolution of the old Government till the Month of November last, a term of fourteen years and upwards—That from the Non-importation Agreement, and various other causes incident to the Revolution, the Income of the Office was inadequate to its disbursements, as will appear by the Schedule hereunto annexed, and in order to accomplish this undertaking, she was obliged to advance hard money to defray the Charges of Post-Riders for several years, when they were not to be procured on any other terms; during which period, the whole of her labour and industry was necessarily unrewarded; therefore, she with great deference hoped, that having thus established and continued the Office when it was worth no Person's acceptance, She would be considered as worthy of being retained whenever it became more valuable.

That She hath been discharged without the smallest imputation of any Fault, and without any previous notice whatever, till an Order arrived from Mr. Burrell whilst at Baltimore, to deliver up the Office to Mr. White, the Bearer of his note, & although he remained several Days in town, yet he did not think proper to indulge her with a personal interview, whereby she might learn (therein) of her removal, or to what motives, it could possibly be ascribed. Such a Procedure contrasted with her conduct in Office, and the approbation of the public, testified by the number and respectability of these, who addressed Messrs. Osgood & Burrell on her behalf, leave no room to question either her inclination or ability to discharge the duties of her appointment.

That sundry public and private applications, prior to the 19th of November last, were made to the above Gentlemen, praying that She might be restored, but no answer was returned, till the latter End of January when a Mr. Osgood wrote to the Merchants of Baltimore, that the Evil was irremediable by him. During this Interval She flattered herself that so long a consideration of the Subject would have infallibly terminated in her favour; but she has since learned that the neglect proceeded more from contempt than a desire of redress.

She also represents that taking her Office, contrary to the sense & Expectation of the whole Community, and delaying a determination of her Fate so long, whether she should be restored or not, has greatly augmented her anxiety and distress—these are but poor rewards indeed for fourteen Years faithful Services, performed in the worst of times, and acknowledged in the most public manner by all her Co-temporaries & Superiors in Office in these words, "that no change could possibly be for the benefit of the public."

And further, as it has been universally understood that no Person should be removed from Office under the present Government, unless manifest misconduct appeared, and as no such charge could possibly be made against her, with the least colour of Justice, she was happy in the Idea of being secured both in her employ & the protect of all those who wished well to the federal Cause: And if it should so happen that she should be obliged to make room for one of more worth or interest, that she would nothwithstanding be allowed a reasonable time to prepare for the Event.

And although Mr. White who has succeeded her might doubtless have been highly meritorious, in the different Offices he has sustained, yet, she humbly conceives, he was not more worthy of public notice & protection in his Station, than She has uniformly been in hers. It must therefore become a matter of serious importance to her, if Government can find no means of rewarding this Gentleman's Services, but by taking her little Office, established by her own Industry in the best years of her life, & whereon depended all her future Prospects of subsistence. In old Countries, People come in & go out, with the Minister of the day & his party; but here She never could suppose that any Minister Party, or Individual, would deign to cast a wishful Eye upon so small an Object, whilst in the Hands of such a Professor. Various reasons have from time to time been assigned & abandoned, to sanction her removal, but the only one worthy of either notice or belief, is to the following Effect, though equally fallacious with the rest; ... That the Deputy at Baltimore will hereaforth be obliged to ride & regulate the Offices to the Southward, but that with great deference to the Post Master General[1] will be found altogether impractiable; because the business of that Office will require his constant attendance, as no other than the Principal alone could possibly be relied on, or give satisfaction to the Merchants who frequently make large remittances by post. If therefore the duties of Mr. Burrell's Office are to be performed by any other than himself, it cannot well be attempted by a Deputy, fully occupied with his own; and if two Persons must be employed, according to his new Plan, She apprehends herself, at least, as well qualified to give the necessary Instructions to the Ride Post Master, as Mr. White, or any other person heretofore unexperienced in such business.

That although it has been suggested that the Income of her Office, for a few years last past, has made her amends for her former assiduity care and expence, yet She would beg leave to observe, that from the many failures which have distressed this Community since the peace, She has met with her Share of losses and misfortunes, a Truth well known to all her Neighbours; And now to deprive her of this Office, to which She has a more meritorious & just claim than any other person, is a circumstance, pregnant with that Species of aggravation, which a Sense of Ingratitude inspires & which is much easier felt than described.

She therefore humbly hopes that the honorable the Senate will take her case into their serious Consideration & grant her such Assistance, as may be in their Power, in restoring her to the public Confidence & the Enjoyment of her former Office, & She will ever pray ...

Baltimore 29th Jan. 1790.

M. K. Goddard

---

1. Samuel Osgood.

"Death-Bed" Declarations

Skate'ne (Choctaw)

There are many solemn and sacred death rites among Native American peoples, but as in Euro-American cultures, there are also many myths and legends about death. The following tale comes from a group of Choctaw who occupied the region identified as Louisiana by early French explorers.

Bibliography: Bushnell.

Skate'ne

Late one afternoon several children were playing near their house when suddenly they saw a woman approaching. She was very old and stooping, and her hair was white. The children were greatly frightened and ran into the house, but soon returned to the old woman, who said to them: "Children, do not be afraid of me, for nothing will harm you. I am your great-great-great-grandmother, and neither you nor your mother has ever seen me. Now, go to the house and tell her that I have come." The children did so. Then they took a deer skin and spread it on the ground for the old woman and carried her food and drink. She then asked the children when their father went to sleep and in which part of the house he lay, and the children told her all.

That night, after all had gone to sleep, the old woman entered the house and cut off the man's head, which she put into a basket she carried for the purpose; then she covered the man's body with his blanket and quietly left the house. The next morning the man's wife was surprised to find him asleep (as she supposed), since it was his custom to go hunting before sunrise. So she spoke to him, and as he did not answer she pulled off his blanket. When she saw his head was missing, she became greatly alarmed.

After cutting off the man's head, Skate'ne, the old woman, immediately left the house and started down the road. Soon she met a large bear, who said to her, "What have you covered up in your basket, old woman?" "You must not

123

see it," said she, "for if you look on it you will lose your eyes; it is poison and bad." The bear was contented and went on his way.

Then she met many other animals, and at last came two wildcats. "Stop, old woman, and show us what you have in your basket," called one of the wildcats, "we must see what you carry." The old woman repeated what she had told the bear and all the others. "But we must look inside your basket, even if we do lose our eyes," replied one of the wildcats, at the same time seizing the basket and raising the cover.

When they saw the man's head they knew it was the old woman who prowled around during the night, killing men and animals and birds, so they determined to kill her. While one held her the other went to find a large club. When he had gone she said to the wildcat holding her, "Over there is a large club. You would do well to get it and kill me before your companion returns, for the one that kills me will always have good luck, and I like you." So the remaining wildcat went to get the club, for he believed what the old woman had told him, and hence wanted to kill her. On his return with the club, he could not find the old woman, for she was Skate'ne, an owl, and had flown away.

Sarah Whipple Goodhue (1641–1681)

The youngest daughter of Susannah and John Whipple, Sarah was born in 1641 into a devout Puritan family in Ipswich, Massachusetts. In 1661 she married Joseph Goodhue, and they raised eight children together. Just prior to the birth of twins in 1681, Sarah had a "strong persuasion" that she would die in childbirth. This was not only a common fear of early American women but a highly plausible one in an era of high infant and pregnant women's mortality rates. She did not tell her husband or other family members about her premonition; rather, she chose to record a "valedictory and monitory" for their edification. Her text follows closely the tenets of the strict Puritan Calvinism to which she faithfully adhered, but it is also a testimony of one woman's desires: for the salvation of her children, for her husband to know of her love for him and of her wishes for their offspring, and also for a sense of control, the opportunity to shape her family's lives even after her passing.

Traditional in form, the document reflects one way in which women who adhered to a submissive role in the family and in society made known their opinions and sought to carry to its fullest the role of spiritual guide. Further, the precise language and insertions of poetic meditations suggest the literary quality for which Whipple Goodhue strove in her writings. Sarah Whipple Goodhue died on July 23, 1681, three days after delivering twins. Her *Vale-*

dictory was published in 1681 in Cambridge and remained a popular document through the eighteenth and nineteenth centuries. It was reprinted in Salem, 1770; Portland, 1805; and Cambridge, 1850.

Works: *A Valedictory and Monitory Writing* (1681). *Bibliography: Publications of the Ipswich Historical Society* 20 (1915), pp. 12–17.

A Valedictory and Monitory Writing

Dear and loving Husband, if it should please the Lord to make a sudden change in thy family, the which I know not how soon it may be, and I am fearful of it:

Therefore in a few words I would declare something of my mind, lest I should afterwards have no opportunity: I cannot but sympathize and pity thy condition, seeing that thou has a great family of children, and some of them small, and if it should please the Lord to add to thy number one more or two, be not discouraged, although it should please the Lord to deprive thee of thy weak help which is so near and dear unto thee. Trust in the living God, who will be an help to the helpless, and a father to the motherless: My desire is, that if thou art so contented, to dispose of two or three of my children: If it please the Lord that I should be delivered of a living child, son or daughter, my desire is, that my father and mother should have it, if they please, I freely bequeath and give it to them. And also my desire is, that my cousin *Symond Stacy* should have *John* if he please, I freely bequeath and give him to him for his own if thou art willing. And also my desire is, that my cousin *Catharine Whipple* should have *Susanna*, which is an hearty girl, and will quickly be helpful to her, and she may be helpful to the child, to bring her up: These or either of these I durst trust their care under God, for the faithful discharge of that which may be for my children's good and comfort, and I hope to deal well by them, answer my desire I pray thee, thou hast been willing to answer my request formerly, and I hope now thou wilt, this being the last so far as I know. . . .

O my children all, which in pains and care have cost me dear; unto you I call to come and take what portion your dying mother will bestow upon you: many times by experience it hath been found, that the dying words of parents have left a living impression upon the hearts of Children; O my children be sure to set the fear of God before your eyes; consider what you are by nature, miserable sinners, utterly lost and undone; and that there is no way and means whereby you can come out of this miserable estate; but by the Mediation of the Lord Jesus Christ: He died a reproachful death, that every poor humble and true repenting sinner by faith on God through him, might have everlasting life: O my Children, the best counsel that a poor dying Mother can give you is, to get a part and portion in the Lord Jesus Christ that will hold, when all these things will fail; O let the Lord Jesus Christ be precious in your sight. . . .

My children, one or two words I have to say to you more, in the first place, be sure to carry well to your father, obey him, love him, follow his instructions and example, be ruled by him, take his advice, and have a care of grieving him: For I must testify the truth unto you . . . that your Father hath been loving, kind, tender-hearted towards you all . . . You that are grown up, cannot but see how careful your father is when he cometh home from his work, to take the young ones up into his wearied arms, by his loving carriage and care towards those, you may behold as in a glass, his tender care and love to you every one as you grow up: I can safely say, that his love was so to you all, that I cannot say which is the child that he doth love best; but further I may testify unto you, that . . . he hath given you many instructions, which hath been to the end your souls might enjoy happiness . . . to attend unto reading God's Word . . . that it might soke into the heart and find entertainment there: and that you should meditate upon it. . . .

My first, as thy name is *Joseph*, labour so in knowledge to increase,
As to be free from the guilt of thy sins, and enjoy eternal Peace.
Mary, labour so to be arrayed with the hidden man of the heart,
That with Mary thou mayest find, thou hast chosen the better part.
William, thou hadst that name for thy grandfather's sake.
Labour so to tread in his steps, as over sin conquest thou mayest make.
Sarah, Sarah's daughter thou shalt be, if thou continuest in doing well,
Labour so in holiness among the daughters to walk, as that thou mayest excel.
So my children all, if I must be gone, I with tears bid you all *Farewell*.
                                    The Lord bless you all.

Now dear Husband, I can do no less than turn unto thee, And if I could, I would naturally mourn with thee. . . . A tender-hearted, affectonate and entire loving husband thou hast been to me several ways . . . thou hast by thy chearful love to me, helped me forward in a chearful frame of spirit. . . .

This twenty years experience of thy love to me in this kind, hath so instamped it upon my mind, that I do think that there never was man more truly kind to a woman: I desire for ever to bless and praise the Lord, that in mercy to my soul, he by his providence ordered that I should live with thee in such a relation, therefore dear husband be comforted in this, (although God by his providence break that relation between us, that he gave being to at first) that in thy place thou hast been a man of knowledge to discharge to God and my soul, that scripture commanded duty, which by the effects in me wrought, through the grace of God, thou mayest behold with comfort our prayers not hindered; but a gracious answer from the Lord, which is of great price and reward. Although my being gone be thy loss, yet I trust in and thro' Jesus Christ, it will be my gain. . . .

If thou couldest ask me a reason why I thus declare myself?—I cannot answer no other but this; that I have had of late a strong persuasion upon my mind, that by sudden death I should be surprised, either at my travail, or soon after it, the Lord fit me for himself: although I could be very willing to enjoy thy company, & my children longer, yet if it be the will of the Lord that I must not, I hope I can say cheerfully, *the will of the Lord be done*, this hath been often my desire and the prayer.

Further if thou could'st ask me why I did not discover some of these particulars of my mind to thee before, my answer is because I knew that thou wert tender hearted towards me, and therefore I would not create thee needless trouble.

O dear husband of all my dearest bosom friends, if by sudden death I must part from thee, let not thy trouble and cares that are on thee make thee to turn aside from the right way.

O dear heart, if I must leave thee and thine here behind,
Of my natural affection here is my heart and hand.

Be courageous, and on the living God bear up thy heart in so great a breach as this.

Sarah Goodhue.

Hannah Hill, Jr. (1703–1714)

Although her life was extraordinarily short, Hannah Hill felt the compulsion to leave a record of her existence. As a Quaker, Hill sought "General Good and Wellfare" for all sects, for "all the Sons and Daughters of Men, under what Denomination soever" and of whatever race. The daughter of devout parents, Hannah and Richard Hill of Philadelphia, Hannah Jr. was encouraged in her religious devotions and her particular opinions were not silenced. Shortly before her death, Hannah had a dream that John Lowdon, a minister in nearby Abington, was dying. News of his death came the next day, and Hannah asked that his body be brought back to Philadelphia for burial. The funeral was described by Hannah to her young cousin, Elizabeth Norris. The sense of prophecy and the death of a close family friend, and especially his notable last words, probably shaped Hannah's own dying thoughts, which were recorded by attending family members and published shortly after her death.

A Legacy for Children includes a long narrative of Hannah's death by an anonymous observer, probably a family member, who recorded her faithful willingness for death, her joy at finally going to see deceased relatives and friends, her devotion to her parents, and her concern for their servants; interspersed are quotations of her "sayings." Hannah sensed her own approaching death "for some Considerable time before she was Seized," and often spoke of it to her family and especially to Elizabeth Norris. Fortified by the accuracy of her premonition about John Lowdon's fate, she left a record of her final thoughts that is traditional in form but unique in its youthful perspective and especially interesting for the comments directed to her mother and only sister. After several days of "a violent Feaver and Flux," the last three of which were filled with the "most Violent Extremity of Pain," Hannah died on July 23, 1714. Her *Legacy* was extraordinarily popular and was published in at least three editions.

Works: A Legacy for Children, Being Some of the Last Expressions, and Dying Sayings, Of Hannah Hill, Junr. of . . . Philadelphia . . . Aged Eleven Years and near Three Months (1714).

From *A Legacy for Children*[1]

Dear Cousin E. Norris;

The Burial of our worthy Friend, *John Lowdon*, was performed in the most Solemn manner, the Corps being carried from our House, first to the Meeting, which was very large and from thence to the Grave, where many exprest their Sorrow, for the Churches Loss: But it must needs be his exceeding gain, who expresly said (a few minutes before his Departure) he had done his days Work in his Day; and that he laid down his head in Peace with God, and in Unity with his People; Which that thee and I may do, is the Earnest desire of

Thy affectionate loving Cousin,
H. Hill, Junior.

Selected Sayings

Am I prepared! Am I prepared! Oh! that I might dye the Death of the Righteous, and be Numbered with them at Thy Right Hand! O Almighty God! Prepare me, Prepare me for thy Kingdom of Glory.

I do freely Forgive all, and have nothing in my Heart but Love, to both White and Black. But Father will every Body Forgive me?

O most Glorious God now give me Patience, I beseech thee, with Humility to bear what it shall please thee to lay upon thy poor Afflicted Hand-Maiden. . . . I had rather dye and go to God, than to continue in this World of Trouble. When will the Messenger come Oh! hasten thy Messenger! . . . Oh! that I could Launch away like a Boat that Sails! So would I go to my Dear Brother, who is gone to Heaven before me.

Why is there so much to do about me, Who am but poor Dust and Ashes? We are all but as Clay, and must Dye; I am going now; Another next Day; And so one after another: The whole World Passes away.

O my Dear Mother! I Fear the Lord is displeased with me again. . . . Because I am continued, thus long, to endure this Extremity of Body, which none knows but my selfe, nor can any think how great my Pains are. . . . My Dear

1. The letter to Hill's cousin is appended to *A Legacy*. No copies are extant of the first (1714) and second (1715) editions of *A Legacy*. The letter and following sayings are from the third edition, published in 1717.

Mother! Pray to God for Direction; Dear Mother! if thou desires it, I'll take another Dose [of medicine].

O my good God, Comfort the Mourners in Sion, and Support their Drooping Heads; Be pleased to provide for the Widdows and Fatherless, and be thou both Husband and Father to them.

Dear Sister! my desires are, that thou mayest Fear God; be Dutifull to thy Parents, Love Truth; Keep to Meetings, and be an Example of Plainness.

The fire would not cease burning, until all the Chaff was consumed, though Men Strive never so much in Vain, to Quench it. . . . Now my Dear Mother! Pray lay thy Head close to mine.

Rebekah Chamblit (?–1733)

Little is known about Rebekah Chamblit's short life other than the sparse details she supplies in her *Declaration*. Chamblit was executed in Boston on September 27, 1733, for the murder of her infant son. Although intended as a warning to other young people against the ways of sin, the *Declaration* is a much more complex document than such an intention suggests. The record of her act of murder is horrifying both for its details of child abuse and for its brevity; only one paragraph, bereft of emotional content, is given to the act itself. The remainder of the text is Chamblit's struggle to express her remorse, first resistant to admitting wrongdoing but ultimately confronting her impending death. But the subtext of the felon's statement is even more informative, since it reveals another struggle—against a society that denies a natural status to sexual desires. As Rebekah notes, young people's "Age peculiarly exposes them to" such desires, but the lack of a means to discuss and understand these desires often leads them into "the Sin of Uncleanness." Equally revealing is Chamblit's psychological insight—that it is less the act than the "Guilt of this undiscover'd Sin lying upon [one's] Conscience" that leads to depravity.

Works: *The Declaration, Dying Warning and Advice of Rebekah Chamblit* (Boston, 1733).

The Declaration, Dying Warning and Advice of Rebekah Chamblit

A Young Woman Aged near Twenty-seven Years. Executed at *Boston September 27th.* *1733.* according to the Sentence pass'd upon her at the Superiour Court holden there for the County of *Suffolk*, in *August* last, being then found Guilty of *Felony*,

129

in concealing the Birth of her spurious Male Infant, of which she was Deliver'd when alone the Eighth Day of *May* last, and was afterwards found Dead, as will more fully appear by the following Declaration, which was carefully taken from her own Mouth.

Being under the awful Apprehensions of my Execution now in a few Hours; and being desirous to do all the Good I can, before I enter the Eternal World, I now in the fear of GOD, give this Declaration and Warning to the Living.

I was very tenderly brought up, and well instructed in my Father's House, till I was Twelve Years of Age; but alass, my Childhood wore off in vanity. However, as I grew in Years, my Youth was under very sensible Impressions from the SPIRIT of GOD; and I was awakened to seek and obtain Baptism, when I was about Sixteen Years of Age; and lived for some time with a strictness somewhat answerable to the Obligations I was thereby brought under. But within two or three Years after this, I was led away into Sin of Uncleannes, from which time I think I may date my Ruin for this World. After this, I became again more watchful, and for several Years kept my self from the like Pollutions, until those for which I am now to suffer.

And as it may be necessary, so doubtless it will be expected of me, that I give the World a particular account of that great Sin, with the aggravations of it, which has brought me to this Shameful Death: And accordingly in the fear of GOD, at whose awful Tribunal I am immediately to appear, I solemnly declare as follows;

That on Saturday the Fifth Day of *May* last, being then some-thing more than Eight Months gone with Child, as I was about my Houshold Business reaching some Sand from out of a large Cask, I received considerable hurt, which put me into great Pain, and so I continued till the Tuesday following; in all which time I am not sensible I felt any Life or Motion in the Child within me; when, on the said Tuesday the Eighth Day of *May*, I was Deliver'd when alone of a Male Infant; in whom I did not perceive Life; but still uncertain of Life in it, I threw it into the Vault about two or three Minutes after it was born; *uncertain*, I say, whether it was a living or dead Child; tho, I confess its probable there was life in it, and some Circumstances seem to confirm it. I therefore own the Justice of GOD and Man in my Condemnation, and take Shame to my self, as I have none but my self to Blame; and am sorry for any rash Expressions I have at any time uttered since my Condemnation; and I am verily perswaded there is no Place in the World, where there is a more strict regard to Justice than in this Province.

And now as a Soul going into Eternity, I most earnestly and solemnly Warn all Persons, particularly YOUNG PEOPLE, and more especially those of my own Sex, against the Sins which their Age peculiarly exposes them to; and as the Sin of Uncleanness has brought me into these distressing Circumstances, I would with the greatest Importunity Caution and Warn against it, being perswaded of the abounding of that Sin in this Town and Land. I thought my self as secure, a little more than a Year ago, as many of you now do; but by woful Experience I have found, that Lust when it has conceived bringeth forth Sin, and Sin when it is finished bringeth forth Death; it exposes the Soul not only to Temporal, but to Eternal Death. And therefore as a Dying Person, let me call upon you to forsake the foolish and live: Do not accompany with those you know to be such, and if Sinners entice you do not consent. I am sensible there are many Houses in this Town, that may be called Houses of Uncleanness, and Places of dreadful Temptations to this and all other Sins. O shun them, for they lead down to the Chambers of Death and Eternal Misery.

My mispence of precious Sabbaths, lies as a heavy burden upon me; that when I might have gone to the House of GOD, I have been indifferent, and suffered a small matter to keep me from it. What would I now give, had I better improv'd the Lord's Day! I tell you, verily, your lost Sabbaths will fit heavy upon you, when you come into the near prospect of Death and Eternity.

The Sin of Lying I have to bewail, and wou'd earnestly caution against; not that I have took so great a pleasure in Lying; but I have often done so to conceal my Sin: Certainly you had better suffer Shame and Disgrace, yea the greatest Punishment, than to hide and conceal your Sin, by Lying. How much better had it been for me, to have confess'd my Sin, than by hiding of it to provoke a hold GOD, thus to suffer it to find me out. But I hope I heartily desire to bless GOD, that even in this way, He is thus entring into Judgment with me; for I have often thought, had I been let alone to go on undiscovered in my Sins, I might have provok'd Him to leave me to a course of Rebellion, that would have ripen'd me for a more sudden, and everlasting Destruction; and am fully convinc'd of this, that I should have had no solid ease or quiet in my mind, but the Guilt of this undiscover'd Sin lying upon my Conscience, would have been a tormenting Rack unto me all my Days; whereas now I hope GOD has discover'd to me in some measure the evil of this, and all my other Sins, and enabled me to repent of them in Dust and Ashes; and made me earnestly desire and plead with Him for pardon and cleansing in the precious Blood of the REDEEMER of lost and perishing Sinners: And I think I can say, I have had more comfort and satisfaction within the Walls of this Prison, than I ever had in the ways of Sin among my vain Companions, and think I wou'd not for a World, nay for ten Thousand Worlds have my liberty in Sin again, and be in the same Condition I was in before I came into this Place.

I had the advantage of living in several religious Families; but alass, I disregarded the Instructions and Warnings I there had, which is now a bitterness to me; and so it will be to those of you who are thus favoured, but go on unmindful of GOD, and deaf to all the Reproofs and Admonitions that are given you for the good of your Souls. And I would advise those of my own Sex especially, to chuse to go into religious Families, where the Worship and Fear of GOD is maintained, and submit your selves to the orders and Government of them.

In my younger Years I maintain'd a constant course of Secret Prayer for some time; but afterwards neglecting the same, I found by experience, that upon my thus leaving GOD, He was provoked to forsake me, and at length suffer'd me to fall into that great and complicated Sin that has brought me to this Death: Mind me, I first left GOD, and then He left me: I therefore solemnly call upon YOUNG PEOPLE to cherish the Convictions of GOD's Holy SPIRIT, and be sure keep up a constant course of fervent Secret Prayer.

And now I am just entring into the Eternal World, I do in the fear of GOD, and before Witnesses, call upon our YOUNG PEOPLE, in particular, to secure an Interest in the Lord JESUS CHRIST, and in those precious Benefits He has purchased for His People; for surely the favour of GOD, thro' CHRIST, is more worth than a whole World: And O what Comfort will this yield you when you come to that awful Day and House I am now arriving unto. I must tell you the World appears to me vain and empty, nothing like what it did in my past Life, my Days of Sin and Vanity, and as doubtless it appears now to you. Will you be perswaded by me to that which will yield you the best Satisfaction and Pleasure here, and which will prepare you for the more abundant Pleasures of GOD's Right Hand for evermore.

> Sign'd and Acknowleg'd in the Presence of divers
> Witnesses, with a desire that it may be
> published to the World, and read at
> the Place of Execution.
> Rebekah Chamblit.

September 26th
  1733.

Emerging Feminist Voices

As noted in the general introduction, Part II is intended to emphasize the emergence of feminist voices in early America and to act as a bridge between Parts I and III in which many other feminist ideas are recorded. Additionally, there were many women for whom we have no extant writings but whose lives and actions demanded equality for women and challenged the gendered nature of colonial life.

Lady Deborah Moody (?–1659?), for instance, settled in Massachusetts in 1639 where the General Court granted her four hundred acres of land. She added to her properties, built a large home, and joined the Salem church. But the restrictive culture in Massachusetts Bay Colony was stifling for Moody (as it was for Roger Williams, founder of Rhode Island). Moody's independent attitudes, especially toward religion, created concerns among the Puritan leaders; John Endecott termed her "a dangerous woeman." Within a few years she left the Bay, settling first in New Netherland with the Dutch and accompanied by a group of followers who were attracted to her Anabaptist leanings. By the mid-1640s she had founded a colony on Long Island in which religious tolerance was the byword.

In Maryland, a similarly independent, land-owning, outspoken woman gained enormous power and recognition: Margaret Brent (c. 1601–c. 1671). Her wisdom, business acumen, and diplomacy in times of political unrest were noted by Governor Calvert, who appointed her executor upon his death. Brent gained power of attorney to act for the Lord Proprietor of Maryland. In this capacity, Margaret Brent gained lasting fame when she became the first woman in the colonies to demand the right to vote. On January 21, 1647/48, she demanded that she be granted *two* votes by the General Assembly: one in her own right as a landowner, and a second in her official capacity as the Proprietor's attorney. Her request was denied, but Brent continued to voice her official opinions and to act as attorney-of-record in numerous court cases. In an era in which most women were denied existence under the law (see the discussion of *feme covert* in Part III), Margaret Brent made an extraordinary mark in the history of women's challenges to patriarchal laws and customs.

It was in the eighteenth century, however, and especially in the Revolutionary and early federal years, that we see the most overt changes in women's attitudes about their roles in society and a keener awareness of the gendered culture of early America. Elizabeth Magawley (fl. 1730–31) was an important and early figure in the process of change. In a letter to the *American Weekly Mercury*, Magawley argued against the stereotypic depiction of women in that newspaper. Writing under the pseudonym "Generosa," Magawley is also notable for pointing out the gendered constructions of "Woman" and "Man." She engaged in an extended poetic exchange with the (male) "Pennsylvania Wits," satirizing their works and visions and presenting her humorous and carefully constructed alternative view. "Aspasia," another pseudonymous author, continued this pattern of openly challenging publications that perpetuated sexist images of women. Significantly, writers such as Magawley and Aspasia brought into the public arena dialogues about women's inscription in early American culture that had previously appeared only in private writings.

Some women, such as Elizabeth Graeme Fergusson (1737–1801) and others who appear throughout the anthology, probably would never have defined themselves as feminists, yet their individual actions advanced changes in women's lives and opportunities. Caught under the belief that a woman's political alliance had to be the same as her husband's, Graeme Fergusson faced the loss of her property and way of life after the war because of her husband's loyalty to the British. In seeking to establish herself as an independent legal entity under the law, Graeme Fergusson, like Margaret Brent and many later women (see especially the "Petitions" section of Part III), began to challenge the androcentric nature of the law itself. Further, early individual acts also prefigured the rise of women's organized political activity during the American Revolution. For instance, the Ladies' Association, headed by Esther DeBerdt Reed and with its manifesto "The Sentiments of an American Woman," and the North Carolina women's 1782 petition to the governor are best understood in the context of the history of women's challenges and contributions to the development of the new political order.

In the last two decades of the eighteenth century, the writings of Judith Sargent Murray emerged in the pages of the *Massachusetts Magazine* and other periodicals. Feminist in theory and content, her writings gained a remarkable acceptance in the post-Revolutionary atmosphere of proposed egalitarianism. Whether as a poet, novelist, dramatist, or essayist, Sargent Murray argued for a liberal education for young women and a national commitment to education in general; for federalist political practices and a strongly nationalistic cultural atmosphere; and for equality of the sexes in all aspects of American life.

In the early national period, as during the Revolution, the press and literary publications gained increasingly powerful roles in the determination of cultural values. How, then, did Sargent Murray, as a woman, attain a position of power in a decidedly patriarchal system that excluded women from virtually all legal and civic rights? Several avenues of exploration may assist a late-twentieth-century audience in determining viable answers to such a question. First, Sargent Murray did not challenge the religiocentrism of eighteenth-century Americans. If secularism was beginning to dominate debates on the establishment of a republican political order, religion still played a vital role in the personal lives of most Americans. Married to the founder of the American Universalist Church and herself a devout participant in that institution,

Sargent Murray brought her religious attitudes to bear upon her writings, thereby creating an atmosphere of familiarity for her audience. Yet under this guise of familiarity, Sargent Murray was able to express radically liberal religious views that not only challenged various theological precepts but, in fact, challenged an entire way of life, especially as it related to women in society.

Second, although Murray used various pen names (Constantia, Honoria) and occasionally published under her own name, in her writings for the *Massachusetts Magazine* she used the narrative persona of a philanthropic man, Mr. Vigilius or "The Gleaner." Undoubtedly, a male narrative voice rendered Sargent Murray's liberal philosophy more palatable to a general audience. Yet in the pages of the *Massachusetts Magazine* Sargent Murray herself repeatedly raised the issue of the real identity of Mr. Vigilius and mocked numerous attempts by precocious readers to discern "his" identity. In an era in which authors such as Benjamin Franklin and Hugh Henry Brackenridge were consciously establishing "Founding Fathers" as the voice of power and reason in the new nation, Sargent Murray created a persona of authority noted for his synthesis of reason *and* sensibility. She used a discourse of discovery to undermine the androcentricity of the narrator's authority and, ultimately, to shift attention from authorial identity to issues of equality among the sexes.

Last, and perhaps most important, to understand how a writer such as Sargent Murray could emerge in patriarchal eighteenth-century America requires an awareness of the proliferation of women's writings over the past two centuries. For early American women, as for men, writing was not simply a matter of economic necessity. For many women, it was a means of cathartic outlet, while for others it became the fulfillment of a desire to express themselves artistically. Writing was also increasingly understood as access to political expression. As Mercy Otis Warren asserts in the prologue to her farce *The Group* (*q.v.*), "What! arm'd for virtue and not point the pen[?]" Like Magawley, Aspasia, Sargent Murray, and Otis Warren, several women chose satire as a means of exposing cultural biases. While all of these women struggled for change in their own lifetimes, they also envisioned a more equitable future for women and men. One of America's earliest utopian visionaries was a noted educator, Sarah Pierce (1767–1852). In a short poem, she dictates a future life of peace, natural ways of existence, and gynocentric equality. Her vision is an important precursor to later feminist utopian ideals as conceived by Mary E. Bradley Lane and Charlotte Perkins Gilman.

Feminist Visions

Elizabeth Magawley (fl. 1730–31)

Elizabeth Magawley was a razor-sharp satirist and, when it came to both politics and letters, a pragmatist. During the early 1730s, her works appeared in the *American Weekly Mercury*, published in Philadelphia. In January 1730/31, under the pseudonym "Generosa," Magawley published a letter to the editor, Andrew Bradford, in which she challenged the repeated depictions of women in his gazette as fools who preferred "Fops and Coxcombs" to "Men of Sense." Magawley astutely notes the biases in such assertions but also is one of the first writers to explicitly challenge the gendering of language, especially in the construction of "Woman," and insisting, "The Word Ladies is an ambiguous Term, to which no single Idea can be affix'd."

Magawley challenged the "Wits and Poets" of the region, a collection of notable male writers who often published in the *Mercury*, to more rationally address issues concerning love and the sexes. Two responses emerged immediately: one from "Generosus," whose extravagant and lavish praise of her wisdom suggests as much mockery as serious admiration, ends in a proposal of marriage, noting that it is a topic she failed to mention; and a second from "Ignavus," who amusingly wants to defend the coxcombs of the world. In a subsequent poem, however, Ignavus strikes out at Generosa, who he implies must be an aging woman. Obviously recognizing in Ignavus's poem the idea that only aging and bitter women would challenge the ways in which men grant attention to women, Magawley responded in a resounding poetic satire of the entire group of male wits who were recognized in the pages of the *Mercury*.

As David Shields has discerned, in "The Wits and Poets of Pennsylvania" Magawley casts herself as the true poet (against the burlesque or simply inadequate styles of the male wits) and as a literary critic. Not only does Magawley satirize the poetic shortcomings of her opponents, but she also challenges their visions of

137

the future of literature in early America. The wits adhered to neo-classical literary values and "the myth of *translatio studii* . . . to envision Philadelphia as the future sanctuary of world art, the 'New Athens,' " but Magawley rejected this vision (Shields, D.S. 100, 142–143). In the use of satire and the refusal to mythologize American arts, Magawley joined forces with several other women writers in early America who sought redress for the imbalances of power in their society and in early American literary arts.

Works: Letter to the editor; "The Wits and Poets of Pennsylvania, A Poem, Part I."
Bibliography: Shields, D. S.

Letter to the Editor[1]

Semper ego Auditor tantum? Juv.[2]

To the Author of the American-Mercury.
Sir,

I have observ'd of late, that our unfortunate Sex have been the Subject of almost all the Satyr[3] that has dropt from your Pen for some Months past; I do assure you notwithstanding, that as I am your constant Reader, so I am your hearty Well-wisher; I am not sorry to find Vice or even Fooleries put in odious Colours; nor more angry to see ill Women expos'd, than a Valiant Soldier would be to see a Cowardly one call'd Coward. But as there is an Insinuation in one of your Papers, which I think is entirely groundless: I hope you will pardon me the Freedom of telling you it is! The Sum of the Charge is, *That Fools and Coxcombs[4] are most acceptable to the Ladies.* The Word Ladies is an ambiguous Term, to which no single Idea can be affix'd; as in your Sex there are the several Classes of Men of Sense, Rakes, Fops, Coxcombs and downright Fools, so I hope, without straining your Complaisance, you will allow there are some Women of Sense comparatively, as well as Coquets, Romps, Prudes and Idiots. If you had said Fools and Coxcombs are most acceptable to Coquets and Romps I readily grant it: Men of Sense value themselves too much to be used as Tools, they cannot stoop to the little Fooleries impos'd on them by their imaginary Goddesses, and their Resentments are too strong to bear Contempt and Insults. As to the Women of Sense, (if you will allow any to be so) you will also own THEY are more delighted with the Conversation of Men of Sense, than with that of Coxcombs or Fools, since the contrary takes away their Character of Sense. But Men of Sense are scarce Sir, very scarce indeed, and those

1. Published in the *American Weekly Mercury*, January 5, 1730/31. I am indebted to David Shields for bringing Magawley's work to my attention.

2. Must I always be only a listener? (Juvenal, Roman satirist).

3. Satire, but the alternative spelling also acts as a pun upon "satyr," drawing upon a Greek mythological figure that had come to be identified with any lecherous male.

4. A coxcomb is literally a jester's cap, but implies any conceited, foolish male.

few that are, are too proud or think their Time ill bestow'd, in the Conversation of the Ladies. They very often think for Want of Trial, that what I argue against is true; the Vulgar Error has impos'd even upon them. This is our lamentable Case, and what must we do? Must we resolve never to Converse with the opposite Sex, or go under the Reproach of favouring Coxcombs? It may be said we love Fops and Fools, because we play with them, and so we do with Parrots, Monkeys and Owls; and if we cannot procure Objects of Admiration and Esteem, we divert our selves with those of Ridicule and Contempt: But, Oh, Sir, if you knew the exquisite Pleasure that we Women receive from the Conversation of a Man of Sense; what Raptures we conceive upon the least Imagination of being belov'd by him, you will confess with me, that Coxcombs are only indulged out of meer Necessity; and the ill Success of Men of Sense, is owing to their Want of Courage.

> *I am, Sir,*
> *with the greatest Respect,*
> *Yours*
>
> GENEROSA.

To the Author of the *American* Weekly-Mercury.
Mr. Bradford,
If you think fit to insert this Piece in your next Mercury, it will be a Favour to,

> *your humble Servant,*
> E.M.[5]

The Wits and Poets of Pennsylvania, a Poem. Part I.[6]

Spiritum Phobus mihi, Phobus Artem
Carminis Nomenque dedit Poetae. Hor.[7]

'Twas when a gloom my pensive Soul e're spread,
And every gay and chearful Though[t] was fled;
As o're the Expanded Fields I cast my Eye,
Two sportive, active Colts[8] I chanc't to spy.

---

5. J. A. Leo Lemay is responsible for identifying Magawley as author of this poem.
6. Part II was never published. The publication of Part I ended the paper war between Magawley and her antagonists that had flourished in the pages of the *Mercury*.
7. "To Phoebus I owe my art and inspiration. Phoebus has conferred upon me the name of poet." (Horace, Roman poet and satirist.)
8. Probably referring to Generosus and Ignavus, whom Magawley believed were Joseph Breintnall and Jacob Taylor, respectively.

A gamesome chace the Challenge first began,
And wanton Whinnies Eccho'd as they ran;
Then with a Wheel they Circled o're the Ground,
And meeting, strove to show the highest Bound;
When Breast to Breast Erect, They paw'd the Air,
And loving Raps, by turns, as freely Share;
Descending then, Each in the Pseudo Fight
Embrac'd so lovingly, and strove to bite;
But biteing hard, The weakest gave a Roar,
Turn'd Tail, Kickt up his Heels, and play'd no more.

Bless Me, says I, so fares it with our *Witts*![9]
These Colts have only acted o're their Tricks.
Strait at the Word, I felt My Bosome glow,
Nor could have Ease, till I those *Witts* should show

For choice of Diction, I would B——int——nl[10] choose,
For just Conceptions, and a ready Muse;
Yet is that Muse too labour'd and prolix,
And seldom, on the Wing, knows where to fix.

So strictly regular is every Rise,
His Poems loose the Beauty of Surprize,
In this, his Flame is like a Kitchen fire.
We see the Billets cast, that mounts it higher:
Yet thro' the whole appear'd an Excellence,
And more of *Wit* would shine, but curb'd to much by Sense.

With Years opprest, and compass'd round with Woes,
A Muse with Fire fraught yet *T——y——lr*[11] shoes.
His Fancy's bold, Harmonious are his Lays,
And were He more correct, He'd reach the Bays:
But Heedless of the Rein, He Ply's the Whip,
'And in's carreer make *Heavenly Mansions* speak;
'Avers, *America's* for this found Out,
'That *W——b*[12] might roar, and sing, and make a rout:
'Then tells us *Georgee* had been born at *Rome*,
'But that like other folks, He dropt at home.
Yet such a Sweetness trills thro' all his Strains,
To have Our Ears so pleas'd, We could away with Brains.

Shew next, the Muse hath Rang'd the distant Spheres,
And when the Gods were speaking, cockt her Ears;

9. That is, the group of recognized Pennsylvania male poets who often published their work in the *Mercury* and elsewhere. They are individually identified and critiqued in subsequent stanzas of the poem. For extended identification of the wits whom Magawley satirizes, see Shields.

10. Joseph Breintnall, often referred to as Philadelphia's "first native poet."

11. Jacob Taylor, the elder of Pennsylvania's recognized poets.

12. George Webb, a younger poet praised by Taylor for a poem, "Bachelors-Hall" (1731), celebrating the pleasures of a gentleman's club.

Heard the decrees of Thunder-stinging Jove,
And then came back, and told Us all for Love:
Twas *Georges* Muse rang'd this untrodden Track,
W——b! Who like *Bantoff*s fam'd for the best Hack;
For thro' the Piece Poetick Genius shines,
Where, Thoughts sublime Meet in harmonious Lines:
Where, hounding *Pegasus*[13] with loosen'd Rein
Proud of the Course shows a well order'd Flame.
Pleas'd with the Event, a second Heat he try'd,
And soar'd its true; but with a lessen'd Pride.
Some say he got a most confounded fall,
And snapt a Leg in two, against the Hall;
Which the *Chimeroans*[14] seeing eas'd his Pain
By Paper Stampt, and sat all right again.

But see! A Poet of another Tribe,[15]
Stalks round *Parnasus*[16] with a sullen Pride.
No Rhymer equal's him in false Sublime,
A Rumbling bombast loads the labouring Line.
Such in his Flights! But when his humbler Flame
Descends to common Sense, none write more plain;
With Sp——ws and Sh——tes he fluffs the savoury Song,
And Beatle like, seems might fond of Dung.

In *Br*——*ks*[17] Capacious Breast the Muses sit
Enrob'd with Sense polite, and poignant Wit;
His lines run smoothly, tho' the Current strong;
He forms with Ease, with Judgment sings the Song.
As th' Awful Elm Supports the Purpling Vine,[18]
So round his Sense his sprightly *Wit* Entwines:
Oh! would oftener write, so should the Town
Or mend their Truths, or lay the Muses down;
For after Manna, who would Garbage Eat!
That hath a Spark of Sense, or Grain of *Wit*.

13. In Greek mythology, Pegasus was a winged horse; the name became synonymous with poetic inspiration.

14. Shields suggests this refers to Benjamin Franklin's Junto, the group of Philadelphia men who studied together and which evolved into the American Philosophical Society. Several of the wits, including Webb, were members of the Junto.

15. Possibly Samuel Keimer, a local printer who had employed both Franklin and Webb, although Magawley may be referring to a poet who published anonymously and whose identity she did not know.

16. In Greek mythology, Parnassus is the mountain that is home to the Muses.

17. Henry Brooke, whom Magawley obviously admires more than the other wits, was author of a poem entitled "On Wit" (1727).

18. Shields has identified this line as a reference to Brooke's poem, "On Wit," which was published in an almanac along with a calendar for the month of September. Above the calendar appears the lines, "Wit, like a Luxuriant Vine/ Unless to a Virtuous prop it joyn . . ./ It lies Deformed and Rotting on the Ground" (136).

"*Aspasia*" (fl. 1776–89)

"Aspasia"[1] was an anonymous female writer who challenged the renowned wit Francis Hopkinson when he contributed to a series entitled "The Old Bachelor" (March–December 1775) in the *Pennsylvania Magazine; or, American Monthly Museum*. In the series, women are often the comic figures or take the brunt of Hopkinson's humor and typically are admired only for their nurturance of men. At one point, Hopkinson as "The Old Bachelor" asserts a desire to have "propagated my species in a numerous offspring, without the help, without the plagues, without the expence of a female assistant—" (Number VI, October 1775). In "The Bachelor, Number VIII," the title character, a bachelor in his fifties, falls in love with a twenty-year-old woman and is so proud of his comportment and appeal that he insists thereafter that he be called "The Bachelor" rather than "The Old Bachelor." Aspasia's response was published in January 1776. She carefully identifies herself against the stereotypes in which women are usually cast: "I am neither one of your female cousins, who shewed their officious assiduity to you, in your late illness; nor am I, in any shape, a puppet moving on their wires; I am no discreet virgin, busy in forming schemes upon your sweet person; nor am I a widow, that has just dried up her tears for her last poor dear; neither have I daughter, sister, or kinswoman, for whom I have formed prudent plans of future settlements. I am myself a married woman, and most sincerely hope, I shall never be flung into a situation, that can admit of my committing matrimony again." Under the guise of great concern about the bachelor's future, she exposes the vast differences in interests that will naturally occur between an elderly husband and a young wife and suggests that he will be cast, by his wife as well as by her friends, in the role of the Old Fool. Aspasia's signature appears again in *American Museum*, reprinted in August 1789, when she responded to another series, "The Visitant." The title author purports to criticize women only in the hope of guiding them to perfection; he also asserts that he greatly admires Aspasia's writing, feeling she is more capable of painting "the ungenerous conduct of men" than he would be able to do, and thus he appends her letter to his essay. She challenges the representations of women presented by The Visitant and other male writers. With wit and outspokenness, she counters the (stereo)typical denigration of women.

Works: Essays.

1. The author's pseudonym refers to the fifth-century Greek Aspasia, who was renowned for her learning, wit, and beauty.

From "The Visitant." Number XI

Mr. Visitant,

The candid and kind manner, in which you treat both the errors and perfections of the female sex, must make every woman, who reads your paper with as good a heart, as you appear to have, when you write it, your admirer and friend.

I do assure you, sir, I am totally ignorant, whether the Visitant is written by one, who appears in a black coat or a red; or one, whose garb does not denote any particular profession. Alas! so excentric a set of beings are writers, that the Visitant may be unsocial, indelicate, and unfriendly—the reverse of every thing he says—Fool he can never be; but I hope the kind advocate of our cause is as agreeable in private life, as in public; and in this he is truly amiable.

Your definition of politeness, and the sources of affectation, in No. IV., I read with peculiar satisfaction; but give me leave, at present, to mention your paper, No. VII., where, among many good things you say, you endeavour to shew, what are the steps [for women] to attain esteem, and what to attain admiration. As far as I am a judge, the means are well calculated to gain their respective ends. But, sir, you must correct some faults in your own sex, before you can brighten the shades of ours. The ways you have pointed out, will, as I have just observed, secure us esteem; but at esteem we shall always stop.

When a worthy young woman, not without a share of sensibility in her composition, has attentively cultivated the virtues of the mind, and has improved herself in the several branches of education, with much resolution, and, on many occasions, with much self-denial—when, thus accomplished, she enters upon life, and mixes in a polite circle of both sexes—must it not give her a sensible mortification, to see a girl of sprightly levity, whose understanding, if she is pretty, is thought brilliant; whose tartness is styled elegant repartee; and rises only to what Pope calls "the pert low dialogue, scarce a degree above Swift's polite conversation"[2]—must it not mortify her to see such a one singled out, and draw the attention of men of merit, while she is passed by without notice? As for the *moths* of the season, that are always buzzing about, their neglect gives no uneasiness.

The men are extremely confined in their notions of our sex. It is true, they do not all express themselves in the coarse, inelegant, trite saying, "give me a wife, that can make a shirt, and a pudding;" but, indeed, mr. Visitant, if you will be as candid as you have hitherto been, you will own, that this sentiment runs through the major part of the lordly race.

One would think, that they were throwing sarcasms[3] on their own sex, when they draw the following conclusions—that the more a woman's understanding is improved, the more apt she will be to despise her husband—

2. Alexander Pope (1688–1744), influential English poet, and Jonathan Swift (1677–1745), renowned Irish-English satirist.
3. The text reads "scarcasms."

that the strengthening of her reason will weaken her affection—that the duties of tenderness and attention, and all the social train, will be disregarded, in proportion as her knowledge is increased—that, to teach her God and nature, will, in the end, destroy all order, and domestic comfort. Good heavens! What subversions of truths are all these assertions! Does not the enlargement of the understanding point out the relative duties? And is not subordination to a husband, one of them? Does not reason as frequently rouse, as damp the affections?—Does not knowledge dilate and expand the finer feelings of the mind, and make it thrill in a thousand vibrations, unknown to the savage and untutored soul?—Do not God and nature lead us to a course of tender affections and pleasing duties, which can be practised only by one, whose mind is touched with ardent piety, and who can observe, with refined delight, the regular and beautiful order of the universe.

However, in gratitude to the generous few, that have condescended to treat us as reasonable beings, let us never forget that an Addison, a Richardson, and a Fordyce,[4] have not thought it beneath them, to point out, what is, and what is not, female excellence.

Hard, indeed, is that medium to be observed, which you mention in your ninth paper; and it only falls to the lot of a happy few, to answer the poet's elegant picture:

> Favours to none, to all she smiles extends:
> Oft she rejects; but never once offends.

Howsoever pleasing timidity and implicit submission in us may be to your sex, yet what lord Halifax[5] observed, is very true; "that a woman who has not too much spirit on some occasions, will run the risque of having too little on others." As maids, as wives, and as widows, we meet with a thousand occasions in life, where fortitude and resolution are absolutely necessary. I would not wish a lady be a Camilla or a Thalestris;[6] but steadiness, to a degree of perseverance, is absolutely requisite in us. Before marriage, it is necessary, in the important point of dismissing or accepting lovers; for you know, sir, that is all a single woman has to do. After marriage, it is necessary in the education of children, and in regulating the more subordinate members of a family; for, as to a husband, it is a virtue, which must never peep out, where his lordly prerogative is concerned. And surely equally essential is it, in the lonely widowed state, where we have to act in so many different capacities.— In which of these classes the writer of this is, cannot be material; let it suffice, that, in your public character of Visitant, she is much your admirer.

ASPASIA.

---

4. Joseph Addison (1672–1719), English essayist and poet; Samuel Richardson (1689–1761), English novelist.

5. Charles Montagu, Earl of Halifax (1661–1715), English statesman.

6. Women warriors of great tenacity in classical mythology. Camilla, for instance, fought with one breast bared so her bow arm would not be hindered.

Elizabeth Graeme Fergusson (1737–1801)

Born on February 3, 1737, in Philadelphia, Elizabeth Graeme was the youngest of nine children of Ann Diggs and Thomas Graeme, a physician and later a state supreme court justice. Graeme was raised on the family estate, Graeme Park, near Philadelphia; her early life was one of wealth and an international association with political and literary figures. When she was twenty, she fell in love with William Franklin, son of Benjamin Franklin,[1] but her father and Benjamin Franklin had been politically opposed since their early days as members of the American Philosophical Society. Two years later, Benjamin took William to London, in effect ending the young people's relationship, to Graeme's despair. In an attempt to recover from her loss, Graeme created several poetic translations (most notably of Fénelon's *Télémaque* and of the Psalms), traveled to London, and began her lifelong association with the world of literature. After her mother's death in 1765, Graeme managed Graeme Park and raised two orphaned relatives. She also established one of the early literary salons in America, held each Saturday evening in her home.

Graeme married Henry Hugh Fergusson, a Scotsman who had recently settled in Philadelphia, on April 21, 1772. It was a disastrous union, both emotionally and financially for Graeme Fergusson. When her father died later that year, he left Graeme Park to her. During the American Revolution, Henry's loyalty to the British and Elizabeth's apparent role as courier in the conveyance of some of his political messages led to reprimands from her friends, including George Washington. But Graeme Fergusson sided with the American cause; their political differences and Henry's political intrigues eventually led to the couple's estrangement. Graeme Park was confiscated after the war under the auspices of belonging to a Loyalist, as Henry was deemed. It is in her role as political protester that Graeme Fergusson raises a voice that would become increasingly central to the early women's rights movement: Graeme Fergusson not only sought legal redress under the argument of her right to own property, but she also challenged the concept that a married couple had one will—the husband's. In several petitions to the General Assembly and in letters to various representatives, she demanded her rights and argued to establish herself as a legal entity separate from her husband and entitled to the property she inherited. Although Graeme Park was, with the help of friends who were prominent citizens of Philadelphia, restored to her, financial

1. See the Deborah Read Franklin entry for details on William Franklin's birth; he later became Governor of New Jersey.

difficulties forced her to sell it 1791. She died ten years later, after an extended illness.

In addition to her legal challenges, Graeme Fergusson's letters also reveal her astute satirical talents (see her selections in the "Poetry" section in Part III as well), which she employed against male writers who denigrated the female sex. Undoubtedly Graeme Fergusson would not have defined herself as a feminist, had the term been available to her at the time; but her actions for legal rights and her demands for respect for all women, especially when rendered by one who was renowned for her literary talents and friendships, are important in the development of feminist goals in early America.

Works: Letters, petitions, translations. Bibliography: Gratz; Griswold; Myers; Stedman and Hutchinson.

Elizabeth Graeme Fergusson's Letters

To the Honourable, Speaker of the House of Assembly of the Commonwealth of Pennsylvania.

Septem^r 4, 1779

Sir

The Petition,[2] which I the Subscriber humbly presented in Person to the Honourable House in the month of February, last past, having been laid aside to another Sessions, and the House being not met, I beg leave to hope that it may be Reviv'd, and I still trust that the House will take the peculiarity of my Situation into their Consideration, and in their great Cander and Clemency will cause a Stop to be put to the Sale of Graeme Park which the Agents for Philadelphia County, have orders to Sell on a forfeited Estate; and are immediatly proceeding There unto; unless those in power will step forth and interfere in behalf of the Petitioner.

The most material points were allegd in the Petition aforesaid; but as Business of much more Consequence to the Public mind have occurd than the Relief of an Insignificant Individual, Î shall briefly touch upon the Heads of that Petition, which was presented; and in so doing Hope that It will not be construed an impertinent peice of Tautoligy, when it really arisses from a Belief that my affairs are not of Consequence sufficent to hold a place in the memory of the Honorable House, to which they are Referd.

First   The Estate in question is a Patrimonial one not made over and Consequentialy the Fee Simple Vested in me.[3]

2. Graeme Fergusson would continue for several years to petition the state legislature for her rights, most notably filing a petition for her property rights with the General Assembly of Pennsylvania in July 1781.

3. The petition states, "The Estate of Graeme Park was devised to your Petitioner in Fee Simple by her late honored Father Doctor Thomas Graeme—and having never been made over by any Conveyance to Mr. Fergusson nor having had any Child by him—The Claim of the State can exist no longer than during their Joint Lives. . . ."

Secondly as I have no Child it can only (if sold at all) be put up during the joint lives of M[r] Fergusson, and myself, and I should think would sell but for little to the State when taken into the Scale that one of the Parties is a Female, in an Indiferent State of Health; betwixt forty and fifty years of age.

Thirdly M[r] Fergusson having left this state ten months before the Declaration of Independence, And absent at the Time, and again afterwards; Could not be deemed in the Eye of the Law a *Traytor* Tho He is proscribd under that Predicament: in consequence of which Proscription, His Personal Estate was all Seizd and Sold last October, This Plea I am encouraged to dwell upon by Gentlemen learned in the Law who judge M[r] Fergusson can not be amenable to this State as he is not Regularly a Subject.

I could here enumerate a list of Names of Gentlemen in, and of Britain, that now hold landed Property here, which have never been Seizd, some of whom are at this time acting in the Military Line, M[r] Fergusson holds no Office at present under the King of Britain, and the transient one he filld during his stay in the City,[4] I was in hopes had not been of a Nature to have drawn down Ruine on me; as I am sure in his Deportment he was not among the Number of them who add Sorrow to the Afflicted.

Graeme park Sept 10 1779

Sir[5]

... In the last place may I be allowd to touch on my own Conduct since this unhappy Contest, I have for my own part Constantly remaind on the Premisses; earnestly praying for Peace But if the Sword must decide our Fates, Sincerly wishing it might be on the Side of *America*; which in my short View of things I look on to be the Injurd Party.

I never went into the City while the Britsh were There without a Pass, I had no Acquaintance with the Military Gentlemen, and my stay but very short; I returnd And Spent my days with one Female friend In Silence and Solitude.

At the time M[r] Fergusson took the Department of Commissary of Prisoners, I wrote to Him; and to two Gentlemen of His acquaintance to endeavor to diswade him from Acting in any Shape under *General Howe*, These Letters could be producd did the showing them answer any Valuable Purpose, The Seizing the Personal Estate and the Rise of all the Articles of Life have renderd my affairs so Embarassd that if I am not Speedily Redressd; Want and Distress must compose the Remaining part of the Days of your Petitioner. ... If M[r] Fergusson is really within the Letter of the Law; I make no doubt but I shall suffer the Full Penalities in my fortune.

The Jewish Proverb is here fully verified "The Parents have Eaten Sour Grapes And the Childrens Teeth are set on Edge." Believe me Sir, I would not Deceive you, I was ever on the Side of my Country. ...

4. For a short period of time, Henry Fergusson held the office of Commissary of Prisoners with the British Army.

5. Addressed to John Dickinson, member of the General Assembly.

Billet, April 20, 96

My Dear Mrs Frazer

I stand indebted to you 3 Letters, one by Dr Tod, one by Mr Worthy, and this Day by *Mr Evans*.[6] As he return early tomorrow morning you will be so good as to pardon any inaccuracies, that will arise in writing in a hurry. The Death of Bishop Seabury is a public and Domestic Loss: It is sd. more people have within this last twelve months Died of apoplexy than was ever known in the same Space of time, whether this is to be traced to natural Causes I leave the the Faculty to decide. As to poor Judge Wicks I think it is a most extraordinary Death, I supose he was on horse-back and that no traces of the Beast nor master could be found is uncomon   I should conclude that he had not fair play for Life if the Body is not found but I know not the Situation of the wood. As to the marriage of Miss Boyls and Mr S——d by what Mrs Tod says of him I pity the girl. I find Dr. Tod was one of the wedding Guests. Mr. Pope Says you know in a frequent quoted line:

"Some men to *Business*, some to *pleasure* take
But every woman is at heart a *Rake*"

I don't know but it might be more just to say

But every woman *has* at *heart* a *Rake*

Dr Young in one of his Satires on our Sex has some very severe lines on this very Error

"The youth of Fire, who has Drank deep, and played"
"And Killed his man, and triumphed o'er his Maid:"
"For him (if yet unhung) she Spreads her Charms,"
"And takes the Dear Distroyer to her Arms."

. . . . perhaps my feelings are more lively than usual as in a Recollection of my pensive *Calendar* I too well remember on this night April 21 of 1772 at nine at wicacoe Church I married the man that has proved the Source of so much Sorrow to me: . . . yet a man one once loved and expected to have passd ones Life with to such a temper as mine cannot be the object of Indiference tho he may be of extreme Resentment. . . . Yours with regard

E. Fer

Judith Sargent Murray (1751–1820)

Judith Sargent Murray's fame today rests on her seminal essay, "On the Equality of the Sexes," written in 1779 and published in 1790 with an appended commentary. While that fame is warranted, it is far too narrow; many other writings by Sargent Murray—including a subsequent extended discussion of women's rights that has long

6. The poet Nathaniel Evans.

been neglected, "Observations on Female Abilities," as well as her dramatic writings and her recently rediscovered body of letters numbering more than two thousand—deserve recognition and critical appraisal. From 1792 until 1794, Judith Sargent Murray published a series of essays in the *Massachusetts Magazine* that afforded her an unusual opportunity for a woman: the space to publicly voice her opinions. The series was "narrated" by the fictitious "Gleaner," Mr. Vigilius; by the time the series was reprinted in a three-volume edition in 1798, however, Sargent Murray's identity was well known and, to emphasize the female creator of the essays, she used her pseudonym "Constantia" on the title page. *The Gleaner* essays are important not only for their blending of nonfictional and fictional genres but also for their synthesis of satire, sensibility, and realism, thus challenging our traditional assumptions about the rise of realism in American literature.

Works: *The Gleaner*, 3 Vols. (1798). Bibliography: Davidson, *Revolution and the Word*; Field; Harris, ed. *Selected Writings of Judith Sargent Murray*; Kerber; Norton; Walker and Dresner.

On the Equality of the Sexes[1]

That minds are not alike, full well I know,
This truth each day's experience will show;
To heights surprising some great spirits soar,
With inborn strength mysterious depths explore;
Their eager gaze surveys the path of light,
Confessed it stood to Newton's piercing sight.
   Deep science, like a bashful maid retires,
And but the *ardent* breast her worth inspires;
By perseverance the coy fair is won.
And Genius, led by Study, wears the crown.
   But some there are who wish not to improve,
Who never can the path of knowledge love,
Whose soul's almost with the dull body one,
With anxious care each mental pleasure shun;
Weak is the leveled, enervated mind,
And but while here to vegetate designed.
The torpid spirit mingling with its clod,
Can scarcely boast its origin from God;
Stupidly dull—they move progressing on—
They eat, and drink, and all their work is done.
While others, emulous of sweet applause,
Industrious seek for each event a cause,
Tracing the hidden springs whence knowledge flows,

1. Originally published in the *Massachusetts Magazine* (Mar.–Apr. 1790): 132–135, 223–226.

Which nature all in beauteous order shows.
　　Yet cannot I their sentiments imbibe,
Who this distinction to the sex ascribe,
As if a woman's form must needs enroll,
A weak, a servile, an inferior soul;
And that the guise of man must still proclaim,
Greatness of mind, and him, to be the same:
Yet as the hours revolve fair proofs arise,
Which the bright wreath of growing fame supplies;
And in past times some men have *sunk* so *low*,
That female records nothing *less* can show.
But imbecility is still confined,
And by the lordly sex to us consigned;
They rob us of the power t'improve,
And then declare we only trifles love;
Yet haste the era, when the world shall know,
That such distinctions only dwell below;
The soul unfettered, to no sex confined,
Was for the abodes of cloudless day designed.
　　Meantime we emulate their manly fires,
Though erudition all their thoughts inspires,
Yet nature with *equality* imparts,
And *noble passions*, swell e'en *female hearts*.

Is it upon mature consideration we adopt the idea, that nature is thus partial in her distributions? Is it indeed a fact, that she hath yielded to one half of the human species so unquestionable a mental superiority? I know that to both sexes elevated understandings, and the reverse, are common. But, suffer me to ask, in what the minds of females are so notoriously deficient, or unequal. May not the intellectual powers be ranged under their four heads—imagination, reason, memory and judgement. The province of imagination has long since been surrendered up to us, and we have been crowned undoubted sovereigns of the regions of fancy. Invention is perhaps the most arduous effort of the mind; this branch of imagination hath been particularly ceded to us, and we have been time out of mind invested with that creative faculty. Observe the variety of fashions (here I bar the contemptuous smile) which distinguish and adorn the female world; how continually are they changing, insomuch that they almost render the whole man's assertion problematical, and we are ready to say, *there is something new under the sun.* Now, what a playfulness, what an exuberance of fancy, what strength of inventive imagination, doth this continual variation discover? Again, it hath been observed, that if the turpitude of the conduct of our sex, hath been ever so enormous, so extremely ready are we that the very first thought presents us with an apology so plausible, as to produce our actions even in an amiable light. Another instance of our creative powers is our talent for slander; how ingenious are we at inventive scandal? what a formidable story can we in a moment fabricate merely from the force of a prolifick imaginaton? how many reputations, in the fertile brain of a female, have been utterly despoiled? how industrious are we at improving a hint? suspicion how easily do we convert into conviction, and conviction, embellished by the power of eloquence, stalks abroad to the surprise and confusion of unsuspecting innocence. Perhaps it will be asked if I furnish these facts as instances of excellency in our sex. Certainly not; but as proofs of a creative faculty, of a lively imagination. Assuredly great activity of mind is thereby discovered, and was this activity properly directed, what beneficial effects would follow. Is the needle and kitchen sufficient to employ the operations of a soul thus organized? I should conceive not. Nay, it is a truth that those very departments leave the intelligent principle vacant, and at liberty for speculation. Are we deficient in reason? We can only reason from what we know, and if opportunity of acquiring knowledge hath been denied us, the inferiority of our sex cannot fairly be deduced from thence. Memory, I believe, will be allowed us in common, since every one's experience must testify, that a loquacious old woman is as frequently met with, as a communicative old man; their subjects are alike drawn from the fund of other times, and the transactions of their youth, or of maturer life, entertain, or perhaps fatigue you, in the evening of their lives. "But our judgment is not so strong—we do not distinguish so well." Yet it may be questioned, from what doth this superiority, in this discriminating faculty of the soul, proceed. May we not trace its source in the difference of education, and continued advantages? Will it be said that the judgment of a male of two years old, is more sage than that of a female's of the same age? I believe the reverse is generally observed to be true. But from that period what partiality! how is the one exalted and the other depressed, by the contrary modes of education which are adopted! the one is taught to aspire, and the other is early confined and limited. As their years increase, the sister must be wholly domesticated, while the brother is led by the hand through all the flowery paths of science. Grant that their minds are by nature equal, yet who shall wonder at the *apparent* superiority, if indeed custom becomes *second nature*; nay if it taketh place of nature, and that it doth the experience of each day will evince. At length arrived at womanhood, the uncultivated fair one feels a void, which the employments allotted her are by no means capable of filling. What can she do? to books, she may not apply; or if she doth, *to those only of the novel kind*, lest she merit the appellation of a *learned lady*; and what ideas have been affixed to this term, the observation of many can testify. Fashion, scandal and sometimes what is still more reprehensible, are then called in to her relief; and who can say to what lengths the liberties she takes may proceed. Meantime she herself is most unhappy; she feels the want of a cultivated mind. Is she single, she in vain seeks to fill up time from sexual employments or amusements. Is she united to a person whose soul nature made equal to her own, education hath set him so far above her, that in those entertainments which are productive of such rational felicity, she is not qualified to accompany him. She experiences a mortifying consciousness of inferiority, which embitters every enjoyment. Doth the person to whom her adverse fate hath consigned her, possess a mind incapable of improvement, she is equally wretched, in being so closely connected with an individual whom she cannot but despise. Now, was she permitted the same instructors as her

151

brother, (with an eye however to their particular departments) for the employment of a rational mind an ample field would be opened. In astronomy she might catch a glimpse of the immensity of the Deity, and thense she would form amazing conceptions of the august and supreme Intelligence. In geography she would admire Jehovah in the midst of his benevolence; thus adapting this globe to the various wants and amusements of its inhabitants. In natural philosophy she would adore the infinite majesty of heaven, clothed in condescension; and as she traversed the reptile world, she would hail the goodness of a creating God. A mind, thus filled, would have little room for the trifles with which our sex are, with too much justice, accused of amusing themselves, and they would thus be rendered fit companions for those, who should one day wear them as their crown. Fashions, in their variety, would then give place to conjectures, which might perhaps conduce to the improvement of the literary world; and there would be no leisure for slander or detraction. Reputation would not then be blasted, but serious speculations would occupy the lively imaginations of the sex. Unnecessary visits would be precluded, and that custom would only be indulged by way of relaxation, or to answer the demands of consanguinity and friendship. Females would become discreet, their judgments would be invigorated, and their partners for life being circumspectly chosen, an unhappy Hymen would then be as rare, as is now the reverse.

Will it be urged that those acquirements would supersede our domestick duties, I answer that every requisite in female economy is easily attained; and, with truth I can add, that when once attained they require no further *mental attention.* Nay, while we are pursuing the needle, or the superintendency of the family, I repeat, that our minds are at full liberty for reflection; that imagination may exert itself in full vigor; and that if a just foundation early laid, our ideas will then be worthy of rational beings. If we were industrious we might easily find time to arrange them upon paper, or should avocations press too hard for such an indulgence, the hours allotted for conversation would at least become more refined and rational. Should it still be vociferated, "Your domestick employments are sufficient"—I would calmly ask, is it reasonable, that a candidate for immortality, for the joys of heaven, an intelligent being, who is to spend an eternity in contemplating the works of Deity, should at present be so degraded, as to be allowed no other ideas, than those which are suggested by the mechanism of a pudding, or the sewing of the seams of a garment? Pity that all such censurers of female improvement do not go one step further, and deny their future existence; to be consistent they surely ought.

Yes, ye lordly, ye haughty sex, our souls are by nature *equal* to yours; the same breath of God animates, enlivens, and invigorates us; and that we are not fallen lower than yourselves, let those witness who have greatly towered above the various discouragements by which they have been so heavily oppressed; and though I am unacquainted with the list of celebrated characters on either side, yet from the observations I have made in the contracted circle in which I have moved, I dare confidently believe, that from the commencement of time to the present day, there hath been as many females, as males, who, by the *mere force of natural powers,* have merited the crown of applause; who *thus unassisted,* have seized the wreath of fame. I know there are those

152

who assert, that as the animal powers of the one sex are superiour, of course their mental faculties also must be stronger; thus attributing strength of mind to the transient organization of this earth born tenement. But if this reasoning is just, man must be content to yield the palm to many of the brute creation, since by not a few of his breathren of the field, he is far surpassed in bodily strength. Moreover, was this argument admitted, it would prove too much, for occular demonstration evinceth, that there are many robust masculine ladies, and effeminate gentlemen. Yet I fancy that Mr. Pope, though clogged with an enervated body, and distinguished by a diminutive stature, could nevertheless lay claim to greatness of soul; and perhaps there are many other instances which might be adduced to combat so unphilosophical an opinion. Do we not often see, that when the clay built tabernacle is well nigh dissolved, when it is just ready to mingle with the parent soil, the immortal inhabitant aspires to, and even attaineth heights the most sublime, and which were before wholly unexplored. Besides, were we to grant that animal strength proved anything, taking into consideration the accustomed impartiality of nature, we should be induced to imagine, that she had invested the female mind with superiour strength as an equivalent for the bodily powers of man. But waving this however palpable advantage, for *equality* only, we wish to contend.

I am aware that there are many passages in the sacred oracles which seem to give the advantage to the other sex; but I consider all these as wholly metaphorical. Thus David was a man after God's own heart, yet see him enervated by his licentious passions! behold him following Uriah to the death, and shew me wherein could consist the immaculate Being's complacency. Listen to the curses which Job bestoweth upon the day of his nativity, and tell me where is his perfection, where his patience—*literally* it existed not. David and Job were types of him who was to come; and the superiority of man, as exhibited in scripture, being also emblematical, all arguments deduced from thence, of course fall to the ground. The exquisite delicacy of the female mind proclaimeth the exactness of its texture, while its nice sense of honor announceth its innate, its native grandeur. And indeed, in one respect, the preeminence seems to be tacitly allowed us, for after an education which limits and confines, and employments and recreations which naturally tend to enervate the body and debilitate the mind; after we have from early youth been adorned with ribbons and other gewgaws, dressed out like the ancient victims previous to a sacrifice, being taught by the care of our parents in collecting the most showy materials that the ornamenting our exterior ought to be the principal object of our attention; after, I say, fifteen years thus spent, we are introduced into the world, amid the united adulation of every beholder. Praise is sweet to the soul; we are immediately intoxicated by large draughts of flattery, which, being plentifully administered, is to the pride of our hearts the most acceptable incense. It is expected that with the other sex we should commence immediate war, and that we should triumph over the machinations of the most artful. We must be constantly upon our guard; prudence and discretion must be our characteristics; and we must rise superior to, and obtain a complete victory over those who have been long adding to the native strength of their minds by an unremitted study of men and books, and who have, moreover, conceived from the loose characters which they have seen portrayed in the extensive variety of their reading, a most contemptible opinion of the sex. Thus unequal, we are, nothwithstanding, forced to the combat, and the infamy which is consequent upon the smallest deviation in our conduct, proclaims the high idea which was formed of our native strength; and thus, indirectly at least, is the preference acknowledged to be our due. And if we are allowed an equality of acquirement, let serious studies equally employ our minds, and we will bid our souls arise to equal strength. We will meet upon even ground, the despot man; we will rush with alacrity to the combat, and, crowned by success, we shall then answer the exalted expectations which are formed. Though sensibility, soft compassion, and gentle commiseration are inmates in the female bosom, yet against every deep-laid art, altogether fearless of the event, we will set them in array; for assuredly the wreath of victory will encircle the spotless brow. If we meet an equal, a sensible friend, we will reward him with the hand of amity, and through life we will be assiduous to promote his happiness; but from every deep-laid scheme for our ruin, retiring into ourselves, amid the flowery paths of science, we will indulge in all the refined and sentimental pleasures of contemplation. And should it still be urged that the studies thus insisted upon would interfere with our more peculiar department, I must further reply that *early hours*, and close application, will do wonders; and to her who is from the first dawn of reason taught to fill up time rationally, both the requisites will be easy. I grant that niggard fortune is too generally unfriendly to the mind, and that much of the valuable treasure, time, is necessarily expended upon the wants of the body; but it should be remembered, that in embarrassed circumstances our companions have as little leisure for literary improvement as is afforded to us; for most certainly their provident care is at least as requisite as our exertions. Nay, we have even more leisure for sedentary pleasures, as our avocations are more retired, much less laborious, and, as hath been observed, by no means require that avidity of attention which is proper to the employments of the other sex. In high life, or, in other words, where the parties are in possession of affluence, the objection respecting time is wholly obviated, and of course falls to the ground; and it may also be repeated that many of those hours which are at present swallowed up in fashion and scandal might be redeemed, were we habituated to useful reflections. But in one respect, O ye arbiters of our fate! we confess that the superiority is undubitably yours; you are by nature formed for our protectors; we pretend not to vie with you in bodily strength; upon this point we will never contend for victory. Shield us then, we beseech you, from external evils, and in return we will transact *your* domestic affairs. Yes, *your*, for are you not equally interested in those matters with ourselves? Is not the elegancy of neatness as agreeable to your sight as to ours, is not the well favored viand equally delightful to your taste; and doth not your sense of hearing suffer as much from the discordant sounds prevalent in an ill regulated family, produced by the voices of children and many *et ceteras*?

Constantia.

By way of supplement to the forgoing pages, I subjoin the following extract from a letter wrote to a friend in the December of 1780.

And now assist me, O thou genius of my sex, while I undertake the arduous task of endeavouring to combat that vulgar, that almost universal errour, which hath, it seems enlisted even Mr. P—— under its banners. The superiority of your sex hath, I grant, been time out of mind esteemed a truth incontrovertible; in consequence of which persuasion, every plan of education hath been calculated to establish this favourite tenet. Not long since, weak and presuming as I was, I amused myself with selecting some arguments from nature, reason and experience, against this so generally received idea. I confess that to sacred testimonies I had not recourse. I held them to be merely metaphorical, and thus regarding them, I could not persuade myself that there was any propriety in bringing them to decide in this *very important debate.* However, as you, sir, confine yourself entirely to the sacred oracles, I mean to bend the whole of my artillery against those supposed proofs, which you have from thence provided, and from which you have formed an intrenchment *apparently* so invulnerable. And first, to begin with our great progenitors; but here, suffer me to promise, that it is for mental strength I mean to contend, for which respect to animal powers, I yield them undisputed to that sex, which enjoys them in common with the lion, the tyger, and many other beast of prey; therefore your observations respecting *the rib, under the arm,* at *a distance from the head, &c.&c.* in no sort militate against my view. Well, but the woman was first in the transgression. Strange how blind *self love* renders you men; were you not wholly absorbed in a partial admiration of your own abilities, you would long since have acknowledged the force of what I am now going to urge. It is true some ignoramuses have, absurdly enough informed us, that the beauteous fair of paradise, was seduced from her obedience, by a malignant demon, *in the guise of a baleful serpent;* but we, who are better informed, know that the fallen spirit presented himself to her view, *a shining angel still;* for thus, saith the criticks in the Hebrew tongue, ought the word to be rendered. Let us examine her motive—Hark! the seraph declares that she shall attain a perfection of knowledge; for is there aught which is not comprehended under one or other of the terms *good* and *evil.* It doth not appear that she was governed by any one sensual appetite; but merely by a desire of adorning her mind; a laudable ambition fired her soul, and a thirst for knowledge impelled the predilection so fatal in its consequences. Adam could not plead the same deception; assuredly he was not deceived; nor ought we to admire his superiour strength, or wonder at his sagacity, when we so often confess that example is much more influential than precept. His gentle partner stood before him, a melancholy instance of the direful effects of disobedience; he saw her not possessed of that wisdom which she had fondly hoped to obtain, but he beheld the once blooming female, disrobed of that innocence, which had heretofore rendered her so lovely. To him then deception became impossible, as he had proof positive of the fallacy of the argument, which the deceiver had suggested. What then could be his inducement to burst the barriers, and to fly directly in the face of that command, which *immediately* from the mouth of Deity *he* had received, since, I say, he could not plead the fascinating stimulus, the accumulation of knowledge, as indisputable conviction was so visibly portrayed before him. What mighty cause impelled him to sacrifice myriads of beings yet unborn, and by one impious act, which *he saw* would be productive of such fatal effect, entail undistinguished ruin upon a race of beings, which he was yet to produce. Blush, yet vaunters of fortitude; ye boasters of resolution; ye haughty lords of the creation; blush when ye remember, that he was influenced by no other motive than a bare pusillanimous attachment to a woman! by sentiments so exquisitely soft, that all his sons have, from that period, when they have designed to degrade them, described as highly feminine. Thus it should seem, that all the arts of the grand deceiver (since means adequate to the purpose are, I conceive, invariably pursued) were requisite to mis-lead our general mother, while the father of mankind forfeited his own, and relinquished the happiness of posterity, merely in compliance with the blandishments of a female. The subsequent subjection the apostle Paul explains as a figure; after enlarging upon the subject, he adds, "*This is a great mystery; but I speak concerning Christ and the church.*" Now we know with what consummate wisdom the unerring father of eternity hath formed his plans; all the types which he hath displayed, he hath permitted *materially* to fail, in the very virtue for which *they* were famed. The reason for this is obvious, we might otherwise mistake his economy, and render that honor to the creature which is due only to the creator. I know that Adam was a figure of him who was to come. The grace contained in this figure is the reason of my rejoicing, and while I am very far from prostrating before the shadow, I yield joyfully in all things the preeminence to the second federal head. Confiding faith is prefigured by Abraham, yet he exhibits a contrast to affiance, when he says of his fair companion, she is my sister. Gentleness was the characteristic of Moses, yet he hesitated not to reply to Jehovah himself; with unsaintlike tongue he murmured at the waters of strife, and with rash hands he brake the tables, which were inscribed by the finger of divinity. David, dignified with the title of the man after God's own heart, and yet how stained was his life. Solomon was celebrated for wisdom, but folly is wrote in legible characters upon his almost every action. Lastly, let us turn our eyes to man in the aggregate. He is manifested as the figure of strength, but that we may not regard him as anything more than a figure, his soul is formed in no sort superior, but every way equal to the mind of her, who is the emblem of weakness, and whom he hails the gentle companion of his better days.

Sarah Pierce (1767–1852)

The youngest of Mary Paterson and John Pierce's seven children, Sarah Pierce was born on June 26, 1767, in Litchfield, Connecticut. Her mother died when Pierce was quite young, and her father remarried; Mary Goodman and John Pierce had at least three children. Sarah was fourteen when her father died; her only brother Colonel John Pierce supported the family and sent Sarah and one sister, Nancy, to New York City for their education. In 1792, Sarah Pierce began her lifelong occupation as founder and head of a girls' school that became nationally recognized for its quality of education. The Litchfield Female Academy (although not incorporated under that title until 1827) was begun in Pierce's home, with only two or three students in attendance. By 1798, Pierce was so successful that the people of Litchfield built a schoolhouse for her.

Under Pierce's leadership, the school maintained its reputation for excellence in female education for nearly forty years, drawing students from throughout the United States and Canada. While she did teach accomplishments, including dancing and sewing, her curriculum was extensive and included reading, writing, composition, arithmetic, geography, history, and science. As enrollments increased, Pierce selected her own best pupils to become teachers at the Academy, thus perpetuating her pedagogical vision through subsequent generations. Her students included Catharine Beecher (Harriet Beecher Stowe also attended Pierce's school). As Pierce remarked in a close-of-school address in 1818, "It is equally important to both sexes that memory should be stored with facts; that the imagination should be chastened and confined within its due and regular limits; that habits of false judgment, the result of prejudice, ignorance or error, should be destroyed or counteracted; that the reasoning faculties should be trained to nice discriminations and powerful and regular research. Hence then all those sciences and all those exercises which serve in our sex for those important purposes should be part of a well regulated female education."

In 1825, when Pierce was fifty-eight, her nephew John Pierce Brace, who had assisted her at the school for more than a decade, became principal of the Litchfield Female Academy. However, Pierce was not ready for retirement; she continued to teach her favorite topic—history—and when Brace moved to the principalship of another school in 1833, she returned, at the age of sixty-six, to her role as head of the Academy and remained in that capacity for another decade. Pierce died in Litchfield on January 19, 1852, having dedicated her life to the education of women.

The following poem by Pierce is one of the earliest recorded utopian visions in American literature, a prototype for many later feminist utopian texts. Lesbian in spirit, the poem was preserved in the papers of Pierce's lifelong friend Elihu Hubbard Smith. In a letter dated December 24, 1795, Smith recounts the circumstances under which the poem was written: "A strict intimacy had subsisted, for some years, between Miss Sally Pierce, & my two eldest sisters. Of these, at the time the 'Verses' were written, Mary, the eldest, was . . . engaged to marry her present husband, Thomas Mumford. Sally Pierce, was, at the time of writing these lines, just beginning to acquire, by her own exertions, some feeble knowledge of Drawing. The three young women were together; it was evening;

Sally had shewn them some of the productions of her pencil; &
they were, sportingly, conversing of their different destinations. The
conclusion was, that, when Mary left them, the other two should
unite, & spend their lives together, 'in single blessedness.' This idea
once started, it received numerous additions, & the whole economy of a house, & of life, was readily arranged & determined on.
Before separating, it was agreed that Sally, should design a house
suitable for each, & sketch the surrounding scenery. . . . Her first
care was directed towards accomplishing a plan for Mary. . . . The
inexperience of Miss Pierce, in the art of design, made her progress
both slow & painful; so that, when she had effected her first picture, by the aid of the pencil, she had recourse to a readier instrument, & relied on the pen for a sketch of the second. And, lo!
this is the landscape which she drew."

*Works: Sketches of Universal History Compiled from Several Authors. For the Use of
Schools.* (4 vols., 1811–18). *Bibliography:* Cott; Cronin; von Frank.

Verses,
    written in the Winter of 1792, & addressed to Abigail
    Smith Jr.—
    by Sally Pierce.[1]

On rising ground we'll rear a little dome;
  Plain, neat, and elegant, it shall appear;
No slaves shall there lament their native home,
  Or silent, drop the unavailing tear.

Content and cheerfulness shall dwell within,
  And each domestic serve thro' love alone;
Coy Happiness we'll strive, for once, to win,
  With meek Religion there to build her throne.

And oft our friends shall bless the lonely vale,
  And, social, pass the wintry eves away;
Or, when soft Summer swells the fragrant gale,
  Delighted mark new beauties as they stray.

Pleased with the scene, by Fancy's pencil drawn,
  The various landscape rushes on my view;
The cultivated farm, the flowery lawn,
  That sucks the fragrance of the honied dew.

The fertile "meadows trim with daisies pied";
  The garden, breathing Flora's best perfumes;

---

1. I am indebted to Albert von Frank for drawing my attention to this poem.

And stored with herbs, whose worth, by Matrons tried,
   Dispels disease, and gives health's roseate blooms.

Here vines, with purple clusters bending low,
   And various fruit-trees loaded branches bear;
There roots of every kind profusely grow,
   Bespeaking plenty thro' the circling year.

See yonder hillock, where our golden corn
   Waves its bright head to every passing breeze;
Yon fruitful fields our sportive flocks adorn,
   Our cows at rest beneath the neighboring trees.

As misty clouds from silent streams arise,
   Yon distant Town attracts the gazer's view;
Yon mount, whose lofty summit meets the skies,
   Shelters the Village on the plain below.

Behind our lot, a Wood defies the storm,
   Like those where Druids wont, in days of yore,
When Superstition wore Religion's form,
   With mystic rites their unknown Gods adore.

Within this grove we'll oft retire to muse,
   Where Contemplation builds her silent seat;
Her soothing influence she will ne'er refuse
   To those who wander in this blest retreat.

A river solemn murmurs thro' the shades,
   The whispering pines, in echoes soft, reply,
Then, hoarse o'er rocks, it seeks the distant glades,
   Forming a rain-bow in the moistened sky—

Nor leaves us here—but thro' the Village winds,
   Where simple elegance, in neat array,
Might teach even pomp that, not to wealth confined,
   Genius & taste might to a cottage stray.

In front, a level grass-plot smooth & green,
   Where neighboring children, pass sweet hours at play,
And Fairies oft, (if Fairies e'er have been,)
   Will featly foot the moonlight hours away.

Our plenteous store we'll freely give to all;
   Want ne'er shall pass, in sorrow, from our door;
With joy we'll seat the beggar in our hall,
   And learn the tale of woe that sunk his store.

But chiefly those who pine, by sickness prest;
   Whose merit, known to few, unheeded lies
How sweet, to banish sorrow from the breast,
   And bid fair hope shine sparkling in the eyes.

Thus, humbly blest, when youthful years are flown,
  (Proud to be good, not wishing to be great,)
And swift-wing'd Time proclaimed our moments run,
  Resign'd to heaven, we'll cheerful bow to fate.

Placed in one grave, beneath a plain, smooth, stone,—
  Where oft the tear unfeign'd shall dew the face,
The sick, the poor, shall long our fate bemoan,
  But wealth & grandeur never mark the place.

This simple Epitaph the stone adorns,—
  Which calls, from artless eyes, the frequent tear—
Matrons & maids shall often stoop to learn,
  And all the Village think it passing rare.

    The Epitaph.

Beneath this stone two female friends interr'd,
  Who past their lives content, in solitutde;
They wish'd no ill, yet oft, thro' ignorance, err'd;
  Reader! depart, reflect, and be as good.

III

Origins, Revolutions, and Women in the Nations

n Part III, women's writings are viewed from several perspectives: over time, from Native peoples and the first settlers to participants in the War for Independence to second- and third-generation Americans; and in terms of the numerous genres that women explored as forms in which to express their personal feelings, religious beliefs, philosophical debates, and literary talents. Although important individually, cumulatively these documents also detail American women's intellectual history in a way that informs our understanding of how someone like Judith Sargent Murray came to write her proclamation on equality. Although many of these accounts are not in traditional literary forms, the letters, diaries, and other modes of personal expression, when combined with published texts (from petitions to plays), challenge our conceptions of what we mean by "literature," by the recording of history, and by women's roles in Native, colonial, revolutionary, and federal America. Cumulatively, these texts also begin to define early women's poetics and therein offer many opportunities for reconceptualizing studies of later women's writings and early American studies in general.

The title of the "First Women" section is intended both as an ironic and a serious designation. In the former mode, it is meant as a satirical juxtaposition with the concept of "First Ladies," that ubiquitous term that identifies women only in relation to their renowned spouses. While some of the women writers in this section may meet that criterion, it is for their own contributions that they have been included in this anthology. In the latter mode, "First Women" is intended specifically to emphasize that the true first women were those who were native to the North American continent for centuries before European settlement. Rather than continue separatist distinctions, however, it also refers to women who recorded their initial responses to resettlement in a foreign region.

There is another level on which the authors included in this section and throughout the anthology need to be understood. The eighteenth century's international redefinition of the concept of genius into a highly gendered and exclusionary realm acted as a major instrument in the exclusion of women from the designation of "first-rate" thinkers and writers. The terminology of "intellectual" or "original" artistry has excluded—and continues to exclude—

women by means of an intellectual class system that preserves that territory for a select(ed) group of dominant-culture males. This remains true, too, for histories of national "founders" and "discoverers," those terms that remain at the heart of literary and historical accounts of early America. This section, then, presents a variety of texts that may encourage reconsiderations of what we mean by "first"—whether it be first-rate intellectual, first to inhabit a region, or first to record one's reflections on a particular region or idea.

Early Americanists have long acknowledged Virginia Dare (1587–?) as the first English person born in America and one of the many settlers of Roanoke Island (North Carolina) who simply disappeared between settlement in 1587 and 1591 when compatriots finally arrived with supplies, only to discover that the settlers had vanished. There has been an ironic parallel in the "disappearance" of women from accounts of early America, and "First Women" (like the anthology as a whole) seeks to work against that erasure. It is appropriate that this section begins with Native American texts. "Sky Woman," an Iroquois origin story, captures the dual-gendered nature of many tribal origin narratives. In the Chinook tale of "The First Ship," we are reminded of the process of colonization and its effects upon native peoples. Juxtaposed against that tale are the texts of early Euro-American women who settled throughout the colonies: Margaret Tyndal Winthrop (c. 1591–1647), whose adherence to Calvinism and Puritan cultural ideals invokes both the consequences and rewards of such adherence; Susanna Moseley (fl. 1649–50) and Katherine Marbury Scott (fl. 1658), whose resistances to cultural norms conversely demonstrate the early dates at which women's challenges to patriarchal ideologies began; and Barbara Smith (fl. 1689) and Mary Herendean Pray (fl. 1675), whose detailed and outspoken descriptions of seventeenth-century colonial life recall the diversity of experiences of early settlers. Accounts by Hannah Callowhill Penn (1671–1726), Mary Stafford (fl. 1711), and Elizabeth Bland (fl. 1735) extend women's descriptions of settlement into eighteenth-century Pennsylvania, South Carolina, and Georgia, respectively.

As important as these women's records are, they must be recognized as representing only a fraction of women's experiences in colonial America. Many alternative experiences have been lost through neglect or, equally common, through the lack of written accounts. The latter is readily recognized in discussions of Native American literatures, but it was equally true for Euro-American women in the lower economic classes. For example, some of the earliest women to arrive in colonial Louisiana were prostitutes who had been removed from prisons and sent to the colony to become wives of the male settlers. Later, beginning in 1728, the India Company of France sent *filles à la cassette*, or "Casket Girls," to the colonies. So named because all of their possessions had to be stuffed into wooden trunks, these young women were also sent in order to become wives, but they were designated as virgins and housed by nuns until appropriate marriages could be enacted. Even though both groups (like their counterparts in early Virginia) were treated as commodities in the marriage market, a distinction emerged between them that played into patriarchal definitions of female virtue and *value*.

Similar issues appear in a quite different form in early America: in the spiritual narrative. Cultural values as well as individual sects' theological perspectives are integral to the production of any spiritual narrative, whether it is the Zuni narrative "Two Girls and the Dancers" or Sophia Wigington Hume's (1702–1744) Quaker vision. In "Two Girls," for instance, the significance of the interaction between the Zuni and their kachinas (spiritual guides) is rendered through a courtship tale. The danger of humans seeking too soon to join their ancestors is emphasized, as is the role of females as spiritual messengers whose words become an integral part of Zuni beliefs and practices.

For early Euro-American women, the spiritual narrative (like poetry) constituted one of the first literary forms through which they were allowed public expression. In the Puritan colonies of seventeenth-century New England, women were subjugated in their spiritual accomplishments in the same manner that they were under civil law. While a woman's attainment of grace (spiritual salvation) was an individual process, the hierarchical nature of the Puritan religious community (God/man/woman) demanded an even stronger sense of abjectness in women's spiritual narratives than it did of the men in the community. If Edward Taylor, the famous Puritan minister and poet, deemed himself a "crumb of dust," he nonetheless retained in the Puritan religious hierarchy a gender-defined status over the female members of his community that personal spiritual humility did not diminish.

For early American scholars this subjugation remains a distinct problem in the study of oral narratives and the processes of transcription. Were women's narrations or legends relating to women transcribed verbatim? or were men's valuations of certain aspects of women's lives privileged over other aspects? and were the less-privileged aspects ignored or diminished in the transcribed texts? Thus although we have Sister Crackbone's spiritual narrative transcribed at the moment of utterance, it is impossible to determine the accuracy of her minister's record of her words. These issues are even more complicated when the transcriber has little familiarity with the cultural experience of the speaker. For Native American oral narratives, transcriptions by late eighteenth- or nineteenth-century non-natives, however well intentioned, have altered the original texts beyond recovery of their original forms. This is a fact we must recognize even as we seek to represent narratives from oral cultures; indeed, representation is all we can garner.

If Sister Crackbone's (fl. 1640) testimony suggests the continuing oppression of women in transplanted cultures, the four subsequent spiritual narratives in this section suggest that our traditional literary histories have, for too long, emphasized stories of sacrifice and ignored women's historical and literary challenges to patriarchal domination. It should not be surprising that the four subsequent spiritual narratives are by Quakers: within the Society of Friends, women's involvement in their community was much broader than in most other Euro-American societies, and Quaker women's voices were not openly silenced by custom or design. The narratives of Mary Traske and Margaret Smith (fl. 1660), Bathsheba Bowers (1672–1718), Sophia Wigington Hume (1702–1774), and Jane Fenn Hoskens (1694–?) range over a century of Quaker settlement in the New World. They capture women's activities in New England, the mid-Atlantic colonies, and the South, and suggest the variety of narrative forms—confrontation or exhortation, individual or collective—in which women chose to express their spiritual journeys. What remains the same throughout these personal narratives, however, is a woman's concern not only for her own salvation but for "saving grace" to be attained by others as well.

As recent feminist scholars have noted, women's autobiographical narratives often de-center the inscription of the Self; that is, as women's lives were subjugated to males in the dominant culture so their autobiographical narratives render, in Patricia Spacks's term, "lives in hiding." Mary Traske and Margaret Smith, for instance, point out to John Endecott, their persecutor: "you cannot see our life which is hid with Christ in God." Thus, while these spiritual narratives, and the works in this anthology as a whole, seek to restore "women's voices" to our literary history, it is done with the recognition that women who dared to voice their opinions and experiences often did so as part of a hidden and repressed subculture. Yet to succumb completely to a hermeneutics of suspicion as a critical approach to these women's writings can, conversely, border dangerously on a preservation of the dominant culture's processes of suppression.

In balance, then, we must recognize the significance of a woman's spiritual narrative as her first step toward finding inroads for a gynocentric "voice" in a phallocentric discourse while at the same time recognizing that, however seemingly egalitarian her community, she was always forced to write from a position of "other," a position that required the resisting woman to engage in textual subterfuge at the same time that she appeared to acquiesce to male literary traditions. It is important to note, too, that, because many women recognized their marginalized status, they sought a sense of community with others who were also marginalized. Thus we often see a progression in women's spiritual narratives from positions of individual isolation and otherness to a growing sense of women's communities. In Jane Fenn Hosken's narrative, for instance, the authored Self remains de-centered but it also embraces—and names—others who helped her attain her goals: Elizabeth Lewis, Abigail Bowles, Rebecca Minshall, and Margaret Churchman—"true yoke-fellows" in Fenn Hoskens's personal and narrative journeys, recalling for twentieth-century readers Alice Walker's term "familiars" for her spiritual foremothers.

Captivity narratives have long been recognized as a genre in which women writers excelled, beginning with Mary White Rowlandson's (1637?–1711) famous and highly influential text. Recent work by Kathryn Zabelle Derounian-Stodola and James Levernier, among others, has greatly expanded our understanding of the breadth and diversity of experience and expression in this unique genre. Elizabeth Meader Hanson's (1684–1741) and Mary Lewis Kinnan's (1763–1848) captivity narratives demonstrate how the genre developed through the eighteenth century. (See also "Novels" for fictionalized representations of captivity narratives.)

In addition to narratives of forced removals, women also wrote many texts that relate the experiences of traveling by choice. Sarah Kemble Knight's (1666–1727) adventurous account of travel for business purposes—and certainly recorded as a means of displaying her talents as a satirist and wit—was unusual by seventeenth-century standards. By the mid-eighteenth century, however, women were often choosing to travel for pleasure, for health reasons, or to begin once again the process of resettlement—this time in the western regions of the continent, as Mary Coburn Dewees (fl. 1787–88) and her family did. Perhaps nothing changed women's perspectives on their lives so radically as exposure (forced or chosen) to new regions and new ways of life. The accounts of travel in this section complement many of the texts about settlement included in the "First Women" section.

Another important genre in early American literature is the letter. Epistolary exchanges by early American women constitute one of the most prolific but least recognized movements by women toward a public voice in social, cultural, and political issues of their day. Extant from as early as the 1630s, written exchanges were a means by which Euro-American women could maintain a sense of community and, in some instances, acted as a testing ground for women's literary and political development, thus prefiguring the early nineteenth-century women's coteries. In the exchanges between the Winthrop women in early seventeenth-century Massachusetts, Margaret Tyndal Winthrop's powerful position within the community acts as a locus for women's attentions, and the women in her family depend upon her for emotional, spiritual, and physical sustenance. There are several collections of women's letters that capture family dynamics in early America: Mehetabel Chandler Coit (1673–1758) of Connecticut maintained a correspondence with her daughters; Anne Huntington (1740?–1790), also of Connecticut, exchanged letters with her daughter, Rachel Huntington Tracy (1779–?); and the Tilghmans, Henrietta (1763–1796) and Mary (?–?) of Maryland, followed the same pattern. Equally common were exchanges between friends. The lively and politically astute letters of Abigail Smith Adams (1744–1818) and Mercy Otis Warren (1728–1814) capture the changing attitudes about women's roles in Revolutionary America and demonstrate the means by which women friends shared and extended their thinking on various sociopolitical topics through the exchange of letters. Many collections of this sort are extant today; in addition to those included in the "Epistolary Exchanges" section, of particular interest are exchanges between the poets Annis Boudinot Stockton (1736–1801) and Elizabeth Graeme Fergusson (1737–1801), or the religious discussions exchanged between the Quaker devotees Sarah Haggar Wheaten Osborn (1714–1796) and Susanna Anthony (1726–1791), or the exchanges between Esther Edwards Burr (1732–1758) and several of her women friends. Young women of the upper classes were especially likely to exchange letters, particularly during their courtship years. The letters included here between Deborah Norris (Logan), the two Sarah Fishers, and Sally Zane capture the delightful humor of youth and the means by which letters allowed the friends (who lived in Pennsylvania and New Jersey) to discuss their many romantic interests and to work out between them a sense of the proper conduct of young women in a period of social crisis and change.

If the exchange of letters allowed women a safe means of exploring personal, social, and political issues, the section including "Petitions, Political Essays, and Organizational Tracts" probably represents the least recognized

means by which women were beginning to focus on and influence public issues. Women's early uses of personal or collective petitions provided an avenue into increased political activity and into claims for their legal rights before, during, and after the Revolution. Throughout colonial history, individual
women had sporadically sought recourse through informal or legal petitions.
One of the earliest on record was a brief notarized petition by "Isabel, the Mu-
latto." On January 8, 1600, she filed the following petition with the mayor of
Querétaro in New Spain:

> as I am going on the expedition to New Mexico and have reason to fear that I
> may be annoyed by some individuals, since I am a mulatto, and as it is proper to
> protect my rights in such an eventuality by an affidavit showing that I am a free
> woman, unmarried, the legitimate daughter of Hernando, a negro, and an Indian
> named Madalena, I therefore request your grace to accept this affidavit, which
> shows that I am free and not bound by marriage or slavery. I request that a prop-
> erly certified and signed copy be given to me in order to protect my rights, and
> that it carry full legal authority. I demand justice. Isabel. (quoted in Hammond
> and Rey 560)

Other early petitions included Sarah Drummond's 1677 filing after the deba-
cle of Bacon's Rebellion in which her husband was killed, and Mary Easty's
(fl. 1692) transcribed petition in response to the Salem witch trials. The individual's petition was especially popular in the Revolutionary years. Perhaps
no period made the gendered nature of the law so evident. Under the legal
status of *feme covert*, a married woman not only transferred all rights to her
property to her husband upon marriage, but—especially important during the
war—her will was assumed to be one with her husband's. Thus, if a woman
supported the American cause but her husband had remained loyal to England, she could be deemed a Loyalist, regardless of her actions during the
war, and her property confiscated. The petition became a popular means of
attempting to distinguish one's self from a spouse's actions. However, rarely
were state governments willing to acknowledge the right to redress. In part,
they were unwilling to challenge the erasure of women under the law; more
often, their refusals were rooted in the economic strain placed upon state cof-
fers during the war. A few notable African-American women recognized this
moment of declared democratic values as an opportunity for raising the issue
of slavery. Two such women, one known only as "Belinda" (fl. 1782) and Elizabeth Freeman (fl. 1791), each filed petitions seeking their freedom. Although
unsuccessful, they made an important inroad in the process of using the legal
system to defeat its racial biases, an inroad that paved the way for later African
Americans to challenge the legal and political system that supported slavery.

Once the power of collective action was recognized, petitions became the
instrument of choice for women who sought change, in early America and
well into the nineteenth century when leaders of the women's movement employed that form of political protest with renewed fervor—and greater success. One group of early women that sought redress was from North Carolina;
protesting the banishment of women whose absent husbands were Loyalists,
they worked together in an important early demonstration of a sense of sis-

terhood to demand justice over political expediency. Collective activities by women were not limited to petitions, however. As early as 1733, widowed business practitioners in New York published a satirical attack on their lesser treatment by the leaders of their community. As noted in "Emerging Feminist Voices," satire became a very effective tool of women seeking an entry into published protest. A group of Young Ladies, supposedly from throughout the newly established states, used the form of a petition to satirize cultural assumptions about marriage and courtship and about political leadership. The most serious—and effective—collective action by women during the Revolution, however, occurred under the leadership of Esther DeBerdt Reed (1747–1780), who published "The Sentiments of an American Woman" as a call for women to become active in supporting the troops. Women from throughout the colonies responded, with financial support and volunteered activism, to organize a system of donating to the cause. It was an extraordinarily successful campaign, tainted only by the resistance of male leadership to *allowing* the women to use the funds raised in the manner they preferred.

The Revolutionary and early federal years also saw the rise of women's published essays, especially texts that were secularly rather than religiously oriented. Letitia Cunningham published a political tract in 1783 protesting what she deemed unfair taxes levied by the U.S. Congress, and a decade later Margaretta V. Bleecker Faugères (1771–1801) published an antislavery essay in a collection of her mother's and her own writings. The courage to produce such outspoken publications—and to sign their own names to the texts—arose out of the changing conditions of women's lives in Revolutionary America. Therefore, although writings by women during the Revolutionary years appear throughout the anthology, a section has been devoted to "Revolutionary War Writings."

The Revolutionary War was the most significant political conflict of the period, but it followed almost two centuries of conflicts—sometimes between colonies, sometimes between tribal societies, but most often between settlers and Native Americans. Susanna Wright's (1697–1784) letters demonstrate a renowned Euro-American woman's role in political contestations in the pre-Revolutionary years. The majority of texts in the "Revolutionary War Writings," however, focus on the period from 1776 to 1783 and constitute unpublished accounts of women's attitudes toward American independence and their experiences during the war. Letters to family members and friends account for the largest body of women's writings during this period. Like the members of the Continental Congress who carefully preserved their writings for posterity, these epistolary writers recognized the significance of events and sought to record them from their own perspectives—and their perspectives were extremely varied. Diaries and journals provided women with a more private means of recording their reactions to the war; not surprisingly, these accounts are often more explicit and opinionated, capturing women's most private reflections upon the war in a way that public exchanges could not. Many women wholeheartedly supported independence from England, but many also had doubts about the costs to human life and the ways of life evoked by war. A number of women were also Loyalists who ardently opposed separation.

As in any war, one's actions were always carefully scrutinized. As Mary Willing Byrd (1740–1814) discovered, proving one's loyalty to America could be extremely difficult. While many women were noted as Loyalists, very few who remained in the country were ever charged with treason. Although Willing Byrd escaped charges (due in large part to her persistent resistance), Mary Philipse Morris (1730–1825) and one of her sisters were charged with treason by the New York legislature in 1778 because of Philipse Morris's husband's alliance with the British. While women like Molly Brant, a Mohawk, and Patience Lovell Wright, a Euro-American, actively participated in acts to support the American military forces, most women participated by supporting relatives who were soldiers or, like Mary Bartlett (?–1789), maintained the family properties while their husbands were at war. Whether young, like Sally Wister (1761–1804), or mature, like Lydia Minturn Post (fl. 1776–83), women wrote about their extraordinary experiences during this period. Though they sometimes struggled with the horrors of war and their own personal losses, they identified themselves as Patriots. This was, in itself, a radical act, as evidenced by the nineteenth-century editing of Dorothy Dudley's (fl. 1775–76) diary from the Revolutionary period. In spite of Dudley's dedicated record of the war's events, the nineteenth-century editor inserted a footnote at the end of the first paragraph of the diary: "Though Miss Dudley carefully attributes her interest in public events to 'patriotism,' the exactness and promptness of her information suggest that some gallant officer gave her intelligence of his movements, and that we owe her details rather to the tender passion than to the love of country." This kind of devaluation of women's patriotism has had a long history. In truth, the town clerk was a friend of Dudley's, and he often supplied her with copies of newspaper reports and government proclamations.

The war brought many women into unanticipated acts of heroism and daring. There were numerous women who deserve the designation of war heroine. While many twentieth-century readers will recognize the name of "Molly Pitcher," few know the real name of this symbolic woman: Mary (Molly) McCauley (1754–1832) of Trenton, New Jersey. While her husband John was fighting in the Battle of Monmouth, McCauley carried water from a nearby well to the wounded, thereby earning her renowned image of "Molly Pitcher." Because of her efforts, the Pennsylvania General Assembly awarded her an annuity for life, aligning her actions with that of the soldiers who received pensions after the war. To note only a few of the women who were cited during the Revolutionary years for their heroic actions in support of independence suggests the numerous ways in which women acted as patriots: Margaret Cochran (1751–1789) and Lydia Barrington Darragh (1728–1789) of Pennsylvania; Deborah Sampson Gannett (fl. 1776) of Massachusetts; Nancy Hart (1735?–1830) of Georgia; Catherine van Rensselaer Schuyler (1733–1804) of New York; Emily Geiger Threrwitz (c. 1760–?) of South Carolina; Tsistunagiska, or "Nancy Ward" (c. 1738–c. 1824), a Cherokee woman from Tennessee; and Prudence Cummings Wright (fl. 1775) of Massachusetts and New Hampshire. The image of Molly Pitcher acknowledges women's actions in battle, but it is also important to remember the real women behind the image.

The final sections of Part III focus on specific literary genres in which women wrote, from their beginnings through 1800. From Anne Dudley Bradstreet (1612–1672) to Annis Boudinot Stockton (1736–1801) to Mercy Otis Warren (1728–1814) to Hannah Webster Foster (1758–1840), early American women consciously aspired to express themselves artistically. Most women in early America found that expression limited to nontraditional forms, such as letters, diaries, and private or locally published autobiographies. As this final section reflects, however, several women openly sought the public arena; and if they worked within conventional genres, they brought decidedly woman-centered intellectual, philosophical, political, and social perspectives to their writings.

Poetry was one of the genres accessible to women from the earliest periods. In tribal societies, songs were integral to cultural practices and the perpetuation of cultural values. In Euro-American cultures, poetry was a more individualized practice but, as Anne Dudley Bradstreet demonstrates, one that could make a significant impact in a community. For many women, poetry writing was experiential, a means of exploring religious and personal events of importance. For others, it was an avenue for political expression; and, of course, there are many ways in which these means overlapped. Poetry was an especially important genre for African Americans, including Lucy Terry (from whom only one poem remains extant and for whom poetry was an oral art form) and Phillis Wheatley (who published a book of poetry during her lifetime and who was internationally recognized as an artist). Whatever the form or practice, poetry was an accessible—and acceptable—genre for early women writers.

The accomplishment of gaining a public voice via poetry writing must be understood in the restrictive cultural context under which women artists labored. By the early eighteenth century, socially constructed ideologies of "femininity" (modest, spiritual, private) and "masculinity" (frank, political, public) perpetuated separate spheres for women and men. In England, the once internationally renowned poet Aphra Behn had been deleted from literary anthologies because of the eroticism and frank wit of her writings. In 1738 a contributor to the *Gentleman's Magazine* (a title that, in itself, suggests the widening gap between women's and men's spheres) mockingly envisioned a demonic and bare-breasted Behn attempting to claim a place among immortal male poets only to be reprimanded with the assertion that "none of her sex has any right to a seat there" (quoted in Todd 2). In the colonies, the separate-spheres ideology had taken hold from the beginnings of European settlement. Yet women's resistant voices did emerge—from Anne Dudley Bradstreet and Phillis Wheatley's attempts to reclaim female historical figures to more outspoken poets, including Judith Sargent Murray (1751–1820), Sarah Wentworth Morton (1759–1846), Hannah Griffitts (1727–1817), and that large cadre of "Anonymous" female poets.

Formal histories by women did not appear until the late eighteenth century. Most notable in the field were the achievements of Mercy Otis Warren, who published a three-volume history of the American Revolution, and Hannah Adams (1755–1831), author of several historical studies, including religious histories. While Otis Warren and Adams followed traditional history-writing styles, revisionist histories also began to appear. Judith Sargent Murray, for example, published a four-part sequel to "On the Equality of the Sexes" that was a history of international literary women.

Women had engaged in historical writings, however, since they appeared on the continent. Early Native American oral cultures depended upon a variety of narrative forms—legends, tales, origin stories, songs, and the like—to record and preserve their histories. "The First Ship" and "Sky Woman," while identifiable as a legend or an origin story, respectively, also constitute histories, and the same crossover nature of many women's written accounts should also be recognized. Eliza Yonge Wilkinson (fl. 1779–82), for example, left an account of the British invasion of Charleston during the war. Although recorded as a letter, its intent was to capture a moment in history, so as "never to forget." Louisa Susannah Wells (c. 1755–1831) used the journal form to recount a Loyalist's view of her passage from America to England in 1778–79. Whether about major cultural events or individual experiences, women's history is evidenced throughout the writings of early women and in a multitude of genres.

Women playwrights did not emerge in America until the eighteenth century. In this genre, women's entry into the field closely paralleled men's, since it was the least developed of artistic forms in early American literature. Due in large part to beliefs that stage productions and acting were questionable if not thoroughly immoral, no drama by an American was produced until the 1760s, although English touring troupes had appeared earlier. Charlotte Ramsey Lennox (1720–1804) should probably be considered one of America's earliest female dramatists. Although she was born in New York, she removed to England at an early age and produced all of her works in her adopted country. Several factors emerged in America during the last half of the eighteenth century to encourage the development of dramatic writings, and especially dramas by women. First, the dialogue had long been a popular poetic form, so aspects of the aesthetics of playwrighting were not completely unfamiliar to American writers. Second, teachers such as Sarah Pierce and Susanna Haswell Rowson (1761–1824) had used dialogues and short sketches as educational tools, creating in their students an interest in and familiarity with the form. Third, Mercy Otis Warren's publication of several plays during the American Revolution was probably the single most important step in opening the door for women dramatists. Although Otis Warren's plays were never produced, their publication under the pseudonym of "A Lady from Massachusetts" and their overt politicization of the form helped to erase some of the stigma surrounding the theater. Fourth, the support of the theater and dramatists by prominent essayists authorized an increased acceptance of the field. As Judith Sargent Murray recognized, acting and playwrighting could especially be made acceptable in the post-Revolutionary years if they were presented as a means of establishing a particularly *American* perspective in literature. Otis Warren, Sargent Murray, and Margaretta V. Bleecker Faugères were major contributors to the development of drama in America.

After the American Revolution, as the country sought in a variety of ways to distinguish itself as a "separate and free" nation, how to establish a body of *American* literature was at the forefront of literary debates, as the early dramatists had recognized. Because of their length and popularity, novels were ultimately seen as the most viable means of achieving this goal. The emphasis on the "truth" of novels written by early American authors was due in part to social attitudes toward the novel that deemed it an immoral and dangerous literary form, especially for young women who might be led away from the norms of propriety by "excessive" engagement of the imagination. To assert that a story was true or based on true events was, therefore, a means of asserting a novel's legitimacy.

Yet this emphasis on factuality also had a political objective for women novelists: to legitimize women's experiences and their modes of communication. In an industry that continually sought to subordinate women's "truths" and in a society that insisted upon "marrying well" as the predominant career for women, the novel became a political forum, both for novelists such as Helena Wells (c. 1760–c. 1809) and Sally Sayward Barrell Wood (1759–1855), whose works perpetuated patriarchal ideals of women's second-class citizenship, as well as for those novelists who used the genre as a means of realistically delineating and ultimately abrogating the injustices of women's status. Susanna Haswell Rowson's *Charlotte Temple*, America's first best-seller, is an important transitional text between those novelists who perpetuated and those who challenged patriarchy's ideologies, especially its inscription of woman's sphere.

As women moved into novel writing in the late eighteenth century, they carried forward into that genre two earlier literary forms (one private and one public) in which they had previously excelled: epistolary exchanges and the captivity narrative. Approximately one-third of early American novels were written in epistolary form. Certainly this style is a reflection of the influence of English novelists such as Samuel Richardson, but it also reflects the culmination of a long tradition of women's development of political and social commentaries through the exchange of letters. In novels of the period by male authors, the epistolary form is often sublimated and the structure of the text almost always gives priority to the male voice; for many women authors, especially Hannah Webster Foster, the appearance of an epistolary exchange remained an integral aspect of the materiality of her text.

Ann Eliza Schuyler Bleecker (1752–1783), who had exchanged many ideas with her female cousins through letters and poetry, structured *The History of Maria Kittle* as a letter to her cousin Susan Ten Eyck. But *The History* is a blending of numerous literary genres—in addition to being an epistolary novel, it acts as a biography of the fictional Maria Kittle; it is also a tribute to the captivity narrative, and it constitutes the beginning of a new literary genre, the frontier romance.

Perhaps the most notable feature of the novels by Ann Eliza Schuyler Bleecker and Hannah Webster Foster, however, is the detailed rendering of the psychological drama of a woman's inner life. For Schuyler Bleecker this inner life is represented through the drama of captivity; several years later, Webster Foster continued the process of rendering psychological realism in *The Coquette* by presenting women's social condition as an acculturized captivity. It has long been recognized that emerging male novelists were asking what it meant to be an American. This was equally true for women writers, although the grounds for debate were somewhat different: novelists such as Charles Brockden Brown and Hugh Henry Brackenridge questioned within their texts the best means by which a citizen should be represented in government. For women, excluded by law from the rights of citizenship, the questions of what status and means of representation, if any, they were to have in the new nation were at the forefront of their concerns. As Webster Foster recognized, women were being sent mixed messages about their responsibilities and roles in the new nation, and, as she also recognized, to challenge the sociocultural status quo was itself a political act.

Probably the most gifted of early American sentimental novelists, Webster Foster exposed the consequences of "polite" society and the limitations of upper-class women's lives at the end of the century. A significant precursor to the rise of realism in early nineteenth-century American women's fiction, *The Coquette* challenges our literary assumptions about sentimentalism and realism at the same time that it presents one of early American literature's most memorable characters, Eliza Wharton. If Eliza is led astray by the rake Peter Sanford, she is equally well led astray by the incongruous teachings of her society.

Tabitha Gilman Tenney's novel *Female Quixotism* pushes the novel form to its outer boundaries. Picaresque in form and carnivalesque in style, the novel exposes the extraordinary diversity of backgrounds, ethnicities, and races of early Americans. If it remains a class- and race-bound novel, it graphically captures the construction of gender in turn-of-the-century American culture.

First Women

Sky Woman (Iroquois)

In terms of power and achievement as well as influence, the Iroquois were one of the most important alliances in early America. Consisting of the Six Nations—originally, the Cayuga, Mohawk, Oneida, Onondaga, and Seneca, and in 1715 joined by the Tuscarora—the Iroquois controlled a region that included western Massachusetts to Lake Erie and from southern Canada into North Carolina. The alliance was a democratically governed entity, with elected representatives. Women actively participated in tribal governance. For instance, Iroquois women not only advised the tribal chiefs but were responsible for nominating the individuals for election to position of chief. The origin story "Sky Woman" reflects the longstanding integrative nature of Iroquois culture.

Bibliography: Converse.

Sky Woman

In the faraway days of this floating island, there grew one stately tree that branched beyond the range of vision. Perpetually laden with fruit and blossoms, the air was fragrant with its perfume, and the people gathered to its shade where councils were held.

One day the Great Ruler said to his people, "We will make a new place where another people may grow. Under our council tree is a great cloud sea which calls for our help. It is lonesome. It knows no rest and calls for light. We will talk to it. The roots of our council tree point to it and will show the way."

Having commanded that the tree be uprooted, the Great Ruler peered into the depths where the roots had guided, and summoning Ata-en-sic, who was with child, bade her look down. Ata-en-sic saw nothing, but the Great Ruler knew that the sea voice was calling, and bidding her carry its life, wrapped around her a great ray of light and sent her down to the cloud sea.

173

Dazzled by the descending light enveloping Ata-en-sic, there was great consternation among the animals and birds inhabiting the cloud sea, and they counseled in alarm.

"If it falls, it may destroy us," they cried.

"Where can it rest?" asked the Duck.

"Only the oeh-da (earth) can hold it," said the Beaver, "the oeh-da which lies at the bottom of our waters, and I will bring it." The Beaver went down but never returned. Then the Duck ventured down, but soon its dead body floated to the surface.

Many of the divers had tried and failed when the Muskrat, knowing the way, volunteered to obtain it and soon returned bearing a small portion in his paw. "But it is heavy," said he, "and will grow fast. Who will bear it?"

The Turtle was willing, and the oeh-da was placed on his hard shell.

Having received a resting place for the light, the water birds, guided by its glow, flew upward and receiving the woman on their widespread wings, they bore her down to the Turtle's back.

And Hah-nu-nah, the Turtle, became the Earth Bearer. When he stirs, the seas rise in great waves, and when restless and violent, earthquakes yawn and devour.

The oeh-da grew rapidly and had become an island when Ata-en-sic, hearing voices under her heart, one soft and soothing, the other loud and contentious, knew that her mission to people the island was nearing.

To her solitude two lives were coming, one peaceful and patient, the other restless and vicious. The latter, discovering light under his mother's arm, thrust himself through, to contentions and strife; the right born entered life for freedom and peace.

These were the Do-ya-da-no, the twin brothers, Spirits of Good and Evil. Foreknowing their powers, each claimed dominion, and a struggle between them began, Hah-gweh-di-yu claiming the right to beautify the island, while Hah-gweh-da-et-gah determined to destroy. Each went his way, and where peace had reigned discord and strife prevailed.

At the birth of Hah-gweh-di-yu, his Sky Mother, Ata-en-sic, had died, and the island was still dim in the dawn of its new life when, grieving at his mother's death, he shaped the sky with the palm of his hand, and creating the sun from her face, lifted it there, saying, "You shall rule here where your face will shine forever." But Hah-gweh-da-et-gah set Darkness in the west sky, to drive the Sun down behind it.

Hah-gweh-di-yu then drew forth from the breast of his Mother, the Moon and the Stars, and led them to the Sun as his sisters who would guard his night sky. He gave to the earth her body, its Great Mother, from whom was to spring all life.

All over the land Hah-gweh-di-yu planted towering mountains, and in the valleys set high hills to protect the straight rivers as they ran to the sea. But Hah-gweh-da-et-gah wrathfully sundered the mountains, hurling them far apart, and drove the high hills into the wavering valleys, behind the rivers as he hunted them down.

Hah-gweh-di-yu set forests on the high hills, and on the low plains fruit-bearing trees and vines to wing their seeds to the scattering winds. But Hah-gweh-da-et-gah gnarled the forests besetting the earth, and led monsters to dwell in the sea, and herded hurricanes in the sky which frowned with mad tempests that chased the Sun and Stars.

The First Ship (Chinook)

This legend is undoubtedly based on an incident in the fifteenth or sixteenth century when Spanish ships sailed along the Pacific Northwest coastline; it constitutes one of the rare Native American stories that presents the other side of Spanish, Dutch, and English explorers' narratives. The legend is notable, too, because it is an elderly Clatsop woman who first espies the seeming monster as it lands on shore and who reports its presence to her community.
Bibliography: Clark, E.; Erdoes and Ortiz.

The First Ship

An old woman in a Clatsop village near the mouth of Big River[1] mourned the death of her son. For a year she grieved. One day she stopped her crying and took a walk along the beach where she had often gone in happier days.

As she was returning to the village, she saw a strange something out in the water not far from shore. At first she thought it was a whale. When she came nearer, she saw two spruce trees standing upright on it.

"It's not a whale," she said to herself, "it's a monster."

When she came near the strange thing that lay at the edge of the water, she saw that its outside was covered with copper and that ropes were tied to the spruce trees. Then a bear came out of the strange thing and stood on it. It looked like a bear, but the face was the face of a human being.

"Oh, my son is dead," she wailed, "and now the thing we have heard about is on our shore."

Weeping, the old woman returned to her village. People who heard her called to others, "An old woman is crying. Someone must have struck her."

The men picked up their bows and arrows and rushed out to see what was the matter.

"Listen!" an old man said.

They heard the woman wailing. "Oh, my son is dead, and the thing we have heard about is on our shore."

All the people ran to meet her. "What is it? Where is it?" they asked.

---

1. Probably the Columbia River, where it feeds into the Pacific Ocean.

"Ah, the thing we have heard about in tales is lying over there." She pointed toward the south shore of the village. "There are two bears on it, or maybe they are people."

Then her people ran toward the thing that lay near the edge of the water. The two creatures on it held copper kettles in their hands. When the Clatsop arrived at the beach, the creatures put their hands to their mouths and asked for water.

Two of the men ran inland, hid behind a log awhile, and then ran back to the beach. One of them climbed up on the strange thing, entered it, and looked around inside. It was full of boxes, and he found long strings of brass buttons.

When he went outside to call his relatives to see the inside of the thing, he found that they had already set fire to it. He jumped down and joined the two creatures and his people on shore.

The strange thing burned just like fat. Everything burned except the iron, the copper, and the brass. Then the Clatsop took the two strange-looking men to their chief.

"I want to keep one of the men with me," said the chief.

Soon the people north of the river heard about the strange thing, and they came to the Clatsop village. The Willapa came from across the river, the Chehalis and the Cowlitz from farther north, and even the Quinault from up the coast. And people from up the river came also—the Klickitat and others farther up.

The Clatsop sold the iron, brass, and copper. They traded one nail for a good deerskin. For a long necklace of shells they gave several nails. One man traded a piece of brass two fingers wide for a slave.

None of them had ever seen iron or brass before. The Clatsop became rich selling the metal to other tribes.

The two Clatsop chiefs kept the two men who came on the ship. One stayed at the village called Clatsop, the other stayed at the village on the cape.

Margaret Tyndal Winthrop (c. 1591–1647)

Margaret Tyndal was raised on a large estate, Great Maplestead, in Essex County, England. Her parents, Sir John and Lady Anne Tyndal, were influential figures in the community, and Sir John was Master in Chancery. Although the Tyndals were wealthier than the Winthrops, the latter were a respected family and John Winthrop's reputation for leading a virtuous, deeply religious life made him a worthy candidate as Margaret's husband. Her character is revealed in a letter from her future father-in-law in which he declared admiration for her "modest behaviour, and mielde nature," requisite attributes for a Puritan woman, but he also admired her because of her "constant minde wch I perceyve to be settled in you towards my sonne." Tyndal Winthrop's father had been murdered in 1616 as the result of a decision he had rendered as Master of Chancery; but, with Lady Anne's approval, Margaret became John's third wife on April 24, 1618. She was supportive of the decision to remove to New England, but her own departure came more than a year after John's because, in 1630 when John sailed on the *Arbella*, Tyndal Winthrop was pregnant with their second child. Their marriage was a Puritan union, which demanded that their piety be placed above their regard for each other and the husband above the wife, but it was a loving relationship. Tyndal Winthrop, her children, and several other family members arrived in Massachusetts in the fall of 1631. To show their respect and to welcome the Governor's wife, the townspeople greeted Margaret with a salute of volleys, formal visits, and gifts for their home—as close to a royal welcome as America was to see for many years. A pious and intelligent woman, Margaret Tyndal Winthrop was at the center of the colony's political and social activities for the remainder of her life. She died in Massachusetts in 1647.

Works: Correspondence. *Bibliography:* Earle, *Margaret Winthrop;* Morgan, *The Puritan Dilemma;* Rutman; Twichell; *Winthrop Papers.*

The Letters of Margaret Tyndal Winthrop

[c. October 1627][1] Most Deare and Loveinge Husband. I can not expres my love to you as I desire. in theese poore livelesse lines, but I doe hartily wish you did see my harte how true and faythfull it is to you, and how much I doe desire to be allwayes wit you. to injoy the sweet comfort of your presence. and those helps from you in sperituall and temperall dutyes which I am so unfite to performe with out you. it makes me to see the want of you and wish my selfe with you. but I desire wee may be gided by god in all our wayes who is able to derect us for the best and so I will wayt upon him with pacience who is all sufficient for me . . . I prayse god we are all heare in health as you left us. and are glad to heare the same of you and all the rest of our frends at London. my mother and my selfe remember our best love to you and all the rest. our children remember theare duty to you. and thus desiringe to be remembred in your prayers I bid my good Husband godnight; littel Samewell[2] thinkes it is time for me to goe to bed, and so I beseech the lord to keepe you in safety and us all heare farwell my sweete husband. Your obediente Wife

1. John was in London on business at the time this letter was written; Margaret was at their family estate, Groton, several miles outside of London.
2. Samuel Winthrop, their first son, was an infant at this time.

[c. early May 1631]   My deare sonne,[3] blessed be our good god for the good newes which we have hard out of n: e: mr. wilson[4] had bin with me before thy letters came to my hands, but brought me no letter. he speakes very well of things thear, so as my hart and thoughts are thear allready. I want but means to carye my bodye after them. I am now fully parswaded that it is the place whearein god will have us to settle in, and I beseech him to fit us for it, that we may be instruments of his glorye thear[5] . . . Your lovinge mother

[c. May 24, 1631]   My deare Sonne, Since it hath pleased god to make a waye for me, and to give me incoragement for my voyage, and upholds my hart that it faynts not, I doe resolve by his assistance to cast my selfe upon him, and to goe for N: E: as spedyly as I can with any convenience   thearfore, my good Sonne, let me intreate thee to take order for our goeinge as soone as thou canst, for winter wil come on apace. yet I doe not knowe howe wee can goe wel before harvest by resone of our provisions of corne. I did heare from my brother Tyndall[6] whose counsell is for to stay till the springe, but I hope to breake through that, and geete his good will. I did speake with mr. wilson, who was very desyrus to knowe when we went, but then I could not tell howe things would falle out at London and could not resolve him. if he goe it must be without his wifes consent, for she is more averce then ever she was.[7] if he goe not it will disharten many that would be wiling to goe. I have bin constrayned to send to the tenants for rent wantinge monye but have receved but a little yet this weeke thay promise to paye. thay complayne of the hardnesse of the time, and would be glad to be forborne, but I tell them that my nesessityes requires it, so I hope to gette in some. . . . your lovinge mother

["Sad Boston" c. November 15, 1637]   Deare in my thoughts,[8] I blush to thinke howe much I have neclected the opertunytye of presenting my love to you. sad thougts posses my sperits, and I cannot repulce them which makes me unfit for any thinge wondringe what the lord meanes by all these troubles amounge us. shure I am that all shall worke to the best, to them that love god, or rather are loved of hime. I know he will bring light out of obcuritye, and make his ritousnesse shine forth as clere as the noune daye. yet I finde in my selfe an aferce spiret, and a tremblinge hart, not so wilinge to submit to the will of god as i desyre. thear is a time to plant and time to pul up that which is planted, which I could desyre mite not be yet. but the lord knoweth what is best, and his wilbe done. . . .

3. Tyndal Winthrop's stepson, John Winthrop Jr., who was in London.

4. Probably the Rev. John Wilson who emigrated to New England where he became pastor of the Boston church and as such supported John Winthrop in his charges against Anne Hutchinson.

5. Tyndal Winthrop's concern for the unity of the new community was as strong as her husband's. In a letter several days later to John Jr., she remarked, "we shall al joyne together I hope, and be of one minde" on the voyage. Her statement reflects the same ideals which her husband had asserted in "A Model of Christian Charity."

6. Tyndal Winthrop's brother, Deane Tyndal.

7. It was not until 1635 that Reverend Wilson was able to convince his wife to join him in New England.

8. Addressed to John Winthrop. Tyndal Winthrop had been in New England for nearly six years at this point. John was in Newtown (later Cambridge), where Anne Hutchinson's trial was being held. The reference to "all these troubles amounge us" is undoubtedly a reference to that event and the Antinomian Controversy as a whole.

[Boston, October 10, 1642]   Lovinge sonne,[9] . . . your wife thinkes longe for your cominge, yet it pleaseth god to help hir to beare it prety cherfully   hir little boye[10] is so mery that it puteth many a sad thought from his mother. When I thinke of the trublesom times and manyfolde destractions that are in our native Contrye I thinke we doe not pryse our happynesse heare as we have case, that we should be in peace when so many troubles are in most places of the world. I wish we ware more sencible of the calamityes of others that we myte crye the more mytylye to god for them. . . . your loving mother

Susanna Moseley (fl. 1649–50)

Susanna Moseley emigrated from Rotterdam, Holland, to Virginia with her merchant husband, William, and their two sons, Arthur and William, in the spring of 1649. They had received grants of land in Lower Norfolk County, Virginia, and there they built an estate called "Rolleston" after the Moseley family estate in Staffordshire, England. William Sr. became Justice of Lower Norfolk County from the time of their settlement until April 1655. The Moseleys thrived in the colony[1] and became one of the leading Virginia families. Little is known about Susanna Moseley, but she was obviously well educated, an astute negotiator, and a leading woman in her community.

Works: Letter.

Susanna Moseley's Letter to Francis Yeardley[2]

Worthy Sir:

My husband havinge some bussines downe the river was gone from home two howers before your servant came, soe I finding what the contents of your letter did import, have in my husband's absence made bould to answer it, and with all I knowe he referrs the sale of them to me. Sir, in regards you cannot

9. Addressed to John Winthrop Jr., who had returned to London on business for the colony.

10. Probably Fitz-John Winthrop, who would have been about four years old at the time and who later became, like his father, Governor of Connecticut.

1. Like most of the early Virginia colonists, the Moseleys owned slaves. In his will, William Moseley Sr. left Susanna Moseley "one negro woman called Mary with her Childe Besse, to be at her disposing during her life" and "all the sheepe with the Increase thereof." In the Moseley family tradition and common for the time, all of the land (800 acres in Virginia and English lands as well) was willed to their sons. Susanna was entitled to "her wearing apparell and her Lifetime upon the plantation where she now lives" (*VMHB* Jan. 1898, 328).

2. Yeardley was the son of Governor Sir George Yeardley and a leading political figure in colonial Virginia.

miss out of your stocke no more then fower younge Cowes and one elder and fower oxen, I will not press you beyond what you are willing to doe, but will accept of your proffer by reason of my greate wante of Cattle, and withall I had rayther your wife should weare them then any gentle woman I yet know in ye country; but good Sir have *no* scruple concerninge their rightness, for I went my selfe from Rotterdam to ye haugh[3] to inquire of the gould smiths and found y't they weare all Right, therefore thats without question, and for the hat band th't alone coste five hundred gilders as my husband knows verry well and will tell you soe when he sees you; for the Juell and the ringe they weare made for me at Rotterdam and I paid in good rex dollars for sixty gilders for the Juell and fivety and two gilders for the ringe, which comes to in English monny eleaven poundes fower shillings. I have sent the sute and Ringe by your servant, and I wish Mrs. Yeardley[4] health and prosperity to weare them in, and give you both thanks for your kind token. When my husband comes home we will see to gett the Cattell home, in the meantime I present my Love and service to your selfe & wife, Mr. Chandler and his wife and the youngue gentle women and old Capt. and commit you all to God, and remaine,

Your friend and servant,
Susan Moseley.

Elizabeth River, this Last July, 1650.

Katherine Marbury Scott (fl. 1658)

Katherine Marbury Scott, like her sister Anne Hutchinson, was an outspoken advocate of religious freedom. She and her husband, Richard, had lived in Boston under the Puritan rule of Governor John Winthrop. Like her sister, Marbury Scott was not merely a follower of male religious and political leadership; according to Governor Winthrop, it was Katherine Marbury Scott who "emboldened" Roger Williams to profess his own dissatisfaction with the Massachusetts Bay Puritans' restrictive practices. She joined Williams when he established Providence, Rhode Island, as a community dedicated to religous tolerance. Later, Marbury Scott became a Quaker and once again she chose to challenge Puritan authority—this time by returning to Boston to speak on behalf of her new faith. Like many other Quakers who spoke out against Calvinism (see, for instance, Mary Traske and Margaret Smith), she was imprisoned and subjected to a whipping for expressing her beliefs. The following letter, addressed to John Winthrop, Jr., then Governor of Massachusetts Bay Colony, captures her heartfelt voice of protest.

Works: Letters. Bibliography: Winthrop Papers.

3. The Hague.
4. Sarah Offley Yeardley.

Katherine Marbury Scott's Letter

For th[e] hand of John Winterup called Governore, at Harvard in New Ingland, theis deliver with trust.

Providence, this 17 of the 4 month, 1658.

John Winterup,—Thinke it not hard to be called soe, seeing Jesus, our Saviour and Governor, and all that were made honorable by him, that are recorded in Scripture, were called soe. I have writ to thee before, but never hard whether they came to thy hand; my last, it may be, may troble thee, conserning my sonne; but truly I had not propounded it to thee but to satisfie his mind, and to prevent his going where wee did more disafect; but I heare noe more of his mind that way. I hope his mind is taken up with the thing wch is the most nessesary, and first to seeke his kingdome, &c.: therefore let y^t be burred in silence: but my later requeist I must reuise, and that is only out of true love and pity to thee, that thou maiest be free, and not trobled, as I have hard thy father was, upon his death bed, at the banishment of my deare sister Hutchenson and others. I ame sure they have a sad cup to drink, that are drunke with the blod of the saints: O my freind, as thou lovest the prosperity of thy soull and the good of thy posterity, taike heed of having thy hand, or hart, or tounge lifted up against those persons that the wise yet follish world in scorne calls quaikers: for they are the messengers of the Lord of Hosts, wch hee hath in his large love and pity sent into theis parts, to gather together his out casts and the distressed of the chilldren of Israell: and they shall acomplish the worke, let the rage of men be never soe great: taike heed of hindering of them, for noe weapen formed against them shall prosper. It is given to them not onely to beleive, but to sufer, &c., but woe to them by whom they sufer. O my freind, try all things, and waiy it by the balence of the sanctuary: how can you try without hearing of them? for the care tries words as the mouth tasts meat. I dare not but beare witnese against the unjust and cruell lawes of my contrymen in this land: for cursed are all they that cometh not out to help the Lord against the mighty; and all that are not with him are against him, &c. Woe be to y^m that gather and not by him, & cover with a covering, and not with his spirit: wch woe I desire thou maiest escape.

Katherine Scott.

Barbara Smith (fl. 1689)

Political rivalries were rampant in early Maryland, and Barbara Smith, a leading citizen of the proprietorship, was an outspoken and notable participant in the disputations. In the late seventeenth century, the English king and administrators were concerned about preserving their proprietorship against both political and religious forces. Fearing incursions from the French, who had aligned themselves with Native American groups in the colonies, and fearing the rise of Catholic rather than Anglican leaders, the English proprietors were wary of all infringements upon their rights. In the midst of these tensions, John Coode led what was deemed a revolution against the provincial leadership and followers of George Calvert, Lord Baltimore, the colonizer who had been granted the region that became Maryland by King James I in 1632. Coode asserted that Calvert had appointed many Catholics to high offices; coupled with news that Native Americans had massacred settlers in Schenectady and rumors that thousands of Native Americans were headed in their direction, many Maryland colonists sided with Coode. Others sought redress against his actions. Residents throughout the Maryland region sent petitions, either collectively or individually, to William and Mary, reigning majesties, protesting Coode's actions. Historians have noted Barbara Smith's protest as one of the most interesting texts in this politically volatile moment.

Works: Letter. Bibliography: Andrews.

Letter Petition of Barbara Smith

[1689]

Upon the 25th of March last, a rumor was spread abroad about the mouth of Puttuxent River that ten thousand Indians were come down to the Western Branch of the said River, whereupon my husband went up to the said Western Branch, where he found no Indians; but there a strong report that nine thousand were at Matapany and at the mouth of Puttuxent and that they had cut off Capt. Bournes' family and had inforted themselves at Matapany,—which was all false.

Upon these rumors the Country rose in arms, but after diligent search and enquiry in all parts of the Province, this rumor was found to be only a sham; and no Indians anywhere appeared to disturb or molest any of the people of our Province.

All which reports I do verily believe were spread abroad to incite the people to rise in arms, as afterwards by the like sham they were induced to do. For the latter end of July following, one Capt. Code, Col. Jowles, Major Beal, Mr. Blackiston, with some others, appeared in arms and gave for their pretence that the Papists had invited the Northern Indians to come down and cut off the Protestants and that their descent was to be about the latter end of August when roasting ears were in season, and that they, therefore, rose in arms to secure the magazine of arms and ammunition and the Protestants from being cut off by the said Indians and Papists.

This was their pretence to those they found very apprehensive of the said Indians. To others they said their design was only to proclaim the King and Queen, but when the aforesaid persons, with some others, had gathered together a great number of people they then came out and seized upon the government, who withstood them first at St. Maryes in the State House where the Records are kept, whom the said Code and his part soon overcame and seized upon the Records. From thence he proceeded with his party to Matapany House, wherein Col. Darnall with some forces, as many Protestants as Papists, had garrisoned themselves, but were soon forced to capitulate, surrender and yield to the said Code and his party.

They having thus possessed themselves of the Government, one Johnson, Master of a Ship being bound for England, they gave him charge he should carry no letters but what was sent for themselves, and my husband they arrested and put in prison for fear he should go for England with the said Johnson to give an account of their proceedings; and as soon as the said Johnson was gone, they released him again. The said Code and his Complices then sent out letters to all the Counties of the Province to choose an Assembly; what was done in the rest of the Counties, besides Calvert and Ann Arrundell, I am not acquainted with; but when the said Letters for the choosing of Burgesses came to our Sheriff to summon the people for that purpose, he refused the same. They then went to Mr. Clegatt, Coroner, and he also refused (who are both Protestants) whereupon Col. Jowles rode about to give the people notice himself.

When the County were come together, most of the House Keepers agreed not to choose any Burgesses, and drew up an abhorrence against such proceedings, the which election was also much opposed by our Sheriff. Whereupon Col. Jowles gathered his soldiers and caused the election to be made by the number he had, which was not above twenty, and of them not above ten that were capable of electing. Col. Jowles himself and Major Beal, his next officer, were returned for two of the Burgesses elected, and because Mr. Taney, the Sheriff, and my husband endeavored to oppose the election, the said Code caused them to put in prison.

Neither for this election nor in their cause did almost any of our County appear that were men of estates, or men of note; but they, to the contrary, published an abhorrence against such proceedings and were themselves as are most of our County Protestants. The County of Ann Arrundell, which is accounted the most populous and richest of the whole Province, and wherein is but one papist family, unanimously stood out and would not elect any Burgesses.

About the 21st of August, the Assembly of their calling met, before whom was brought Mr. Taney, our Sheriff, and my husband; and Capt. Code and his Complices having pretended they had the King's Proclamation for what they did, my husband demanded to see the same; but their answer was, 'take him away, Sheriff.' Mr. Taney likewise asking them by what authority he was called before them, Code answered, 'What! this is like King Charles and you are King Taney, take him away!' Notwithstanding upon the said Code's rising (as before is said), their pretense was chiefly to secure the Country against the Indians, yet all this while not until my coming away which was the 26th of September last, there was not the least appearance of any foreign or home Indians coming to disturb us. What was their further proceedings in their Assembly I am not able to give any account of, but Mr. Taney and my husband were detained prisoners at my coming away.

Mary Herendean Pray (fl. 1675)

Mary Pray was a resident of Providence, Rhode Island, when she wrote to her friend Captain James Oliver of Boston. Virtually nothing is known of Pray's life; her first marriage was to Benjamin Herendean (or Hearndale), and she was probably married to Ephraim Pray at the time of her correspondence with Oliver. What is evident about Pray's letter is the role that rumors played during the early years of the settlement of Rhode Island; she also speaks pointedly about the controversy that surrounded the colony's founder, Roger Williams, during King Philip's War.

Works: Correspondence. *Bibliography*: *Winthrop Papers*.

Mary Herendean Pray's Letter

[Providence, October 20, 1675]

Cap. Oliver, Sir,—After dew respects, these lines. I canot forbear to writ, I am so ful of grife for our frinds and conterymen. These fals trecherus imps, the Naraganset Indians, about 4 dayes sinc, exultingly tel there asociates of Warwick that Captain Mosley an 3 hundred men with him are al cut ofe.[1] We hope there joy is without such a caus. We here are al amased to see how things are carried, that no cours is teken with these vilans who thus insult as they doe; this fals peac hath undon this contery; these rouges are undoubtedly they that maintain the war westward against the English. Mr Roger Wilims hath an Indian boy who chose his master hous rather than his mothers; his brother told John Inman that Mosop gave Nononottonut 20 bushel of corn which he divided to fourscore Indians and sent them out, but he would not tel whether, an I ve herd he made them up 3 hundred and sent them al away, but neither wil that infermer tel whether. An Indian that hath much convers with Cap. Fenner[2] saith the Indians doe not desier to fight this winter, but when the leaves are green then they wil be for us; this we so wel beliv that we know that if the Lord refus to give them into our hands this winter we cannot live here, nor many hundreds moer as wel as we. It is to much to writ to troubl

---

1. Herendean Pray is writing during the bitterest days of King Philip's War. The incident she reports concerning Captain Samuel Moseley of Dorchester proved to be false.
2. Probably Arthur Fenner of Providence.

you to read our sad condition; our poer nation are neerely ensnaered, and betrayed by mens privat intrest and trusting Indians. The Indians boast and say those Indians that are caled praying Indians never shut at the other Indians, but up into the tops of the trees or into the ground; and when they make shew of going first into the swamp they comonly give the Indians noatis how to escape the English. Sir, we have experienc of them that they are as bad as any other; and it is report by the Indians them selves tha[t] Cap. Gucking[3] helps them to powder, and they sel it to those that are imployed by Philip to bye for him. This we have ground to belive. It grives us al to here of the downfal of our contremen by these savage beasts. The Naragasets say that our English soulders canot kil Indians, for they put a bandalere of powder in at once and that mounteth there shoot over the Indians heads. Divers great men, for ther trade and gain-sake, delude the counsel and say peac; but God I hope wil reward there deceit, who if they have but there gain they caer not what becoms of the contery. I did not here him say it, but I herd a report that Rich. Smith[4] said, about 2 months sinc, that he hoped to have one hundred barels of pork of the Indians for al what was past. Som here conclud he staved of war with them for his porkes sake; but if he did, be it upon him after his deserts. It is deemed by al here that now is the time to try what the Lord God of power an mercy wil do for us against them. Shortly the wether wil be cold that men canot bear it; one fortnight is past of brave wether sinc the leaves are fallen. Sir, if a spedy dispach be not, provision will be so scers that men wil not be able to goe out and fight, and then the contery wil be lost. Were I not made sencablely able to see Gods hand in al this, it would amase any one to think what is now com to pas, and how things might have been prevented at first. Ohe what caus hath Cap. Huchesons family[5] and hundreds moer to rue the treatings with Indians. Had the contery as one man broke out like a fier upon them, in an ordanary way we might have known the worst and best by this time. These fals imps at Naraganset, we here, take the swine out of the pens of our English, and, to provok them, tel them that they kil there cattel and take there other fruits from them at there plesuer. We every day expect to be asalted by them, and look for nothing but trechoury from them. They very latly refrain there great resort to Warwick and Pawtucset. What mischif they are in hand with now we know not, but many here do think they wil draw down to them al or moast of the rout of rougs that Cap. Moesley is gon after, or run to them or have them very neer them, if any armey come up against them. Now they know ther is a considerable force out, we think they wil run al down upon us and upon what forces you send against thes vilans of Naraganset. The Lord in much mercy petie us and arise for his great name. The

---

3. Daniel Gookin, a member of the House of Representatives in Massachusetts Bay Colony for nearly twenty-five years. In 1676, however, he was expelled from office because of his concern for those Native Americans who had been friendly with the English.

4. Smith was one of Rhode Island's most prominent citizens and chief magistrate of the Narragansett region.

5. Edward Hutchinson Jr., the eldest son of Anne Hutchinson, had died from battle wounds on August 19.

Lord I hop wil look upon us and rebuke these wreches, not for our sakes but for his great names sake. Moast certain it is God exactes les of us then our pride and our many-fold goings astray from his deserveth; but I hope though Asirya be the rod of his wrath, and the stafe in his hand Gods indignation, yet he doth purpos uterly to destroy these wreches. Lt us al intreat his guidance and counsel, and he is able to over throw there contrivances what ever they be.

I was bold to desier you to send me tow cutlashes an belts for my to sons. Though John hath lost his whol estat I wil not fail to pay you in fethers or sheeps wool, if I canot get mony. If you wil send them by John Harker I hope he wil bring them safe, or by any of Seconk. I hope your helth with yours, and desier to here from you by the first.

Yours in any service to my power
Mary Pray.

Rich. Wilams very privatly told us your governor doth intend to send up an army to Naraganset. The Lord grant they may not be deluded to spaer them by flatery; a vollum might be writ of there vilany. I pray Sir, let me here from you what tidings are there, and whether these rouges must live or not. We here this rouges brother Narganset Sachim burnt Springfeeild. This day we had newes from Warwick, that som of the praying Indians are lately come to a plantation 14 mil from us, who do perswad the Naragansets forthwith to fall upon the English, teling them that they are suer that if they doe not the English will fall upon them sudenley. Sir, the whol contery hath caus to abhor al sorts of Indians but the Mohegings; there fidelity to the English wil be evidenced by 30 of Providenc, if need be, who were with them at Nipsachuck fight; and we here they are discouraged by the English making peac with the Naragansets. Sir, hath not the Lord made a winter for us, as wel as a sumer for the Indians? They tooke there opertunity, why doe we thus neglect ours? My soul knoweth exprinctialy that the race is not to the swift, nor the battel to the strong, but the lot is cast into the lap and the disposing therof is of the Lord. He is the God of Battel; he is wise and just in all his dealing with us. The cause of our deliveranc must be his mere mercy. Our condition is sad: we are every way at a lose, and know not what to do; but our eyes are upward. Sir, can you think we can subsist another sumer? No, we canot, if these live. We are forced now then men to goe about tow mens work. We have lost our crap, many of us our hay time. We are forced to desroy al or most of our cattel and hoges, becaus we have not corne and hay for to keep them alive, and if som few remain what hope can we have of enjoyin them the next sumer or our own lives? These wreches are so fleshed with the last sumers enjoyments, we conclud the next sumer wil be far wors then this hath been; and the sucses these have had wil encourage al the rest to joyn with them, and then it wil son com to Philipes threat, that he would make us English eat one another. It would grive you, I know, to see our ruins. Are our frinds of Boston satesfied that Naragansets are not true by detaining those murderus wreches? We have been certainly informe that som of Naraganset, who, if they had not been with Philip, had not been hurt then. Jeremiah Roads, a man of sober life and conversation, to[ld] me an Indian to[ld] him that the Indians purpose was this winter to come down in the night by 8 or 10 in a company, and fier our town, or as much of it as might be, and so run away again, and not ours onely but other towns; and this, said he, I know they wil do, or else do you hang mee up. This, said he, wil be when you English think you are at quiet.

Hannah Callowhill Penn (1671–1726)

Hannah Callowhill was born in Bristol, England, on February 11, 1671, into an upper-middle-class Quaker family. Her mother, Hannah Hollister, was a leader in the Women's Meeting of the Bristol Friends' Society, a tradition of leadership that was passed on to Hannah at an early age and that served her well in her future life in Pennsylvania. Her father, Thomas Callowhill, was a well-to-do shipping exporter-importer who encouraged his daughter's business education apparently because she was the only one of their nine children to survive to adulthood. On March 5, 1696, Hannah married the widower William Penn, future Proprietor of Pennsylvania. Three years later, on September 3, 1699, Hannah and William sailed for Philadelphia aboard the *Canterbury* to begin their new endeavor. William had already established a 6,000-acre manor, Pennsbury, several miles north of Philadelphia. Hannah was pregnant with their first child when they left England, and she always remembered "the extreame trouble of the sea," which included treacherous weather conditions and the possibility of pirate attacks. They landed at New Castle, Delaware, in December 1699. Hannah gave birth to John Penn (the first of seven children) on January 28, 1700.

As wife of the Proprietor and Governor of Pennsylvania, Hannah was an active participant in the affairs of the commonwealth. Though her sojourn in America lasted only until 1701, when the Crown's threat to abolish proprietorships required that both she and William return to Bristol, she continued to participate actively in the running of the Province. She was known to have a far better mind for business than her husband, and her letters reveal her constant concern for the economic welfare of Pennsylvania and of her own family. Callowhill Penn's biographer notes that when William suffered a stroke in 1712, Hannah "served Pennsylvania as acting proprietor and governor" for the next fourteen years. She died in Bristol on December 20, 1726.

Works: Correspondence. *Bibliography*: Drinker; *The Papers of William Penn*.

The Letters of Hannah Callowhill Penn

[c. September 1700][1]

James,[2] my husband has been for some time, espesially the 2 days past, much Indispos'd wth a feavourish cold . . . wch has prevaild wth him to stay till to morrow w[he]n, if better he intends not to faile of being in town. wherefore he would have the councell adjourn from day to day till they see him. also would have thee tell Tho: Story[3] to read over the laws carefully and observe their shortnes or other defects, wth memorandums of direction, espesially those about courts of Justice. Marriage. law of Property. unreasonable Alienation of fines. &c & what time thou can well spare he would have thee Imploy on the same Subject. for after the rising of this Assembly he determines to send the laws for England & desire T. S to show Judge Gest[4] his draught[5] for Regulating courts. also do thou by the first oppertunity send to R. Parmeter[6] for his draught upon the same subject, (it may help.) and be sure to mind the buisness of the Maryl[an]d sloop. & speak to the councell or Magestrates {to consider of} a place for the Generall assembly. the Governour understands Jos: Shippen[7] gives in reallity but 7l 10 [a ton], to N. Puckle,[8] & hopes thou gives not more I desire thou will not faile to return that mony due to my father at least one halfe by first good oppertunity to Barbadoes or otherwise. not else at presant from   thy frd   Hannah Penn

Philadelphia 6th 1st month [March] 1700[/1]

Dear Friend,[9]   the love which has long lived in my heart to thee, has very often (even in this desolate land,) brought thee into my remembrance; wth true desires to the God of all our mercys, that he would be pleasd to Continue his blessings to thee, and give thee an increase of spirituall & tomperoll[10] Comforts, in the room of those wch he in his wisdom has thought fit to deprive thee of (as to the outward: I mean thy dear & honourable father[11] whose Memory is sweet, & pleasant to us, and I doubt not, but Your, & our, Loss is his eternall gain. I often think on thy Dear Mother[12] under her divers afflictions, espe-

---

1. This letter appears to have been written when William Penn was preparing for the next General Assembly meeting, held in October 1700.

2. Addressed to James Logan, William Penn's secretary and a family friend. Logan later became Chief Justice of Pennsylvania.

3. Thomas Story had been a friend of the Penns in London. He later became Master of the Rolls and Keeper of the Seal.

4. John Guest was Chief Justice of the Pennsylvania Supreme Court and a member of the Provincial Council.

5. *draught*: draft, here referring to a legislative bill.

6. Parmeter was a relative of William's. Apparently William was seeking to establish Parmeter as Attorney General.

7. Son of Edward Shippen, Joseph was a Boston merchant.

8. Nathaniel Puckle, a Quaker, was captain of the ships *Bristol Trader* and *Philadelphia*.

9. Addressed to Elizabeth Vickris Taylor, a close friend of Callowhill Penn's who resided with her husband, James, in Bristol.

10. *tomperoll*: temporal.

11. Vickris Taylor's father, Richard Vickris, had recently died.

12. Elizabeth Bishop Vickris (1655–1724).

sially that of Loosing so tender & affectionate a husband, as he was to her. . . . And now my dear friend tho, I have been backward in writing, I do assure thee I have not in wishing, thy happyness & wellfare in this thy Married estate, which as it is the greatest comfort in this world, so is it mixt with greatest exercises, a proof of which I hear thou hast already experienc'd, in the Loss of thy dear little daughter,[13] which I was truly sorry for, but hope it will please the lord to give thee more,[14] wch may be a comfort & pleasure to thee in days to come; but as in this, so in all other things, our Comforts are in his hand, who can withhold, or distribute, as he pleases; & we must not say unto him what does'd thou; I have been a witness of his [great power &] deliveran[ce] t[h]rough many exercises, & have cause to bless his name, who in his own due time, was pleasd to turn his hand, & make me partaker of his mercys, beyond what I could even have expected, which I desire I may always remember wth a thankfull heart while I have a being in this world; now dear betty, as to perticulars know, that I have had my health much better than in england, my dear Husband is pretty well also, but exceedingly prest in business partly by his too long stay in england, which will I fear occasian his stay here to be too long also; I know his dear love is to thee & thine, and to the faithfull every where. the Country has Injoyd health in a great degree since we came hither, and my dear little boy[15] grows bravely, he's very pleasant & lively, much like his father, in whom he takes great delight, is well belov'd of his sister,[16] and indeed proves a great comfort & divertion to us all, I have Suckled him my selfe hitherto but think of Weaning him in a little time   he has five teeth, and can go alone very well if he pleases   Our friend Sarah Climent[17] is here & well, she has had good service in new england, Rhoad, & long Island, &c and intends for Maryland about 2 months hence   she desires her dear love to thee & thy relations as oppertunity offers. pray give mine also, and to thy husband in perticular. I wish you comfort & happyness in each other, for I am as I have always been

Thy reall & Affectionate Friend Hanh Penn. . . .

Mary Stafford (fl. 1711)

The following letter is the only information we have about Mary Stafford. Written to a relative who was identified only as "Mrs. Randall," the letter and its description of life in early eighteenth-

13. Vickris Taylor's four-month-old daughter, Elizabeth, had died on January 7, 1701.

14. The Taylors had at least eight more children.

15. Callowhill Penn is referring to her son John, now thirteen months old. Since the Penns' other children were all born in England, John was always referred to as "John the American."

16. Laetitia Penn (1678–1746) was William's daughter with his first wife, Gulielma Springett, who had died in 1694. Laetitia had accompanied Hannah and William on their journey to Pennsylvania in 1699.

17. Sarah Clements was a traveling Quaker minister who came to Pennsylvania in the summer of 1699. It is her signature that appears on John's birth certificate.

century South Carolina might have been lost except that Stafford wished James Petiver, a London apothecary whose interests in the natural features of the region were well known, to see her letter. Unlike many women of the period whose works survive, Stafford was not from the upper classes, and her financial struggles are undoubtedly far more representative of early settlers' experiences and their hopes for a better future in America.

Works: Letter. *Bibliography*: Childs.

Mary Stafford's Letter

For Mrs. Randall London

Dear Couzen

I am soe much ashamed I know not how to write to you but I am sensible of your good humour & therefore makes me rely upon it, therefore first I beg your pardon that I left England without seeing you that I was assured was my freind & that would really pity me, & assist me in the distracted condition I was in. Nothing, Dear Couzen, should have kept me from it, but the Debt I had contracted to you made me ashamed to show my face to you, & now I have set pen to paper I beg your patience to hear the inducements that occasioned my leaving England and all the circumstances that has or doth attend us. One true reason and the greatest, my husband's very earnest desire as well as my own to be just to all the world, endeavouring to pay our debts which I earnestly beg of God I may see done before I dye. Another, alas, is how tender allmost to mention and a sting to my conscience. I mean my dear Mother. The thoughts of her doth most sadly afflict me. I pray God and her to forgive me whatever hath been amiss upon that score. I cannot mention that and my home without the greatest regret imaginable   a very sad companion to me in my passage hither attened with bad weather & allmost constant stormes, such as the Captaine said that in 6 and thirty years' trade to sea, he but once met with the like, and nothing to support such a Voyage. Indeed the Sailers were very kind to us or it had been impossible to have lived. Then when I saw our selves put on Shore in a Country that looked so little inhabited and little to be seen but tress, noe Money & not known by any body, I will leave you to judge whether any thing upon Earth could be more dismall I could have no other thought but the good God that had preserved us in our passage would allso raise some Freinds to have some pity for us & accordingly happening to lodge in a Gentlewoman's house, that was sensible of our very low condition & seeing us inquire for any thing of business whatsoever to get an honest living took nothing for our being there. In which time Mr. Wigfalls brother of Swapthorpe, hearing some of his country people had come, invited us to his house till we could fall into some business; and his sister which is married [till we could fall in] to a house, took my two Children to her house with intention to have had Will prentice but I am very glad that we did not for poor Charles Goodalls sake that served his time with them, but I refer you to the inclosed.[1] I shall now proceed to tell you that we could hardly tell what business we could doe but I undertook to clear starch dress heads & make linen which I continue still to doe, & my husband having provided himself with lancetts in England resolved upon practiseing Physick & Surgery which he has done with sucess beyond his expectations. The dry bellyach[2] is a sad distemper in this Country so as to take away the use of all their limbs, and the flux of which abundance of new comers dyed last Summer, and my husband was soe bad of a feaver for two months I did not expect his life. It is what they call the Seasoning to the country.[3] But I must return to my subject which is to tell you that Mrs. Susannah Wigfall that was before marriage,[4] her neighbour the next plantation a Gentleman had been a Captain of Ships, happened to have a fall from his horse & broke his thigh, my husband was sent to either to undertake it, or goe up and take some care of him till he was better which he did not venturing to set it least it should not succeed well. In the time of his sickness he took a likeing to him altho a great humourist, and sent for me & proposed to put us in a house & plantation of his & there to practise Phisick to teach a school & take Children to board which we doe. He lent us money to buy Medecines, and of the parents of the Children we took we had little necessarys for our house and provision although I must tell you, by the by, is no very high keeping for we are resolved to shift any how if it be possible to accomplish the Main end of our coming; and now my hand is in I care not if I tell you our diet   First I begin with breake[fast] and a dish you meet not with in England: it is Indian Corn ground upon a steel Mill and boiled stiff, and eaten with mil, it is called homony; that is the most plentyfull food in the Country. Sall Beef but very little muttons or indeed fresh meat and that nine pence a pound, and that which is the greatest punishment of all to me is the drinking allmost allways water, for we cannot afford wine, it is dear, and there no bear but what is made of treacle and that but now and then to be met with all, but I take myself as easy as is possible, hoping I shall return home to England where there is no want of any thing. I do assure you the last year it was very hard with me, I have known the want of many a meal but God has supported me. I cannot say but is a good Country for many things and has good comodities in it as I believe soe young a Country can be, soe little inhabited or cultivated, but any place is good to the fortunate, I pray God ours may be reversed. Here is good incouragement for handy crafts men or for husband men that can manage the Land and get a few slaves and can beat them well to make them work hard, here is no living here without. I am not yet worth one, they are solf for Fifty pound a head, I have one I hire for twelve pound a year to doe my work and a White girl I have taken prentice

---

1. No enclosure is extant.

2. Also called "dry gripes," the condition was rampant in the colonies. Its symptoms suggest it may have been lead poisoning (see Childs 3n).

3. Locally, "Seasoning to the country" meant an ailment many newcomers suffered until they adjusted to the new climate and conditions; as Childs suggests, it is more likely that the settlers suffered from infection due to malaria parasites.

4. Susan Wigfall had married David Maybank and lived in Christ Church Parish, indicating this may have been the region in which the Staffords also settled.

for 3 years. I wish I had brought my own Maid with me. I have but 13 boarders yet but believe I shall have more, they are peoples Children of good Fashion and are very kind to us.

Pray, Good Couzen, give our Service to Coz: Woodcock and their Family and please to tell Coz: Ned I beg his pardon for making that distinction, that if it lay in his way or any of his acquaintance to get my husband any Commission here it would doe us a great deal of Service and we should be highly obliged to him. All sorts of English goods sell well here @ 150 or 200 Per Cent. Pray give my humble service to Coz. Petiver & tell him we have the same intention to pay him as well as any body else so soon as please God to make us able; pray tell him I often think of him when I am in the Woods and meet with such swarms of Insects and some very troublesome, there is great quantitys of Snakes allsoe. Be soe kind to give my service to Mrs. Stackden when you see her or any body we are indebted our intentions of paying them. When that is done, I care not how soon I return home and able to assist my dear Mother, and my Children put prentice at home I am then arrived to the height of my wishes. I cannot have one thing to my apprehension to encourage them to their staying hear, but quite the contrary, I hope by that time they are fit to send effects to put them out, for money is but very scarce here as well as in England. I had like to have forgott to tell you that we was offerd by a Landgrave threescore pound a Year and the keeping of our Children, but we was advised to be M[aste]r of our selves, and a little rather then be as servants, indeed Severall Gentlemen since we have been known have been soe kind to offer us their assistance in case we wanted. I have given you an account of our very bare beginning the world a second time and our little creeping on till it please God to throw any else in our way to our advantage, if not I must still be contented. I chose, my dear Coz: to be thus troublesome to you because the same kindness you have formerly done me in writing to me, I hope you will continue to me allthough I have acted soe, and be assured it will be a thousand times more welcome and is more convenient then it is for those in the Country not hearing of oppertunities, which I hope is the only reason I have not heard this year past, which has exceedingly troubled me, for I have not received one little but the spice which my good Freinds were soe kind to gather for to supprot us in our passage; missing of us it came by the next vessels, and was our first beginning here. I pray God to bless them for it, and may he preserve them and theirs, that none of our relations may be such miserable unhappy poor wretches as we, and must have been much more soe if we had not taken this course, fir I saw nothing but misery and ruine on every side, not a possibility to get a piece of Bread, a Gaol for my husband, and want to my self and Children or relying upon my Freinds which I knew would not doe. And the greife it would be to my dear Mother to see all this, and ye reflections of the world upon this, and indeed I could not look upon my Mother without being almost at my wits end. The thoughts are very terrible at this distance, and them though I knew I must undergoe a great deal, none could soe immediate be sensible of it, and might put us in a possability of living at home. I despaired of it; my grief was so great I cared not what did become of me, only my poor Children I always had a dread upon me for them, for I should have thought myself their Murderer, but I hope it will be for their good as well as my own, if please God they get well home, I hope the worst is past. . . .

Mary Stafford

P.S. You may see my, Dear Coz:, by the Date of this I intended it long before this, it should have been at your hand but the Vessell sailed before they went on board, and was taken by the Enemie,[5] soe hope it will beet a surer pasage. . . . our business goes on with Courage. I have increased my lodgers or boarders, to seventeen and with very hard struling compassed half a dozen Cows, and purchased a Negroe man which cost me 55 pound, indeed we were very bare of Cloaths which we were forct to furnish at the extravagant prises they goe at in this Country which has been a great hindrance to us but hope to struggle through all if please to spare us Life and health which has not been good this hot season, which has been much hotter then last summer for we have been as if we were baked inan Oven and Multitudes of People died. The heat occasions me swelled Legs, pains in my Back and indeed disorders all over me, but the greatest is very weak Eyes, upon any little Cold scarce able to look up they are soe sore, in short it is allmost impossible to live if people live not extreamly temporate, but I hope it will please God to spare us one, 2, or 3 years, that I may return with my poor Children prentice and with a little to put me in a way of living, and hope then my husband will then get what will make us easy and himself too, when he will have little charge otherwise. . . . I am Dear Coz: allways your ever obliged

Mary Stafford

Mr. Stafford presents his Service
Augt. 23, 1711

Elizabeth Bland (fl. 1735)

As with many of the earliest settlers who did not hold military commissions, nothing is known of Elizabeth Bland's life other than as recorded in her only extant letter. Bland was a widow with one child, James, who settled in Savannah, Georgia, in the early 1730s. Her unhappiness at conditions in Georgia led her to request to return to England. Bland's financial status was questionable in 1735, but her ability to write and certain class assumptions that are revealed in her letter suggest she may have been of the middle or upper classes at one time. Further, her son came to Georgia with a letter of recommendation from James Oglethorpe, the British general who founded

5. The letter was written during Queen Anne's War.

the colony of Georgia in 1733.[1] Elizabeth Bland directed her appeal for the right to depart from Georgia to Thomas Causton, First Bailiff and Storekeeper, and thereby the most important official in the colony during Oglethorpe's absence. Causton refused her request under the claim that she had come to America at the expense of the colony's Trustees, which she denied (although it may have been true). Bland continued her appeal in the following letter of June 14, 1735, to Oglethorpe. What Bland could not have known was that Causton had identified her to Oglethorpe as a troublemaker and, in an age-old tradition for women who refuse to "know their place," raised questions about her sanity: "she is very troublesom to the whole Place and every one believes her to be mad."[2] Bland's letter is that of a determined, but hardly insane, woman.

Work: Letter. *Bibliography*: Coleman and Ready.

Letter of Elizabeth Bland

Savannah June the 14th 1735

Good S[r]

After a ten weeks dissogreable Voyage in a very bad Ship & rude Commander wanting every thing in this life wee Arriv'd at Charls town from whence the passinger that wou'd goe were Conveyd in a pettyauger to Georgia but I and Some others remain at Charls town being very ill for meer want because had not eat nor drinkd nothing but bisket & watter for Seven week & three days before I landed   I not being able to lay in fresh provissions & my Stomach cou'd not bear the Ships provission & the litle Licqure mr Spooner laid in we was rob'd of by the Sailers So that when we Caim out to See we had notthing but Watter to drink, & the barberouse Company & Capt that was in the Cabin took all occassions to pick quarills with us & by that means to Avoid Assisting us which they thought they must doe if wee remain all friends &c.   the litle Goods I brought as well as all the passingers was quite Spoild by reason of the badness of the Vessill which was but a one deck Vessel & indeed So Small that it Seemd a presumption to take Such a voyage in her. at Carolina I heard So terable a Charicter of Georgia that I resolv'd never to See it & had gott a pasage for England in a very good Ship but hearing my Son was not well at Georgia I was resolvd to go & see him before I left the Country[3] the Ship I was to go in

1. This region was originally inhabited by the Creek and Cherokee. In the sixteenth century, De Soto visited the region, and it was an area of dispute between the Spanish and English when Oglethorpe's followers settled there.

2. Letter from Thomas Causton to James Oglethorpe, dated July 7, 1735, from Savannah (*Colonial Records* 437–441).

3. James, still a minor, had purportedly been separated from his mother upon landing. In the July 7, 1735, letter, Causton indicated to Oglethrope that he had set out a lot for James Bland and found a German family to work as servants for him; however, James's last known whereabouts were in May 1737 when he was listed as part of a company that had settled at Fort Argyle. Thereafter, the only official notation about him is that he "Ran away."

Not being to Sail under a fortnight or three weeks time when I came to Georg^a Mr Causton promisd not to detain me against my Will but to my great Surprise I have lost my liberty & must not return home to my Native Land without leav from the Trusttees when Sr You are Sencable I had Nothing from them either for my passage or otherwise neither woud I have Sold my freedom for ten thousand pounds Sterling & as I have done Nothing to forfeit my liberty hope I am not to Loose it there Can be no greater Injurry to the Success of the Colloney then my letters wou'd be Shoud I acquaint the world of my Loss of liberty but I hear them not whilst I have good Mr Oglethorp to Apply to for redress S^r the Country is so very hott I am not Capable of any industry in it & it is so very Sickly that Such Numbers Of all aiges dye dayly which terrfyes me So much I am not able to injoy the least thought of life hear oh S^r had I thought of the least restraint all the Land in amerreca Should not have purchas'd my freedom I therefore beg Your positive Command to these people in power to let me go & hope a Check into the bargain for detaining me who am a free woman & no ways Confinde by lott or otherwise I have taken nothing from Stores neither will I & Caustin will not pay me the five pound You was pleased to order me I pitty my poor Son & wish him in the place of Your meanest Servant for they are in a Land of health liberty & property but did king Georg Use his people as they are Used here he woud Soon loose his Crown Such lying Such Scandle & false Swearing as I never heard in my life in Short its a very hell upon Earth & I beg & intreat Your orders for my deliverance as soon as possible I cou'd inform You of a great many Affairs You woud be Glade & very Sorry to hear but dair not write them in Short I tremble all the time I writ this for Shou'd I be ketch'd writing this I should be made a Close prissoner & allowd Nothing oh Cou'd dear Mr Oglethorp See & hear the Complaints of people hear it wou'd greiv You to the very Soul & it is impossible my Son Shou'd do any thing hear without four or five Servants he will not be able to work himselfe in this Country if he lives he is now very ill of the bloody flux but wont write You of it oh S^r send for us home or we Shall Certainly loose our lives in this terable place, there is differant Sort of people fitt for it but God know wee are not & Sence I can be of no Service to the Colony I hope You will take Such Cair to Send we May not loose our life hear provissions are very indiferant but they Say much Mended I can't Eat with any Satisfacttion my Stomach is very bad You was pleasd to order me to be very perticularr therefor hope You will pardon this long Scrole which tho I am very ill my liberty is so much at hart I can't for beer repetition & from this Moment Shall never enjoy life till I hear from my only friend & deliverer & May God Allmighty the rewarder of all Good Send You long life & every blessing Added to itt is & Shall be the Constant prayers of

> Dear S^r
> Your Most Obbliged
> & Obedient Servant
> E BLAND

Caustin hass put me into a house instead of a Lodging I told him You only Mentiond a lodging I thought but he Says he Shall have a great Many people

Coming & he must have rooms for them So that I am to be Stuff'd in with all Sorts Sick & well when they come   the house is without a Chimney & I see no Sign of any   for my Son they Say he can't build without Money & indeed the best favour You can do my poor Son is to Send for him when You Send for me for we Shall do no Good hear & I would serve my betters in England rather than be a Slave to such ville wretches as govern hear
(To James Oglethorp, Esqr In Old Palace Yard
Westminster.)

Spiritual Narratives

The Ghost Bride and The Ghost Wife (Pawnee)

Before the nineteenth century, the Pawnees were an agricultural people and part of a federation of plains tribes that lived in the area of the Platte River in what is now the state of Nebraska. The religion of the Pawnee, like many other tribal religions, reflected the dual-gendered nature of their deities. Tirawa Atius, their main deity, was a father figure; but corn, their foremost means of subsistence, was a sacred mother figure. The Pawnees believe in a powerful supernatural world, and the two stories that follow explain how the tribe learned that there was a spiritual world and an afterlife.

Bibliography: Grinnell.

The Ghost Bride

In a place where we used to have a village, a young woman died just before the tribe started on a hunt. When she died, they dressed her up in her finest clothes, and buried her, and soon after this the tribe started on a hunt.

A party of young men had gone off to visit another tribe, and they did not get back until after this girl had died and the tribe had left the village. Most of the party did not go back to the village, but met the tribe and went with them on the hunt. Among the young men who had been away was one who had loved this girl who had died. He went back alone to the village. It was empty and silent, but before he reached it, he could see, at a distance, someone sitting on top of a lodge. When he came near, he saw that it was the girl he loved. He did not know that she had died, and he wondered to see her there alone, for the time was coming when he would be her husband and she his wife. When she saw him coming, she came down from the top of the lodge and went inside.

197

When he came close to her, he spoke and said, "Why are you here alone in the village?" She answered him, "They have gone off on the hunt. I was sulky with my relations, and they went off and left me behind." The man wanted her now to be his wife, but the girl said to him, "No, not yet. Later we will be married." She said to him, "You must not be afraid. To-night there will be dances here; the ghosts will dance." This is an old custom of the Pawnees. When they danced they used to go from one lodge to another, singing and dancing. So now, when the tribe had gone and the village was deserted, the ghosts did this. He could hear them coming along the empty streets, and going from one lodge to another. They came into the lodge where he was and danced about, and whooped and sang, and sometimes they almost touched him, and he came pretty near being scared.

The next day, the young man persuaded the girl to go on with him, and follow the tribe, to join it on the hunt. They started to travel together, and she promised him that she would surely be his wife, but not until the time came. They overtook the tribe; but before they got to the camp, the girl stopped. She said, "Now we have arrived, but you must go first to the village, and prepare a place for me. Where I sleep, let it be behind a curtain. For four days and four nights I must remain behind this curtain. Do not speak of me. Do not mention my name to anyone."

The young man left her there and went into the camp. When he got to his lodge, he told a woman, one of his relations, to go out to a certain place and bring in a woman, who was waiting there for him. His relative asked him, "Who is the woman?" To avoid speaking her name, he told who were her father and mother. His relative, in surprise, said, "It cannot be that girl, for she died some days before we started on the hunt."

When the woman went to look for the girl, she could not find her. The girl had disappeared. The young man had disobeyed her, and had told who she was. She had told him that she must stay behind a curtain for four days, and that no one must know who she was. Instead of doing what she had said, he told who she was, and the girl disappeared because she was a ghost. If he had obeyed the girl, she would have lived a second time upon earth. That same night this young man died in his sleep.

Then the people were convinced that there must be a life after this one.

The Ghost Wife

One time there were living together a man and his wife. They had a young child. The woman died. The man was very sad, and he mourned for his wife.

One night he took the child in his arms, and went out from the village to the place where his wife was buried, and he stood over the grave, and mourned for his wife. The little child was very helpless, and cried all the time. The man's heart was sick with grief and loneliness. Late in the night, he fell asleep, fainting and worn out with sorrow. After awhile he awoke, and when he looked up, there was a form standing by him. The form standing there was the one who had died. She spoke to her husband, and said, "You are very unhappy here. There is a place to go where we would not be unhappy. Where I have been, nothing bad happens to one. Here, you never know what evil will come to you. You and the child had better come with me."

The man did not want to die. He said to her, "No. It will be better if you can come back to us. We love you. If you were with us, we would be unhappy no longer."

For a long time they discussed this, to decide which one should go to the other. At length the man by his persuasions overcame her, and the woman agreed to come back. She said to the man, "If I am to come back, you must do exactly as I tell you for four nights. For four days the curtain must remain let down before my sleeping place; it must not be raised; no one must look behind it."

The man did as he had been told, and after four days had passed, the curtain was lifted, and the woman came out from behind it. Then they all saw her, first her relations, and afterward the whole tribe. Her husband and her child were very glad, and they lived happily together.

A long time after this, the man took another wife. The first wife was always pleasant and good-natured, but the new one was bad-tempered, and after some time she grew jealous of the first woman, and quarreled with her. At length, one day the last married woman became angry with the other, and called her bad names, and finally said to her, "You ought not to be here. You are nothing but a ghost, anyway."

That night when the man went to bed, he lay down, as was his custom, by the side of his first wife. During the night he awoke, and found that his wife had disappeared. She was seen no more. The next night after this happened, the man and the child both died in sleep. The wife had called them to her. They had gone to that place where there is a living.

This convinced everybody that there is a hereafter.

Two Girls and the Dancers (Zuni)

The search for a guardian spirit was a common rite of passage. Although finding one's spiritual intercessor was typically considered more important for males, many legends, such as the following Zuni tale, present the process of finding a guardian spirit as an integral part of young females' maturation as well. Unlike many other societies, the Zuni allowed women to join some of their secret religious orders, and the Kotikili order required a priestess as its leader. Each new priestess was carefully selected by the elderly priestess, who taught her protégé the masked dances in which she was personified as the goddesses of the Zuni religion.

Bibliography: Clark, E.; Niethammer; Zuni People.

Two Girls and the Dancers

Years ago when the supernatural beings came to earth as kachinas they danced during a feast as the villagers gathered around to watch them. The kachinas were the rain dancers and in the group there were two handsome young men who danced without masks. When all the kachinas were finished with their dance they started to file out of the plaza. Two young maidens had been watching the dances and were very taken by the dancers who performed without the shield of masks.

When the kachinas began to leave the plaza to depart for their own land, the two maidens ran up behind them. Eventually the kachinas noticed the girls and asked them if they wished to come along. Of course the girls wanted to go, so the kachinas consented to take them to their homeland.

The girls stayed with the kachinas for some time and were well cared for. But one day the kachinas approached them and told them, "Our children, we think it will be better if you return to your own land. We do not think it best for you to stay among us. You still have a long life span ahead of you."

The kachinas told the girls that they would perform all the dances for them so the girls should watch closely and memorize what they saw so they could take the information back to their people. The kachinas did this because they decided they should no longer go to the villages, for more people might wish to leave with them.

The next day the kachinas took the girls to the edge of their village. The maidens were greeted by their relatives, who asked where they had been. The girls replied, "We were sent back because we have a long time before we can join our ancestors. But we were shown all of the dances, and we remember every detail. You will make replicas of the dancers we have seen, and from now on we will preserve them. The supernaturals will come by breath in the winds and join us. When the dancing stops, the spirits alone will return to the land of our ancestors, and that way the lives of our people will remain on this land until their time comes."

So it was at that time the kachinas of today were created from the detailed descriptions of the two girls. From that time on the people asked for blessings with prayer and rituals carried out by the kachina cult.

Sister Crackbone (fl. c. 1640)

During the years 1637 to 1645, Thomas Shepard recorded conversion narratives as professed by the working-class members of his congregation in Newtown (Cambridge), Massachusetts. Among the members were Gilbert Crackbone and his wife, for whom Shepard designated no name other than "Brother Crackbone's Wife." The Crackbones probably came to New England in early 1637, and they thrived in Shepard's community, owning land and a home on

Garden Street. If, like so many women in the early years of the Massachusetts Bay Colony, Sister Crackbone remains a nearly anonymous figure for us, we can detect in her narrative a decidedly woman-centered perspective on coming to grace. The narrative was given publicly shortly after a fire had destroyed her home, and the psychological consequences of that experience for Crackbone are embedded in the text. Although the conversion narratives were expected to conform to a specified pattern (confession of sin, profession of faith, and finally the embracing of the Covenant), they were also, as Patricia Caldwell has demonstrated, the earliest form of public expression for lay citizens in the New World.

Works: Conversion narrative. Bibliography: Caldwell.

Sister Crackbone's Conversion Narrative

Her brother sending for her to London in a good house, there I considered my course and ways especially of one sin.[1] And thought the Lord would never accept me more and was terrified and out of hope. And hearing I Isaiah—white as snow[2]—I had some hope. And hearing out of Mr. Smith's book[3] what Lord required viz. the heart and if heart given then eye and foot were given. And so I wished my parents knew me. And so being married and having poor means and having afflictions on my child and took from me and so troubled what became of my children. And to hell I thought it was because I had not prayed for them. And so came to New England. I forgot the Lord as the Israelites did and when I had a new house yet I thought I had no new heart. And means did not profit me and so doubted of all Lord had done, yet hearing when Lord will do good He takes away all ornaments. And so thought of seeking after the ordinances but I knew not whether I was fit. Yet heard I was under wings of Christ, one of them yet not under both. And so saw sloth and sluggishness so I prayed to the Lord to make me fit for church fellowship and Lord. And the more I prayed the more temptation I had. So I gave up and I was afraid to sing because to sing a lie, Lord teach me and I'll follow thee[4] and heard Lord will break the will of His last work. And seeing house burned down, I thought it was just and mercy to save life of the child and that I saw not after again my children there. And as my spirit was fiery so to burn all I had, and hence prayed Lord would send fire of word, baptize me with fire.[5] And since the Lord hath set my heart at liberty.

1. Since the narratives were transcribed by Thomas Shepard, it is (as with all oral narratives) impossible to know if the shifts in pronouns are Crackbone's or Shepard's. Another woman in the collection does appear to speak of herself entirely in the third person.

2. Isaiah 1:18.

3. Four "Smiths" published works at this time with which Crackbone may have been familiar: Henry Smith, John Smith, Miles Smith, and Samuel Smith.

4. Psalm 86:11. Churches in the Massachusetts Bay Colony used The Whole Book of Psalmes (London, 1562) as their hymnal until The Bay Psalm Book was published at Cambridge, Massachusetts, in 1640.

5. Matthew 3:11; Luke 3:16.

Mary Traske and Margaret Smith

(fl. 1660)

In a co-authored letter written while they were imprisoned, Mary Traske and Margaret Smith delineated one of the great paradoxes of the settlement of New England: having left Old England under the guise of seeking the right to practice Calvinism in their own fashion, the Puritans subsequently denied similar rights to other religious sects and oppressed dissenters with a harshness often equivalent to that perpetrated against them in their native country. This early Quaker document also furnishes us with a record of the determination, intelligence, and highly literate status of these two seventeenth-century women.

Works: Correspondence. *Bibliography*: Stedman and Hutchinson.

Joint Letter from Mary Traske and Margaret Smith, Written in 1660

To thee, John Endicott,[1] and the rest of the rulers of this jurisdiction, who are given up to fight against the Lord and his truth in this day wherein it is springing forth, and by the comeliness of it hath the Lord our God constrained us to take up the cross and follow him through great trials and sufferings as to the outward. And herein we can rejoice that we are counted worthy and called thereunto to bear a testimony against a cruel and hard-hearted people, who are slighting the day of their visitation and foolishly requiting the Lord for his goodness, and shamefully entreating his hidden ones whom he hath sent amongst you to call you from the evil of your ways, that ye might come with them to partake of his love and feel his life and power in your own hearts; that with us ye might have been brought to be subject to the higher power, Christ Jesus; whom you should have been obedient unto, and hearkened to his judgments while he stood at the door and knocked (for he will not always strive with man), and then it should have been well with you. But seeing you are gone from this that leadeth into tenderness, love and meekness, and to do unto all as you would be done unto; therefore you are given up unto a Spirit of Error and hardness of heart and blindness of mind; the eye of your minds being blinded by the god of this world; so that you cannot see our life which is hid with Christ in God, who is become our light and life, and hope of glory, and our exceeding great reward; in whom we do rejoice. Yea, surely the God of Jacob[2] is with us whatever you may be able to say against us; for behold the Lord

---

1. Endecott was a Puritan magistrate.
2. Biblically, Jacob is a symbol of faith and obedience (Gen. 29:18); ultimately, he became the founder of the Hebrew nation (Gen. 49:1–28).

our God is arising as a mighty and terrible one to plead the cause of his people and to clear the cause of the innocent; but surely He will in nowise acquit the guilty who have shed the blood of the innocent; and you shall assuredly feel his judgments who have wilfully put forth your hands against his Chosen. You have cut off the righteous from amongst you and are still taking counsel against the Lord, to proceed against more of his people, but this know, the Lord our God will confound your counsel and lay your glory in the dust. Unto whom will you flee for help, and whither will ye go to hide yourselves? For verily the Lord will strip off all your coverings, for you are not covered with the Spirit of the Lord, therefore the woe is gone out against you; for your place of defence is a refuge of lies and under falsehoods you have hid yourselves.

Woe, woe unto you, for you have forsaken the Lord, the fountain of living waters, and are greedily swallowing the polluted waters that comes through the stinking channel of your hireling masters, unclean spirits, whom Christ cries woe against and who cannot cease from sin, having hearts exercised with covetous practices. Woe unto them (saith the Scripture), for they have run greedily after the error of Balaam[3] who loved the wages of unrighteousness; and are seeking enchantments against the seed of Jacob; their divinations against Israel the Lord will confound; and all your wicked counsel bring to naught. Woe unto you that decree unrighteous decrees and write grievousness, which you have prescribed to turn away the poor and needy from their right. Have you not sold yourselves to work wickedness, and are strengthening yourselves in your abominations till the measure of your iniquity be full? Surely the overflowing scourge will pass over you and sweep away your refuge of lies, and your covenant with hell shall be disannulled; for lo, destruction and misery is in your way and the way of peace you do not know, for you are gone from the good old way after your own ways, therefore the way of holiness is hid from your eyes. Oh, that you had owned the day of your visitation before it had been too late, and had hearkened to the voice of his servants whom He hath sent unto you again and again in love and tenderness to your souls; but ye would not hearken unto the Lord when He called, therefore when ye cry and call He will not hear you. Although you may call unto him yet He will not answer; He will laugh at your calamity when it cometh, for you have set at naught all his counsel, and have chosen rather to walk in your own counsel. But this know, that if ye had hearkened to the counsel of the Lord, the light, which is now your condemnation, and had waited there to know his will, then you should have known it; and then these wicked laws had never been made nor prosecuted by you, which you have made in your own wills, contrary to the law of God, which is pure and leadeth all that yieldeth obedience to it into purity and holiness of life. And for our being obedient to this law which the Lord hath written in our hearts, we are hated and persecuted by you who are in Cain's nature[4] murdering the just; yea, surely the cause is

3. Balaam, a biblical prophet who advocated natural morality, predicting God would curse Israel for its evilness; later Christians believed that Balaam's error was in not recognizing the higher morality through which God may redeem a sinner, without forfeiting His own justice (Rom. 3:26).

4. As the first murderer recorded in the Bible, Cain is a symbol of man's natural desperate state that needs grace and atonement (Eph. 1:7; Col. 1:14).

the Lord's, for which we have suffered all this time, and the battle is the Lord's, and He will arise and stand up for them that faithfully bear forth their testimony to the end. And ye shall be as broken vessels before him, which cannot be joined together again; therefore fear and tremble before the Lord, who is coming upon you as a thief in the night; from whom you shall not be able to hide yourselves, and will reward you according to your works; whose judgments are just; and He is risen to plead with the unjust rulers, priests and people, who are joined together in a profession of godliness, and of glorying in it, but denying the power thereof in them where it appears. But your glorying will be turned into shame and confusion of face, and your beauty will be as the fading flower which suddenly withereth away; and this you shall find to be true in the day when the Lord shall accomplish it upon you. And we have written to clear our consciences, and if ye account us your enemies for speaking the truth, and heat the furnace of our affliction hotter, yet know we shall not fall down and worship your wills; neither esteem all the dumb idols, after which you are led, of no other use but to be thrown aside to the moles and the bats; for what are the shadows, if it were of good things to come, to the substance? And that which seemed glorious hath no glory in respect of that which excelleth; and all the sufferings that we have endured from you for Christ have not at all marred his visage to us, but we still see more beauty in him; well knowing, that as they did unto him so they do unto us, and how they are come to pass, we remember that He said these things.

Mary Traske,
Margaret Smith.

From your house of Correction where we have been unjustly restrained from
our children and habitations, one of us above ten months, and the other
about eight; and where we are yet continued by your oppressors that
know no shame;
Boston, 21st of the 10th Month, 1660.

Bathsheba Bowers (c. 1672–1718)

Born in Charlestown, Massachusetts, probably in 1672, Bathsheba Bowers was the third daughter of Elizabeth Dunster and Benanuel Bowers's twelve children. Her parents were English Quakers who had emigrated to New England before her birth. Little is known of Bathsheba's life other than what is revealed in her one extant manuscript, *An Alarm Sounded*, which was published in 1709. Her niece, Ann Bolton, resided for some time with Bowers and Ann's remembrances of her aunt have added some insights into the author's life. Although Bowers's parents chose to confront the persecution they were suffering at the hands of the Massachusetts Puritans, they sent Bathsheba and her sisters to live in Philadelphia.

A highly religious woman with distinct writing talents, Bathsheba chose not to marry but rather to establish her own home in the Quaker City and to seclude herself therein. She preferred a simple life of gardening, reading, and, especially, writing. The following excerpt from her spiritual autobiography exhibits her extraordinary strength of character, her frustration over the criticism of publishing women's writings, and her insistence upon the validity of her own spiritual experiences. Bowers died in South Carolina in 1718.

Works: *An Alarm sounded to prepare the inhabitants of the World to meet the Lord in the way of his judgment* (1709). *Bibliography:* Cowell; Potts; Shea; Watkins; Wright, L.

An ALARM Sounded . . .

. . . Why it pleased the Almighty to bend his Bow and set me as a Mark for his Arrow, not only from my Youth, but even from my very Infancy up, I know not but even so it has been; for to the best of my remembrance I was but about six or seven years of Age when first I had strange and numerous Apprehensions of a future state, and a fear to dye, and after to be cast into Hell, would make such strong Impressions of Horror upon my Spirit, which caused me to weep and tremble, and often to wish I had never been born. And the weight and inward sence and feelings of those things keeps me in great awe before the Lord. Well, I arrived to the age of about fourteen years, and then Pride, the chief evil I was naturally inclined to, became a very potent Enemy against me; and tho' I was but young I found I was in an evil case, by the strong propensity and inclination to the Influences of evil, not that I was sensible of the Deformity of evil it self, no. but because I was smitten, pincht and restrained in my Libertine progress; for I really believed that Pride and Luxury, and abundance of outward Riches to uphold it, was the chiefest good; and on the other hand, to be limited to Obedience, Humility and taking up the Cross, was an intolerable Confinement, but under this, considered, I was afraid going to Hell was worse, so I continued in this Condition some years, being extreamly addicted to decking up my self, going abroad and keeping of wild Company; but this state was rendered very uncomfortable to me, because I was still followed with a secret terror what the evil would be. Sometimes I should wish and hope there was no God, and sometimes pray, that if there was, he would by any means bring me nearer to himself. Thus it was with me till I entered into the 19th year of my Age. And then at the latter end of the Summer, I was visited with a violent Feaver, which brought very extream pain upon me. . . .[1] I thought now was the time that I had from my Infancy feared: now I must dye, and to Hell I must go, as the reward of my Pride; that was chief thing presented before me; and in this condition I made many Protesta-

---

1. Bowers had reason for concern; a smallpox epidemic was devastating the area. Her brother died from the disease shortly after the onset of her illness.

tions and Promises to my self, if God would graciously grant me a Reprieve, and give me a little longer time, which I thought I had no reason to expect; but as my Terrors within, so my Distemper without continually increased, tho' I had been urgent for the assistance of the Doctor, and the application of what might be proper for my Relief, but it was so violent that I expected no other but in a few hours or minutes to be choaked, being in extream thirst, and every thing I took forcing its passage thorow my Nose. And in this Distress I earnestly desired some finall Beer to be given me, promising to my self, that if I could swallow that, it should be a sign to me that God had not forsaken me. And when I came to try the experiment, this found passage down very comfortably, which was an exceding joy to me, insomuch that it forced my feeble Body upon my knees, to give thanks to him who I did not know but might have mercy on my Soul, which I supposed to be in a very dangerous Condition at that time; but this spark was soon blown out by the returns of my fear, terror and anguish of Spirit, which remained strong upon me for many days, having blindness without and darkness within, every night I expected to dye; and in my slumbers thought I was actually in Hell; but his Judgments he mixt with Mercy, and lifted me out of the horrible Pit, and gave respit for a time.

And after some time, when I was pretty well recovered of my Distemper, only I remained weak, as I was one morning lying in my Bed, ruminating in my mind, and hoping the bitterness of Death was past, on a suddain, before I was aware, I found my self overcome with a divine Sweetness, which all my life before I had been a stranger to, this made me say, in the words of *David*, *O Lord, if ever I forget thee, let me be forgotten by thee; and if I prefer thee not above my chiefest joy, let my Tongue cleave to the roof of my Mouth.* But my pleasant Theam soon folded up, and the divine Ray withdrew, leaving this word with me, to wit, *Obedience is better than Sacrifice;* and also, a strong Injunction upon me to leave off my little Fineries, and vain Complements, and to take up the much despised saying *Thee* and *Thou* to a single Person. This again brought a strange Impression of horror over me, and raised a great unwillingness and strong Reasonings offered themselves, and a foolish shame got the dominion over me, which altogether brought me even within a hairs breadth of rebelling; but I awakened not long before upon good ground; I submitted, tho' it was not without Tears. But soon after I found it was to double advantage; for whereas I took delight in nothing but reading Romances,[2] decking up and receiving and giving Visits, (not that by my saying this I am about to represent my self as a Gentlewoman by Birth, which had nothing else to do; No, for my Mother found me other imployment beside, tho' it was often sore against my will; but now I was under a total alteration; for having been kept from visiting by reason of my illness, about half a year, my propencity to that exercise was pretty much abated, tho' I suppose it would soon have renewed its strength; but I was ashamed to see or to be seen of my former Acquain-

2. Ann Bolton, describing Bathsheba's collection of books, remarked: "She had several wrote by a female hand filled with dreams and visions and a thousand Romantic Notions of her seeing Various sorts of Beasts and Bulls in the Heavens" (quoted in Potts 112).

tance and Companions, because I durst do no other than appear in a way that was very contemptible in my own eyes, and I suppose no less in the eyes of others; but it was not long before this Cross lost its sting, and I became not only easy, but pleased with my great Change of affairs; and I began to take delight in Gardening, and applyed my self, with pleasure, to the Contemplation of Matters Philosophical and Divine. But this was not the end of my progress in trouble, as by the sequel you will find. For soon after the old Accuser and Troubler was let loose against me, and represented before me, That now I had submitted to this Light within, I must be obedient and perform all the preposterous Actions, but above other things, the fear of going Naked[3] was sharp upon me; this was like a Sword to my Nature, which from my Childhood had been bashful, to an extream; but I soon got over this Terror; but it continued with me to be mighty full of Thoughts and Considerations, passing and repassing in a perpetual Motion, sometimes one fear wou'd be uppermost, and sometimes another; but at length it was fixt upon me to believe, I was still short in the faith of Christ crucified, and my work not yet finished; the whole systim of Religion was become a very intricate knotty thing to me, and if I might, I should have been very willing to have let it all alone, but I was entered in the list, and cou'd by no means free my self; and since it was so that I cou'd not get out, I thought it was best for me to be industrious to get Instruction; but I found that Men nor Books cou'd not do it, and to apply my self to God I was afraid, remembring the smart of that teaching I had received. . . . And then I considered I had heard great talk of great matters in *Pennsilvania*, and being willing to try that experiment, I prepared my self, and came over. . . .

Jane Fenn Hoskens (1694–?)

Jane Fenn was born in London in 1694 to religious parents. Although "strictly educated" in the Church of England, her early years were relatively happy and a time during which she developed her singing and musical talents. At age sixteen, however, beset with a near fatal illness, she made a contract with God: if her life was spared, "the remaining part of my days should be dedicated to his service." Thereafter, she began the extraordinary life that led her to the "New World," to a new religion, and to untold public attention for a young woman in the eighteenth century. Her intelligence, independence, and dedication to fulfilling her promise also led her into controversy. Although the 1771 publication of her life as a public preacher was undoubtedly prepared as an answer to her critics, it is surprisingly free of defensive rhetorical gestures.

3. A practice among some early Quakers; their nakedness was meant to signify the spiritual "nakedness" of the times.

As one observer noted, Hoskens was "of a tender spirit, but weighty and awful in prayer," and that powerful presence and dedication to her profession is evidenced in her autobiography, as is her careful attention to the deeds of the women who worked beside her.

Works: *The Life and Spiritual Sufferings of That Faithful Servant of Christ, Jane Hoskens, A Public Preacher among the People called Quakers* (Philadelphia, 1771). *Bibliography:* Davis, R. H.

The Life and Spiritual Sufferings of . . . Jane Hoskens

. . . *Pennsylvania* was still in my mind, the thought continued that if I was among strangers, I could better serve God (though I had no thought of leaving the profession[1] I was brought up in, nor had I any acquaintance with Friends or knowledge of their principles.) But my friends being all so averse to my going, put me upon making several attempts to get away, unknown to them, but was prevented; hereupon my mother took occasion to lay before me the danger and difficulties of one of my years and circumstances might be subjected to, in such an undertaking, which had such weight with me, that I was again diverted from it. But after some time I grew very uneasy . . . that I was made willing to forego every thing else, to pursue what I believed to be my duty, and concluded, that whatever I suffered, I would not delay any longer, but embrace the first opportunity of going to *Pennsylvania*, provided the Almighty would go with me, and direct my steps, which like a little child I humbly begged he might be graciously pleased to do. In a little time the way was opened. One *Robert Davis*, a Welchman, with his wife and two daughters, were going to settle in *Philadelphia;* a friend in whom I could confide told me of their going, and went with me to them; we soon agreed, in the following manner. That he should pay for my passage, and wait 'till I could earn the money on the other side of the water, for which he accepted my promise without note or bond, or my being bound by indenture in the usual manner.

Under these circumstances I came into this land. . . . We arrived in *Philadelphia* the sixteenth day of the third month, 1712, in the nineteenth year of my age; as soon as I was landed I was provided a place, among people of repute, of my own society . . . [but] the enemy of all good, was still unwearied in his attempts against me, for having learned in my native country to sing, he stirred up those with whom I now lived, to draw me into that vain amusement, which, as I plainly saw it was a snare of his, it brought trouble and uneasiness over my mind, and after I had been in *Philadelphia* somewhat more than a quarter of a year, *Robert Davis* insisted I should sign indentures, binding myself a servant for four years, to a person that was an utter stranger to me, by which means he would have made considerable advantage to himself; but as this was contrary to our agreement before-mentioned, (which I was willing to comply with to the utmost of my power) . . . I thought it best to withstand him in it,

---

1. That is, her professed faith, the Church of England.

let the consequences be what it would; whereupon he had recourse to the law, and by process laid me under confinement: this was a trying circumstance. I was a poor young creature among strangers, and being far separated from my natural friends they could not redress my grievances nor hear my complaints: But the Lord heard my cries and raised me up many Friends, who visited me in this situation and offered me money to pay *Davis* for my passage, according to contract, but I could not accept even of this kindness, because I was well assured *Philadelphia* was not to be the place of my settlement. . . . The principal of four families living at *Plymouth*, who had several children, agreed to purchase a sober young woman, as a school-mistress to instruct them in reading, &c. And on their applying to their friends in town, I was recommended for that service. When we saw each other, I perceived it my place to go with them, wherefore, on their paying *Davis* twelve pounds currency, being the whole of his demand against me, I bound myself to them by indenture, for the term of three years, and went chearfully with them to the aforesaid place. . . .[2]

It was in the year 1719, I came to *David Loyd's*, but did not travel far abroad until the year 1722, when having the consent of friends, and their certificate for that purpose, between that time and the year 1725, I accompanied my before mentioned friend *Elizabeth Lewis*, on a religious visit to friends in *Maryland*, *Virginia*, and *North-Carolina*, then returning home, we afterwards went to *Barbadoes*, and from thence took shipping and landed on *Rhode-Island*, and visited that place, *Nantucket*, *New-England*, *Long-Island*, the *Jersies*, our own province, the counties of *New-Castle*, *Kent*, and *Sussex* on *Delaware*, the eastern shore of *Maryland*, and again into Virginia.

It was in the year 1725, that we visited *Barbadoes*, in all which journeys and voyages we were true yoke-fellows; sympathizing with each other in, and under, the various exercises whether of body or mind, which we had to pass through. She was sound in the ministry, and wherever we were led, she was of great and good service. I always preferred her for the works sake; her conduct out of meetings, was exemplary, which preached aloud. I must add, she was no busy body; we meddled not with other peoples concerns, whether in or out of meeting; she was of great service to me, and I hope the love which subsisted between us when young, will remain to each other forever; mine is as strong to her as then, for which I am truly thankful to the author of all goodness.

In the year 1726, I travelled with *Abigail Bowles* (from *Ireland*) through the lower counties on *Delaware*, the eastern shore of *Maryland*, *Virginia*, *Cape-May*, the *Egg-harbours*, and other parts of *New Jersey*, and through this province; in which journeys we travelled about one thousand seven hundred miles. . . . On the fourteenth of the second month 1728, I came to *Whitehaven*, and on the 16th went on board the ship *Reserve*, *John Nicholson*, master, bound for *Dublin*, *Ireland*, where we arrived safe the eighteenth. I was at most of the

2. These people were Quakers; during her three years in their community, Hoskens learned their religious principles, met Grace and David Lloyd, with whom she stayed in Chester, and was supported by her friend, Elizabeth Lewis, in her endeavors to speak in Meeting. The Lloyds "adopted" Jane and granted her "liberty to go wherever truth leads."

meetings of that kingdom, had meetings in many places where no friends lived, and visited friends in their families, within the city of *Dublin*. Generally in many opportunities which I had, both among friends and others, it evidently appeard that counsel was unfolded to the people. The doctrine of truth descended as the small rain upon the tender grass, whereby many were refreshed, and a living greenness appeared; those of other societies were many of them tender, and well satisfied with the visits, and some among them appeared ripe for information into friends principles, so that the faithful had frequently cause to rejoice in the wonderful condescension and loving kindness of the merciful creator of heaven and earth, from whom all good comes. . . .

In the year 1742–3, I went a second time to *Barbadoes*, in company with *Rebecca Minshall;* from *Barbadoes* we took shipping for *Rhode-Island*, and visited that place and *New-England*. In the year 1744, I had a certificate to go a second time to *Maryland, Virginia* and *Carolina*, in company with *Margaret Churchman*, concerning which visit I could say much, but it may suffice to remark that it appeared to me to be a time of gathering, and great openess among people of various ranks, who followed us from meeting to meeting, treating us with respect, and the marks of real love and affection; but knowing we had nothing valuable of ourselves, I attribute all to divine goodness, who opened the way for us, and is alone worthy. *Margaret* sometimes appeared in public, and I thought to good purpose, and was to me a good companion. In the year 1747 I performed a second visit to the churches of Christ in *England* and *Ireland;* I had hitherto underwent many close trials and provings in my pilgrimage through life, but *this* visit was attended with some of the heaviest and most painful exercises of any I had ever before experienced, and yet I have to believe the good hand, though often concealed, was near under all, and he did enable me at times to speak to the conditions of the people, so that the witness was reached, and by his own almighty power the seed raised and brought into dominion; of this, time hath brought undeniable proofs, so that this was a painful journey both to body and mind, yet as the infinitely wise being was pleased to bless it to some, to the honour of his own great name, I dare not repine, but hope humbly to submit to what he hath permitted or may permit to attend for the refining of my faith, and making it more pure than gold. . . .

Sophia Wigington Hume (1702–1774)

Sophia Wigington was born into a prosperous South Carolina family that valued education; ironically, the early intellectual challenges to which she was exposed later acted as impetus for her own departure from paternal strictures. At the age of nineteen Sophia married a prominent South Carolinian lawyer, Robert Hume. They raised two children and led an active life in Charleston until Robert's death in 1737, an event which precipitated a religious as well as emotional crisis for Sophia. For the first time, she felt that her Anglican faith offered little sustenance. As she recounts in her "Exhortation," this was the religion of her father, Henry Wigington; but her mother, Susanna Bayley Wigington, was a Quaker and her maternal grandmother had been the well-known Quaker preacher, Mary Fisher. It was to this tradition that Hume turned; her departure for England, where she joined the Society of Friends, became not only a literal but a symbolic separation from her early education and lifestyle.

When Wigington Hume returned to her "native Country" of South Carolina in 1747, she was a woman with a mission. In the following year Wigington Hume published "Exhortation to the Inhabitants of the Province of South Carolina" as a challenge to her neighbors, especially the women, to return to a simpler, more pious lifestyle. Wigington Hume eventually returned to England, where she continued her Quaker ministry and published several religious tracts. If she had once felt the abuse of her native region, she lived to see herself "justly celebrated." Most notable was her concern for the literary heritage of the Quakers; in 1766 she published a collection of early Friends' writings, "Extracts from Divers, Antient Testimonies," as a means of preserving the spiritual history of the faith she had come to embrace. Sophia Wigington Hume died in London on January 26, 1774.

Works: *An Exhortation to the Inhabitants of the Province of South Carolina . . .* (1748); *A Caution to Such As Observe Days and Times . . .* (1763); *Extracts from Divers, Antient Testimonies* (1766); *The Justly Celebrated Mrs. Sophia Hume's Advice* (1769). Bibliography: Bowden; Gummere.

An Exhortation to the Inhabitants of the Province of South-Carolina . . .

My Friends and Neighbours,

After an Absence of near six Years from this Province (my native Country) and my Arrival among you, I have beheld the Faces of many of the Inhabitants whom I have known, and been known to, some Years: But the Novelty of my religious Sentiments, and Meanness of my Appearance, has, I find, render'd me despicable in your Eyes; which has been obvious, when a Few of us, called *Quakers*, have met to worship the Supreme Being in a Manner agreeable to the best of our Understanding and Knowledge: And tho' some perhaps may stile our Principles[1] and Tenets by the hard Name of *Herisy*, and our Mode or Manner of Worship, ridiculous or absurd; nevertheless, we are humbly of Opinion, they are neither *unscriptural* nor *unchristian*, having, as we think, the Sanction and Authority of our Lord himself, the Example of primitive Believers, and right Reason, on our Side.

1. In a footnote, Hume refers her readers to *Robert Barclay's Apology* as a guide to Quaker principles.

. . . I am not insensible, that the Reason I have offered for writing, as well as the Subject itself, may probably be considered as the Production of a distemper'd and enthusiastick Brain; as it is possible, on such a novel and uncommon Occasion, as a Woman's appearing on the Behalf of God and Religion, you may (as others have done in the like Circumstances) be induced to consider such an One under some unaccountable Delusion, or affected with Religious Madness; and more especially, as the Things recommended to your Consideration, are offered by a simple Female of your own Country: Some, in this Case, I expect, will afford me a Smile of Contempt, while others (acted by a more generous Passion) pity my Folly, and kindly wish me a Return of my Senses: But however this may be, I have considered, that from the earliest Ages of Christianity, and indeed in all preceding Time, those who refused to conform to the Usage and wicked Customs of the Age, and lived a Self-denying Life, "Their Lives were counted Madness by the World, and their End to be without Honour:" Not considering that religous Minds despise and contemn all worldly Honour, and earthy Preferment, seeking that only which comes from God, and which he is pleased to distinguish those by, who honour him (by walking in Conformity to his Laws and Precepts) as he himself declares, *Those who honour me, I will honour; but those who despise me, shall be lightly esteemed.*

. . . But to proceed; I have told you that this Voyage to my native Place, was undertaken in Pursuance of what I verily believed was the Will of God concerning me, and required of me by him (I make no Doubt) as one amongst the many Trials I have been exercised with, of my Faith, Love and Obedience; wherein I believe it my Duty openly and freely to confess Christ before Men whose operating Power on my Heart I had fearfully and cowardly endeavour'd to conceal before I left this Province; and I take this Occasion to declare to you, that I am not ashamed of the Gospel of Christ, which I have in Measure experienced to be the Power of God to Salvation to all them who believe, and continue to obey it: And the more numerous the Testimonies, and greater the Cloud of Witnesses, to the Efficacy of the Grace and Power of God, the more will the Truths and Evidences proposed and produced, be strengthen'd and corroborated. . . .

When I was (by Marriage) remov'd from my Mother's Care and Direction, I continued in my Father's Profession of Religion, for no other Reason that I remember, but that it allowed me most Liberty in Dress and Recreations, tho' my Father, as well as my Mother, did not fail to inculcate a Just Abhorrence of the Evils the moral Law condemns. However, when I consider'd and examin'd religious Matters with more Seriousness, Sincerity and Attention than was usual with me, I found the little Religion (or rather the Profession of it) that I had, was that of my Education, which I could not properly call my own, as it was not the Religion of my Judgment, which I find absolutely necessary, and highly reasonable to be concern'd for. . . . But upon perusing the [*Articles of the Church of England*] (as well as considering the Opinion of most dissenting Sects) I could not reconcile some Opinions therein contain'd with Scripture Doctrine and Testimonies. . . .

I would now observe to you who indulge yourselves in the false Pleasures, vain Amusements and Recreations, of the Age, which once I had a Fondness for, as well as you now have. . . . Some are apt to think all is well, and they have done their Duty to God, when they neglect not customary times of formal Prayer, or Devotion (as it is falsely called) or their Diversions don't interfere with this Formality, which by some is punctually perform'd. This brings to my Remembrance the absurd as well as impious Character a certain Author gives of a Woman of this preposterous Composition of Diversion and Devotion; or, in his own Words, of Religion and Cards; he presents her, in some Interval of her Game, just recollecting it was her Hour of Devotion and Prayer, upon which she rises in great Precipitation, and desires her Neighbour to hold her Cards till she steps and says her Prayers. To mention this Character, is sufficient to shew the Absurdity of it. Again, the Description another Writer gives of a Woman at her Gaming Table, is enough, one would imagine, to make the hardest Forehead blush: And to say no more, than that it renders her unamiable in the Eyes of reasonable People, one would judge, this would be a great Reason for her to decline the Diversion; but when she is represented accusing her ill Fortune, as she calls it, in terms of Fury and Absurdity, the Portrait is horrid and shocking, unbecoming a rational Mind, and most unworthy any Person who professes Christianity. Compare this Character with humble *Mary's* sitting at her Lord's Feet, waiting to hear the gracious Words that proceeded out of his Mouth—compare it with the Apostle's Description of a Woman professing Godliness, whose Mind is adorn'd with *Meekness, Quietness and Modesty;* and see if you can discover one similar Line in the Characters. Again, describe a Woman dancing at a Ball, and adorn'd with all the Luxury and Pomp of Dress, tending, according to the Opinion of a pious Writer, to excite a Passion I forbear to name; and Country Dances, some of 'em, you know, are condemn'd by a Writer much admir'd by the polite and fashionable Part of the World, who peruse him, I have thought, to very little Purpose: Examine, I say, the Characters I have mentioned, and see if you can observe the least Trace of Christianity in them: In short, a dancing, gaming, masquerading Christian, appears as a great Contradiction. . . . But, further, tho' some Recreations, properly chosen and adapted may be lawful to a Christian; yet I have found those the Generality of People allow themselves in, are pernicious and hurtful in their Consequences, and therefore unlawful to, and inconsistent with the Life of a Christian. . . .

Jemima Wilkinson (1752–1819)

Jemima Wilkinson was born in Cumberland, Rhode Island, on November 29, 1752, the eighth of twelve children born to Amey Whipple and Jeremiah Wilkinson. Jemima Wilkinson became a renowned religious leader (known as "The Publick Universal Friend") and founder of a religious community in western New York State. Her independent actions seemed fitting for a family that could trace four generations of religious activists back to a colonial leader who had joined Roger Williams in Rhode Island in the 1650s. Little is known of her early life except that she harbored a passion for reading theological and historical texts. In 1776, when George Whitefield made his last visit to the United States, Wilkinson attended the New Light Baptist meetings in Cumberland; her actions caused her to be dismissed from the Quaker society to which she had belonged all her life.

After a severe illness later that year, Wilkinson asserted that she had had a vision both of her death and of God's determination to return her to the earthly world so she might preach His word. Thereafter, she refused to identify herself as Jemima Wilkinson, preferring "The Publick Universal Friend" or simply "the Friend." At first she was a traveling preacher, traversing throughout New England during the American Revolutionary years. She began to have a significant following, including several prominent citizens from around New England and many who held a messianic view of her. She advocated pacificism, opposed slavery and all forms of violence, preferred celibacy although she did not insist upon it for her married followers or deny marriage to members of her flock; in these tenets, she was adhering largely to the Quaker beliefs with which she had been raised. In 1788 she established The Friend's Settlement in New York, in a village she called Jerusalem (near what is now known as Seneca, New York). For her outspokenness and her power as a religious leader, she was attacked by many and stories were propagated about her in attempts to discredit her and her community. In reality, she practiced her faith. She created a community open to religious freedom, accepted both the power and responsibility contingent upon her role as leader of a religious sect, acted as doctor and educator to her followers, and extended her religious hospitality to all who traveled through the isolated area in which The Friend's Settlement was located.[1]

Wilkinson was a prolific correspondent and published several religious tracts. *The Universal Friend's Advice* was published in 1784; it became a kind of handbook for her followers. The excerpt included here from *An Advertisement* (1779) is one of her earliest proclamations. Jemima Wilkinson died on July 1, 1819. Without her strength and personal charisma, The Friend's Settlement lost its appeal and lasted for less than two decades after her death.

Works: Letters, sermons, tracts, journals. *Bibliography:* Earle, *Colonial Dames.*

---

1. This included Native American tribes, with whom she maintained a peaceful relationship, in spite of the growing animosities between the indigenous peoples of the region and the colonists.

An ADVERTISEMENT *to the Powers and People of this Nation.*

Because of my dear love to my native country, and because of the dregs of that cup which the Lord hath already caused it to drink of, which cannot be spared unless the Lord's will be effected without, which dregs are so bitter, terrible and dreadful, as will make the stoutest hearts to faint, and the most confident countenance wax pale: I say for this cause, in love am I constrained to add these few lines,—that if it be possible this nation may apply itself, in the fear and dread of the eternal majesty and power, to make its peace with him against whom it hath long warred, not only by much outward wickedness, looseness, vanity, and profaneness, but more especially by setting up an invented form of godliness, and persecuting the power, and to whom it is not yet reconciled in this matter, nor found so much as willing to be reconciled.

The Lord God of heaven and earth, of glory, of majesty, of everlasting power, victory and dominion over all, who made both heaven and earth, and hath the common of all things therein, he disposeth of nations, of governments, of earthly powers, according to his pleasure, and who may say unto him, what doest thou? Who may implead him for making a rich nation poor? A strong nation weak? Or for bringing down the high and mighty, the strong, stout, honorable, and noble in a nation, and exalting the poor, the mean, the persecuted? And if he turn his hand again, and lay them flat whom he had lifted up, and exalt the other even unlooked for, who can withstand him, or who can contradict him? Now what is in the Lord's heart, who is thus mighty and absolute, he will certainly bring to pass, how unlikely, how contrary, how impossible soever it seem to the eye of man; if he will exalt his despised truth, which always was so to the eye of the great and wise ones of this world, or give his people liberty to fear, worship and obey him, if he will have truth and righteousness have the dominion in men's hearts, and in the nation's, and not in the wills and lusts of men, how great and powerful soever; I say, if this be his intent, though generation should rise up after generation to oppose him herein, it will be too hard for them all, and they will all fall before him; and his truth, his people, his holy eternal counsel, will he raise up, and cause to triumph over them all.

It is man's way to settle himself by outward strength against outward strength, and then he thinks he is safe; not eyeing the invisible hand which turns the wheels, and delights to overturn that which is outwardly strong, and seemeth unremovable, when it forgetteth him, and opposeth itself against him. The Lord God loves to take his enemies at the strongest, when they are most wise, most mighty, even when nothing seems able to deal with them but himself. This was it overthrew the foregoing powers one after another; they were courting worldly interest, and strengthening themselves that way; but overlooked God who raised them, and the work which he had raised them to accomplish. This turned the hand against them which had been for them; and how then could they maintain their standing?

Oh! that the present generation could see the ticklishness of their standing, and consider that this is their day of trial, and the Lord's eye is upon them, to observe their ways, to see whether they will now mind righteousness and the liberty of his people, better than formerly they did; and that his truth may in its life and powers, and not in such a form or way of worship as they may think good to prescribe, have its scope in the nation. The Lord's eye and heart are upon his truth and upon his people; and as nations or powers deal with that, so will he deal with them. Oh! therefore be not deceived; for though the Lord hath oftentimes long suffered his people to lie under reproach and persecution, as he did Israel in Egypt for divers ages, yet at length he hath faith [?] heard their groans, and hath arisen to deliver: And though Pharaoh afterwards with all his strength went after them, and made no question but to bring them back again under his subjection, and there was nothing in appearance able to deliver them from him, yet he could not, but overthrow himself and his strength utterly. Ye know not what strong cries and tears were put up to the Lord before these late changes; that righteousness might be established in the nation, and that his people might have liberty to worship him in his fear, and according to the leadings of his spirit, without being yoked under any form of worship which their hearts could not own to be of God. . . .

Captivity Narratives and Travel Journals

Mary White Rowlandson (1637?–1711)

Mary White was born in Somerset, England, around 1637; she emigrated to Salem, Massachusetts, with her parents, Joan and John White, and her nine siblings. Little is known of her life until 1656 when she married Reverend Joseph Rowlandson of Lancaster, Massachusetts. They had three surviving children. White Rowlandson's life was radically altered during King Philip's War (1675–1678). On February 10, 1676, Narragansett warriors attacked the settlement of Lancaster. White Rowlandson and her three children (Joseph, 14 years; Mary, 10 years; and Sarah, 6 years) were taken captive. Sarah died shortly after their capture, and White Rowlandson was separated from Joseph and Mary. After she was ransomed by her husband on May 2, the family resided in Boston for five years and then moved to Wethersfield, Connecticut where her husband soon died, and she married Captain Samuel Talcott in August 1679.

Three years later, Mary White Rowlandson published a narrative of her captivity experiences. Although the *Narrative* became one of the first best-sellers in America, it was the only literature White Rowlandson ever wrote. She graphically detailed her experiences and recounted her spiritual struggles during her ordeal as well as the poignant realities of her psychological state after her return. If the *Narrative* dramatically relates one woman's courage under horrendous conditions, its depiction of the Algonkian people as savages and monsters is typical of Puritan representations of a race that they never acknowledged as equals. Mary White Rowlandson died in Wethersfield on January 5, 1711.

Works: *The Soveraignty and the Goodness of GOD, Together With the Faithfulness of His Promises Displayed; Being a Narrative of the Captivity and Restauration of Mrs. Mary Rowlandson* (1682). Bibliography: Breitwieser; Derounian, "The Publication . . . of Mary Rowlandson's Indian Captivity Narrative"; Greene; Lang, "Introduction."

... A Narrative of the Captivity and Restauration of Mrs. Mary Rowlandson

On the tenth of February 1675, Came the *Indians* with great numbers upon Lancaster; Their first coming was about Sun-rising; hearing the noise of some Guns, we looked out; several Houses were burning, and the Smoke ascending to Heaven. . . .

At length they came and beset our own house, and quickly it was the dolefullest day that ever mine eyes saw. The House stood upon the edge of a hill; some of the *Indians* got behind the hill, others into the Barn, and others behind any thing that could shelter them; from all which places they shot against the House, so that the Bullets seemed to fly like hail; and quickly they wounded one man among us, then another, and then a third, About two hours (according to my observation, in that amazing time) they had been about the house before they prevailed to fire it. . . . Now is the dreadfull hour come, that I have often heard of (in time of War, as it was the case of others) but now mine eyes see it. Some in our house were fighting for their lives, others wallowing in their blood, the House on fire over our heads, and the bloody Heathen ready to knock us on the head, if we stirred out. Now might we hear Mothers and Children crying out for themselves, and one another, *Lord, what shall we do?* Then I took my Children (and one of my sisters, hers) to go forth and leave the house: but as soon as we came to the dore and appeared, the *Indians* shot so thick that the bullets rattled against the House, as if one had taken an handfull of stones and threw them, so that we were fain to give back. . . . No sooner were we out of the House, but my Brother in Law[1] (being before wounded, in defending the house, in or near the throat) fell down dead, wherat the *Indians* scornfully shouted, and hallowed, and were presently upon him, stripping off his cloaths, the bulletts flying thick, one went through my side, and the same (as would seem) through the bowels and hand of my dear Child in my arms.[2] One of my elder Sisters Children, named William, had then his Leg broken, which the *Indians* perceiving, they knockt him on the head. Thus were we butchered by those merciless Heathen, standing amazed, with the blood running down to our heels. . . .

I had often before this said, that if the *Indians* should come, I should chuse rather to be killed by them then taken alive but when it came to the tryal my mind changed; their glittering weapons so daunted my spirit, that I chose rather to go along with those (as I may say) ravenous Beasts, then that moment to end my dayes; and that I may the better declare what happened to me during that grievous Captivity, I shall particularly speak of the severall Removes we had up and down the Wilderness.[3]

. . . I sat much alone with a poor wounded Child in my lap,[4] which moaned night and day, having nothing to revive the body, or cheer the spirits of her,

1. Her sister's husband, John Divoll.
2. Sarah Rowlandson.
3. They camped and moved ("removes") twenty times during the three months that White Rowlandson was held captive.
4. This part of the narrative occurs during the third remove.

but, in stead of that, sometimes one Indian would come and tell me one hour, that your Master[5] will knock your Child in the head, and then a second, and then a third, your Master will quickly knock your Child in the head.

This was the Comfort I had from them, miserable comforters are ye all, as he said.[6] Thus nine dayes I sat upon my knees, with my Babe in my lap, till my flesh was raw again; my Child being even ready to depart this sorrowfull world, they bade me carry it out to another Wigwam (I suppose because they would not be troubled with such spectacles) Whither I went with a very heavy heart, and down I sat with the picture of death in my lap. About two houres in the night, my sweet Babe like a Lambe departed this life, on Feb. 18, 1675. It being about six yeares, and five months old. It was nine dayes from the first wounding, in this miserable condition, without any refreshing of one nature or other, except a little cold water. I cannot, but take notice, how at another time I could not bear to be in the room where any dead person was, but now the case is changed; I must and could ly down by my dead Babe, side by side, all the night after. I have thought since of the wonderfull goodness of God to me, in preserving me in the use of my reason and senses, in that distressed time, that I did not use wicked and violent means to end my own miserable life. . . .

. . . But a sore time of tryal, I concluded, I had to go through,[7] My master being gone, who seemed to me the best friend that I had of an *Indian*, both in cold and hunger, and quickly so it proved. Down I sat, with my heart as full as it could hold, and yet so hungry that I could not sit neither; but going out to see what I could find, and walking among the Trees, I found six Acorns and two Chesnuts, which were some refreshment to me. Towards Night I gathered me some sticks for my own comfort, that I might not ly a-cold: but when we came to ly down they bade me go out and ly some-where-else, for they had company (they said) come in more than their own: I told them, I could not tell where to go, they bade me go look; I told them, if I went to another *Wigwam* they would be angry, and send me home again. Then one of the Company drew his sword, and told me he would run me thorough if I did not go presently. Then was I fain to stoop to this rude fellow, and to go out in the night, I knew not whither. Mine eyes have seen that fellow afterwards walking up and down Boston, under the appearance of a *Friend-Indian*, and severall others of the like Cut. I went to one *Wigwam*, and they told me they had no room. Then I went to another, and they said the same; at last an old *Indian* bade me come to him, and his Squaw gave me some Ground-nuts; she gave me also something to lay under my head, and a good fire we had: and through the good providence of God, I had a comfortable lodging that night. . . .

I can remember the time, when I used to sleep quietly without workings in my thoughts, whole nights together, but now it is other wayes with me.[8] When all are fast about me, and no eye open, but his who ever waketh, my thoughts

5. The Native American who claimed White Rowlandson as his property after her capture.
6. Job 16:1–2.
7. White Rowlandson is in the twelfth remove.
8. White Rowlandson has now been ransomed and reunited with her family.

are upon things past, upon the awfull dispensation of the Lord towards us; upon his wonderfull power and might, in carrying of us through so many difficulties, in returning us in safety, and suffering none to hurt us. I remember in the night season, how the other day I was in the midst of thousands of enemies, and nothing but death before me: It is then hard work to persuade my self, that ever I should be satisfied with bread again. But now we are fed with the finest of the Wheat, and, as I may say, With honey out of the rock:[9] In stead of the Husk, we have the fatted Calf.[10] The thoughts of these things in the particulars of them, and of the love and goodness of God towards us, make it true of me, what *David* said of himself, *Psal.6.5.*[11] *I watered my Couch with my tears.* Oh! the wonderfull power of God that mine eyes have seen, affording matter enough for my thoughts to run in, that when others are sleeping mine eyes are weeping.

I have seen the extrem vanity of this World: One hour I have been in health, and wealth, wanting nothing: But the next hour in sickness and wounds, and death, having nothing but sorrow and affliction.

Before I knew what affliction meant, I was ready sometimes to wish for it. When I lived in prosperity, having the comforts of the World about me, my relations by me, my Heart cheerfull, and taking little care for any thing; and yet seeing many, whom I preferred before my self, under many tryals and afflictions, in sickness, weakness, poverty, losses, crosses, and cares of the World, I should be sometimes jealous least I should have my portion in this life, and that Scripture would come to my mind. *Heb.* 12.6 *For whom the Lord loveth he chasteneth, and scourgeth every Son whom he receiveth.* But now I see the Lord had his time to scourge and chasten me. The portion of some is to have their afflictions by drops, now one drop and then another; but the dregs of the Cup, the Wine of astonishment, like a sweeping rain that leaveth no food, did the Lord prepare to be my portion. Affliction I wanted, and affliction I had, full measure (I thought) pressed down and running over; yet I see, when God calls a Person to any thing, and through never so many difficulties, yet he is fully able to carry them through and make them see, and say they have been gainers thereby. And I hope I can say in some measure, As *David* did, *It is good for me that I have been afflicted.*[12] The Lord hath shewed me the vanity of these outward things, that they are the *Vanity of vanities, and vexation of spirit;*[13] that they are but a shadow, a blast, a bubble, and things of no continuance. That we must rely on God himself, and our whole dependance must be upon him. If trouble from smaller matters begin to arise in me, I have something at hand to check my self with, and say, why am I troubled? It was but the other day that if I had had the world, I would have given it for my freedom, or to have been a Servant to a *Christian.* I have learned to look beyond present and smaller troubles, and to be quieted under them, as *Moses* said, *Exod.* 14.13. *Stand still, and see the salvation of the Lord.*

9. Psalm 81:16.
10. Luke 15:23.
11. Actually, Psalm 6:6.
12. Psalm 119:71.
13. Ecclesiastes 1:2.14

Sarah Kemble Knight (1666–1727)

The eldest daughter of Elizabeth Trerice and Thomas Kemble, Sarah Kemble was born in Boston in 1666. When she was in her early twenties, she married Richard Knight, apparently an older man and a shipmaster. They had one daughter, Elizabeth, born in 1689. The sketchy data on the Knights indicate that Richard died around 1706 and that Sarah had already begun to take over his business operations before his death. In addition to the family business in Boston, Kemble Knight was known to take on legal tasks such as selling estates and she may have run a writing school as well. In 1704–5, Kemble Knight traveled from Boston to New York, apparently to settle an estate for her cousin Caleb Trowbridge. On this trip, Kemble Knight recorded her experiences in journals that might best be understood as an extended narrative in which she is the central, heroic figure. Filled with humor (as well as with her class biases), Kemble Knight's journal has become a classic text in early American literature.

Works: *The Journals of Madam Knight* (written 1704–05, published by Theodore Dwight, *The Journals of Madam Knight . . .*, New York, 1825). Bibliography: Bush; Derounian-Stodola, "The New England Frontier. . . ."

From the Journals of Madam Knight[1]

Monday, Octb'r. ye second, 1704. . .

When we had Ridd about an how'r, wee come into a thick swamp, wch. by Reason of a great fogg, very much startled mee, it being now very Dark. But nothing dismay'd John:[2] Hee had encountered a thousand and a thousand such Swamps, having a Universall Knowledge in the woods; and readily Answered all my inquiries wch. were not a few.

In about an how'r, or something more, after we left the Swamp, we come to Billinges,[3] where I was to Lodg. My Guide dismounted and very Complasantly help't me down and shewd the door, signing to me wth his hand to Go in; wch I Gladly did—But had not gone many steps into the Room, ere I was Interogated by a young Lady I understood afterwards was the Eldest daughter of the family, with these, or words to this prupose, (viz.) Law for mee—what in the world brings You here at this time a night?—I never see a woman on the Rode so Dreadfull late, in all the days of my versall[4] life. Who are You? Where are You going? I'me scar'd out of my witts—with much now of the same Kind. I stood aghast, Prepareing to reply, when in comes my Guide—to

1. From the 1825 edition; the original manuscripts are not extant.
2. Her guide.
3. Billings Inn, Dorchester, Massachusetts.
4. *versall*: universal, entire.

him Madam turn'd, Roreing out: Lawfull heart, John, is it You?—how de do! Where in the world are you going with this woman? Who is she? John made no Ansr. but sat down in the corner, fumbled out his black Junk,[5] and saluted that instead of Debb; she then turned agen to mee and fell anew into her silly questions, without asking me to sitt down.

I told her shee treated me very Ruidely, and I did not think it my duty to answer her unmannerly Questions. But to get ridd of them, I told her I come there to have the post's[6] company with me to-morrow on my Journey, &c. Miss star'd awhile, drew a chair, bid me sitt, And then run up stairs and putts on two or three Rings, (or else I had not seen them before,) and returning, sett herself just before me, showing the way to Reding, that I might see her Ornaments, perhaps to gain the more respect. But her Granam's new Rung[7] sow, had it appeared, would affected me as much. I paid honest John with money and dram according to contract, and Dismist him, and pray'd Miss to shew me where I must Lodg. Shee conducted me to a parlour in a little back Lento,[8] wch was almost fill'd wth the bedsted, wch was so high that I was forced to climb on a chair to gitt up to ye wretched bed that lay on it; on wch having Stretcht my tired Limbs, and lay'd my head on a Sad-colourd pillow, I began to think on the transactions of ye past day.

Tuesday, October ye third. . . . Now was the Glorious Luminary,[9] with his swift Coursers arrived at his Stage, leaving poor me with the rest of this part of the lower world in darkness, with which *wee* were soon Surrounded. The only Glimering we now had was from the spangled Skies, Whose Imperfect Reflections rendered every Object formidable. Each lifeless Trunk, with its shatter'd Limbs, appear'd an Armed Enymie; and every little stump like a Ravenous devourer. Nor could I so much as discern my Guide, when at any distance, which added to the terror.

Thus, absolutely lost in Thought, and dying with the very thoughts of drowning, I come up wth the post, who I did not see till even with his Hors: he told mee he stopt for mee; and wee Rode on Very deliberately a few paces, when we entred a Thickett of Trees and Shrubbs, and I perceived by the Hors's going, we were on the descent of a Hill, wch, as wee come neerer the bottom, 'twas totaly dark wth the Trees that my Guide told mee was the hazzardos River he had told me off; and hee, Riding up close to my Side, Bid me not fear—we should be over Imediatly. I now ralyed all the Courage I was mistriss of, Knowing that I must either Venture my fate of drowning, or be left like ye Children in the wood. So, as the Post bid me, I gave Reins to my Nagg; and sitting as Steady as Just before in the Cannoo, in a few minutes got safe to the other side, which hee told mee was the Narragansett country.

Here We found great difficulty in Travailing, the way being very narrow, and

---

5. A pipe.
6. Messenger who carries the mail through the region.
7. That is, having a ring through the nose.
8. A lean-to, a makeshift room.
9. The moon. Kemble Knight is now with her third guide and has just crossed a treacherous waterway by canoe, and she has been informed that an even more dangerous crossing lies ahead.

on each side the Trees and bushes gave us very unpleasent welcomes with their Branches and bow's, wch wee could not avoid, it being so exceeding dark. My Guide, as before so now, putt on harder than I, wth my weary bones, could follow; so left mee and the way beehind him. Now Returned my distressed apprehensions of the place where I was: the dolesome woods, my Company next to none. . . . Now, coming to ye foot of a hill, I found great difficulty in ascending: But being got to the Top, was there amply recompenced with the friendly Appearance of the Kind Conductress of the night, Just then Advancing above the Horisontall Line. The Raptures wch the Sight of that fair Planett produced in mee, caus'd mee, for the Moment, to forgett my present waryness and past toils; and Inspir'd me for the most of the remaining way with very divirting tho'ts, some of which, with the other Occurrances of the day, I reserved to note down when I should come to my Stage. My tho'ts on the sight of the moon were to this purpose:

Fair Cynthia,[10] all the Homage that I may
Unto a Creature, unto thee I pay;
In Lonesome woods to meet so kind a guide,
To Mee's more worth than all the world beside.
Some Joy I felt just now, when safe got or'e
Yon Surly River to this Rugged shore,
Deeming Rough welcomes from these clownish Trees,
Better than Lodgings wth Nereidess.[11]
Yet swelling fears surprise; all dark appears—
Nothing but Light can disipate those fears.
My fainting vitals can't lend strength to say,
But softly whisper, O I wish 'twere day.
The murmur hardly warm'd the Ambient air,
E're thy Bright Aspect rescues from dispair:
Makes the old Hagg her sable mantle loose,
And a Bright Joy do's through my Soul diffuse.
The Boistero's Trees now Lend a Passage Free,
And pleasant prospects thou giv'st light to see.

. . .

Saturday, Oct. 7th. . . . about two a clock in the afternoon we arrived at New Haven, where I was received with all Posible Respects and civility. Here I discharged Mr. Wheeler[12] with a reward to his satisfaction, and took some time to rest after so long and toilsome a Journey; And I Inform'd myselfe of the manners and customs of the place, and at the same time employed myselfe in the afair I went there upon.

They are Govern'd by the same Laws as wee in Boston, (or little differing,) thr'out this whole Colony of Connecticut, And much the same way of Church Government, and many of them good, Sociable people, and I hope Religious

10. The moon, represented as a goddess.
11. Nereides: sea nymphs.
12. Her most recent guide.

too: but a little too much Independant in their principalls, and, as I have been told, were formerly in their Zeal very Riggid in their Administrations towards such as their Lawes made Offenders, even to a harmless Kiss or Innocent merriment among Young people. Whippings being a frequent and counted an easy Punishment, about wch as other Crimes, the Judges were absolute in their Sentences. They told mee a pleasant story about a pair of Justices in those parts, wch I may not omit the relation of.

A negro Slave belonging to a man in ye Town, stole a hogs head from his master, and gave or sold it to an Indian, native of the place. The Indian sold it in the neighbourhood, and so the theft was found out. Thereupon the Heathen was Seized, and carried to the Justices House to be Examined. But his worship (it seems) was gone into the feild, with a Brother in office, to gather in his Pompions.[13] Whither the malefactor is hurried, And Complaint made, and satisfaction in the name of Justice demanded. Their Worships cann't proceed in form without a Bench: whereupon they Order one to be Imediately erected, which, for want of fitter materials, they made with pompions—which being finished, down setts their Worships, and the Malefactor call'd, and by the Senior Justice Interrogated after the following manner. You Indian why did You steal from this man? You sho'dn't do so—it's a Grandy wicked thing to steal. Hol't Hol't, cryes Justice Junr, Brother, You speak negro to him. I'le ask him. You sirrah, why did You steal this man's Hoggshead? Hoggshead? (replys the Indian,) me no stomany. No? says his Worship; and pulling off his hatt, Patted his own head with his hand, sais, Tatapa—You, Tatapa—you; all one this. Hoggshead all one this. Hah! says Netop, now me stomany that. Whereupon the Company fell into a great fitt of Laughter, even to Roreing. Silence is comanded, but to no effect: for they continued perfectly Shouting. Nay, sais his worship, in an angry tone, if it be so, *take mee off the Bench.* . . .

Elizabeth Meader Hanson (1684–1741)

The desire of New England Puritans to usurp the land of the French and Native Americans brought the two latter forces together against the Puritans. The bloody disputes between the two groups often took place in the vicinity of Dover, New Hampshire, where Elizabeth Meader Hanson resided. As Quakers, Meader Hanson and her husband John did not take sides in the ongoing disputes, but in 1724 their home was attacked by the French and Native Americans and Elizabeth was taken captive. She was held by the Native Americans for several months and then was left "amongst the French," from whom her husband was able to negotiate her release after more than a year in captivity. Meader Hanson's eldest daugh-

13. *Pompions*: pumpkins.

ter, Sarah, had been captured at the same time as she; however, because Sarah was of marriageable age, her Native American captors
refused to release her with her mother. John Hanson died before
he was able to effect his daughter's release, but with the help of
relatives, Elizabeth continued those efforts. Sarah was eventually
transferred to the French, one of whom (Jean Baptiste Sabourin)
she married and with whom she settled in Canada, in spite of her
mother's protests. Elizabeth Meader Hanson's narrative was published in 1728.[1]

Works: *God's Mercy Surmounting Man's Cruelty, Exemplified in the Captivity and Re-
demption of Elizabeth Hanson* (1728). Bibliography: Vaughan and Clark.

God's Mercy Surmounting Man's Cruelty

. . . Now having kill'd two of my Children, they scalp'd 'em (a Practice com-
mon with these People, which is, when-ever they kill any *English* People, they
cut the Skin off from the Crown of their Heads, and carry it with them for a
Testimony and Evidence that they have kill'd so many, receiving sometimes a
Reward of a Sum of Money for every Scalp) and then put forward to leave the
House in great Haste, without doing any other Spoil than taking what they
had pack'd together, with my self and little Babe Fourteen Days old, the Boy
Six, and two Daughters, the one about Fourteen and the other about Sixteen
years, with my Servant Girl.

It must be considered that I having lain-in but 14 days, and being but very
tender and weakly, being removed now out of a good Room well accommo-
dated with Fire, Bedding, and other Things suiting a Person in my Condition,
it made these Hardships to me greater than if I had been in a strong and healthy
Frame; yet for all this, I must go or die. There was no Resistance.

In the Condition aforesaid we left the House, each *Indian* having something;
and I with my Babe and three Children that could go of themselves. The Captain, tho' he had as great a Load as he could well carry, and was helped up
with it, did for all that, carry my Babe for me in his Arms, which I took to be
a Favour from him. Thus we went thro' several Swamps and some Brooks,
they carefully avoiding all Paths of any Track like a Road, lest by our Foot-
steps we should be followed. . . .

. . . my daily Travel and hard Living[2] made my Milk dry almost quite up,
and how to preserve my poor Babe's Life was no small Care on my Mind, having no other Sustenance for it, many Times, but cold water, which I took in
my Mouth and let it fall on my Breast (when I gave it the Teat,) to suck in,
with what it could get from the Breast; and when I had any of the Broth of
the Beaver or other Guts, I fed my Babe with it, as well as I could: By which

1. This excerpt is from the 1728 American edition, published by Thomas Keimer in
Philadelphia. An English edition was also published, but it was erroneously attributed to Samuel
Bownas, an English Quaker; later English editions contained unauthorized revisions.

2. Almost one month of daily movement has occurred at this point.

Means, thro' care to keep it as warm as I could, I preserved its Life till I got to *Canada*, and then I had some other Food, of which more in its Place.

Having by this Time got considerably on the Way, the *Indians* part; and we must be divided amongst them. This was a sore Grief to us all: But we must submit, and no Way to help ourselves. My eldest Daughter was first taken away, and carried to another Part of the Country far distant from us, where for the present, we must take Leave of her, tho' with a heavy Heart. . . .

We had not been long at home[3] ere my Master went ahunting, and was absent about a Week, he ordering me in his Absence to get in Wood, gather Nuts, &c. I was very diligent, cutting the Wood, and putting it in Order, not having very far to carry it. But when he returned, having got no Prey, he was very much out of Humour, and the Disappointment was so great, that he could not forbear revenging it on us poor Captives. However he allowed me a little boyled Corn for self and Child, but with a very angry Look threw a Stick or Corn-Cob at me, with such Violence as did bespeak he grudged our Eating. At this his Squaw and Daughter broke out in a great Crying.[4] This made me fear Mischief was hatching against us: And on it, I immediately went out of his Presence into another Wigwam; upon which he comes after me, and in great Fury tore my Blanket off my Back, and took my little Boy from me and struck him down as he went along before him;[5] But the poor Child . . . ran away without crying; then the *Indian* my Master left me: but his Wife's Mother came and sat down by me, and told me, *I must sleep there that Night.* She then going from me a little Time, came back with a small Skin to cover my Feet withal, informing that my Master intended now to kill us . . . as well as I could, I made her sensible how unreasonable he was. Now, tho' she could not understand me, nor I her, but by Signs, we reasoned as well as we could: She therefore makes Signs that I must die, advising me, by pointing up with her Fingers, in her Way, to pray to God, endeavouring by her Signs and Tears to instruct me in that which was most needful, *viz.* to prepare for Death which now threated me; the poor old Squaw was so very kind and tender that she would not leave me all that Night, but laid her self down by my Feet, designing what she could to assuage her Son-in-law's wrath. . . .

I having been about five Months amongst the *Indians*, in about one Month after I got amongst the *French*, my dear Husband, to my unspeakable Comfort and Joy, came to me, who was now himself concerned to redeem his Children, two of our Daughters being still-Captives, and only my self and two little ones redeemed; and thro' great Difficulty and Trouble he recover'd the younger Daughter: But the eldest we could by no Means obtain from their

3. Meader Hanson and her captors have now arrived at their destination, "the *Indian* Fort," as Hanson called it. Her second daughter and her servant had been separated from her. Her "Master" refers to the Native American who had control over her.

4. Many Native American women assisted women captives. The tradition was so ingrained in cultural knowledge that as late as 1873 Rebecca Harding Davis reiterated it in a short story, "A Faded Leaf of History," chronicling the colonial period.

5. This was Meader Hanson's six-year-old son; only this son and her infant remained with her at this point in her captivity.

Hands, for the Squaw, to whom she was given, had a Son which she intended my Daughter should in Time be prevailed with to marry; the *Indians* being very civil toward their captive Women, not offering any Incivility by any indecent Carriage (unless they be much overgone in Liquor,) which is commendable in them so far.

However, the Affections they had for my Daughter made them refuse all Offers and Terms of Ransom; so that after my poor Husband had waited and made what Attempts and Endeavors he could, to obtain his Child, and all to no Purpose, we were forced to make homeward, leaving our Daughter to our great Grief, behind us, amongst the *Indians*, and set forwards over the Lake, with Three of our Children, and Servant-Maid, in Company with sundry others, and by the Kindness of Providence, we got well home on the first Day of the Seventh Month 1725. . . .

Thus, as well, and as near as I can from my Memory (not being capable of keeping a Journal,) I have given a short but true Account of some of the remarkable Trials and wonderful Deliverances, which I never purposed to expose; but that I hope thereby the merciful Kindness and Goodness of God may be magnified, and the Reader hereof provoked with more care and fear to serve Him in Righteousness and Humility, and then my designed End and Purpose will be answered.   E.H.

Mary Lewis Kinnan (1763–1848)

Little is known of Mary Lewis's early life. She was born on August 22, 1763, and in 1778 she married Joseph Kinnan; they had three children, Lewis, Joseph Jr., and Mary. Mary Lewis Kinnan is best known to us through her captivity narrative, which comes at the end of the religious tradition in captivity tales and the beginning of their incorporation into sentimental fiction. Yet Lewis Kinnan's ordeal was real, and like so many sentimentalists, she subverted that genre at the same time that she adhered to its formulas. Lewis Kinnan and her husband, Joseph, had left Basking Ridge, New Jersey, and settled in Randolph County, Virginia, in 1787. On May 13, 1791, Lewis Kinnan was captured by Shawnees at her Virginia home; later traded to the Delawares, Lewis Kinnan's captivity lasted for more than three years. She was released on August 16, 1794. Today, her memoir is often admonished for its melodramatic overlay on a real event; however, a careful review of Lewis Kinnan's life after captivity offers a new sense of her choice of narrative and lifestyles.

Sentimentalism was the mode of choice for many authors who wished to record the events of the domestic arena; in Lewis Kinnan's situation, its use highlights the shattering of that seemingly secure realm but also the possibilities of survival outside of "woman's sphere," even under the most horrendous conditions. More important, Lewis Kinnan's text does not offer an extended restoration "scene," requisite in the earlier narratives; this subversion of the tradition was in keeping with her own experiences. Unlike Mary White Rowlandson's classic restoration to the old ways of life, Lewis Kinnan never returned to her home in Virginia; her husband and daughter had been killed in the raid, and she chose to remain in New Jersey where she was taken after her brother gained her release. For Lewis Kinnan, the romantic vision of the traditional "woman's sphere" had been eradicated; what was left were visions of her "child, scalped and slaughtered . . . my husband, scalped and weltering in his blood." Lewis Kinnan had also survived much more personal violence than many of the other narrators of captivities. The consequent recognition of her own capabilities for survival were echoed in her postcaptivity decisions: the bucolic home-scene could not be restored; she established herself in New Jersey and remained there until her death, thirty years later, on March 12, 1848.

Works: *A True Narrative of the Sufferings of Mary Kinnan, who was Taken Prisoner by the Shawanee Nation of Indians on the Thirteenth Day of May, 1791, and Remained with them till the Sixteenth of August, 1794* (Elizabethtown, NJ: Kollock, 1795). Bibliography: Stutler; VanDerBeets.

A True Narrative of the Sufferings of Mary Kinnan

Whilst the tear of sensibility so often flows at the unreal tale of woe, which glows under the pen of the poet and the novelist, shall our hearts refuse to be melted with sorrow at the unaffected and unvarnished tale of a female, who has surmounted difficulties and dangers, which on a review appear romantic, even to herself. . . .

On the 29th of June we approached the Shawanee towns; when we arrived within about half a mile of them they fired their guns, stripped the bark from five trees, painted themselves and me in a most horrid manner, and commenced the scalp-whoop: never did I hear a sound so calculated to inspire terror: my blood curdled within me at the sound, and fear took possession of all my faculties.[1] This they repeated five times: they then seated themselves, until a vast number of people, attracted by the well-known and pleasing sound, came from the town and shook hands with them: each persen then struck me with great violence over the head and face, till I could not see, and till I finally dropt down senseless. They then recovered me and as-

1. As VanDerBeets notes, the number of scalp-whoops indicates the number of deaths among the enemies and the five stripped trees is an act of recording victories.

sisted me to walk into the town, having previously explained to me, that all the abuse which had been so liberally bestowed upon me, was to welcome me amongst them.

During my journey, the sense of present danger blunted the remembrance of past misery, and prevented me from indulging in gloomy anticipations of future woe;—but now the whole weight of my affliction pressed heavily on my heart. The picture of my life was deeply, too deeply dashed with shade, and but a few faint strokes of light were intermingled with the numerous touches of the *sombre* pencil. But when my spirits were surcharged with sorrow's dew, I breathed out a fervent prayer to heaven, and relied on the beneficence of the Father of All. Uniformly my efforts were successful, and a calm resignation diffused itself through my frame, or the rays of hope danced sweetly round my heart. I lived during four days with the sister of the savage who tore me from my peaceful home, and often contemplated with a sigh the depth of degradation, of which the human character is capable. On the third of July I was bought by a Delaware squaw, and by her was put to the most menial and laborious offices.

One of the principal objects of my attention, whilst I lived amongst the Indians, was the humiliating condition of their women. Here the female sex, instead of polishing and improving the rough manners of the men, are equally ferocious, cruel, and obdurate. Instead of that benevolent disposition and warm sensibility to the sufferings of others, which marks their characters in more civilized climes, they quaff with extatic pleasure the blood of the innocent prisoner, writhing with agony under the inhuman torments inflicted upon him—whilst his convulsive groans speak music to their souls. . . .

In November the Indians began to be weary of war, and, in the beginning of January, sent in a talk to General Wayne[2] by a Robert Wilson, an Indian trader, together with three Indians. General Wayne insisted, as a preliminary article, that all the prisoners should be delivered up: accordingly they came home, and collected a great number of us, unfortunate sufferers, and prepared to set out the next day to General Wayne at Fort Jefferson. But previously to our departure, one of the British agents came to them, and persuaded them, that perfidy was a leading trait in the character of the people of the United States; that they had placed ambuscades for them; and that they would never return alive. By these and other arts, they persuaded the Indians to persevere in their warfare, and we were again dismissed to our laborious occupations.

O Britain! how heavy will be the weight of thy crimes at the last great day! Instigated by thee, the Indian murderer plunges his knife into the bosom of innocence, of piety, and of virtue; and drags thousands into a captivity, worse than death. The cries of widows, and the groans of orphans daily ascend, like a thick cloud, before the judgment-seat of heaven, and

"Plead like angels, trumpet-tongued,
"For your damnation:

2. General Anthony Wayne, commander of the U.S. Army.

"And pity, like a naked, new-born babe,
"Striding the blast, or heav'n's cherubin, hors'd
"Upon the sightless couriers of the air,
"Shall blow your horrid deeds in every eye,
"That tears shall drown the wind."[3]

I had by this time witnessed so many disappointments, that I yielded myself up entirely to despondency, and endeavored to stifle the few scattered rays of hope, which faintly twinkled, like the glimmerings of a lamp just ready to expire. . . .

[Kinnan was reunited with her friends on October 7, 1794.] If my history has been marked with woe-worn incidents;—if I have been in a peculiar manner the child of misfortune;—if my cup of life has been deeply mixed with gall;—if despair has brooded over my soul, with all its horrors—and finally, if I have been obliged to dismiss even dear delusive hope, having so often felt "what kind of sickness of the heart that was, which proceeds from hope deferred:"—yet, by these very woes, I have been led to place my dependence on the beneficent dispenser of good and evil, and to withdraw my affections from that world, where the ties by which mankind are in general so firmly bound are indissolubly broken. Since the consequences of my affliction have been so beneficial, I repine not at it; ye, who are pierced by the darts of misfortune, imitate my example, and like me recline on the bosom of your Father and your God.

Mary Coburn Dewees (fl. 1787–88)

In 1787 Mary Coburn Dewees and her family traveled from Philadelphia to Kentucky where they intended to settle; the journey took a little more than five months. The Kentucky lands had opened up to settlement by white colonists because of the defeat of the local Shawnees in 1774 by the Virginia militia in Lord Dunmore's War. The Shawnees retained only hunting and fishing rights to the lands over which they had once had complete control. In spite of numerous hardships and initial illness that Coburn Dewees experienced, she noted the beauty of the western regions and embodied throughout her travels the spirit of heading toward "better days." Although changing locales, Coburn Dewees maintained her traditional class values: several times she "preferred" to sleep in her wagon than to have the shelter of a cabin if it meant sharing with other travelers or being "crouded with frenchmen and Ne-

---

3. *Macbeth*, I.xii.19–25. Lewis Kinnan's revision (or conversion, as it were) of the opening lines of this passage emphasize the culpability of the British.

groes on an earthen floor." It was the "genteel" society that she sought at each community, refusing at one point to accept an invitation because "we in our travelling dress [are] not fit to make our appearance in that Gay place."

Coburn Dewees's travel journal was probably compiled from notes taken while she traveled across several states and was intended for family and friends who remained in Philadelphia. In addition to the diary's revelations about a woman's travel experiences in the late eighteenth century, one physical detail of the journal adds a touching note to the personal nature of leaving one region to explore the possibilities of a new region: inside the front cover of the diary, Mary appended a photograph with the notation, "My Mother Mrs. Rachel Dewees Wilson."

Works: Journal. Bibliography: Blair; Cochran.

From the Journal of Mary Coburn Dewees

September 27th, 1788[1] Left Philadelphia about 5 O'Clock in the afternoon and tore our selves from a number of dear friends that assembled to take a last farewell before we set off for Kentucky. Made our first stage 6 Miles from the city, being very sick the greatest part of the way. . . .

29th Left the United States and Arrived at the Waggon 40 Miles from Philad that place which contains so many valu'd friens. Sister[2] and the Childern very hearty, the Childern very diverting to all but poor Maria who was as sick as it was possible to be.[3] We took up lodging at the Compass. . . .

October 1st. Crost the Conostogo, a good deal uneasie for fear my sickness should return. The Conostogo is a beautifull creek with fine prospects arround it. After refreshing ourselves we tooke a walk up the Creek and I think I never saw a more beautifull prospect. You cant imagine how I long'd for you my friends to join our little Party and to be partakers of the Beauties of nature that now surround us. We are seated beneath the shade of intermingling trees, that grow reeling oer the creek and entirely shades us from the noon day sun. Several since I sat here has crossed some on horse back others in boats, whilst a fall of water at a little distance adds dignity to the scene and renders it quite romantic. As the sun was setting we rode through Lancaster a Beautifull inland town, with some Elegant Houses in it. I was quite delighted with the view we have from the Corner of the street where the prison stands of the upper

1. Coburn Dewees's date; however, the following January is noted as 1788 also. It is unclear if Coburn Dewees traveled in 1787–88 or 1788–89.

2. Eliza (Betsy) Coburn Rees, who traveled with the Dewees family and was later joined by her husband.

3. Coburn Dewees occasionally refers to herself in the third person by use of her family nickname, Maria.

part of the town which at once presents to your sight a sudden rise with houses, trees, and gardens, on either side that has a very pleasing effect.

2nd 'Tho but a few days since my friends concluded I could not reach Kentucky, will you believe me when I tell you I am sitting on the Bank of the Susquehanah, and can take my bit of ham and Biscuit with any of them.

> "Returning health has made the
> "face of nature gay,
> "Given beauty to the sun
> "and pleasure to the day.

Just cross'd the river in company with Mrs. Parr and her daughter. Not the least sick. What gratitude is owning from me to the great Author of nature who in so short a time has restored me from a state of Languishment and Misery to the most enviable Health. . . .

7th Set off for the north mountain which we find so bad we are Obliged to foot it up, and could compair ourselves to nothing but a parcel of Goats climbing up some of the Welch Mountains that I have read of. Sally very desirous to know whether this Mountain is not the one thats in Mr. Adgates song.[4] Find this the most fatiguing days Journey we have had, the roads so very bad and so very steep that the horses seem ready to fall backwards. In many places, you would be surprised to see the Childern, Jumping and Skiping, some times quite out of Sight some times on horse back some times in the Waggon, so you see we have variety, 'tho sometimes would very willingly dispence with some of it. Believe me my dear friends the sight of a log house on these Mountains after a fatiguing days Journey affords more real pleasure than all the Magnificent buildings your city contains. Took up our lodging at the foot of the Mountain and met with very good entertainment. . . .

14th Set out for Chestnut ridge. Horrid roads and the Stony's land in the world. I believe, every few hundred yards, rocks big enough to build a small house upon. We arrived at Chenys Mill towards the middle of the day and parted with our Company. Chenys Mill is a beautifull situation, or else the scarcity of such places make us think it more so than it really is. We were overtaken by a family who was going our way, which renders it more Agreeable travelling than by ourselves. I think by this time we may call ourselves Mountain proof. At the close of the day we arrived at a house and thought it prudent to put up for the night. The people are Scotch Irish, exceedingly Kind but Surprizingly dirty. We concluded (as the Company that was with us Made up 18 besides the family) to lodge in our Waggon which we did. It rained very hard in the night but we laid pretty Comfortably. . . .

---

4. In 1784 Andrew Adgate had founded the Institute for the Encouragement of Church Music (later the Uranian Academy of Philadelphia), through which he published numerous music books and gave occasional choral concerts. At least two of Coburn Dewees's daughters (Sally and Rachel) and two sons (Sammy and Johnny) traveled with their mother.

19th[5] ... The water very low. I am much afraid we shall have a tedious passage. Our boat is 40 foot long, our room 16 by 12 with a Comfortable fireplace. Our Bed room partioned off with blankets, and far preferable to the Cabbins we met with after we crossed the Mountains. . . . The Monongahela with the many coulored woods on each side is Beautiful, and in the Spring must be delightfull. We are now longing for rain much as we dreaded it on the land for it is impossible to get down untill the water raises. We live entirely Independant, and with that there is a pleasure which Dependants can never be partakers of. . . .

[November] 20th   Just as the day broke, got aground on a sandbar, at the beach Bottom. Just at that time a small Kentucky Boat, that was ashore endeavoured to alarm us by firing of a gun and Accosting us in the Indian tongue But our people could just discern the boat which quieted our fears. At sun rise we passed through Norris Town on the Indian Shores[6] a Clever little Situation with ten Cabbins pleasantly situated. Saw another Kentucky Boat and passed by Wheeling a place where a Fort was kept and attacked last war. . . . An excessive hard gale of wind Obliged us to put to Shore. After the wind Abated, we again put out in the Channal and were Obliged again by a fresh gale to put to Shore on the Indian Coast which caused some disagreeable Sensations, as it is not long since the Indians have done some mischief hereabouts. After the wind lulled they thought proper to put out again 'tho it still continued to rain very hard which made it very dark and disagreeable, as it was imposible to discern where the rocks and ripples lay. . . . The weather being too bad to proceed, we laid all night ashore, it still continued very Stormy: many large trees blew down on the Bank; we expect'd every moment the boat would leave her Anchor. . . .

. . . on the first of December arrived at Lexington, [Kentucky] . . . we were politly receiv'd and welcomed by Mrs. Coburn.[7] We all staid at my Brothers 'till 11th December when Betsy Rees left us to begin house Keeping, her house not being ready before.[8]

Jany 1788   We Still continue at my Brothers and have altered our determination to go to Buckly farm, and mean to go down to south elk horn as soon as the place is ready. Since I have been here I have been visited by the genteel people in the place and receivd several Invitations both in town and Country. The Society in this place is very agreeable and I flatter myself I shall see many happy days in this Country. Lexington is a clever little Town with a court house and Jail and some pretty good buildings in it Chief Log. . . .

5. The Deweeses now began the portion of their trip that had to be traveled by water. Coburn Dewees remarked that the boat "resembl[ed] Noahs Arks not a little." The low water remained a problem; it became so low they were forced to remain docked at McKees Island from October 26 until November 18.

6. The north bank of the Ohio River was referred to locally as "the Indian shore" because it had been the scene of many conflicts between Native Americans and settlers; the other side of the river was denominated "the Virginia shore."

7. Coburn Dewees's sister-in-law.

8. Mr. Rees had joined the party on November 30.

29th   I have this day reach south Elk horn, and am much pleased with it. Tis a snug little Cabbin about 9 Mile from Lexington on a pretty asscent surrounded by Sugar trees, a Beautifull pond a little distance from the house, with an excellent Spring not far from the door. I can assure you I have enjoyed more happiness the few days I have been here than I have experienced these four or five years past. I have my little family together And am in full expectations of seeing better days.

Epistolary Exchanges

The Winthrop Women (1630s–1640s)

Certainly Margaret Tyndal Winthrop (*q.v.*) is the best known of the Winthrop family women; however, her prolific sister-in-law, Lucy Winthrop Downing (1600/01–1679), is an equally important early American writer and one who was much less willing to couch her ideas in the submissive discourse typical of early seventeenth-century Puritan women. This was especially true when she was corresponding with her brother John, Governor of Massachusetts Bay Colony. Other Winthrop women include Mary Winthrop Dudley, Margaret's stepdaughter (Mary's mother, Mary Forth, was John Winthrop's first wife); Martha Fones Winthrop, Margaret's daughter-in-law; and Martha Downing Peters, Lucy's daughter. The Winthrop women of all ages viewed epistolary exchanges as a kind of refuge from the conundrums of domesticity in what was then a sparsely populated region.

Works: Correspondence. *Bibliography*: Downing; Earle, *Margaret Winthrop*; *Winthrop Papers*.

The Winthrop Women's Letters

Margaret Tyndal Winthrop to her daughter-in-law, Martha Fones Winthrop, c. April 10, 1631

Lovinge daughter,[1] I am sory that time did so prevent me, as I could not right to thee by the caryer, but haveinge nowe another mesenger I must needs right a word or to, thought I have no matter of wayte to impert to you, onely an intercorce of love betwene us which will take all ocasions to shewe it selfe, where it finds good entertainment. I doe very much and often, [wish] for my

---

1. Martha had married John Winthrop Jr. on February 8, 1630/31. They were staying at their aunt and uncle Downings's residence "near fleete condite" in London.

deare sonne and your selfe, for my owne comfort, but in regard of his many-foulde imployments[2] I must the more paciently beare his longe abcence   I think now the time the longer the nearer it aproches, for newes from new ingland. I shalbe the more joyfull when it comes if it be good, or if it be bad the more oppressed with grefe. . . . Your lovinge mother

Lucy Winthrop Downing to Margaret Tyndal Winthrop, c. March 1636/37[3]

Moste worthy Sister, Thes tedious passages bares us of all commerce: further then the unlimeted wishes of each others hapynes, wich allthough I have noe power to procure: yet it glads all my spirits to hear it: and blesed be god that hath so tenderd you in this infancie of a plantation, when theer was so small hopes of support or comfort. god still preacheth the life of fayth to his: and discovers himselfe in the mount. Ohe that thees experiences of his faythfullnes maye make us able to doe all things throwhe christ: to live hapylie and to dye comfortable: and all knowinge that ouer dayes heare are but a moment be they sweet or bitter . . . I hartylie thank you for all the expressions of your love, and desiers of our company. I know not yet how it will pleas god to dispose of us. wee are in many distractions: my present condition is unfit for changes:[4] and both this plauge and plaugs approach, and increas, and maye well affright: as beinge the arguments of the allmighties controversie with us: and provo-cations increasinge to such heyghts:[5] what can wee expect: if the sonne of god must suffer, rather then his Justis be unsatisfied. Lend us all your faythfull prayers: knowinge the head is the same, wherever the members are: and if god pleas to afford us the presence of each other in this life, I shall hope of much comfort therin. but if he denyes that, and bringe us together in heaven, wee shall not have much cause of complaint. . . . Yours in reallitie rather then in subscription

L. Downinge

Mary Winthrop Dudley[6] to Margaret Tyndal Winthrop, c. January 1635/36[7]

Deare Mother, my humble dutie remembred to you. It rejoyceth me to heare of your recoverie out of your dangerous sicknes, and should be glad to heare

2. John was to arrange supplies for the colony and to prepare the way for Margaret and her children to make the journey to New England.

3. Margaret had been in New England since 1631. Lucy is still in London at this time; she was much more reluctant in her anticipation of coming to the "New World" than Margaret had been.

4. Lucy was pregnant at the time, probably with her sixth child.

5. Lucy is probably referring to the undercurrents fomenting in England that would lead, in just a few years, to civil war.

6. In 1633 Mary Winthrop had married the Reverend Samuel Dudley, newphew of Anne Dudley Bradstreet (q.v.)

7. Mary and her husband lived in Cambridge and later in Ipswich; Margaret resided in Boston for the remainder of her life.

how your health is continued to you by a letter from your selfe. . . . I thought it convenient to acquaint you and my father, what a great affliction I have met withal by my maide servant, and how I am like through god his mercie to be freed from it; at her first comminge to me she carried her selfe dutifully as became a servant; but since through mine and my husbands forbearance towards her for small faults, shee hath got such a head and is growen soe insolent, that her carriage towards us especially myselfe is unsufferable. if I bid her doe a thinge shee will bid me to doe it my selfe, and she sayes how shee can give content as wel as any servant but shee will not, and sayes if I love not quietnes I was never so fitted in my life, for shee would make me have enough of it. If I should write to you of all the reviling speeches, and filthie language shee hath used towards me I should but greive you. my husband hath used all meanes for to reforme her, reasons and perswasions, but shee doth professe that her heart and her nature will not suffer her to confesse her faults; If I tell my husband of her behaviour towards me, upon examination shee will denie all that shee hath done or spoken: so that we know not how to proceede against her: but my husband now hath hired another maide and is resolved to put her away the next weeke. . . .[8]

Lucy Winthrop Downing to Margaret Tyndal Winthrop, May 19, [1636]

Moste Dear Sister,—ther is such a distance betwixt my letters, and my memory is so short that I maye fear troubleinge you with totaligie; but in a waye of thankfullnes I am sure not to writ superfluouslie: your favors doe so aboundantlie exceed the utmost extent of my expressions, and are so frequentlie repeated. I have littell news to impart to you . . . Mrs Fowle is dead of a consumtieon: my sister Gostlin, God be praysd, is very well abroad againe. But they are very like to los Msr. Lea. The Bishope of Norwige, whose name is Wren, doth impose a hundred and 32 articles to the clergy in his diocess, some wheerof they fear will put by both Msr Lea and divers others wich thought themselves very conformable men. Msr. Gourden is questioned for not bowinge and knellinge att buriall prayers. Sir Hary Millmay and my Lady are in towne, and well, and doe earnestlie wish your wellfear. Mr. Arksden is maryed. My lord Carliell is buried as statelie as he lived. I should be very glad to see my dear brother and your selfe and all our good frinds with you; but wee can not yet bringe all ends together. I doupt not but He that apoints the end apoints the time, and means. . . . wee are in much fear of both famine and plauge, wee have had noe raine hear this 6 or 7 weeks. God make us wise ere his decree be irrevocable.

Yours affectionatlie   Lucie Downinge.

8. Mary's difficulties with this maid (and subsequent servants she hired) lasted through the summer and possibly after. These letters reveal class differences in the Massachusetts Bay Colony on a uniquely everyday level.

Lucy Winthrop Downing to Margaret Tyndal Winthrop, c. May 1640[9]

My moste honerd sister, I maye well blush att my longe silence beinge your deptor for so many noble favors both when I was with you and since.

it is truth I sometimes forbear you trouble by writinge, because I see it pleaseth you better to pleasure your frinds in acsions then in words. I could wish my selfe mrs. of that faculltye allso, but barrennes in both is a bleamish intollerable. I hope I shall studiouslie desire to doe you better servis: my frequent and exquisit messeryes I presume you have often heard of. they keept me in a habit of complayninge, but I bles god I have had much remission for 4 dayes past, and should be moste glad if it would pleas the lord to give me strenght to wayt apon you, but rather that I maye ever submit to his will that makes all conditions blesings, to whom I pray commend your unworthy sister and servant
L.D.

your lemmons wear allmost as rare as drops of life. I am the more sensible of your deprivement of them.

Lucy Winthrop Downing to Margaret Tyndal Winthrop, 1640–41

Worthylie Honerd,—I humble thank you for all your favors whearin both I and myne are sempiternally ingaged, allso I humble thank you for the mayde. I have good hopes of her. My cosen Nab and she wear fellow travillers in the ship from Eng: Nab. gives her the report of a very good carigd theer: allso my brother Got and his wife wear near neighbours to hir frinds in Eng. and they repute them to be people of a very godly conversation, and many times hereditary blesings are perpetuated and vertue folowes them. My mayd Abygall is suddaynlie to be maryed to Robert Moulton of this towne: and I hope it maye prove a blessinge of comfort to her, for the parents and sonne are people of a religious peacable life, and pruident in their estates. I have felt more generall weaknes within this fortnight then ever formerly without violent distemper. But I suppose age and constant infermitye can produce noe less. . . .

Lucy Winthrop Downing to her daughter, Martha Downing Peters, September 9, 1662[10]

Dear Daughter,—I doe see thy husband, and all thy freinds there are unwilling to be the messingers of sad nuse to me, but I know if my deare nephew had bene living I should have had letters from him, in all this time. He is a publick lose, and a greate lose unto his family, and what unto myseulf is more then I can expres; but Gods will must be don, and it is ouer

9. Lucy and her husband came to New England in November 1638. She was residing in Salem, Massachusetts, at the time this letter was written.

10. Martha was Lucy's only daughter to return to England, where she resided in Westminster. No letters are extant from Martha after her marriage to Captain (John?) Peters. Only the address and a postscript are in Downing's handwriting; the letter may have been copied or, more likely, she was not well enough to write it herself.

dutyes to learne to suffer, and to labour to be fitted for ouer owne chang, for both scriptuer and dayly experiens tells us that death will cum wen we lest exspeckt it. I should have bene very glad to have sene the heare, if with conveniency; and my journy for London is yet unsertayne. I am sory for the lose, but I beleve they were not so good but they may esily be recruted, but me thinkes with a little care, that garden would be safe. I am glad you have my cossen Saulters company. She is a good body, but if he be so neare you still I marvell he never sent me a letter, nor any answer of mine. I pray commend me to them both. I wish her a good home, and I pray commend me to my sonne Peters, and to littell Jacke. Ower girls are well, I bles God, and present you there duty. So with my deare afecktions and best wishes for the.

I am Youer loving mother   Lucie Downinge

Abigail Smith Adams (1744–1818) *and Mercy Otis Warren* (1728–1814)

Both Abigail Smith Adams ("Portia") and Mercy Otis Warren ("Marcia") were born into prominent Massachusetts political families. Precocious young women, they took advantage of the exceptional at-home educations they were afforded and continued processes of self-education for the remainder of their lives. Although Smith Adams's concerns did not carry her outside the domestic sphere, she wielded what power she could from her limited environment. Otis Warren, an adamant patriot, was a far more outspoken and public woman. The letters of Abigail Smith Adams and Mercy Otis Warren remain a vital contribution to American literature; they not only remind us of how early the movement for women's rights began, but they also give us insiders' perspectives on the domestic and political history of the Revolutionary and federal periods.

Works: Correspondence. *Bibliography:* Butterfield; Rossi; *Warren-Adams Letters.*

The Letters of Abigail Smith Adams and Mercy Otis Warren

Abigail Smith Adams to Mercy Otis Warren

Braintree April 27 1776[1]

He is very sausy to me in return for a List of Female Grievances which I transmitted to him. I think I will get you to join me in a petition to Congress.

---

1. In March 1776, Smith Adams had written John Adams: "in the new Code of Laws . . . I desire you would Remember the Ladies and be more generous and favourable to them than your ancestors." John's response, "As to your extraordinary code of laws, I cannot but laugh," was the impetus for this letter to Otis Warren.

I thought it was very probable our wise Statesmen would erect a New Government and form a new code of Laws. I ventured to speak a word in behalf of our Sex, who are rather hardly dealt with by the Laws of England which gives such unlimitted power to the Husband to use his wife Ill.

I requested that our Legislators would consider our case and as all Men of Delicacy and Sentiment are averse to Excercising the power they possess, yet as there is a natural propensity in Humane Nature to domination, I thought the most generous plan was to put it out of the power of the Arbitrary and tyranick to injure us with impunity by Establishing some Laws in our favour upon just and Liberal principals.

I believe I even threatned fomenting a Rebellion in case we were not considerd, and assured him we would not hold ourselves bound by any Laws in which we had neither a voice, nor representation.

In return he tells me he cannot but Laught at My Extrodonary Code of Laws. That he had heard their Struggle had loosned the bands of Government, that children and apprentices were dissabedient, that Schools and Colledges were grown turbulant, that Indians slighted their Guardians, and Negroes grew insolent to their Masters. But my Letter was the first intimation that another Tribe more numerous and powerfull than all the rest were grown discontented. This is rather too coarse a complement, he adds, but that I am so sausy he wont blot it out.

So I have help'd the Sex abundantly, but I will tell him I have only been making trial of the Disintresstedness of his Virtue, and when weigh'd in the balance have found it wanting.

It would be bad policy to grant us greater power say they since under all the disadvantages we Labour we have the assendancy over their Hearts.

And charm by accepting, by submitting sway.

Abigail Smith Adams to Mercy Otis Warren

[Braintree, post-January 22, 1779]

... I sympathize with my Friend that she is again and so soon call'd to mourn a departed relative[2] cut of in the midst of her days, witherd in her Bloom at a time when the young charge require the maternal watchfulness and precepts. This is a much more trying Dispensation than resigning those who according to the course of Nature have done the work assignd them and like a shock of corn are gathered.

> As those who love decay, we dye in part
> String after string is sever'd from the Heart
> Till loosen'd life, at last but breathing clay
> Without one pang is glad to fall away,
> Unhappy those, who latest feel the blow
> Whose Eyes have wept o'er every Friend laid low,

2. Otis Warren's sister-in-law, Elizabeth Gray Otis, had died on January 22, 1779, leaving a husband, Samuel Allyne Otis, and five children. Otis Warren's father had also died in November of the previous year.

Drag'd ling'ring on from partial Death to Death
Till, dying, all they can resign is Breath.

At a late hour I must bid a good Night to Marcia and close her affectionate
Portia

Mercy Otis Warren to Abigail Smith Adams

Plimouth March 15 1779

. . . You ask what I think of the Late Dispute among the higher powers of America. I know Little of it Except what is in the public papers, where I think may be Discovered the precipitation and timidity of Guilt in a Certain Indiscreet writer.[3] But it is not unusual in the infancy of states, for some of the most unworthy characters to justle themselves by fortunate accidents into the most capital departments of office:—and when by their atrocious conduct, they have thrown every thing into confusion, they make efforts to escape punishment and often impeach the most worthy, and cast an odium on the best concerted plans. I think time must unravel some misteries which *authority* at present thinks best should be hushed in silence.

To your second question I answer, there is no calculating on the termination of military rencountres, yet, I do not fear much from the sword of Britain. I believe her to be more haughty than powerful, and more malevolent than politic, and that she will endeavour to do much by *intrigue.*

Heaven will restrain the arms and defeat the councels of a corrupt Court, but not for our sakes. The Lord of the universe will disappoint the projects of our foe, to carry on the system of his own government: and while he protects, will chastise us if necessary, and will punish an ungrateful people, in ways more analegous to the usual doings of providence, than to suffer a new formed nation to be trodden down e'er it arrives to maturity.

America is a theatre just erected—the drama is here but begun, while the actors of the old world have run through every species of pride, luxury, venality, and vice—their characters will become less interesting, and the western wilds which for ages have been little known, may exhibit those striking traits of wisdom, and grandeur and magnificence, which the Divine oeconomist may have reserved to crown the closing scene. . . .

Mercy Otis Warren to Abigail Smith Adams

Eleriver August 6 1779

My Dear Friend

"And are you sure the News is true,
And are you sure He's Come."[4]

---

3. The "Indiscreet writer" was Silas Deane. A private letter of Deane's, highly critical of John Adams and John Quincy Adams, had been published by the British in *Lloyd's Morning Post* (London, 16 August 1778).

4. John Adams had just returned home after being unceremoniously relieved of his duties in Europe as a commissioner for the newly formed United States, a service he had performed since February 1778.

... When I participate the Family Happiness, and take a part in the Felicity of my Friends, I Flatter myself it is an Emenation of Benevolence.

But There is not a spark of patriotism in the Cordial Gratulation in the Larger scale which is the Measure of patriotic Merit. What are the Little streams of social affection, the Heart felt pleasure of the Wife, the parent and the Friend, who would not sacrifice without a sigh these smaller Considerations when *pro bono publico* Requires, always assured of the Gratitude and applause of the *unchanging* Multitude.

But to be serious both you and I wish well to our Country, and will hope that some Good may result Even from the Mistakes of Her Rulers.

It is strongly impressed on my mind that the Return of a Gentleman Rather unexpectedly to his American Friends, May Give a New turn to the state of parties, and Eventually be productive of Happy Consequences. But my design is to say Little of public affairs. The full Heart Enwrapt (after the Anxieties and impatience of a Long abscence) in the tender scenes of Mutual affection has no Room, at pre[sent for]⁵ Forreign Cares. . . .

Abigail Smith Adams to Mercy Otis Warren

Febry. 28 1780

How does my Dear Mrs. Warren through a long and tedious Winter? in which I have never been honourd with a single line from her hand. Possibly she may think me underserving of her favours; I will not presume to lay claim to them upon the score of merit, but surely she should have charitably considered my lonely State, and Brightned the Gloomy hour with the Benign Rays of her Friendship dispenced through her elegant pen. . . .

I have heard this winter of a Letter from a Lady to her son containing Strictures upon Lord Chesterfields Letters.⁶ I have not been favour'd with a sight of it, tho I have wished for it. A collection of his Lordships Letters came into my Hands this winter which I read, and tho they contain only a part of what he has written, I found enough to satisfy me, that his Lordship with all his Elegance and graces, was a Hypocritical, polished Libertine, a mere Lovelace, but with this difference, that Lovelace was the most generous Man of the two, since he had justice sufficient to acknowledge the merit he was distroying, and died penitently warning others, whilst his Lordship not content himself with practiseing, but is in an advanced age, inculcateing the most immoral, pernicious and Libertine principals into the mind of a youth whose natural Guardian he was, and at the same time calling upon him to wear the outward Garb of virtue knowing that if that was cast aside, he would not be so well able to succeed in his persuits.

I could prove to his Lordship were he living that there was one woman in the world who could act consequentialy more than 24 hours, since I shall

5. Manuscript torn by seal.

6. The letter was by Otis Warren, dated December 24, 1779. Otis Warren attacked Chesterfield as a man of "finished Turpitude"; Smith Adams agreed so thoroughly with her friend's sentiments that she had the letter published in a Boston newspaper.

dispise to the end of my days that part of his character. Yet I am not so blinded by his abuse upon our sex, as not to allow his Lordship the merrit of an Elegant pen, a knowledge of *Mankind* and a compiler of many Excellent maxims and rules of Libertinism that I believe they will do much more injury than benifit to Mankind. . . .

Mercy Otis Warren to Abigail Smith Adams

Plimouth March 10th 1780

I have to thank my Friend Mrs. Adams for a very agreable Letter Received a few days since. I shall make no other Apology for my long silence, but a Frank acknowledgment that I have layed asside my pen in Complesance to her, supposing her time and Attention taken up in more profitable correspondencies. But shall Fail at no time to shew myself Equally ready to Resume it. I Rejoice in the Happy opportunity to Congratulate you on Mr. Adams's arrival in Europe. . . .

I am obliged for the Communication of some Extracts from Mr. Adams's Friends in France. I think they shew both the spirit of the times and the Industry of our Enemies, but I think they Contain nothing to enhaunce your fears.

The probity of the best of Men may for a time be suspected. But when there is a uniform principle of Integrity, a Man May bid Defiance to the stings of Columny, for the General sense of Truth still Remaining among mankind will in time do justice to his Character.

Curiosity burns not so high in my Bosom as it has done in Former Days. I feel more Indiferent to the transactions on a Theatre which will soon be taken down, or the actors Removed to more permanent scenes. Yet if there is anything Communicable in your Late letters, it may be an amusement of a solitary Moment, and prolong the Obligations of Friendship. . . .

Abigail Smith Adams to Mercy Otis Warren

September 1 1780

My dear Madam

From your Hospitable Mansion of Benevolence and Friendship, I reachd my own Habitation,[7] the day I left you, and found my family well, but the Scenes arround me wore a dismal aspect—the dyeing Corn, the Barren pastures and the desolated Gardens threaten us with distress, and Hunger. Not a vine that had modestly and silently crept along the Ground unasspiring of a nearer approach to the Burning God, but had crumbled to dust beneath his scorching Rays.

Ceres witherd Head reclines, Virtumnus is fled, and Pomona is scattering here and there the half Grown fruit e'er she too bids us adieu. To the Father

---

7. Smith Adams had just visited Otis Warren in Plymouth.

of the rain, and the Mercifull dispencer of the dew Drops, must we lift up our Beleiving hearts, for that releif which he does not refuse to the young Ravens when they cry, nor to the more important works of his Hands, but to oblige them to confess from whence cometh every good and perfect gift.

How happy should I be my dear Madam, Honourd as I am with your Friendship, if I could often join a sister mate, instead of sitting in my own solitary chamber the representitive of the lonely dove. Methinks we might coo, to each other, in accents which might Mitigate pain and illude the Solitary Hour, but when this is deliverd you that Idea will vanish from your mind, yet whilst you felicitate your own happier Lot, lend a pittying Sigh of commisiration to a sufferer. . . .

The Norris-Fishers-Zane Circle (1780s)

The correspondence between two cousins, Sarah Fisher of Duck Creek Cross-Roads (Delaware) and Sarah Fisher of Philadelphia, and their friends Deborah Norris and Sally Zane, both of Philadelphia, captures the thoughts and lives of a circle of young women friends in the mid-eighteenth century. The Delaware Sarah ("Sally") Fisher (1758–1789) was the center of the corresponding circle and the individual to whom most of the extant letters are addressed. The daughter of Mary Holliday and Fenwick Fisher, Sally was a popular young woman among both sexes and eventually married William Corbit, a well-to-do widower with two young children who was thirteen years older than she. They had one child together, but Sally died at the age of thirty, only five years after her marriage.

Her cousin Sarah ("Sally") Fisher (1759–1789) was the daughter of Sarah Rowland and Joshua Fisher; the Fishers were one of the most prominent Quaker families in Philadelphia (Joshua Fisher and Sons), whose wealth came from the shipping and mercantile trades. Sally was the youngest of six Fisher children; in 1785 she married Abijah Dawes, a local merchant with whom she had two children. Like her cousin Sarah Fisher Corbit, she died in 1789.

Deborah Norris (1761–1839) is probably the best known of the correspondents, known affectionately as "Debby" among her relatives and as "Ardelia" among her select female correspondents. Her parents, Mary Parker and Charles Norris, were from well-established Philadelphia families. Mary Parker Norris was widowed when Debby was young; she educated her daughter at home and then sent her to Anthony Benezet's female academy. At the age of twenty, Debby Norris married George Logan, a wealthy physician, an activist in federalist politics, and grandson of James Logan,

William Penn's secretary (see Hannah Callowhill Penn). Deborah Norris Logan's home became one of the centers of Philadelphia intellectual and political life.

Norris's friend Sally Zane (1754–1807) completes the circle of four correspondents. Zane was the eleventh child of Sarah Elfreth and Isaac Zane. She remained single, but little is known of her later life. All four women were active and well-to-do members of the regional Quaker society. They traveled often between Delaware and Pennsylvania, maintaining lifelong friendships.

Works: Letters. Bibliography: Sweeney.

The Norris-Fishers-Zane Letters

Sarah Fisher (Delaware) to Deborah Norris, March [?] 1780

My Dearest Debby

I just now sit down to write a short letter to my much lov'd and admir'd Debby Norris and must beg her to excuse the long silence of her friend and not attribute it to the least decrease of that tenderness which I have ever felt for thee since our happy acquaintance I have ventur'd to call it so from my own feeling (if I do not compliment my self too highly) whose mind was tun'd in unison with my own   how endearing was thy tender pathetic Letter relative to my poor destress'd cousins[1]   I thought then as well as at many other times that nothing so exalts the human soul except the genuine flame of piety as the sweet emotions of humanity which affords a kind of pleasing pain and leaves serenity almost divine—It was a maxim of the wisest of men that it was better to go to the house of mourning than to the house of mirth   I acquiesce with him it is more instructive for there we may learn lessons of the frailty of all sublunary enjoyments which would teach a thoughtfull mind to endeavor to lay up an immortal treasure that nothing earthly can destroy—

The family thee writes so affectionately of are indeed as shorn lambs and shorn to thy very quick but the being who has wounded them can alone bind them up for ever I have a particular sympathy with my poor old Uncle[2]   his age seems to have render'd him less able to resist such an alarming shock of fate but I believe he has a supernatural aid which has strengthened to stand the tempests of these boisterous times—do my Dear girl inform me in thy next how the poor Dear girl[3] my Departed Cousin was eng[age]d to bears the separation I think her affliction must be as great as if the ceremony had been pass'd as their affection were united   When such friends part tis the survivor dies—I really am in a serious mood but I cannot well help telling thee a secret I have had a new declaration   I must not let thee into the whole affair

1. Fisher is referring to the death of her relative, Jabez Maud Fisher, an employee of Joshua Fisher and Sons; Jabez had been in England on business and died suddenly while in London.
2. Joshua Fisher.
3. Jabez Fisher had been engaged to Hannah Redwood (1759–1796) of Newport, Rhode Island.

now I have not time I have a curiosity to know who that was went by with the Dr. that desir'd to be acquainted with thee likewise what a person said of Dan Mifflin[4] and me—

... Adieu my Dearest Debby I entertain the tenderst affection I have confided in the[e] in one part of this letter in particular

Sally Zane to Sarah Fisher (Delaware), April 6, 1780

The Acceptable favour of 31st inst. was handed me To day by thy Ameable Frd. Debby Norris—I am far my dr. Sally from Doubting thy Veracity in any point—But I really began to Think that some particular Engagement divert'd thy Attention from this Quarter, as there has been so long a silence on thy side, I lose no Time in Answering thine. Therefore permit me to Insist upon a Testimony of thy Remembrance more frequent for the future, That we may Experience that "Valuable Priviledge of Absent Friends"—With thy lively sentiments I unite in Allowing that Act of duelling, Unchristian & Inhuman and feel great satisfifaction in Assuring thee there was not the least foundation for that Invidious Report—My Dearest Girl, I should at Once imagine myself in a Great Degree Happy (if I may be Allowed the Expression) To find myself Encircled in Your "Sweet little Village" for such, it must be, Where harmonious disposition's Consist—Our first scheme to procure me There I fear will not succeed if not I must attempt Another (i.e.) as I Expect my Br. Isaac in Town Next week I must lay my Command's upon him to spend some time in this City then we really must make a visit a[s] I have the greatest Inclination to have a real Acquaintance of that Agreeable Situation as well as the Amiable Character of its Inhabitants of which thou has given me so Expert a Description of—My Dear Girl I fear thee has put a Misconstruction upon a Paragraph in my last I do not at Present recollect what it was I aim'd at but be assur'd if there had been anything in what I Apprehend thee hinted at I should at once land it in the secure Repository of my dr. Sally's bosom without Hesitation, Therefore I claim the Same Confidence from thyself as I Esteem that Trust Inviolable therefore by no Means to be Disclos'd— ...

Believe me Dear Sally To be Thy sincere

Sally Zane

Deborah Norris to Sarah Fisher (Delaware), May 6, 1780

Thy wellcome letter which put me out of that disagreeable state suspence, came safe to me this afternoon, with an apology from Danl Mifflin for not sending it sooner;—indeed my dear it seems to me that we shall neither of

4. Daniel Mifflin (1754–1812) was from Virginia; the previous year he had married Debby Howell of Philadelphia. In later years, the Mifflins used a significant inheritance to establish Mifflin's Cross Roads, a flourishing settlement which later became Camden.

us marry; but for reasons rather differant, thee from not having an offer thee approves, I, from having no offers to disapprove; so I think we may as well be before hand with our destiny and agree upon living Old Maids, by the way, I think it is a situation that may be supported with great dignity; And I always thought it a striking impropriety for any person, especially one of our own Sex, to speak in that Contemptuous way of Old Maids which is sometimes common, And which too many practise, but my dear to return to the Love affair, depend upon my fidelity   was it the Youth I mentioned in my last? if it was, only put "Yes Debby," in thy next letter And I will be no furthur importunate—How much do I, my beloved Girl, admire thy sentiments on evry subject; I strive as I read thy letters to catch some Emanation of thy Virtues, And I am desirous of possessing in reallity those good qualities which thy partiallity attributes to me already—this much I can say for myself, that I Am Above flattery—I am very glad to hear that thy Aunt Rowland is so well, I hope her little ones will live, do give my respects to her, and sincere Congratulations on her safety.—How sweetly amiable and pleasing in sensibility, how beautifully does it gild and add lustre to other accomplishments; like the sun beam to the trembling dew drop! these were my reflections when I read that part of thy letter which Concerned thy Aunt.—I am obliged to thee in a way that I cannot express, for wishing me to come to Kent again, Ah! how rejoiced I should be to do it, I declare the idea of seeing thee, came to me so forcibly just now, that my Heart jumped and beat quick for two or three minutes   I have spent an afternoon with Hannah Redwood, and one with thy Cousin Sally, since I wrote to thee and indeed my love, I experienced that it is better to go to the house of mourning than to the House of mirth, for I felt much more satisfaction in being there than in several Gay visits and Circles which I have lately been engaged in—I sometimes wonder of what jumblement of materials my mind is composed of, I well remember, that I could not be said to perfectly relish any parties where the J.s[5] were excluded their society seemed in a manner nessessary to my happiness, And yet their behaviour has some how estranged them from my mind in a way unaccountable to me, I am not very intimate with any Girls here, now; 'tho I have a large Acquaintance, I cannot easily form New friendships. at length the Dr.[6] has sailed my dear, they were to have sailed a fortnight before they did, he took leave of all his Acquaintance, I believe he drank tea with me about a week ago And when he went away, wishd me a great share of Health and Happiness, And I in return wishd him a prosperous Voyage And a safe return;—but the last and most tender Adieu was with Bell Marshall[7]   he was particularly Attached to her; (to use his own expressions on such an occasion) and I dare say cried Adieu! with a very good grace.—

---

5. Sweeney suggests that this may refer to the Jones sisters of Virginia, daughters of Susanna Evans and Owen Jones. What caused the breach between Norris and the sisters is unknown.

6. Probably John Foule (1757–1796), who left in May 1780 to study abroad.

7. Isabella Marshall (Wistar) (1763–1790).

Sarah Fisher (Philadelphia) to Sarah Fisher (Delaware), December 16, 1781

8 oClock first day evening—

Well my Dear the leterary Converse, is again Commenced, but after so much Verbal Communication as we have had my mind seems more fit for retirement than for any other employment—there has been quite a female party of us—only think five fine girls and one Maried Lady, without one male attendant—thee must know the girls—Maria & Lucretia, with the others I mentioned before—Matrimony has been made the subject—and I have not a little shared in their banter, they have heard strange reports concerning me, but they are without foundation, Billy Lewis was married last fifth day Evening,[8] he beeing Leontine's[9] uncle it has engross'd much of the attention of our Circle, and the girls have been giving me an account of the appearance, as I am confined and did not go to the meeting—

whether Debby Logan[10] can find time to write thee I do not know, I have been thinking she may say with Rosalinda in Elizabeth Rowe[11]—"the romance is now finish'd, the drama is come to a conclusion. I have been Maried these three Months and from the sober regular way of life I am now in thee must expect no more Epistles—" it seems she is perfectly domestic, stays much at home, and employs her mind in the useful study of family affairs—contrary to my expectation, I thought she would have enjoy'd the polite Circle with more pleasure than when her situation was different—She is an amiable woman may find the Doct. in every respect worthy of her is my sincere wish—no retirement is attainable the family have all enterd the room, and Johny with them, so it will not be in my power to say much more—

thee must take an excuse to Joshua tho I do not think one is necessary, as I think he might have wrote me, tho Ceremony would not have prevented me—Cleora's[12] kind love attends thee she says the weather is so cold she cannot yet write—but intends doing it soon—my very kind love attends all your family, for whom I feel a strong affection—and shall esteem it a pleasure when ever its in my power any way to evince it—this letter was intended to have been quite in the longness—but it is out of my power, do let me hear from thee soon—give my affectionate love to thy worthy parents, tell Cousin Fenwick I shall write him yet for all I have left it so long—

I want much to hear if our friend Eusebus has been yet at Dover; and how

8. William Lewis and Rachel Wharton were married on December 13, 1781.

9. The young correspondents had code names for many of the bachelors in their circle. Leontine is unidentified, but he appears several times in the Philadelphia Sarah Fisher's letters.

10. Deborah Norris had married on September 9, 1781.

11. Elizabeth Rowe (1674–1737), the renowned English author of epistolary works, including *Letters Moral and Entertaining* (1729–33).

12. Cleora, Emma, and Peggy Plesants, three sisters from Virginia, were visiting Fisher's family.

our little Creek lad[13] comes on—if thee does not tell me something after I have Communicated thus freely I shall be much offended with thee—

I have sent some tokens of my remembrance of which I beg your acceptance—give my love to I[saac?]—tell him I often think of him—and a letter from him will please me—do not let him see this letter I request of thee, but if thee tells him I desire it he will,

Daddy and Sister Hetty desire their kind love may be handed you all—and accept a large share from thy ever affectionate

Cousin
Sally Fisher

"Eternal blessings crown my Dearest friend,
"And round her dwelling guardian saints attend,
    first day evening—
dont mention to any person living what I have mentioned,

---

13. "Eusebus" and "our little Creek lad" are two more pseudonyms for the young men in the circle of friends.

Petitions, Political Essays, and Organizational Tracts

Mary Easty (fl. 1692)

Little is known of Mary Easty's early life. She has become a part of American literary history and of American history itself through her victimization during the Salem witch trials of 1692. Like all of those who were executed, Easty maintained her innocence throughout the proceedings, and her petition reflects a tremendous sense of personal dignity and a belief in justice that transcends her individual circumstances. The petition was submitted to Governor Phips on May 20, 1692. She was executed by hanging that summer.

Works: Petition. *Bibliography*: Boyer and Nissenbaum; Burr; Heimert and Delbanco; Woodward.

The Petition of Mary Easty

The humble petition of Mary Easty unto his Excellencies Sir William Phips, and to the Honored Judge[1] and bench now sitting in judicature in Salem, and the Reverend Ministers, humbly sheweth:

That whereas your poor and humble petitioner, being condemned to die, do humbly beg of you to take it in your judicious and pious considerations that your poor and humble petitioner, knowing my own innocencie—blessed be the Lord for it—and seeing plainly the wiles and subtility of my accusers, by myself cannot but judge charitably of others that are going the way of myself, if the Lord steps not mightily in. I was confined a whole month upon the same account that I am condemned now for, and then cleared by the afflicted persons, as some of your Honors know. And in two days time I was cried out upon by them and have been confined and now am condemned to die. The Lord above knows my innocencie then and likewise does now, as at the great day will be known to men and angels. I petition to your Honors not for my own life, for I know I must die and my appointed time is set, but (the Lord

---

1. Samuel Sewall (1652–1730) was the presiding judge at the Salem witch trials; in later years, historians often referred to him as "the hanging judge" of the trials.

knows it is) that if it be possible, no more innocent blood may be shed, which undoubtedly cannot be avoided in the way and course you go in. I question not but your Honors does to the utmost of your power in the discovery and selecting of witchcraft and witches, and would not be guilty of innocent blood for the world; but by my innocencie I know you are in the wrong way. The Lord in his infinite mercy direct you in this great work, if it be blessed will that no more innocent blood be shed. I would humbly beg of you that your Honors would be pleased to examine these afflicted persons strictly and keep them apart some time, and likewise to try some of these confessing witches, I being confident there is several of them has belied themselves and others, as will appear if not in this world I am sure in the world to come, whither I am now a-going. And I question not but you'll see an alteration of these things they say myself and others, having made a league with the devil, we cannot confess. I know and the Lord knows, as will shortly appear, they belie me and so I question not but they do others. The Lord above, who is the searcher of all hearts, knows that as I shall answer it at the tribunal seat that I know not the least thing of witchcraft—therefore I cannot, I dare not, belie my own Soul. I beg your Honors not to deny this my humble petition from a poor dying innocent person, and I question not but that the Lord will give a blessing to your endeavors.

To his Excellency Sir William Phips, Governor, and to the Honored Judge and magistrates now sitting in judicature in Salem.

New York Widows (1733)

The following petition was submitted for publication to John Peter Zenger, editor of the *New-York Weekly Journal*. Using the petition format, the text satirizes the very real differences in treatment that widowed businesswomen received from the political leaders of New York as compared to their male counterparts.

"We the Widows . . ."[1]

We the Widows of this City, have had a Meeting and as our case is something Deplorable we beg you will give it Place in your *Weekly Journal*, that we may be Relieved, it is as follows.

We are House keepers, Pay our Taxes, carry on Trade, and most of us are she Merchants, and as we in some measure contribute to the Support of Government, we ought to be Intituled[2] to some of the Sweets of it; but we find

1. The petition appeared in the *New-York Weekly Journal* 1 n.s. (21 January 1733), pp. 3–4.
2. That is, entitled.

our selves intirely neglected, while the Husbands that live in our Neighbour-hood are daily invited to Dine at Court: we have the Vanity to think we can be full as Entertaining, and make as brave a Defence in case of an Invasion, and perhaps not turn Taile so soon as some of them; and tho' we don't un-derstand the Law, we do the Gospel, witness the seven first Verses of the 23d Chapter of *Proverbs* lately put up near the Markett Place.[3]

Belinda (fl. 1782)

All that is known about the African slave Belinda is revealed in her orally narrated petition; the transcriber is unknown.[1] The text has obvious political significance, but it is also important in literary history from several perspectives—as a rendering of oral literature; as an example of Romantic aesthetics beginning to appear in Amer-ican narratives;[2] and, as Joanne Braxton has noted, as an impor-tant contribution to the rise of African-American women's autobi-ographical narratives.

Works: Petition. *Bibliography:* Braxton; Dove; Kaplan.

Petition of an African Slave[3]

Petition of an African Slave, to the Legislature of Massachusetts.
To the honourable the senate and house of representatives, in general court
    assembled:
The petition of Belinda, an African,
    Humbly shews,
    That seventy years have rolled away, since she, on the banks of the Rio de Valta, received her existence. The mountains, covered with spicy forests—the vallies; loaded with the richest fruits, spontaneously produced—joined to that happy temperature of air, which excludes excess, would have yielded her the

---

3. Proverbs 23:1–7 reads, "When you sit down to eat with a ruler, observe carefully what is before you; / and put a knife to your throat if you are a man given to appetite. / Do not desire his delicacies, for they are deceptive food. / Do not toil to acquire wealth; be wise enough to desist. / When your eyes light upon it, it is gone; for suddenly it takes to itself wings, flying like an eagle toward heaven. / Do not eat the bread of a man who is stingy; do not desire his delicacies; / for he is like one who is inwardly reckoning, 'Eat and drink!' he says to you; but his heart is not with you."

1. I am following Sidney Kaplan's and Joanne Braxton's leads in assuming this is an "as-told-to" narrative; it is also possible that Belinda was literate and wrote her petition in the third person.

2. See also, for example, Phillis Wheatley's "On Reflection" and "On Imagination" as well as Ann Eliza Schuyler Bleecker's *History of Maria Kittle.*

3. Published in *The American Museum* 1 (June 1787): 538–540.

most complete felicity, had not her mind received early impressions of the cruelty of men, whose faces were like the moon, and whose bows and arrows were like the thunder and the lightning of the clouds. The idea of these, the most dreadful of all enemies, filled her infant slumbers with horror, and her noon-tide moments with cruel apprehensions! But her affrighted imagination, in its most alarming extension, never represented distresses equal to what she has since really experienced: for before she had twelve years enjoyed the fragrance of her native groves, and ere she realized that Europeans placed their happiness in the yellow dust, which she carelessly marked with her infant foot-steps—even when she, in a sacred grove, with each hand in that of a tender parent, was paying her devotion to the great Orisa, who made all things, an armed band of white men, driving many of her countrymen in chains, rushed into the hallowed shades! Could the tears, the sighs, and supplications, bursted from the tortured parental affection, have blunted the keen edge of avarice, she might have been rescued from agony, which many of her country's children have felt, but which none have ever described. In vain she lifted her supplicating voice to an insulted father, and her guiltless hands to a dishonoured deity! She was ravished from the bosom of her country, from the arms of her friends, while the advanced age of her parents, rendering them unfit for servitude, cruelly separated her from them for ever.

Scenes which her imagination had never conceived of, a floating world, the sporting monsters of the deep, and the familiar meetings of billows and clouds, strove, but in vain, to divert her attention from three hundred Africans in chains, suffering the most excruciating torment; and some of them rejoicing that the pangs of death came like a balm to their wounds.

Once more her eyes were blest with a continent: but alas! how unlike the land where she received her being! How all things appeared unpropitious. She learned to catch the ideas, marked by the sounds of language, only to know that her doom was slavery, from which death alone was to emancipate her. What did it avail her, that the walls of her lord were hung with splendor, and the dust trodden under foot in her native country, crouded his gates with sordid worshippers! The laws rendered her incapable of receiving property: and though she was a free moral agent, accountable for her own actions, yet never had she a moment at her own disposal! Fifty years her faithful hands have been compelled to ignoble servitude for the benefit of an Isaac Royall, until, as if nations must be agitated, and the world convulsed, for the preservation of that freedom, which the Almighty Father intended for all the human race, the present war commenced. The terrors of men, armed in the cause of freedom, compelled her master to fly, and to breathe away his life in a land, where lawless dominion sits enthroned, pouring blood and vengeance on all who dare to be free.

The face of your petitioner is now marked with the furrows of time, and her frame feebly bending under the oppression of years, while she, by the laws of the land, is denied the enjoyment of one morsel of that immense wealth, a part whereof hath been accumulated by her own industry, and the whole augmented by her servitude.

Wherefore, casting herself at the feet of your honours, as to a body of men, formed for the extirpation of vassalage, for the reward of virtue, and the just returns of honest industry—she prays that such allowance may be made her, out of the estate of colonel Royall, as will prevent her, and her more infirm daughter, from misery in the greatest extreme, and scatter comfort over the short and downward path of their lives: and she will ever pray.

BELINDA.

Boston, February, 1782.

Esther DeBerdt Reed (1747–1780)

"The Sentiments of an American Woman" is one of the most renowned petitions written by a woman in early America. Written by Esther DeBerdt Reed, who became the first president of the Ladies Association, "Sentiments" was intended as a collective statement of women's support for the Revolutionary War effort. As DeBerdt Reed wrote to her father in 1775, "I think the cause . . . so just, so glorious, and I hope will be so victorious, that private interest and pleasure may and ought to be given up, without a murmur."[1]

The 1780 publication of "Sentiments" was DeBerdt Reed's central effort—and the first of its kind in the nation—to organize a large group of Philadelphia women (thirty-six in all) to solicit contributions from women throughout the nation. First published in Philadelphia, "Sentiments" was reprinted in newspapers throughout the thirteen colonies. Collectively, the women donated more than $300,000 for the U.S. soldiers. Money was to be directed to Martha Custis Washington, and supporters included Sarah Franklin Bache (cf. Deborah Read Franklin), Martha Wayles Jefferson, and Hannah Lee Corbin. Contributions were received from 1,645 women, and the contributors were from all economic classes, including an African-American woman, Phillis,[2] and the Marchioness de Lafayette.

DeBerdt Reed wrote to George Washington, informing him of the collection and the women's desire to give the money directly to the soldiers to use as they individually wished; however, Washington preferred that the money be used for clothes for the soldiers or deposited in the National Bank, which, he asserted, would be "serviceable to the Bank and advancing its operations."[3] DeBerdt Reed resisted Washington's suggestion, arguing that the

---

1. William B. Reed, *The Life of Esther DeBerdt* (Philadelphia: C. Sherman, 1853), p. 228.

2. William Reed identifies these contributors (319). I have been unable to confirm that this is Phillis Wheatley, but it seems probable that the donator was she.

3. George Washington to Esther DeBerdt Reed, July 20, 1780 (*The Life* 321–322).

money was intended as a means of conveying more directly "the idea of a reward for past services, and an incitement to future duty."[4] Washington continued to pressure DeBerdt Reed into what he (like most men in the colonies) considered more appropriate contributions from women: the making of shirts for the soldiers. Eventually DeBerdt Reed acquiesced, and when she died shortly thereafter (a victim of a city-wide dysentery epidemic), Sarah Franklin Bache continued with the shirts project.

"The Sentiments" not only calls upon "Women and Girls" to take action in support of the war but it does so by invoking an international array of historically renowned women who set the precedent for such action. DeBerdt Reed thereby challenged historical as well as contemporary renderings of women as uninvolved in patriotic endeavors and recast women as activists and organizers in the national cause by calling upon them to form a national Ladies Association. If their efforts were thwarted by George Washington's sense of appropriate women's work, they recognized the significance of their own efforts—indeed, each shirt had the name of its producer sewn into it. By such an act, women from throughout the colonies literally inscribed their contributions into the material history of the American Revolution.

Bibliography: Kerber; Norton; Reed.

The Sentiments of an American Woman

On the commencement of actual war, the Women of America manifested a firm resolution to contribute as much as could depend on them, to the deliverance of their country. Animated by the purest patriotism, they are sensible of sorrow at this day, in not offering more than barren wishes for the success of so glorious a Revolution. They aspire to render themselves more really useful; and this sentiment is universal from the north to the south of the Thirteen United States. Our ambition is kindled by the fame of those heroines of antiquity, who have rendered their sex illustrious, and have proved to the universe, that, if the weakness of our Constitution, if opinion and manners did not forbid us to march to glory by the same paths as the Men, we should at least equal, and sometimes surpass them in our love for the public good. I glory in all that which my sex has done great and commendable. I call to mind with enthusiasm and with admiration, all those acts of courage, of constancy and patriotism, which history has transmitted to us: The people favoured by Heaven preserved from destruction by the virtues, the zeal and the resolution of Deborah, of Judith, of Esther! The fortitude of the mother of the Macchabees, in giving up her sons to die before her eyes: Rome saved from the fury of a victorious enemy by the efforts of Volumnia, and other Roman Ladies: So

4. Esther DeBerdt Reed to George Washington, July 31, 1780 (*The Life* 323).

many famous sieges where the Women have been seen forgeting the weakness of their sex, building new walls, digging trenches with their feeble hands, furnishing arms to their defenders, they themselves darting the missile weapons on the enemy, resigning the ornaments of their apparel, and their fortune, to fill the public treasury, and to hasten the deliverance of their country; burying themselves under its ruins; throwing themselves into the flames rather than submit to the disgrace of humiliation before a proud enemy.

Born for liberty, disdaining to bear the irons of a tyrannic Government, we associate ourselves to the grandeur of those Sovereigns, cherished and revered, who have held with so much splendour the scepter of the greatest States, the Batildas, the Elizabeths, the Maries, the Catharines, who have extended the empire of liberty, and contented to reign by sweetness and justice, have broken the chains of slavery, forged by tyrants in the times of ignorance and barbarity. The Spanish Women, do they not make, at this moment, the most patriotic sacrifices, to encrease the means of victory in the hands of their Sovereign. He is a friend to the French Nation. They are our allies. We call to mind, doubly interested, that it was a French Maid who kindled up amongst her fellow-citizens, the flame of patriotism buried under long misfortunes: It was the Maid of Orleans who drove from the kingdom of France the ancestors of those same British, whose odious yoke we have just shaken off; and whom it is necessary that we drive from this Continent.

But I must limit myself to the recollection of this small number of achievements. Who knows if persons disposed to censure, and sometimes too severely with regard to us, may not disapprove our appearing acquainted even with the actions of which our sex boasts? We are at least certain, that he cannot be a good citizen who will not applaud our efforts for the relief of the armies which defend our lives, our posssessions, our liberty? The situation of our soldiery has been represented to me; the evils inseparable from war, and the firm and generous spirit which has enabled them to support these. But it has been said, that they may apprehend, that, in the course of a long war, the view of their distresses may be lost, and their services be forgotten. Forgotten! never; I can answer in the name of all my sex. Brave Americans, your disinterestedness, your courage, and your constancy will always be dear to America, as long as she shall preserve her virtue.

We know that at a distance from the theatre of war, if we enjoy any tranquility, it is the fruit of your watchings, your labours, your dangers. If I live happy in the midst of my family; if my husband cultivates his field, and reaps his harvest in peace; if, surrounded with my children, I myself nourish the youngest, and press it to my bosom, without being affraid of seeing myself separated from it, by a ferocious enemy; if the house in which we dwell, if our barns, our orchards are safe at the present time from the hands of those incendiaries, it is to you that we owe it. And shall we hesitate to evidence to you our gratitude? Shall we hesitate to wear a cloathing more simple; hair dressed less elegant, while at the price of this small privation, we shall deserve your benedictions. Who, amongst us, will not renounce with the highest pleasure, these vain ornaments, when she shall consider that the valiant defenders of America will be able to draw some advantage from the money which she may have laid out in these, that they will be better defended from the rigours of the seasons, that after their painful toils, they will receive some extraordinary and unexpected relief; that these presents will perhaps be valued by them at a greater price, when they will have it in their power to say: *This is the offering of the Ladies.* The time is arrived to display the same sentiments which animated us at the beginning of the Revolution, when we renounced the use of teas, however agreeable to our taste, rather than receive them from our persecutors; when we made it appear to them that we placed former necessaries in the rank of superfluities, when our liberty was interested; when our republican and laborious hands spun the flax, prepared the linen intended for the use of our soldiers; when exiles and fugitives we supported with courage all the evils which are concomitants of war. Let us not lose a moment; let us be engaged to offer the homage of our gratitude at the altar of military valour, and you, our brave deliverers, while mercenary slaves combat to cause you to share with them, the irons with which they are loaded, receive with a free hand our offering, the purest which can be presented to your virtue.

By An AMERICAN WOMAN.

IDEAS, relative to the manner of forwarding to the American Soldiers, the presents of the American Women.

ALL plans are eligible, when doing good is the object; there is however one more preferable; and when the operation is extensive, we cannot give it too much uniformity. On the other side, the wants of our army do not permit the slowness of an ordinary path. It is not in one month, nor in eight days, that we would relieve our soldiery. It is immediately; and our impatience does not permit us to proceed by the long circuit of collectors, receivers and treasurers. As my idea with regard to this, have been approved by some Ladies of my friends, I will explain them here, every other person will not be less at liberty to prepare to adopt a different plan.

1st. All Women and Girls will be received without exception, to present their patriotic offering; and, as it is absolutely voluntary, every one will regulate it according to her ability, and her disposition. The shilling offered by the Widow or the young Girl, will be received as well as the most considerable sums presented by the Women who have the happiness to join to their patriotism, greater means to be useful.

2d. A Lady chosen by the others in each county, shall be the Treasuress; and to render her task more simple, and more easy, she will not receive but determinate sums, in a round number, from twenty hard dollars to any greater sum. The exchange forty dollars in paper for one dollar in specie.

3d. The Women who shall not be in a condition to send twenty dollars in specie, or above, will join in as great a number as will be necessary to make this or any greater sum, and one amongst them will carry it, or cause it to be sent to the Treasuress.

4th. The Treasuress of the county will receive the money, and will keep a register, writing the sums in her book, and causing it to be signed at the side of the whole by the person who has presented it.

5th. When several Women shall join together to make a total sum of twenty dollars, or more, she amongst them who shall have the charge to carry it to the Treasuress, will make mention of all their names on the register, if her associates shall have so directed her; those whose choice it shall be, will have the liberty to remain unknown.

6th. As soon as the Treasuress of the county shall judge, that the sums which she shall have received, deserve to be sent to their destination, she will cause them to be presented with the lists, to the wife of the Governor or President of the State, who will be the Treasuress-General of the State; and she will cause it to be set down in her register, and have it sent to Mistress Washington. If the Governor or President are unmarried, all will address themselves to the wife of the Vice-President, if there is one, or of the Chief-Justice, &c.

7th. Women settled in the distant parts of the country, and not chusing for any particular reason as for the sake of greater expedition, to remit their Capital to the Treasuress, may send it directly to the wife of the Governor, or President, &c. or to Mistress Washington who, if she shall judge necessary, will in a short answer to the sender, acquaint her with the reception of it.

8th. As Mrs. Washington may be absent from the camp when the greater part of the bank shall be sent there, the American Women considering, that General Washington is Father and Friend of the Soldiery; that he is himself, the first Soldier of the Republic, and that their offering will be received at its destination, as soon as it shall have come to his hands, they will pray him, to take the charge of receiving it, in the absence of Mrs. Washington.

9th. General Washington will dispose of this fund in the manner that he shall judge most advantageous to the Soldiery. The American Women desire only that it may not be considered as to be employed, to procure the army, the objects of subsistence, arms or cloathing, which are due to them by the Continent. It is an extraordinary bounty intended to render the condition of the Soldier more pleasant, and not to hold place of the things which they ought to receive from the Congress, or from the States.

10th. If the General judges necessary, he will publish at the end of a certain time, an amount of that which shall have been received from each particular State.

11th. The Women who shall send their offerings, will have in their choice to conceal or to give their names; and if it shall be thought proper, on a fit occasion, to publish one day the lists, they only, who shall consent, shall be named; when with regard to the sums sent, there will be no mention made, if they so desire it.

Letitia Cunningham (fl. 1783)

Letitia Cunningham is known only by a political tract, "The Case of the Whigs," that she published in Philadelphia in 1783. The tract runs fifty-one pages in length, and its style and wit suggest she was a highly educated woman. Cunningham begins the text with a philosophical argument, employs an astute political voice, and delights in using puns to expose the political machinations and ineptitude of her opponents (both unfair taxes and political "fallibility" are satirized, for instance, in her recognition that one critic "fairly taxes our Congress" for their lack of wisdom).

Works: *The Case of the Whigs* (Philadelphia, 1783).

The Case of the Whigs, &c.

Time has been, and that not very long since, when had the rectitude of some of the decisions of Congress, and some of our other legislative bodies, been as freely discussed, and as fairly proved to have been strongly tinctured with fallibility, as they have of late been, not only in private conversation, but also in some publications in our newspapers, neither the author nor publishers of such daring truths would have escaped the imputation of political heresy; and it would have been their peculiar good fortune, if they had not likewise been enquired after, in order to undergo the severities of political excommunication.

Nor will this account of matters seem at all surprising to any one who considers the natural ardor of the human heart in all national contentions for what men esteem their dearest rights and privileges; a very respectable kind of enthusiasm being closely connected with such ideas, no wonder that the multitude should look up to those who are their leaders and counsellors, in their opposition to what they deem tyrannical impositions, with esteem and gratitude. In this case all their defects and blemishes are viewed in a favourable light, they find it difficult to separate the man from his cause; and therefore an endeavour to find fault with, or to represent any of their measures as pernicious to public safety, is sure to be interpreted by such people as inimical to the cause in which the public are engaged; at such times prudent people may think it best to keep silence, at least for some time.

But political phrensy is not generally of very long continuance. History will inform us of some who were for a while revered and obeyed as demi-gods, who were afterwards dragged to the tribunal of justice, in order to suffer for their crimes when in power; in some, indeed, it lasts until the last moment of their lives, and such choice spirits I believe we have among ourselves, upon whom neither reason nor the ties of humanity have the least influence; but it is not I say generally so, for many, as has been observed in the first paragraph, throwing off the fetters of servility, have nobly dared to point out real grievances occasioned by the determinations of our rulers, and have submitted their remarks to public examination, and have also demanded redress, hitherto, it must be confessed, without success; yet still it is the duty of him who aspires to the illustrious name of patriot, persist in his endeavours to have the grievances of his fellow men and fellow citizens redressed; a name this which reflects more solid glory on any character than the most valiant achievements or most brilliant victories obtained in the field without a view to it; and it is to be hoped and wished for, that many more will employ the talent committed to them in this way.

I have been led into these reflections upon perusing a paper in The Freeman's Journal of July 24th, where a writer under the signature of Vox Populi hath, with manly freedom publicly spoken a great many salutary truths. As I intend to pursue the path marked out by him much farther than he has done, I must beg to remind the reader of some of his sentiments in his own words; he there, speaking on the design of stopping the interest on loan office certificates hitherto paid by bills of exchange upon France, says, "They must be tame spirits indeed, who will submit to it, and unworthy the name of freemen;" and in another place, "There is a certain degree of public injustice which no free people, from love of country or any other motive will submit to," and there fairly taxes our Congress with want of wisdom, and with what is much worse, with breach of honour and public faith, and I think he fairly proved it too; but certainly there are many more instances of this odious charge being fixed upon our public rulers, than that which he hath adduced, which it shall be the business of the present papers to lay before the public for their impartial consideration. One remark more I shall quote from this writer, which ought, I think, to be engraved on tablets, and so exposed to the view of every free citizen of these states, he says, "Whether we are oppressed as heretofore by the arbitrary edicts of a British parliament, or, as at present, by the unjust ordinances of Congress, we may be equally sufferers, and are equally called upon to redress ourselves." Very true, sir; in this sentiment, I think every one who has the smallest spark of liberty alive in his breast must concur, and many will think you might with equal truth have added, that we never did suffer the twentieth part by any edict of the British parliament, as no inconsiderable number of the good people of these states have suffered by some unjust ordinances of Congress, and other legislative bodies under their influence. The truth of this shall be submitted to the impartial judgment of the unprejudiced, when they have considered what is hereafter presented to their review.

I cannot, however, help wishing, that the writer above quoted had taken this task upon himself, as his subject led him naturally to it; he has confined his remarks upon the broken faith and violated contracts of these states by their Congress, solely to the case of those who funded their property prior to the first of March, 1778, of which number I suppose he is one; but surely it was not quite generous to confine his remarks to one sett of public creditors, when every circumstance of distress which he paints as the consequences of the stoppage of the interest on funded money, must apply with as much or rather greater force, in the case of those who funded after that period, and yet never received any interest at all. It certainly must be evident to every enquiring person, that in this latter class of funders, are those pitiable objects the widow and the fatherless, whose impending distress, as a consequence of the measure he reprobates, he so pathetically laments, as also those "who having placed their money in the public funds, are deprived of the means of increasing their capital by personal efforts of industry," and to these let me add also the aged and infirm, who are incapable of increasing their capital by any personal efforts, and who formerly subsisted by the interest of this same money, which is now most unrighteously and barbarously witheld from them; it must also be known to every one who is in any degree conversant in our affairs, that to these was as often and as solemnly pledged the public faith for the payment both of this principle and interest as to the others, that the times for the payment of both were stipulated by Congress in the original contract, that it was in virtue of this contract they funded their property, and yet in both cases hath this contract been violated. . . .

Women of Wilmington, North Carolina (1782)

In 1782 twenty-one women from Wilmington, North Carolina, submitted a petition to Governor Alexander Martin asserting their patriotism, their advocacy of women's right to fair treatment, and their support of "the independent State of North Carolina." As *feme coverts*, some women in North Carolina at the end of the Revolution were being punished because of their "Absentee" husbands' political alliances with the British. The petitioners, women who had been forcibly removed from Wilmington by the British during the war, argued that if the State of North Carolina was to view their own removal by the British as wrong, then they must not duplicate such actions against women who were "old friends and acquaintances." Explicitly understanding that this was a new and equally significant form of "warfare," the petitioners demanded honorable treatment for honorable actions—"It is beneath the character of the independent State of North Carolina to war with women and children." The text is a blend of demands for women's rights and acquiescence to the idea that women needed to be legally protected, a synthesis that reflects the very precarious legal situation in which many women found themselves during the years of Revolution. But more important, it is a public act of sisterhood: an act by women for other women in which they refuse to let war shatter friendships and destroy the lives of innocent women and children.

Works: Petition.

To His Excellency Gov. Alex. Martin
and the Members of the Honorable Council

We, the subscribers, inhabitants of the town of Wilmington, warmly attached to the State of North Carolina, and strenuously devoted to our best wishes and endeavours to the achievement of its independence, feeling for the honor of, and desirous that our Enemies should not have the smallest pretext to brand them as cruel or precipitate, that the dignity of our public characters may not be degraded to the imitation of examples of inhumanity exhibited by our Enemies.

Humbly shew to His Excellency, the Governor, and the Honorable Council, that we have been informed that orders have issued from your honorable board that the wives and children of Absentees should depart the State with a small part of their property in forty eight hours after notice given them.

It is not the province of our sex to reason deeply upon the policy of the order, but as it must affect the helpless and innocent, it wounds us with the most sincere distress and prompts our earnest supplication that the order may be arrested, and the officers forbid to carry it into execution. If it is intended as retaliation for the expulsion of some of us, the subscribers, by the British from the Town of Wilmington, and to gratify a resentment which such inhumanity to us may be supposed to have excited, its object is greatly mistaken.

Those whom your proclamation holds forth as marks of public vengeance, neither prompted the British order nor aided the execution of it. On the contrary, they expressed the greatest indignation at it, and with all their power strove to mitigate our sufferings. Still some instances attended which made the execution of it less distressing to us than yours must be to those upon whom it is intended to operate. We were ordered without the British Lines and then our friends were ready to receive us. They received us with a cordial welcome, and ministered to our wants with generosity and politeness. With pleasure we bear this public testimony. But our Town women now ordered out must be exposed to the extreme of human wretchedness. Their friends are in Charles Town; they have neither carriages nor horses to remove them by land, nor vessels to transport them by water, and the small pittance allotted them of their property, could they be procured, would be scarce equal to the purchase of them. It is beneath the character of the independent State of North Carolina to war with women and children. The authors of our ill treatment are the proper subjects of our own and the resentment of the public. Does their barbarity strike us with abhorrence? Let us blush to imitate it; not justify by our own practice what we so justly condemn in others. To Major Craig, and him alone, is to be imputed the inhuman edicts, for even the British Soldiers were shocked at it.

If we may be allowed to claim any merit with the public for our steady adherence to the Whig principles of America; if our sufferings induced by that attachment have given us favor and esteem with your honorable body, we beg leave to assure you that we shall hold it as a very signal mark of your respect for us if you will condescend to suffer to remain amongst us our old friends and acquaintances whose husbands, though estranged from us in political opinions, have left wives and children much endeared to us, and who may live to be an honor to the State and to Society if permitted to continue here. The safety of this State, we trust in God, is now secured beyond the most powerful exertions of our Enemies, and it would be a system of abject weakness to fear the feeble efforts of women and children.

And as in Duty bound we shall ever pray.

Anne Hooper,	Ann Towkes,
Mary Allen,	M. Hand,
Sarah Nash,	S. Wilkings,
Mary Nash,	M. Lord,
Mary Moore,	Isabella Read,
E. Nash,	Sally Read,
Sarah Moore,	Mary Granger,
M. Loyd,	Jane Ward,
Catharine Young,	Hannah Ward,
J. M. Drayton,	Kitty Ward,
E. Wilkings.	

Petition of the Young Ladies (1787)

Like the petition of the New York widows, the following political satire uses the petition format in order to lambast the arrogance of some of the gentlemen delegates to Congress, the stereotype of young women's desperation for suitable marriage partners, and the political system of patronage ("the sunshine of preferment").

The Petition of the Young Ladies . . .[1]

To the honourable the Delegates of the United States in Congress assembled.

The petition of the young ladies of Portsmouth, Boston, Newport, New-London, Amboy, New-Castle, Williamsburgh, Wilmington, Charleston and Savannah,

Most ardently sheweth,

That your petitioners possess the qualities of youth, health and beauty, in an eminent degree.

That notwithstanding these advantages, they see with great pain but little prospect of getting good husbands, owing to the passion the pretty fellows have of going abroad and marrying in other countries, thereby leaving a great disproportion between the sexes at home.

That population is the true source of national wealth and power.

That in all countries, population increases, in proportion as marriages are frequent.

1. Originally published in *The American Museum* 1 (Apr. 1787): 347–348.

That without marriage, even the object of the Almighty, in creating them, must be defeated, and his first and great command disobeyed.

That your petitioners have been informed of the many marriages that have taken place in New-York, since your residence in that city, and that even some of your own members have to their great honour, become husbands.

That delegates in congress ought to be all bachelors, and a new election ordered in consequence of marriage, domestic duty being a good excuse from public service.

That with due deference to their New-York sisters, they cannot allow them any just preference in the requisite qualities to make the married state happy.

That as the first motive for appointing a congress was, to promote the welfare of humanity, they presume the daughters, as well as the sons of America, have an equal right to a participation of the blessings arising therefrom.

That for these reasons, your petitioners earnestly request you would annually remove the seat of federal government into the metropolis of each state, in due rotation; leaving Maryland, Pennsylvania and New-York the three last upon the list, you having already resided in each of their capitals.

That if your petitioners' request be granted, they hope, from the number of foreigners and other fine fellows, who keep themselves in the sunshine of preferment, as well as from your own body, to have at least a chance of bringing their accomplishments and good qualities into their destined use, and of thereby improving as well as augmenting society.

And your petitioners, as by inclination prompted, shall ever with, &c. &c. &c.

Margaretta Van Wyck Bleecker Faugères (1771–1801)

Born October 11, 1771, in Tomhanick, New York, Margaretta Bleecker was the daughter of Ann Eliza Schuyler, the poet (*q.v.*), and John J. Bleecker, Esq. As a child Margaretta suffered greatly as a consequence of the war years. Her younger sister died when Margaretta and her mother fled British troops in the area, and Ann Schuyler Bleecker suffered severe depressive bouts thereafter until her death in 1783. In spite of a superb education and her father's return to a prosperous lifestyle, Bleecker rejected the aristocratic intellectual traditions of her parents, advocating instead Jacobin tenets. Her political bent was exemplified in her decision to marry on Bastille Day in 1791; her spouse was a French physician, Peter Faugères.

Bleecker Faugères was instrumental in preserving her mother's works, collecting and publishing them in 1793 along with a memoir of her mother and other selections of her own writings. Included in this collection is the following essay, representing Faugères's democratic values and the growing objection to slavery in the new republic. In her own life, however, Faugères did not succeed in establishing the egalitarian relationship that her marriage had seemed to proffer. Peter Faugères was apparently an abusive husband who squandered the family money. When her husband died in 1798, Bleecker Faugères and her young daughter were left in near poverty; to survive, she turned to teaching at several schools in the New England region. Her demise rapidly followed. She died in Brooklyn on January 14, 1801; her personal history became a tragic echo of her mother's depression and early death. Yet, also like her mother, in her short lifetime Bleecker Faugères produced a significant body of work. In addition to being an essayist, she was a poet, publishing in the *New-York Magazine* and elsewhere, often under the pen name "Ella"; she was also a dramatist (*q.v.*); and in 1797 she published *The Ghost of John Young*, in which she argued against capital punishment. Bleecker Faugères's death at age twenty-nine represented a significant loss to intellectual life in early America.

Works: *The Posthumous Works of Ann Eliza Bleecker . . . To Which is Added, a Collection of Essays, Prose and Poetical, by Margaretta V. Faugères* (1793); *Belisarius: A Tragedy* (1795); *The Ghost of John Young* (1797). Bibliography: Griswold.

Fine Feelings Exemplified in the Conduct of a Negro Slave[1]

Notwithstanding what the learned Mr. Jefferson has said respecting the want of finer feelings in the blacks,[2] I cannot help thinking that their sensations, mental and external, are as acute as those of the people whose skin may be of a different coulour; such an assertion may seem bold, but facts are stubborn things, and had I not *them* to support me, it is probable I should not attempt to oppose the opinions of such an eminent reasoner.

In the interior parts of this state lived (a few years ago) a man of property, who owned a number of blacks; but formed in Nature's most savage mould, his chief employment was inventing punishments for his unfortunate dependants, and his principal delight in practising the tortures he had invented. Among the number of his slaves was an old Negro, who, in his younger days, had been a faithful servant; but captivity and sorrow had at length broken his spirit, and destroyed that ambition which actuates the free, and gives energy and life to all they perform. This was a proper subject for the cruelty of Mr.

1. Written in 1791, this essay was published in *The Posthumous Works* (1793), pp. 268–270.

2. In spite of his public statements against the slave trade, most notably in the draft of the Declaration of Independence, Thomas Jefferson's racist attitudes emerged in several public and private writings.

A—— to act upon. Upon the commission of the smallest fault, or the most trifling neglect, he would himself tic MINGO, (as butchers do sheep intended for slaughter) and after having beaten him till the blood followed every stroke of the whip, he would retire, leaving the wretch weltering in his gore, exposed to the burning rays of summer or the gelid gales of winter. When rested he would return, and after a repetition of his amusement, would release the sufferer, lest a few more minutes of such extreme agonies should shorten the period of MINGO's woes, and his master's felicity. However, this mode of punishment becoming a little troublesome to Mr. A——, he thought of another which he believed would answer nearly as well: he caused a large ox-chain to be made, and putting it about MINGO's waist, he brought it round his neck, and there fastened it again, leaving an end of about four yards, to which he nailed a piece of wood weighing upwards of forty weight. With this clog the slave was obliged to work—and this at night was placed in the master's chamber, (the chain passing through a hole in the door) while MINGO slept on the ground out side of the house, from which uncomfortable couch nothing but the most bitter cold excused him.

Seven long years did the miserable being groan under this load, when the captain of a vessel, hearing of his hard fate, out of pity bought him.

After having paid the money he went home, and sending for MINGO, told him he was free:—"You are your own master," said the humane sailor; "but you are old, and helpless—I will take care of you."—Overpowered with joy, the old man clasped the captain's knees; he wept aloud—he raised his swimming eyes to heaven—he would have spoken his thanks;—but his frame was too feeble for the mighty conflict of his soul—he expired at his benefactor's feet!

Revolutionary War Writings

Susanna Wright (1697–1784)

Susanna Wright was born in Warrington, England, on August 4, 1697, one of eight children born to Patience Gibson and John Wright. Wright's family settled in America in 1714, and she joined them shortly thereafter, having stayed behind long enough to complete her education. When her mother died in 1722, Wright began a twenty-year career of running Hempfield, the family homestead in the Susquehanna Valley region (now Columbia) of Pennsylvania, where the family ran a ferry business. Later in her life she settled in a large house left to her by Samuel Blunston. Like the Wrights, Blunston was a pioneer settler; he and Wright were rumored to have been in love for many years, but they never married.

In spite of the hardships of a frontier life, Wright was recognized throughout the region for her intellectual and artistic abilities. She was a talented manufacturer, raising thousands of silkworms at Wright's Ferry and producing silk that she spun into fancy dresses; she was called upon by neighbors and travelers for her talents as a scrivener; she was recognized as a talented arbitrator in land disputes; and she acted as both physician and apothecary for the region. Only the silk production was a paying enterprise, but her contributions to the community were many. An ardent bibliophile, Wright was fluent in four languages and learned in science as well as being a prolific correspondent with many women and men in the intellectual circles of Philadelphia. She was also an accomplished poet. It is little wonder that this extraordinary woman came to be known as "the celebrated Susanna Wright." She died on December 1, 1784, at the age of eighty-eight.

Works: Correspondence, poetry. *Bibliography*: Biddle and Lowrie; Cowell; Lopez and Herbert; McElroy.

The Letters of Susanna Wright

To James Pemberton, Philadelphia merchant

Esteemed Friend

My Brother Jimmy was Obliged without any previous notice, to set out very Early this morning towards paxton, partly to see what flour could certainly be got ready in time for the British troops, and partly to assist Wm Franklin in procuring horses &c for their use, And Directed me to write to thee to the following purpose, that Benjamin Franklin (who is now in these parts) thought it absolutely wrong to send down any more flour, till the quantity wanted at the camp, could be ascertained to be got ready in time, which there is great reason to believe will not be done; and that if any misfortune should happen to that Expedition, to whatever cause it may be owing, it wil be attributed to their march being hindred for want of this flour, he was told at Winchester there was no more then two loads at the mouth of Conagochage last week, and it is a question whether half the wheat is yet ground, or a third part of the casks made and as the troops Purpose to Begin their march about the middle of may, Benj^a Franklin says they were very Loud in their Exclamations; he is now Endeavouring to procure horses and Waggons for them, what Success he will meet with is yet unknown————I Inclose one of his Advertisements————he likewise says the Officers were prejudiced in a most Extraordinary manner against that people of the province; that they were quite Strangers to this flour being a present from this Gov^t, and thought they were to pay for it; that they had never heard of the £10000 Given to N England, or of the last bill offered by the Assembly to the Gov^t, that he had done Every thing in his power to remove their prejudices, which he had a good Opportunity for, as he Staid some time with them after the rest of the company were come away—Since I sealed this I rec^d two letters to my brother, one from Hess & one from [illegible] Morgan—I Know it was his oppinion when he left here that no more of this flour must be sent to you And if he finds it otherwise what is to be sent will be sent with the utmost dispatch, he Expected to return in 2 or 3 days and will Inform thee by some person from the Court held at Lancaster[1] what you may Certainly depend upon in relation to it

I am thy assured friend

April the 27th 1755   S: Wright

To Mary Park in Chester, Pennsylvania

Dear Polly

as I know not what exuse to make that will appear a Sufficient one, I shall not attempt to make any at all; I know I ought long agoe, to have returned my hearty thanks to thy Worthey father & thy self, for the great kindness you were pleased to show us when we were in Philadelphia & Chester, but I have not done it, and

---

1. Illegible words added above the line. See also Franklin's *Autobiography* on this event.

now If you will accept my late acknowledgm^{ts}, I shall take it as a further favour; often reflect with vexation that I did not spend more time with my old & Good friends in chester, when I was so near them, but the Circumstances of our family would not then permit it, and want of Inclination was no part of the reason.– – –we live in perpetual alarm about Indians, and hear of mischeifs done much nearer to us then when we left home last fall, but I beleive being more used to the, and particularly learning the Indians have not cannoes to come upon us by water, is the reason we are not under the same apprehensions we had then and we further hope devine providence will Continue to preserve us, I should take a letter from thee as a favour, to hear of your health, I know thou can write readily, and has not those disquiets & disturbances to devert thy mind from obliging a friend, as any person must have who lives in a Situation like ours

My Brothers are in Phil^a, the rest of our family Joyn in
Kind Respects and Complim^{ts} to thy father & thy Self

I am my Dear friend thy truly obliged fr^d
S:Wright

To Isaac Whitelock in Lancaster, Pennsylvania

Jan 16th [1764]

My Respected Friend

I received the disagreable account from your town this night, that the Govr of N:York would not Suffer the Indians to be taken into that Gov^t, But had ordred them to be brought back to Phil^a, where it was Suppos'd they were arrivd by this time; and that the Rioters, Instigted to mischief, from within, and without, would Imediatly colect themselves, and go in search of them,—this report, whether true or false, gives me great anxiety, more Especialy, as we are told they are still roving about in companys, and that in all their Revels, they Breath vengeance against Js Pemberton, Jos Fox and my Brother, By name, as well as against many others who they do not name, I hope devine Providence will protect them, but if the Indians are realy returnd, and these wretches pursue their Purposes, I wish they might be apprisd of these threats—I would fain hope this report is without foundation, John Blackburn & a friend from Phil^a, left that Citty last 6th day morning, when they had heard nothing of the Kind, but suposd the poor defenceles creatures were on their way to Sr Wm Johnson,—I shall take it as a favor, if thou will oblige me with a line, of whatever thou knows about it, which given to Anne Marsden or Johny Bowne, will be Safely sent me by the boy who carrys this

I am thy assured fr^d
S:Wright

Mary Willing Byrd (1740–1814)

Born in Philadelphia on September 10, 1740, Mary Willing was one of ten children. Her mother, Anne, was a member of the renowned Shippen family of Philadelphia, and her father, Charles, was mayor of the city; Mary's writing talents and intellectual skills suggest she was very well educated. On January 29, 1761, she married Colonel William Byrd III of Westover, Virginia, a member of the famous Virginia family. It was Mary's first marriage and her husband's second. Although William had established an appearance of wealth in Virginia and maintained a magnificent estate on the James River, his gambling habits left his wife and eight children with little means of support upon his death. Through determination and hard labor, the widowed Willing Byrd reestablished the plantation as a profitable enterprise.

Mary Willing Byrd's literary and historical significance actually begins during the American Revolution when British troops landed several times at Westover. Although apparently a trustworthy patriot herself, she came under suspicion of passing communications for the enemy, in large part because of her acquaintances in the British forces (her husband had been aligned with the British and one of his sons by his first marriage was serving in that army) and because of her family connections (a cousin, Margaret Shippen, was married to Benedict Arnold). During the Revolution and subsequently, no proof of Willing Byrd's collaboration with the British army was ever substantiated; however, in February 1781 Colonel John Nicholas had his officers seize all of her papers. Arthur Lee, of the Virginia Lee family, and others came to her support, and no record remains of further action against her. What does remain is Willing Byrd's own determination to clear her name and to seek restitution of her property—a determination that she took directly to the then-Governor of Virginia, Thomas Jefferson. Her letters to Jefferson and Colonel (Baron) Friedrich Wilhelm von Steuben reveal her sense of honor and determination—and a considerable literary talent.

Works: Correspondence. Bibliography: The Correspondence of The Three William Byrds of Westover, Virginia; The Papers of Thomas Jefferson.

Letter of Mary Willing Byrd

To Thomas Jefferson, Governor of Virginia
Sir,   *Westover, February 23, 1781.*
Having heard from Major Turberville,[1] that he had sent to inform you of the arrival of Mr. Hare, and the business on which he came; and that the answer he received was, you left that matter to the commanding officer, I thought it unnecessary for me to give you the trouble, at that time, of writing to you

1. Major George Lee Turberville was regional commander during the "Westover Affair," as Willing Byrd's experience was termed by the military officials. It was at Sandy Point, near Westover, that Lieutenant Charles Hare and his ship were detained by Turberville.

on the subject of his business, for two reasons; it was my determination not to keep the things brought by Mr. Hare in the Flag, without first consulting the Executive. This Mr. Meade[2] and many other persons had often heard me say. In a letter I wrote immediately on his coming up to the Baron,[3] I informed him some articles were brought for me, and assured him I had not the least inclination to keep them, if the Executive did not approve of it. The other reason was, I did not know the whole amount of the articles, and wished when I wrote, to be able to write fully on the subject. Think not, sir, that I had anything to do with Mr. Hare's coming from Sandy Point to Westover. I knew nothing of it, and beg the favor of you to suspend your opinion of my conduct, until I have an opportunity of vindicating it.

The officers have acted so confusedly that I dare believe you have had but a very imperfect account of the whole affair, and I am by no means capable of giving a proper one of it, I think.

I think I am called on [to] say something on the subject, as a duty I owe myself, the public in general, and you in particular as Supreme Magistrate of this State. Baron Steuben thinks me accountable to the civil, and not to the military power for my conduct; and to that I appeal for justice. Mr. Hare came up by the Baron's permission, on a Flag,[4] granted by General Arnold,[5] for the purpose of bringing up such negroes as he chose to return.[6] This permission was given before your order was sent to General Nelson, respecting negroes.[7] I flattered myself that I could have served my neighbors, and with this view, wrote by a flag, and by the advice of one of your most particular friends, a man of most excellent judgment, and express approbation of every person I have seen.

I hear Mr. Hare has forfeited his flag, been made a prisoner and searched. Among his papers was found a letter written by myself, while the fleet lay at Westover, I think in answer to a message I received from Captain Evans, by a little gentleman whom he was very fond of, a relation of his. I do not recollect the contents of this letter, but am easy about it, for my heart never dictated aught that was dishonorable, so my pen could never have expressed anything that I could not justify. If policy had not forbid it, I owe too much to my honor to betray my Country.

2. Colonel Richard Kidder Meade of Virginia; he had been General Washington's aide-de-camp from 1777 to 1780.

3. Baron Friedrich Wilhelm von Steuben was a Prussian army officer who trained the Continental Army during the American Revolution.

4. Flagship, a ship that transports the commander of a fleet and flies his flag.

5. Benedict Arnold was a general in the American army during the Revolution. In 1780, after failing to receive what he felt was a deserved promotion, he betrayed the West Point military post to the enemy. Escaping after his traitorous act, he joined the British forces and was acting in that capacity at the time of this letter.

6. Like many other Southern estate owners, Willing Byrd maintained a large number of slaves as the chief work force on her plantation.

7. In a letter dated February 21, Steuben informed Jefferson that "previous to the Order of Government that no partial requisitions should be made for Property taken by the Enemy; I granted Mrs. Byrd a flag for the purpose of receiving her Negro's &c. I informed the person who went with the flag, that if Arnold would not send them, he might send a flag when he pleased, with Mrs. Byrds Property, and that I would give his flag a passport" (*Papers* 4:680). Jefferson's order concerning the requisitions had been written on January 10, 1781.

Indeed, sir, you may rely on my veracity when I assure you, that no action of my life has been inconsistent with the character of a virtuous American.

I cannot express violent, enthusiastic opinions, and wish curses [and] distruction on the meanest individual on earth. It is against my religion. I wish well to all mankind, to America in particular. What am I but an American? All my friends and connexions are in America; my whole property is here—could I wish ill to everything I have an interest in?

My honor is dearer to me than my life; let not my Countrymen attempt to injure me further. The All-seeing eye of our gracious God, will revenge the innocent and the helpless. I pray that he will forgive my persecutors, and enable them to show as much virtue as I have done when they have as great a tryal. He that will show more let him cast the first stone. I flatter myself I have raised myself in the esteem of the British, by showing them that I had a perfect love for my country.

I hope you will pardon the trouble I give you. I mean to address you not only as the Governor, but as an acquaintance, whom I have experienced kindness and some friendship from, to ask your advice . . . what will be the proper steps for me to take in this affair. I know a law passed sometime ago, which I looked over in a cursory manner, importing what was treason.[8] I never conceived that there was an object up the river, to lead the enemy near my habitation, therefore I did not attentively read the law. No person gave me warning of their approach. I had no time to send anything out of the way of the privateers, which were what I was afraid of.

When the officers landed, I received them according to my idea, with propriety. I consulted my heart and my head, and acted to the best of my judgment, agreeable to all laws, human and divine. If I have acted erroneously, it was an error in judgment and not of the Heart. As Pope expresses it, "One self-approving hour will outweigh the praises of millions." The force of this sentiment I now fully experience. I mean not by this to show contempt for the good opinion of the public. I value it highly, but would rather know I merited it, than know I had it.

If you, sir, will have the goodness to furnish me with that law, and your opinion of it, I shall be extremely obliged to you. I hope to prove myself worthy of your kindness. If any unavoidable things have happened that the law forbids, I cannot doubt the justice of the legislative body, that they will pass another in my favor, when I have an opportunity of making my innocence appear.

Every good man must have been shocked when they heard of the *savage* treatment I have met with. This cannot be called *Liberty*. I do not know who has been in fault. I am convinced, sir, that you have had no share in these bare [base?] actions; and [I] should not do that great man, Baron Steuben, justice, if I did not declare that I was convinced, that the whole of his con-

8. An act defining treason had been passed by Congress in October 1776 in which the consequences of giving "aid and comfort" to the enemy were stipulated as loss of property and life. On the first of March, Jefferson responded that he had only one copy of the law but informed Willing Byrd of the gist of the act. Although careful to note that he had no authority to rule on the situation, Jefferson indicated his belief that Willing Byrd's incident would be considered a misdemeanor.

duct was perfectly amiable, and that he was incapable of giving orders that would authorize such rash, such indecent, horrid conduct, as I have met with.

I have the honor to be, sir, your most obedient, humble servant, M Byrd[9]

Mary Bartlett (?–1789)

Mary Bartlett was born in Newton, New Hampshire, the daughter of Sarah Hoyt and Joseph Bartlett. Little is known of her early life, but in 1754 she married her cousin, Dr. Josiah Bartlett, and settled in Kingston, New Hampshire. Thereafter, Bartlett's life becomes representative of the alterations that the War for Independence brought to so many women's lives. While her husband (who later became Governor of New Hampshire) attended the first Continental Congress, Bartlett accepted full responsibility for their economic survival: she ran the household, directed the planting and harvesting of their crops, and supervised the servants who worked the estate. Although Josiah acknowledged "the Greatest uneasiness" over leaving his family, he had left the estate in good hands. During her husband's absence Bartlett also cared for their children and gave birth to and buried a daughter born during Josiah's absence. In an exceptional national cause, she rose to the occasion; yet her exceptionalism aligns her with numerous other women who supported the Revolution through similar economic means, in spite of personal hardships.

Works: Correspondence. *Bibliography:* Bartlett, J.; Bartlett, L.; Maier.

The Letters of Mary Bartlett[1]

My Dear

. . . I hope by this time You have arrived as far as Philadelphia in health & without Difficulty & may You be kept from all Evil; tho I hear Some British Lords have Laid a Plan to attack Philadelphia by Land if Impracticable by Sea however I Believe they can Plan more than they will be Suffer'd to accomplish . . .

Lieut Pearson is Better of all His Disorders . . . —no Deaths in this Parish

9. Throughout February, Willing Byrd continued to correspond with Jefferson; ultimately, the record dwindles away, and no charges of treason were filed.

1. All of Bartlett's letters included here are addressed to her husband, Josiah, who was attending the Continental Congress in Philadelphia.

Except the widow fowler Who was buried last Sunday—their has been near 30 Persons Sick with the Canker & all like to Recover—[2] . . .

the weather very much alter'd Since you left us warm Rains & Shines by turns which has Brought the peach trees Cherry & other Plumb trees in full Blossom apple trees Begining to Blossom they Do not appear to Bloom So thick as they Did Last Year—we have almost Done Plantain[g]

I wrote to you last week & Shall write ev[ery] week if I have an opertunity to Send I Shall be Glad to hear from you as often as I can— . . .

no more at Present
I remain Yours &c

Kingstown may 17th 1776 Mary Bartlett
8 oclock in the evening 2nd Letter[3]

My Dear *June 10th 1776*

. . .the People in general are more healthy no funaral this week I take it a favour your writeing and sending a book and newspapers; indeed I and the People among us Saw an account of the ingagements of the Roebuck and liverpool men of war with the Gondaloes but we did not know they were so near Philadelphia you gave us an account of great Chains being Drawn acrost the river Deleware and it is a mistry to us how they got up the river I Shall be glad if you can write to me how it was the frost with us the last of may was very Great it froze Ice upon the water it cut Down beans Pumkins Cucumbers and Such tender Plants Cool mornings with us yet indian corn very bacward among us begining to weed worms have not eat very much corn yet—

the bigest part of the apple trees did not bloom but I hope the frost did not hurt them that did I See the apples hang on very well I will Give you more account about it by the leave of divine Providence nothing Strange among us

I am yours &c
Mary Bartlett

Kingstown July 13th 1776

My Dear

These Lines Leave me much better in health than when I wrote to you Last; the Sick headach I mentioned Last week held me three Days & nights without Intermition; the Rest of the family are very well at this time; Levi came

---

2. Kingston residents had been suffering from a rash of illnesses and deaths due to "Canker," often combined with scarlet fever. Bartlett is probably referring to the stomach ailment, although "canker" was often used synonymously with "cancer" during this period. The town also feared the spread of smallpox from Boston, and her letters are rife with accounts of deaths and burials, due in large part to such epidemics although the traditional mortality factors of consumption and childbirth also are in wide evidence.

3. Because of the uncertainty of mail deliveries, Bartlett numbered her early letters and requested that her husband do the same.

home Last wednsday; he is very well & Likes the School very much—our People met here for trainings & town meetings three Days this week to List men to Go to Canada; and have Listed almost Enough   old Mr. Proctor and old Willim Collins of this town & Several younger men have listed; they are to march next week I hear

we have had plenty of rain about ten Days past & I beleive hay will be vastly better than our fears Some time ago; English Corn I beleive will be very Good; flax will be better than our fears were in times past; Indian Corn we Cannot tell what Crops we shall have Yet, it Grows very fast—People among us Dont mow yet as they think the Grass Grows faster now than it has this Summer before; they Say it is a quarter better now that it was a week or ten Days ago; apples will be Scarce with us this year

... I Beleive Biley & Peter[4] manages your farming business very well—Peter is more Steady now than he was when you left him Before—I am under Some Difficulty to Send my Letters to the Post office; I wrote you last week & Sent it by Coll. Gales son;[5] he went Down to Dummers School Early a tuesday morning to bring up his Brother and Levi; & he forgot to leave the Letter in the Post office till he Came back. . . .

Kingstown July 20th 1776

My Dear
... I Should be glad to know if you think you Can Come home the beginning of the fall as you Gave us Some Encouragement you hoped you Should be at home in September   we have not had our healths so well Since you left us this last time as we had when you left us before   I have been Poorly this ten Days Past   I am now better   Ezra[6] was taken last monday in the afternoon (after we had Dated a letter to you that we were well) with the Canker and Scarlet fever   he has had a very high fever & broke out red all over till friday morning   he is now Some better   he has kept his bed from monday night till this morning. . . .

the men among us are very backward about Going into the war they are not Contented with the Province bounty   our men have had a town meeting & have voted to raise their bounty to fifty Dollars a man beside their wages   They are to begin their march to Day & meet at Esqr websters at Chester   David Quimby of hawk is Captn   Jacob Webster first Lieut   John Eastman Second Lieut   old mr Proctor is Gone   mr wheeler is a Going[7]

I wrote to you last week about the farming business   our menfolks have Done hilling of indian corn and begin to mow Some of the thinest Grass   we have not began to Reap yet   the weather wet and a fine growing time. . . .

4. Biley and Peter were the Bartletts' servants and field hands.
5. Probably James Gale, son of Colonel Jacob Gale.
6. Ezra was born September 13, 1770; despite serious childhood illnesses, he lived to be seventy-eight years old.
7. John Webster, a storekeeper who became colonel of the Chester regiment; David Quimby of Hawke (Danville), a lumber merchant; John Eastman, a cooper; James Proctor; Abner Wheeler; the second Webster volunteer is unidentified.

we hear of wars and tumults from one end of the Continent to the other; I Should be glad to Know if Your courage holds out yet about keeping & Defending america

I Remain Yours &c.
Mary Bartlett

Kingstown August 9th 1776

My Dear

... mr John Noyes Says he has been in england & Several of the west Indie Islands   But he Says america is the only Place for living Comfortably if we can enjoy our Liberty   he Says Some of the people in england is almost as Stuped as the Brute creation; they are so Ignorant they could hardly Beleive he was an american because, they Said he Lookd & Spoke So much like an English man

The people among us is very hurried Gitting in the English harvest; I beleive they will Chiefly finish this week; we have cut all our Grain; Something Late Gitting in hay; we have not half Done as the Grass Grew very fast of late— Plenty of rains; the weather not very hot—we have not had much Sharp Lightning and thunder with us of late—a fine growing Season Indian corn Look exceeding well   a general time of health—. . . .

from Yours &c.
Mary Bartlett

Kingstown September 9th 1776

My Dear

... Major Philbrick was here yesterday and Said he Saw Col. Whipple at Exeter last week and he Said he had Some money for me which he left at Portsmouth, he forgot to bring it up   as for the farming Business you wrote you Should be glad to know about   our men Folk are Some Belated about their work, so much wet weather for Six weeks every few Days Rain Except one week no Rain, I hired a man one week about hay—help is So Scarce we Could not git one Days work about Reaping upon any account & none about mowing   But what I Paid the money for—   we have almost Done haying   Biley Says he beleives we Shall have about Sixteen Load when it is all in—our English corn is not threshd yet. . . .

... I Do not write this by way of Complaint   I Believe Biley & Peter has Done as well as Can be expected & other People you Know will take Care of Self first

Pray Do come home before Cold weather as you Know my Circumstances will be Difficult in the winter If I am alive[8]

In hast from Yours &c.
Mary Bartlett

8. Bartlett was pregnant. Conceived when her father had returned to Kingston in the spring, Hannah Bartlett was born on December 13, 1776. Unlike her brothers Ezra (1770–1848), Josiah Jr. (1768–1838), and Levi (1763–1823) who lived to adulthood, Hannah died at the age of four months.

Mary ("Molly") Brant (?–1796)

Molly Brant was a Canienga (Mohawk[1]) woman who was probably born in Ohio. She and her brother, Joseph Brant, who was later named Chief of the Six Nations, were raised in the Mohawk Valley region of what is now New York State. As that region links Canada and the United States, so too did Brant's activities as negotiator between her people (the Iroquois, known as the Confederation of the Six Nations of the Longhouse) and the British whom they supported during the American Revolution. Although few details are known of Brant's early years, as the daughter of a sachem, she came into contact with many prominent Euro-American settlers and thereby learned her skills in English. Sir William Johnson was the Superintendent of Indians Affairs for the Province of New York, and during the pre-Revolutionary years had maintained excellent relations with the Iroquois. Johnson's first wife died in 1759, and he later married Brant in an Indian ceremony. Brant retained her family customs and name, and retained her right to participate in the Mohawk council and her prominent position in the community. She and Johnson had nine children (one died as an infant).

Brant's training as negotiator began in 1764 during the Peace Council of the Western Nations, at which Johnson met with all of the Nations' representatives. Her skills were honed a decade later when white traders slaughtered several Native Americans who lived along the Ohio River. In June 1774 as many as six hundred members of the Iroquois gathered at the Brant-Johnson home to hold a council and offer their support of the embattled Ohio tribes. Johnson, who had been ill off and on for several years, died during the council. A year later, as the beginnings of the Revolution were felt in the area, several Loyalist settlers were taken prisoner; the now-destitute Brant and her children escaped to Canajoharie, a Native American settlement. It was at this point that Brant's strength of character and courage became evident as she worked for the security of her people. In a letter dated 1780, a member of the military stationed in the area wrote, "Miss Molly Brant's influence over [her people] is far Superior to that of all the Chiefs put together."

Chief Joseph Brant allied the Six Nations with the British during the Revolution, and it was during these years that Molly Brant continued to move between her people and the British in order to offer support to the British and to work for the safety of her people. When the British lost the war, the Mohawks' land along the

---

1. "Mohawk" is standard usage today, but as Jean Johnston reminds us, it is the name the English used for Brant's people, who termed themselves Canienga or "People of the Flint" (107n). The Canienga, like all Iroquois, are matrilineal.

Mohawk River was confiscated. With her people, Brant settled in Ontario. A remarkable life ended in disillusionment and a sense of betrayal; Brant died on April 16, 1796. Although she was instrumental in the Iroquois-British negotiations during the war and a pioneer in the settlement of Ontario, she is today a controversial figure among her people. Whereas the Brants placed their faith in the British, that faith was never fulfilled: England's loss in the war had great effects on the Six Nations' people, but even in their Canadian resettlement they faced the establishment of British Canada at the expense of their own culture. The following dictated letters (Brant apparently did not write in English) reveal her astute assessments of military actions during the Revolution and her concern for her people during the conflict.

Works: Narrated letters. *Bibliography*: Crary; Johnston, J.

The Letters of Molly Brant to Judge Daniel Claus

Niagara, 23 June 1778

Dear Sir

I have been favor'd with Yours and the Trunk & parcels by Mr. Street: everything mentioned in the Invoice You sent me has come safe, except the pair of gold Earrings which I have not been able to find.

We have a report of Joseph having had a brush with the Rebels, but do not know at what place. A Cayuga Chief is said to be Wounded, and Schohary Indian (Jacob) killed, & one missing since when it's reported that Col° Butler, & Joseph have Joined; Every hour we look for a confirmation of this news.

I am much obliged to You for the care, & attention in sending me up those very necessary articles, & should be very glad if you have any accounts from New York that you would let me know them, as well as of the health of George, & Peggy, whom I hope are agreably settled: My Children are all in good health, & desire their loves to You, Mrs. Claus, Lady, & Sir John Johnson. I hope the Time is very near, when we shall all return to our habitations on the Mohawk River.

I am Dr Sir ever
affectionately Your
Mary Brandt

Carleton Island, 5th October 1779

Sir

We arraived here the 29th last month after Tedaous and dissagreable Voyage; where we remain and by all Appearance may for the winter   I have rote to Col° Butler and my brother Acquainting them of my Situation, desireing there advice, as I was left no Directions Concerning my self or family. Only when a Vessel Arraived, I Could get a passage to Niagara—I have been promised by

Col° Johnson at Montreal that I Should hear from the Gen¹ [Haldimand] and have his directions & order to be provided at whatever place my little service should be wanted which you know I am always ready to do, Should you think proper to speak to the Gen¹ on that head will be much Oblidged to You. the Indians are a Good deele dissatisfied on accᵗ of the Col°.s hasty temper which I hope he will soon drop   Otherwise it may be Dissadvantageous   I need not tell You whatever is promised or told them it ought to be perform'd—

Those from Canada are much Dissatisfied on Account of his taking more Notice of those that are suspected than them that are known to be Loyal, I tell this only to you that you advise him on that head—Meantime beg leave to be remembred to all Your family from Sir—

Your wellwisher
Mary Brant

Patience Lovell Wright (1725–1786)

An internationally noted wax sculptor, Patience Lovell Wright was born in Bordentown, New Jersey, in 1725. Like her future friend Benjamin Franklin, she resisted her family's early strictures and fled to Philadelphia to begin a new life for herself. In 1748 she married Joseph Wright, a Philadelphia craftsman, and for twenty years she lived a rather typical life for residents of an eighteenth-century urban area. When Joseph died in 1769, however, Lovell Wright did not choose to retire into widowhood. Her talents as a wax sculptor led her to the formation of a traveling wax museum noted for likenesses of famous or socially prominent individuals. In 1772, after fire destroyed most of the contents of the museum during a showing in New York, Lovell Wright moved to London. She was introduced into London society by prominent Philadelphians, including Benjamin Franklin, and she immediately became a success. Accounts of the period always note her extraordinary skills as a conversationalist with wide knowledge. Eventually, she became acquainted with King George III and his family, but when war between England and America broke out, Lovell Wright shifted her activities from polite entertainment to espionage. It is believed that some of her information, gathered as a companion of London society, was hidden in wax sculptures that were sent to America. A dedicated patriot, Patience Lovell Wright was in the process of arranging to return to America when she died from a fall in 1786. As her letters to Franklin reveal, she felt it was imperative that the male leaders of the Revolution understand "that women are usful" in the cause of liberty as well.

Works: Letters. *Bibliography*: Lopez and Herbert.

Letters of Patience Lovell Wright
to Benjamin Franklin in Paris

My Much Honoured Friend   *Pall-mall March 7, 1777*
  Sir / your thorow knowledge of me and my Princeples and actions makes
it not necessery for me to apoligize for writing to you——

  I was very anxious for a opertunity to be of some use in the great work of
doing good to mankind But now I See and behold god ordreth all things by
His wise Provedence and things are all in the universal Course set in order by
him—and all I can do is only Pray for you as the means to bring about a Wise
and Safe Peace——

  My daughter wrote to you informing you of the case of m[r] Platt now in
Newgate for Rebelion comitted in Savannah in Georgia in year 1775 7 month
before the Coloney was Declared Rebels the wondrful method taken to convince us of our Safe Situation——I make no doubt but your real knowledge
of human nature and humane temper with a desire to do all the good you can
you will so ordr that Either Platt be Imeadatly Set at liberty or Exchangd for
another person or some money be sent to Support him in His unjust confinement——a Letter from you to the alldman of London or to some other of
those who have Power it will Spirit [illegible word] those good honest men
(for Some this are) who will se that Justice be done if he be Brot to trial—we
are now impatient for your advise how to proced as youl see from the news
paper his Case and the procedings against him——We keept in the Dark with
all the movements of govrment and hope light to brake in upon us by some
divine spark kindled [by] you or those providence makes his agents—

  ... My vanity promps me to think I can entertain you if permited to
write   Pray Sir suffer me to troubel you with my Scraps of paper as I formaly
did in Craven Street—Small begining and some time a slight hint to a wise
man from a honest heart may do wonders—. . . .

                                        Your faithful humble srvt
                                        Patience Wright

                                        Pall-mall waxwork
Honoured Sir/   *March 29th 1778*
  as mr Platts history, his marage to my daughter and their return to america
is already Laid before you for your assistance,[1] &c. The most Sincere grat-
itu[d]e to God for making *YOU* the gardian angel of us, who are so farr from
our Native Contry, notwithstanding I meet with the greatest politeness and se-
vility from the people of England yet, the distress which is already come and
must follow to this once *great littel* Island give me such pain I cannot Content my Self to Behold any more   I began with the Boston Port Bill and I have
travild through all the *diferent* ways of profdence to Bring about the grand and
most extrordany Revolutions by the most unlikly means—that I now belive
that all my romantick Education Joynd with my Father old Lovells Courage

---

1. In the margin, preceding "assistance" is the word "Councell."

Can be Servisable yet farther to Bring on the Gloriouse Cause of Sivil and religious Liberty   5 years ago I drempt a dream Concerning Doctr Frankling   I wrote down [the] dream and told numbers now readg to-day that all those wonderful Events wont happen and as only one half is yet come to Pass I most solemly believe I shall live to see the other Part Compleated—your Publick Entry to the Court of France is a prelude to the same honour done you at the Court of London with the addition of being the Glorious Deliver &c. when the great god who governs the wo[r]ld and rules in the heart of princes he Raises up a Frankling to do his great work and that America should be honourd with her Son Benjaman the Youngest of his Father Famaly—and the man whome I have been taught to look on with the highest hopes to my Contry It has made me determine to make you a visit to take your Bosto[2] to send to the Empror of Germany,—the Queen France and other Such Likeness, as you shall aprove—word cannot Express the honour your letter has done me   When you say you love me as well as ever which is say Mrs Wright has the Friendship of the greatest man in the whole world and her study has and shall be to deserve it by a faithful eye to His honour, and her Contry by paying due honour to the now great philospher doct Frankling acknowledgd so by all the known Christian people

I Intend seting out for Fance as soon as the [illegible] begins which must happen by mid sumer

I shall bring some of my performance with me and

from the same etc   Patience Wright

Ann Gwinnett (?–post-1780)

Unlike Elizabeth Bland, who came to the Georgia colony apparently because of financial exigency, Ann Gwinnett was part of the small but influential colonial upper class. She came to Georgia from England, arriving on January 14, 1765, a few years after her spouse, Button Gwinnett (?–1777), had come to the colony. She spent only a year in Georgia at that time, she returned again from England some time before the spring of 1771. Button first sought his livelihood as a merchant (his trade in England) but soon was able to purchase St. Catherine's Island, a 6,200-acre estate. Button Gwinnett became President of Georgia and later was one of the Georgia representatives who signed the Declaration of Independence. He died in 1777 in a duel with his political antagonist, General Lachlan McIntosh. The general had been charged with profiting from trade with the British, and he had brought countercharges against Button Gwinnett for meddling in military matters. Their

---

2. That is, Lovell Wright wanted to create a bust of Franklin.

case came before Georgia's Assembly in May 1777. While the Council found in favor of Gwinnett, McIntosh publicly asserted his enemy was "a scoundrel and a lying rascle," assertions that led to the fatal duel on May 16th. Both men were wounded and Button Gwinnett died within a few days, leaving Ann Gwinnett and their child, Elizabeth, in a small and contentious colony.

Ann Gwinnett petitioned John Hancock, President of the Continental Congress, to remove McIntosh from the army under court-martial. In a subsequent petition to Congress and in a private letter to Hancock, Gwinnett recorded the details of the event that has remained notable in Georgia's early history. The petitions and other papers of Ann Gwinnett were read before Congress on October 1, 1777. After considerable debate, Congress voted to try McIntosh, but he had supporters in the assembly as well and they apparently blocked the trials. Eventually he was assigned to General George Washington's troops at Valley Forge. In July 1778 Ann Gwinnett left Savannah and settled in Charleston where Elizabeth was attending boarding school. Gwinnett died in South Carolina; the date of her death is unknown, but her last recorded document was dated 1780.

Works: Petitions, letters. *Bibliography*: Jenkins.

The Writings of Ann Gwinnett

To the Honourable JOHN HANCOCK Esq[r]. President & other Members
    of the Honourable Continental Congress

    The Humble Petition of Ann Gwinnett Widow of Button Gwinnett Deceased, late President of Georgia Sheweth to your Honour that Brigadier General McIntosh calld said Gwinnett, your petitioners Deceased Husband, a Scoundrel, & used other insulting Language to Him in the House of Assembly in the State of Georgia, for no other reason than for acquiting Himself to that House of some Charges the General laid against Him—& also for supporting some charges He brought against the General as from His conduct Mr Gwinnett had good reason to apprehend the General was far from being a real friend to the cause of the United States in general & this State in Particular—on which a Duel ensued in which your Petitioners Husband Lost His Life, Your petitioner also informs Your Honours, that Josep Habersham Colonel of the first Georgia Battalion—& George Wells said to be a Colonel of Militia were seconds— & so cruel & Bloodthirsty did they appear to be, that they measured the distance from each other (when they were to fire) to be only ten feet   Your Honours petitioner is informd that by the Articles of War, the General & Colonel Habersham may be Cashiered—as the first was a principle & the second carried the Message, & acted as second to the General   Your petitioner craves leave to inform Your Honours that probably the civil Law will acquit them, but hopes Your Honours will take proper notice of them—& do justice

to the United States by removing them from Command, which will in some measure Satisfie a disconsolate Widow & Daughter and Your Petitioner will ever Pray   Ann Gwinnett
Savannah 1777
August 1st

To the Honourable the President & other Members of the Grand
    Continental Congress
MOST HONOURABLE GENTLEMEN:
Next to Heaven I apply to your August Body for redress, on the Melancholy sufferings I undergo, on account of the cruel Death of my Husband, Button Gwinnett now no more—the late President of Georgia, by whom it has been preserved (& for exerting Himself to do it) they seekt His Life various ways, ever since He executed the Honourable John Hancock's order on George McIntosh, on rect. of that order, He directly without consulting Council (for that He knew wou'd prevent His being taken) caused said George McIntosh to be taken Prisoner, & put in the common jail—& ordered Him to have Iron handcufs on, for being a Traitor to the United States of America & this State in Particular—& directly sent one Colonel Sandiford, to Seize the Estate Real & Personal of said George McIntosh, the State Prisoner. It was said George McIntosh was indisposed & the Irons injurious to His health & Council at their own risque took the Irons of[f] & wou'd have Baild Him—but Mr Gwinnett refus'd that, & wou'd by no means take any sort of Bail for Him—the Expedition soon calld Mr Gwinnett from Savannah—then the Vice President so calld, the Honourable Jonathan Bryan Esqr. & His Council, took, or rather gave Bail for said George McIntosh, & gave Him back His effects—the Vice President I think is one of His Bail—the Agent for this State I am sure is one, & John Houston Esqr. a Lawyer here another of His Bail—a Brother of Sr Patrick Houstons that was partner with Mr George McIntosh in the Rice sent of[f] last Year[1]—this Lawyer Houston is one of the Council at this time. George McIntosh Married this Gentlemans Sister—sure none but Tories wou'd Bail a State Prisoner, & one that had been in the Council too—but tis plain He only got in to betray it—really they are all so much alike they will all bail one another, take any oath, do anything to put the Continental Money in their Pocket, & do nothing for it but Sacrifice the State & any Person in it that is true to it, in it. Theres one good & able Friend to the Cause left yet, & His Life they have seekt—the depositions are given in of it before a Magistrate, & the Tories do strive to do Him all the injury they can—none else dislike him—He is the best Friend to the Liberty Cause it now has left—His Name is Wood. He is appointed a Delegate to go to Congress—the Tories endeavouring to prevent His going. But to return to my sad & dismal tale; which my every thought is bent on. Honourable Gentlemen pray give me leave to ask if the Speaker of the Georgia House of Assembly ought not when Mr Gwinnett was so basely

---

1. McIntosh had been charged with aiding his brother in the shipment of rice to the starving British garrison at St. Augustine.

affronted by Brigadier General McIntosh (that it conjurd Him to fight) to order the General to the Bar of the House, & make him ask Mr Gwinnett pardon. This wou'd have sav'd Mr Gwinnetts Life—as a public concession repairs a public affront—(but no) no such thing was requir'd from the General & only Mr Gwinnetts Life fell a sacrifice for striving to save the Country. How grating must this be to Mr Gwinnett to be thus insulted by the Brigadier General. He resig'd His Colonelship in favor of, when He went to Deligate to Congress last year—so deceived was He in the Man—Oh He proves a very Traitor, it wou'd fill Volumes to relate His trecherous Villany. His Brothers & His own chicanery shine in Georgia—His Eldest Brother William behav'd so ill last year it brought Him to a tryal, but by the Artifice of the General & His good friends the tories brought him of[f] clear, I cannot help wishing to live to see the day when no McIntosh is in pay here. The People are true if they had good officers—three of the Generals Sons, & two of His Brother Williams are Officers now—tis well known here at the Engagement here last year, they might have taken all the Kings troops had not General McIntosh preserv'd them—when the men were going to fire He said they must not wat the powder—another party further of[f] sent for a Swivel gun to fire at a Vessell that was aground—& He sent one & the Balls was so large it cou'd not be chargd—& kept out of the way till the tide rose & the Vessell floated, then appear'd & sent Balls proper to load the Gun with—if He & all His Family (or say connections) are not sent out of Georgia, it will always be betray'd & the enemy supplyd with provisions, & be what it really is, a compleat Tory State under Continental pay.—Extract of a letter to Genl Howe:

> I have Substantial reasons to be more & more convinced of the propriety of the present Expedition & I cannot help suggesting that the immediate removal of General McIntosh out of this State will tend to the safety of this & the United States: I just mention these things to your Excellency & perhaps hereafter you will be fully convinced of the Expediency of them signd March 14th 1777. To General Howe—B. Gwinnett

The above request not even Noticed—no General Howe from Carolina did not heartily join the Liberty side. He feasted with the Tories—at Mr McGilverys & Mr Telfairs both noted Tories—was at their dances several Evenings & spent His time mostly with them, tho' in time of War the cause of His being sent for one Fusilier invaded Georgia, & took great quantities of Cattle & some of our men from the frontiers, & much escaped him but seeing the then President Archibald Bulloch Esqr. true, & the Militia resolute He retreated—this good & worthy President was taken of in a very bad way indeed. I heard a Do[c]tor say He was poisoned but to return to General Howe, when He came here Mr Gwinnett was President & seeing a favourable opportunity offer to take Augustine was going to try to take it—& General Howe refus'd to go over the line & wou'd not join to go against it, by any means whatever—but said Georgia was not invaded—indeed Fusilier was retreated & General Howe wou'd not join the Expedition but return'd back to Carolina. He left one Colonel Sumpter here a little while & then sent for him away. How Mr Gwinnett did wish for one General Moor. He said He knew He wou'd have gone over the line any where. Tis plain Fusilier did not stand on that complement with Georgia—it was thought He was invited here, I heard Mr Gwinnett say, the General said after He knew of their coming or expected them to come—twas thought He did. The Great Father of truth knows all I relate to be so, concerning the cruel ill treatment Mr Gwinnett met with in this State, for Daring to be true to the United States in this State & I cannot doubt but the most worthy President & other Members of the Honourable Continental Congress, will do every justice to His Memmory. Tis there I seek redress, theres such a junto here none can be expected. tho the Blood of the Slain cries for vengeance, the widow & orphan in unutterable & inexpressible Grief seek to you in the midst of it for relief. Theres no justice to be had here for liberty people yet.

The Honourable & August Body of the United States at the Grand Continental Congress, Condescending to Notice this, will be esteem'd a Tribute to the Deceasd Button Gwinnett, by His Widow, who begs leave to subscribe Herself your Honours, most disconsolate & very sincerely griev'd Hble Servt.

A Gwinnett

Savannah 1777
August 1st.

Dorothy Dudley (fl. 1775–76)

Young Dorothy Dudley's diary has long fascinated the American public. In 1876 the Ladies Centennial Committee of Cambridge, Massachusetts, published a history of the city that prominently included Dudley's diary and selected correspondence. William Dean Howells appended to the text a dedicatory poem to Dudley, "Fair maiden, whom a hundred summers keep / Forever seventeen." It is little wonder that the young patriot has remained such an engaging figure from the past: her diary is a detailed and impassioned firsthand account of the Revolutionary War.

Works: Diary and correspondence. *Bibliography*: *Theatrum Majorum*.

From the Diary of Dorothy Dudley

April 20th [1775].—It has come. The long expected blow has been struck, and by the British arm. How can I nerve myself to write of the horrors of yesterday; but I will do it.

At midnight of Tuesday we were awakened by the ringing of bells and beating of drums and the hurried tread of men arming for battle. The air was filled with cries of frightened women and children. "The regulars are out. To arms!" was the shout which, with lightning speed, went from mouth to mouth. Then we knew that the purposes of General Gage[1] had ripened into deeds, and war was fairly upon us. Our minutemen were ready for action, and as the sun arose set off in the direction of Lexington, where the British troops had gone. For us at home there was the most terrible suspense to be endured. At noon came a body of Redcoats, led by Lord Percy, over the bridge from Boston, to reenforce the troops which went through our town Tuesday night. It was not till toward evening that our anxiety and suspense could be relieved by any certain news. Then the King's troops were re-treating in most ignominious haste before the pursuing militia of Lexington, Concord, and Cambridge. As they ran over the road they had so proudly marched over the night before, the slaughter among them was terrible. Several of our brave Cambridge men are killed. Mrs. Hicks sent her eldest boy to look for his father as night came on. He found him lying dead by the roadside, and near him Mr. Moses Richardson and Mr. William Marcy. These three were brought home and hastily buried in one common grave in the churchyard. Ah, the sorrows of that night! How near it brought war to our doors, this first burial of victims of British tyranny. It was no time for funeral ceremonies; and as the terrified and sorrowing friends stood around the rude grave in which was put all that was mortal of these brave men, Dr. Warren[2] tried to comfort them with hopeful words. "It will soon be over," he said, "then rightful honors will be paid to these who fell in defence of our country." I cannot forget it. The lurid glare of the torches, the group in the graveyard, the tender but hurried burial without service or even coffins, and Elias Richardson's act of filial love in carefully spreading the cape of his father's overcoat upon the dead man's face, lest the cold earth should fall directly upon it. . . .

April 21st.—Our little town is the seat of war. An army is gathering in our midst in response to the call of the Committee of Safety. Yesterday immediately after the affair at Lexington and Concord, a proclamation to the Colonies was issued, urging them to do all in their power to raise an army. "Our all is at stake. Death and devastation are the certain consequences of delay. Every moment is infinitely precious. An hour lost may deluge your country in blood and entail perpetual slavery upon the few of our posterity that may survive the carnage." But the Colonies have not waited for the call. One spirit animates all—the determination to stand by our country in its hour of need—and the universal cry is Liberty or Death. Volunteers come from all quarters, many with nothing but the clothes on their backs, no money, no provisions. Our houses are thrown open to accommodate as far as possible the great throng of men who have rushed to the cause of liberty. General Ward has taken the chief command and is doing his best to bring order out of this chaos. The Committee of Safety have taken up their quarters at Mr. Hasting's house, and General Ward is also there.

1. General Thomas Gage, commander of the British forces in North America from 1763 to 1775. His measures, most notably the "Intolerable Acts" limiting the colonists' geographic and political freedoms, are credited with bringing about the battles of Lexington and Concord that began the American Revolution.

2. Joseph Warren, a general in the American forces. On June 18, Dudley records "the great and terrible loss which has come to us in the death of our beloved Dr. Warren" at Bunker Hill.

Orders are issued that [Harvard] college be removed to Concord, and the students are going; the library has already been partly carried to Andover. The college buildings are to be used as barracks for the soldiers. The Common is the rendezvous for military; and a busy scene it is, with its groups of excited minutemen and thousand signs of warlike preparations. A great many of our townspeople have run away, as this influx of soldiers has come. Tory Row is nearly deserted. The widow of Major Henry Vassall has left her house and sought a place of safety. Colonel Stark has his property in charge. All that cannot be made of use to our army is sent to Boston. The barns will be used to store forage for our cavalry horses. Mr. John Borland has abandoned his home and it is taken by the Committee of Safety. Major Phipps, too, thinks discretion the better part of valor, and has departed. We have but little of the Tory element among us now. The Tories who remain are lukewarm in their principles.

August 1st.—There is a young man in camp whom I have noticed again and again as he passes the house. He is striking in appearance, though quite small and boyish. His eyes are piercing in their brightness, and there is something winning in his manner. His name is Aaron Burr, a son of Rev. Aaron Burr, formerly President of Princeton College, N.J., and grandson of Rev. Jonathan Edwards. . . .[3]

December 1st.—Winter is fairly upon us. Snow several inches deep. Mrs. John Adams[4] is in town. I met her at Mrs. Mifflin's last evening. Mrs. Adams is a charming woman, combining ease and grace of manner, and sweetness of temper, with great strength and decision of character. I have the warmest admiration for her. Had a delightful evening. . . . General Lee was there.[5] . . . The General is a most singular man, very unprepossessing in appearance, tall and thin, with large features, eyes that are never at rest, and a certain air of carelessness, as if he gave not a thought to his dress or manner of life. He has a great fondness for dogs, and is rarely seen without one or more. Last night, "Mr. Spada," a large, shaggy, bearish-looking animal, was with him, and was the source of some annoyance as well as amusement to the guests. He insisted upon the dog's presenting his paw to Mrs. Adams, who, as a stranger, was entitled to every mark of attention. "Love me, love my dog," this whimsical man might well say to his friends. He has lived among the Indians long enough to acquire their confidence, and be honored by appointment as chief, and in their expressive way they called him from his passionate nature, "Boiling Water." . . . He speaks and writes several languages, fluently, and Mrs. Adams says with truth, "the elegance of his pen far exceeds that of his person. . . . Brattle's Mall[6]

---

3. Aaron Burr struck many Americans as notable; he became Vice President of the United States after a tie vote with Thomas Jefferson for the presidency. Burr was tried for treason in 1807 for attempting to colonize the Southwest, but he was acquitted.

4. Abigail Smith Adams (*q.v.*).

5. Charles Lee. In 1776 Lee was captured by the British and, unknown to the Americans, provided the enemy with information to defeat the local troops. His treason then and at the Battle of Monmouth was not discovered until much later. He was dismissed from the American army in 1780.

6. The Mifflin family's temporary residence.

is a place of wonderful attraction, moonlight evenings in summer. The graceful play of the shadows upon the velvety lawns and well-kept paths, the murmuring hum of the river, the glad rush of the ice-cold water as it bursts from its prison in the marble grotto—all these are so many magnets, each drawing to the Brattle grounds a goodly number of pleasure-seekers. Now, the promenade is wrapt in a soft white dress, which clothes all nature—and dazzling in its purity, hides beneath its veil of charity all the blemishes of our mother earth.

December 18th.—Mrs. Washington was at church yesterday with the General.[7] She is a fine-looking lady, with regular features, dark chestnut hair and hazel eyes, and a certain gravity in her carriage which becomes her position. She was a widow when General Washington married her, rich and attractive, and he was taken captive at first sight. They say General and Mrs. Gates came with them, and occupied a pew near. Dr. Appleton prayed most earnestly for our country and its defenders, alluding pointedly and affectionately to the chief officer of the army.[8] For some time it has not been customary to pray for the King. Independence is much thought and talked of, and any sign of allegiance to the mother country is very offensive. Mrs. Washington has expressed a wish that Christ Church may be put in readiness for services, and orders have gone forth to that effect.

January 2d [1776].—Yesterday a union flag was raised on Prospect Hill. It has thirteen stripes of alternate red and white, emblematic of the thirteen united colonies . . . and on a blue ground in the corner are the united red and white crosses of St. George and St. Andrew. As it was flung to the breeze and tossed and spread itself in graceful glee, a volley of thirteen guns thundered forth a glad greeting to our national banner. If one can trust the index of patriotism and determination and bravery, unswerving in the face of dreadful discouragements, this our national flag will ere long proudly wave over a free country. There it is now, flaunting defiantly in the very eyes of his Majesty's troops, who are bewildered by the loud huzzas which fill the air. . . .

January 30th.—Madame Washington has enlivened the monotony of her winter among us by a reception, on the seventeenth anniversary of her wedding day. The fine old Vassall mansion was in gala dress, and the coming and going of guests brightened the sober aspect of the General's headquarters. The General and his wife stood in the drawing-room at the left of the front entrance, and there received the company. General Washington's study is the room opposite, and opening out of this, the one set apart for his military family. These of course were all thrown open for the accommodation of the guests. There was much chatting and walking to and fro, and easy and social manners were the rule. The General does not talk much, but is gracious and courteous to all. His lady is

---

7. Martha Dandridge Custis Washington had arrived in Cambridge a week earlier, but this was probably her first public appearance after what Dudley described as a "long, tedious journey from Mount Vernon."

8. George Washington who, in June, had been appointed by Congress as commander-in-chief of the United Colonies.

very unceremonious and easy like other Virginia ladies, though there is no lack of dignity in her manner. Of course simplicity of dress was noticeable,—no jewels or costly ornaments,—though tasteful gowns, daintly trimmed by their owner's fingers, were numerous. The occasion was a most enjoyable one.

July 19th.—Independence is declared at last! The glorious document which proclaims our Colonies to be free and independent States, has been read from the balcony of the State House and in Faneuil Hall, and greeted with cheers of welcome from thousands of patriotic throats. The thought of independence has been a familiar one for many months, and the fiery enthusiasm which now flames forth from all quarters tells of the universal joy of the nation. . . .

Margaret Hill Morris (1737–1816)

Margaret Hill, daughter of Deborah Moore and Richard Hill, was born in South River, Maryland. In 1739, because of severe financial difficulties and in spite of the fact that Deborah Hill had recently died, Margaret's father left the family and settled on the island of Madeira, hoping to recoup his losses in the wine business. Hannah Hill Moore, only fifteen but already married, became the sole parental figure for six of her seven siblings, including Margaret, who was two years old, and their youngest sister, who became the poet Milcah Martha Moore, and was only eighteen months old at the time. Out of this early hardship, the Hill children formed a lasting bond.

In 1758 Margaret married William Morris, Jr., a Philadelphia dry-goods merchant. William died in 1766 when Margaret was pregnant with their fifth child, Gulielma.[1] She struggled for several years to provide for her four children, the oldest of whom was six at William's death; but in 1770 she was able to purchase a home near her sister Sarah Hill Dillwyn in Burlington, New Jersey. It was while she was living in this house on the "Green Back," which overlooked the Delaware River, that Hill Morris began keeping a journal of the momentous events occurring literally before her eyes. As a Quaker, she was against all acts of war, lamenting "what sad havoc will this dreadful war make in our land!" and attempting to aid any who needed her assistance. Hill Morris also refused to rely solely on her relatives for support. Well acquainted with medical practices,[2] she put her knowledge to work, treating the wounded

---

1. The three older children were John (whose twin, Richard, had died before the age of one), Deborah, and Richard.

2. Hill Morris undoubtedly gained much of her medicinal knowledge from her father, who was a physician. For a brief period in 1780, she ran her own business—a retail shop from which she distributed medicines.

as well as aiding the ill during a smallpox epidemic and the yellow fever epidemic in 1793. Little is known of Hill Morris's later life, although she lived to the age of seventy-nine. Margaret Hill Morris died at Burlington on October 10, 1816.

Works: Journal, private diary (1751–1768), letters. Bibliography: Jackson; Morris, M. H.; Smith, J. J.

From Margaret Hill Morris's Journal

December 6th 1776—Being on a visit to my frd. M.S. at Haddonfield. I was preparing to return to my Family, when a person from Philad told us the people there were in great Commotion, that the English fleet was in the River & hourly expected to sail up to the City;[3] that the inhabitants were removing into the Country & that several persons of considerable repute had been discoverd to have formd a design of setting fire to the City, & were Summoned before the Congress and strictly injoined to drop the horrid purpose—when I heard the above report my heart almost died within me, & I cried surely the Lord will not punish the innocent with the guilty, & I wished there might be found some interceeding Lotts & Abrahams amongst *our People.* On my Journey home I was told the inhabitants of our little Town were going in haste into the Country, & that my nearest neighbours were already removed—when I heard this, I felt myself quite Sick I was ready to faint—I thought of my S.D.[4] the beloved Companion of my Widowed State—her Husband at the distance of some hundred miles from her—I thought of my own lonely situation, no Husband to cheer, with the voice of love, my Sinking spirits. My little flock too, without a Father to direct them how to Steer,—all these things crouded into my mind at once, & I felt like one forsaken—a flood of friendly tears came to my relief—& I felt an humble Confidence that he, who had been with me in six troubles would not forsake me now—. . . .

[*December*] 12th—The people of the gallies, Suspecting that some troops were yet either conceald in Town or the Neighborhood of it,[5] have been very Jealous of the inhabitants, who have been often alarmd with reports, that the City would be Set on fire, Many have gone in haste & great distress into the Country, but we still hope, no Mischief is Seriously intended—A Number of Men landed on our Bank this Morning,[6] & told us it was thier settled purpose to set fire to the Town—I begd them not to set my house afire—they askd which was my House, I showd it to them, & they said they knew not what hinderd them from fireing on it last Night, for seeing alight in the Chambers, they thought there were Hessians in it, & they pointed the Guns

3. Probably Philadelphia; Burlington is usually referred to in the journal as "the Town."

4. Sarah Hill Dillwyn (1738/9–1826) and her husband, George Dillwyn (?–1820).

5. After days of rumors, the British troops had entered the town on December 11; though there was some firing, no one had been injured.

6. Situated on the Green Bank, the house was far enough from town that Hill Morris and her family had not heard the cannonade of the previous night.

at it Several times, I told them my Children were Sick, which obligd me to burn alight all Night[7]—Tho they did not know what hinderd them from fireing on us, I did, it was the Guardian of the Widow & the Orphan, who took us into his Safe keeping, & preservd us from danger, oh—that I may keep humble, & be thankful for this, as other favors Vouch safed to my little flock—

. . . from the 13th to 16th we had various reports of the advancing & retireing of the Enemy—Parties of Armd Men rudely enterd the Houses in Town, & diligent search made for Tories, the 2 last taken releasd & sent on Shore—some of the Gondola Gentry broke into & pillagd R Smiths House[8] on the bank— Mem° to give a more pticular account the manner by & by—about noon this day, (the 16) avery terrible account of thousands coming into Town—& now actually to be seen on Gallows Hill—My incautious son [John] catchd up the Spy Glass, & was running to the Mill to look at them. I told him it w[d] he liable to misconstruction, but he prevaild on me to let him gratify his curiosity, & he went, but returnd much dissatisfyd, for no troops coud he see as he came back, poor Dick took the glass & resting it against a tree, took a view of the fleet—both of these was observd by the people on board, who suspected it was an Enemy that was watching thier Motions—They Mannd aboat & sent her on Shore—aloud knocking at my door brought me to it—I was a little flutterd & kept locking and unlocking that I might get my ruffled face, a little composd, at last I opend it, & half adozen Men all Armd, demanded the keys of the empty House—I asked them what they wanted there they said to Search for a D——d tory who had been spy[G] at them from the Mill—the Name of a Tory so near *my own door*, seriously alarmd me—for a poor refugee dignifyd by that Name, had claimd the shelter of my Roof & was at that very time conceald, like a thief in an Auger hole[9]—I rung the bell violently, the Signal agreed on, if they came to Search, & when I thought he had crept into the hole—I put on avery simple look & cryd out, bless me I hope you are not Hessians—say, good Men are you the Hessians? do we look like Hessians? askd one of them rudely—indeed I dont know; Did you ever see a Hessian? no never in my life but they *are Men*, & you are Men & may be Hessians, for any thing I know—but Ill go with you into Col C°[10] house, tho indeed it was my Son at the Mill, he is but a Boy & meant no harm, he wanted to see the Troops—so I marchd at the head of them, opend the door, & searchd every place but we could not find the tory—strange where he coud be—we returnd; they greatly disappointed, I pleasd, to think *my house* was not Suspected—. . . .

7. Her daughters had been ailing with a fever.

8. Richard Smith, a distant relative through marriage. After the galley had confronted Hill Morris at her home on the 12th, she had written her sister Milcah that "though I place no confidence in the arm of flesh, yet I have abundant cause for humble gratitude, that those hardy men did not treat me roughly."

9. The "refugee" was Dr. Jonathan Odell, an Episcopal minister and physician, who had professed allegiance to the British. Earlier in the month Odell had been asked by citizens of Burlington to act as interpreter between the Americans and the Hessians. An auger-hole is a secret chamber, usually in a distant section of the house so that a bell can be rung as a warning and not be heard in the main house.

10. Colonel Cox, one of Hill Morris's neighbors.

[December] 27th—a letter from Gen Read to his B^r—informing him that Washington had had an engagement with the Regulars on the 25th early in the Morning, taking them by surprize, killd fifty, & took 900 prisoners.[11] The loss on our side not known, or if known, not sufferd to be publick.—It seems this heavy loss to the Regulars was oweing to the prevailing custom among the Hessians of getting drunk on the eve of that great day which brought peace on Earth and good Will to Men—but oh, how unlike Christians is the Manner in which they Celebrate it, can, we call ourselves Christians, while we act so Contrary to our Masters rules— ... instead of good will, envy & hatred seem to be the ruling passions in the breasts of thousands. ... An Officer [in the Philadelphia militia] spent the Evening with us, & appeard to be in high spirits, & talkd of engaging the English as a very trifling affair, Nothing so easy as to drive them over the North River &c—not considering that there is a God of Battle, as well as a God of peace, who may have given them the late advantage, in order to draw them out to meet the Chastisement that is reservd for them.

[January] 14th [1777]— ... I hear Gen: Howe sent arequest to Washington desireing 3 days Cessation of Arms, to take care of the Wounded, & bury the Dead—which was refused, What a Woeful tendency War has, to harden the human heart against the tender feelings of humanity; Well may it be called *a horrid Art*, thus to change the Nature of Man—I thought that even Barbarous Nations had asort of Religious regard for their Dead—A fr^d from trenton tells me poor A[nthony] Morris, died in 3 hours after he was wounded, & was buryd in frd^s burying ground at Stony Brook—also Capt [William] Shippen was buryd by him—the same friend told us a Man was killd in his Bed at the House of Stacey Potts in Trenton in the time of the engagement there, and that Potts's Daughter, a Young Woman about the Age of Mine, went from Home to lodge, the Night preceeding the Battle, & returning in the Morning. Just as she stept into her Fathers door, a Ball met her, (& being directed by the unerring hand of Providence) & took the Comb out of her hair, & gently Grazed the Skin of her head, without doing her any further injury—who shall dare to say they are shot at Random—

[June] 14th— ... by a person from Borden Town, we hear 12 expresses came in there to day from Camp— ... Some of the Gondola Men & thier Wives being Sick, & no Doctor in Town to apply to, they were told that Mrs M— was a Skillful Woman—& kept Medicines to give to the poor—& not withstanding thier late attempt to Shoot my poor boy—they Ventured to come to me—& in a very humble manner begd me to come and do something for them—At first I thought they might have a design to put a trick on me & get me aboard their Gondolas—& then pillage my house, as they had done to some others—but on Asking where the Sick folks were, was told they were lodged in the Governor house so I went to see them—there was several both men and Women very ill with a fever, some said the Camp or putrid fever— They were broke out in blotches, & on close examination, it appeard to be

11. Colonel Joseph Reed of Pennsylvania; the occurrence was George Washington's surprise attack on the British at Trenton on Christmas Day.

the itch fever—I treated them according to art, & they all got well—I thought I had received all my pay when they Thankfully acknowledged my kindness—but lo—in a Short Time afterwards, a very rough ill looking Man came to the door & askd for me—when I went to him, he drew me aside, & askd if I had any frd^s in Philad^a the question alarmd me—supposing there was some mischief meditated against that poor City—however—I calmly said, I have an Ancient Father[-in-law]—some Sisters—& other near frd^s there—Well—said the Man—do you wish to hear from them—or to send any thing by way of refreshment to them—if you do, I will take charge of it—& bring you back any thing you may send for—I was very much surprisd—& thought to be sure he only wanted to get provisions to take to the Gondolas—When he told me—his Wife was one of those I had given Medicine to—& this was the only Thing he coud do to pay me for my kindness—My heart leapd with Joy—& I set about preparing something for my dear absent frd^s. . . .

Lydia Minturn Post (fl. 1776–83)

The daughter of an Anglican clergyman, Lydia Minturn Post remained a patriot throughout the American Revolution; but, owing to prolonged exposure to the devastating horrors of war, she ultimately turned her attentions more directly to her faith in God than in "the warrior's craft." Minturn Post's husband was an army officer, a position that demanded his continued absence from their Long Island home, even when the British troops occupied the region and their Hessian supporters lodged in the Posts' house. Lydia Minturn Post's journal reveals her astute recognition of political and military issues. As a record maintained throughout the war years for her husband, Edward, its recounting of daily experiences that she and her neighbors had to endure is also a testimony to the sacrifices made by women who did not participate on the battlefield but who faced the calamities of war literally within their own occupied homes.

Works: Journal. *Bibliography: Personal Recollections of the American Revolution* (1859).

From the Journal of Lydia Minturn Post

September 1776. Still at the Parsonage with my three precious children: already heart-weary at your absence,[1] but striving to keep up courage. . . . In

---

1. Minturn Post's husband had departed, probably in August, to join General Washington's command.

this little nook where we had hoped to find peace and safety, we shall have disturbance, fear, and danger; since the enemy have possession of the island, there can be no doubt of it, but to some extent my father's neutral stand, and sacred profession, will protect us.

As we have moved to this place, dear Edward, since you left us, I think it will be agreeable to you to have some little description of it. It is a low-roofed, Dutch style of house, with its gable to the road; white-washed and covered with sweetbriar and creeping vines of many kinds; and my father has planted the ivy, which came from his dear Old England. It grows slowly, and the children love to pick its glossy leaves, and carry them to grandpa. At the sight of them, his heart of tenderness reverts to early days; he tells them of the old castles, and grey ruins it mantles over the sea, and of the one which overgrew the cottage where he was born. The thoughts of my dear, honored parent remind me of a brave old tree torn up by its roots, and transplanted into a foreign soil; it may not die, but it has a sickly appearance, and its leaves have lost their living green, and are pale and yellow. . . . His breast is, I think, agitated by contending emotions. He is attached to the land of his adoption, and can sympathize in her distress, but naturally his first, his dearest affections, were given to the land of his birth. Can we censure this? call it infatuation, blindness? Oh no! I honor my father for the sentiment. Do not condemn it, Edward. We love this, our native land, the native country of my mother, of both your parents. Her cause seems to us a righteous one. She is over-taxed, oppressed, insulted. . . .

October 3d. Dear, dear husband! was there ever anything so sorrowful, so dreadful, as young Nathan Hale's fate?[2] . . . In the performance of this duty, the flower of the army has fallen a victim to British wrath and brutality.

Rhoda Pemberton wrote me that at the time when Colonel Knowlton first made known to the officers, the wish of the Commander-in-Chief, a dead silence prevailed; and then Captain Hale looked up and said, "I will undertake it." It seemed, she said, against right and nature to all his friends, and even to strangers, that so young and gallant an officer should go out on such service. But young Hale said, "Every kind of service for his country became honorable. It was desired by the Commander of her armies." . . . "I only regret," he said, just before he ascended to the gibbet, "that I have but one life to lose for my country."

Rhoda gave me this account. She says that Prevost Cunningham (the inhuman wretch!) called out, "Swing the Rebel off!"

I cannot write this without weeping. It was a noble testimony, but a bitter necessity. So likely, so young, so brave.

Wednesday [October 1776]. Charles[3] accompanied John Harris home from school, with my permission, last night. He returned this morning with a story of the night, which he related to me in breathless excitement.

---

2. Hale had been sent to Long Island by George Washington to obtain information about British movements; he was captured and hanged without trial.

3. Minturn Post's only son; she had two daughters, Marcia and Grace.

A family living a mile from us were quietly sitting together in the evening, when a noise was heard at the door like that of a sharp instrument thrust into it. On opening the door, there stood a redcoat with his sabre in his hand, which he had stuck into the wood an inch or two. He was backed by a dozen men. They pushed their way in, and were very unruly, rummaging and ransacking every drawer and closet. . . .

The redcoats, highly enraged at finding nothing, began to threaten terrible things. . . . Mr. W. told them, that if they dared do any violence he would report them to the commanding officer; whereupon they actually went into the kitchen, kindled some light wood, came out, and set a burning brand at each corner of the house. The family were exceedingly alarmed. In great terror, Sarah, the youngest daughter, rushed out. She is famed through all the north side for her comeliness. I can well imagine that she must have appeared to them like a lovely apparition, with her flashing eye and glowing cheek. The ringleader, astonished, stood with a torch in his hand, gazing at her.

At length he said, "Angel!"

"Stop, I entreat you," said Sarah. His looks were riveted upon her in ardent admiration, which embarrassed her.

"I will, on one condition," said he.

"What is it?" said she.

"Will you grant it?"

"If I can," replied Sarah.

"It is, that you will allow me to kiss you."

"Oh, if that is all," said her father, "comply, my daughter." So, as she made no resistance, the rough soldier planted a fervent kiss on her lips, expressed himself satisfied, and departed.

They found before her baby-house that the soldiers had stuck the dolls on their bayonets, and railed among themselves and laughed. . . .

Monday [December 1776].   Henry Pattison, the nearest neighbor, has eight sturdy sons, and one little timid daughter. He belongs to the Society of Friends, is a fine specimen of humanity, owns a valuable farm, yet has a pretty hard struggle to bring up his large family. He was beginning to prosper a little, when the war began; but he is a mild, patient, pious man, consulted in all troubles and difficulties the whole country round; has prevented much going to law; visits the sick in soul and in body, and relieves them by his judicious advice, temporal and spiritual. He is called hereabouts The Peace-Maker.

Friend Pattison appears to have neither "part nor lot" in the struggle in which the country is engaged. How strange! *To be a man, and remain neutral!* His soul abhors War. This principle of their sect is enrooted in his breast. Yet he is a severe sufferer from it. Six Hessians are quartered upon him. They took possession of the kitchen; swung up their hammocks; cook his (the farmer's) food, and hang about, smoking and drinking the live-long day. Dear, how annoying! When shall we be rid of them?

Tuesday [a week later].   Edith Pattison came over the Parsonage to-day for the first time. She is a sweet young Quakeress; her pure, lovely, and attractive looks are indeed winning. . . . She is very fair, though her hair and eyes are dark; her aspect is mild, gentle, and pensive. I can describe to you the outline of Edith's features, but not the spiritual expression of her face. She is made a perfect lady of by her eight doting brothers. They will fetch, and carry, and run for their beautiful sister, as though she were a queen. And when you look at her, you do not think it strange, her air and mien are so serene, and dignity sits enthroned upon her brow.

Doubtless when you read my Journal, penned for your eye, you will exclaim, "How *could* she calmly write these details in stirring times like these?" But remember, Edward, I must be occupied about something; it beguiles the attention, and keeps off sad thoughts of you, which, when I give way to them, rend my heart. My precious father's peace is disturbed, and even the dear children appear to participate in the foreboding gloom.

Tuesday [December 1776]. ... Oh, dear husband, war is a weariness! Its effects sicken the soul. Every hour some fresh account of murder, robbery, wounding, destroying, depredating!

When will this unnatural warfare be at an end?

Wednesday. Major Musgrave[4] is very ill to-day, but yet considerate, and full of the thoughtful courtesy of the gentleman. What a blessed thing it is, that national animosity can be lost sight of, forgotten, in sorrow and compassion for a fellow-creature's distress! It leads me constantly to bring home to my own thoughts and feelings the idea of a beloved husband, child, or brother, in such a situation, away from me and all that he loved; amid those against whom his hand had been raised in warfare; sounded, ill, in pain, and anguish of spirit. Should I not cherish, in the deep places of my heart, an everlasting gratitude? And should I not teach it religiously to my children, to those who had *thus* ministered unto mine own?

Friday ... What is this struggle of the Colonies? Is it a war of aggression, of cupidity, of conquest, of fierce passion, for tyranny and despotic sway? No— it is the noble endeavor, the strong purpose, founded in inalienable right, to throw off a galling yoke unjustly and perseveringly imposed. It is the cry of humanity against oppression, usurped power, insolence, and rapacity. Will it prevail, or will it be smothered? Will those evils, from which our fathers fled to this new-found country, like hydra-headed monsters, raise *here* their heads, nor be smitten?

[November 1777]. To-day took Edith into Major Musgrave's room, he having expressed a wish to see the kind lady who had sent him so many delicacies made by her own hand. She has many admirers; soldiers and ploughmen, lettered and unlearned, the peaceful disciple of her own quiet sect, and the officer with epauletted shoulder and sword on side. She is lovely and captivating but

> "Securely she smiles on the forward and bold,
> They feel what they owe her, and feel it untold."

---

4. One of the soldiers occupying the Parsonage.

Yesterday I saw her pass the window with a gallant at her side. The contrast between them—*she* in her little close bonnet, grey dress, and sober mien, and the gay officer in scarlet regimentals—was very striking. Edith's eyes were cast down to the ground, while his were fixed upon her sweet face pleadingly. I heard him say, in a low tone, "Oh Edith, how *shall* I win your favor?"

I can tell him; he will not win it unless he relinquish the warrior's craft. To Edith, all "the pomp and circumstance of glorious war" is shrouded in gloom. "The shrill fife and spirit-stirring drum" drowneth not in *her* ear the groan of the wounded, the cry of the dying. Amid the din of arms, she listeneth to the widow's wail; and when the shout of victory rises, she sees the orphan's tears!

Do you know, dear husband, that papa and I are much of her way of thinking of late? although it needed not Edith's eloquent defence of peace to convince us. I long for the hastening of the day when "the nations shall not learn war any more, nor lift up sword against nation; but the sword shall be turned into the ploughshare, and the spear into the pruning hook."

I suppose you will say, "So be it"—after our independence is secured!

Sarah Wister (1761–1804)

Sarah ("Sally") Wister was born in 1761 into a prominent Philadelphia family. Her parents, Lowry Jones and Daniel Wister, sent her to Anthony Benezet's distinguished Quaker Girls School. It was there that Wister met Deborah Norris (*q.v.*), who became her best friend. Like many of the young burgeoning intellectuals in her social circle, Wister honed her writing talents through journal-writing, correspondence, and poetry. Some of her early poetry appeared in the *Philadelphia Port-Folio* under the signature of "Laura." The Wisters lived several miles outside Philadelphia during the Revolutionary years; and Sally, sixteen when she began her epistolary journal in 1777, recorded her thoughts about her life and the events of the war with her friend Deborah Norris as the intended recipient. When the British entered the region, soldiers camped near the Wisters' home and used their house as necessary. Sally Wister captures both the horrors of the British invasion and the allure of the young soldiers. Later in her life, Wister, who remained single, became deeply religious, using her journal as a spiritual narrative. But in the years of the war, it is the sixteen-year-old's voice that prevails.

Works: Journal, poetry. *Bibliography*: Derounian, *Journal*; Wister.

From the Journal of Sally Wister

To Deborah Norris[1]

Tho' I have not the least shadow of an opportunity to send a letter if I do write I will keep a sort of journal of the time that may expire before I see thee, the perusal of it may some time hence give pleasure in a solitary hour to thee and our Sally Jones,[2] yesterday, which was the 24th September two Virginia officers call'd at our house, and inform'd us that the British Army had cross'd the Schuylkill   presently after another person stop'd and confirm'd what they had said and that Genl Washington and Army were near Pottsgrove.[3] well thee may be sure we were sufficiently scar'd   however the road was very still till evening   about seven o'clock we heard a great noise to the door we all went, a large number of Waggons with about three hundred of the Philadelphia Militia   they beg'd for drink and several push'd into the house   one of those that enter'd was a little tipsy and had a mind to be saucy   I then thought it time for me to retreat so figure me (mightyly scar'd as not having presence of mind eneough to face so many of the Military) running in at one door and out another all in a shake with fear. but after a while seeing the officers appear gentlemanly and the Soldiers civil I call'd reason to my aid   my fears were in some measure dispell'd tho' my teeth rattled and my hand shook like an aspen leaf. they did not offer to take their quarters with us. so with many blessings and as many adieus they march'd off   I have given thee the most material occurrences of yesterday faithfully.

5th day septm 26th [1777][4]   we were unusually silent all the morning no passengers came by the house except to the Mill & we don't place much dependence on Mill news, about 12 oclock our cousin Jesse[5] heard that Gen Howe's Army had moved down towards Philadelphia, Then my dear our hopes & fears were engag'd for you however my advice is summon up all your resolution call Fortitude to your aid dont suffer your spirits to sink. my dear theres nothing like courage tis what I stand in need of myself but unfortunately have little of it in my composition   I was standing in the kitchen[6] about 12 when somebody came to me in a hurry screaming Sally Sally here [are the light horse. This was the greatest fright] I had endur'd   fear tack'd wings to my feet. I was at the house in a moment at the porch I stopt and it really was the light horse   I run immediatly to the western door w[h]ere the family were assembled anxiously waiting for the event. they rode up to the door and halted, and enquir'd

1. This entry is undated; it is probably from September 1777. See also Norris, "Epistolary Exchanges."

2. Wister's aunt, Sarah Jones; born on May 30, 1760, Sarah was only one year older than her niece.

3. The Battle of Brandywine had been fought on September 11; Washington was preparing to defend the Philadelphia area against General Howe's advance.

4. Wister's dates are incorrect at the beginning of her journal; this date should read September 25.

5. Jesse Foulke (1742–1821), a relative of Wister's by marriage.

6. The kitchen and house were separated by "a small distance." Thus, she had to cross an open area in order to rejoin her family.

if we had horses to sell. he was answer'd, negatively, have not you sir to my father, two black horses, yes. but have no mind to dispose of them, my terror had by this time nearly subsided. the officer and men behav'd perfectly civil, the first drank two glasses of wine. rode away bidding his men follow which after adieus in number they did. the officer was Lieutenant L Lindsay,[7] of Blands regiment Lee's troop. to our great joy [they] were Americans and but 4 in all. what made [us] imagine them British they wore blue and red. which with us is [not] common. it has rain'd all this afternoon, and to present appear will all night. in all probability the english will take possession of the city to morrow or next day what a change will it be. may the almighty take you under his protection for without His divine aid all human assistance is vain.

May heavens guardian arm protect my absent friends
From danger guard them and from want defend.

forgive my dear the repetition of these lines but they just darted into my mind. nothing worth relating has occur'd this afternoon now for trifles. I have set a stocking on the needles and intend to be mighty industrious. this evening some of our folks heard a very heavy cannon we supposed it to be fir'd by the english the report seem'd to come from Philad[elphi]a we hear the American army will be within five mile of us to night the uncertainty of our [pos]ition engrosses me quite. perhaps to be in the midst of War and ruin and the clang of arms. But we must hope for the best. . . .

Oct the 19th [20th] 1777 seconday, now for new and uncommon scenes. as I was laying in bed. and ruminating on past and present events, and thinking how happy I shou'd be if I cou'd see you. Liddy come running into the room. and said there was the greatest drumming fifing and rattling of Waggons that ever she had heard, what to make of this we were at a loss. we dress'd and downstairs in a hurry, our wonder ceas'd the british had left Germantown[8] and our Army was marching to take possession. it was the general opinion they wou'd evacuate the capitol, sister Betsy[9] myself and GE.[10] went about half a mile from home. where we cou'd see the army pass, thee will stare at my going, but no impropriety in my *opine*, or I wou'd not have gone. we made no great stay but return'd with excellent appetites for our breakfast. several officers call'd to get some refreshment, but none of consequence till the afternoon. cousin Prissa[11] and myself were sitting at the door I in a green skirt dark short gown, &c. two genteel men of the military order rode up to the door. your servant ladies, &c ask'd if they cou'd have quarters for Genl Smallwood.[12] aunt Foulke[13] thought she cou'd accomodate them as well as most of

7. William Lindsay, a Cornet in Colonel Bland's Regiment of the Virginia Light Dragoons.
8. The Battle of Germantown had been waged on October 4, 1777.
9. Elizabeth Wister (1764–?).
10. George Emlen (1741–1812), husband of Sarah Fishbourne, both of whom were Quakers and family friends of the Wisters.
11. Priscilla Foulke (1744–1821) was not related to Wister. "Cousin" was an often used appellation of courtesy and affection.
12. William Smallwood (1732–1792), colonel of the Maryland regiment.
13. Hannah Jones Foulke, mother of Prissa Foulke.

her neighbours said they cou'd, one of the officers dismounted, and wrote Smallwoods quarters over the door which secur'd us from straggling soldiers, after this he mounted his steed and rode away. when we were alone dress and lips were put in order for conquest and the hopes [of] adventures gave brightness to each before passive countenance   thee must be told of a Dr Gould[14] who by accident had made an acquaintance with my father a sensible conversible man. a carolinian and had come to bid us adieu on his going to that State   daddy had prevail'd upon him to stay a day or two with us, in the evening his Gen'ralship came with six attendants, which compos'd his family, a large guard of soldiers, a number of horses and baggage Waggons. the yard and house were in confusion, and glitter'd with military equipments. Gould was intimate with Smallwood and had gone into Jesse's to see him   while he was there, there was great running up and down stairs, so I had an opportunity of seeing and being seen. the former the most agreable, to be sure. one person in particular attracted my notice. he appear'd cross and reserv'd, but thee shall see how agreeably disappointed I was. Dr Gould usher'd the gentleman in to our parlour and introduc'd them. Genl Smallwood Capt Furnival Major Stodard Mr. Prig Capt Finley and Mr. Clagan. Col Wood and Col Line[15] these last two did not come with the Genl they are virginians and both indispos'd, the Genl and suite are Marylanders be assur'd I did not stay long with so many men but secur'd a good retreat heart safe so far. some sup'd with us. others at Jesse's   they retir'd about ten, in good order. how new is our situation, I feel in good spirits tho surrounded by an Army the house full of officers, yard alive with soldiers. very peaceable sort of men tho', they eat like other folks, talk like them, and behave themselves with elegance, so I will not be afraid of them. that I won't. adieu I am going to my chamber to dream I suppose of bayonets and swords, sashes, guns, and epaulets.

14. David Gould (?–1781), a surgeon with the Continental Army.

15. Alexander Furnival, William Stoddard, Ebenezer Finley, Horatio Claggett, James Wood, George Lyne; Mr. Prig is unidentified.

Poetry

Native American Songs

(Omaha, Hopi, Ojibway, and Osage)

Within virtually all tribal societies, songs were an important part of many facets of tribal life. Songs constitute one of the earliest oral forms of poetry, crossing many racial and cultural boundaries. The Native American poem-songs that follow reflect both formal spiritual ceremonies and fundamental facets of women's everyday lives. "Prayer for Infants" is an Omaha song to celebrate the birth of a child; as Carolyn Niethammer has explained, the ceremonial song was performed on the eighth day of the child's life to assure "it would have an accepted place in the life force that united all nature, both animate and inanimate" (11–12). The second song, from the Hopi, demonstrates how integrated were a Hopi woman's sense of self and her work in the community. Grinding corn was a process much like sewing in Euro-American culture: it was a skill passed from mother to daughter; whenever women gathered, their hands were busy with the grinding of corn, and exceptional skill could bring special acknowledgment for a young girl. The Ojibway songs reflect moments in individuals' lives while the Osage lamentation captures the strong sense of community that was a part of all tribal societies.

Bibliography: Burton; Densmore; Fletcher and La Flesche; La Flesche; Niethammer; Qoyawayma.

Prayer for Infants (Omaha)

Ho! Ye Sun, Moon, Stars, all ye that move in the heavens,
   I bid you hear me!
Into your midst has come a new life.
   Consent ye, I implore!
Make its path smooth, that it may reach the brow of the first hill!

Ho! Ye Winds, Clouds, Rain, Mist, all ye that move in the air,
   I bid you hear me!
Into your midst has come a new life.
   Consent ye, I implore!
Make its path smooth, that it may reach the brow of the second hill!

Ho! Ye Hills, Valleys, Rivers, Lakes, Trees, Grasses, all ye of the earth,
   I bid you hear me!
Into your midst has come a new life.
   Consent ye, I implore!
Make its path smooth, that it may reach the brow of the third hill!

Ho! Ye birds, great and small that dwell in the forest,
Ho! Ye insects that creep among the grasses and burrow in the ground,
Into your midst has come a new life.
   Consent ye, I implore!
Make its path smooth that it may reach the brow of the fourth hill!

Ho! All ye of the heavens, all ye of the air, all ye of the earth:
   I bid all of you to hear me!
Into your midst has come a new life.
   Consent ye, consent ye all, I implore!
Make its path smooth—then shall it travel beyond the four hills.

Corn Grinding Song (Hopi)

Oh, for a heart as pure as pollen on corn blossoms,
And for a life as sweet as honey gathered from the flowers,
May I do good, as Corn has done good for my people
Through all the days that were.
Until my task is done and evening falls,
Oh, Mighty Spirit, hear my grinding song.

A Woman's Song (Ojibway)

You are walking around
Trying to remember
What you promised,
But you can't remember.

I Am Arrayed Like the Roses (Ojibway)

What are you saying to me?
I am arrayed like the roses
And beautiful as they.

I can charm the man.
He is completely fascinated with me

In the center of the earth
Wherever he may be
Or under the earth.

The Weaver's Lamentation (Osage)[1]

You have left me to linger in hopeless longing,
Your presence had ever made me feel no want,
You have left me to travel in sorrow.
Left me to travel in sorrow; Ah! the pain,
Left me to travel in sorrow; Ah! the pain, the pain, the pain.

You have left me to linger in hopeless longing,
In your presence there was no sorrow,
You have gone and sorrow I shall feel, as I travel,
    Ah! the pain, the pain, the pain.

You have gone and sorrow I shall feel as I travel,
You have left me in hopeless longing.
In your presence there was no sorrow,
You have gone and sorrow I shall feel as I travel;
    Ah! the pain, the pain, the pain.

Content with your presence, I wanted nothing more,
You have left me to travel in sorrow;
    Ah the pain, the pain, the pain!

Anne Dudley Bradstreet (1612–1672)

Long distinguished as the first Euro-American poet but often studied only as an anomaly, Anne Dudley Bradstreet has recently gained
her deserved critical attention. Married at sixteen to Simon Bradstreet, Anne and her family came from England with John Winthrop
aboard the *Arbella* in 1630. In spite of the rigors of establishing a
new home in an unknown environment and raising eight children,
the artistic spirit in Dudley Bradstreet could not fail to be expressed.
Most anthologies, however, eliminate Dudley Bradstreet's most
women-centered poems, thus suppressing her more radical per-

1. This is a ritual song in which the singer is addressing beloved relatives who have died.

spectives. For instance, much has been made of Dudley Bradstreet's elegiac dedication to her father, but rarely has her elegy to her mother been anthologized, nor has her political poetry. In her religious poetry, Dudley Bradstreet envisioned human beings' "native qualities" as feminine, not simply in the tradition of pronoun references but in the sense that, when God had created human beings in his image, He established a balance of masculine and feminine traits. In her political poetry, Dudley Bradstreet repeatedly casts women as figures of physical and political power. Paradoxically an orthodox Puritan and an outspoken individualist in her poetry, Dudley Bradstreet remains the major woman poet of seventeenth-century America.

Works: *The Tenth Muse* (1650); *The Works of Anne Bradstreet*, ed. Jeannine Hensley. *Bibliography:* Cowell and Stanford; Schweitzer; Stanford.

Of the Four Humours in Man's Constitution[1]

The former four now ending their discourse,[2]
Ceasing to vaunt their good, or threat their force,
Lo! other four step up, crave leave to show
The native qualities that from them flow:
But first they wisely showed their high descent,
Each eldest daughter to each element.
Choler was owned by Fire, and Blood by Air,
Earth knew her black swarth child, Water her fair:
All having made obeisance to each mother,
Had leave to speak, succeeding one the other:
But 'mongst themselves they were at variance,
Which of the four should have predominance.
Choler first hotly claimed right by her mother,
Who had precedency of all the other;
But Sanguine did disdain what she required,
Pleading herself was most of all desired.
Proud Melancholy, more envious than the rest,
The second, third, or last could not digest.
She was the silentest of all the four,
Her wisdom spake not much, but thought the more.
Mild Phlegm did not contest for chiefest place,
Only she craved to have a vacant space.
Well, thus they parle and chide; but to be brief,
Or will they, nill they, Choler will be chief.
They seeing her impetuosity
At present yielded to necessity. . . .

1. All of the poems included here appeared in the first edition (1650) of *The Tenth Muse, Lately Sprung Up In America.*
2. In *The Tenth Muse*, this poem followed "The Four Elements."

A Dialogue Between Old England and New;
Concerning Their Present Troubles, Anno, 1642

New England

Alas, dear Mother, fairest queen and best,
With honour, wealth, and peace, happy and blest;
What ails thee hang thy head and cross thine arms?
And sit i' th' dust, to sigh these sad alarms?
What deluge of new woes thus overwhelm
The glories of thy ever famous realm?
What means this wailing tone, this mournful guise?
Ah, tell thy daughter, she may sympathize.

Old England

Art ignorant indeed of these my woes?
Or must my forced tongue these griefs disclose?
And must myself dissect my tattered state,
Which 'mazed Christendom stands wond'ring at?
And thou a child, a limb, and dost not feel
My fainting weak'ned body now to reel?
This physic purging potion I have taken
Will bring consumption or an ague quaking,
Unless some cordial thou fetch from high,
Which present help may ease my malady.
If I decease, doth think thou shalt survive?
Or by my wasting state dost think to thrive?
Then weigh our case, if't be not justly sad;
Let me lament alone, while thou art glad. . . .

An Epitaph on My Dear and Ever-Honoured Mother
Mrs. Dorothy Dudley, Who Deceased December 27, 1643 . . .

Here lies,
A worthy matron of unspotted life,
A loving mother and obedient wife,
A friendly neighbor, pitiful to poor,
Whom oft she fed and clothed with her store;
To servants wisely awful, but yet kind,
And as they did, so they reward did find.
A true instructor of her family,
The which she ordered with dexterity.
The public meetings ever did frequent,
And in her closet constant hours she spent;

307

Religious in all her words and ways,
Preparing still for death, till end of days:
Of all her children, children lived to see,
Then dying, left a blessed memory.

In Honour of That High and Mighty Princess Queen Elizabeth of Happy Memory

The Proem

Although, great Queen, thou now in silence lie
Yet thy loud herald Fame doth to the sky
Thy wondrous worth proclaim in every clime,
And so hath vowed while there is world or time.
So great's thy glory and thine excellence,
The sound thereof rapts every human sense,
That men account it no impiety,
To say thou wert a fleshly deity.
Thousands bring offerings (though out of date)
Thy world of honours to accumulate;
'Mongst hundred hecatombs of roaring verse,
Mine bleating stands before thy royal herse.
Thou never didst nor canst thou now disdain
T' accept the tribute of a loyal brain.
Thy clemency did erst esteem as much
The acclamations of the poor as rich,
Which makes me deem my rudeness is no wrong,
Though I resound thy praises 'mongst the throng.

The Poem

No Phoenix[3] pen, nor Spenser's[4] poetry,
No Speed's nor Camden's[5] learned history,
Eliza's works, wars, praise, can e'er compact;
The world's the theatre where she did act.
No memories nor volumes can contain
The 'leven Olympiads of her happy reign.
Who was so good, so just, so learn'd, so wise,
From all the kings on earth she won the prize.
Nor say I more than duly is her due.
Millions will testify that this is true.

---

3. A legendary bird that rises from its own ashes, renewed and youthful.
4. Edmund Spenser (1552?–1599), English poet.
5. William Camden (1551–1623), English historian.

She hath wiped off th' aspersion of her sex,
That women wisdom lack to play the rex.
Spain's monarch, says not so, nor yet his host;
She taught them better manners, to their cost.
The Salic law,[6] in force now had not been,
If France had ever hoped for such a queen.
But can you, doctors, now this point dispute,
She's argument enough to make you mute.
Since first the Sun did run his ne'er run race,
And earth had, once a year, a new old face,
Since time was time, and man unmanly man,
Come show me such a Phoenix if you can.
Was ever people better ruled than hers?
Was ever land more happy freed from stirs?
Did ever wealth in England more abound?
Her victories in foreign coasts resound;
Ships more invincible than Spain's, her foe,
She wracked, she sacked, she sunk his Armado;
Her stately troops advanced to Lisbon's wall,
Don Anthony in's right there to install.
She frankly helped Frank's brave distressed king;
The states united now her fame do sing.
She their protectrix was; they well do know
Unto our dread virago, what they owe.
Her nobles sacrificed their noble blood,
Nor men nor coin she spared to do them good.
The rude untamed Irish, she did quell,
Before her picture the proud Tyrone fell.
Had ever prince such consellors as she?
Herself Minerva[7] caused them so to be.
Such captains and such soldiers never seen,
As were the subjects of our Pallas queen.[8]
Her seamen through all straits the world did round;
Terra incognita[9] might know the sound.
Her Drake[10] came laden home with Spanish gold;
Her Essex[11] took Cadiz,[12] their Herculean hold.
But time would fail me, so my tongue would too,
To tell of half she did, or she could do.

6. Rules of succession that, in many European families of nobility, precluded the succession of women or those members who were descended from the female line. While France maintained Salic laws, Spain rescinded them in order to instate Isabella II; the law still prevented Queen Victoria from succeeding in Hanover, however.
7. Roman goddess of wisdom.
8. Athena, Greek goddess of war.
9. Unknown territory.
10. Sir Francis Drake (1540?–1596), English admiral.
11. Robert Devereux (1566–1601), 2d Earl of Essex.
12. Spanish province.

Semiramis[13] to her is but obscure,
More infamy than fame she did procure.
She built her glory but on Babel's walls,
World's wonder for a while, but yet it falls.
Fierce Tomris (Cyrus' headsman) Scythians' queen,
Had put her harness off, had she but seen
Our Amazon in th' Camp of Tilbury,[14]
Judging all valour and all majesty
Within that princess to have residence,
And prostrate yielded to her excellence. . . .
She was a Phoenix queen, so shall she be.
Her ashes not revived, more Phoenix she.
Her personal perfections, who would tell
Must dip his pen in th' Heleconian well,
Which I may not, my pride doth but aspire
To read what others write and so admire.
Now say, have women worth? or have they none?
Or had they some, but with our Queen is't gone?
Nay masculines, you have thus taxed us long,
But she, though dead, will vindicate our wrong.
Let such as say our sex is void of reason,
Know 'tis a slander now but once was treason.
But happy England which had such a queen;
Yea happy, happy, had those days still been.
But happiness lies in a higher sphere,
Then wonder not Eliza moves not here.
Full fraught with honour, riches and with days
She set, she set, like Titan in his rays.
No more shall rise or set so glorious sun
Until the heaven's great revolution;
If then new things their old forms shall retain,
Eliza shall rule Albion[15] once again. . . .

Martha Wadsworth Brewster (fl. 1725–57)

Little is known of Martha Wadsworth Brewster's life other than
what she reveals in her single published book, *Poems on Divers Subjects* (1757). She lived part of her life in Goshen, Massachusetts,
and her writing reflects her Calvinist Puritanism. One of her earliest poems, for example, is addressed to the "Opposers" of "the

13. Mythical Assyrian queen said to have founded Babylon.
14. Southeastern English seaport.
15. England.

special Grace of *God*"; composed in August 1741, the poem reflects her alignment with the evangelicals of the Great Awakening.
Some time around 1745, Wadsworth moved to Lebanon, Massachusetts; separation from her friends in Goshen was a painful experience, but she found comfort, then as later, by expressing her
responses to her life experiences through poetry. The move to
Lebanon, perhaps for marriage, occurred one year after the death
of her father. She and her husband, Oliver Brewster, had two children, Ruby and Wadsworth. When her daughter married Henry
Bliss, Martha Wadsworth Brewster poignantly lamented this third
"loss" in a poetic letter to Ruby.

Wadsworth Brewster's collected poems were published, but not
without a conflict similar to that faced by Phillis Wheatley years
later. The quality of Wadsworth Brewster's literary output caused
more than the normal questioning of a woman's talent: she was accused of "borrowing" her poetry from male poets of the period.
Her indignation and body of work were insufficient rebuttals, however; she was presented with a passage from Scripture and asked
to translate it into verse "Extempore" as proof of her poetic skills.
She produced a twenty-eight-line poem in a matter of minutes, "as
vindication from that Aspersion" of plagiarism. Because of the time
constraints, it certainly is not her best work, but the inclusion in
Poems on Divers Subjects of the poem and explanatory notes as to
its composition suggests Wadsworth Brewster's subtle but unfal-
tering assertion of her talents and her right to a public voice, as
does the title page of her text, which, unlike many women's publications of the era, includes her name on the cover in bold print.

Works: *Poems On divers Subjects* (1757).   Bibliography: Cowell; Watts.

Preface to Martha Wadsworth Brewster's *Poems on Divers Subjects* (untitled)

PARDON her bold Attempt who has reveal'd
Her Thoughts to View, more fit to be conceal'd;
Since thus to do was urged vehemently,
Yet most no doubt will call it Vanity;
Condemn the Stile you may without Offence,
Call it insipid, wanting Eloquence.
I Blush to Gaul so delicate an Ear,
Which to sublimer Sonnets do adhere;
For why my Muse had but a single Aim,
Myself and nearest Friends to entertain;
But since some have a Gust for Novelty,
I here presume upon your Clemency,
For rare it is to see a *Female Bard*,
Or that my *Sex* in *Print* have e're appear'd:

311

Let me improve my Talent tho' but small,
And thus it humbly wait upon you shall.

March 9th, 1757.

On the last *Judgment*.

ABOUT the middle of the Night,
   When all securely slept,
The Dead, the Risen, Reigning Lord,
   His Armies musters up.
Hark! High, beyond these Crystal Orbs,
   An Herald strong Proclaims,
The great Assize,[1] my radiant Guards,
   March down, attend the same.
Ye Courtiers of this lower House,
   Lift up your raptur'd Eyes,
Behold, the Bridegroom's on his Way,
   Behold, he tares the Skys.
The lofty Battlements of Heav'n,
   In vast Confusion hurl'd,
The Sun with his refulgent Rays,
   Drops down to burn the World.
All Nature is at once Unhing'd,
   And in Convulsions thrown;
What panick Hearts, horrendous Cries?
   What Tears, and bursting Groans?
Hark! the shrill Trumpet soundeth long,
   Hail, dearly purchas'd ones,
With trimmed Lamps and gorgeous Robes,
   Draw near the great White Throne.
The Saints that come with CHRIST, descend,
   Bright Angels guard their way,
To reap the World, set ope' their Graves,
   Revive their sleeping Clay.
Rise, says the Soul, my Body rise,
   Embrace thy Consort Dear,
Our LORD's preserved ev'ry Dust,
   And wip'd of ev'ry Tear.
Saints, Quick and Dead, now Glorious made,
   On CHRIST's right Hand advance,
While all around, behold them Crown'd,
   T' inhabit Holiness.
Then Sinners Grudge, Blaspheme their Judge,

---

1. Session of the English court.

And Gnashing gnaw their Tongues;
Too late they ask for pardoning Grace,
　　But straight with Guilt are stung.
Feign would they Delve, each dang'rous Shelve,
　　To quit the Judges Face,
But nought can Screen, or change his Mein,
　　Hell is their proper Place.
The Devils too, their Rage Renew,
　　Their Doom being now compleat,
Who string and drive those wretched Ghosts,
　　Their Curs'd Remains to meet.
Sleep on our Rueful Wretched Dust,
　　Our Torment don't Augment:
We that have Partners been in Sin,
　　Must Share in Punishment.
With trembling Joints, and visage Grim,
　　Crawl forth against their Wills;
Hast found us oh, our hateful Souls,
　　Our Lusts shall Plague you still.
Thus ev'ry Member, ev'ry Sense,
　　And ev'ry Faculty,
Fill'd with GOD's Wrath, and scourg'd with Fiends
　　Seeks Death, but cannot Die.
Thus hellish Feuds and wretched Wights,
　　Into the Lake are turn'd,
Seal'd down with Ire in vengeful Fire,
　　Eternally are Burn'd.
The magnificent Judge Returns,
　　Homewards his Chariots rise;
Cherubick Legions sweetly Sound,
　　Each Emulating tries.
To touch the highest String of Praise,
　　And accent ev'ry Note,
While ev'ry Victim crown'd with Bay's,
　　Incircle him about.
With palms in Hand, and golden Harps,
　　The Trophies of his Grace,
Unite the Choir and all resound,
　　The Great *Redeemer's* Praise.
Thus they attend their Glorious Head,
　　'Till He ascends the Throne,
And to His *Father* doth Resign,
　　The Kingdom he has won.
And GOD be all, in all, yea all,
　　His Creatures Happiness;
And their Desire and Glory too,
　　The Source of all their Bliss.

The God-head Smiles, welcome he says,
　　To Mansions Fair and Bright,
Each loud Proclaim their *Lord* the *Lamb*,
　　And Glory in the Height.

A Letter to my Daughter *Ruby Bliss*[2]

My only Daughter Dear, my Hearts Delight,
Since cruel Distance keeps thee from my Sight:
I breath forth Sighs into the empty Air,
My best Desires pursue thee ev'ry where.
My ardent Love can reach thee where thou art,
And mingle with thy sympathizing Heart.
My Breast a Magazine of tend'rest Passions,
Pregnant with Grief, seeks Vent in sev'ral Fashions:
Sometimes the optick Fountains up do break,
And liquid Salts do deluge o'er my Cheek:
Each Filial due Performance strikes my Heart,
And mournful Pleasure shoots through ev'ry Part;
[?] Fancies o'er the Mind still Float,
Sometimes your Joys, and prosp'rous State I doat,
But grim Distrust soon rifles my Repose,
Presents you Sick, Bereav'd and full of Woes:
O Absence! Absence! sharper than a Thorn,
The tender Sian from the Stock is Torn:
But sure my fond Affections wildly Rove,
My nobler Pow'rs in higher Orbs should move.
Then Grant me Grace, to bear much Fruit to Thee.
My pleasant Branchy, which thou hast Grafted, *Lord*,
Make her the charge of Angels, and afford,
Thy special Benediction while Alive,
Then to some Glorious Mansion her Receive;
But while she's Station'd here, let her obtain,
Such precious Fruit as shall embalm her Name:
Let Bud, and Branch, and Tree securely stand,
Drest by the Culture of thy Gracious Hand:
Planted by purling Streams, crystial Founts,
In Gospel Soil, and circle-ed about,
With a bright Rainbow of the Promises,
A sure Defence and costly purchas'd Peace.
Chear up my drooping Heart, shake of thy Woes,
Tho' cruel Distance means to Interpose.
There is a Place where we may Daily meet,

---

2. Ruby Brewster had married Henry Bliss before this poem was written. Brewster's wedding-day poem to Ruby was joyous and celebratory, unlike the "Letter," which was composed after Ruby and her husband had settled in a distant region.

With joynt Request, before the Mercy Seat;
In hopes of which your tender Mother rests,
Until your Countenance her Eyes shall Bless.

Hannah Griffitts (1727–1817)

Hannah Griffitts was born in Philadelphia in 1727. Her parents were
notable figures in the community: Mary Norris, a Quaker, was part
of a distinguished family in the region; and Thomas Griffitts was a
noted public official. Griffitts was one of the most prolific writers
of her era; more than two hundred of her manuscript poems (typically signed "Fidelia") are extant. She also wrote numerous essays
and maintained correspondence with an extended group of women,
including the poets Susanna Wright (q.v.) and Elizabeth Graeme
Fergusson (q.v.). A devout Quaker, Griffitts struggled to keep her
poetry as an "amusement," that is, sublimated to her religious duties; though she asserted at an early age that "the Muse [had been]
long banished and disused" and her poetry "consecrate[d]" to God,
her careful writing and rewriting of her works suggest the seriousness with which she shaped her literary endeavors. Nor was she
only a religious poet. Her writings from about age ten until her
death at age ninety reflect her intellectual involvement with the religious, political, and social issues of some of America's most volatile
years. Griffitts refused to publish her poetry during her lifetime,
preferring to exchange it only among the community of women
with whom she corresponded. Hannah Griffitts remained single
throughout her life; she died in Philadelphia on August 24, 1817.

Works: Poetry, correspondence, essays. *Bibliography:* Cowell.

On Reading Some Paragraphs in "The Crisis," April, '77

Pane[1]—Though thy tongue may now run glibber,
   Warm'd with thy independent glow,
Thou art indeed the coldest fibber,
   I ever knew, or wish to know.
Here page and page, even num'rous pages,
   Are void of breeding, sense or truth;
I hope thou don't receive thy wages,
   As tutor to our rising youth.

1. Thomas Paine, author of *The American Crisis*, a collection of pamphlets published during the
American Revolution. The first "Crisis" paper had been published in the *Pennsylvania Journal* on
December 19, 1776, and immediately made Paine one of the leading political essayists of the Revolution.
In April 1777, Paine was appointed Secretary to the Committee on Foreign Affairs of Congress, a
position created so he could devote himself to his writings in support of the American cause.

Of female manners, never scribble,
   Nor with thy rudeness wound our ear;
Howe'er thy trimming pen may quibble,
   The delicate is "not thy sphere."

And now, to prove how false thy stories,
   By facts which won't admit a doubt,
Know there are "conscientious tories,"
   And one poor whig, at least, without.

Wilt thou permit the muse to mention
   A whisper, circulated round;
Let Howe[2] increase the scribbler's pension,
   No more will Pane a whig be found;

For not from principle, but lucre,
   He gains his bread from out the fire;
Let Court and Congress both stand neuter,
   And the poor creature must expire.

To the Memory of My Late Valuable Friend Susannah Wright, who Died Decr 1st, 1784 (In the 88th Year of Her Age)

Shall thou, whose gentle muse in softest strain
   Wept others' sorrow with a feeling breast,
Ah shall Veneria close her lot of pain,
   Nor leave a muse, her virtues to attest.

Not so; the muse once favor'd and belov'd
   Shall trace her mild benignity of heart,
The soul that wish'd each human ill remov'd,
   The hand that every comfort would impart.

And though with innate powers superior blest,
   The striking sense and energy of mind,
How veil'd their luster, while her form express'd
   The humble, courteous, diffident, and kind.

While o'er the "tomb of friendship" sorrow flow'd
   In feeling grief, and deep reflection strong,
How with the theme her gentle bosom glow'd,
   How sweet her powerful harmony of song.

For genius, thus distinguish'd and admir'd,
   Above ambition's low contrasted care,
She walk'd with wisdom, in the "vale retir'd,"
   And left the world its tinsel and its glare.

2. General William Howe of the British army.

Warm to the ties of nature and of love,
    She own'd their influence and cementing power,
(And in this sphere of duty, fond to move)
    From them, the pleasing and the painful hour.

Did suffering wound, or death remove the friend,
    She felt the anguish of its keenest dart;
Did brighter fancy, the social-hour attend,
    She shared the pleasure, with a grateful heart.

Nor to this narrow spot alone confin'd,
    (Virtue, more wide, will all its powers expand)
She pour'd the balm, compassionately kind,
    On human sufferings, with a healing hand.

Thus through each period of a lengthen'd day,
    (Fulfill'd the tender claim, the social tie)
"She kept the noiseless tenor of her way,"[3]
    Yet sigh'd for the good the world could not supply.

Till nature droop'd beneath the waste of years,
    Panted for life, and long'd to be undress'd:
A life beyond these sublunary spheres,
    A life distinguish'd by eternal rest.

Perfected thus, may thou, departed friend,
    The full fruition of thy bliss enjoy,
A bliss that fears no change, decrease or end,
    A portion time nor death can e'er destroy.

And while this bosom, once to friendship dear,
    In artless verse embalms its kindred clay,
Center'd in God, releas'd from sorrowing care,
    "Thy mortal shall surpass thy natal day."[4]

Lucy Terry (Prince) (1730–1821)

Kidnapped from her homeland of Africa and brought to Rhode Island at about age five, Lucy Terry was purchased by a Massachusetts landowner, Ebenezer Wells, who transported her to his home in Deerfield. It was there, among the community of slaves on Wells's estate, that Lucy crafted her artistry in the oral tradition of her na-

3. Griffitts's note: "Gray's Church-Yard."
4. Griffitts's note: "See a piece she wrote on her own birthday, which closes with the above last line."

tive land. In 1756, Lucy married an emancipated man, Abijah Prince, who probably purchased Lucy's freedom as well. The couple settled in Vermont, becoming landowners and raising six children. Yet Terry Prince did not settle into complacency once freed; when a white neighbor sought to usurp some of the Princes' land, she and her husband took legal action to stop their neighbor, having to fight the case through several state courts and finally to the state Supreme Court where it is believed Lucy Terry Prince presented the family's case before the court. "Bars Fight" is her only extant poem, but its date of 1746 signifies Terry Prince as the earliest known African-American poet.

Works: "Bars Fight" (1746). *Bibliography*: Cowell; Foster; Holland; *An Introduction to Black Literature*.

Bars Fight[1]

August, 'twas the twenty-fifth,
Seventeen hundred forty-six;
The Indians did in ambush lay,
Some very valiant men to slay,
The names of whom I'll not leave out.
Samuel Allen like a hero fout,
And though he was so brave and bold,
His face no more shall we behold.
Eleazer Hawks was killed outright,
Before he had time to fight,—
Before he did the Indians see,
Was shot and killed immediately.
Oliver Amsden he was slain,
Which caused his friends much grief and pain.
Simeon Amsden they found dead,
Not many rods distant from his head.
Adonijah Gillett, we do hear,
Did lose his life which was so dear.
John Sadler fled across the water,
And thus escaped the dreadful slaughter.
Eunice Allen see the Indians coming,
And hopes to save herself by running,
And had not her petticoats stopped her,
The awful creatures had not catched her,
Nor tommy hawked her on her head,
And left her on the ground for dead.
Young Samuel Allen, Oh lackaday!
Was taken and carried to Canada.

1. "Bars" is slang for a meadow.

Sarah Parsons Moorhead (fl. 1741–42)

Little is known of Sarah Parsons Moorhead's early life. She was married to the Reverend John Moorhead, and she lived in Boston during the Great Awakening, when religious revivalism flourished in America. Her adept poetic skills in the heroic couplet and her knowledge of the theological debates of her day suggest an unusually acute education. Each of her extant poems cautions against "the zeal" that fired too many emotional and doctrinal excesses during the Great Awakening; yet she also cautions "scoffers" to consider the possibilities afforded by "this blest Fountain" of opportunity. In the following excerpt from her address to the Reverend James Davenport, Parsons Moorhead acknowledges Davenport's qualities and contributions as a minister, but questions the itinerant evangelicalist's need to criticize local ministries. In Parsons Moorhead's poem, it is only when Davenport removes himself from the tumult of his zeal (ll. 19ff) that he can clearly assess his own actions, and Parsons Moorhead's text inserts that same "Shade" of "Gentle checks" into a community of discourse too often fraught with emotional upheaval.

Works: "Lines . . . Dedicated to the Rev. Mr. Gilbert Tennent," *New England Weekly Journal* (March 17, 1741), p. 1, rpt. by Benjamin Franklin in *General Magazine and Historical Chronicle* 1 (April 1741), pp. 281–282; "To the Reverend Mr. James Davenport on his Departure from Boston, By Way of a Dream . . ." (Boston, 1742). *Bibliography*: Cowell; Hornstein.

To the REVEREND MR. JAMES DAVENPORT
on his Departure from Boston . . .[1]

Assist celestial Powers my grieved Heart,
For Love and Sorrow bear an equal Part;
I love the Zeal that fires good DAVENPORT's Breast,
But his harsh censures give my Soul no rest;
Our worthy *Guides* whom GOD has much inflam'd,
As unexperienc'd Souls, alas, he nam'd;
Hence giddy Youth a woful Licence take;
A mock at reverend hoary Heads they make,
Despite the blest Instructions of their Tongue,
Conversion is become the Drunkard's Song;
GOD's glorious Work, which sweetly did arise,
By this unguarded sad Imprudence dies;
Contention spreads her Harpy Claws around,
In every Church her hateful Stings are found

1. The complete title of the text is "To the REVEREND MR. JAMES DAVENPORT on his Departure from Boston, By Way of a DREAM: With a Line to the *Scoffers* at Religion, who make an ill improvement of his naming out our worthy Ministers. To which is added, A Postscript to the Rev. Mr. A——d——w C——w——ll."

But as these Thoughts my troubled Mind opprest,
Sleep sweet Cessation instantly refresh'd,
My Tumults calm, and new-born Pleasure rise,
A charming VISION swims before my Eyes.
   The sacred Man is to his Shade convey'd,
On Cammomile his aking Temples laid;
Here Roses, Honey-Suckles, Jessamine
In beauteous Arches o'er the Champion twine;
Here Nature does her flowery Glories spread,
Sheets of white Lillies dress the lovely Bed,
With rich Cor'nations for his Coverlid;
Here pretty Birds employ each smiling Hour
In noble Toyls to deck the charming Bower;
Arabia Trace for Spices in the Bloom,
And with enamel'd Branches straw the Room.
Here gilded Clouds *Ambrosia* Drops distill,
And all the Air with matchless Odors fill;
Here gentle Zephyrs fan the fragrant Flowers,
While singing Angels guard his sleeping Hours:
Now as the shining Warriors watch his Bed,
These *gentle Checks* they whisper in his Head;
'Favorite of Heaven! How came it in thy Mind?
'That Grace was so much to thy self confin'd;
'Crush the proud Thought, and kill it in the Bud;
'Too long you have in this sad Error stood;
'Let Charity unclose thy drowsy Eyes;
'You'll see a Train of faithful Pastors rise,
'Thousands of happy Souls surround their Feet,
'Which you in Realms of Glory soon shall meet;
'The timorous Christian to his great Surprize,
'Sees himself there, tho' he himself despis'd;
'So the censorious Wonders when he views
'Souls there he thought GOD surely would refuse:
'What has the Enemy provok'd you too?
'Success is not confin'd, dear Man, to you,
'O let not Fancy turn thy Zeal aside,
'Free Grace in others must not be deny'd;
'No more attempt to touch the Judgment Throne,
'*Soul Secrets* to the LORD alone are known.'
   The Heraulds rise & touch him with their Wings;
Now in his Breast a holy Shame there springs;
He starts with rosy Blushes in his Face,
And weeping sweetly sings to sovereign Grace;
'Praise to Free Grace, that kept my erring Breath,
'Nor sent me, swiftly to eternal Death:'
Down his Cheeks the chrystal Showers flow,
He wrings his Hands in penitential Woe,

Cryes, 'What have I vain-glorious Mortal done,
'Strove to Eclipse the Influence of the Sun,
'Made false Report a Bandage for my Eyes,
'And boundless Grace in Numbers vast despise;
'The very End my Zeal pursu'd the most,
'The glorious End untemper'd Zeal has lost:[']
In lovely Language here his Lips impart
The blest Contrition of his pious Heart;
His shining Guardians listen to his Tongue,
And smiling upwards bear his mournful Song:
I'll hearken too, as yet he does not cease;
'FATHER, he cries, Creator of my Peace,
'Forgive my Guilt, I'll censure so no more,
'Thy Pardon on my Knees I here implore;
'Unite the Churches I have rashly rent,
'To heal the Breaches O let some be sent;
'My Error in my Mind I ever keep,
'Unhappy Shepherd thus to scatter Sheep;
'COLMAN and SEWALL[2] I in hast exprest,
'I clasp as first rank Worthies to my Breast;
'Now all I've wrong'd, or have too rashly nam'd,
'Freely forgive, as I myself have blam'd:'
In folded Arms of Love the Prophets meet,
GOD's Work goes on by Unity most sweet.

. . .

But I must leave the Pleasures of my Dream,
And turn my Thoughts to a more awful Theme,
To Souls immers'd in the black Gulph of Sin,
Who sporting drink the deadly Poison in;
Pleas'd with the fancy'd Freedom of their Will,
They seek their crying Conscience to still;
Nor can they bear dear Nature to deface,
Pride will not Beggar be to sov'reign Grace;
Array'd in moral Duties, gaudy shew,
They for a Saviour little have to do;
They wonder any such Complaints should make,
In Reformation they a Shelter take:
Dare you appear before th' eternal Throne
In this vile Cob-webb Garment of your own!
Oh no! my Friends, repent, reform ye must,
And trust Free-Grace, or be for ever curst:

. . .

2. Benjamin Colman had been a renowed Boston minister since his installation at the Brattle Street Church in 1699. The Reverend Joseph Sewall was, as Perry Miller termed him, "a disciple" of Cotton Mather (*New England Mind* 2:184), that is, like Colman, an "Old Light."

Now let the Scoffers at the Word of GOD,
Tremble, for *Gabriel* brandishes his Sword;
Your raging Hearts shall feel the burning Steel,
And GOD his Terrors in your Soul reveal;
Think not the Frailties of a Man forgiv'n,
Gives you a Licence thus to storm at Heav'n;
Turn your dire Hissings into Songs of Praise,
Leave off your Railings, and amend your Ways;
Fly to the purple Streams on Calv'ry shed,
There bathe your Souls, or Vengeance strikes you dead:
But ah, in vain I bid you thither go,
Of this blest Fountain yet ye nothing know;
Poor blinded Nature can't her Danger see,
Unless the optick Scale removed be,
Much less descry the blessed Remedy.
   O glorious JESUS! the poor Sinner's Friend,
Our Sins, black Mountains, come and condescend
To show the charming Beauties of thy Face,
And stop the Rebels in their woful Race;
In sleeping Conscience fix thy piercing Spear,
And make them bow to thee with trembling Fear.

. . .

Elizabeth Graeme Fergusson (1737–1801)

In addition to poetic translations, Elizabeth Graeme Fergusson wrote several poems that appeared in Nathaniel Evans's *Poems on Several Occasions* (1772), which she helped to some degree to co-edit after Evans's death. Evans had been a long-time friend of Graeme Fergusson and had attended many of her Saturday evening literary gatherings. When she wrote "A Parody," satirizing Pope, they began what they termed a "poetical *Raillery*," an exchange of a series of poems. It is this exchange that is appended to Evans's book. Graeme Fergusson's poems are signed "Laura"; Evans used "Strephon" as a pen name. [For additional biographical data, see entry in Part II.]

Works: Poetry; letters; translations. *Bibliography*: Cowell; Evans, N.; Gratz; Griswold; Lopez and Herbert; *Papers of Benjamin Franklin*; Stedman and Hutchinson.

Invocation to Wisdom[1]

Grave Wisdom, guardian of the modest youth,
Thou soul of knowledge and thou source of truth,

---

1. This poem is prefixed to Fergusson's translation of Fénelon's *The Adventures of Télémachus* (1769).

Inspire my muse, and animate her lays,
That she harmonious may chant thy praise.
  O could a spark of that celestial fire,
Which did thy favored Fénelon inspire,
Light on the periods of my fettered theme,
And dart one radiant, one illumined beam,
Then struggling Passion might its portrait view,
And learn from thence in tumults to subdue.
  This was the pious prelate's great design:
As rays converged to one bright point combine,
So do the fable and the tale unite
The path of Truth by Fancy's torch to light;
Each to one noble, generous aim aspires,
And the rich galaxy at once conspires
To catch the fluttering mind and fix the sense
The end can justify the fine pretence,
For youthful spirits abstract reasonings shun,
And from grave precept void of life they run.
Though heathen gods are introduced to sight,
'Tis one Great Being radiates every light;
Seen through the medium of a lesser guide,
From one pure fount is each small rill supplied;
Then, rigid Christian, be not too severe,
Nor think great Cambray in an error here.
  In parable the holy Jesus taught—
Unwound the clue with mystic knowledge fraught.
He knew the frailties of man's earthly lot,
That truths important were too soon forgot;
He screened his purpose in the pleasing tale,
Then tore aside the heavenly-woven veil,
Showed his design—the perfect, sacred plan—
And raised to angel what he found but man;
By nice gradation in this scale divine
The glorious meaning did illustrious shine.
Like his great Master, pious Cambray taught,
And all the good of all mankind he sought:
Through his Télémachus he points to view
What youth should fly from and what youth pursue.
He makes pure Wisdom leave the realms above
To screen a mortal from bewitching love,
To lead him through the thorny ways below,
And all those arts of false refinement show
Which end in fleeting joy and lasting wo;
He pains gay Venus in tumultuous rage,
Yet shows her baffled by the guardian sage,
Who draws his pupil from Italian groves,
From blooming Cyprus and from melting loves.

323

Passion and Wisdom hold perpetual strife
Through the strange mazes of man's chequered life
Of all the evils our frail nature knows,
The most acute from Love's emotions flows.
The utmost efforts of the brave are seen,
To check the transports of the Paphian queen;[2]
Minerva[3] gives an energy of soul
Which does the tide of Passion's rage control,
Nor damps that fire which generous youth should feel,
But only tempers the high-finished steel:
For metal softened, polished, and refined,
Is like th' opening of the ductile mind.
Moulded by flame, made pliant to the hand,
Turned in the furnace to each just command:
This fire is disappointment, grief, and pain,
Which, if the soul with fortitude sustain,
The furnace of affliction makes more bright;
Yet higher burnished in Jehovah's sight,
And it at last shall joyfully survey
The tangled path to where perfection lay,
And bless the briers of life's thorny road
That led to peace, to happiness, and God!

A Parody On the foregoing Lines,[4] by a Lady, assuming the Name of LAURA

How happy is the country Parson's lot?
Forgetting *Bishops*, as by *them* forgot;
Tranquil of spirit, with an easy mind,
To all his *Vestry's* votes he sits resign'd:
Of manners gentle, and of temper even,
He jogs his flocks, with easy pace, to heaven.
In Greek and Latin, pious books he keeps;
And, while his Clerk sings psalms, he—soundly sleeps.
His garden fronts the sun's sweet orient beams,
And fat church-wardens prompt his golden dreams.
The earliest fruit, in his fair orchard, blooms;
And cleanly pipes pour out tobacco's fumes.
From rustic bridegroom oft he takes the ring;
And hears the milk-maid plaintive ballads sing.
Back-gammon cheats whole winter nights away,
And Pilgrim's Progress helps a rainy day.

2. Paphos was an ancient town in southwestern Cyprus.
3. Roman goddess of wisdom.
4. A parody on Pope's Lines, printed in Evans's *Poems on Several Occasions* (1772).

Ann Eliza Schuyler Bleecker (1752–1783)

Ann Eliza Schuyler was born in 1752, the daughter of aristocratic New Yorkers, Margareta Van Wyck and Brandt Schuyler. Raised by her mother (her father died shortly before she was born), Ann was encouraged as a young woman to pursue her interests in the literary arts. In 1769 she married John J. Bleecker, Esq.; they first lived in Poughkeepsie and then settled in the small village of Tomhanick, near Albany. Schuyler Bleecker's early life had ill prepared her, however, for the harrowing realities of her adult life.

After nearly a decade of peace and comfort, the American Revolution swept through the New York region in which the Bleeckers resided. Raids by Native Americans and Tories threatened their home several times, and in 1777 General John Burgoyne led his British troops into the area. John was away from home on business, and Schuyler Bleecker was forced to flee her home with her two children. She found the difficulties of this surreptitious travel and of finding shelter for her children devastating; the journey eventually resulted in the death of her youngest child, Abella. Schuyler Bleecker's subsequent lifelong despair over this loss is evident in much of her poetry and fiction. Nor was that the end of her troubles. In 1781 John was captured by Tories, and Schuyler Bleecker set out, once again, to attempt his rescue. Though John was eventually released, Schuyler Bleecker suffered numerous health problems thereafter, including bouts of severe depression during which, according to her daughter, the poet Margaretta V. Bleecker Faugères (*q.v.*), she destroyed some of her writings. Her depression is poignantly evident in letters she wrote after the death of Abella: "You are to look upon my letters as coming from the ends of the earth...," she wrote in 1780, "Alas! the wilderness is within." Schuyler Bleecker died on November 23, 1783; she was thirty-one years old. None of her works were published during her lifetime.

Works: *The History of Maria Kittle* (1791); *The Posthumous Works of Ann Eliza Bleecker*, ed. Margaretta Bleecker Faugères (New York, 1793). *Bibliography*: Cowell; Griswold; Kettell; May.

Written in the Retreat from BURGOYNE[1]

Was it for this, with thee, a pleasing load,
I sadly wander'd through the hostile wood;
When I thought Fortune's spite could do no more,
To see thee perish on a foreign shore?

1. Dated October 29, 1777, the poem was first published in the *New-York Magazine* in March 1790; this text is taken from the *Posthumous Works*.

Oh my lov'd babe! my treasure's left behind,
Ne'er sunk a cloud of grief upon my mind;
Rich in my children—on my arms I bore
My living treasures from the scalper's pow'r:
When I sat down to rest beneath some shade,
On the soft grass how innocent she play'd,
While her sweet sister, from the fragrant wild,
Collects the flow'rs to please my precious child;
Unconscious of her danger, laughing roves,
Nor dreads the painted savage in the groves!
   Soon as the spires of *Albany* appear'd,
With fallacies my rising grief I cheer'd:
'Resign'd I bear,' said I, 'heaven's just reproof,
'Content to dwell beneath a stranger's roof;
'Content my babes should eat dependent bread,
'Or by the labor of my hands be fed:
'What tho' my houses, lands, and goods are gone,
'My babes remain—these I can call my own.'
But soon my loved *Abella* hung her head,
From her soft cheek the bright carnation fled;
Her smooth transparent skin too plainly shew'd
How fierce thro' every vein the fever glow'd.
—In bitter anguish o'er her limbs I hung,
I wept and sigh'd, but sorrow chain'd my tongue;
At length her languid eyes clos'd from the day,
The idol of my soul was torn away;
Her spirit fled and left me ghastly clay!
   Then—then my soul rejected all relief,
Comfort I wish'd not, for I lov'd my grief:
'Hear, my *Abella!*' cried I, 'hear me mourn,
'For one short moment, oh! my child return;
'Let my complaint detain thee from the skies,
'Though troops of angels urge thee on to rise.'
All night I mourn'd—and when the rising day
Gilt her sad chest with his benignest ray,
My friends press round me with officious care,
Bid me suppress my sighs, nor drop a tear;
Of resignation talk'd—passions subdu'd,
Of souls serene and christian fortitude;
Bade me be calm, nor murmur at my loss,
But unrepining bear each heavy cross.
   'Go!' cried I raging, 'stoick bosoms go!
'Whose hearts vibrate not to the sound of woe;
'Go from the sweet society of men,
'Seek some unfeeling tyger's savage den,
'There, calm—alone—of resignation preach,
'My Christ's examples better precepts teach.'

Where the cold limbs of gentle *Laz'rus* lay
I find him weeping o'er the humid clay;
His spirit groan'd, while the beholders said
(With gushing eyes) 'see how he lov'd the dead!'
And when his thoughts on great *Jerus'lem* turn'd,
Oh! how pathetic o'er her fall he mourn'd!
And sad *Gethsemene's* nocturnal shade
The anguish of my weeping Lord survey'd:
Yes, 'tis my boast to harbour in my breast
The sensibilities by God exprest;
Nor shall the mollifying hand of time,
Which wipes off common sorrows, cancel mine.

To Miss M.V.W.[2]

Peggy, amidst domestic cares to rhyme
I find no pleasure, and I find no time;
But then, a Poetess, you may suppose,
Can better tell her mind in verse than prose:
True—when serenely all our moments roll,
Then numbers flow spontaneous from the soul:
Not when the mind is harassed by cares,
Or stunn'd with thunders of intestine wars,
Or circled by a noisy, vulgar throng,
(Noise ever was an enemy to song.)
   What tho' the spiral pines around us rise,
And airy mountains intercept the skies,
Faction has chas'd away the warbling Muse,
And Echo only learns to tattle news,
Each clown commences politician here,
And calculates th' expenses of the year;
He quits his plow, and throws aside his spade,
To talk with *squire* about decrease of trade:
His tedious spouse detains me in her turn,
Condemns our measures and neglects her churn.
Scarce can I steal a moment from the wars
To read my Bible, or to say my pray'rs:
Oh! how I long to see those halcyon days
When Peace again extends to us her rays,
When each, beneath his vine, and far from fear,
Shall beat his sword into a lab'ring share.

---

2. Possibly Margaret Van Wyck. In the introduction to Schuyler Bleecker's collected writings, her daughter maintains the anonymity of this person by also referring to her and her sister as "the Miss V** W***'s" who corresponded with Schuyler Bleecker.

Then shall the rural arts again revive,
Ceres[3] shall bid the famish'd rustic live:
Where now the yells of painted sons of blood
With long vibrations shake the lonely wood,
All desolate, *Pomona*[4] shall behold
The branches shoot with vegetable gold:
Beyond the peasant's sight the springing grain
Shall wave around him o'er the ample plain;
No engines then shall bellow o'er the waves,
And fright blue *Thetis*[5] in her coral caves,
But commerce gliding o'er the curling seas,
Shall bind the sever'd shores in ties of peace.
    Then WASHINGTON, reclining on his spear,
Shall take a respite from laborious war,
While *Glory* on his brows with awful grace
Binds a tiara of resplendent rays.
How faint the luster of imperial gems
To *this immortal wreath* his merit claims!
See from the north, where icy mountains rise,
Down to the placid climes of southern skies,
All hail the day that bids stern discord cease,
All hail the day which gives the warrior peace:
Hark! the glad nations make a joyful noise!
And the loud shouts are answer'd from the skies;
Fame swells the sound wrapt in her hero's praise,
And darts his splendors down to the latest days.

Phillis Wheatley (c. 1753–1784)

Born perhaps in the Cambia River region of Africa, brought to America as a slave when she was about seven years old, and apparently named after the slave ship *Phillis* that carried her to North America, Phillis Wheatley became this country's first major African-American poet and a figure of renown in her own lifetime, publishing a collection of poems in 1773. But if Anne Bradstreet was studied for so long as an anomaly because of her era and gender, Wheatley was similarly classified because of her race and circumstances. She was an extraordinary woman, committing herself to her art in spite of her enslavement. Only re-

---

3. The Roman goddess of agriculture.
4. Ancient Italian goddess of fruit trees.
5. In Greek mythology, one of the Neriads, or sea nymphs.

cently has scholarship begun to address Wheatley in her complexities, as an African enslaved in the new republic *and* as an artist.

Works: Poems on Various Subjects, Religious and Moral (London, 1773); *The Collected Works of Phillis Wheatley*, ed. John Shields. *Bibliography*: Robinson; Shields, J.

On Recollection[1]

MNEME[2] begin. Inspire, ye sacred nine,
Your ventr'rous *Afric* in her great design.
Mneme, immortal pow'r, I trace thy spring:
Assist my strains, while I thy glories sing:
The acts of long departed years, by thee
Recover'd, in due order rang'd we see:
Thy pow'r the long-forgotten calls from night,
That sweetly plays before the *fancy's* sight.

Mneme in our nocturnal visions pours
The ample treasure of her secret stores;
Swift from above she wings her silent flight
Through *Phoebe's*[3] realms, fair regent of the night;
And, in her pomp of images display'd,
To the high-raptur'd poet gives her aid,
Through the unbounded regions of the mind,
Diffusing light celestial and refin'd.
The heav'nly *phantom* paints the actions done
By ev'ry tribe beneath the rolling sun.

Mneme, enthron'd within the human breast,
Has vice condemn'd, and ev'ry virtue blest.
How sweet the sound when we her plaudit hear?
Sweeter than music to the ravish'd ear,
Sweeter than *Maro's*[4] entertaining strains
Resounding through the groves, and hills, and plains.
But how is *Mneme* dreaded by the race,
Who scorn her warnings, and despise her grace?
By her unveil'd each horrid crime appears,
Her awful hand a cup of wormwood bears.
Days, years mispent, O what a hell of woe!
Hers the worst tortures that our souls can know.

1. Written in 1711, when Wheatley was approximately eighteen years old. All of the poems in this selection are from the 1773 edition of *Poems on Various Subjects*.
2. The Muse of remembrance, or recollection.
3. Goddess of the moon.
4. Virgil (70–19 B.C.), Roman poet.

Now eighteen years their destin'd course have run,
In fast succession round the central sun.
How did the follies of that period pass
Unnotic'd, but behold them writ in brass!
In Recollection see them fresh return,
And sure 'tis mine to be asham'd, and mourn.

O *Virtue*, smiling in immortal green,
Do thou exert thy pow'r, and change the scene;
Be thine employ to guide my future days,
And mine to pay the tribute of my praise.

Of *Recollection* such the pow'r enthron'd
In ev'ry breast, and thus her pw'r is own'd.
The wretch, who dar'd the vengeance of the skies,
At last awakes in horror and surprize,
By her alarm'd, he sees impending fate,
He howls in anguish, and repents too late.
But O! what peace, what joys are hers t' impart
To ev'ry holy ev'ry upright heart!
Thrice blest the man, who, in her sacred shrine,
Feels himself shelter'd from the wrath divine!

On Imagination

THY various works, imperial queen, we see,
How bright their forms! how deck'd with pomp by thee!
Thy wond'rous acts in beauteous order stand,
And all attest how potent is thine hand.

From *Helicon's*[5] refulgent heights attend,
Ye sacred choir, and my attempts befriend:
To tell her glories with a faithful tongue,
Ye blooming graces, triumph in my song.

Now here, now there, the roving *Fancy* flies,
Till some lov'd object strikes her wand'ring eyes,
Whose silken fetters all the senses bind,
And soft captivity involves the mind.

Imagination! who can sing thy force?
Or who describe the swiftness of thy course?
Soaring through the air to find the bright abode,
Th' empyreal palace of the thund'ring God,

---

5. One of the earthly mountain homes of the Greek muses.

We on thy pinions can surpass the wind,
And leave the rolling universe behind:
From star to star the mental optics rove,
Measure the skies, and range the realms above.
There in one view we grasp the mighty whole,
Or with new worlds amaze th' unbounded soul.

Though *Winter* frowns to *Fancy's* raptur'd eyes
The fields may flourish, and gay scenes arise;
The frozen deeps may break their iron bands,
And bid their waters murmur o'er the sands.
Fair *Flora*[6] may resume her fragrant reign,
And with her flow'ry riches deck the plain;
Sylvanus[7] may diffuse his honours round,
And all the forest may with leaves be crown'd:
Show'rs may descend, and dews their gems disclose,
And nectar sparkle on the blooming rose.

Such is thy pow'r, nor are thine orders vain,
O thou the leader of the mental train:
In full perfection of all thy works are wrought,
And thine the sceptre o'er the realms of thought.
Before thy throne the subject-passions bow,
Of subject-passions sov'reign ruler Thou;
At thy command joy rushes on the heart,
And through the glowing veins the spirits dart.

Fancy might now her silken pinions try
To rise from earth, and sweep th' expanse on high;
From *Tithon's*[8] bed now might *Aurora*[9] rise,
her cheeks all glowing with celestial dies,
While a pure stream of light o'erflows the skies.
The monarch of the day I might behold,
And all the mountains tipt with radiant gold,
But I reluctant leave the pleasing views,
Which *Fancy* dresses to delight the *Muse*;
Winter austere forbids me to aspire,
And northern tempests damp the rising fire;
They chill the tides of *Fancy's* flowing sea,
Cease then, my song, cease the unequal lay.

6. Goddess of flowers.
7. God of the woods.
8. Possibly Tithonus; in Greek mythology Tithonus was granted immortality but not immortal youth. He fathered Aurora's Ethiopian son, Memnon.
9. Goddess of the dawn.

To the Right Honourable William,
Earl of Darmouth, His Majesty's Principal
Secretary of State for North America, &c.

Hail, happy day, when, smiling like the morn,
Fair *Freedom* rose *New-England* to adorn:
The northern clime beneath her genial ray,
Dartmouth, congratulates thy blissful sway:
Elate with hope her race no longer mourns,
Each soul expands, each grateful bosom burns,
While in thine hand with pleasure we behold
The silken reins, and *Freedom's* charms unfold.
She shines supreme, while hated *faction* dies:
Soon as appear'd the *Goddess* long desir'd,
Sick at the view, she languish'd and expir'd;
Thus from the splendors of the morning light
The owl in sadness seeks the caves of night.

  No more, *America*, in mournful strain
Of wrongs, and grievance unredress'd complain,
No longer shall thou dread the iron chain,
Which wanton *Tyranny* with lawless hand
Had made, and with it meant t' enslave the land.

  Should you, my lord, while you peruse my song,
Wonder from whence my love of *Freedom* sprung,
Whence flow these wishes for the common good,
By feeling hearts alone best understood,
I, young in life, by seeming cruel fate
Was snatch'd from *Afric's* fancy'd happy seat:
What pangs excruciating must molest,
What sorrows labour in my parent's breast?
Steel'd was that soul and by no misery mov'd
That from a father seiz'd his babe belov'd:
Such, such my case. And can I then but pray
Others may never feel tyrannic sway? . . .

NIOBE in Distress for her Children slain by
Apollo, from *Ovid's* Metamorphoses, Book VI.
and from a view of the Painting of Mr. *Richard Wilson*[10]

. . .

Niobe[11] comes with all her royal race,
With charms unnumber'd, and superior grace:

10. Wilson was a Welsh landscape artist who at least three times depicted Niobe in his paintings.

11. In Greek legend, Niobe was turned to stone while weeping for her slain children, but she continued to weep.

Her *Phrygian*[12] garments of delightful hue,
Inwove with gold, refulgent to the view,
Beyond description beautiful she moves
Like heav'nly *Venus*, 'midst her smiles and loves:
She views around her graceful head with stern disdain,
Proudly she turns around her lofty eyes,
And thus reviles celestial deities:
"What madness drives the *Theban*[13] ladies fair
"To give their incense to surrounding air?
"Say why this new sprung deity preferr'd?
"Why vainly fancy your petitions heard?
"Or say why *Coeus*'[14] offspring is obey'd,
"While to my goddesship no tribute's paid?
"For me no altars blaze with living fires,
"No bullock bleeds, no frankincense transpires,
"Tho' *Cadmus*'[15] palace, not unknown to fame,
"And *Phrygian* nations all revere my name.
"Where'er I turn my eyes vast wealth I find.
"Lo! here an empress with a goddess join'd.
"What, shall *Titaness* be deify'd,
"To whom the spacious earth a couch deny'd?
"Nor heav'n, nor earth, nor sea receiv'd your queen,
" 'Till pitying *Delos*[16] took the wand'rer in.
"Round me what a large progeny is spread!
"No frowns of fortune has my soul to dread.
"What if indignant she decrease my train
"More than *Latona's*[17] number will remain?
"Then hence, ye *Theban* dames, hence haste away,
"Nor longer off'rings to *Latona* pay?
"Regard the orders of *Amphion's* spouse,[18]
"And take the leaves of laurel from your brow."
Niobe spoke. The *Theban* maids obey'd,
Their brows unbound, and left the rights unpaid. . . .

Anna Young (Smith) (1756–1780)

Anna Young was born November 5, 1756, the daughter of Jane
Graeme and John Young of Philadelphia. Anna's mother died when

12. Native to ancient Phrygia.
13. Native to the ancient Egyptian city of Thebes.
14. A Titan; all Titans were giants.
15. A Phoenician prince who slew a dragon, the teeth from which were transformed into armed men.
16. An Aegean island.
17. Daughter of Coeus and Phoebe, the moon goddess.
18. Niobe, who married Amphion, King of Thebes.

she was an infant, so she and her brother John were raised by their maternal aunt Elizabeth Graeme Fergusson (q.v.), a poet and intellectual who encouraged Anna's imaginative and creative explorations. It was under Graeme Fergusson's tutelage and before her marriage to Dr. William Smith in 1775 that Anna Young wrote most of her poems. Many of these poems were published in *Pennsylvania Magazine* and the *Universal Asylum and Columbia Magazine*, under the pseudonym of "Sylvia." A "warm Whig," as her aunt identified her, Young Smith's poetry addresses political issues, but it also includes numerous themes about women's lives and often from a feminist perspective. Anna Young Smith died on April 3, 1780, in childbirth.[1]

Works: Poetry. *Bibliography*: Cowell.

On Reading Swift's Works.[2]
Written by a *Young Lady* of *eighteen*, who was born and educated in *Philadelphia*; and who died some years ago.

Ungenerous bard, whom not e'en *Stella's* charms
Thy vengeful satire of its sting disarms!
Say, when thou dipp'st thy keenest pen in gall,
Why must it still on helpless woman fall!
Why must our "*dirt* and *dulness*" fill each line,
Our love of "*follies*, our desire to shine!"
Why are we drawn as a whole race of *fools*,
Unsway'd alike by sense or virtues rules!
Oh! had thy heart with generous candour glowed,
Hadst thou alone on vice thy lash bestowed,
Had there fair Purity her form imprest,
And had the milder virtues filled thy breast;
Thy sprightly page had been by all approved,
And what we now admire we then had loved.
But thy harsh satire, *rude*, *severe*, *unjust*,
Awakes too oft our anger or disgust.
Such are the scenes which still thy pen engage,
That modesty disdains the shameless page.

1. As Pattie Cowell notes, there is confusion over the exact date and whether or not this was Young Smith's third child; I agree with Cowell's determination that Elizabeth Graeme Fergusson's dating of these events should receive preference.

2. The source of this poem is the *Universal Asylum and Columbian Magazine* 5 (Sept. 1790), p. 185. It was published in the magazine's poetry column, "The Columbian Parnassiad." Jonathan Swift (1667–1745) was an Anglo-Irish author and satirist.

'Tis true, we own thy wit almost divine,
And view the *diamond* 'midst the *dunghill* shine:
Oh, had it sparkled on the breast of youth,
To charm the sage, and to instruct with truth;
To chace the gloom of ignorance away,
And teach mankind with wisdom to be gay;
Thy perfect style, thy wit serenly bright,
Would shed through distant climes their pleasing light,
Mankind would grateful to thy muse attend,
And after ages hail thee as their friend!
But now, so oft filth choaks thy sprightly fire,
We loath one instant, and the next admire—
Even while we *laugh*, we *mourn* thy wit's abuse,
And while we *praise* thy talents, *scorn* their use.

An Ode to Gratitude[3]

Oh gratitude thou power benign,
Who does such warmth impart!
Teach my unskillful mind to sing
The feelings of my heart.
   Teach me to thank the gracious maid,
Who rear'd my infant years;
That gives me every useful aid,
And mourns my faults with tears.
Nor tenderness I can't repay,
Nor half her love recount;
That worth like his I should approve;
But still I thought not it was love.
   When e'er I heard his angel tongue,
On all his words I fondly hung;
With ev'ry sound my heart would move,
But yet I knew not it was love.
   Though soft compassion I betray'd,
With joy the anxious youth survey'd:
His artless sighs my bosom mov'd,
I pity felt and own'd I lov'd.
   Since that blest day no doubts molest
No jealous fears disturb my breast,
Convinc'd my Damon ne'er will rove,
But still deserve his Sylvia's love.[4]

---

3. This poem is dedicated to Young Smith's aunt, and is dated 1770 by the poet.
4. Renowned in legend, Damon and Sylvia were noted Sicilian lovers.

I feel no wish my bosom swell,
But still in Damon's heart to dwell:
This tender wish may Heaven approve,
And kindly bless our mutual love.

An Elegy to the Memory of the American Volunteers, who Fell in the Engagement Between the Massachusetts-Bay Militia, and the British Troops. April 19, 1775.[5]

Let joy be dumb, let mirth's gay carol cease,
See plaintive sorrow comes bedew'd with tears;
With mournful steps retires the cherub peace,
And horrid war with all his train appears.
  He comes, and crimson slaughter marks his way,
Stern famine follows in his vengeful tread;
Before him pleasure, hope, and love decay,
And meek-eye'd mercy hangs the drooping head. . . .
  Where e'er the barb'rous story shall be told,
The British cheek shall glow with conscious shame;
This deed in bloody characters enroll'd,
Shall stain the luster of their former name.
  But you, ye brave defenders of our cause,
The first in this dire contest call'd to bleed,
Your names hereafter crown'd with just applause,
Each manly breast with joy-mixt woe shall read;
  Your memories, dear to every free-born mind,
Shall need no monument your fame to raise,
Forever in our grateful hearts enshrin'd,
And blest by your united country's praise.
  But O permit the muse with grief sincere,
The widow's heart-felt anguish to bemoan,
To join the sisters, and the orphans tear,
Whom this sad day from all they lov'd has torn. . . .
  O grant us, Heaven, that constancy of mind
Which over adverse fortune rises still,
Unshaken faith, calm fortitude resign'd,
And full submission to thy holy will.
  To Thee, Eternal Parent, we resign
Our bleeding cause and on thy wisdom rest;
With grateful hearts we bless thy power divine,
And own resign'd "Whatever is, is best."

5. Originally published in *Pennsylvania Magazine* 1 (June 1775), pp. 278–279.

Sarah Wentworth Apthorp Morton (1759–1846)

Born August 1759 to Sarah Wentworth and James Apthorp, Sarah entered the upper-class realm of New England at birth, but she revealed her independent nature when the American Revolution demanded personal moral commitments: in spite of her family's Loyalist inclinations, Sarah proclaimed herself a Patriot and, in 1781, married Perez Morton, a Patriot and statesman in the reorganized state government. Together, the Mortons dominated Boston's sociopolitical scene during the post-Revolutionary years. Their seeming marital happiness, however, was soon shattered by the suicide of Sarah's sister, Frances; the impetus to Frances's act was an affair with Perez Morton. Nor was Wentworth Morton allowed to bear these tragedies in private; the circumstances were used by William Hill Brown as the plot of the first American novel, *The Power of Sympathy* (1789). Looking beyond the melodrama of Wentworth Morton's life, however, we find a dedicated, intelligent contributor to early national life and ideas. An early supporter of the theater, a patron for younger authors, and an abolitionist, Sarah Wentworth Morton published many of her writings in *Massachusetts Magazine* under the pseudonym "Philenia." Her poetry and essays revealed her astute analysis of the major literary and political movements of the late eighteenth century.

Works: *Ouabi . . . An Indian Tale in Four Cantos* (1790); *Reanimation* (1791); *Beacon Hill: A Local Poem . . .* (1797); *The Virtues of Society: A Tale Founded on Fact* (1799); *My Mind and Its Thoughts, in Sketches, Fragments, and Essays* (Boston: Wells & Lily, 1823; rpt. Delmar, NY: Scholars' Facsimiles, 1975). Bibliography: Cowell; Pendleton and Ellis; Watts.

Ouabi: or the Virtues of Nature,
An Indian Tale. In Four Cantos.[1]
By PHILENIA, a Lady of Boston.

CANTO I.

'Tis not the court, in dazzling splendor gay,
Where soft luxuriance spreads her silken arms,
Where garish fancy leads the soul astray,
And languid nature mourns her slighted charms;

---

1. *Ouabi* was originally published in 1790 (Boston: Thomas & Andrews) and is the source for these excerpts. In the following year, the *Universal Asylum & Columbia Magazine* (6 [Feb. 1791], pp. 105–107) published a review and excerpts from the tale.

'Tis not the golden hill, nor flow'ry dale,
Which lends my simple muse her artless theme;
But the black forest and uncultur'd vale,
The savage warrior, and the lonely stream.

Where MISSISSIPPI[2] rolls his *parent flood*,
With slope impetuous to the surgy main,
The desert's painted chiefs explore the wood,
Or with the thund'ring *war-whoop*[3] shake the plain.

There the fierce *sachems* raise the battle's din,
Or in the stream their active bodies lave,
Or midst the flames their fearless songs begin[4]—
PAIN HAS NO TERRORS TO THE TRULY BRAVE.

There young CELARIO, Europe's fairest boast,
In hopeless exile mourn'd the tedious day;
Now wand'ring slowly o'er the oozy coast,
Now thro the wild woods urg'd his anxious way.

Where the low stooping branch excludes the light,
A piercing shriek assail'd his wounded ear;
Swift as the winged arrow speeds its flight,
He seeks the piteous harbinger of fear.

There a tall *Huron* rais'd his threat'ning arm,
While round his knees a beauteous captive clung,
Striving to move him with her matchless form,
Or charm him by the magic of her tongue.

Soon as *Celario* viewed the murd'rous scene,
Quick from his vest the deathful tube he drew;
Its leaden vengeance thunder'd o'er the green,
While from the savage hand the ling'ring hatchet flew.

Low at his feat the breathless warrior lies;
Still the soft captive sickens with alarms,
Calls on OUABI's name with streaming eyes,

While the young victor lives upon her charms.
Her limbs were straighter than the mountain pine,
Her hair far blacker than the raven's wing;
Beauty had lent her form *the waving*[5] *line*,
Her breath gave fragrance to the balmy spring.

2. *Mississippi*, an Indian name, signifying the great father of rivers. It is subject to no tides, but from its source in the north of the American Continent flows with rapid force, till it empties itself into the Gulph of Mexico. [Morton's note.]

3. *War-whoop*, the cry of battle, with which they always make their onset. [Morton's note.]

4. The American Indians, after exhausting every species of cruelty and torture upon their most distinguished prisoners, burn them by a distant fire; who expire singing songs of glory and defiance. [Morton's note.]

5. See Hogarth's Line of Beauty. [Morton's note.]

Each bright perfection open'd on her face,
Her flowing garment wanton'd in the breeze,
Her slender feet the glitt'ring sandals[6] grace,
Her look was dignity, her movement ease.

With spendid beads her braided tresses shone,
Her bending waist a modest girdle bound,
Her pearly teeth outvi'd the cygnet's down—
She spoke—and music follow'd in the sound.

SHE.

Great ruler of the winged hour,[7]
AXÂKIA trembles at thy pow'r;
While from thy hand the thunders roll,
Thy charms with lightnings pierce the soul;
Ah! how unlike our sable race,
The snowy lustre of thy face!
That hair of beaming Cynthia's[8] hue,
Those shining eyes of heav'nly blue!
Ah! didst thou leave thy blissful land,
To save me from the murd'rer's hand?

And is *Ouabi* still thy care,
The dauntless chief, unknown to fear?

HE.

Cease to call *Ouabi's* name,
Give *Celario* all his claim.
No divinity is here:
Spare thy praises, quit thy fear:
Bend no more that beauteous knee,
For I am a slave to thee:
Let my griefs thy pity move,
Heal them with the balm of love.
Far beyond the orient main,
By my rage a youth was slain;
He this daring arm defied,
By this arm the ruffian died:
Exil'd from my native home,
Thro the desert wild I roam;
But if only blest by thee,
All the desert smiles on me.

6. The sandals are ornamented either with little glistening bells, or with a great variety of shining beads and feathers. [Morton's note.]

7. It is presumed that *Axâkia* had never before seen a European, or heard the report of a pistol, as she considers one a deity, and the other his thunder. [Morton's note.]

8. Roman goddess of the moon.

SHE.

See a graceful form arise![9]
Now it fills my ravish'd eyes,
Brighter than the morning star,
'Tis *Ouabi*, fam'd in war:
Close before my bosom spread,
O'er thy preference casts a shade,
Full on him these eyes recline,
And his person shuts out thine.
Let us to his home retire,
Where he lights the social fire;
Do not thro the desert roam,
Find with me his gen'rous home;
There the *Illinois* obey
Great *Ouabi's* chosen sway.

. . . .

THE AFRICAN CHIEF.

See how the black ship cleaves the main,
  High bounding o'er the dark blue wave,
Remurmuring with the groans of pain,
  Deep freighted with the princely slave!

Did all the Gods of Afric sleep,
  Forgetful of their guardian love,
When the white tyrants of the deep,
  Betrayed him in the palmy grove.

A Chief of *Gambia's* golden shore,
  Whose arm the band of warriors led,
Or more—the lord of generous power,
  By whom the foodless poor were fed.

Does not the voice of reason cry,
  Claim the first right that nature gave,
From the red scourge of bondage fly,
  Nor deign to live a burdened slave.

Has not his suffering offspring clung,
  Desponding round his fettered knee;

---

9. The Indian women of America are very chaste after marriage, and if any person makes love to them, they answer, "*The Friend that is before my eyes, prevents my seeing you.*" [Morton's note.]

On his worn shoulder, weeping hung,
   And urged one effort to be free!

His wife by nameless wrongs subdued,
   His bosom's friend to death resigned;
The flinty path-way drenched in blood;
   He saw with cold and phrenzied mind.

Strong in despair, then sought the plain,
   To heaven was raised his stedfast eye,
Resolved to burst the crushing chain,
   Or mid the battle's blast to die.

First of his race, he led the band,
   Guardless of danger, hurling round,
Till by his red avenging hand,
   Full many a despot stained the ground.

When erst *Messenia's*[10] sons oppressed,
   Flew desperate to the sanguine field,
With iron cloathed each injured breast,
   And saw the cruel Spartan yield.

Did not the soul to heaven allied,
   With the proud heart as greatly swell,
As when the *Roman Decius* died,
   Or when the *Grecian* fell[11] victim.

Do later deeds quick rapture raise,
   The boon *Batavia's William*[12] won,
Paoli's[13] time-enduring praise
   Or the yet greater *Washington*!

If these exalt thy sacred zeal,
   To hate oppression's mad controul,
For bleeding *Afric* learn to feel,
   Whose Chieftain claimed a kindred soul.

Ah, mourn the last disastrous hour,
   Lift the full eye of bootless grief,
While victory treads the sultry shore,
   And tears from hope the captive Chief.

10. The Messinians were enslaved by the conquering Spartans.

11. Leonidas.

12. The Netherlands, conquered by the French during the French Revolution, was reconstituted as the Batavian Republic (1795–1806); during the war, the Dutch army was led by William I (1772–1843).

13. Pasqale Paoli (1725–1807) was a Corsican patriot who led a revolt in 1755 that ousted the Genoese rulers and established Corsica as a republic with Paoli as its first president.

While the hard race of *pallid hue*,
   Unpracticed in the power to feel,
Resign him to the murderous crew,
   The horrors of the quivering wheel.

Let sorrow bathe each blushing cheek,
   Bend piteous o'er the tortured slave,
Whose wrongs compassion cannot speak,
   Whose only refuge was the grave.

Anonymous Women Poets

The Lady's Complaint[1]

Custom, alas! doth partial prove,
   Nor gives us equal measure;
A pain for us it is to love,
   But is to men a pleasure.

They plainly can their thoughts disclose,
   Whilst ours must burn within:
We have got tongues, and eyes, in vain,
   And truth from us is sin.

Men to new joys and conquests fly,
   And yet no hazard run:
Poor we are left, if we deny,
   And if we yield, undone.

Then equal laws let custom find,
   And neither sex oppress;
More freedom give to womankind,
   Or give to mankind less.

The Maid's Soliloquy[2]

It must be so—Milton, thou reas'nest well,
Else why this pleasing hope, this fond desire,
This longing after something unpossess'd?

1. Originally published October 22, 1736, in the *Virginia Gazette*, with several reprints thereafter.
2. Written by a young woman from South Carolina, per the headnote, and published February 25, 1751, in the *South Carolina Gazette*.

Or whence this secret dread and inward horror
Of dying unespous'd? Why shrinks the soul
Back on itself, and startles at the thought?
'Tis instinct! faithful instinct stirs within us,
'Tis nature's self that points out an alliance,
And intimates an husband to the sex.
   Marriage! thou pleasing and yet anxious thought!
Through what variety of hopes and fears,
Through what new scenes, and changes, must we pass:
Th' important state in prospect lies before me,
But shadows, clouds and darkness, rest upon it.
Here will I hold—if Nature prompts the wish,
(And that she does is plain, from all her works)
Our duty and our interest, bid indulge it:
For the great end of nature's law, is bliss.
But yet—in wedlock—women must obey:
I'm weary of these doubts—the priest must end them.
   Thus, rashly do I venture loss and gain,
Bondage and pleasure, meet my thoughts at once;
I wed—my liberty is gone for ever:
If happy—then I'm still secure in life.
Love, will then recompense my loss of freedom;
And when my charms shall fade away, my eyes
Themselves grow dim, my stature bend with years,
Then virtuous friendship, shall succeed to love.
Then pleas'd, I'll scorn infirmities, and death,
Renew'd immortal, in a filial race.

The Young Lady's Choice[3]

Let the bold youth, who aims to win me, know
I hate a fool, a clown, a sot, a bean:
I loath a sloven, I despise a cit,——
I scorn a coxcomb, and I fear a wit.
   Let him be gentle, brave, good-humor'd, gay,
Let him, in smaller things, with pride obey;
Be wise enough in great ones to command;
Produce but such a youth, and here's my hand.

Address to the Moon[4]

While wandering through the dark blue vault of Heaven,
   Thy trackless steps pursue their silent way,

---

3. Originally published February 4, 1797, in the *South Carolina Weekly Museum*.
4. Orginally published February 17, 1798, in *The Weekly Magazine* (Philadelphia).

And from amongst the starry host of even,
   Thou shed'st o'er slumb'ring earth a milder day;
And when thou pour'st abroad thy shadowy light,
   Across the ridgy circles of the stream,
With raptur'd eyes, O! changeful nymph of night,
    I gaze upon thy beam.

Great was the Hand that form'd thy round, O Moon!
   That mark'd the precincts of thy steady wheel;
That bade thee smile on night's oblivious noon,
   And rule old Ocean's solemn swell.
Great was the Pow'r that fill'd with radiant light,
   Those worlds, unnumber'd, which from pole to pole,
Hang out their golden lamps to deck thy flight,
   Or gild the planets, which around thee roll.

From realms of love, beyond where rolls the sun,
   Whose distant beams create our brightest day;
Beyond where stars their ceaseless circles run;
   Or lucid night emits her opaque ray,
Mounted on the dark'ning storm,
On the strong whirlwind's ragged pinions borne;
With glory circumfus'd, the source of bliss
Sublime, came flying o'er the vast abyss.

His voice was heard—in dire dismay,
The shades of darkness fled away;
While bursting waves of light the flight beheld,
And all the spacious void triumphant fill'd.

Without delay, this restless ball,
Uprose obedient to His call;
(But that He spake it into light,
It still had slumber'd in eternal night).
The mountains rear'd their verdant head;
The hills, their destin'd places found;
And as the fountains pour'd their waters round,
Ocean submissive wander'd to its bed.
The Sun up rose, with beams benign he shone,
And Terra cheer'd with splendors, all his own,
   "Go gild the morn," his Maker said;
    Impatient to obey,
   O'er half the globe his rays were spread,
    And blaz'd along the day.
Then wast thou form'd, and all the starry train,
   That decorate the evening skies;
Some made to travel o'er the sapphire plain,
   And some forbid to set or rise.

Long hast thou reign'd, and from thine amber throne,
The various changes of this world hast known;
  Hast seen its myriads into being rise,
Shine their short hours, and then their life resign;
  New generations seize the fickle prize,
And like their fires, but strengthen to decline.
Yet be not vain, tho' since thy natal day,
  Some thousand years their circling course have made;
For lo! the era hastens on apace,
  When all thy glory shall forever fade.
Earth shall the revolution feel,
  The change of seasons, shall be o'er;
Time shall forget to guide his wheel,
  And thou, O Moon, shall set to rise no more.

Ella.

"Address to the Moon" represents an instance in which we can examine an anonymous poet's published work versus her original manuscript. The poem was actually written in 1792 by Margaretta V. Bleecker Faugères (see "Petitions . . ." for biographical data) and published in 1793 in a collection of writings by Bleecker Faugères and her mother, Ann Eliza Schuyler Bleecker (q.v.). Whether the numerous changes were made by Bleecker Faugères or the editor of *The Weekly Magazine* is impossible to know, but it is probable that they were editorial changes. The style of the poem as it appeared in *The Weekly Magazine* is consistent with poems by other authors published in the magazine, while the 1793 version, edited by Bleecker Faugères herself, is consistent with the style of Bleecker Faugères's other published poems. The 1793 version follows:

To the MOON[5]

April, 1792.

While wand'ring through the dark blue vault of heav'n,
  Thy trackless steps pursue their silent way,
And from among the starry host of ev'n,
  Thou shed'st o'er *slumbering earth* a milder day;
And when thou pour'st abroad thy shadowy light
  Across the ridgy circles of the stream,
With raptur'd eyes, O changeful nymph of night!
  I gaze upon thy beam.

---

5. Published in *The Posthumous Works of Ann Eliza Bleecker, in Prose and Verse. To which is added, A Collection of Essays, Prose and Poetical,* by Margaretta V. Faugères. Ed. Margaretta V. Faugères. New York: T. and J. Swords, 1793. 319–322.

GREAT was the *hand* that form'd thy round, O Moon!
　　That mark'd the precincts of thy steady wheel,
That bade thee smile on *Night's* oblivious noon,
　　And rule old *Ocean's* solemn swell;
GREAT was the POWER, that fill'd with radiant light
　　Those *Worlds* unnumber'd, which from pole to pole
Hang out their golden lamps to deck thy flight,
　　Or gild the *Planets* which round thee roll.

From realms of Love, beyond where moves the *Sun,*,
　　Whose distant beams create our brightest day,
Beyond where *Stars* their ceaseless circles run,
　　Or *lurid Night* emits his opaque ray;
　　　　Mounted on the dark'ning storm,
On the strong whirlwind's ragged pinions borne,
With *glory* circumfus'd, the *Source* of *Bliss*
Sublime, came flying o'er the vast abyss.

　　　　His voice was heard—in dire dismay
　　　　Chaotic *Darkness* fled away,
While bursting waves of *Light* the flight beheld,
And all the spacious void triumphant fill'd.
　　　　Without delay, this restless ball
　　　　Uprose, obedient to his call;
　　But that he spake it into light,
It still had slumber'd in eternal night:
　　The *mountains* rear'd their verdant head,
　　The *hills* their destin'd places found,
And as the *fountains* pour'd their waters round,
　　Ocean submissive wander'd to her bed;
The *Sun* arose—with beam benign he shone,
And *terra* cheer'd with splendours all his own.
　　"Go gild the morn," his maker said.
　　　　Impatient to obey,
　　O'er half the globe his rays he spread,
　　　　And blaz'd along the day.

Then wast *thou* form'd with all the starry train
　　That decorate the ev'ning skies;
Some made to travel through the sapphire plain,
　　And some forbid to set or rise.

Long hast thou reign'd, and from thine amber throne
The various changes of *this world* hast known;
Hast seen its *myriads* into being rise,
　　Shine their short hour, and then their *life* resign;
New generations seize the fickle *prize*,
　　And like their fires, but strengthen to decline:
Yet be not vain, (though since thy natal day

346

Some thousand years their circling course have made)
For lo! the *aera* hastens on apace,
   When all thy glory shall for ever fade.
  Earth shall the *revolution* feel,
     The *change* of seasons shall be o'er,
  Time shall forget to guide his wheel,
And *thou*, O Moon, shalt *set* to *rise* no more!

On Reading the Poems of Phillis Wheatley, the African Poetess[6]

His servile lot the beast of burden bears,
Unstung by memory, and unvext with cares,
With glad release returning evening smiles,
And food and slumber closes all his tolls.
  If Afric's sable sons be doom'd to know
Nought but long bondage and successive woe,
Why did just Heav'n their sun-born souls refine
With passions, virtues, as our own, divine?
What tho' the sanguine flushes that adorn
Our limbs with tinges like the roseate morn,
Ah, partial Nature! on the race be lost;
Yet leave them peace and freedom still to boast:
For, as a just gradation still we find,
Up from the grov'ling to the enlighten'd mind,
And all the graces of the human form
Allied, in system, to the meanest worm;
The unfavor'd race in shade are meant to be
The link between the brutal world and we.
  In flowers we see that beauteous order rise
From earth to purest substance of the skies;
Rough and unformed in its first degree,
More polish'd verdue in the next we see;
The third claims perfect beauty to its share,
And breathes its fragrant soul in kindred air.
  Free and impartial still, the gifts of Heaven
In just degrees to all mankind are given:
This boasts of mental, that corporeal grace,
Or the vain merits of a beauteous face;
And these no grace, no scientific art,
But all the nobler virtues of the heart;
As our's their souls with great ambition glow,
Or melt in softer sympathy of woe.

  6. Published in *New York Magazine*'s "The American Muse" poetry column, under the section noted as "Original Poetry" in October 1796.

Long did the hapless race in bondage groan,
In grief unheeded, and in worth unknown,
And long in vain their weeping genius bore
The sighs of sorrow to the eternal shore.
Oft when the Lover in some fav'rite grove,
Told the soft raptures of successful love,
Rude ruffian force the guiltless youth would tear
From all that love and nature render'd dear,
To unrelenting Rigour's cruel sway,
To drudge his fond unhappy soul away.
  'Tis done! at length the long-withheld decree
Goes forth, that Afric shall be blest and free;
A PHILLIS rises, and the world no more
Denies the sacred right to mental pow'r;
While, Heav'n-inspir'd, she proves *her Country's* claim
To Freedom, and *her own* to deathless Fame.

New-York.   MATILDA.

Histories

Mercy Otis Warren (1728–1814)

Renowned for major contributions to early America drama (*q.v.*), Mercy Otis Warren produced equally impressive work in the field of history. The involvement of Otis Warren and her family in the events of the Revolution was impetus for her move into the writing of history. She completed her three-volume *History . . . of the American Revolution* in 1791 but did not publish it until 1805; the *History* remains today a fascinating study in republican expostulation on the era. Written over a twenty-five-year period, the *History*'s characterizations of the renowned male figures who shaped the new Republic offer us memorable insights into early political leaders from an eyewitness to their careers. The text reveals this remarkable woman's talents as a writer as well as a historian.

Works: *History of the Rise, Progress, and Termination of the American Revolution . . . with Biographical and Moral Observations* (3 Vols., 1805). *Bibliography*: Adams; Baym, "Between Enlightenment and Victorian"; Cohen; Oreovicz; Smith, W.

History . . . of the American Revolution

From *Vol. 1, Chapter IX. 1776*

. . . Yet they wisely judged, that this was a proper period to break the shackles, and renounce all political union with the parent state, by a free and bold declaration of the independence of the American States. This measure had been contemplated by some gentlemen in the several colonies, some months before it took place. They had communicated their sentiments to the individual members of congress, but that body had been apprehensive, that the people at large were not prepared to unite in a step so replete with important consequences. But the moment of decision had now arrived, when both the congress and the inhabitants of the colonies advanced too far to recede. . . .

Richard Henry Lee, Esq., a delegate from the state of Virginia, a gentleman of distinguished abilities, uniform patriotism, and unshaken firmness and integrity, was the first who dared explicitly to propose, that this decided measure, on which hung such mighty consequences, should no longer be delayed. This public and unequivocal proposal, from a man of his virtue and shining qualities, appeared to spread a kind of sudden dismay. A silent astonishment for a few minutes seemed to pervade the whole assembly: this was soon succeeded by a long debate, and a considerable division of sentiment on the important question.

After the short silence just observed, the measure proposed by Mr. Lee was advocated with peculiar zeal by John Adams, Esq., of the Massachusetts Bay. He rose with a face of intrepidity and the voice of energy, and invoked the *god of eloquence*, to enable him to do justice to the cause of his country, and to enforce this important step in such a manner, as might silence all opposition, and convince every one of the necessity of an immediate declaration of the independence of the United States of America.

Mr. John Dickinson, of Pennsylvania, took the lead in opposition to the boldness and danger of this decided measure. He had drawn the petition to the king forwarded by Mr. Penn,[1] and though no man was more strenuous in support of the rights of the colonies, he had always been averse to a separation from Britain, and shuddered at the idea of an avowed revolt of the American colonies. He arose on this occasion with no less solemnity than Mr. Adams had recently done, and with equal pathos of expression, and more brilliance of epithet, he invoked the *Great Governor* of the *Universe*, to animate him with powers of language sufficient to exhibit a view of the dread consequences to both countries, that such a hasty dismemberment of the empire might produce. . . .

From *Vol. 2, Chapter XVI. 1780*

The outrage of innocence in instances too numerous to be recorded, of the wanton barbarity of the soldiers of the King of England, as they patrolled the defenceless villages of America, was evinced nowhere more remarkably than in the burnings and massacres that marked the footsteps of the British troops as they from time to time ravaged the State of New Jersey.

In their late excursion they had trod their deleterious path through a part of the country called the Connecticut Farms. It is needless to particularize many instances of their wanton rage and unprovoked devastation in and near Elizabethtown. The places dedicated to public worship did not escape their fury; these were destroyed more from licentious folly than any religious frenzy or bigotry, to which their nation had at times been liable. Yet through the barbarous transactions of this summer nothing excited more general resentment and compassion than the murder of the amiable and virtuous wife of a Presbyterian clergyman, attended with too many circumstances of grief on the one side and barbarism on the other to pass over in silence.

This lady was sitting in her own house with her little domestic circle around her and her infant in her arms, unapprehensive of danger, shrouded by the

1. William Penn, Proprietor of Pennsylvania. See also Hannah Callowhill Penn.

consciousness of her own innocence and virtue, when a British barbarian pointed his musket into the window of her room, and instantly shot her through the lungs. A hole was dug, the body thrown in, and the house of this excellent lady set on fire and consumed with all the property it contained.

Mr. Caldwell, her affectionate husband, was absent; nothing had ever been alleged against his character, even by his enemies, but his zeal for the rights, and his attachment to his native land. For this he had been persecuted, and for this he was robbed of all that he held dear in life, by the bloody hands of men in whose benevolence and politeness he had had much confidence until the fated day when this mistaken opinion led him to leave his beloved family, fearless of danger and certain of their security, from their innocence, virtue, and unoffending amiability.

Mr. Caldwell afterward published the proofs of this cruel affair, attested on oath before magistrates by sundry persons who were in the house with Mrs. Caldwell and saw her fall back and expire immediately after the report of the gun. "This was," as observed Mr. Caldwell, "a violation of every tender feeling; without provocation, deliberately committed in open day; nor was it ever frowned on by the commander." The catastrophe of this unhappy family was completed within two years by the murder of Mr. Caldwell himself by some ruffian hands.

His conscious integrity of heart had never suffered him to apprehend any personal danger, and the melancholy that pervaded all on the tragical death of his lady, who was distinguished for the excellence and respectability of her character, wrought up the resentment of that part of the country to so high a pitch that the most timid were aroused to deeds of desperate heroism. They were ready to swear, like Hannibal against the Romans, and to bind their sons to the oath of everlasting enmity to the name of Britain.

From *Vol. 3, Chapter XXVII. 1783*

... No country has produced men more learned and liberal, of more comprehensive genius, virtue, and real excellence, than England; yet the contrast may as justly be exhibited there, as in any part of the world. But the balance of real merit, both individual and national, must be left to the all pervading eye, which, with a single glance, surveys the moral and intellectual system of creation. We now leave them to the rotations of time, and the re-action of human events, to the period which shall be pointed by the providential government of HIM, to whom a thousand years are as one day. . . .

. . . A dead and dreary silence reigns. . . . Nor will we dwell longer on any of the proud projects of conquest in the cabinet of Great Britain, either in the East or the West; but carry the mind forward, and indulge a pleasing anticipation of peace and independence to the *United States of America.*

From *Chapter XXVIII. 1783*

The discordant sounds of war that had long grated the ears of the children of America, were now suspended, and the benign and heavenly voice of harmony soothed their wounded feelings, and they flattered themselves the dread summons to slaughter and death would not again resound on their shores. The independence of America acknowledged by the first powers in Europe, and even Great Britain willing to re-sheathe the sword on the same honorable terms for the United States, every prospect of tranquillity appeared.

These were events for which the statesman had sighed in the arduous exertions of the cabinet; for which the hero had bared his breast, and the blood of the citizens had flowed in copious streams on the borders of the Atlantic, from the river St. Mary's to St. Croix, on the eastern extreme of the American territory. Peace was proclaimed in the American army by order of the commander in chief, on the nineteenth of April, one thousand seven hundred and eighty-three. This was just EIGHT YEARS from the memorable day, when the first blood was drawn in the contest between the American colonies and the parent state, in the fields of *Concord* and *Lexington*.

The operation and consequences of the restoration of peace, were now the subject of contemplation. This opened objects of magnitude indeed, to a young republic, which had rapidly passed through the grades of youth and puberty, and was fast arriving to the age of maturity:—a republic consisting of a number of confederated states, which by this time had received many as inhabitants, who were not originally from the stock of England. Some of them, indeed, were from more free governments, but others had fled from the slavery of despotic courts; from their numbers and abilities they had become respectable, and their opinions weighty in the political scale. From these and other circumstances it might be expected, that in time, the general enthusiasm for a republican system of government in America, might languish, and new theories be adopted, or old ones modified under different names and terms, until the darling system of inhabitants of the United States, might be lost or forgotten in a growing rabiosity for monarchy.

Symptoms of this nature, already began to appear in the language of some interested and ambitious men, who endeavored to confound ideas, and darken opinion, by asserting that *republicanism* was an indefine term. In social circles they frequently insinuated, that no precise meaning could be affixed to a word, by which the people were often deceived and led to pursue a shadow instead of an object of any real stability. This was indeed, more the language of art than principle, and seemed to augur the decline of public virtue in a free state.

It required the utmost vigilance to guard against, and counteract designs thus secretly covered. It was not unexpected by the judicious observers of human conduct, that many contingencies might arise, to defeat or to render fruitless the efforts that had been made on the practicability of erecting and maintaining a pure, unadulterated, republican government.

Time must unfold the futility of such an expectation, or establish the system on a basis, that will lead mankind to rejoice in the success of an experiment that has been too often tried in vain. Those who have been nurtured in the dark regions of despotism, who have witnessed the sale of the peasantry with the glebe they have cultivated from infancy, and who have seen the sire and son, transferred with the stables and the cattle, from master to master, cannot realize the success of a theory that has a tendency to exalt the species, and elevate the lower grades of mankind to a condition nearer to an equality with adventitious superiority. It is not wonderful, that a people of this description and education, should be incredulous of the utility of more free modes of government. They are naturally tenacious of old customs, habits, and their own fortuitous advantages; they are unable to form an idea of general freedom among mankind, without distinction of ranks that elevate one class of men to the summit of pride and insolence, and sink another to the lowest grade of servility and debasement.

Hannah Adams (1755–1831)

The daughter of Eleanor Clark and Thomas Adams, Hannah was born in Medfield, Massachusetts, on October 2, 1755. Like most upper-class young women in the eighteenth century, she was educated at home, but her family's status and her prodigious intellect afforded her the status of being the first woman allowed into that male enclave, the Boston Athenaeum. Adams remained single all her life; when sewing did not supply sufficient income, she turned to writing as a career and became one of the first professional women writers in the United States. Her chosen field was history, and she produced five carefully researched and well-documented histories between 1784 and 1812 as well as writing her *Memoirs.* Her contributions to the professionalization of historical writings in the United States deserve far greater notice than she has received to date, especially since Adams was attentive to women's and the common person's contributions to history.

Works: *Alphabetical Compendium of the Various Sections* . . . (1784); *A Summary History of New England* . . . (1799); *The Truth and excellence of the Christian Religion Exhibited* (1804); *Abridgement of the History of New England for the Use of Young People* (1807); *The History of the Jews* . . . (1812); *Narrative of the Controversy between the Rev. Jedidiah Morse, D.D., and the Author* (1814); *A Concise Account of the London Society* . . . (1816); *Letters of the Gospels* (1824); *Memoir of Miss Hannah Adams* (1832). Bibliography: Brooks; Vella.

A Summary History of New-England . . .
By Hannah Adams[1]

1635.

The settlers of Massachusetts purchased their lands of the native proprietors, and gave what was deemed by those savages an adequate compensation.

---

1. Adams was one of the few women at the time who published under her own name rather than pseudonymously. All subsequent notes are by Adams, unless otherwise noted.

The soil was to them of small value, as they subsisted chiefly by hunting, and did not possess that patient industry, which agriculture requires. In the year 1633, the colony passed an act, prohibiting the purchase of the lands from the natives, without having previously obtained a licence from government.[2]

After the governor and company removed from London to Massachusetts, the change of place and circumstances induced them to vary in certain instances from the directions of the charter. "They apprehended themselves subject to no other law or rule of government, than what arose from natural reason and the principles of equity, except any positive rules from the word of God."[3] Influential characters among them maintained, that birth was no necessary cause of subjection; for that the subject of any prince or state had a natural right to emigrate to any other state, or quarter of the world, when deprived of liberty of conscience, and that upon such removal his allegiance ceased. They called their own a voluntary civil subjection, arising merely from a mutual compact between them and the king, founded upon the charter. They acknowledged that this compact obligated them not to be subject to, or seek protection from, any other prince, nor to enact laws repugnant to those of England, &c. On the other hand, they maintained, that they were to be governed by laws made by themselves, and by officers of their own electing.[4]

When the Massachusetts colony completed their system of government, instead of making the laws of England the foundation of their code, they preferred the laws of Moses. They also created a representative body of their own motion in six years after the grant of their charter, which was wholly silent upon so important an institution. And although it gave them no power to judge and determine capital offences, the judicatories they established assumed this act of sovereign authority. In the same manner they supplied a defect of authority to erect judicatories for the probate of wills; to constitute courts with admiralty jurisdiction; to impose taxes on the inhabitants, and to create towns and other bodies corporate.[5] . . .

1636.

. . . Soon after the settlement was begun in Providence, [Rhode Island,] the commonwealth of Massachusetts was disturbed by intestine divisions. The male members of the church in Boston had been accustomed to convene, in order to repeat and debate on the discourses which were delivered on Sundays. Mrs. Anne Hutchinson, a very extraordinary woman, established a similar meeting for her own sex, founding her practice on Titus ii.4. Her custom was to repeat passages of Mr. Cotton's[6] sermons, and make her remarks expositions. These lectures for some time were received with general approbation, and were attended by a numerous audience. At length it appeared, that she distinguished

---

2. *Sullivan's History of the District of Maine,* p. 140.
3. *Hutchinson's Letter of December 7, 1762.*
4. *Gordon's History of the American War,* Vol. I. p. 50.
5. *Hutchinson,* Vol. II. p. 5.
6. John Cotton, Puritan minister who was largely responsible for expelling Hutchinson from Massachusetts Bay Colony. [Editor's note.]

the ministers, and members of churches through the country, a small part of whom she allowed to be under a covenant of grace, and the others under a covenant of works. The whole colony was soon divided into two parties, differing in sentiment, and still more alienated in affection. They stiled each other Antinomians and Legalists. Mrs. Hutchinson was charged with maintaining, that "the Holy Ghost dwells personally in a justified person; and that sanctification is not an evidence to believers of their justification."[7]

1637.

The Antinomians exerted themselves to keep in office Sir Henry Vane, who adopted their sentiments, and protected their preachers. On the other hand, the opposite party used every effort to discontinue him, and substitute John Winthrop, Esq. After some difficulty, they succeeded in the election of this gentleman. . . .[8]

Mrs. Hutchinson was next cited to her trial before the court,[9] and a large number of the clergy. Her sentence upon record is as follows: "Mrs. Hutchinson, the wife of Mr. William Hutchinson, being convented for traducing the clergymen and their ministry in the country, she declared voluntarily her revelations, and that she should be delivered and the court ruined with their posterity; and thereupon was banished, and in the mean time was committed to Mr. Joseph Weld, of Roxbury, until the court should dispose of her." Having received her sentence from the court, she was obliged to undergo a further trial in the church. She was first admonished, and presented to the church a recantation of the errors with which she was charged; yet at the same time professed she never maintained any other sentiments than what were there exhibited. Upon this she was excommunicated as a lyar by the church of Boston, to which she belonged.[10]

Mrs. Hutchinson, with a large number of the Antinomian party, some of whom had been banished, and others disfranchised, removed from the jurisdiction of the Massachusetts colony. Mr. Roger Williams[11] received and entertained them with the most friendly attention at Providence. . . .

[Concluding chapter]

. . . After independence was obtained by the sword, and acknowledged by the neighboring nations, a spirit of anarchy threatened the subversion of our recently acquired liberty. The interposition of Providence was visible, at this alarming crisis, in causing those tumults finally to terminate in the establishment of the federal constitution, which placed the privileges of the United States on a permanent foundation.

7. *Hutchinson*, Vol. II. p. 482.
8. Vol. I. p. 67.
9. Hutchinson's brother, Reverend John Wheelright, was the first Antinomian to be brought to trial. [1799 editor's note.]
10. *Hutchinson*, Vol. I. p. 70. *See Mrs. Hutchinson's trial in Appendix to Hutchinson's History.*
11. Founder of Rhode Island, a colony recognized for its religious tolerance.

Exalted from a feeble state to opulence and independence, the federal Americans are now recognized as a nation throughout the globe. From a comparison of their former with their present circumstances, the mind is expanded to contemplate scenes of future grandeur, and is led to conclude, that the United States are advancing in knowledge and happiness, while the wealth and power of more ancient governments is rapidly declining. The highly favored Americans ought to raise their minds in grateful aspirations to Heaven, that the fair prospect may never be reversed, by a spirit of anarchy prevailing among the people; but that GENUINE LIBERTY, *united with* ORDER *and* GOOD GOVERNMENT, may continue to diffuse their blessings through the widely extended nation.

Louisa Susannah Wells (Aikman)

(c. 1755–1831)

Louisa Susannah Wells was the daughter of a South Carolina newspaper publisher. Like her father, Wells was an ardent Loyalist, and when he had to abandon his trade and leave the country, she continued to run their Charleston newspaper until she also felt the need, in 1778, to seek exile in London. Accompanied by an uncle and his son, Robert and Charles Rowand, a female companion, Frances Thorney, and a maid, "Bella," Wells set sail on June 27 aboard the *Providence*; the ship's course took it to Rotterdam and then to London. In the following year, Wells wrote an account of her journey in order to have a record of the purpose and events of that significant period in her own life and in the history of the Revolution. The explicitness of the account, running to more than 120 pages, makes it an exemplar of the informal histories that many women recorded in this era. In 1782 Wells married Alexander Aikman, a printer to the House of Assembly and King's Printer for Jamaica. She died in 1831.

Works: *The Journal . . . Charlestown, S.C., to London . . . Written from Memory only in 1779.*

London, May 3rd 1779.[1]

. . . I cannot help here relating a trifling circumstance as it will show you to what necessity we were reduced for the want of British Manufactures. With much difficulty and trouble I obtained three eighths of a yard of black serge; I purchased a pair of clumsy shoe heels of a Jew; and in an obscure Lane, I found out a Negro Shoe Maker, who said he could make for Ladies. I deny that he could fit them. My shoes had no binding, were lined with French sail-Duck, and the heels were covered with Leather. On stepping out of the Boat,

1. Wells is discussing events of June 17, 1778, as she boarded the *Providence* at Charleston.

to go up the side of the ship, one of my dear-bought shoes slipped off. I exclaimed, "then I must go barefooted to Europe"! Our Captain[2] declared he would go to the bottom of the sea first, and almost leaping over the stern, he saved my shoe. Our fears for his safety were not small. On coming on board one of the ladies lent me a Morocco Slipper, two she could not spare. I used to darn my stockings with the ravellings of another, and we flossed out our old Silk Gowns to spin together with Cotton to knit our gloves. In the Country the Ladies were forced to use the thorns of the Orange Tree instead of Pins.

On this day many boats were employed in carrying up Palmetto Trees and Boughs to celebrate, in Town, the Anniversary of the ever inglorious 28th of June 1776! We saw the ruins of the Palmetto Fort on Sullivan's Island, now, Fort Moultrie. The Cannon Balls of the Ships under Sir Peter Parker, lodged in the logs as in a sponge.

On the 1st of July, the wind proving fair, we weighed Anchor, having a Black Pilot on Board, to whom we promised a hundred dollars, Congress, if he would carry us safely over the Bar. As we passed the Point at Fort Johnston, a providential escape I had of being drowned occurred to my memory. I was but ten years old when I attended my Mother with two Infant Sisters, both ill of the Hooping-Cough. We had an apartment in the Governor of the Fort's house, Col. Robert Howarth. I was tired of a Sick-room, and slipped out one day after dinner to walk on the Beach, and seeing the Point uncovered, I imagined it reached to Sullivan's Island, and I thought I might go thither with ease, and be back before dark. The Governor happened luckily to be looking over the Battery, and called out as loud as possibly he could through a Speaking Trumpet, to run as fast as I could or I would be swallowed up in the Sea. He dispatched a Soldier to my assistance, and in a quarter of an hour I saw the Sand-Bank covered with surf! Before that, I had escaped drowning in a Pond in King Street, being pushed off a narrow bridge, of two planks, by a mischievous girl, who wanted to get before me: but saved by the presence of mind of another, a girl about 12 years old, the eldest daughter of Cato Ash; who ran home to her Mother and told her my disaster, who sent a man to take me out. My other comrades were wringing their hands lamenting my untimely fate. I fell on my side, but should soon have been suffocated as the mud had got into one Nostril. The sequel of my voyage will prove that, a watery Grave is not yet ready for me.

Perhaps you do not know what gave rise to the name the Sea-Island[3] called Coffin Land? I will tell you. When the Hudson's Bay Company obtained so much interest with the then existing Ministry as to have the flourishing Scots Colony of Darien broke up, and its inhabitants recalled: Three large Ships were purchased and fitted up for the reception of such a cargo and sent. One of them was called the "Rising Sun." For what reason she anchored on our Coast I know not, perhaps for provisions or Water, but one of their Clergymen, the Revd. Stobo hearing there was a Scots Presbyterian Meeting House and Con-

2. Richard Stevens.

3. The Sea Islands are a chain of more than one hundred islands off the Atlantic coast of South Carolina, Georgia, and Florida.

gregation on John's Island, came on shore with his wife, the next day, being Sunday and preached to them. A Storm arose in the night, and wrecked the ship on "Coffin Land." Between three and four hundred souls perished. Many of the dead bodies were washed on shore, Women with their infants clasped to their breasts were found cast up on this Island. Mr Stobo soon after was preacher to that Meeting, and I knew his Daughter, old Mrs. Joseph Stanyarne. His great-grand daughter Miss E. Stobo is amongst the number of my correspondents in Carolina. Another of these ships was lost on another part of the American Coast, and only one arrived safe to Scotland to carry the melancholy news. The wreck (of the Rising Sun) was very lately seen by my Uncle and he drew from it several great Nails which are now to be seen in the Live Oak Tree near his house at Stone-Landing.

Every person on board the "Providence" were banished except Captain Stevens. Never did any of us experience joy, so truly, as when we found ourselves in the wide Ocean, out of the dominion of Congress. You know the many difficulties the poor Tories had to encounter in procuring ships, getting Men &c. The poor Pilot by whose skill we were indebted for safety, seemed to enjoy our happiness, independent of our contribution, above his Master's fee. The Pilot boat sailed ahead and tracked our way, notwithstanding which we struck twice on this dangerous Bar. We had just reason to suspect that the Pilot of the "True Briton," Jamaica Ship (afterwards the "Prosper" Man of War, and purchased by Sir Edmund Head and Mr Kincaid, who restored her original name) had been bribed to run that unfortunate vessel on the Shoals. These Tories were obliged to return to Town, unload the Cargo, and the bottom of the ship to be repaired, which detained them many months. For this reason we chose a Negro Pilot, their's was a White man. Never shall I forget poor Bluff's (the name of the Pilot) anxiety when our Hay-Stack of a ship missed Stays on the Bar! He said he was a true friend to British Manufactures and that was as much Loyalty as he durst own, but these Revolution times was not so good as before for poor Negroes.

London, May 5th 1779.

Captain Stevens, too, had been ill used in Charlestown. We therefore turned our backs on the Land, which soon disappeared and Captain Stevens sinking a ballast stone said "When that rises, I return." I really joined him from my heart.

London, Sunday Evening.[4]

... During the tedious period of eight foggy days, what were my reflections! They almost bordered on impiety. Often-times did I think myself tantalized, by being permitted to accomplish that wish, which I had, for so many years indulged, namely of coming to England: but that the door was now shut against me! No wonder, said I, to the Captain one day, that I was in my despondency, "that English people begin to hang and drown themselves in the gloomy month of November" One day more and I should have been tempted to jump out of the cabin window.

A dreadful storm was brooding, and our Commodore knowing that the

---

4. It is the end of November; they are heading for the English Channel.

'Leviathan'[5] could stand no more bad weather, crowded sail, and hasted for Plymouth, leaving us, with six other sail, to the care of Providence—five of these were wrecked that night and the following day!

In the afternoon we saw the Lofty Coast of Cornwall, happy sight to us, poor fugitives and Exiles. We soon made the two Lights of the Lizard, and before bed time passed the Eddy Stone and other Lights. On the 26th the wind rose higher. The Iron bound Coast of England, our Lee shore; and with all our skill could not keep three miles to windward of it: but I came upon deck. My heart leaped when I saw a little Fishing Town near Dongenness. Here were a great number of Dutch Ships riding. The Avarice of these people make them thus expose their Lives and Property, and they will not go into a safer Port, for the expense of paying the Lights, which they must necessarily pass. We saw several Dutch Wrecks lying near this place, which were as safe as their neighbours but a week before.

We drove up the Channel at an amazing rate under close reefed courses. My uncle wished to have landed at Portsmouth, but it was impossible to accomplish it. Whilst on deck I saw the Race of Portland. The prospect we had of soon being in the Downs cheering our drooping spirits, for the Dead Lights were generally in and our candles used to appear like the faint glimmering of sparks in a cavern, as I came from above.

As I had not had a sound sleep for many nights; about 12 o'clock I resigned my wearied mind and body to calm repose. Happy me! Little did I know our danger! At one o'clock the Captain and all hands were called to turn out: None were able to steer the Ship but Bernard, and he was lashed to the Tiller, otherwise he would have been washed overboard, as the Waves were continually breaking over the Quarter. A thick fog arose to "cheer the hopes" or rather to depress the spirits of the desponding Mariners. I did not awake until nine o'clock next morning, and asked, as usual, for my breakfast, which was generally brought to my bedside. A sullen silence prevailed in the Cabin. At length Mrs Weir answered me from her State room that "as I never had been afraid before, it was now high time" Charles awakened upon this, and asked me "why I had not called him before to get his breakfast" so true is the observation that 'those who know no danger, fear none' A dreadful noise above, occasioned by the hauling of ropes with the attendant *Chaunt*; the whistling of the Wind, the dashing of the waves against the sides of the Ship, all convinced me that every thing was not as it should be; and the only assistance which I could give, must be negatively, viz: to ly still and say nothing! No sooner had I formed this resolution, that I heard the Captain call out, "Try the Pumps" O! thought I, 'tis all over now, as I had never heard any Pumping during the voyage before. I comforted myself with this reflection, that I could never die with more indifference to the world than at that time, or even now.

August 29th 1779.

In about two hours every thing underwent a total transformation. The Wind changed, which cleared away the fog and discovered Beachy Head, only one league to leeward! Happily for us, we did not know we were so near the shore. Had the Storm or Fog continued half an hour longer, we should have been

5. An accompanying ship.

wrecked on this dreadful Rock! We soon found the way to the Deck, and we were glad to find our Caboose was not carried away by the Seas we had shipped. *Fifty-six hours* had elapsed since a fire had been lighted, and a dish of Lob-scouse, made of stale meat and fowl, with some sliced potatoes, required no sauce but hunger to make it relish. . . .

We soon made Dover, and, at 4 o'clock in the afternoon of the 27th of November anchored in the Downs. . . .

Eliza Yonge Wilkinson (fl. 1779–82)

In 1779, when Eliza Yonge Wilkinson recorded for an unidentified woman friend her impressions of the British invasion of Charleston, South Carolina, she was already a young widow living at Yonge's Island, about five miles south of Charleston. In the twelve letters that remain, Wilkinson satirizes her own preinvasion ignorance of the horrendous realities of war and depicts the conversion of a passive observer to an ardent Patriot. Her home was ransacked both by the invaders and by their local Tory sympathizers, and she was eventually forced to flee to the countryside for safety. Through a powerful narrative style ("my historical manner"), Wilkinson was able to convey both the personal consequences and the political implications of the Revolution for a Southern community. Like so many women of the era, she also acts as a local historian; her letters were written three years after the invasion because, as she told her friend, "I mean never to forget."

Works: Correspondence. *Bibliography*: Wilkinson, E.

The Letters of Eliza Yonge Wilkinson

To Miss M—— P——.   *Yonge's Island, 1782.*

As I mean never to forget the *loving-kindness and tender mercies* of the renowned Britons while among us, in the ever-memorable year 1779, I shall transmit you a brief account of their *polite* behavior to my Father and family, where you will find me sufficiently punished for being something of an unbeliever heretofore. You know we had always heard most terrible accounts of the actions of the British troops at the northward; but, (fool that I was,) I thought they must be exaggerated, for I could not believe that a nation so famed for humanity, and many other virtues, should, in so short a time, divest themselves of even the least trace of what they once were.

. . . I was so infatuated with what I had formerly heard and read of Englishmen, that I thought humanity, and every manly sentiment, were their inherent qualities;—though I cannot but say that, much as I had admired the former lustre of the British character, my soul shrunk from the thought of having any communication with a people who had left their homes with a direct intention to imbrue their hands in the blood of my beloved countrymen, or derive them of their birthright, Liberty and property. . . .

Now, the time drew near when this State was to have her day of suffering in sympathy with her sister States. Oh, how I dreaded the approaching enemy! I had thoughts (with my other friends,) to go higher up the country to avoid them; but as my Father, with many others of my relations, had not conveniences ready to carry off their effects with them, and as the enemy approached rapidly, they agreed to stay. It was a melancholy sight to see such crowds of helpless, distressed women, weeping for husbands, brothers, or other near relations and friends, who were they knew not where, whether dead or alive. When the enemy were at Ashepoo, or somewhere thereabouts, my sister and sister-in-law were then at my Father's, when one Sunday morning a negro wench, who had been out visiting, came running home in a violent hurry, informing us that a party of British horse were then at Mr. W.'s, not above five or six miles from us.

. . . This created such confusion and distress among us all as I cannot describe. A boat was immediately pushed off. My sister Yonge, my sister Smilie, and myself, were desirous of putting the evil day afar off; so we went over the river to Mr. Smilie's. . . .

We had but just got over, when a scene presented itself to us, enough to move the hardest heart in the British army could they have seen it. This was a large boat-load of women and children on their way to Charlestown, as that place promised more safety than any other. They called at Mr. Smilie's, and staid a day or two. I pitied them all greatly, (though we were much in the same situation;) one lady especially, who had seven children, and one of them but a fortnight old; thus, in her weakly situation, to venture her life and that of her babe, rather than fall into the hands of an enemy, whose steps have been marked with cruelty and oppression. . . .

[From Letter III.] . . . I could not think of staying at Father's, as he lived on the river, and we very often saw boat-loads of red-coats pass and repass; so I went and staid with my sister at the plantation. She had another lady with her too; one Miss Samuells. While we staid there, we used to see parties of our friends—mostly the Willtown hunters, pass the avenue, towards Stono Ferry, where they rode daily in search of adventures, and would frequently call on us. O! how sweet, how comforting, the presence of a friend in such distressing times; especially those we look on as the protectors, the prop of their country. And yet, with a tender anxiety for their welfare, we beheld them; the poorest soldier, who would call at any time for a drink of water, I would take a pleasure in giving it to him myself, and many a dirty ragged fellow I have attended, with a bowl of water, or milk and water; and with the utmost compassion beheld their tattered raiment and miserable situation; they really merit every thing who will fight from principle alone; for, from what I could learn, these poor creatures had nothing to protect them, and seldom get their pay. . . .

We grew melancholy and unhappy on our friends disappearing, and hourly expected unwelcome visitors; but seeing nor hearing nothing of them, only that they were erecting forts at the Ferry, I began to be in hopes they would not be so free in obtruding their company on us, as they had done elsewhere; but at length the time arrived. The 2d of June, two men rode up to the house; one had a green leaf, the other a red string in his hat; this made us suspect them as spies (for we hear M'Girth's men wore such things in their hats.) They were very particular in their inquiries "if there were any men in the house?" (Foolish fellows! if there were, they would not have had time to have asked us that question.)— "If any had been there?" "No." "Did any go from here this morning?" Impertinents, thought I; do you think that we are bound to answer to all your interrogations! but I must not say so. "Well," says one, "do you know Col. M'Girth will be along here presently with two hundred men? You may expect him in an hour or two." Ah! thought I—I'd far rather (if I must see one) see old Beelzebub; but here are some of his imps—the forerunners of his approach. "Why," (said my friend, Miss Samuells,) "if Col. M'Girth should come, I hope he wont act ungenteelly, as he'll find none but helpless women here, who never injured him!" "O!" says one, "he'll only take your clothes and negroes from you." After a little farther chat, they rode off, leaving us in a most cruel situation, starting [at] every noise we heard, and dreading the enemy's approach. . . .

Well, now comes the day of terror—the 3d of June. (I shall never love the anniversary of that day.) . . . I heard the horses of the inhuman Britons coming in such a furious manner, that they seemed to tear up the earth, and the riders at the same time bellowing out the most horrid curses imaginable; oaths and imprecations, which chilled my whole frame. Surely, thought I, such horrid language denotes nothing less than death; but I'd no time for thought—they were up to the house—entered with drawn swords and pistols in their hands; indeed, they rushed in, in the most furious manner, crying out, "Where're these women rebels?" (pretty language to ladies from the *once famed Britons!*) That was the first salutation! The moment they espied us, off went our caps, (I always heard say none but women pulled caps!) And for what, think you? why, only to get a paltry stone and wax pin, which kept them on our heads; at the same time uttering the most abusive language imaginable, and making as if they'd hew us to pieces with their swords. But it's not in my power to describe the scene: it was terrible to the last degree; and, what augmented it, they had several armed negroes with them, who threatened and abused us greatly. They then began to plunder the house of every thing they thought valuable or worth taking; our trunks were split to pieces, and each mean, pitiful wretch crammed his bosom with the contents, which were our apparel, &c. &c. &c. . . .

[from Letter VI.] . . . After dinner our friends began to move towards camp; my brother persuaded us not to stay an hour longer, for the enemy, upon hearing what had been done, might come out, and use us worse then they had done already. Father had the same thoughts, and sent for us; but having not a horse left, he only sent umbrellas to shelter us from the sun, which was exceedingly warm. My sister packed up a few things, and gave the Negroes to carry, and then we went off. . . . Two of Father's Negro men attended us, armed with great clubs; one walked on before, the other behind, placing us in the centre.

It was not long before our guard had some use for their clubs; we were crossing a place they call the Sands, when one of the enemy's Negroes came out of the woods. He passed our advance guard with nothing but the loss of his smart Jocky cap, which was snatched from his head. He turned round, and muttering something, then proceeded on; when, attempting to pass our rear-guard, he was immediately levelled to the earth; he arose, and attempted to run off, when he received another blow, which again brought him down. I could not bear the sight of the poor wretch's blood, which washed his face and neck; it affected me sensibly. "Enough, Joe! enough," cried I; "don't use the creature ill, take him at once, I wont have him beaten so." "Let me alone, Mistress, I'll not lay hand on him till I have stunned him; how do I know but he has a knife, or some such thing under his clothes, and when I go up to him, he may stab me. No, no,—I know Negroes' ways too well." With that he fetched him another blow. I was out of all patience; I could not help shedding tears. I called out again; "Inhuman wretch, take the Negro at once, he cannot hurt you now if he would; you shall not—I declare you shall not beat him so." With that he took him, tied his hands behind him, and gave him to the fellow who went before; he himself stayed behind with us; but the poor wretch was sadly frightened. The fellow who had him in custody, walked on very fast, but he kept looking back on us. At last he said to me, "Do, Mistress, let me walk by you." "Don't be afraid," said I, "they shan't hurt you again, I wont let them." But he looked on me so pitifully—his head continually turning round towards me, with such terror in his countenance, that I felt for the poor crea-ture, and, to make him easy, walked, or rather ran, close behind him; for, to keep up with them I was obliged to go in a half run, the fellow who had hold of him walking at a great rate, for fear of being overtaken by the enemy. . . .

Yonge's Island, July 14th. . . . The day the last vessel sailed,[1] some British offi-cers came to the house where I staid. I was sitting very melancholy, and did not alter my position on their entrance. They sat for some time; at length they broke silence with—"You seem melancholy, Madam!" "I am so, Sir; I am thinking how suddenly I am deprived of my friends, and left almost alone in the midst of"—

"Do not say enemies, Madam," (interrupting me,)—"there is not one in this garrison but would protect and serve you to the utmost of his power, as well as those whose absence you lament."

"I have no further business in this garrison, Sir; those on whose account I came down are now gone, and I shall very shortly return to the country; or you may send me off, too—will you?"

"No, no, Madam; I will enter a *caveat* against that—I am determined to con-vert you."

"That you never shall, for I am determined not to be converted by you."

"Why, then, you shall convert me."

"I shall not attempt it, Sir"—and I turned about, and spoke to a lady by me. Some time after I was asked to play the guitar,—"I cannot play, I am very dull."

---

1. Several ships, carrying prisoners as well as passengers seeking refuge in England, sailed from Charleston while Yonge Wilkinson was visiting the city.

"How long do you intend to continue so, Mrs. Wilkinson?"
"Until my countrymen return, Sir!"
"Return as what, Madam?—*prisoners* or *subjects?*"
"As *conquerors!* Sir." . . .

Judith Sargent Murray (1751–1820)

As in so many other endeavors, Judith Sargent Murray was at the forefront of the writing of revisionist history. In a four-part series, "Observations on Female Abilities," originally published in the *Massachusetts Magazine* and collected in *The Gleaner* (1798, vol. 3, numbers 88–91), Sargent Murray explicitly aligned the rewriting of history with her earlier essay, "On the Equality of the Sexes" (*q.v.*). Tracing women's active participation in historical events and in the production of literature, from ancient times and across international borders, Sargent Murray reinscribed women in the national consciousness. Her goal was straightforwardly acknowledged: "the establishment of the female intellect, or the maintaining of justice and propriety of considering women, as far as relates to their understanding, in *every respect*, equal to men." The following excerpts from parts three and four of the essay suggest the range of women Sargent Murray studied and the talents—from letters to botany—that they brought to their respective cultures.

Works: *The Gleaner* (1798). Bibliography: Harris, ed., *Selected Writings of Judith Sargent Murray.*

"Observations on Female Abilities," Part III.

'Tis joy to tread the splendid paths of fame,
Where countless myriads mental homage claim;
Time honour'd annals careful to explore,
And mark the heights which intellect can soar.

. . . In the thirteenth century, a young lady of Bologna, pursuing, with avidity, the study of the Latin language, and the legislative institutions of her country, was able, at the age of twenty-three, to deliver, in the great church of Bologna, a Latin oration, in praise of a deceased person, eminent for virtue; nor was she indebted for the admiration she received, to the indulgence granted to her youth, or Sex. At the age of twenty-six, she took the degree of a Doctor of Laws, and commenced her career in this line, by public expositions of the doctrines of Justinian: At the age of thirty, her extraordinary merit raised her to the chair, where she taught the law to an astonishing number of pupils, collected from various nations. She joined to her profound knowledge, sexual modesty, and every feminine accomplishment; yet her per-

sonal attractions were absorbed in the magnitude and splendor of her intellectual abilities; and the charms of her exterior only commanded attention,
when she ceased to speak. The fourteenth century produced, in the same city,
a like example; and the fifteenth continued, and acknowledged the pretensions of the Sex, insomuch that a learned chair was appropriated to illustrious women.

Issotta Nogarolla[1] was also an ornament of the fifteenth century; and
Sarochisa of Naples was deemed worthy of comparison with Tasso.[2] Modesta
Pozzo's[3] defence of her Sex did her honour; she was, herself, an example of
excellence. Gabrielle,[4] daughter of a king, found leisure to devote to her pen;
and her literary pursuits contributed to her usefulness and her happiness. Mary
de Gournai[5] rendered herself famous by her learning. Guyon,[6] by her writings and her sufferings, have evinced the justice of her title to immortality.
Anna Maria Schuman of Cologne, appears to have been mistress of all the useful and ornamental learning of the age which she adorned: She was born in
1607; her talents unfolded with extraordinary brilliancy: In the bud of her life,
at the age of six years, she cut, with her scissors, the most striking resem-
blances of every figure which was presented to her view, and they were finished with astonishing neatness. At ten, she was but three hours in learning
to embroider. She studied music, painting, sculpture and engraving, and made
an admirable proficiency in all those arts. The Hebrew, Greek and Latin languages were familiar to her; and she made some progress in the oriental
tongues. She perfectly understood French, English and Italian, and expressed
herself eloquently in all those languages; and she appropriated a portion of
her time, to the acquirement of an extensive acquaintance with geography, astronomy, philosophy, and the other sciences: Yet she possessed so much feminine delicacy, and retiring modesty, that her talents and acquirements had
been consigned to oblivion, if Vassius, and other amateurs of literature, had
not ushered her, in opposition to her wishes upon the theatre of the world:
But when she was once known, persons of erudition, of every description, corresponded with her; and those in the most elevated stations, assiduously sought
opportunities of seeing and conversing with her.

Mademoiselle Scudery,[7] stimulated by necessity, rendered herself eminent
by her writings. Anna de Parthenay[8] possessed great virtues, great talents, and
great learning; she read, with facility and pleasure, authors in the Greek and
Latin languages; she was a rationale theologician; she was a perfect mistress
of music; and was as remarkable for her vocal powers, as for her execution of

1. Issotta Nogarola (1420?–1466), poet and letter-writer.
2. Torquato Tasso (1544–1595), Italian poet and dramatist.
3. Pozzo (1555–1592) used the pen name of "Moderata Fonte"; she published dramas and
religious essays.
4. Unidentified.
5. Marie de Jars Gournay (1565–1645), essayist who was noted for her advocacy of equality
between the sexes.
6. Madame Guyon (1648–1717) was noted for her religious writings.
7. Marie-Madeleine du Moncel de Martinval Scudery (1627–1711) was best known as a novelist
and letter-writer.
8. Sixteenth-century poet and musical composer.

the various instruments which she attempted. Catharine de Parthenay,[9] niece to Anna, married to Renatus de Rohan, signalized herself by her attention to the education of her children; and her maternal cares were crowned with abundant success: Her eldest son was the illustrious Duke of Rohan, who obtained immortal honour by his zeal and exertions in the Protestant cause; and she was also mother to Anna de Rohan, who was as illustrious for her genius and piety, as for her birth. She was mistress of the Hebrew language; her numbers were beautifully elegant; and she supported, with heroic firmness, the calamities consequent upon the siege of Rochelle.

Mademoiselle le Fevre,[10] celebrated in the literary world by the name of Madame Dacier, gave early testimonies of that fine genius which her father delighted to cultivate. Her edition of Callimachus was received with much applause. At the earnest request of the Duke of de Montansier, she published an edition of Florus, for the use of the dauphin; she exchanged letters with Christina, queen of Sweden; she devoted herself to the education of her son and daughter, whose progress were proportioned to the abilities of their interested preceptress: Greek and Latin were familiar to her; and she was often addressed in both those languages, by the literati of Europe. Her translation of the Iliad was much admired. She is said to have possessed great firmness, generosity, and equality of temper, and to have been remarkable for her piety. Marie de Sevigne[11] appropriated her hours to the instruction of her son and daughter; she has enriched the world with eight volumes of letters, which will be read with pleasure by every critic in the French language. The character of Mary II. Queen of England, and consort to William of Nassau,[12] is transcendently amiable. She is delineated as a princess, endowed with uncommon powers of mind, and beauty of person. She is extensively acquainted with history, was attached to poetry, and possessed a good taste in compositions of this kind. She had a considerable knowledge in architecture and gardening; and her dignified condescension, and consistent piety, were truly admirable and praiseworthy— Every reader of history, and lover of virtue, will lament her early exit. The Countess of Pembroke[13] translated from the French, a dramatic piece; she gave a metrical edition of the Book of Psalms, and supported an exalted character.

Anna Killigrew, and Anna Wharton,[14] were eminent, both for poetry and painting; and their unblemished virtue, and exemplary piety, pointed and greatly enhanced the value of their other accomplishments. Catharine Phillips[15] was, from early life, a lover of the Muses; she translated Corneille's Tragedy of Pompey into English; and in this, as well as the poems which she published, she

9. Parthenay (?–1631) was a poet, dramatist, and translator; Viscount Rene de Rohan was her husband.

10. Anne LeFevre Dacier (1651–1720), editor and pamphleteer.

11. Marquise de Sevigne (1626–1696), letter-writer.

12. Mary II (1662–1694) and William of Nassau, Prince of Orange, ruled jointly.

13. Mary Sidney, Countess of Pembroke (1561–1621), translator.

14. Anna Killigrew (c.1660–1685) and Anna Wharton (1659–1685).

15. Katherine Fowler Philips (1631–1664) was a dramatist, translator, and founder of the literary salon, Society of Friendship. Pierre Corneille (1606–1684), whose work Philips translated, was a dramatist.

was successful. Lady Burleigh, Lady Bacon, Lady Russell, and Mrs. Killigrew,[16] daughters of Sir Anthony Cook, received from their father a masculine education; and their prodigious improvement was an ample compensation for his paternal indulgence: They were eminent for genius and virtue, and obtained an accurate knowledge of the Greek and Latin languages. The writings of the Dutchess of Newcastle[17] were voluminous; she is produced as the first English lady who attempted what has since been termed polite literature. Lady Halket[18] was remarkable for her erudition; she was well skilled, both in physic and divinity. Lady Masham, and Mary Astell,[19] reasoned accurately on the most abstract particulars in divinity, and in metaphysics. Lady Grace Gethin[20] was happy in natural genius and a cultivated understand; she was a woman of erudition; and we are informed that, at the age of twenty, "*she treated of life and morals, with the discernment of Socrates, and the elegance of Xenophon*"[21]—Mr. Congreve[22] has done justice to her merit. Chudleigh, Winchelsea, Monk, Bovey, Stella, Montague[23]—these all possess their respective claims. Catharine Macauley[24] wielded successfully the historic pen; nor were her exertions confined to this line—But we have already multiplied our witnesses far beyond our original design; and it is proper that we apologize to our readers, for a transgression of that brevity which we had authorized them to expect.

Part IV.

Nor are the modern Fair a step behind,
In the transcendent energies of mind:
Their worth conspicuous swells the ample roll,
While emulous they reach the splendid goal.

. . . But while we do homage to the women of other times, we feel happy that nature is no less bountiful to the females of the present day. We cannot, indeed, obtain a list of the names that have done honour to their Sex, and to humanity, during the period now under observation: The lustre of those minds,

16. Mildred Burghley, wife of Lord Burghley; Anne Cooke Bacon (1528–1610), translator and letter-writer; Elizabeth Cooke Russell (1540–1609), poet and translator; Killigrew is unknown. Their father, Sir Anthony Cooke (1504–1576), was Edward VI's tutor.

17. Margaret Lucas Cavendish (1623–1673), Duchess of Newcastle, was a noted philosopher and essayist.

18. Lady Ann Halkett (1623–1699), memoirist and educator.

19. Masham (1658–1708), religious essayist; Mary Astell (1666–1731), poet, political essayist, recognized for her attacks on the oppression of women in English society.

20. Gethin (1676–1697) was an essayist.

21. Xenophon (c.430–c.355 B.C.), a noted Greek historian.

22. William Congreve (1670–1729), Restoration dramatist.

23. Mary Lee, Lady Chudleigh (1656–1710), poet and activist against women's oppression; Anne Kingsmill Finch, Countess of Winchilsea (1661–1720), poet; Mary Molesworth (?–1715), poet; Catharina Bovey (1669–1726), philanthropist; Lady Mary Wortley Montagu (1689–1762), letter-writer and essayist.

24. Catharine Macauley (1731–1791), a radical feminist activist, historian, and philosopher; she was a recognized proponent of women's education.

still enveloped in a veil of mortality, is necessarily muffled and obscure; but the curtain will be thrown back, and posterity will contemplate, with admiration, their manifold perfections. Yet, in many instances, fame has already lifted her immortalizing trump. Madame de Genlis[25] has added new effulgence to the literary annals of France. This lady unites, in an astonishing degree, both genius and application! May her indefatigable exertions be crowned with the success they so richly merit—May no illiberal prejudices obstruct the progress of her multiplied productions; but, borne along the stream of time, may they continue pleasurable vehicles of instruction, and confer on their ingenious author that celebrity to which she is indisputably entitled. France may also justly place among her list of illustrious personages, the luminous name of Roland.[26] Madame Roland comprised, in her own energetic and capacious mind, all those appropriate virtues, which are characterized as masculine and feminine. She not only dignified the Sex, but human nature in the aggregate; and her memory will be held in veneration, wherever talents, literature, patriotism, and uniform heroism, are properly appreciated.

The British Isle is at this moment distinguished by a constellation of the first magnitude. Barbauld, Seward, Cowley, Inchbald, Burney, Smith, Radcliffe, Moore, Williams, Wollstonecraft, &c. &c.[27]—these ladies, celebrated for brilliancy of genius and literary attainments, have rendered yet more illustrious the English name.

Nor is America destitute of females, whose abilities and improvements give them an indisputable claim to immortality. It is a fact, established beyond all controversy, that we are indebted for the discovery of our country, to female enterprize, decision, and generosity. The great Columbus, after having in vain solicited the aid of Genoa, France, England, Portugal, and Spain—after having combated, for a period of eight years, with every objection that a want of knowledge could propose, found, at last, his only resource in the penetration and magnanimity of Isabella of Spain, who furnished the equipment, and raised the sums necessary to defray the expenses, on the sale of her own jewels; and while we conceive an action, so honourable to the Sex, hath not been sufficiently applauded, we trust, that the equality of the female intellect to that of their brethren, who have so long usurped an unmanly and unfounded superiority, will never, in this younger world, be left without a witness. We cannot ascertain the number of ingenious women, who at present adorn our country. In the shade of solitude they perhaps cultivate their own minds, and superintend the education of their children. Our day, we know, is only

25. Comtesse de Genlis (1746–1830) was a novelist, dramatist, and memoirist.

26. Marion Philipon Roland (1754–1793) was the author of letters, essays, and memoirs, in addition to being a noted political activist.

27. Anna Laetitia Aikin Barbauld (1743–1825), poet, essayist; Anna Seward (1742–1809), poet, novelist, letter-writer; Hannah Parkhouse Cowley (1743–1809), poet and dramatist; Elizabeth Inchbald (1753–1821), actress, dramatist, essayist, and novelist; Fanny Burney (1752–1850), novelist, memoirist; Charlotte Turner Smith (1749–1806), novelist; Ann Radcliffe (1764–1823), novelist; Jane Elizabeth Moore (1738–?), poet; Helen Maria Williams (1762–1827), poet, novelist, translator; Mary Wollstonecraft (1759–1797), essayist and novelist, arguably the most renowned woman of the age based upon the publication of her controversial (and now classic) feminist text, *A Vindication of the Rights of Woman* in 1792.

dawning—But when we contemplate a Warren, a Philenia, an Antonia, a Eu-phelia,[28] &c. &c. we gratefully acknowledge, that genius and application, even in the female line, already gild, with effulgent radiance, our blest Aurora.

But women are calculated to shine in other characters than those adverted to, in the preceding Essays; and with proper attention to their education, and subsequent habits, they might easily attain that independence, for which a Wollstonecraft hath so energetically contended; the term, *helpless widow*, might be rendered as unfrequent and inapplicable as that of *helpless widower*; and al-though we should undoubtedly continue to mourn the dissolution of wedded amity, yet we should derive consolation from the knowledge, that the infant train had still a remaining prop, and that a mother could *assist* as well as *weep* over her offspring.

That women have a talent—a talent which, duly cultivated, would confer that independence, which is demonstrably of incalculable utility, every atten-tive observer will confess. The Sex should be taught to depend on their own efforts, for the procurement of an establishment in life. The chance of a mat-rimonial coadjutor, is no more than a probable contingency; and if they were early accustomed to regard this *uncertain* event with suitable *indifference*, they would make elections with that deliberation, which would be calculated to give a more rational prospect of tranquility. All this we have repeatedly as-serted, and all this we do invariably believe. To neglect polishing a gem, or obstinately to refuse bringing into action a treasure in our possession, when we might thus accumulate a handsome interest, is surely egregiously absurd, and the height of folly. The *united efforts of male and female* might rescue many a family from destruction, which, notwithstanding the efforts of its *individual* head, is now involved in all the calamities attendant on a dissipated fortune and augmenting debts. It is not possible to educate children in a manner which will render them *too beneficial* to society; and the more we multiply aids to a family, the greater will be the security, that its individuals will not be thrown a burden on the public.

An instance of *female capability*, this moment occurs to memory. In the State of Massachusetts, in a small town, some miles from the metropolis, resides a woman, who hath made astonishing improvements in agriculture. Her mind, in the early part of her life, was but penuriously cultivated, and she grew up almost wholly uneducated: But being suffered, during her childhood, to rove at large among her native fields, her limbs expanded, and she acquired a height of stature above the common size; her mind also became invigorated; and her understanding snatched sufficient information, to produce a consciousness of the injury she sustained in the want of those aids, which should have been furnished in the beginning of her years. She however applied herself diligently to remedy the evil, and soon made great proficiency in writing, and in arith-metic. She read every thing she could procure; but the impressions adventi-tiously made on her infant mind still obtained the ascendency. A few rough acres constituted her patrimonial inheritance; these she has brought into a state of high cultivation; their productions are every year both useful and or-

---

28. Mercy Otis Warren (*q.v.*); Sarah Wentworth Morton (q.v.); the other women are unidentified.

namental; she is mistress of agricolation, and is at once a botanist and a florist. The most approved authors in the English language, on these subjects, are in her hands, and she studies them with industry and success.

She has obtained such a considerable knowledge in the nature of soils, the precise manure which they require, and their particular adaptation to the various fruits of the earth, that she is become the oracle of all the farmers in her vicinity; and when laying out, or appropriating their grounds, they uniformly submit them to her inspection. Her gardens are the resort of all strangers who happen to visit her village; and she is particularly remarkable for a growth of trees, from which, gentlemen, solicitous to enrich their fruit-gardens, or ornament their parterres, are in the habit of supplying themselves; and those trees are, to their ingenious cultivator, a considerable income. Carefully attentive to her nursery, she knows when to transplant, and when to prune; and she perfectly understands the various methods of inoculating and ingrafting. In short, she is a complete *husbandwoman*; and she has, besides, acquired a vast stock of general knowledge, while her judgment has attained such a degree of maturity, as to justify the confidence of the villagers, who are accustomed to consult her on every perplexing emergency.

In the constant use of exercise, she is not corpulent; and she is extremely active, and wonderfully athletic. Instances, almost incredible, are produced of her strength. Indeed, it is not surprising that she is the idol and standing theme of the village, since, with all her uncommon qualifications, she combines a tenderness of disposition not to be exceeded. Her extensive acquaintance with herbs, contributes to render her a skilful and truly valuable nurse; and the world never produced a more affectionate, attentive, or faithful woman: Yet, while she feelingly sympathizes with every invalid, she is not herself subject to imaginary complaints; nor does she easily yield to real illness. . . .

Although far advanced in years, without a matrimonial connexion, yet, constantly engaged in useful and interesting pursuits, she manifests not that peevishness and discontent, so frequently attendant on *old maids*; she realizes all that independence which is proper to humanity; and she knows how to set a just value on the blessings she enjoys.

From my treasury of facts, I produce a second instance, equally in point. I have seen letters, written by a lady, an inhabitant of St. Sebastian, (a Spanish emporium) that breathed the true spirit of commerce, and evinced the writer to possess all the integrity, punctuality and dispatch, which are such capital requisites in the mercantile career. This lady is at the head of a firm, of which herself and daughters make up the individuals—Her name is *Birmingham*. She is, I imagine, well known to the commercial part of the United States. She was left a widow in the infancy of her children, who were numerous; and she immediately adopted the most vigorous measures for their emolument. Being a woman of a magnanimous mind, she devoted her sons to the profession of arms; and they were expeditiously disposed of, in a way the best calculated to bring them acquainted with the art of war. Her daughters were educated for business; and, arriving at womanhood, they have long since established themselves into a capital trading-house, of which, as has been observed, their respectable mother is the head. She is, in the hours of business, invariably to be found in her compting-house; there she takes her morning repast; her daughters act as clerks, (and they are adepts in their office) regularly preparing the papers and letters, which pass in order under her inspection. She signs herself, in all accounts and letters, *Widow Birmingham*; and this is the address by which she is designated. I have conversed with one of our captains, who has often negociated with her the disposal of large and valuable cargoes. Her consignments, I am told, are to a great amount; and one of the principal merchants in the town of Boston asserts, that he receives from no house in Europe more satisfactory returns. Upright in their dealings, and unwearied in their application, these ladies possess a right to prosperity; and we trust that their circumstances are as easy, as their conduct is meritorious. . . .

Drama

Judith Sargent Murray (1751–1820)

Although Judith Sargent Murray is best known for her feminist essay "On the Equality of the Sexes" (*q.v.*), she was a political theorist and philosopher whose interests ranged from economic issues to models of industriousness, modes of philanthropy, and reflections on both religion and "Heathen mythology." Equally diverse in her attention to literary styles and genres, Sargent Murray wrote several essays on the emergence of *American* literature. One of her most significant articles was "Panagyric on the Drama," in which she details the rise of American drama and, with satiric flourish, defends not only the writing of dramas but public performances as being appropriate to the times: a new age demands new modes of literary representation just as it demands new laws. Sargent Murray wrote several works of drama, including *The Medium; or, Virtue Triumphant* (1795) and *The Traveller Returned* (1796),[1] but her most significant contributions to American drama may be her early critical assessments of the emerging genre. As in all of Sargent Murray's writings, her specific interest is in women's attitudes toward and contributions to the arts. Thus she extends her study of American drama in a later essay, "Observations of the Tragedies of Mrs. Warren"; this essay constitutes an early example of literary criticism by a woman, and it reflects Sargent Murray's concern that women's contributions to literature not be lost to future generations.

Works: The Gleaner: A Miscellaneous Production. 3 Vols. Boston: Thomas & Andrews, 1798, rpt., ed., Nina Baym; Harris, ed., *Selected Writings of Judith Sargent Murray.*

---

1. Complete texts of Sargent Murray's two plays are included in *The Gleaner* (1798) and the complete text of *The Traveller Returned* is in *Selected Writings of Judith Sargent Murray,* ed. Harris.

No. XXIV. Panegyric on the Drama . . .

Leaning on morals when the Drama moves,
Friendly to virtue when the vision proves—
Lessons adopting form'd to mend the heart,
Truths meliorated, potent to impart;
Her splendid fictions wisdom will embrace,
And all her scenic paths enraptur'd trace.

The various parterres, now putting forth their promising buds, in many sections, in this our country, looks with a very favourable aspect upon a man of my profession;[2] and I cannot but hope, that in the occupation of a Gleaner, I shall be able to cull many a fragrant flower, wherewith to compose a bouquet, that may throw an agreeable perfume over the leisure hours of the sentimental speculator.

To *express myself less technically.* The progress of the Drama, in this new world, must assuredly interest the feelings of every observer; and, being under the pleasing necessity, in the routine of my excursions, of visiting many parts of the United States, and thus, having frequent opportunities of presenting myself in our several theatres, from the elegant house in Philadelphia to the temporary resorts of itinerant companies, in those little towns, which will invariably copy the examples they receive from the metropolis, I naturally, in the course of my perambulations, pick up many observations, that may possibly serve for the amusement of my readers.

The great question which does, and *ought* to occupy the mind of every patriotic moralist, is the *utility* of licensed stage-playing. Perhaps I may as well withdraw the word *licensed;* for, in the present enlightened era and administration of liberty, the citizen would hardly consent to an abridgment of those amusements, the evil tendency of which could not be unequivocally demonstrated to his understanding; and the late struggle in the State of Massachusetts, evinces the futility of erecting barriers, not substantiated by reason.

The law in that State was outrage in its very face: the flimsy subterfuge of *moral lectures* deceived no one;[3] and though, as I am informed, the theatrical prohibition is but *partially repealed respecting the Bostonians, and remains in full force upon the rest of the State,* yet is it notorious, that itinerant players are constantly marching and counter-marching from town to town, to the no small diversion of the good people of this very respectable member of the Union. But, without presuming to intermeddle with the policy of the legislature, my design is, to hazard a few remarks upon the subject in general.

As I abhor the domination of prejudice, and, upon the strongest conviction, regard it as a tyrant, that if once brought to the guillotine, would (*provided it*

2. Sargent Murray used a male persona as author of *The Gleaner.* The last essay in Volume 3 teasingly asserts to "unmask" the author, but fails to do so. At the same time that she employs the freedom inherent in the use of a male persona, she also satirizes the language and attitudes of the dominant culture. Her pseudonym "Constantia" was on the title page.

3. To evade the restrictive laws against theatrical productions, some companies had advertised themselves as presenting "moral lectures."

is not of the Hydra kind) leave an opening for the introduction of an era far more friendly to the progress of *genuine* and *corrected* liberty, than the murder of all the *humane, virtuous,* and *religious princes in the universe*; so I most sincerely deprecate its despotism; and whenever I seat myself, with the pen of inquiry, I am solicitous to raise a rebellion against encroachments, that, however sanctioned by time, cannot, in my opinion, be considered in a court of equity, as legal or natural. The objections to theatrical amusements are many and plausible. I pretend not to decide for others; I would only investigate.

If I mistake not—*Waste of time—Imprudent expenditures—Encouragement of idleness*—and, *Relaxation of morals*, stand foremost in the catalogue of objections.

Prodigality of time, is indeed an irremediable evil; and if it can be proved, that an hour devoted to the theatre would certainly have been appropriated to any beneficial employment, for which no moment of leisure will in future present, I, for one, shall be impelled to allow the validity of the allegation; and, I do hereby invest such plea with full authority to detain every such person from all dramatical representations whatever: But, with the same breath I contend, that those evenings which are immolated at the shrine of Bacchus, which are loitered in a tavern, in unnecessary gossiping, cards, scandal, and the numerous vagaries of fashion, will be *comparatively redeemed*, if marked by an entertainment so incontrovertibly rational.

The complaint of exorbitant expenditures, is of a similar description. A friend of mine, who resided for some time abroad, once informed me, that he had frequently been stopped, when in full career to the play-house, by a consideration that the indulgence he was about to procure himself, would supply some tearful sufferer with bread, for at least one whole week. Now, all such persons, provided they can make it appear, they are not in the use of any *as expensive and more superfluous gratification*, shall be released, upon their parole given, that they will absolutely and *bona fide* employ their six shillings to the aforesaid purpose.

To the third objection I cannot allow the smallest weight: *Who, I would ask, are the Idlers?* Perhaps there is no mode of life which requires more assiduous and laborious application, than that of a *good* and *consistent* actor. School exercises are certainly not the most *pleasurable* employments of adolescence; and every adult can tell, how much more easy he could imprint the memory of his early years, than that retention which is the accompaniment of his matured life. But the *ambitious* and *principled* actor hath past the age of flexibility, and still his days are, almost unceasingly, devoted to study: By frequent repetitions, such is the constitution of the mind, the finest sentiments too often pall; and the will informed, ingenious and meritorious performer is in danger of losing his taste for the highest mental enjoyments; while the entertainment which he produces for others, is the result of unremitted and painful labour to himself.

Why then, permit me to ask, if he is solicitous to blend, with our amusements, the highest possible improvement; if his manners and his morals are unblemished; and if, by becoming stationary, he in effect takes rank with our citizens—why, I ask, is he *so lightly esteemed?* Surely, if, under the influence of reason, of gratitude and impartiality, I must unhesitatingly acknowledge, persons ardently engaged in procuring for us a *rational entertainment*, are entitled to a *degree of genuine respect*, to encouragement, and even to patronage.

It is asserted, and the assertion does not appear unfounded, that a *virtuous theatre* is highly influential in regulating opinions, manners, and morals of the populace.

Here we are naturally led to the fourth and last division of our subject.

Relaxation of morals.—And I ask, Doth not a *virtuous theatre* exemplify the lessons which the ethic preacher labours to inculcate? I take it for granted, that none but a *virtuous and well regulated theatre* will be tolerated. In the southern and middle States, Philadelphia particularly, no performance can make its appearance upon the stage, without passing under the previous examination of the governor and two other respectable magistrates, who, by their avowed approbation, become responsible to the public for the merit of the piece. Similar restrictions will, perhaps, be adopted, wherever the Drama shall progress; and my confidence in the trustees of the Boston Theatre, represents to my view every apprehension, not only as superfluous, but absolutely injurious.

. . . If it may be presumed, that the stated objections, thus considered, are obviated, I conceive it will not be denied that, from a *chaste and discreetly regulated* theatre, many attendant advantages will indisputably result. Young persons will acquire a refinement of taste and manners; they will learn to think, speak, and act, with propriety; a thirst for knowledge will be originated; and from attentions, at first, perhaps, constituting only the amusement of the hour, they will gradually proceed to more important inquiries.

Clarinda Meanwell, the daughter of a gentleman whom I highly respect, whose education hath been upon the very best plan, continued nevertheless, for the first twenty-five years of her life, without manifesting the smallest literary curiosity. It was impossible to interest her, even in the pages of a novel; and whatever she learned, was more the result of a disposition naturally conceding; the night of exhibition was announced, *every body*, as they phrased it was going; but Miss Clarinda could not be animated to a wish for the entertainment; her accustomed complacency of disposition yielded her, however, the companion of her associates; the piece was interesting; it forcibly seized her faculties; it possessed, to *her*, in every sense, the charms of novelty; for the world she would not be absent upon any future occasion. In the course of the day preceding a theatrical entertainment, that she might the better comprehend the several parts, the play-book was in her hand, a laudable spirit of inquiry obtained in her bosom, and with amazing rapidity she ran through, and compassed the sense of every volume within her reach. History, geography, astronomy—in all these, her proficiency is prodigious; and, in one word, I hardly know a better informed, or more amiable young woman in the circle of my acquaintance. But Clarinda Meanwell is not a solitary instance; and as I have very frequently observed the good effects of dramatical presentations, I trust that my readers are enough acquainted with a heart, the feelings of which I have, upon various occasions, essayed to sketch, to give me full *credit*, for that throb of deep-felt complacency, which I experienced upon receiving information of the elegant and superb theatre, which hath so recently been erected for the reception of the Drama, in the State of Massachusetts. . . .

No. XCVI. ". . . Observations on the tragedies of Mrs. Warren"[4]

Were I at liberty my plans to choose,
My politics, my fashions, and my muse
Should be American—Columbia's fame
Hath to Columbia's meed a righteous claim;
Her laws, her magistrates I would revere,
Holding this younger world supremely dear.

Hardly a day passes that does not furnish some new instance of the paucity of national attachment in our country. We regret much the frequent occasions which impel us to reiterate expressions of concern, on account of an evil so truly alarming. The real patriot must necessarily lament the present aspect of affairs. French men and measures—English men and measures. These do in fact divide the majority of the people; while those who rally round the standard of America are reduced to a very inconsiderable party.

We are far removed from the elder world; the wide Atlantic is our barrier. Persons of information affirm, that we possess within ourselves the sources of independence; and it is certainly true, that the interior of our country, reduced to a state of cultivation, would become amply productive, largely supplying every *essential article of life*. Necessity is pronounced the mother of invention—Improvement follows; and these elegancies, or superfluities, to which we are attached, would, by a natural process, become the growth of America. Why then do we not *radically throw off every foreign yoke*—asset ourselves, and no longer delay to fill our ranks as free, sovereign, and independent States?

While I am writing, a circle of ladies in the next room are discussing this very subject, and a respectable female, in an elevated tone of voice, declares, she had rather take the fashion of her garments from an American presidentress, than from any princess in Europe. We wish this idea was adopted, from the State of New-Hampshire, to those far distant and extensive banks, whose verdant borders are washed by the waters of the Ohio; and that American habiliments, politics, and sentiments of every description, might hence forward receive an American stamp.

Perhaps our deficiency in national partiality is in nothing more apparent than in the little taste we discover for American literature. Indigenous productions are received with cold neglect, if not contempt, or they are condemned to an ordeal, the severity of which is sufficient to terrify the most daring adventurer. Mortifying indifference, or invidious criticism—these, in

---

4. Mercy Otis Warren, dramatist, poet, and historian (*q.v.*).

their respective operations, chill the opening bud, or blast its expansive leaves, and the apathy with which we regard the toils of intellect, is truly astonishing. An original genius hath produced a sentiment of the following nature: *If the first rate abilities, cloathed in the habiliments of morality, were passing through the streets of our metropolis, they would be elbowed by the crowd, knocked down by a truckman, or rode over by a hackney coach.* And we add—better so, than if they were consigned to the lingering tortures of the rack, or condemned to suffer death under the axe of a mangling and barbarous executioner.

We do not say that the office of a *candid critic* is not beneficial, and even *essential:* But when an author, or his productions, are to be dissected, in the name of every principle of humanity let a *man of feeling preside*—let the operation be conducted by an artist, who, possessing the abilities to discriminate, will be governed by the admonitions of decency. An informed, judicious, and well disposed critic, will not wholly reject the influence of sympathy; and his feelings will induce him, when calling into view a glaring absurdity, to produce, if possible, some pleasing selection, which may soothe the bosom he is thus necessitated to lacerate. When a work is to be analyzed, if the plot is deficient in conception, and in adjustment—if the ideas are extravagant, the events tragical, and the catastrophe improbable—the critic, if he is not a *usurper*, if he is legally invested with the robes of office, will, however, find something to admire in the style; and if it abounds with just sentiments, and classical allusions, he will produce them, not only with marks of decided approbation, but with triumph.

The stage is undoubtedly a very powerful engine in forming the opinions and manners of a people. Is it not then of importance to supply the American stage with American scenes? I am aware that very few productions in this line have appeared, and I think the reason is obvious. Writers, especially dramatic writers, are not properly encouraged. Applause, that powerful spring of action, (if we except the ebullitions of the moment) is withheld, or sparingly administered. No incentives are furnished, and indignant genius, conscious of its own resources, retires to the intellectual banquet, disdaining to spread the feast for malevolence and ingratitude.

If productions, *confessedly indifferent*, were from the ascendency of local preferences, *endured in their turn, and received with manifest partiality*, it would, perhaps, stimulate to more polished efforts, and the Columbian Drama might at length boast the most finished productions. But so far are we from evincing this predilection that even performances, decidedly meritorious, are almost forgotten. Tyler's[5] plays are strangely neglected; and the finished scenes of the correct and elegant Mrs. Warren, have never yet passed in review before an American audience. Was the American taste decidedly in favour of native worth, the superintendants of the Drama would find it for their interest to cherish indigenous abilities, and the influence of patronage would invigorate and rear to maturity the now drooping plant.

5. Royall Tyler (1757–1826), best known today for his comedy *The Contrast* (1787).

To the celebrity of Mrs. Warren, it is beyond the power of the Gleaner to add: Yet, accustoming himself to join issue with those who yield the palm to genius, he is constrained to say, that her excellent tragedies abound with the pathetic, the beautiful, and the sublime, and that they apparently possess sufficient scenic merit and variety of situation to bestow those *artificial advantages* which are necessary to insure their *stage effect*. Camps, palaces, cities— a view of the orb of day, just emerging from the shades of night—assembled senators—citizens passing up and down—a procession of priests, senators, and nobles, addressing, in the attitude of supplication, a Vandal tyrant— gardens, grottos—a wilderness, an alcove—shouts of victory—a prison, a battle—repeated acts of suicide. A succession of these objects, would, it is presumed, completely gratify the wishes, even of the most visionary audience; and we should assuredly attend with heightened and inexpressible pleasure to that energetic, beautiful, and soul affecting actress, Mrs. S. Powell, while in the characters of Edoxia, or Eudocia in the Sack of Rome, and of Donna Louisa in the Ladies of Castile,[6] she delivered sentiments truly interesting, highly wrought, and tenderly pathetic: We have often in imagination listened to the language of Louisa, from our favourite performer, and most admirably has she pointed every sentence.

We conceive that Mrs. Warren, while delineating Donna Maria, traced in her own strong and luminous intellect the animated original which she presented; and, making up a judgment from information, which we presume accurate, we have not hesitated to pronounce our celebrated countrywoman the *Roland* of America.[7] The address of Donna Maria to Louisa, in page 119, is truly beautiful.[8] The character of Gaudentius in the Sack of Rome is finely conceived, strongly interesting, and well supported; his reflections on discovering his murdered father, are natural and highly finished; and it is impossible to read without a degree of pensive solemnity his soliloquy in the grotto. Maximus mourning his Aredelia dead, must command the sympathetic gush; and while the story of the empress is replete with instruction, her accumulated woes pierce the bosom of sensibility. Don Juan, in the Ladies of Castile, exhibits virtues which announce him the kindred spirit of his Maria; and his native independence, his valour and his magnanimity are uniformly exemplified. The virtues of Condes Haro we spontaneously revere; and we listen, with peculiar satisfaction, to sentiments resulting from benevolence and a just idea of the rights of man, as they are delivered by the adverse chief, while the woes of Don Francis and Donna Louisa excite our tenderest feelings.

Contemplating these specimens of our drama, confessedly excellent, a very natural inference presents—If compositions of this description find no place

6. *The Sack of Rome* and *The Ladies of Castile* (q.v.) are plays by Otis Warren. "Louisa" and "Donna Maria" are characters in *Castile*.

7. Roland, one of Charlemagne's commanders, was the hero of the French medieval *Song of Roland* (11th–12th century).

8. Sargent Murray's pagination refers to Warren's *Poems, Dramatics and Miscellaneous* (1790), which included *Ladies of Castile*. The passage Sargent Murray refers to is Maria's speech in which she asserts, "I ne'er will yield, / Nor own myself a slave."

on the American stage, what can the more humble adventurer expect? Are not the present arrangements highly impolitic? Is it not probable that talents, now dormant, might by proper encouragement be called into action? Is it not possible that paths, yet untrodden in the regions of nature and of fancy, remain to be explored? and that under the fostering smiles of a liberal and enlightened public, Columbian Shakespeares may yet elevate and adorn humanity? . . .

Mercy Otis Warren (1728–1814)

Born on September 25, 1728, Mercy Otis was the third of thirteen children born to Mary Allyne and James Otis of Barnstable, Massachusetts. Mercy's intelligence and independence were encouraged by her politically active family, and she was educated in the same manner as her brothers—by her uncle, the Reverend Jonathan Russell. Her literary skills were deeply influenced by Russell's sermons, but there is also evidence of a keen knowledge of Dryden, Pope, Shakespeare, Milton, and Molière. Her political allegiance was formulated from an adherence to John Locke's philosophy as presented in his *Essay on Government*. In 1754 Mercy married James Warren; their marriage was apparently an especially loving and intellectually stimulating relationship. Although Otis Warren gave birth to five sons in the early years of her marriage, she also began to develop her poetic skills during this period.

In the 1770s, as war with Britain became imminent, Otis Warren joined her husband and her brother James in political activism. Her dramas were political satires intended to belittle the British position and inflame the Patriot spirit for the American cause. She later used the pen name of "A Columbian Patriot" to oppose the Federalists' position on the American Constitution, an attitude that is also evident in her dramatic work; she argued for the necessity of "a union of the states on the free principles of the late Confederation." By the time of her death, on October 19, 1814, at Plymouth, Massachusetts, Mercy Otis Warren had attained a national reputation for her literary and political achievements.

Works: *The Adulateur: A Tragedy* (1772); *The Defeat: A Play* (1773); *The Group: A Farce* (1775); *The Motley Assembly* (1779); *Observations on the New Constitution, and on the Federal Conventions* (1788); *Poems, Dramatic, and Miscellaneous* (1790). Bibliography: Anthony; Baym, "Mercy Otis Warren's Gendered Melodrama of Revolution"; Earle, *Colonial Dames*; Franklin V; Kerber; Kern; Oreovicz, "Heroic Drama for a Uncertain Age"; Walker and Dresner.

From *The Group*

Act I. Scene I.

Scene, a little dark parlour, guards standing at the door.
[Lord Chief Justice] Hazelrod, Crusty Crowbar, Simple-Sapling, [Brigadier]
   Hateall, and Hector Mushroom.[1]

SIMPLE.

I know not what to think of these sad times,
The people arm'd—and all resolv'd to die
E're they'll submit.—

CRUSTY CROWBAR.

I too am almost sick of the parade
Of honours purchas'd at the price of peace.

SIMPLE.

Fond as I am of greatness and her charms
Elate with prospects of my rising name,
Push'd into place, a place I ne'er expected,
My bounding heart leapt in my feeble breast
And extasies entranc'd my slender brain.—
But yet, e're this I hop'd more solid gains,
As my low purse demands a quick supply.—
Poor Sylvia weeps,—and urges my return
To rural peace and humble happiness,
As my ambition beggars all her babes.

CRUSTY.

When first I listed in the desp'rate cause,
And blindly swore obedience to his will,
So wise, so just, so good I thought Rapatio,
That if salvation rested on his word
I'd pin my faith and risk my hopes thereon.

HAZLEROD.

And why not now?—What staggers thy belief?

CRUSTY.

Himself—his perfidy appears—
It is too plain he has betray'd his country.
And we're the wretched tools by him mark'd out
To seal its ruins—tear up the ancient forms,
And every vestige treacherously destroy,
Nor leave a trait of freedom in the land.
Nor did I think hard fate wou'd call me up

---

1. Below the "Dramatis Personae," Otis Warren has indicated that the group is "Attended by a swarm of court sycophants, hungry harpies, and unprincipled danglers, collected from the neighbouring villages, hovering over the stage in the shape of locusts, led by Massachusettensis in the form of a basilisk; the rear brought up by proteus, bearing a torch in one hand, and a powder-flask in the other: The whole is supported by a mighty army and navy, from blunder-land, for the laudible purpose of enslaving its best friends."

From drudging o'er my acres,—
Treading the glade, and sweating at the plough,
To dangle at the tables of the great;
At bowls and cards, to spend my frozen years;
To fell my friends, my country, and my conscience;
Prophane the sacred sabbaths of my God;
Scorn'd by the very men who want my aid
To spread distress o'er this devoted people.

HAZLEROD.

Pho—what misgivings—why these idle qualms
This shrinking backwards at the bugbear conscience?
In early life I heard the phantom nam'd.
And the grave sages prate of moral sense
Presiding in the bosom of the just;
Or panting thongs about the guilty heart.
Bound by these shackles, long my lab'ring mind
Obscurely trod the lower walks of life,
In hopes by honesty my bread to gain;
But neither commerce, or my conjuring rods,
Nor yet mechanics, nor new fangled drills,
Or all the Iron-mongers curious arts,
Gave me a competence of shining ore,
Or gratify'd my itching palm for more;
Till I dismiss'd the bold intruding guest,
And banish'd conscience from my wounded breast.

CRUSTY.

Happy expedient!—Could I gain the art,
Then balmy sleep might sooth my waking lids.
And rest once more refresh my weary soul.— . . .

Act II. Scene III. . . .

[JUDGE] MEAGRE.[2]

Let not thy soft temidity of heart
Urge thee to terms, till the last stake is thrown.
Tis not my temper ever to forgive
When once resentment's kindled in my breast.
I hated Brutus for his noble stand
Against the oppressors of his injur'd country.
I hate the leaders of these restless factions,
For all their gen'rous efforts to be free.
I curse the senate which defeats our bribes,
Who Hazlerod impeach'd for the same crime.
I hate the people, who, no longer gull'd,

---

2. The Judge is addressing Secretary Dupe.

See through the schemes of our aspiring clan,
And from the rancour of my venom'd mind,
I look askance on all the human race,
And if they'r not to be appall'd by fear,
I wish the earth might drink that vital stream
That warms the heart, and feeds the manly glow,
The love inherent, planted in the breast,
To equal liberty, confer'd on man,
By him who form'd the peasant and the King!
   Could we erase these notions from their minds,
Then (paramount to these ideal whims,
Utopian dreams, of patriotic virtue,
Which long has danc'd in their distemper'd brains[)]
   We'd smoothly glide on midst a race of slaves,
Nor heave one sigh tho' all the human race
Were plung'd in darkness, slavery and vice.
If we could keep our foot-hold in the stirrup,
And, like the noble Claudia of old,
Ride o'er the people, if they don't give way;
Or wish their fates were all involv'd in one;
For Iv'e a *Brother*, as the roman dame,
Who would strike off the rebel neck at once.
        SECRETARY.
   No all is o'er unless the sword decides,
Which cuts down Kings, and kingdoms oft divides.
By that appeal I think we can't prevail,
Their valour's great, and justice holds the scale.
They fight for freedom, while we stab the breast
Of every man, who is her friend profest.
They fight in virtue's ever sacred cause,
While we tread on divine and human laws.
Glory and victory, and lasting fame,
Will crown their arms and bless each Hero's name!
        MEAGRE.
   Away with all thy foolish, trifling cares,
And to the winds give all thy empty fears;
Let us repair and urge brave Sylla on,
I long to see the sweet revenge begun.
As fortune is a fickle, sportive dame,
She may for us the victory proclaim,
And with success our busy ploddings crown,
Though injured justice storm and solemn frown.
   Then they shall smart for ev'ry bold offence,
Estates confiscated will pay th' expense;
On their lost fortunes we a while will plume
And strive to think there is no after doom.   *Ex. Om——;*
   As they pass off the stage the curtain draws up, and discovers to the audience

*a Lady nearly connected with one of the principal actors in the group, reclined in
an adjoining alcove, who in mournful accents accosts them—thus—*

What painful scenes are hov'ring o'er the morn,
When spring again invigorates the lawn!
Instead of the gay landscape's beautious dies,
Must the stain'd field salute our weeping eyes,
Must the green turf, and all the mournful glades,
Drench'd in the stream, absorb their dewy heads,
Whilst the tall oak, and quiv'ring willow bends
To make a covert for their country's friends,
Deny'd a grave!—amid the hurrying scene
Of routed armies scouring o'er the plain.

Till British troops shall to Columbia yield,
And freedom's sons are Masters of the field;
Then o'er the purpl'd plain the victors tread
Among the slain to seek each patriot dead,
(While Freedom weeps that merit could not save
But conq'ring Hero's must enrich the Grave)
An adamantine monument they rear
With this inscription—*Virtue's sons lie here!*

F I N I S.

From *The Ladies of Castile: A Tragedy*[3]

Act II. Scene I: An Alcove in an artificial Wilderness.

DONNA LOUISA, sola.
The burnish'd hills o'erlook the verdant dales,
And nature's deck'd in all her bright array.
The whispering breeze plays o'er the dappled mead,
And fans the foliage on the flowery bank:—
The towering wood lark trills her tender note,
And soft responsive music cheers the lawn;
Yet here I wander wilder'd and alone,
Like some poor banish'd fugitive who seeks
The meagre comfort of a moss grown cave.
              Enter DONNA MARIA.
        MARIA.
Awake fond maid—nor thus supinely waste
Thy youth—thy bloom. Thy matchless beauty fades
Mid'st sorrow, sighs, and unavailing tears.

3. Otis Warren had focused her dramatic writings in the mode of satire, but at the request of a
friend, she wrote this tragedy, which he had designated should not have an American setting. Thus
Otis Warren decided "to [recur] to an ancient story in the annals of Spain, in her last struggles for
liberty, previous to the complete establishment of despotism by the family of Ferdinand." The tragedy
was written in 1784 and published in *Poems, Dramatic and Miscellaneous* (1790).

LOUISA.

Thought feeds my woes, nor can my reason aid
To calm the passions of my grief torn breast,
'Till concord weaves again her palmy wreath,
To deck the face of this distracted land.

MARIA.

Though weak compassion sinks the female mind,
And our frail sex dissolve in pity's tears;
Yet justice' sword can never be resheath'd,
'Till Charles is taught to know we will be free;
And learns the duty that a monarch owes,
To heaven—the people—and the rights of man.

Let him restore the liberties of Spain—
Dismiss the robbers that arrest his ear—
Those pension'd plunderers that rudely seize
What nature gave, and what our fathers won.

LOUISA.

I retrospect, and weep Spain's happier days—
Survey the pleasures once we call'd our own,
When harmony display'd her gentle wand,
And every peasant smil'd beneath his vine—
'Till nature sickens at the sad reverse,
And my swoln bosom heaves with smother'd sighs,
Too big to be repress'd.—I yield to grief
'Till floods of tears relieve my tortur'd soul.

MARIA.

Maria has a bolder part to act—
I scorn to live upon ignoble terms—
A supple courtier fawning at the feet
Of proud despotic nobles, or of kings.

LOUISA.

Had I thy firmness, yet my heart would bleed
To see my country torn by civil feuds.
Each hero hurls a javelin at the breast
His heart reveres, and friendship's soul recoils
When the bold veteran urges home the blow,
To pierce the man he venerates and loves;
While the brave patriot parries back the shaft
Against a life that virtue's self would save.

MARIA.

This sad necessity—this painful strife,
Should reunite the citizens of Spain;
And rouse each languid arm with tenfold zeal
To point the thunder at a tyrant's head,
Ere yet the lingering mind indignant sinks,
Debas'd and trembling at a despot's frown.

Rather let cities that support his reign,

Like Torbolatan yesterday reduc'd,
Be storm'd and sack'd before tomorrow's dawn;
And thus be taught the weakness of the mind
That dare a moment balance in the scale,
A crown for kings—with liberty to man.

LOUISA.

But ah, Maria!—this little self obtrudes;
I cannot boast disinterested grief;
Louisa's tears can never cease to flow.
If brave Don Juan wins a glorious day,
My father—friends—and family are lost;
If victory for loyalty declares—
Or if Don Francis—noble Francis, falls—
Is there a name from Castile to the Rhone,
So wretched as thy friend—thy lov'd Louisa!

MARIA.

Thou should'st have liv'd in mild and gentler times,
And breath'd, and slumber'd in the lap of peace,
As innocent and soft as infant love,
When lull'd to rest by a fond mother's song:
The smiling babe, wak'd by the wind's rude breath,
The pearly dew drop trickles from its eye,
'Till sooth'd to quiet by its favourite toy;
But for myself—though famine, chains, and death
Should all combine—nay, should Don Juan fall—
Which Heav'n forbid—I ne'er will yield,
Nor own myself a slave. . . .

Margaretta Van Wyck Bleecker Faugères (1771–1801)

Born October 11, 1771, in Tomhanick, New York, Margaretta Van Wyck Bleecker was the daughter of the poet Ann Eliza Schuyler (*q.v.*) and John Bleecker. Rather than continuing in the aristocratic and intellectual traditions of her parents, however, Bleecker advocated Jacobin tenets, and she chose to marry on Bastille Day in 1792; her husband was a French physician, Peter Faugères. Margaretta was instrumental in preserving her mother's works, collecting and publishing them with a memoir of her mother in 1793 that also included some of Bleecker Faugères's own writings.

Bleecker Faugères turned in 1795 to drama as a new literary field of exploration. Publishing *Belisarius: A Tragedy* by subscription that year, she incorporated her admiration for the French and American struggles for freedom in her representative man, Belisarius, who, as L. W. Koengeter has noted, "is the just man caught between corrupt courtiers on the one hand, and heartless cruel revolutionists on the other. Belisarius represents uncompromising human values" (Faust I:207). Like many political plays of the era, however, the setting is ancient Rome during the reign of Justinian and Theodora.

Bleecker Faugères's career was hindered by her abusive marriage, which, when it ended in 1796, left her and her young daughter in near poverty. To survive, she turned to teaching at several schools in the New England region. Her demise rapidly followed, and her history becomes a tragic echo of her mother's depression and early death. Bleecker Faugères's death at age twenty-nine represents a significant loss to intellectual life in early America.

Works: *The Posthumous Works of Ann Eliza Bleecker . . . To Which is Added, a Collection of Essays, Prose and Poetical, by Margaretta V. Faugères* (1793); *Belisarius: A Tragedy* (1795). Bibliography: Griswold.

Belisarius: A Tragedy

Act III, Scene I

SCENE—*The Tent of the Prince of Bulgaria*

. . .[1]

BELISARIUS. Yes, when the battle burns, and *maniac Rage*
Bites the hot earth, and like a *daemon* roars,
While clouds of dust inshrou'd his [the warrior's] starting eyes,
And streams of blood spout from his mangled limbs,
Oh! then, amid the horror, sonorous notes,
Peal'd from an hundred brazen mouths at once,
Drown the deep groans of those who dying fall,
And bear their cries, on Clamour's wings, to heaven:
But music, such as lulls *my* wayward cares,
Is often heard within the peasant's hamlet,
What time grey Twilight veils the eastern sky,
When the blight[2] maiden carols rustic songs
To soothe the infirmities of peevish Age,
Or (when the moon shines on the dew-gem'd plain)
Attunes her voice to chant some lightsome air
For those who dance upon the tufted green.

1. Though Belisarius is blind and aged, the Prince of Bulgaria attempts to recruit him once again in battle against the Byzantines by reminding Belisarius of his past glories and "the thoughts that warm the warrior's bosom." Belisarius's reply follows.
2. The 1795 edition has "blight"; Griswold suggests "blithe" is the intended word.

Such are the strains I love, and such as float
On the cool gale from a far mountain's side,
Where some lone *shepherd* fills his simple pipe,
Calling the *echoes* from their dewy beds,
To chase mute sleep away. Ah! bless'd is he
If his choice melody be ne'er disturb'd
By the death-breathing trumpet's woeful tone.
    PRINCE. If thou wert ever thus averse to war,
General, why did'st thou fight?
    BELISARIUS. To purchase *peace*, not to extend dominion.
Peace was the crown of *conquest*. He who fought
And screen'd his country from the invading foe,
Returning, sheath'd his sword, and reap'd his grain,
Eating his fruits in safety and content;
Nor wip'd his shield, nor burnished his spear,
Till outrage call'd him to the field again—
Such is the triumph of humanity!

Act III, Scene II

SCENE—*The Palace Hall of Justinian.*
Enter Theodora
    THEODORA. Things go on well; my ancient prying foe[3]
Is now dismist, with all his cares of state,
And now may ruminate in solitude
How oft he thwarted me in my designs,
While he his own accomplished. Had he done
As other courtiers, *honour'd* and *obey'd*,
He had been *General* still, but he was proud,
And still oppos'd, or slighted my bequests,
Till he work'd up my anger to a storm,
And fram'd his own destruction.
And yet, methinks I do not feel reveng'd,
While he in haughty stubbornness of soul
Looks on his punishment with cool contempt,
Or rather, an *indifference* that shocks me.
Can I believe, that, stript of courtly honours,
Blinded, and sunk in abject poverty,
Cast in a dungeon, cumbered there with fetters,
He should be happy still? It cannot be;
'Till all hypocrisy——a base invention;
The last resource of mortified *ambition*,
That still would lift itself above the crowd
For the fool world to gaze at.

---

3. That is, Belisarius.

Enter Barsames[4]

What news Barsames?

BARS. None, Madam, save that JULIA is return'd
From the Bulgarian court.

THEO. What says she of her hero?[5]

BARS. Storms and rages—sometimes she sits and weeps,
Calls herself *fool*, and says she will forget him;
Then, starting in the wildness of despair,
Tears off her locks and casts them to the winds;
And in the horrid phrenzy of her soul,
With broken speech, utters such imprecations
As makes one's blood grow chilly.

THEO. Whom does she curse?

BARS. Dreadful to tell, your majesty and the EMPEROR.

THEO. Base, vile, rebellious wretch! are these the thanks
For all my sisterly attentions to her?
Did I not take her from obscurity,
A poor illiterate orphan, train her up
As an own child, and loaded her with honours?
And yet, because I sent her from BYZANTIUM,
To shield her from the ruin I saw would fall
And crush the traitor, now she curses me.
Were it not for TIBERIAS, her brother,[6]
This night my dungeon's heaviest iron doors
Should close on her forever.   (*Makes a long pause.*)
Barsames, have you seen the cells to-day?

BARS. I have, and saw the stubborn EUCHUS die.

THEO. Ha! Made he no confession?

BARS. None, for soon as they brought him to the torture,
He call'd on HEAVEN, and swore an awful oath,
That neither scourge, nor fiercest fires, nor racks,
Should e'er compel him to disturb the silence
That then should seal his lips.
They tortur'd him, and though his pangs were keen,
His heart disdain'd to utter even a groan:
But as his life began to lose its hold,
Sinking upon the *skeleton* of his father,
He kiss'd the bones, and laying his scorch'd hand
Upon his shrivelled mouth, look'd up, and died.

THEO. Then have I lost all hopes of a discovery.
Oh! this conspiracy, how it gnaws my bosom!
Euchus I stole from out a dismal prison;

---

4. Barsames is High Treasurer and a favorite of the Empress.
5. Julia was in love with Belisarius.
6. Tiberias is Julia's brother and the Emperor's nephew.

I singled him from all the rest, and life,
With riches, honours, and my choicest gifts,
I proffered him, but proffer'd all in vain.
    BARS. Are they all dead?
    THEO. None of the band remain save the vile head,
And he perhaps secure drinks of my cup,
And saunters unmolested in my chamber.
Did you see Phaedrus?
    BARS. Yes; but he did not know me:
He sat upon a heap of mouldering bones,
With his shrunk hands, thus, folded on his breast,
And his sunk eyes were fix'd upon the ground
Half shut, and o'er his bosom stream'd his beard,
Hoary and long. I twice accosted him
Ere he regarded me; then looking up,
He eyed me with a vague and senseless gaze,
And heaving a most lamentable sigh,
Drop'd his pale face upon his breast again.
    THEO. I'll go myself this moment and give orders
For his removal to some cheerful place,
Where kind attendance, and my best physician,
May woo his scattered senses back again;
For *thus insane* he loses sense of woe.
This MANIA is a *balm*, a sovereign *cure*
For all the ills that fetter in the heart;
It sets the warring passions all asleep,
Blotting out good and evil—'tis peace—'tis bliss,
And *that* my vengeance meant not to bestow:
I meant him *anguish* and *eternal pangs*,
But this the mad feel not—therefore, when life,
Fraught with rich vigor, through his arteries rolls,
And reason rises cloudless in his brain,
Embracing courteous hope, then will I go
And break the vain enchantment: galling chains
Shall load his shivering limbs, and shocking curses
Pursue him to his lurid den again.
This will be sweet revenge—there let him try
If the bright wit that jeer'd a woman's *foibles*
Will light the dungeon where her *fury* dwells.   [*Exit hastily.*]
        BARSAMES *solus,* (*after a long pause.*)
    BARS. Dwells there beneath thine arch immense, O sky!
Another heart so strain'd with shameful crimes?
Black as the caverns where her victims suffer—
Devil incarnate, scourge of this wide empire—
Her's is the task to plan deep cruelties,
Horrid as hell! and *mine* to execute them;
Nightly to wander, thief-like, through the streets,

And bid my sabre drink the bosom's blood
Of him she deems offending;
Or basely lurking in some fated mansion,
To watch till Midnight's soporific bands
Have lull'd the willing world in sweet repose,
Then rushing like a tiger from his den,
To burst where the devoted victim sleeps,
And tear him from his frighted consort's arms,
Who faintly screams and swoons, while he, aghast,
Clasps her cold body in a dumb embrace,
And *looks* a last adieu. Most horrible!
This is *my* mission—Oh! my heart revolts
From the infernal ministry—blood—blood!
Yet soft—thou dust, and ye encircling walls
Hear not these overflowings of my soul,
Lest they transpire, and I this awful night
Groan in the prison with those whose fate I mourn.   [*Exit.*]

> Enter TIBERIAS *and* JULIA.

JULIA. Begone—I say begone! let me alone,
I am no child—I will not be controul'd—
I tell thee I will see her.

TIB. Nay, but the Emperor—

JUL. The Emperor! who cares? what of him pray?
Think'st thou I fear to whisper in his ear,
Or tell the Empress of her faults before him?
Or think'st though that I *love* his Majesty,
That thus his name is offered as a charm?

TIB. But hear me sister—

JUL. I swear TIBERIAS, though thou art my brother,
If still thou thwart'st my bosom's fix'd design,
I'll plunge this dagger to thy very soul.
This instant quit thy hold!

TIB. A dagger—ha! no, then you shall not go.

JUL. Help! murder! help!

> Enter the EMPEROR, THEODORA, BARSAMES, *and others*

THEODORA. Who dares make this outcry so near my chamber?

JUL. *I* made it, Madam, for I wish'd to enter,
And this, my lordly brother, did prevent me;
He hath learn'd tyranny within these walls,
A goodly school I tro.

TIB. Madam, a mania hath possess'd her brain;
I pray you heed her not. (*Kneels.*)

THEO. Rise, gentle youth, I—

JUL. No, 'tis no *mania* that directs *my* tongue;
It is proud *Reason*, who, defying danger,
Dares lift her angel voice, and trumpet forth
The cruelties of *power*—yes, and dares tell

How easy Emperors, hoodwink'd by their minions,
Stab their best friends, and clasp polluted *Ruin*
To their own bosoms.
   TIB. My sister, let me lead you to your chamber.
   JUL. Avaunt, nor till I've told the hideous tale
That weeping *Truth* pour'd in my startled ear,
Think to decoy me hence. Thou, JUSTINIAN,
Hast from my heart torn every bleeding nerve
Sacred to *love* or *pity*. The stern *mandate*
That bore me *mad* from my deluded lover,
Stamp'd on its seal the horrors of my fate,
And doom'd me to a life of ceaseless woe,
And thou, vile woman, impious THEODORA,
Who dar'd to break the ligaments of affection,
What though thou now mayest steep thine hands in blood,
Yet think, oh! think, remorseless, fiend-like woman,
The day of retribution is at hand.
   THEO. Guards, lead her off—Tiberias, go with her.
   JUL. Off, monsters off! (*They take her off*, Tib. *follows.*)
. . . .

Novels

Susanna Haswell Rowson (1761–1824)

Born in Portsmouth, England, Susanna Haswell came to America
with her parents, Susanna Musgrave and William Haswell, in 1768.
Her early education in the classics and a life of comfort were halted
by the onset of the Revolutionary War. William Haswell's Tory sympathies led first to the confinement of the Haswell family and later
to their removal to England. Impoverished by these events, the
family struggled to regain its economic stability, and Susanna aided
the family by working as a governess until her marriage to the merchant William Rowson in 1786.

Marriage, however, did not bring economic security; when her husband failed in his business ventures, Haswell Rowson supported the
family through her writings and on the stage. In 1792 she settled in
Boston, her home for the next quarter century. While directing a
school for young women, she continued to write novels, poetry, plays,
short stories, and textbooks. Her early novels are rarely acknowledged
today, but Haswell Rowson's fourth novel, *Charlotte Temple* (1791),
became America's first best-selling novel. Susanna Haswell Rowson
died in her adopted city of Boston on March 2, 1824.

Selected Works: *Victoria* (1786); *The Inquisitor; or, Invisible Rambler* (1788); *Mary; or, The
Test of Honor* (1789); *Charlotte Temple: A Tale of Truth* (1791); *Mentoria; or, The Young
Ladies Friend* (1791); *Rebecca; or, The Fille de Chambre* (1792); *Trials of the Human Heart*
(1795); *Reuben and Rachel; or, Tales of Old Times* (1798).   *Bibliography*: Castiglia; Davidson, introduction to *Charlotte Temple*; Davidson, *Revolution and the Word*; Weil.

From *Charlotte Temple*[1]

Chapter VI. An Intriguing Teacher.

Madame Du Pont was a woman every way calculated to take the care of
young ladies, had that care entirely devolved on herself; but it was impos-

---

1. Chapters II through V of the novel outline Charlotte's ancestors; in Chapter VI she has been
sent to Madame Du Pont's finishing school.

sible to attend the education of a numerous school without proper assistants; and those assistants were not always the kind of people whose
conversation and morals were exactly such as parents of delicacy and refinement would wish a daughter to copy. Among the teachers at Madame Du
Pont's school, was Mademoiselle La Rue, who added to a pleasing person
and insinuating address, a liberal education and the manners of a gentlewoman. She was recommended to the school by a lady whose humanity over-
stepped the bounds of discretion: for though she knew Miss La Rue had
eloped from a convent with a young officer, and, on coming to England, had
lived with several different men in open defiance of all moral and religious
duties; yet, finding her reduced to the most abject want, and believing the
penitence which she professed to be sincere, she took her into her own family, and from thence recommended her to Madame Du Pont, as thinking the
situation more suitable for a woman of her abilities. But Mademoiselle possessed too much of the spirit of intrigue to remain long without adventures.
At church, where she constantly appeared, her person attracted the attention of a young man who was upon a visit at a gentleman's seat in the neighbourhood: she had met him several times clandestinely; and being invited
to come out that evening and eat some fruit and pastry in a summer-house
belonging to the gentleman he was visiting, and requested to bring some of
the ladies with her, Charlotte being her favourite, was fixed on to accompany her.

The mind of youth eagerly catches at promised pleasure: pure and innocent
by nature, it thinks not of the dangers lurking beneath those pleasures, till too
late to avoid them: when Mademoiselle asked Charlotte to go with her, she
mentioned the gentleman as a relation, and spoke in such high terms of the
elegance of his gardens, the sprightliness of his conversation, and the liberal-
ity with which he ever entertained his guests, that Charlotte thought only of
the pleasure she should enjoy in the visit,—not on the imprudence of going
without her governess's knowledge, or of the danger to which she exposed
herself in visiting the house of a gay young man of fashion.

Madame Du Pont was gone out for the evening, and the rest of the ladies
retired to rest, when Charlotte and the teacher stole out at the back gate, and
in crossing the field, were accosted by Montraville, as mentioned in the first
chapter.[2]

Charlotte was disappointed in the pleasure she had promised herself from
this visit. The levity of the gentlemen and the freedom of their conversation
disgusted her. She was astonished at the liberties Mademoiselle permitted them
to take; grew thoughtful and uneasy, and heartily wished herself at home again
in her own chamber.

Perhaps one cause of that wish might be, an earnest desire to see the contents of the letter which had been put into her hand by Montraville.

2. Montraville is an army lieutenant, stationed at Portsmouth while his regiment awaits
transport to America. In Chapter I, Montraville's interest in Charlotte was established, and he had
slipped a letter into her hand. Mademoiselle La Rue had assisted Montraville's interests by agreeing
to bring Charlotte into the field on the evening described in this chapter.

Any reader who has the least knowledge of the world, will easily imagine the letter was made up of encomiums on her beauty, and vows of everlasting love and constancy; nor will he be surprised that a heart open to every gentle, generous sentiment, should feel itself warmed by gratitude for a man who professed to feel so much for her; nor is it improbable but her mind might revert to the agreeable person and martial appearance of Montraville.

In affairs of love, a young heart is never in more danger than when attempted by a handsome young soldier. A man of an indifferent appearance, will, when arrayed in a military habit, shew to advantage; but when beauty of person, elegance of manner, and an easy method of paying compliments, are united to the scarlet coat, smart cockade, and military sash, ah! well-a-day for the poor girl who gazes on him: she is in imminent danger; but if she listens to him with pleasure, 'tis all over with her, and from that moment she has neither eyes nor ears for any other object.

Now, my dear sober matron, (if a sober matron should deign to turn over these pages, before she trusts them to the eye of a darling daughter,) let me intreat you not to put on a grave face and throw down the book in a passion and declare 'tis enough to turn the heads of half the girls in England; I do solemnly protest, my dear madam, I mean no more by what I have here advanced, than to ridicule those romantic girls, who foolishly imagine a red coat and silver epaulet constitute the fine gentleman; and should that fine gentleman make half a dozen fine speeches to them, they will imagine themselves so much in love as to fancy it a meritorious action to jump out of a two pair of stairs window, abandon their friends, and trust entirely to the honour of a man, who perhaps hardly knows the meaning of the word, and if he does, will be too much the modern man of refinement, to practice it in their favour.

Gracious heaven! when I think on the miseries that must rend the heart of a doating parent, when he sees the darling of his age at first seduced from his protection, and afterwards abandoned, by the very wretch whose promises of love decoyed her from the paternal roof—when he sees her poor and wretched, her bosom torn between remorse for her crime and love for her vile betrayer—when fancy paints to me the good old man stooping to raise the weeping penitent, while every tear from her eye is numbered by drops from his bleeding heart, my bosom glows with honest indignation, and I wish for power to extirpate those monsters of seduction from the earth.

Oh my dear girls—for to such only am I writing—listen not to the voice of love, unless sanctioned by paternal approbation: be assured, it is now past the days of romance: no woman can be run away with contrary to her own inclination: then kneel down each morning, and request kind heaven to keep you free from temptation, or, should it please to suffer you to be tried, pray for fortitude to resist the impulse of inclination when it runs counter to the precepts of religion and virtue.

Chapter XVIII. Reflections[3]

"And am I indeed fallen so low," said Charlotte, "as to be only pitied? Will the voice of approbation no more meet my ear? and shall I never again possess a friend, whose face will wear a smile of joy whenever I approach? Alas! how thoughtless, how dreadfully imprudent have I been! I know not which is most painful to endure, the sneer of contempt, or the glance of compassion, which is depicted in the various countenances of my own sex: they are both equally humiliating. Ah! my dear parents, could you now see the child of your affections, the daughter whom you so dearly love, a poor solitary being, without society, here wearing out her heavy hours in deep regret and anguish of heart, no kind friend of her own sex to whom she can unbosom her griefs, no beloved mother, no woman of character will appear in my company, and low as your Charlotte is fallen, she cannot associate with infamy."

These were the painful reflections which occupied the mind of Charlotte. Montraville had placed her in a small house a few miles from New-York: he gave her one female attendant, and supplied her with what money she wanted; but business and pleasure so entirely occupied his time, that he had little to devote to the woman, whom he had brought from all her connections, and robbed of innocence. Sometimes, indeed, he would steal out at the close of evening, and pass a few hours with her; and then so much was she attached to him, that all her sorrows were forgotten while blest with his society: she would enjoy a walk by moonlight, or sit by him in a little arbour at the bottom of the garden, and play on the harp, accompanying it with her plaintive, harmonious voice. But often, very often, did he promise to renew his visits, and, forgetful of his promise, leave her to mourn her disappointment. What painful hours of expectation would she pass! She would sit at a window which looked toward a field he used to cross, counting the minutes, and straining her eyes to catch the first glimpse of his person, till blinded with tears of disappointment, she would lean her head on her hands, and give free vent to her sorrows: then catching at some new hope, she would again renew her watchful position, till the shades of evening enveloped every object in a dusky cloud: she would then renew her complaints, and, with a heart bursting with disappointed love and wounded sensibility, retire to a bed which remorse had strewed with thorns, and court in vain that comforter of weary nature (who seldom visits the unhappy) to come and steep her senses in oblivion.

Who can form an adequate idea of the sorrow that preyed upon the mind of Charlotte? The wife, whose breast glows with affection to her husband, and who in return meets only indifference, can but faintly conceive her anguish. Dreadfully painful is the situation of such a woman, but she has many comforts of which our poor Charlotte was deprived. The duteous, faithful wife, though

3. Charlotte and Montraville have continued to see one another secretly. Montraville has been attempting to lure Charlotte to America with him; she is both drawn to the adventure and repelled by it. When she met him on the night of his departure, she resisted his pleas but was pushed into the chaise by Mademoiselle La Rue—and then fainted, so that she was unable to determine her own fate after that point. The group has reached New York, but Montraville has not married Charlotte, as promised.

treated with indifference, has one solid pleasure within her own bosom, she can reflect that she has not deserved neglect—that she has ever fulfilled the duties of her station with the strictest exactness; she may hope, by constant assiduity and unremitted attention, to recall her wanderer, and be doubly happy in his returning affection; she knows he cannot leave her to unite himself to another: he cannot cast her out to poverty and contempt; she looks around her, and sees the smile of friendly welcome, or the tear of affectionate consolation, on the face of every person whom she favours with her esteem; and from all these circumstances she gathers comfort: but the poor girl by thoughtless passion led astray, who, in parting with her honour, has forfeited the esteem of the very man to whom she has sacrificed every thing dear and valuable in her life, feels his indifference in the fruit of her own folly, and laments her want of power to recall his lost affection; she knows there is no tie but honour, and that, in a man who has been guilty of seduction, is but very feeble: he may leave her in a moment to shame and want; he may marry and forsake her for ever; and should he, she has no redress, no friendly, soothing companion to pour into her wounded mind the balm of consolation, no benevolent hand to lead her back to the path of rectitude; she has disgraced her friends, forfeited the good opinion of the world, and undone herself; she feels herself a poor solitary being in the midst of surrounding multitudes; shame bows her to the earth, remorse tears her distracted mind, and guilt, poverty, and disease close the dreadful scene: she sinks unnoticed to oblivion. The finger of contempt may point out to some passing daughter of youthful mirth, the humble bed where lies this frail sister of mortality; and will she, in the unbounded gaiety of her heart, exult in her own unblemished fame, and triumph over the silent ashes of the dead? Oh no! has she a heart of sensibility, she will stop, and thus address the unhappy victim of folly—

"Thou had'st thy faults, but sure thy sufferings have expiated them: thy errors brought thee to an early grave; but thou wert a fellow-creature—thou hast been unhappy—then be those errors forgotten."

Then, as she stoops to pluck the noxious weed from off the sod, a tear will fall, and consecrate the spot to Charity.

For ever honoured be the sacred drop of humanity; the angel of mercy shall record its source, and the soul from whence it sprang shall be immortal.

My dear Madam, contract not your brow into a frown of disapprobation. I mean not to extenuate the faults of those unhappy women who fall victims to guilt and folly; but surely, when we reflect how many errors we are ourselves subject to, how many secret faults lie hid in the recesses of our hearts, which we should blush to have brought into open day (and yet those faults require the lenity and pity of a benevolent judge, or awful would be our prospect of futurity) I say, my dear Madam, when we consider this, we surely may pity the faults of others.

Believe me, many an unfortunate female, who has once strayed into the thorny paths of vice, would gladly return to virtue, was any generous friend to endeavour to raise and re-assure her; but alas! it cannot be, you say; the world would deride and scoff. Then let me tell you, Madam, 'tis a very unfeeling world, and does not deserve half the blessings which a bountiful Providence showers upon it.

Oh, thou benevolent giver of all good! how shall we erring mortals dare to look up to thy mercy in the great day of retribution, if we now uncharitably refuse to overlook the errors, or alleviate the miseries, of our fellow-creatures.

Ann Eliza Schuyler Bleecker (1752–1783)

For a biography of Schuyler Bleecker, see the "Poetry" section.

Ann Eliza Schuyler Bleecker wrote two novels, *The History of Maria Kittle* and *The Story of Henry and Anne*, both of which were published in *The Posthumous Works of Ann Eliza Bleecker* (1793). Both novels engage significant cultural issues of the new republic—*Maria Kittle*, an epistolary novel, fictionalizes the ever-popular captivity narrative and the relations between settlers and Native Americans and *Henry and Anne* depicts German immigrants who settle in the "New World."

The HISTORY of MARIA KITTLE

In a Letter to Miss Ten Eyck.

Tomahanick, December, 1779.

Dear Susan,

However fond of novels and romances you may be, the unfortunate adventures of one of my neighbours, who died yesterday, will make you despise that fiction, in which, knowing the subject to be fabulous, we can never be so truly interested. While this lady was expiring, Mrs. C——— V———, her near kinswoman, related to me her unhappy history, in which I shall now take the liberty of interesting your benevolent and feeling heart.

MARIA KITTLE was the only issue of her parents, who cultivated a large farm on the banks of the *Hudson*, eighteen miles above *Albany*. They were persons of good natural abilities, improved by some learning; yet, conscious of a deficiency in their education, they studied nothing so much as to render their little daughter truly accomplished.

MARIA was born in the year 1721. Her promising infancy presaged a maturity of excellencies; every amiable quality dawned through her lisping prattle; every personal grace attended her attitudes and played over her features. As she advanced through the playful stage of childhood, she became more eminent than a Penelope[1] for her industry; yet, soon as the sun declined, she always retired with her books until the time of repose, by which means she soon

---

1. Penelope was Odysseus's wife in Homer's *The Odyssey*.

informed her opening mind with the principles of every useful science. She was beloved by all her female companions, who, though they easily discovered her superior elegance of manners, instead of envying, were excited to imitate her. As she always made one in their little parties of pleasure on festival days, it is no wonder that she soon became the reigning goddess among the swains. She was importuned to admit the addresses of numbers, whom she politely discarded, and withdrew herself awhile from public observation. However, the fame of her charms attracted several gentlemen of family from *Albany*, who intruded on her retirement, soliciting her hand. But this happiness was reserved for a near relation of her's, one Mr. KITTLE, whose merits had made an impression on her heart. He, although not handsome, was possessed of a most engaging address; while his learning and moral virtues more particularly recommended him to her esteem. Their parents soon discovered their reciprocal passion, and highly approving of it, hastened their marriage, which was celebrated under the most happy auspices.

MARIA was fifteen when married. They removed to his farm, on which he had built a small neat house, surrounded by tall cedars, which gave it a contemplative air. It was situated on an eminence, with a green inclosure in the front, graced by a well cultivated garden on one side, and on the other by a clear stream, which, rushing over a bed of white pebble, gave them a high polish, that cast a soft gleam through the water.

Here they resided in the tranquil enjoyment of that happiness which so much merit and innocence deserved: the indigent, the sorrowful, the unfortunate were always sure of consolation when they entered those peaceful doors. They were almost adored by their neighbours, and even the wild savages themselves, who often resorted thither for refreshments when hunting, expressed the greatest regard for them, and admiration of their virtues.

In little more than a year they were blessed with a daughter, the lovelier resemblance of her lovely mother: as she grew up, her graces increasing, promised a bloom and understanding equal to her's; the Indians, in particular, were extremely fond of the smiling ANNA; whenever they found a young fawn, or caught a brood of wood-ducks, or surprised the young beaver in their daily excursions through the forests, they presented them with pleasure to her; they brought her the earliest strawberries, the scarlet plumb, and other delicate wild fruits in painted baskets.

How did the fond parents hearts delight to see their beloved one so universally caressed! When they sauntered over the vernal fields with the little prattler wantoning before them collecting flowers and pursuing the velvet elusive butterfly, MARIA's cheek suffusing with rapture, "Oh, my dear," she would say, "we are happier than human beings can expect to be: how trivial are the evils annexed to our situation! may God avert that our heaven be limited to this life!"

Eleven years now elapsed before Mrs. KITTLE discovered any signs of pregnancy: her spouse silently wished for a son, and his desires were at length gratified; she was delivered of a charming boy, who was named, after him, WILLIAM.

A French and Indian war had commenced sometime before; but about eight months after her delivery, the savages began to commit the most horrid depredations on the English frontiers. Mr. KITTLE, alarmed at the danger of his brothers, who dwelt near *Fort-Edward*, (the eldest being just married to a very agreeable young woman) invited them to reside with him during the war. . . .

[While hunting, Peter, one of William's brothers, is killed by Native Americans; William then goes to a neighbor's house, against Maria's wishes, to get a wagon so the family can be moved to the safety of Albany.]

MARIA . . . having assembled the family in a little hall, closed and barred the doors. Mrs. COMELIA KITTLE, MARIA's sister-in-law, was far advanced in her pregnancy, which increased her husband's uneasiness for her; and they were debating in what manner to accommodate her at *Albany*, when the trampling of feet about the house, and a yell of complicated voices, announced the Indians arrival. Struck with horror and consternation, the little family crouded together in the center of the hall, while the servants at this alarm, being in a kitchen distant from the house, saved themselves by a precipitate flight. The little BILLY, frightened at such dreadful sounds, clung fast to his mother's throbbing breast, while ANNA, in a silent agony of amazement, clasped her trembling knees. The echo of their yells yet rung in long vibrations through the forest, when, with a thundering peal of strokes at the door, they demanded entrance. Distraction and despair sat upon every face. MARIA and her companions gazed wildly at each other, till, upon repeated menaces and efforts to break open the door, COMELIA's husband, giving all for lost, leisurely advanced to the door. COMELIA feeling this, uttered a great shriek, and cried out, "O god! what are you doing, my rash, rash, unfortunate husband! you will be sacrificed!" Then falling on her knees, she caught hold of his hand and sobbed out, "O pity me! have mercy on yourself, on me, on my child!"—"Alas! my love," said he, half turning with a look of distraction, "what can we do? let us be resigned to the will of God." So saying he unbarred the door, and that instant received a fatal bullet in his bosom, and fell backward writhing in agonies of death; the rest recoiled at this horrible spectacle, and huddled in a corner, sending forth the most piercing cries: in the interim the savages rushing in with great shouts, proceeded to mangle the corpse, and having made an incision round his head with crooked knife, they tugged off his bloody scalp with barbarous triumph. While this was perpetrating, an Indian hideously painted, stroked ferociously up to COMELIA, (who sunk away at the sight, and fainted on a chair) and cleft her white forehead deeply with his tomahack. Her fine azure eyes just opened, and then suddenly closing for ever, she tumbled lifeless at his feet. His sanguinary soul was not yet satisfied with blood; he deformed her lovely body with deep gashes; and, tearing her unborn babe away, dashed it to pieces against the stone wall; with many additional circumstances of infernal cruelty.

During this horrid carnage, the dead were stripped, and dragged from the house, when one of the hellish band advanced to MARIA, who circling her babes with her white arms, was sending hopeless petitions to heaven, and bemoaning their cruelly lost situation: as he approached, expecting the fatal stroke, she endeavoured to guard her children, and with supplicating looks, implored for mercy. The savage attempted not to strike; but the astonished ANNA sheltered herself behind her mamma, while her blooming suckling quitting her breast, gazed with a pleasing wonder on the painted stranger.—MARIA soon recognized her old friend that presented her with the belt, through the loads of shells and feathers that disguised him. This was no time, however, to irritate him, by reminding him of his promise;[2] yet, guessing her thoughts, he anticipated her remonstrance. "MARIA," said he, "be not afraid. I have promised to protect you; you shall live and dance with us around the fire at *Canada*: but you have one small incumbrance, which, if not removed, will much impede your progress thither." So saying he seized her laughing babe by the wrists, and forcibly endeavoured to draw him from her arms. At this, terrified beyond conception, she exclaimed, "O God! leave me, leave me my child! he shall not go, though a legion of devils should try to separate us!" Holding him still fast, while the Indian applied his strength to take him away, gnashing his teeth at her opposition; "Help! God of heaven!" screamed she, "help! have pity, have mercy on this infant! O God! O Christ! can you bear to see this? O mercy! mercy! mercy! let a little spark of compassion save this inoffending, this lovely angel!" But this time the breathless babe dropt its head on its bosom; the wri[s]ts were nigh pinched off, and seeing him just expiring, with a dreadful shriek she resigned him to the merciless hands of the savage, who instantly dashed his little forehead against the stones, and casting his bleeding body at some distance from the house, left him to make his exit in feeble and unheard groans.—Then indeed, in the unutterable anguish of her soul, she fell prostrate, and rending away her hair, she roared our her sorrows with a voice louder than natural, and rendered awfully hollow by too great an exertion. "O barbarians!" she exclaimed, "surpassing devils in wickedness! so may a tenfold night of misery enwrap your black souls, as you have deprived the babe of my bosom, the comfort of my cares, my blessed cherub, of light and life—Oh hell! are not thy flames impatient to cleave the center and engulph these wretches in thy ever burning waves? are there no thunders in Heaven—no avenging Angel—no God to take notice of such Heaven defying cruelties?" Then rushing to her dead infant with redoubled cries, and clapping her hands, she laid herself over his mangled body; again softened in tears and moans, she wiped the blood from his ghastly countenance, and prest him to her heaving bosom, alternately caressing him and her trembling ANNA. . . . but their melancholy endearments were soon interrupted by the relentless savages, who having plundered the house of every valuable thing that was portable, returned to MARIA, and rudely catching her arm, commanded her to follow them. . . . Meanwhile the lovely ANNA, terrified at the hostile appearance of the enemy, left her mamma struggling to disengage herself from the Indians, and fled precipitately to the house. She had already concealed herself in a closet, when Mrs. KITTLE pursuing her, was intercepted by flames, the savages having fired the house. . . . Then turning to the calm villains who attended her, she cried, "Why do you not attempt to rescue my sweet inno-

2. When the French and Indian War began, this elderly Native American had promised Maria that, as "a true man," he would honor their friendship and ensure her safety.

cent? can your unfeeling hearts not bear to leave me one—a solitary single one?" Again calling to her ANNA, she received no answer, which being a presumption of her death, the Indians obliged MARIA and her brother HENRY[3] to quit the house, which they effected with some difficulty, the glowing beams falling around them and thick volumes of smoke obscuring their passage. The flames now struck a long splendor through the humid atmosphere, and blushed to open the tragical scene on the face of heaven. They had scarce advanced two hundred yards with their reluctant captives, when the flaming structure tumbled to the earth with a dreadful crash. Our travellers by instinct turned their eyes to the mournful blaze; and MARIA, bursting afresh into grievous lamentations, cried, "There, there my brother, my children are wrapt in arching sheets of flames, that used to be circled in my arms! They are entombed in ruins that breathed their slumbers on my bosom! yet, oh! their spotless souls even now rise from this chaos of blood and fire, and are pleading our injured cause before our God, my brother!" He replied on in sighs and groans, he scarcely heard her; horror had froze up the avenues of his soul; and all amazed and trembling, he followed his leaders like a person in a troublesome dream. . . .

Hannah Webster Foster (1758–1840)

Hannah Webster, the daughter of Hannah Wainwright and Grant Webster of Salisbury, Massachusetts, was born on September 10, 1758. When her mother died four years later, Hannah was placed in a boarding school (which became the milieu for her second novel).[1] Married in 1785 to the Reverend John Foster with whom she raised six children, Webster Foster did not begin her literary career until she was almost forty years old; yet she was recognized by her contemporaries as the most gifted of early American sentimental novelists. In *The Coquette*, Webster Foster draws upon the real-life tragedy of Elizabeth Whitman to expose the consequences of "polite" society's hypocrisy and the limitations that social customs place upon all women, even those who are well educated. A significant precursor to the rise of American realism, this novel challenges our literary assumptions at the same time that it presents one of early American literature's most memorable characters, Eliza Wharton. Webster Foster's talent became a legacy to two

---

3. One of William's brothers.

1. The popularity of this novel, *The Boarding School* (1798), is evident from the numerous times it is mentioned in diaries. Julia Cowles, for instance, notes that she read it in 1799 while she was attending Sarah Pierce's Academy. The impact of the novel did not end with Cowles's early education, however. Later, she recorded in her diary a long poem on "Columbia's Daughters" from *The Boarding School*, noting that "Pope among all his admired poetry has not six lines more beautifully expressive."

of her daughters, Harriet Vaughan Cheney and Eliza Lanesford Cushing, both of whom became popular authors during the early nineteenth century. Hannah Webster Foster died in Montreal, at her daughter Eliza's home, on April 17, 1840.

Works: *The Coquette; or, The History of Eliza Wharton* (1797); *The Boarding School; or, Lessons of a Preceptress to Her Pupils* (1798). Bibliography: Davidson, introduction to *The Coquette*; Davidson, *Revolution and the Word*; Harris, *Redefining the Political Novel*; Pettingill.

From *The Coquette; or, The History of Eliza Wharton*

Letter XIV, from Eliza Wharton to her friend, Miss Lucy Freeman:[2]

I have received, and read again and again, your friendly epistle. My reason and judgment entirely coincide with your opinion; but my fancy claims some share in the decision: and I cannot yet tell which will preponderate. This was the day fixed for deciding Mr. Boyer's cause.[3] My friends here[4] gave me a long dissertation on his merits. Your letter, likewise, had its weight, and I was candidly summing up the *pros* and *cons* in the garden, whither I had walked (Gen. Richman and lady having rode out) when I was informed that he was waiting in the parlor. I went immediately in. . . . It is needless for me to recite to you, who have long been acquainted with the whole process of courtship, the declarations, propositions, protestations, intreaties, looks, words and actions of a lover. They are, I believe, much the same, in the whole sex, allowing for their different dispositions, educations, and characters. But you are impatient I know for the conclusion. You have hastily perused the preceding lines, and are straining your eye forward to my part of the farce; for such it may prove after all. Well then, not to play too long with the curiosity, which I know to be excited, and actuated by real friendship, I will relieve it. I think you would have been pleased to have seen my gravity, on this important occasion. With all the candor and frankness which I was capable of assuming, I thus answered his long harangue, to which I had listened, without interrupting him. Self-knowledge, sir, that most important of all sciences, I have yet to learn. Such have been my situations in life, and the natural volatility of my temper, that I have looked but little into my own heart, in regard to its future wishes and views. From a scene of constraint and confinement, ill suited to my years and inclination, I have just launched into society. My heart beats high in expectation of its fancied joys. My sanguine imagination paints, in alluring colors, the charms of

2. Eliza, drawn to the rake Major Sanford more than to the very proper Reverend Boyer, had written to her friend asking for advice. Lucy, the voice of mainstream morality in the novel, counseled Eliza to abandon the dangerous Sanford and recognize the virtue and social acceptability of Boyer.

3. Boyer had been pressuring Eliza to become engaged to him.

4. General and Mrs. Richman, with whom Eliza is staying in New Haven.

youth and freedom, regulated by virtue and innocence. Of these I wish to partake. While I own myself under obligations for the esteem which you are pleased to profess for me, and in return, acknowledge, that neither your person nor manners are disagreeable to me, I recoil at the thought of immediately forming a connection, which must confine me to the duties of domestic life, and make me dependent for happiness, perhaps too, for subsistence, upon a class of people, who will claim the right of scrutinising every part of my conduct; and by censuring those foibles, which I am conscious of not having prudence to avoid, may render me completely miserable. While, therefore, I receive your visits, and cultivate towards you sentiments of friendship and esteem, I would not have you consider me as confined to your society, or obligated to a future connection. Our short acquaintance renders it impossible for me to decide what the operations of my mind may hereafter be. You must either quit the subject, or leave me to the exercise of my free will, which perhaps may coincide with your present wishes. Madam, said he, far is the wish from me to restrain your person or mind. In your breast I will repose my cause. It shall be my study to merit a return of affection; and I doubt not, but generosity and honor will influence your conduct towards me. I expect soon to settle among a generous and enlightened people, where I flatter myself I shall be exempt from those difficulties, and embarrassments, to which too many of my brethren are subject. The local situation is agreeable, the society refined and polished; and if, in addition, I may obtain the felicity which you are formed to bestow, in a family connection, I shall be happy indeed.

He spoke with emphasis. The tear of sensibility sparkled in his eye. I involuntarily gave him my hand, which he pressed with ardor to his lips. Then rising, he walked to the window to conceal his emotion. I rang the bell and ordered tea. . . . He tarried to supper, and took his leave. I retired immediately to my chamber, to which I was followed by Mrs. Richman. I related to her the conversation, and the encouragement which I had given to Mr. Boyer. She was pleased; but insisted that I should own myself somewhat engaged to him. This, I told her I should never do to any man, before the indissoluble knot was tied. That, said I, will be time enough to resign my freedom. . . .

Letter XX, from Eliza Wharton to her mother:[5]

From the conversation of the polite, the sedate, the engaging and the gay; from corresponding with the learned, the sentimental and the refined, my heart and my pen turn with ardor and alacrity to a tender and affectionate parent, the faithful guardian and guide of my youth; the unchanging friend of my riper years. The different dispositions of various associates, sometimes perplex the mind, which seeks direction; but in the disinterested affection of the maternal breast, we fear no dissonance of passion, no jarring interests, no dis-

5. Although all of Eliza's associates have encouraged her relationship with Boyer, she still has doubts about the alliance, which are exacerbated when Sanford discourages her interest in Boyer and tells her that she deserves a more pleasurable and "elevated sphere of life." In this state of confusion, Eliza writes to her mother.

union of love. In this seat of felicity is every enjoyment which fancy can form, or friendship, with affluence, bestow; but still my mind frequently returns to the happy shades of my nativity. I wish there to impart my pleasures, and share the counsels of my best, my long tried and experienced friend. At this time, my dear mamma, I am peculiarly solicitous for your advice. I am again importuned to listen to the voice of love; again called upon to accept the addresses of a gentleman of merit and respectability. You will know the character of the man, when I tell you, it is Mr. Boyer. But his situation in life! I dare not enter it. My disposition is not calculated for that sphere. There are duties arising from the station, which I fear I should not be able to fulfil; cares and restraints to which I could not submit. *This* man is not disagreeable to me; but if I must enter the connubial state, are there not *others*, who may be equally pleasing in their persons, and whose profession may be more comfortable to my taste? You, madam, have passed through this scene of trial, with honor and applause.[6] But alas! can your volatile daughter ever acquire your wisdom; ever possess your resolution, dignity and prudence? . . .

Letter XXVII, from Major Peter Sanford to his friend, Charles Deighton:

I go on finely with my amour. I have every encouragement that I could wish. Indeed my fair one does not verbally declare in my favor; but then, according to the vulgar proverb, *that actions speak louder than words,* I have no reason to complain; since she evidently approves my gallantry, is pleased with my company, and listens to my flattery. Her sagatious friends have undoubtedly given her a detail of my vices. If, therefore, my past conduct has been repugnant to her notions of propriety, why does she not act consistently, and refuse at once to associate with a man whose character she cannot esteem? But no; that, Charles, is no part of the female plan: our entrapping a few of their sex, only discovers the gaiety of our dispositions, the insinuating graces of our manners, and the irresistible charms of our persons and address. These qualifications are very alluring to the sprightly fancy of the fair. They think to enjoy the pleasures which result from this source; while their vanity and ignorance prompt each one to imagine herself superior to delusion; and to anticipate the honor of reclaiming the libertine, and reforming the rake! I dont know, however, but this girl will really have that merit with me; for I am so much attached to her, that I begin to suspect I should sooner become a convert to sobriety than lose her. I cannot find that I have made much impression on her heart as yet. Want of success in this point mortifies me extremely, as it is the first time I ever failed. Besides, I am apprehensive that she is prepossessed in favor of the other swain, the clerical lover, whom I have mentioned to you before. The chord, therefore, upon which I play the most, is the dissimilarity of their dispositions and pleasures. I endeavor to detach her from him, and disaffect her towards him; knowing, that if I can separate them en-

---

6. Mrs. Wharton's husband (and Eliza's father) had been a minister.

tirely, I shall be more likely to succeed in my plan. Not that I have any thoughts of marrying her myself; that will not do at present. But I love her too well to see her connected with another for life. I must own myself a little revengeful too in this affair. I wish to punish her friends, as she calls them, for their malice towards me; for their cold and negligent treatment of me whenever I go to the house. I know that to frustrate their designs of a connection between Mr. Boyer and Eliza would be a grievous disappointment. I have not yet determined to seduce her, though, with all her pretensions to virtue, I do not think it impossible. And if I should, she can blame none but herself, since she knows my character, and has no reason to wonder if I act consistently with it. If she will play with a lion, let her beware of his paw, I say. . . .

Letter XXXI, from Lucy Freeman to Eliza Wharton:[7]

I am very happy to find you are in so good spirits, Eliza, after parting with your favorite swain [Sanford]. For I perceive that he is really the favorite of your fancy, though your heart cannot esteem him; and, independent of that, no sensations can be durable.

I can tell you some news of this strange man. He has arrived, and taken possession of his seat.[8] Having given general invitations, he has been called upon and welcomed by most of the neighboring gentry. Yesterday he made an elegant entertainment. Friend George[9] (as you call him) and I were of the number, who had cards. Twenty one couple went, I am told. We did not go. I consider my time too valuable to be spent in cultivating acquaintance with a person from whom neither pleasure nor improvement are to be expected. His profuseness may bribe the unthinking multitude to show him respect; but he must know, that though

> "Places and honors have been bought for gold,
> Esteem and love were never to be sold."

I look upon the vicious habits, and abandoned character of Major Sanford, to have more pernicious effects on society, than the perpetrations of the robber and the assassin. These, when detected, are rigidly punished by the laws of the land. If their lives be spared, they are shunned by society, and treated with every mark of disapprobation and contempt. But to the disgrace of humanity and virtue, the assassin of honor; the wretch, who breaks the peace of families, who robs virgin innocence of its charms, who triumphs over the ill placed confidence of the inexperienced, unsuspecting, and too credulous fair, is received, and caressed, not only by his own sex, to which he is a reproach, but even by ours, who have every conceivable reason to despise and avoid him. Influenced by these principles, I am neither ashamed nor afraid openly to avow my sentiments of this man, and my reasons for treating him with the most pointed neglect.

---

7. Lucy has just received a letter from Eliza in which she admits the allure of Sanford's charm and has flippantly referred to the stuffiness of Boyer's professions of affection.

8. That is, his newly purchased home in Hartford, where Lucy resides.

9. Lucy's fiance.

I write warmly on the subject; for it is a subject in which I think the honor and happiness of my sex concerned. I wish they would more generally espouse their own cause. It would conduce to the public weal, and to their personal respectability. I rejoice, heartily, that you have had resolution to resist his allurements, to detect and repel his artifices. Resolution, in such a case, is absolutely necessary; for,

> "In spite of all the virtue we can boast,
> The woman that deliberates is lost."

As I was riding out, yesterday, I met your mamma. She wondered that I was not one of the party at our new neighbor's. The reason, madam, said I, is that I do not like the character of the man. I know nothing of him, said she; he is quite a stranger to me, only as he called at my house, last week, to pay me his respects, as he said, for the sake of my late husband, whose memory he revered; and because I was the mother of Miss Eliza Wharton, with whom he had the honor of some little acquaintance. His manners are engaging, and I am sorry to hear that his morals are corrupt.

This, my dear, is a very extraordinary visit. I fear that he has not yet laid aside his arts. Be still on your guard, is the advice of your sincere and faithful friend,

Lucy Freeman

Tabitha Gilman Tenney (1762–1837)

Born in Exeter, New Hampshire, on April 7, 1762, Tabitha Gilman was the eldest of seven children born to Lydia Robinson Giddings and Samuel Gilman. Little biographical information is available, and the author left no autobiographical records. At the age of twenty-six, she married Samuel Tenney, a physician and later a senator from New Hampshire. Her writing career began after her marriage. An anonymous reader aimed at young women, *The New Pleasing Instructor* (1799), has been attributed to Gilman Tenney, but she is best known for her rollickingly satirical novel *Female Quixotism* (1801), also published anonymously. Although she lived until 1837, Gilman Tenney published no other works after *Female Quixotism*. The novel, written at the turn of the century, is indebted to the picaresque tradition but also stands at the forefront of the seriocomic novel tradition in America, which would be followed by women writers such as Fanny Fern and Marietta Holley.

Works: *The New Pleasing Instructor* (1799); *Female Quixotism: Exhibited in the Romantic Opinions and Extravagant Adventures of Dorcasina Sheldon* (1801). Bibliography: Davidson, *Revolution and the Word*; Harris, "Lost Boundaries"; Nienkamp and Collins; Quinn, *American Fiction*.

From Female Quixotism

Book I, Chapter I.

... Little Dorcas, for so was our heroine called after her paternal grandmother, was too young to be sensible of the loss she had sustained. ...[1] [Mr. Sheldon] attended to her education with the utmost care and assiduity; procuring her suitable instructors of every kind, and frequently executing the pleasing office himself, for which his native good sense and various acquirements eminently fitted him. In every branch of her education, Miss Sheldon made great proficiency. She had received from nature a good understanding, a lively fancy, an amiable cheerful temper, and a kind and affectionate heart. What a number of valuable qualities were here blended! But it is a mortifying truth that perfection is not to be found in human nature. With all these engaging endowments, she was unfortunately of a very romantic turn, had a small degree of obstinancy, and a spice too much of vanity.

Now I suppose it will be expected that, in imitation of sister novel writers (for the ladies of late seem to have almost appropriated this department of writing) I should describe her as distinguished by the elegant form, delicately turned limbs, auburn hair, alabaster skin, heavenly languishing eyes, silken eyelashes, rosy cheeks, aquiline nose, ruby lips, dimpled chin, and azure veins, with which almost all our heroines of romance are indiscriminately decorated. In truth she possessed few of those beauties, in any great degree. She was of a middling stature, a little embonpoint, but neither elegant nor clumsy. Her complexion was rather dark; her skin somewhat rough; and features remarkable neither for beauty nor deformity. Her eyes were grey and full of expression, and her whole countenance rather pleasing than otherwise. In short, she was a middling kind of person; like the greater part of her countrywomen. ...

Book I, Chapter IV.[2]

... At any other time, or upon any other occasion, her upright soul would have despised the meanness and duplicity of a conduct totally unworthy of her character. But to such a degree was she infatuated by the insinuating addresses of O'Connor, that, by his influence, she now declined from the straight path of rectitude, which, till this time, she had trodden with undeviating steps.

1. Dorcas Sheldon is three years old when the novel begins. She has just lost her mother, who, the narrator cautions, "would have pointed out to her the plain rational path of life" and restricted her reading of novels, which *Female Quixotism* presents as the source of Dorcas Sheldon's numerous misadventures.

2. Dorcasina (as she now calls herself, believing it a more romantic appellation than Dorcas) is now thirty-four years old. In spite of earlier failed romances, she has not learned that life—and especially love—is not as it is depicted in novels. She has fallen in love with a twenty-two-year-old fortune-hunter, Patrick O'Connor. They have had several secret meetings; in this scene, Dorcasina has just received a letter from O'Connor, who styles himself as her "Most ardent, And almost distracted lover."

She passed the day in impatient expectation of the arrival of the hour, which was to bless her with an interview with the beloved of her soul. . . .[3]

Mr. Sheldon had a large garden, and well stocked with every kind of fruit which the season and climate afforded. The servant who had the care of it was a tall stout negro, called Scipio. The boys here, as in every other village, were troublesome and mischievous. Mr. Sheldon frequently gave them fruit; but, not satisfied with this, they would often go in the night and help themselves; trampling down every thing in their way, to the great detriment of the garden, which Scipio valued himself on keeping in excellent order. The night before that upon which our lovers were to meet, the garden had been robbed of some fine melons, and the vines greatly injured. This put the gardener into a great passion, and determined him to watch in the summer-house, at the bottom of the garden, upon this ill-fated night. Having a favourite in the village, of his own colour, he imparted to [Miss Violet] his design, and she kindly agreed to keep him company.

Scipio, not happening to mention his plan to any of the family, Dorcasina was, unfortunately, ignorant of it. At the appointed hour, therefore, when she thought the family all asleep, she softly descended the stairs, and opening the door which led to the garden, went directly to the summer-house. Scipio, who had previously taken his station there, had unluckily fallen asleep; and, when Dorcasina arrived, was snoring loud enough to be heard all over the garden. Thinking it to be her lover, and feeling some degree of mortification at the circumstance, she stood a few minutes irresolute. But at length, determining not to disturb him, she approached him softly, sat down by his side, and, putting one arm round his neck and resting her cheek against his, resolved to enjoy the sweet satisfaction which this situation afforded her, till he should of himself awake. This liberty, in his waking hours, her modesty would have prevented her from taking; but, with a heart thrilling with transport, she blessed the accident, which, without wounding her delicacy, afforded her such ravishing delight.

While she was thus indulging herself in these blissful sensations, O'Connor and Miss Violet entered the garden at the same time, but at different places; and, both taking their way to the summer-house, encountered each other at a little distance from it. O'Connor, seeing a person in white advancing toward him, thought, naturally enough, that it could be no other than his mistress. As soon, therefore, as he approached her, he dropped on one knee, and poured forth a torrent of words in the usual style, blessing his supposed angelic mistress, for her goodness and condescension, in thus favoring him with an interview. Miss Violet was at first struck with astonishment, and could not divine the meaning of those fine compliments; but, perceiving by his manner and address, that it was a gentleman who thus humbled himself before her, and having a spice of the coquette in her disposition, she had no objection to obtaining a new lover; but, being totally at a loss what to reply to such a profusion of compliments, delivered in a style so new to her, she very prudently remained silent. Thinking her silence occasioned by her fear of being heard

3. O'Connor has asked her to meet him that night in the summer-house.

in the house, as they were then pretty near it, O'Connor rose from the ground, took her hand, which he kissed and squeezed all the way, and led her in silence to the summer-house.

Scipio and Dorcasina were seated at the back side and our Hibernian,[4] having placed his sable mistress just at the entrance, began again to pour forth his expressions of gratitude and love. Dorcasina, knowing his voice, was lost in amazement; but she had not time to wonder long; for Scipio, dreaming of thieves, and being waked by the voice of O'Connor, started suddenly up, and, darting towards the door, seized him by the collar, held him fast with one hand, and cuffed him at a most unmerciful rate with the other; bawling all the time, "You dog, take dat; next time come teal our melon. I teach you better manners." O'Connor was greatly enraged at finding himself so roughly handled, but having discretion enough not to expose himself by speaking, he only struggled, in vain, to disengage himself. Poor Dorcasina, overcome by surprise and terror, jumped out of the window at the back side of the summer-house, and fainted upon the turf. Miss Violet sat a silent spectator of the scene; and, after Scipio had taken ample revenge upon the supposed thief, he let him go; telling him at the same time, that if ever he caught him there again, he should not come off so easily. Exasperated beyond measure, but glad to get out of the hands of a fellow so much stronger than himself, our unlucky adventurer sneaked to his lodgings, cursing alternately Mr. Sheldon, his daughter, Scipio, and himself; vowing, if possible, to be revenged on them all, for his disgrace. Not that he suspected his mistress to have had any hand in it; but such was the violence of his temper, when once raised, that every person who came in his way, was sure to feel the effects of it. After he had left the garden, Miss Violet, who could as easily change a white lover for a black, as receive the addresses of a new one, simply told Scipio, upon his interrogating her, that she met a man in the garden, who immediately fell on his knees and began "to talk fine ting" to her, but that she would not listen to him, and took her way directly to the summer-house; whither he followed, close behind her, and had just entered as Scipio attacked him. "Ah! good for noting dog!" said Scipio, "I bang him well; he no come again arter Violet, nor arter melon!" They then made themselves very merry with the reception he had met with.

In the midst of their glee, Dorcasina, who had hitherto been senseless, began to recover; and, listening a few minutes to the conversation of the African lovers, soon discovered how matters were situated. Mortified and disappointed beyond measure, she crept into the house, and got to bed undiscovered; where, between her own personal chagrin, and distress for her lover, she lay the whole night in sleepless agitation. . . . Her delicate mind could hardly bear to reflect on her familiarity with her father's servant; much less could she endure the idea of its coming to the knowledge of any other person; and least of all, to O'Connor's. . . .

In the mean while, Dorcasina had taken [to] her bed, with marks of as great sorrow as ever was experienced for the death of a lap-dog, or favourite parrot; and, refusing all sustenance, she gave herself up to sighs, tears and lamen-

4. That is, Patrick O'Connor, who is from Ireland or "Hibernia."

tations. Towards evening, however, a scheme entered her mind, which seemed to afford her a small ray of comfort. This was one of the most extravagant that had ever yet entered the romantic imagination of a love-sick girl, and such as no lady, in her sense, would have attempted to execute, who was not blinded to all sense of propriety, and regard to reputation. She was, however, so far gone with the novel-mania, that it appeared a proper attention to a lover, who had suffered so much for her sake. This was no other than to pay him a visit, in the evening, at his lodgings. . . .

As soon as it was dark, she sent Betty[5] out of the way, on an errand; and, calling Patrick[6] to her, she gave him a piece of money, telling him that she wanted his assistance, in a secret expedition, which he must be sure not to reveal to any living person. She then dressed herself in Betty's clothes; and, to disguise herself the better, she wore a strange old-fashioned bonnet, which had been her mother's; to which she added a veil of black gauze, that entirely concealed her face. Thus equipped, she sallied out, attended by Patrick, and took her way directly to the inn.

Being arrived, she sent Patrick to tell the hostess that Betty wanted to speak with Mr. O'Connor alone. . . . [She] followed the hostess, in silence, to the chamber of O'Connor. Our adventurer was sitting in an arm-chair, wrapped in a gown; his head was swathed with so many bandages, that only one eye, his nose and mouth were visible; and his whole head was swelled to an enormous size. Dorcasina could hardly persuade herself that it was her identical handsome lover. Her affection was not, however, in the least degree abated, at seeing him in this disgusting situation. It was rather increased, by being mingled with sentiments of pity and kind concern.

She advanced directly up to him, before she discovered herself by throwing back her veil. His surprise was equal to his pleasure, at the unexpected visit. . . . He even went so far, encouraged by the imprudent step she had taken, as to propose to her, not to return again to her father's house; but to take an apartment in the inn, have the banns[7] published the next Sunday; and go to Philadelphia and have the nuptial knot tied, with all practical dispatch. This business performed, he proposed to get the proper recommendations to her father, and then return, and, throwing themselves at his feet, humbly impore his forgiveness.

Dorcasina listened to him in silent pleasure. This manner of proceeding was so comfortable to many instances which she had read in her favourite authors, that she was upon the point of giving her consent. But, happily, for her, the idea of her father, who had not yet recovered his strength, since his late indisposition, grieved at her having quitted his house, and taken a step of such importance without his knowledge, presented itself to her imagination. She reflected also that a few days could make but little difference, either to herself or her lover. These ideas, fortunately, gave her resolution enough to resist his importunity; and all he could obtain of her, in this interview, was, a solemn promise never to marry another man . . .

5. Betty is Dorcasina's personal maid.
6. This Patrick is a young servant boy.
7. Banns are a public announcement of a proposed marriage.

Book I, Chapter X.

There had arrived, that day, at the inn, a gentleman from Philadelphia, attended by a shrewd Irish servant, possessed of as much impudence as his countryman, O'Connor. Unfortunately for Dorcasina, he was standing in the entry, when she arrived. Seeing a woman of such a strange appearance, his curiosity was excited, and he determined to watch her closely. Consequent upon this determination, he heard the message delivered to the hostess by Patrick, and saw the former shew Dorcasina the way to O'Connor's chamber. . . .

Thinking that he might insult with impunity, one, who had been so long alone with a man, in a chamber of a public house, he followed her out, and, catching her round the waist, addressed her in the most indecent terms. Dorcasina, wholly unused to such treatment, and fearing to cry out, lest she should be discovered, found herself in a more disagreeable situation than even that she had been in the night before, when, with her snowy arms, she encircled Scipio's ebony neck. Her fright and terror were indeed extreme; and she struggled, with all her strength to disengage herself. This rencounter, attracting the attention of a number of small boys, who were at play at a little distance, they advanced, to see more distinctly what was going forward. The fellow, upon their approach, quitted his hold. . . . Dorcasina rejoiced to find herself free from the rude attacks of this unmannerly stranger, sat out immediately upon the run, with all the boys in her train, halloing, and endeavouring with all their might to overtake her. Not being so well accustomed to the exercise as they were, she was soon obliged to slacken her pace, upon which they overtook her; and, on seizing her gown, another her handkerchief, and a third her bonnet, they stript her in an instant of the two latter, and left her only some tattered remains of the former. To add to the disasters of this unlucky night, in running through some mud, she lost both her shoes. In this forlorn condition, she reached the house of her friend, Mrs. Stanly. . . .

Notable Early American Women

Note: Identified women are Euro-American unless otherwise noted. Parenthetic surnames indicate subsequent married names, but by which the individual is less well known.

Adams, Abigail Smith (1744–1818), Massachusetts; letterwriter
Adams, Hannah (1755–1831), Massachusetts; historian, essayist, memoirist
Alexander, Mary Spratt Provoost (1677–1734), New York; businesswoman
Alice (1686–1802), Pennsylvania; African-American oral historian
Almy, Lydia Hill (fl. 1797–99), Rhode Island; diarist
Almy, Mary Gould (1735–1808), Rhode Island; diarist
Ambler, Mary Cary (fl. 1770), Virginia; diarist
Amory, Katherine (1731–1777), Massachusetts; diarist
Anthony, Susanna (1726–1791), Rhode Island; diarist, letter-writer
Ashbridge, Elizabeth (1713–1755), Pennsylvania; autobiographer
Ashburn, Rebecca (fl. 1790), Pennsylvania; essayist
"Aspasia" (fl. 1776–89), Pennsylvania(?); essayist
Austin, Ann (?–1665), Massachusetts; missionary
Bache, Catherine Wistar (1770–1820), Pennsylvania; letter-writer
Bache, Margaret H. (fl. late 18th c.), Pennsylvania; newspaper publisher
Bache, Sarah Franklin (1744–1808), Pennsylvania; letter-writer
Bailey [Bayley], Abigail Abbott (1746–1815), New Hampshire; diarist
Ballard, Martha Moore (1735–1812), Maine; midwife, diarist
Bancroft, Elizabeth (1773–1867), Massachusetts; diarist
Bartlett, Mary (?–1789), New Hampshire; letter-writer
Bates, Ann (fl. Rev.), Pennsylvania; teacher, Loyalist spy, petitioner
Belinda (fl. 1782), Massachusetts; African-American oral narrator, petitioner
Benbridge, Laetitia Sage (?–c.1780), Pennsylvania; artist
Berkeley (Ludwell), Lady Frances Culpeper Stephens (1634–1695?), Virginia; political
    activist, letter-writer
Blair, Anne (pre-Rev.), Virginia; letter-writer
Bland, Elizabeth (fl. 1735), Georgia; letter-writer
Bleecker, Ann Eliza Schuyler (1752–1783), New York; poet, novelist, letter-writer
Bodfish, Mercy Godwin (1752–1803), Maine; diarist
Bolling, Mary Jefferson (1741–1817), Virginia; letter-writer
Bolton, Ann (fl. 1739), Pennsylvania; diarist
Bowen, Elizabeth (1735–c. 1808), Massachusetts; diarist
Bowers, Bathsheba (c. 1672–1718), Pennsylvania; autobiographer

Bowne, Eliza Southgate (1783–1809), Maine; letter-writer

Bradford, Cornelia Smith (fl. 1754), Pennsylvania; printer

Bradford, Elizabeth (1663?–1731), Pennsylvania; poet

Bradstreet, Anne Dudley (1612–1672), Massachusetts; poet, meditations-writer

Brainard, Huldah Foote (fl. 1780), Connecticut; letter-writer

Brant, Mary (?–1796), New York/Ontario; Native American, negotiator between Mohawks and British

Brayton, Patience (fl. 1771ff), Rhode Island; Quaker traveling minister

Brent, Margaret (1601–1671), Maryland; businesswoman, political activist, landowner, attorney

Brewster, Martha Wadsworth (fl. 1725–57), Massachusetts; poet

Broughton, Anne (fl. 1715–16), South Carolina; letter-writer

Brown, Elizabeth Brown (1753–1812), Massachusetts; letter writer

Bryant, Sarah Snell (1766–1847), Massachusetts; diarist

Buffin, Ann (fl. 1752), Massachusetts; essayist

Bulfinch, Hannah (1768–1841), Massachusetts; diarist, letter writer

Burr, Esther Edwards (1732–1758), Connecticut/New Jersey; diarist, letter-writer

Burr, Theodosia Prevost (fl. 1790s), New York; letter-writer

Butterworth, Mary Peck (1686–1775), Massachusetts; inventor

Byrd, Mary Willing (1740–1814), Virginia; letter-writer

Callender, Hannah (1737–1801), Pennsylvania; diarist

Carter, Frances Ann Tasker (1737–1797), Virginia; agronomist

Carter, Maria (pre-Rev.), Virginia; letter-writer

Carter, Mary (fl. 1787–91), Massachusetts; letter-writer

Cary, Margaret Graves (1719–1762), Massachusetts; diarist

Cary, Sarah (?–1824), Massachusetts; letter-writer

Challoner, Martha Church (1723–?), Rhode Island; diarist

Chambers, Charlotte (?–1821), Pennsylvania/Ohio; diarist

Chamblit, Rebekah (?–1733), Massachusetts; confessional essayist

Champion, Deborah (1753–1845), Connecticut; letter-writer

Chichester, Ellen (pre-Rev.), Virginia; letter-writer

Churchill, Mrs. George (fl. 1796), Massachusetts; poet

Clarke, Aletta (fl. 1789–93), Delaware; diarist

Cleaveland, Mary (1722–?), Massachusetts; diarist

Cocks, Judith (fl. 1795), Connecticut; African-American letter-writer

Coit, Mehitable Chandler (1673–1758), Connecticut; diarist, letter-writer

Colden (Farquher), Jane (1724–1766), New York; botanist

Coming, Affra Harleston (?–1699), South Carolina; agronomist, letter-writer

Condict, Jemima (1754–1779), New Jersey; diarist

Cooper, Mary Wright (1714–1778), New York; diarist

Coosaponakessa, aka Mary Musgrove Matthews Bosomworth (c. 1700–post-1760), Georgia; Native American letter-writer, trader, land negotiator

Corbin, Hannah Lee (fl. 1770s), Virginia; letter-writer

Corbin, Margaret Cochran (1751–1789), Pennsylvania; war heroine

Cortlandt, Catharine Ogden (fl. 1776–77), New York; Loyalist letter-writer

Cotton, An. (fl. 1676), Virginia; essayist

Cowles, Julia (1785–1803), Connecticut; diarist

Crackbone, Sister (fl. 1640), Massachusetts; oral narrator

Cranch (Norton), Elizabeth (1763–1811), Massachusetts; diarist

Cresson, Sarah (fl. 1771–1829), Pennsylvania; diarist

Cunningham, Letitia (fl. 1783), Pennsylvania; essayist

Dare, Eleanor White (?–c.1587), Virginia; pioneer settler

Darragh, Lydia Barrington (1728–1789), Pennsylvania; war heroine

Davenport, Elizabeth Wooley (?–post-1660), Connecticut; colonial agent

Deming, Sarah Winslow (1722–1788), Massachusetts; letter-writer

Dennie, Abigail Colman (1715–1745), Massachusetts; poet

Dewees, Mary Coburn (fl. 1787–88), Pennsylvania/Kentucky; diarist

Dickinson, Rebecca (1738–1815), Massachusetts; diarist

Doughty, Ann Graves Cotton Eaton (fl. 1625), Virginia; historian

Douglass, Sarah Hallam (?–1773), South Carolina/New York; actress

Downing, Lucy Winthrop (1600/01–1679), Massachusetts; letter writer

Downing, Mary (fl. 1630s), Massachusetts; letter-writer

Draper, Margaret (c. Rev.), Massachusetts; newspaper publisher

Drew, Abigail Gardner (1777–1868), Massachusetts; diarist

Drinker, Elizabeth Sandwith (1734–1807), Pennsylvania; diarist

Drummond, Sarah Prescott (fl. 1670), Virginia; petitioner

Duchesne, Philippine (1769?–1852); frontier missionary

Dudley, Dorothy (fl. 1775–76), Massachusetts; diarist

Dudley, Mary Winthrop (post-1610–?), Massachusetts; letter-writer

Dunlap, Jane (fl. 1771), Massachusetts; poet

Dyer, Mary (?–1660), Massachusetts; missionary

Easty, Mary (?–1692), Massachusetts; petitioner, executed for witchcraft

Eaton, Mrs. Nathaniel (17th c.), Massachusetts; diarist

Edwards, Sarah Pierpont (1710–1758), Connecticut; essayist, letter-writer

Emerson, Eleanor Read (?–1808), Massachusetts; diarist, letter writer

English, Mary (1652?–1694), Massachusetts; poet, accused of witchcraft

Eppes, Elizabeth Wayles (fl. 1787), Virginia; letter-writer

Estaugh, Elizabeth Haddon (1680–1762), New Jersey; pioneer settler

Eve, Sarah (1749/50–1774), Pennsylvania; diarist

Fages, Doña Eulelia de Callis y (fl. 1783), California; pioneer settler

Fairfax, Sally Cary (fl. 177172), Virginia; diarist

Farmar, Eliza (fl. 1774–75), Pennsylvania; letter-writer

Faugères, Margaretta V. Bleeker (1771–1801), New York; poet, dramatist, essayist, letter-writer

Fenno, Jenny (fl. 1791), Massachusetts; essayist, poet

Ferguson, Catherine (c. 1749–1854), New York; African-American Sunday-school founder

Fergusson, Elizabeth Graeme (1737–1801), Pennsylvania; poet, letter-writer

Fisher (Dawes), Sarah Logan (1751–1796), Pennsylvania; letter-writer, diarist

Fiske, Sarah Symmes (1627–1692), Massachusetts; essayist

Fleet, Mary (1729–c. 1803), Massachusetts; diarist

Fletcher, Bridget Richardson (1726–1770), Massachusetts; hymnist

Foote, Elizabeth (1750–?), Connecticut; diarist

Foster, Hannah Webster (1758–1840), Massachusetts; novelist

Franklin, Anne Smith (1696–1763), Rhode Island; printer

Franklin, Deborah Read Rogers (1708–1774), Pennsylvania; letter-writer

Franks, Abigail Levy (1696–1756), Pennsylvania; pioneer settler, letter-writer

Franks, Rebecca (fl. 1778–81), Pennsylvania; letter-writer

Frazier, Jane Ball McClain (1735?–1815?), Maryland; captivity narrator

Frazier, Mary (c. Rev.), Pennsylvania; letter-writer

Freeman, Elizabeth ("Mumbet") (fl. 1781), Massachusetts; African-American petitioner

French, Mary (fl. 1703), Massachusetts; poet

French, Rebecca Brown (1763–1813), Vermont; letter-writer

Frost, Sarah (1754–1817), Connecticut; diarist

Fuller, Elizabeth (1775–1856), Massachusetts; diarist

Galloway, Grace Growden (?–1782), Pennsylvania; diarist

Gamsby, Dorothea (fl. 1775), New Hampshire; oral narrator

Gill, Sarah Prince (1728–1771), Massachusetts; essayist, letter-writer

Goddard, Mary Katherine (1738–1816), Maryland; printer, postmaster, newspaper editor, petitioner

Goddard, Sarah Updike (c.1700–1770), Maryland/Rhode Island; editor, publisher

Goodhue, Sarah Whipple (1641–1681), New Hampshire; essayist

Graham, Isabella Marshall (1742–1814), New Jersey/New York; letter-writer

Grant, Anne MacVicar (1755–1838), New York; poet, memoirist

Greene, Catherine Ray (1731?–1794), Rhode Island; letter-writer

Griffitts, Hannah (1727–1817), Pennsylvania; poet, letter-writer

Gutridge, Molly (fl. 1778), Massachusetts; poet

Gwinnett, Ann (?–post-1780), Georgia; petitioner

Hanson, Elizabeth Meader (1684–1741), New Hampshire; captivity narrator

Harrison, Anna Symmes (1775–1864), Ohio; letter-writer

Hart, Nancy Morgan (fl. 1776), Georgia; war heroine

Hayden, Anna Tompson (1648–1720), Massachusetts; poet

Hayden, Esther (c.1713–1758), Massachusetts; poet

Heath, Betsey (1769–1853), Massachusetts; diarist

Heaton, Hannah (1721–1794), New York; autobiographer

Heck, Barbara Ruckle (1734–1804), New York; cofounder of Methodism in American colonies

Henshaw (Miles) (Bascom), Ruth (1772–1846), Massachusetts; diarist

Hibbens, Ann (fl. 1640–1692), Massachusetts; trial transcript

Hill, Frances Baylor (fl. 1797), Virginia; diarist

Hill, Hannah Jr. (c. 1703–1714), Pennsylvania; death-bed confessional

Hillhouse, Sarah Potter (late 18th c.), Georgia; editor, publisher

Hinestrosa, Francisca (?–1534), Florida; pioneer settler

Hodgkins, Sarah Perkins (1750?–1803), Massachusetts; letter-writer

Holyoke, Mary Vial (1737–1802), Massachusetts; diarist

Hook, Elizabeth (?–c. 1844), Massachusetts; diarist

Hooker, Mary Treadwell (1755–?), Connecticut; diarist

Hoskens, Jane Fenn (1694–?), Pennsylvania; minister, autobiographer

Hume, Sophia Wigington (1702–1773), South Carolina; minister, essayist

Huntington, Anne Huntington (1740?–1790), Connecticut; letter-writer

Huntington, Hannah (fl. 1791–1811), Ohio; letter-writer

Huntington (Tracy), Rachel (1779–?), Connecticut; letter-writer

Inman, Elizabeth Murray Campbell Smith (c. 1724–1785), Massachusetts; diarist, letter-writer

Jefferson, Martha Wayles Skelton (1748–1782), Virginia; letter-writer

Johnson, Mary Watts (fl. 1776), New York; petitioner

Johnston, Henrietta (?–1729), South Carolina; artist

Jones, Rebecca (fl. 1770s–80s), Pennsylvania; teacher, letter-writer

Kennett, Margaret Brett (fl. 1725), South Carolina; letter-writer

Kinnan, Mary Lewis (1763–1848), Virginia; captivity narrator

Knight, Sarah Kemble (1666–1727), Massachusetts; diarist, businesswoman

Lady of Cofitachique (fl. 1540), Georgia/South Carolina; Native American leader

La Tour, Frances Mary Jacqueline (?–1645), Maine; pioneer settler

Leach, Christiana (?–post-1796), Pennsylvania; diarist

Leadbetter, Mary (1758–1826), Pennsylvania; diarist

Lee (Standerin), Ann (1736–1784), New York; founder of Shakers

Lee (Orr), Lucinda (fl. 1787), Virginia; diarist

Leininger, Barbara (fl. 1759), Pennsylvania; captivity narrator

Lennox, Charlotte Ramsey (1720–1804), New York/England; novelist, dramatist, translator

Leonard, Elizabeth Dow (late 18th c.), New Hampshire; diarist

Letort, Ann (?–1728), Pennsylvania; trader, letter-writer

L'Hommedieu, Abigail (1774–1851), Connecticut; diarist

Livingston, Alida Schuyler van Rensselaer (1656–1727), New York; businesswoman, letter-writer

Livingston, Catharine (fl. Rev.), Massachusetts; letter-writer

Lloyd, Mary Clarke Pemberton Campbell (1681–1749), Massachusetts; religious essayist

Logan, Deborah Norris (1761–1839), Pennsylvania; letter-writer

Logan, Martha Daniell (1704–1779), South Carolina; horticulturist, essayist, letter-writer

Lyman, Abigail Brackett (1779–1803), Massachusetts; letter-writer

Madison, Dolley Payne Todd (1768–1849), North Carolina/Virginia; letter-writer

Magawley, Elizabeth (fl. 1730s), Pennsylvania; essayist

Manigault, Ann Ashby (1703–1782), South Carolina; diarist

Manigault, Judith Giton Royer (?–1711), South Carolina; agronomist, letter-writer

Mason, Priscilla (fl. 1793), Pennsylvania; essayist

Masters, Sybilla (?–1720), Pennsylvania/New Jersey; inventor

Mather, Maria (?–1714), Massachusetts; spiritual narrativist

May, Abigail (1775–1800), Maine; diarist

McCauley, Mary (1754–1832), New Jersey/Pennsylvania; known as "Molly Pitcher," war heroine

McGinn, Sarah Cass (fl. 1777), New York; essayist, interpreter between Native Americans and colonists

Mecom, Jane Franklin (1712–1794), Massachusetts; letter-writer

Meredith, Gertrude Gouveneur Ogden (fl. 1790s–1800), Pennsylvania; letter-writer

Mifflin, Anne Emlen (18th c.), Pennsylvania; essayist

Mixer, Elizabeth (fl. 1707–20), Massachusetts; spiritual autobiographer

Montour, Madame Catherine (c. 1684–c. 1752), New York/ Pennsylvania; Native American interpreter, agent

Moody, Lady Deborah Dunche (1600–1660), New York; colonial leader

Moore, Ann (fl. 1756–68), Pennsylvania; diarist

Moore, Hannah Hill (1745–1833), Maryland/Pennsylvania; essayist

Moore, Milcah Martha (1740–1829), Pennsylvania; poet

Moorhead, Sarah Parsons (fl. 1741–42), Massachusetts; poet

Morris, Margaret Hill (1737–1816), New Jersey; diarist

Morton, Sarah Wentworth Apthorp (1759–1846), Massachusetts; poet

Moseley, Susanna (fl. 1649–50), Virginia; letter-writer

Motte, Rebecca Brewton (1737–1815), South Carolina; war heroine

Murray, Judith Sargent (1751–1820), Massachusetts; poet, essayist, dramatist, novelist, letter-writer

Nelson, Mary (fl. 1769), Pennsylvania; poet

Nuthead, Dinah (fl. 1695), Maryland; printer

Nutt, Anna Rutter Savage (1686–1760), Pennsylvania; businesswoman

Osborn, Sarah Haggar Wheaten (1714–1796), Rhode Island; religious revivalist, diarist, letter-writer, spiritual autobiographer

Palmer, Abigail (fl. 1777), New Jersey; court testimony

Palmer, Esther (?–1714), Rhode Island/Pennsylvania; travel diarist

Papegoija, Armegot Printz (?–1695), Pennsylvania; pioneer settler and landowner

Parker, Margaret (fl. 1779), Virginia; letter-writer

Parkman, Anna Sophia (1755–1783), Massachusetts; diarist

Parrish, Anne (1760–1800), Pennsylvania; philanthropist, educator

Paterson, Cornelia Bell (1755–1783), New Jersey; letter-writer

Patten, Ruth (fl. 18th c.), Connecticut; letter-writer

Penn, Hannah Callowhill (1671–1726), Pennsylvania; businesswoman, letter-writer, colonial leader

Phelps, Elizabeth Porter (1747–1817), Massachusetts; diarist

Phillipse, Margaret Hardenbroek de Vries (?–1690), New York; businesswoman

Pierce, Sarah (1767–1852), Connecticut; educator, poet, letter-writer

Pinckney, Eliza Lucas (c. 1722–1793), South Carolina; diarist, businesswoman

Porter, Sarah (fl. 1791), Massachusetts; poet

Post, Lydia Minturn (fl. 1776–83), New York; diarist

Pray, Mary Herendean (fl. 1675), Rhode Island; letter-writer

Prince, Deborah (fl. 1744), Massachusetts; memoirist, poet

Pritchett, Lucretia (fl. 1776), Virginia; petitioner

Provoost, Maria de Peyster Schrick Spratt (?–1700), New York; businesswoman

Ramsay, Martha Laurens (1759–1811), South Carolina; horticulturalist, diarist, letter-writer

Ratcliff, Mildred Morris (1773–1847), Virginia/Ohio/Pennsylvania; minister, diarist, letter-writer

Rawle (Clifford), Anna (fl. 1781), Pennsylvania; diarist

Read, Catherine (fl. 1798), South Carolina; letter-writer

Reed, Esther DeBerdt (1747–1780), Pennsylvania; political activist, letter-writer

Rensselaer, Maria van Cortlandt van (1645–1689), New York; colonial leader, letter-writer

Richardson, Rebecca (fl. 1738), Pennsylvania; poet

Riedesel, Frederika Von Massow (1746–1808), Germany/New York; diarist

Roberts, Mary (?–1761), South Carolina; artist

Rogers, Martha "Patty" (fl. 1785), New Hampshire; diarist

Rogers, Susanna (fl. 1725), Massachusetts; poet

Rosehill, Lady Margaret Cheer (18th c.), Pennsylvania; actress

Rowlandson, Mary White (1637?–1711), Massachusetts; captivity narrator

Rowson, Susanna Haswell (1761–1824), Massachusetts; educator, actress, novelist, dramatist

Russell, Mary (1768–1839), Connecticut; diarist

Schuyler, Catherine Van Rensselaer (1733–1804), New York; war heroine

Schuyler, Margaret Schuyler (1701–1782), New York; literary critic

Scott, Katherine Marbury (fl. 1658), Rhode Island; letter-writer

Sellers, Elizabeth Coleman (1751–1832), Pennsylvania; letter-writer

Seton, Elizabeth Ann Bayley (1774–1821), Maryland; founder of religious charity, diarist, letter-writer

Sheldon, Charlotte (1780–c. 1840), Connecticut; diarist

Shepard, Hety (1660–?), Rhode Island; diarist

Shippen (Livingston), Anne ("Nancy") (1763–1841), Pennsylvania; diarist

Sinkler, Elizabeth (fl. 1782), South Carolina; letter-writer

Smith, Abigail Adams (1765–1813), Massachusetts; letter-writer

Smith, Anna Young (1756–1780), Pennsylvania; poet

Smith, Barbara (fl. 1689), Maryland; letter-writer

Smith, Eunice (1757–1823), Massachusetts; essayist

Smith, Grace (fl. 1712), Massachusetts; death-bed writer

Smith, Margaret (fl. 1660), Massachusetts; letter-writer
Spaulding, Anna Brown (1761–1825), Vermont; letter-writer
Sprigs, Elizabeth (fl. 1756), Maryland; indentured servant, letter-writer
Springfield, Laodicea Langston (1760–?), South Carolina; war heroine
Stafford, Mary (fl. 1711), South Carolina; letter-writer
Starbuck, Mary Coffin (1645–1717), Massachusetts; community leader
Steuart, Jenny (fl. 1777–79), Virginia; letter-writer
Stockton, Annis Boudinot (1736–1801), New Jersey; poet
Stone, Virlinda Cotton Burdett Boughton (fl. 1650), Maryland; diarist
Stoothoff, Saartze Roelof Kierstede von Borsum (?–1693), New York; interpreter
Storrs, Lucinda Howe (1757–1839), Connecticut/New Hampshire; diarist
Swett, Mary Howell (fl. 1797–99), Pennsylvania; diarist
Symmes, Susan Livingston (fl. 1794–1808), New Jersey/Ohio/New York; letter-writer
Tenney, Tabitha Gilman (1762–1837), Massachusetts; novelist
Terry (Prince), Lucy (1730–1821), Massachusetts; African-American poet
Thomson, Hannah (fl. 1785–88), New York; letter-writer
Threrwitz, Emily Geiger (c. 1760–?), South Carolina; war heroine
Tiffany, Consider (1733–1796), Connecticut; poet
Tilghman, Henrietta Maria (1763–1796), Maryland; letter-writer
Timothy, Ann Donovan (1727–1792), South Carolina; printer
Tranchepain, de Saint Augustine, Sister Marie (?–1733), Louisiana; religious founder
Traske, Mary (fl. 1660), Massachusetts; letter-writer
Turrell, Jane Colman (1708–1735), Massachusetts; poet
van Cortlandt, Catharine Ogden (fl. 1776–77), New York; letter-writer
Waite, Eliza (fl. 1786–91), Massachusetts; letter-writer
Wall, Rachel (fl. 1789), Massachusetts; criminal confessor
Ward, Nancy (c. 1738–c. 1824), Tennessee; Native American war heroine
Ward, Susanna (1779–1860), Massachusetts; diarist
Warder, Ann Head (c. 1758–1829), Pennsylvania; diarist
Warren, Mercy Otis (1728–1814), Massachusetts; dramatist, poet, letter-writer, historian
Washington, Martha Dandridge Custis (1732–1802), Virginia; letter-writer, community leader
Waters, Abigail Dawes (18th c.), Massachusetts; memoirist
Watteville, Benigna Zinzendorf de (1725–1789), Pennsylvania; educator
Webb, Elizabeth (fl. 1781), Pennsylvania; letter-writer
Wells, Helena (c. 1760–c. 1809), Massachusetts; novelist
Wells (Aikman), Louisa Susannah (c. 1755–1831), South Carolina; diarist
Wheatley (Peters), Phillis (c. 1753–1784), Massachusetts; African-American poet, letter-writer
Wheeler, Mercy (fl. 1733), Massachusetts; advice writer
Whitall, Ann Cooper (1716–1797), New Jersey/Pennsylvania; diarist
White, Nancy (fl. 1781–86), Massachusetts; diarist
Whitmore, Mrs. (fl. 1760), Vermont; midwife
Wildes, Elizabeth (1765–1844), Maine; diarist
Wilkinson, Eliza Yonge (fl. 1779–82), South Carolina; letter-writer
Wilkinson, Jemima (1752–1819), Rhode Island; religious leader, preacher, essayist
Williams, Hannah English (1692–1722), South Carolina; biologist, letter-writer
Willis, Lydia Fish (1709–1767), Massachusetts/New Hampshire; letter-writer, poet
Wilson, Elizabeth (fl. 1786), Pennsylvania; criminal confessor
Wilson, Rachel (fl. 1769), New York; essayist
Winslow, Anna Green (1759–1779), Massachusetts; diarist

Winslow, Sarah (fl. 1780–1815), Massachusetts; letter-writer

Winthrop, Margaret Tyndal (c. 1591–1647), Massachusetts; community leader, letter-writer

Wister, Sarah (1761–1804), Pennsylvania; diarist

Wood, Sally Sayward Barrell (1759–1855), Massachusetts; novelist

Wright, Patience Lovell (1725–1786), New Jersey; artist, letter-writer

Wright, Prudence Cummings (fl. 1775), Massachusetts/New Hampshire; war heroine

Wright, Susanna (1697–1784), Pennsylvania; businesswoman, poet, letter-writer

Yardley, Lady Temperance Flowerdew Yardley West (1593–1636), Virginia; community leader

Zenger, Anna Catherina Maul (c. 1704–1751), New York; printer, editor

Zinzendorf, Anna Caritas Nitschmann (1715–1760), Pennsylvania; educator

Selected Bibliography

Adams, Charles F., ed. *Correspondence between John Adams and Mercy Otis Warren, Including . . . Specimen Pages from the History.* New York: Arno, 1972.

Allen, Paula Gunn. *Grandmothers of the Light: A Medicine Woman's Source Book.* Boston: Beacon, 1991.

———. *The Sacred Hoop: Recovering the Feminine in American Literary Traditions.* Boston: Beacon, 1986.

Altman, Janet Gurkin. *Epistolarity: Approaches to a Form.* Columbus: Ohio State UP, 1982.

American Imprints, 1648–1797, in the Huntington Library, Supplementing Evans' American Bibliography. Comp. Williard O. Waters. Cambridge: Harvard UP, 1933.

Anderson, Rufus, ed. *Memoirs of Katherine Brown, a Christian Indian of the Cherokee Nation.* Philadelphia: American Sunday School Union, 1832 [1824].

Andrews, Matthew Page. *The Founding of Maryland.* Baltimore: Williams & Wilkins, 1933.

Andrews, William L., et al., eds. *Journeys in New Worlds: Early American Women's Narratives.* Madison: U of Wisconsin P, 1990.

Anthony, Katharine. *First Lady of the Revolution: The Life of Mercy Otis Warren.* Garden City, NY: Doubleday, 1958.

Armes, Ethel. *Nancy Shippen: Her Journal Book.* Philadelphia: Lippincott, 1935.

Axtell, James, ed. *The Indian Peoples of Eastern America: A Documentary History of the Sexes.* New York: Oxford UP, 1981.

Bacon, Margaret Hope. *Mothers of Feminism: The Story of Quaker Women in America.* New York: Harper & Row, 1986.

Bailyn, Bernard. *Education in the Forming of American Society: Needs and Opportunities for Study.* Chapel Hill: U of North Carolina P, 1960.

Ballard, Martha Moore. "Diary, 1785–1812," in *The History of Augusta [Maine].* Ed. Charles Elventon Nash. Augusta, ME: Charles Nash and Sons, 1904. 229–464.

Barbour, Hugh, comp. and ed., Arthur O. Roberts, ed. *Early Quaker Writings, 1650–1700.* Grand Rapids: Eerdmans, 1973.

Bartlett, Josiah. *The Papers of Josiah Bartlett.* Ed. Frank C. Mevers. Hanover: For New Hampshire Historical Society by UP of New England, 1979.

Bartlett, Levi. *Genealogical and Biographical Sketches of the Bartlett Family in England and America.* Lawrence, MA, 1876.

Bataille, Gretchen M., and Kathleen M. Sands. *American Indian Women: A Guide to Research.* New York: Garland, 1991.

———. *American Indian Women: Telling Their Lives.* Lincoln: U of Nebraska P, 1984.

Baym, Nina. "Between Enlightenment and Victorian: Toward a Narrative of American Women Writers Writing History." *Critical Inquiry* 18 (Autumn 1991): 22–41.

———. "Mercy Otis Warren's Gendered Melodrama of Revolution." *South Atlantic Quarterly* 90 (Summer 1991): 531–554.

Beasley, Maurine H., and Sheila J. Gibbons. *Taking Their Place: A Documentary History of Women and Journalism*. Washington, D.C.: American UP, 1993.

Begay, Shirley M. *Kinaalda, A Navajo Puberty Ceremony*. Rev. ed. Rough Rock, AZ: Navajo Curriculum Center, 1983.

Bennett, Lerone Jr.. *Before the Mayflower: A History of Black America*. Exp. ed. New York: Penguin, 1982.

Benson, Mary Sumner. *Women in Eighteenth-Century America*. New York: Columbia UP, 1935.

Benstock, Shari, ed. *The Private Self: Theory and Practice of Women's Autobiographical Writings*. Chapel Hill: U of North Carolina P, 1988.

Biddle, Gertrude B., and Sarah D. Lowrie, eds. *Notable Women of Pennsylvania*. Philadelphia: U of Pennsylvania P, 1942.

Biemer, Linda; trans. Hugh Uyttenhove. "Business Letters of Alida Schuyler Livingston, 1680–1726." *New York History* 63 (1982): 183–207.

Blair, John L. "Mrs. Mary Dewees's Journal from Philadelphia to Kentucky." *Register of the Kentucky Historical Society* 63.3 (1965): 195–218.

Blassingame, John W., ed. *Slave Testimony: Two Centuries of Letters, Speeches, Interviews, and Autobiographies*. Baton Rouge: Louisiana State UP, 1977.

Blumenthal, Walter Hart. *Women Camp Followers of the American Revolution*. New York: Arno, 1974.

Boles, John B. *Black Southerners 1619–1869*. Lexington: UP of Kentucky, 1984.

Bond, Beverley W. Jr., ed. *The Intimate Letters of John Cleves Symmes and His Family*. Cincinnati: Historical and Philosophical Society of Ohio, 1956.

Bottorff, William B., and Roy C. Flannagan. Introduction to "The Diary of Frances Baylor Hill." *Early American Literature Newsletter* 2 (1967): 4–53.

Bowden, J. *The History of the Society of Friends in America*. Philadelphia, 1850.

Boyer, Paul, and Stephen Nissenbaum, eds. *Salem Village Witchcraft*. Belmont, CA: Wadsworth, 1972.

Brandt, Ellen. *Susanna Haswell Rowson: America's First Best-Selling Novelist*. Chicago: Zebra, 1977.

Braxton, Joanne M. *Black Women Writing Autobiography: A Tradition Within a Tradition*. Philadelphia: Temple UP, 1989.

Breitwieser, Mitchell. *American Puritanism and the Defense of Mourning: Religion, Grief, and Ethnology in Mary Rowlandson's Captivity Narrative*. Madison: U of Wisconsin P, 1990.

Brodzki, Bella, and Celeste Schenck, eds. *Life/Lines: Theorizing Women's Autobiography*. Ithaca: Cornell UP, 1988.

Brooks, Van Wyck. *The Flowering of New England 1815–1865*. Boston: Houghton Mifflin, 1936.

Brown, Herbert Ross. *The Sentimental Novel in America 1789–1860*. Durham, NC: Duke UP, 1940.

Brumble, H. David III. *American Indian Autobiography*. Berkeley: U of California P, 1988.

———. *An Annotated Bibliography of American Indian and Eskimo Autobiographies*. Lincoln: U of Nebraska P, 1981.

Buchanan, Kimberly Moore. *Apache Women Warriors*. (Southwestern Studies Series No. 79.) El Paso: Texas Western P, 1986.

Bulfinch, Ellen Susan, ed. *The Life and Letters of Charles Bulfinch, Architect, with Other Family Papers*. 1896; rpt. New York: Burt Franklin, 1973.

Burr, George L., ed. *Narratives of the Witchcraft Cases*. New York: Scribner, 1914.

Burton, Frederick. *American Primitive Music*. New York: Moffat, 1909.

Bush, Sargent Jr. Introduction to *"The Journals of Madam Knight"* in Andrews, *Journeys in New Worlds*, 69–83.

Butterfield, L. H. *Adams Family Correspondence*. Cambridge: Harvard UP, 1963.

Calder, Isabel, ed. *Colonial Captivities, Marches, and Journeys*. New York: Macmillan, 1935.

Caldwell, Patricia. *The Puritan Conversion Narrative: The Beginnings of American Expression*. Cambridge: Cambridge UP, 1983.

Callender, Hannah. "Extracts from the Diary of Hannah Callender." *Pennsylvania Magazine of History and Biography* 12 (1888): 432–456.

Castiglia, Christopher. "Susanna Rowson's *Reuben and Rachel*: Captivity, Colonization, and the Domestication of Columbus," in Harris, *Redefining the Political Novel*, 23–42.

Chapman, Clayton Harding. "Benjamin Colman's Daughters." *New England Quarterly* 26 (1953): 169–192.

Childs, St. Julien R. "A Letter Written in 1711 by Mary Stafford to her Kinswoman in England." *South Carolina Historical Magazine* 81 (1980): 1–7.

Clark, Alice. *Working Life of Women in the Seventeenth Century*. New York: Dutton, 1919.

Clark, Ella E. *Indian Legends of the Pacific Northwest*. Berkeley: U of California P, 1953.

Cochran, Samuel P. "Mrs. Mary Dewees's Journal from Philadelphia to Kentucky, 1787–1788." *Pennsylvania Magazine of History and Biography* 28 (1904): 182–198.

Cohen, Lester H. "Mercy Otis Warren: The Politics of Language and the Aesthetics of Self." *American Quarterly* 35 (Winter 1983): 481–498.

Coleman, Kenneth. *Colonial Georgia: A History*. New York: Scribner, 1976.

Coleman, Kenneth, and Milton Ready, eds. *The Colonial Records of the State of Georgia: Original Papers, Correspondence to the Trustees, James Oglethorpe, and Others*. Vol. 20. Athens: U of Georgia P, 1982.

Converse, Harriet M. "Myths and Legends of the New York State Iroquois." *New York State Museum Bulletin* 125 (1908): 5–195.

Conway, Jill K. *The Female Experience in 18th and 19th Century America: A Guide to the History of American Women*. Princeton: Princeton UP, 1982.

Cook, Clarence, ed. *A Girl's Life Eighty Years Ago: Selections from the Letters of Eliza Southgate Bowne*. New York: Scribner, 1888.

Cooper, Mary. *The Diary of Mary Cooper: Life on a Long Island Farm 1768–1773*. Ed. Field Horne. Oyster Bay, NY: Oyster Bay Historical Society, 1981.

Cott, Nancy F. *The Bonds of Womanhood: "Woman's Sphere" in New England, 1780–1835*. New Haven: Yale UP, 1977.

Cowell, Pattie. *Women Poets in Pre-Revolutionary America 1650–1775: An Anthology*. Troy, NY: Whitston Publishing, 1981.

Cowell, Pattie, and Ann Stanford. *Critical Essays on Anne Bradstreet*. Boston: G. K. Hall, 1983.

Crary, Catherine S. *The Price of Loyalty: Tory Writings from the Revolutionary Era*. New York: McGraw-Hill, 1973.

Cronin, James E., ed. *Diary of Elihu Hubbard Smith*. Philadelphia: American Philosophical Society, 1973.

Culley, Margo, ed. and intro. *A Day at a Time: The Diary Literature of American Women from 1764 to the Present*. New York: Feminist P, 1985.

Cushing, Frank Hamilton. *Zuni Breadstuff*. (Indian Notes and Monographs 8.) New York: Heye Foundation, 1920.

Davidson, Cathy N. Introduction to *Charlotte Temple*. New York: Oxford UP, 1986. xi–xxxiii.

———. Introduction to *The Coquette*. New York: Oxford UP, 1986.

————. *Revolution and the Word: The Rise of the Novel in America.* New York: Oxford UP, 1986.

————, ed. *Reading in America: Literature & Social History.* Baltimore: Johns Hopkins UP, 1989.

Davis, Gwenn, and Beverly A. Joyce, comp. *Personal Writings by Women to 1900: A Bibliography of American and British Writers.* London: Mansell Publishing, 1989.

Davis, Rebecca Harding. "Old Philadelphia," *Harper's New Monthly Magazine* 52 (April/May 1876): 705–21, 868–82.

Davis, Richard Beale. *Intellectual Life in the Colonial South 1585–1763.* 3 Vols. Knoxville: U of Tennessee P, 1978.

Densmore, Frances. *Chippewa Music.* Bureau of American Ethnology, Bulletin 45, 1910.

DePauw, Linda Grant. *Founding Mothers: Women of America in the Revolutionary Era.* Boston: Houghton Mifflin, 1975.

Derounian [Stodola], Kathryn Zabelle. "The Publication, Promotion, and Distribution of Mary Rowlandson's Indian Captivity Narrative in the Seventeenth Century." *Early American Literature* 23 (1988).

Derounian-Stodola, Kathryn Zabelle. "The New England Frontier and Picaresque in Sarah Kemble Knight's Journal." *Early American Literature and Culture: Essays Honoring Harrison T. Meserole.* Ed. Kathryn Zabelle Derounian-Stodola. Newark: U of Delaware P, 1992. 122–131.

Derounian [Stodola], Kathryn Zabelle, ed. *The Journal and Occasional Writings of Sarah Wister.* Rutherford: Fairleigh Dickinson P, 1987.

Derounian-Stodola, Kathryn Zabelle, and James Levernier. *The Indian Captivity Narrative, 1550–1900.* New York: Twayne, 1993.

Dove, Rita. "Belinda's Petition" in *Selected Poems.* New York: Pantheon, 1993. 28.

Downing, Lucy Winthrop. "Letters of Lucy Downing." *5 Collections* (MHS) 1 (1871): 3–69.

Drinker, Sophie Hutchinson. *Hannah Penn and the Proprietorship of Pennsylvania.* Philadelphia: International Printing Co., 1958.

Dwight, Sereno E. *The Life of President Edwards.* New York: G. & C. & H. Carvill, 1830.

Earle, Alice Morse. *Colonial Dames and Good Wives.* Boston: Houghton Mifflin, 1895.

————. *Margaret Winthrop.* New York: Scribner, 1895; rpt. 1972.

————, ed. *Diary of Anna Green Winslow, A Boston School Girl of 1771.* 1894; rpt., Williamstown, MA: Corner House, 1974.

Ellet, Elizabeth F. L. *The Women of the American Revolution.* 2nd ed. 3 Vols. New York: Baker and Scribner, 1848–1850; rpt., New York: Haskell House, 1969.

Enright, Brian J. "An Account of Charles Town in 1725." *South Carolina Historical Magazine* 61 (1960): 13–18.

Erdoes, Richard, and Alfonso Ortiz, eds. *American Indian Myths and Legends.* New York: Pantheon, 1984.

Evans, Charles. *American Bibliography: A Chronological Dictionary of All Books, Pamphlets and Periodical Publications Printed in the United States of America from the Genesis of Printing in 1639 Down to and Including the Year 1820.* 14 Vols. New York: Peter Smith, 1941; UP of Virginia, 1970.

Evans, Nathaniel. *Poems on Several Occasions with Some Other Compositions.* 1772; rpt. New York: Fordham UP, 1976.

Familiar Letters Written by Mrs. Sarah Osborn, and Miss Susanna Anthony. Newport, RI: Newport Mercury, 1807.

Faragher, John Mack, ed. *The Encyclopedia of Colonial and Revolutionary America.* New York: Facts on File, 1990.

Faust, Langdon Lynne. *American Women Writers: A Critical Reference Guide from Colonial Times to the Present.* 2 Vols. New York: Frederick Unger, 1983.

Field, Vena Bernadette. *Constantia: A Study of the Life and Works of Judith Sargent Murray, 1751–1820*. Orono, ME: University P, 1931.

Fizer, Irene. "Signing the Republican Mother: The Letters of Eliza Southgate." Paper presented at the Modern Language Association Conference, Chicago, December 1990.

Fletcher, Alice C., and Francis La Flesche. "The Omaha Tribe." *Twenty-Seventh Annual Report of the Bureau of American Ethnography, 1905–06*. Washington, D.C.: Smithsonian, 1910.

Foner, Philip S. *Blacks in the American Revolution*. (Contributions in American History, No. 55.) Westport, CT: Greenwood, 1975.

Foster, Frances Smith. *Written by Herself: Literary Production of African American Women, 1746–1892*. Bloomington: Indiana UP, 1993.

Franklin, Benjamin. *Reflections on Courtship and Marriage*. Philadelphia: B. Franklin, 1746.

———. *The Papers of Benjamin Franklin*. 26 Vols. Ed. Leonard W. Labaree, et al. New Haven: Yale UP, 1959–87.

Freibert, Lucy M., and Barbara A. White, eds. *Hidden Hands: An Anthology of American Women Writers, 1790–1870*. New Brunswick, NJ: Rutgers UP, 1985.

Gelles, Edith B. "The Abigail Industry." *William and Mary Quarterly* 45 (Oct. 1988): 656–683.

Goodfriend, Joyce D. *The Published Diaries and Letters of American Women: An Annotated Bibliography*. Boston: G. K. Hall, 1987.

Grant, Anne. *Memoirs of an American Lady: With Sketches of Manners and Scenery in America, as They existed Previous to the Revolution*. London: Longman, Hurst, Rees & Orme, etc., 1808.

Gratz, Simon. "Material for a Biography of Mrs. Elizabeth Fergusson, nee Graeme." *Pennsylvania Magazine of History and Biography* 39.3 (1915): 257–321; 39.4 (1915): 385–409; 41.4 (1917); 385–398.

Green, Rayna. *Native American Women: A Bibliography*. Wichita Falls, TX: Ohoyo Resource Center, 1981.

Greene, David L. "New Light on Mary Rowlandson." *Early American Literautre* 20.1 (1985).

Grinnell, George Bird. *Pawnee Hero Stories and Folk-Tales*. New York: Forest and Stream, 1889.

Griswold, Rufus Wilmot. *The Female Poets of America*. 1848; rev. ed. New York: James Miller, 1877.

Gummere, Amelia M., ed. *The Journal and Essays of John Woolman*. New York: Macmillan, 1922.

Gunn, John M. *Schat-Chen: History, Traditions, and Narratives of the Queres Indians of Laguna and Acoma*. 1917; rpt. New York: AMS, 1977.

Gura, Philip. *A Glimpse of Sion's Glory: Puritan Radicalism in New England, 1620–1660*. Middletown, CT: Wesleyan UP, 1984.

Hakluyt, Richard. *Voyages to the Virginia Colonies*. Ed. and intro. A. L. Rowse. London: Century, 1986.

Hall, Edward Hagman. *Margaret Corbin: Heroine of the Battle of Fort Washington, 16 November 1776*. New York: American Scenic & Historic Preservation Society, 1932.

Hallenbeck, Chester T. "The Life and Collected Poems of Elizabeth Graeme Fergusson." Master's thesis, Columbia U, 1929.

Haller, Mabel. *Early Moravian Education in Pennsylvania*. Nazareth, PA: Moravian Historical Society, 1953.

Hammond, George P., and Agapito Rey, eds. *Don Juan de Oñate, Colonizer of New Mexico 1598–1628*. 2 Vols. Albuquerque: U of New Mexico P, 1953.

Harris, Sharon M. "Lost Boundaries: The Carnivalesque in Tabitha Tenney's *Female Quixotism*" (forthcoming).

———, ed. *Selected Writings of Judith Sargent Murray*. New York: Oxford UP, 1995.

———, ed. *Redefining the Political Novel: American Women Writers 1797–1901*. Knoxville: U of Tennessee P, 1995.

Heimert, Alan, and Andrew Delbanco. *The Puritans in America: A Narrative Anthology*. Cambridge: Harvard UP, 1985.

Hendrickson, James. "Ann Eliza Bleecker: Her Life and Works." Master's thesis, Columbia, 1935.

Hensley, Jeannine, ed. *The Works of Anne Bradstreet*. Cambridge: Belknap, 1981.

Hoffman, Nancy, ed. *Woman's True Profession: Voices from the History of Teaching*. Old Westbury, NY: Feminist P, 1981.

Hoffman, Walter J. *The Menomini Indians*. 14th Annual Report of the Bureau of American Ethnology. Washington, D.C. 1896.

Holland, J. G. *History of Western Massachusetts*. 2 Vols. Springfield: S. Bowles, 1855.

Hopkins, Samuel, ed. *The Life and Character of Miss Susanna Anthony*. Worcester, 1796.

Hornstein, Jacqueline. "Literary History of New England Women Writers: 1630–1800." Ph.D. thesis, New York U, 1978.

Hudak, Leona M. *Early American Women Printers and Publishers, 1639–1820*. Metuchen, NJ: Scarecrow, 1978.

Hungry Wolf, Beverly. *The Ways of My Grandmothers*. New York: William Morrow, 1980.

An Introduction to Black Literature in America, from 1746 to the Present. Comp. Lindsay Patterson. New York: Publishers Co., 1968.

Jackson, John W. *Margaret Morris: Her Journal with Biographical Sketch and Notes*. Philadelphia: George S. MacManus, 1949.

James, Edward J., ed. *Notable American Women 1607–1950: A Biographical Dictionary*. 3 Vols. Cambridge: Harvard UP, 1971.

Jefferson, Thomas. *The Papers of Thomas Jefferson*. 21 Vols. Princeton: Princeton UP, 1950–.

Jenkins, Charles Francis. *Button Gwinnett, Signer of the Declaration of Independence*. New York: Doubleday, 1926.

Jernegan, Marcus Wilson. *Laboring and Dependent Classes in Colonial America 1607–1783*. Chicago: U of Chicago P, 1931.

Johnston, Jean. "Molly Brant: Mohawk Matron." *Ontario History* 56.2 (1964): 105–24.

Jones, Eva Eve. "Extracts from the Journal of Miss Sarah Eve." *Pennsylvania Magazine of History and Biography* 5.1–2 (1881): 19–36, 191–205.

Jordan, Winthrop. *White Over Black: American Attitudes Toward the Negro, 1550–1812*. Chapel Hill: U of North Carolina P, 1968.

Kaplan, Sidney. *The Black Presence in the Era of the American Revolution 1770–1800*. Greenwich, CT: New York Graphic Society, 1973.

Karlsen, Carol F., and Laurie Crumpacker, eds. *The Journal of Esther Edwards Burr, 1754–1757*. New Haven: Yale UP, 1984.

Katz, Jane B., ed. *I Am the Fire of Time: The Voices of Native American Women*. New York: Dutton, 1977.

Kerber, Linda. *Women of the Republic: Intellect and Ideology in Revolutionary America*. New York: Norton, 1986.

Kern, Jean B. "Mercy Otis Warren: Dramatist of the American Revolution," in *Curtain Calls: British and American Women and the Theater, 1660–1820*. Athens: Ohio UP, 1991. 247–59.

Kettell, Samuel. *Specimens of American Poetry*. 3 Vols. 1829; rpt., New York: Benjamin Blom, 1967.

Kibbey, Ann. *The Interpretation of Material Shapes in Puritanism: A Study of Rhetoric, Prejudice, and Violence.* Cambridge: Cambridge UP, 1986.

Kolodny, Annette. *The Land Before Her: Fantasy and Experience of the American Frontiers, 1630–1860.* Chapel Hill: U of North Carolina P, 1984.

Lacey, Barbara E. "The World of Hannah Heaton: The Autobiography of an Eighteenth-Century Connecticut Farm Woman." *William & Mary Quarterly* 45 (Apr. 1988): 280–304.

La Flesche, Francis. *The Osage Tribe: The Rite of Vigil.* 39th Annual Report of the Bureau of American Ethnology. Washington, D.C., 1925.

Lane, Mills, ed. *General Oglethorpe's Georgia: Colonial Letters 1733–1743.* 2 Vols. Savannah, GA: Beehive, 1975.

Lang, Amy Schrager. Introduction to *"The Captivity and Restoration of Mrs. Mary Rowlandson"* in Andrews, *Journeys in New Worlds,* 13–26.

———. *Prophetic Woman: Anne Hutchinson and the Problem of Dissent in the Literature of New England.* Berkeley: U of California P, 1987.

Leonard, Eugenie Andruss, Sophie Hutchinson Drinker, and Miriam Young Holden. *The American Woman in Colonial and Revolutionary Times, 1565–1800: A Syllabus with Bibliography.* Philadelphia: U of Pennsylvania P, 1962.

Levernier, James A., and Douglas R. Wilmes, eds. *American Writers Before 1800: A Biographical and Critical Dictionary.* 3 Vols. Westport, CT: Greenwood, 1983.

Ling, Amy. *Between Worlds: Women Writers of Chinese Ancestry.* New York: Pergamon, 1990.

Lopez, Claude-Anne, and Eugenia W. Herbert. *The Private Franklin: The Man and His Family.* New York: Norton, 1975.

Lossing, Benson J. *Eminent Americans.* New York: John B. Alden, 1885.

Maier, Pauline. *The Old Revolutionaries: Political Lives in the Age of Samuel Adams.* New York: Knopf, 1980.

Mainiero, Lina, ed. *American Women Writers: A Critical Reference Guide from Colonial Times to the Present.* 4 Vols. New York: Frederick Ungar, 1979–82.

Mason, Emily V., ed. *Journal of a Young Lady of Virginia 1782.* Baltimore: John Murphy & Co., 1871.

Mason, Lizzie Norton, and James Duncan Phillips. "The Journal of Elizabeth Cranch." *Essex Institute Historical Collections* 80 (1944): 1–36.

Mather, Cotton. *Magnalia Christi Americana, or the Ecclesiastical History of New England.* Ed. Raymond J. Cunningham. New York: Frederick Ungar, 1970.

Matthews, William. *American Diaries: An Annotated Bibliography of American Diaries Written Prior to the Year 1861.* Berkeley: U of California P, 1945.

May, Caroline. *The American Female Poets.* Philadelphia: Lindsay & Blakiston, 1848.

McElroy, Janice H., *Our Hidden Heritage: Pennsylvania Women in History.* Washington, D.C.: American Association of University Women, 1983.

Montgomery, David. "The Working Classes of the Pre-Industrial American City, 1780–1830." *Labor History* 9 (1968): 3–22.

Mooney, James. *Myths of Cherokees.* 19th Annual Report of the Bureau of American Ethnology, Washington, D.C., 1900.

Morgan, Edmund S. *The Puritan Dilemma: The Story of John Winthrop.* Boston: Little, Brown, 1958.

———. *The Puritan Family: Essays on Religion and Domestic Relations in Seventeenth Century New England.* Boston: Trustees of the Public Library, 1944.

Morison, Samuel Eliot. *The European Discovery of America.* 2 Vols. New York: Oxford UP, 1971, 1974.

Morris, Margaret Hill. "The Revolutionary Journal of Margaret Morris." *Bulletin of Friends' Historical Society of Philadelphia* 9 (May 1919): 2–14, 65–75, 103–14.

Morris, Richard B. *Studies in the History of American Law, with Special Reference to the Seventeenth and Eighteenth Centuries*. [1930] 2nd ed. New York: Octagon Books, 1963.

Moseley, Laura Hadley, ed. *The Diaries of Julia Cowles: A Connecticut Record, 1797–1803*. New Haven: Yale UP, 1931.

Mulford, Carla. *"Only for the eye of a friend": The Poetry of Annis Boudinot Stockton*. Charlottesville: U of Virginia P, 1995.

Murray, Judith Sargent. *The Gleaner*. 3 Vols. Boston: I. Thomas and E. T. Andrews, 1798.

Myers, Andrew Breen, ed. *George Washington's Copy of POEMS ON SEVERAL OCCASIONS, by Nathaniel Evans*. New York: Fordham UP, 1976.

Nienkamp, Jean, and Andrea Collins. Introduction to *Female Quixotism*. New York: Oxford UP, 1992. xiii–xxvi.

Niethammer, Carolyn. *Daughters of the Earth: The Lives and Legends of American Indian Women*. New York: Macmillan, 1977.

Norton, Mary Beth. *Liberty's Daughters: The Revolutionary Experience of America, 1750–1800*. Boston: Little, Brown, 1980.

O'Meara, Walter. *Daughters of the Country: The Women of the Fur Traders and Mountain Men*. New York: Harcourt, Brace & World, 1968.

Oreovicz, Cheryl Z. "Heroic Drama for an Uncertain Age: The Plays of Mercy Otis Warren." *Early American Literature and Culture: Essays Honoring Harrison T. Meserole*. Ed. Kathryn Zabelle Derounian-Stodola. Newark: Delaware UP, 1992. 192–210.

———. "Mercy Warren and 'Freedom's Genius.' " *U of Mississippi Studies in English* 5 (1984–87): 215–230.

Osborn, Sarah. "Sarah Osborn Papers," manuscripts at the Newport Historical Society, Newport, RI, unpublished.

Parker, Patricia L. *Early American Fiction: A Reference Guide*. Boston: G. K. Hall, 1984.

Parsons, Elsie Clews. "Tewa Tales." *Memoirs of the American Folklore Society* 19 (1926): 191–192.

Pendleton, Emily, and Milton Ellis. *Philenia: Life and Works of Sarah Wentworth Morton*. Orono, ME, 1931.

Penn, William. *The Papers of William Penn*. 5 Vols. Ed. Richard S. Dunn and Mary Maples Dunn. Philadelphia: U of Pennsylvania P, 1981–.

Perkins, Mary E. *Old Houses of the Antient Town of Norwich*. Norwich, 1895.

Personal Recollections of the American Revolution: A Private Journal. Prepared from Authentic Domestic Records. . . . Ed. Sidney Barclay [pseud.]. New York: Rudd & Carlston, 1859.

Petter, Henri. *The Early American Novel*. Columbus: Ohio State UP, 1971.

Pettingill, Claire C. "Sisterhood in a Separate Sphere: Female Friendship in Hannah Webster Foster's *The Coquette* and *The Boarding School*," *Early American Literature* 27.3 (1992): 185–203.

Pinckney, Elise, ed. *The Letterbook of Eliza Lucas Pinckney, 1739–1762*. Chapel Hill: U of North Carolina P, 1972.

Pond, E., ed. *Memoirs of Miss Susanna Anthony . . . extracts from her writings. . . .* Portland, ME, 1844.

Potts, William John. "Bathsheba Bowers." *Pennsylvania Magazine of History and Biography* 3 (1879): 110–11.

Qoyawayma, Polingaysi. *No Turning Back: A True Account of a Hopi Girl's Struggle. . . .* Albuquerque: U of New Mexico P, 1964.

Quinn, Arthur Hobson. *American Fiction: An Historical and Critical Survey*. New York: Appleton-Century, 1936.

———. *A History of the America Drama, from the Beginning to Civil War*. New York: F. S. Crofts, 1943.

Ramsay, David, ed. *Memoirs of the Life of Martha Laurens Ramsay.* 3rd ed. Boston: Samuel T. Armstrong, 1812.

The Records of the Virginia Company of London. Ed. Susan Myra Kingsbury. Washington, D.C.: U.S. Government Printing Office, 1933.

[Reed, William B.] *The Life of Esther DeBerdt.* Philadelphia: C. Sherman, 1853.

Reninger, Marion Wallace. *Famous Women of Lancaster County Pennsylvania.* n.p.: Lancaster County Historical Society.

Rich, Adrienne. "Anne Bradstreet and Her Poetry" in *The Works of Anne Bradstreet.* Ed. Jeannine Hensley. Cambridge: Belknap, 1967.

Riedesel, Baroness Fredericke. *Letters and Journals.* Trans. William L. Stone, 1867; rpt. New York: New York Times & Arno, 1968.

The Rise and Progress of the Young-Ladies' Academy of Philadelphia. Philadelphia: Stewart and Cochran, 1794.

Robinson, William H., ed. *Critical Essays on Phillis Wheatley.* Boston: G. K. Hall, 1982.

Rohr, Sara. "Margaret Cochran Corbin, Revolutionary Heroine." *Papers Read Before the Society.* Vol. 15. Chambersburg, PA: Kittochtinny Historical Society, 1970. 28–31.

Rossi, Alice S., ed. *The Feminist Papers.* New York: Columbia UP, 1973.

Ruether, Rosemary Radford, and Rosemary Skinner Keller, eds. *Women and Religion in America.* 2 Vols. San Francisco: Harper & Row, 1983.

Rutman, Darrett B. "My beloued and good Husband." *American Heritage* 13 (Aug. 1962): 24–27, 94–96.

Sasson, Diane. *The Shaker Spiritual Narrative.* Knoxville: U of Tennessee P, 1983.

Schilpp, Madelon Golden, and Sharon M. Murphy, eds. *Great Women of the Press.* Carbondale: Southern Illinois UP, 1983.

Schweitzer, Ivy. "Anne Bradstreet Wrestles with the Renaissance." *Early American Literature* 23.3 (1988): 291– 312.

Seton, Elizabeth. *Letters of Mother Seton to Mrs. Julianna Scott.* Ed. Joseph B. Code. 2nd ed. New York: Father Salvator M. Burgio Memorial Foundation in Honor of Mother Seton, 1960.

———. *Memoir, Letters and Journal, of Elizabeth Seton, Convert to the Catholic Faith, and Sister of Charity.* Ed. Robert Seton. 2 Vols. New York: P. O'Shea, 1869.

Shea, Daniel B. Jr. *Spiritual Autobiography in Early America.* Princeton: Princeton UP, 1968.

Shields, David S. "The Wits and Poets of Pennsylvania: New Light on the Rise of Belles Lettres in Provincial Pennsylvania, 1720–1740." *Pennsylvania Magazine of History and Biography* (1985): 99–143.

Shields, John C. "Phillis Wheatley's Struggle for Freedom in Her Poetry and Prose." *The Collected Works of Phillis Wheatley.* Ed. John C. Shields. New York: Oxford UP, 1988. 229–270.

Sipe, Hale. *History of Butler County Pennsylvania.* n.p.: Historical Publishing Co. n.d.

Smith, John Jay, ed. *Letters of Doctor Richard Hill and His Children.* Philadelphia: Privately printed, 1854.

Smith, William Raymond. *History as Argument: Three Patriot Historians of the American Revolution.* The Hague: Mouton and Co., 1960.

Smith-Rosenberg, Carroll. *Disorderly Conduct: Visions of Gender in Victorian America.* New York: Oxford UP, 1985.

Spacks, Patricia Meyer. *Imagining a Self: Autobiography and Novel in Eighteenth-century England.* Cambridge: Harvard UP, 1976.

Spalding, Phinizy. *Oglethorpe in America.* Chicago: U of Chicago P, 1977.

Sprigg, June. *Domestick Beings.* New York: Knopf, 1984.

Spruill, Julia Cherry. *Women's Life & Work in the Southern Colonies.* 1938; rpt., New York: Norton, 1972.

Stanford, Ann. *Anne Bradstreet: The Worldly Puritan*. New York: Burt Franklin, 1974.

Starling, Marion Wilson. *The Slave Narrative: Its Place in American History*. Boston: G. K. Hall, 1981.

Stedman, Edmund Clarence, and Ellen Mackay Hutchinson, comps. and eds. *A Library of American Literature from the Earliest Settlement to the Present Time*. 11 Vols. New York: Charles L. Webster & Company, 1891.

Sweeney, John A. H. "The Norris-Fisher Correspondence: A Circle of Friends, 1779–82." *Delaware History* 6 (Mar. 1955): 187–232.

Taves, Ann, ed. *Religion and Domestic Violence in Early New England: The Memoirs of Abigail Abbot Bailey*. Bloomington: Indiana UP, 1989.

Taylor, William R. *Cavalier and Yankee: The Old South and American National Character*. New York: George Braziller, 1961.

Temple, Sarah B. Gober, and Kenneth Coleman. *Georgia Journeys*. Athens: U of Georgia P, 1961.

Terrell, John Upton, and Donna M. Terrell. *Indian Women of the Western Morning: Their Life in Early America*. New York: Dial, 1974.

Theatrum Majorum. The Cambridge of 1776 . . . with which is incorporated the Diary of Dorothy Dudley, Now first published. . . . 1876; rpt. New York: New York Times and Arno, 1971.

Thickstun, Margaret Olofson. *Fictions of the Feminine: Puritan Doctrine and the Representation of Women*. Ithaca: Cornell UP, 1988.

Tiffany, Nina Moore, ed. *Letters of James Murray, Loyalist*. 1901; Boston: Gregg, 1972.

Tinling, Marion, ed. *The Correspondence of The Three William Byrds of Westover, Virginia*. 2 Vols. Charlottesville: U of Virginia P, 1977.

Todd, Janet, ed. Introduction to *Oroonoko, The Rover and Other Works* by Aphra Behn. New York: Penguin, 1992. 1–22.

Twichell, Joseph Hopkins, ed. *Some Old Puritan Love Letters: John and Margaret Winthrop, 1618–1638*. New York: Dodd, Mead, 1893.

Ulrich, Laurel Thatcher. *Good Wives: Image and Reality in the Lives of Women in Northern New England, 1650–1750*. New York: Oxford UP, 1982.

———. *A Midwife's Tale: The Life of Martha Ballard, Based on Her Diary, 1785–1812*. New York: Knopf, 1990.

VanDerBeets, Richard, ed. *Held Captive by Indians*. Knoxville: U of Tennessee P, 1973.

Vanderpoel, Emily N., comp. *Chronicles of a Pioneer School From 1792 to 1833 Being the History of Miss Sarah Pierce and Her Litchfield School*. Ed. Elizabeth C. Barney Buel. Cambridge: Printed at the University P, 1903.

Van Doren, Carl, ed. *The Letters of Benjamin Franklin and Jane Mecom*. Philadelphia: American Philosophical Society, 1950.

van Laer, A. J. F., trans. and ed. *Correspondence of Maria van Rensselaer, 1669–1689*. Albany: U of the State of New York, 1935.

Vaughan, Alden T., and Edward W. Clark, eds. *Puritans among the Indians*. Cambridge: Belknap, 1981.

Vella, Michael. "Theology, genre, and gender: The Precarious Place of Hannah Adams in American Literary History." *Early American Literature* 28.1 (1993): 21–41.

von Frank, Albert J. "Sarah Pierce and the Poetic Origins of Utopian Feminism in America." *Prospects* 14 (1990): 45–63.

Walker, Nancy, and Zita Dresner, eds. *Redressing the Balance: American Women's Literary Humor from Colonial Times to the 1980s*. Jackson: UP of Mississippi, 1988.

Wallace, Ernest, and El Adamson Hoebel. *The Comanches, Lords of the South Plains*. Norman: U of Oklahoma P, 1952.

Ward, Nathaniel. *The Simple Cobler of Aggawam in America*. Ed. P. M. Zall. 1647; Lincoln: U of Nebraska P, 1969.

Warren–Adams Letters. Collections of the Massachusetts Historical Society 73 (1925), vol. 2.

Washburn, Wilcomb E., ed. *Narratives of North American Indian Captivities*. Vol. VIII. New York: Garland Publishing, 1975.

Watkins, Owen C. *The Puritan Experience: Studies in Spiritual Autobiography*. New York: Schocken, 1972.

Watts, Emily Stipes. *The Poetry of American Women from 1632 to 1945*. 2 Vols. Austin: U of Texas P, 1977.

Wegelin, Oscar. *Early American Poetry*. 2 Vols. Gloucester, MA: Peter Smith, 1930.

Weil, Dorothy. *In Defense of Women: Susanna Rowson (1762–1824)*. University Park: Pennsylvania State UP, 1977.

Wells, Seth Y., ed. *Testimonies of the Life, Character, Revelations and Doctrines of Our Ever Blessed Mother Ann Lee, and the Elders with Her*. Hancock, MA: n.p., 1816.

Wheatley, Phillis. *The Collected Works of Phillis Wheatley*. Ed. John C. Shields. New York: Oxford UP, 1988.

Wheeler, Joseph T. *The Maryland Press, 1777–1790*. Baltimore: Maryland Historical Society, 1938.

Wilcoxen, Charlotte. *Seventeenth Century Albany: A Dutch Profile*. Albany: Albany Institute of History and Art, 1984.

Wilkinson, Eliza. *Letters of Eliza Wilkinson*. Ed. Caroline Gilman. New York: Samuel Colman, 1839; rpt. New York: Arno, 1969.

Winship, George P. *The Cambridge Press, 1638–1692*. Philadelphia: U of Pennsylvania P, 1945.

Winslow, Ola Elizabeth. *American Broadside Verse from Imprints of the 17th & 18th Centuries*. New Haven: Yale UP, 1930.

———. *Master Roger Williams: A Biography*. New York: Macmillan, 1957.

Winthrop Papers. 5 Vols. New York: Russell & Russell, 1929.

Wissler, C., and D. C. Duvall. *Mythology of the Blackfoot Indians*. Anthropological Papers of the American Museum of Natural History. Vol. 2, 1908.

Wister, Sarah. *Sally Wister's Journal: A True Narrative. . . .* Ed. Albert Cook Myers. Philadelphia: Ferris & Leach, 1902.

Woodward, William A. *Records of Salem Witchcraft*. 2 Vols. New York: DeCapo, 1969.

Wray, Lady Mary. *The Ladies' Library*. 3 Vols. Ed. Sir Richard Steele. London, 1714.

Wright, Luella. *The Literary Life of the Early Friends, 1650–1725*. New York: Columbia UP, 1932.

Wright, Thomas Goddard. *Literary Culture in Early New England, 1620–1730*. 1920; rpt., New York: Russell & Russell, 1966.

The Zunis—Self Portrayals. Trans. Alvina Quam. Albuquerque: U of New Mexico P, 1972.

Index